POVERTY IN CANADA

POVERTY IN CANADA

Implications for Health and Quality of Life

Dennis Raphael

Forewords by
Rob Rainer
Jack Layton

Canadian Scholars' Press Inc.
Toronto

Poverty in Canada: Implications for Health and Quality of Life, Second Edition
Dennis Raphael

Second edition published in 2011 by
Canadian Scholars' Press Inc.
180 Bloor Street West, Suite 801
Toronto, Ontario
M5S 2V6
www.cspi.org

Every reasonable effort has been made to identify copyright holders. CSPI would be pleased to have any errors or omissions brought to its attention.

Canadian Scholars' Press gratefully acknowledges financial support for our publishing activities from the Government of Canada through the Canada Book Fund.

Library and Archives Canada Cataloguing in Publication

Raphael, Dennis
    Poverty in Canada : implications for health and quality of life / Dennis Raphael. — 2nd ed.

Originally publ. under title: Poverty and policy in Canada.
Includes bibliographical references and index.
ISBN 978-1-55130-394-9

1. Poverty—Canada—Textbooks. 2. Poor—Canada— Textbooks. 3. Canada—Social conditions—1991- —Textbooks. 4. Canada—Economic conditions—1991-   —Textbooks. 5. Canada—Social policy— Textbooks. 6. Canada—Economic policy—1991-   —Textbooks. I. Raphael, Dennis. Poverty and policy in Canada. II.Title.

HC120.P6R36 2011   362.5'0971   C2011-904666-0

Text design by Brad Horning
Cover design by Gordon Robertson
Cover image: © Suzanne Tucker/Shutterstock.com

Printed and bound in Canada

MIX
Paper from
responsible sources
FSC® C004071

Table of Contents

Part III
Poverty, Health, and Quality of Life

Part IV
Politics, Public Policy, and Poverty

Foreword to the Second Edition

Foreword

You are holding in your hands the single most valuable reference on poverty in Canada, a book whose dog-eared copy sits prominently on the bookshelf in my office.

Valuable because of the breadth of this book's content, stretching from:

- definitions and measurements of poverty;
- to the experience of poverty ("the worst form of violence," Gandhi called it);
- to poverty's massive, multi-dimensional impact on people and society;
- to the politics of poverty;
- to the very future of the Canadian welfare state—formally but nicely defined in these pages as "the governmental structures that assure the entitlements of citizenship: meeting basic needs, providing resources for participation in society, and minimizing forces that systematically exclude citizens from these activities."

Valuable because of the provocative questions at the end of each chapter, encouraging you to dig deeper (which I hope you will do).

Valuable because of the extensive lists of resources placed throughout, aiding you in your quest for greater understanding and insights.

And, valuable because of the person behind this work.

As will be evident as you read further, Professor Dennis Raphael has encyclopaedic knowledge about poverty in Canada. He has developed this from making the study of poverty central to his life's work. But unlike some academics who are content to study and publish, study and publish, treating their subject matter (and human subjects) with curiosity but not necessarily a passion for social change and social justice, backed by action, Professor Raphael goes beyond publishing to be a scholar (uncommonly) determined to be and unafraid of speaking truth to power—in this case the truth that poverty, more than anything else, is a social construct, a result of how resources and therefore influence are distributed in society.

We know this construct to be true. How else to explain the phenomenon of persistent and, in many ways, worsening poverty in Canada, within the fourth wealthiest nation in 2011, one that has over a million "millionaire households" and a growing number of billionaires? How else to explain the existence of food banks and homeless shelters among the high-end restaurants and mansions, the glitter and gloss of our cities, the symbols of power and privilege?

Conversely, we know—definitively—that poverty is not the result of sloth, the failure to pull oneself up by the proverbial bootstraps. Yes, some may be poor because of disinclination to "work" (though ask yourself, "What is work?") and a preference for "the dole." But, in my travels across this "unfinished country" (as the late, great journalist Bruce Hutchinson called Canada), I've rarely—very rarely—encountered the person who, in the eyes of some, might fit the widespread but utterly false and malicious image of the "lazy welfare bum." Far more frequently, and likely, I meet the woman or man who expresses only an intense desire to escape his or her condition of poverty, to escape what often amounts to be their literal entrapment in deprivation and destitution due to the barriers before them:

- the Aboriginal women in Whitehorse, still reeling in addictions from the physical and mental scarring of the horrendous "Indian" residential school system, with insufficient supports around them to be able to move forward with their lives;
- the immigrant couple in Toronto, unable to apply their credentials from the university at which they studied in their native country, and thus forced to take part-time, low-paying jobs with combined income insufficient to make ends meet for themselves and their three children;
- the single mom with two-year-old twins in Victoria, with weak family support and who has no access to affordable child care so that she can return to the labour market;
- the man in Regina whose episodic, invisible disability makes it seemingly impossible for him to qualify for social assistance support, but even if he does eventually qualify would receive a level of income insufficient to meet his needs.

If you have not experienced poverty yourself, I hope you will spend some time with those who have. Ask them to share, within their comfort range, their stories of trial and survival. You will receive astonishing evidence of courage and resilience in the face of immense barriers—economic, social, and political—to healthier, freer, more socially secure lives. You will come away from your listening with deeper insights into the problem of poverty, and deeper respect for the people enduring its ugliness.

One of the greatest barriers, as Professor Raphael covers in these pages and as I have indicated above, is the inequitable distribution of income and wealth. "Poverty results," he writes, "as more and more of the resources of the society are provided to the wealthy and powerful—to those who control the means of production" (and, one can add, those in the upper echelons of political corridors and of "financial services," e.g., banking, insurance).

Hence, we can understand why, on one side of the equality ledger, 720,231 people drew on food banks for food support in March 2007 (an 8.4% increase since 1997 and a 91% increase since 1989) while, on the other side, the richest 1% of Canadians had by 2007 taken in 32% of all the growth in incomes since 1997.

As the saying goes, "it takes a lot of money to create poverty."

But even more important than unjust income and wealth distribution is the barrier of social indifference to this problem, in turn ensuring inaction to address it by the governments of our day. Or, rather, at the least, a widespread lack of awareness among Canadians of just how wide the chasm has become and continues to spread between the have-nots, the haves, and the "have-yachts"—at troubling risk to the fabric of our society, and our very democracy.

That's not to say that governments in Canada are doing nothing on poverty. They surely are, such as the six provinces (MB, NB, NL, NS, ON, QC) that, as of March 2011, are implementing province-wide poverty "reduction" strategies.

(Permit me to digress to the questions: Why just "reduction"? To what level? Is such a level acceptable? Can we not do better? Is it acceptable to you that even one person in Canada lives in poverty? What if that person is your relative? Your friend? Your neighbour?)

But as Professor Raphael aptly states:

> These anti-poverty strategies and programs have modest poverty-reducing effects because **they fail to address the sources of the unequal distribution of resources**. These broader issues are intricately related to existing inequalities in influence and power associated with Canada being a liberal welfare state. In a nation where the economic marketplace serves to distribute economic resources with rather little intervention from governments, high poverty rates continue to exist since these inequalities in power and influence persist. (emphasis added)

So there we have the heart of the matter: unless we, as Canadians, are prepared to address the inequitable distribution of resources—the income and wealth we collectively generate—we can expect poverty and its devastating impact and cost to be a virtually permanent fixture of our society.

The good news is that we know how to address inequality and have the tools for this at our disposal. Inequality can be reduced (and income poverty addressed) through:

- ensuring living wages for those in the paid labour market, such that any lone adult or couple working full-time can earn enough to meet the basic needs of his, her, or their household (in the mid-2000s, Denmark and Norway achieved a 0% poverty rate for two-parent families with both parents working);
- rebuilding and maintaining strong progressivity and sufficiency in our taxation systems, ensuring that those who can afford to contribute more to the public good, do so, and that the pool of public revenue is deep enough to ensure the "adequate standard of living" and "social security" that are human rights under international law to which Canada is bound;
- through our tax and cash transfer systems, more fully redistributing the pooled income from "those who have much to those who have little" to eliminate the

"poverty gap"—the amount of money needed to bring all people living in poverty up to their poverty lines. This gap, based on the Low Income Cut-Off After Tax proxy measure of poverty, was $12.3 billion in 2007. That, by the way, amounted to only 1.5% of the total market income earned by all Canadians in 2007. In that same year, Canada's gross domestic product was $1.5 trillion, 124 times higher than the poverty gap.

So keep this in mind the next time anyone tells you that Canada cannot afford to fix the problem of poverty.

Some other really good news is this: nations that strive for greater income and wealth equality can expect to yield better social and economic outcomes. In a landmark paper published by the Canadian Centre for Policy Alternatives in 2006, tax law and policy experts Neil Brooks and Thaddeus Hwong found that the Nordic countries, with their comparatively higher rates of taxation and more robust social development and social protection systems, have significantly better social and economic performance than Canada, the United States, and other "Anglo-American" countries. Key findings included that Nordic countries have:

- significantly more income equality;
- significantly lower rates of poverty across almost all social groups;
- significantly more gender equality;
- significantly lower infant mortality rates;
- longer life expectancy;
- lower homicide rates;
- significantly less drug use;
- significantly more leisure time;
- more freedom, according to a widely referred to index of economic freedom;
- more life satisfaction as reported by individuals; and
- significantly more trust among individuals and for public institutions.

Poverty in Canada will help you consider what Canada can do to equal or surpass the Nordic countries in social and economic performance. And we can do much more than what we've done to date: indeed, eliminating poverty should be within the top five if not at the very top of the public policy priorities of every political party in the land.

In *Poverty in Canada*, Professor Raphael encourages you to reflect upon many excellent questions. I would like to add just one more:

What contribution shall I make to the elimination of poverty in my lifetime?

Your answer shall be known toward the end of whatever time you have remaining on this troubled yet still beautiful planet. But whatever contribution you ultimately may make, know throughout your journey that the elimination of poverty is attainable.

For, as Nelson Mandela has so well said, in words inspiring our work, day in and day out, at Canada Without Poverty:

Like slavery and apartheid, poverty is not natural. It is man-made and it can be overcome and eradicated by the actions of human beings. And overcoming poverty is not a gesture of charity. It is an act of justice. It is the protection of a fundamental human right, the right to dignity and a decent life.

Rob Rainer
Executive Director, Canada Without Poverty
March 2011

Foreword to the First Edition

Canadians, overwhelmingly, believe in justice and equality. These are values we trust, and we want to bring them to life in our communities. Our vision of a just society forms the core of our sense of identity *as Canadians*.

But rejecting poverty in our national heart hasn't stopped poverty from festering. Our society enters this new millennium with open wounds and a poverty rate that stands among the worst in the developed world. Does this seem hard to believe? Certainly, it can be hard to reconcile stubborn poverty with our deep sense of who we are as Canadians.

It's a serious problem, because we won't effectively address what we don't collectively see. Just as the gulf between rich and poor widens, so does the cleft between citizens' values and social reality. It seems a cruel paradox that an admirable sense of national self could help blind us to deprivation in our midst. On the other hand, I believe those Canadian values are what will also drive positive and far-reaching change in this country.

This volume explores social and political forces that conspire to allow poverty to continue unabated. At the simplest level, poverty's sheer invisibility keeps it off the national radar. Difficult lives unfold quietly, their everyday grit and greyness hidden from broader view. In cities like Toronto, we see the injustice erupt into visible, undeniable homelessness—but even this can't convey the sheer scale of the deprivation that also weighs the poorly housed, the working poor, the just-getting-by.

That's why Professor Raphael's work is so necessary. This book will strengthen our struggle to make poverty visible, to thereby make it politically *real*, and ultimately to make poverty history.

This year, I mourned the 10th anniversary of a death and an epiphany. One January night in 1996, my wife Olivia and I were walking along Spadina Avenue toward our Toronto home. It was late and bitterly cold. Along the way, we checked on two homeless men huddled in sleeping bags in doorways. They seemed okay, but we pondered hard over what exactly we'd do if someone was not okay. The next morning, the CBC brought news that a man had frozen to death overnight in a bus shelter—two blocks from our home. We'd walked past without seeing him. Eugene Upper died that night in the winter-moon shadows of the bank towers rising over Canada's richest city. Soon after, two more men died, and homelessness and poverty became more real for more Torontonians. It certainly steeled my resolve to make progress on city council, and now on a national level. And I often feel the memory of Eugene Upper, the man I didn't see, pressing me to take more responsibility, to get more done.

In recalling this story, I underline two points. First, we should not need this kind of tragedy to keep poverty in our society's radar! Second, as Professor Raphael's work makes so vividly clear, the homelessness that Eugene Upper struggled with is one face of a wider experience of poverty. A holistic approach to poverty calls us to treat the most critical symptoms as well as the underlying progressive disease—the social processes that produce poverty.

Poverty and Policy in Canada is a work with scholarly integrity. It's also very openly *engaged* with a Canadian anti-poverty movement that aims to achieve concrete results. This generation. This year. Right now.

Canada's NDP, the party I have led since 2003, counts itself as part of this movement. You may also recognize civil society organizations such as the National Anti-poverty Organization, Campaign 2000, and the Centre for Social Justice. And there are many more groups, unions, researchers, and advocates who struggle for economic justice nationally, regionally, and in the smallest of communities. What they share is tremendous commitment and resilience. What they do without is moneyed access to levers of power, or even regular acknowledgment for the critical work they do. I expect all will welcome *Poverty and Policy in Canada* both as a resource and as validation of this tough, common struggle.

I hope that you, too, will count yourself part of this movement—today, or once you've worked through this book.

What is poverty in Canada? Poverty is an index of an unjust society, both a sign of failure and a challenge to do better as a community. Poverty is about the stark denial of both hope and freedom. Poverty spawns social exclusion and desperation, and it's the single most significant predictor of individual and community health. Professor Raphael is a leader among researchers exploring this connection that Canadian governments still stubbornly fail to grasp.

I especially appreciate how Professor Raphael frames poverty as *"a barrier to citizens and communities achieving their full potential."* The inverse, expanding opportunities for people to prosper, is how Canada's NDP frames its mission. We believe that building opportunity and security for people in general is the most enduring way to eradicate poverty.

So we fight for affordable education and training that empowers young people to broaden their choices, without being caged by family income. We continue to work for a legislated national system of affordable early learning and child care—so parents can work or study, and kids get a valuable head start in their most formative years.

We fight for more affordable housing—as a response to homelessness, and because millions of Canadians pay so much for housing that they sacrifice other basic needs. We fight for progressive taxation and labour rights, empowering working people to balance employers and demand living wages. We're renewing our campaign to mend a crumbling social safety net—from social assistance to employment insurance to pension protection.

These ideas support internationally recognized principles of social democracy. Where they're pursued most vigorously, these ideas enrich people, communities, and nations.

In Chapter 11, Professor Raphael reviews research that should open the eyes of every "trickle-down" economist: *Globally, social democratic influence on government directly correlates with lower poverty rates.*

In Canada, last generation's New Democrats worked in minority Parliaments to build pillars of our welfare state—including universal public health care, public pensions, and affordable housing. In the last minority Parliament, the NDP used its influence to stop the government's surprise plan to waste billions on needless tax cuts for profitable corporations. We put that money toward badly needed re-investment in priorities like social housing, education, training, and the environment.

That Liberal government had claimed these priorities as its own, but utterly ignored them through three majority Parliaments. It took social democratic influence in a minority situation to get results. Minus that influence, that same government had spent 12 majority years dismantling Canada's welfare state and social programs—under the approving eye of bond traders and multinational capital.

Through the 1990s, majority Liberal governments withdrew from cost-shared social assistance, with the predictable result that benefits and standards have eroded in most provinces. What else? They axed Canada's national affordable housing program altogether, made Employment Insurance rules so tight that most workers no longer qualify for benefits (but still pay premiums), cut billions from college and university funding (driving tuition fees up 300%), destabilized public health care to the delight of corporate privatization advocates, and did nothing to deliver on their marquee promise of national child care (borrowed from social democrats).

The government said the austerity was needed to battle a "Great Deficit." But when the federal budget deficit yielded to record surpluses by 2000, they didn't reinvest a penny into the programs they'd cut. Instead, they spent billions on the most sweeping corporate tax cuts in this country's history.

This book examines the most distressing result of these policies: the growing gap between the richest and the poorest Canadians. This book also visualizes a way forward politically.

More social democratic influence in government is essential. And as social democrats, we will continue engaging citizens with the argument that eradicating poverty enriches us all. Ethically as well as socially and economically. A people-first program that expands opportunity for the poorest opens doors for all working families. This approach, in turn, provides lasting solutions to so much of what preoccupies people. For instance, while conservatives respond to crime with repressive "law and order" measures, addressing the poverty that spawns such desperations will do more to make our communities safer.

I believe Canadians want to "make poverty history." Even though most call themselves "centrist" in surveys, Canadians are far more progressive than the governments they elect. I believe people are growing ever more impatient with politicians who voice social democratic ideals but end up serving other interests. The past two federal elections saw millions more Canadians choose social democracy through the NDP, and my optimism keeps growing.

At the same time, Professor Raphael is right to target Canada's outdated federal electoral system. It repeatedly subverts Canadians' voting intentions and under-represents social democracy in Parliament. Most democracies have already moved on by incorporating some form of proportional representation. Professor Raphael's arguments add weight to the growing Canadian call to catch up to the world.

At the end of the day, I am an incurable optimist. I believe in Canadians and their values. I believe that once people have the power to drive politics, they'll choose to say "no" to poverty and "yes" to a more just and prosperous Canada.

Jack Layton
Leader, New Democratic Party of Canada
and Leader of the Opposition in Parliament
August 2006

Preface

It has been known since the mid-19th century that living conditions are the primary determinants of health and well-being. The term *poverty* has come to stand for the situation whereby these living conditions produce material and social deprivation that seriously threaten health and reduce quality of life. It has also been known over this time that the incidence of poverty is primarily a result of how a society organizes and distributes its economic, social, and political resources. A century and a half of research and lived experience have confirmed these understandings. There exists no research study that demonstrates that living in conditions of poverty is good for individuals, communities, or societies. Indeed, thousands of accumulated studies have come to the same basic conclusion: The incidence of poverty is a severe—if not the most severe—threat to the health and quality of life of individuals and communities in wealthy developed societies such as Canada.

This truism is recognized by decades of Canadian government and public health association statements, resolutions, and reports. It is found in many international covenants on human rights and human and social development to which Canada is a signatory. Indeed, an all-party resolution on child poverty—passed unanimously by the House of Commons on November 24, 1989, stated: *"This House seek(s) to achieve the goal of eliminating poverty among Canadian children by the year 2000."* More than 10 years after this deadline, Canada's child poverty rate continues to be among the highest in the developed world.

According to the Organisation for Economic Co-operation and Development, Canada's child poverty rate during the mid-2000s was 15%. This is the case even though Canada is a wealthier nation—using the total value of goods and services or its Gross Domestic Product —than most other wealthy developed nations. As an example, Denmark is not as wealthy a nation as Canada, yet its child poverty rate during the mid-2000s of 3.0% represents a virtual elimination of child poverty. This is also the case in many other European nations. There is evidence that Canadians appreciate that eliminating poverty is a worthwhile goal. Politicians and elected governments of every political stripe assure the public that poverty reduction is an important goal, and promise to address it. Indeed, many provinces have developed "anti-poverty" strategies. Why, then, is so little being accomplished?

An increasing body of research finds that poverty rates cannot be attributed to failings of individuals who live in poverty. There are particular identities that make some individuals more susceptible to falling into poverty than others. These identities include being Aboriginal, having less education, living with a disability, being female, being a recent immigrant to Canada (especially one of colour), or being a lone parent. But these identities do not by themselves create the situation of poverty. Poverty is more likely when these identities are present because the political and economic systems do not provide employment wages or social assistance benefits at a level for these individuals that allow for a life outside of poverty. And these situations are worsened when public policy does not provide affordable housing, child care, and responsive health and social services, thereby further straining the economic and social resources available to these vulnerable groups.

Poverty rates do not even depend upon the presence or absence of well-meaning intentions of policy-makers. Rather, rates reflect the general operation of the economy—heavily influenced by the politics—of a nation. Some indicators of these processes are wage levels, the percentage of low-paid workers within a nation, and the percentage of national resources or revenues invested in health and social services, education, employment and training, and other social infrastructure. In international comparisons, Canada performs poorly on all of these indicators.

More specifically, poverty rates reflect how a nation addresses key public policy issues of income distribution, employment security and working conditions, housing, income, and food security, and the creation and preservation of a network of health and social services. This basket of issues has come to be known as the social determinants of health. But once such an analysis is done and Canada is found to be lacking, the question arises: *Why is this the case?* And to answer this, we need to understand the politics and economics—the political economy—of a society.

The title of this volume, *Poverty in Canada: Implications for Health and Quality of Life,* provides a roadmap for this exploration. First, I examine the nature and meaning of poverty in a wealthy industrialized nation such as Canada. Second, I consider the lived experience of poverty and what it means to those who live in poverty. Third, I answer the question of how the experience of poverty comes to shape the health and quality of life of individuals, communities, and societies. Fourth, my analysis focuses on how the incidence of poverty—and these health and quality-of-life outcomes—result from public policy decisions made by governments and what can be done to improve the situation.

Central to this exploration is analysis of how Canada's political economy supports these public-policy decisions. Also important is the extent to which the public holds attitudes and values consistent with this political economy and the public-policy decisions that result from it. All of these factors will determine whether alternative visions for Canada—and the means of implementing these visions—are possible.

This second edition of *Poverty in Canada* updates the data on poverty rates in Canada and elsewhere and includes information on newly developed Canadian measures of deprivation. It expands analysis of how race and gender are increasingly coming to be associated with the incidence of poverty and places these developments in the context of the globalization of Canada's economy. The impacts of the recession of 2008–2009 are identified.

A new chapter examines various "anti-poverty" strategies being implemented by the provinces and examines their potential for reducing the incidence of poverty and its adverse effects upon Canadians' health and quality of life. A revised final chapter concludes with an analysis of how poverty can be reduced through the building of social and political movements that will *force* elected leaders and policy-makers to enact public policy that reduces the incidence of poverty through action on the social determinants of health.

Recent political developments provide some grounds for optimism. Many provinces have established "anti-poverty" strategies and the Canadian Senate and House of Commons have produced extensive reports that identify the importance and means by which poverty can be reduced in Canada. These reports complement a recent Senate report on the social determinants of health. A private member's anti-poverty bill has been introduced in the House of Commons.

Against this, the ruling Conservative government in Ottawa has refused to even acknowledge that poverty in Canada is worthy of attention. The prospect of a more receptive minority federal government following a 2011 election is uncertain. The growing interest in proportional representation as means of sending elected officials to Canada's legislatures has the potential to produce more-poverty-sensitive members of governing legislatures. Since minority governments and the institution of proportional representation would probably lead to the enactment of progressive public policy in Canada that addresses the incidence of poverty and its adverse effects, such developments are to be encouraged.

In the first edition of *Poverty in Canada*, I suggested that Canada may be on the verge of adopting a societal vision that would reduce, if not eliminate, poverty in Canada. To date, the opposite—the institution of policies that maintain or increase levels of poverty—has been the case. Hopefully, this volume will assist in the reversal of our current course of action and lead to the reduction, and possibly the elimination, of poverty in Canada.

Dennis Raphael
Toronto, Ontario
March 2011

A Note from the Publisher

Thank you for selecting *Poverty in Canada: Implications for Health and Quality of Life*, written by Dennis Raphael. The author and publisher have devoted considerable time and careful development (including meticulous peer reviews at proposal phase and first draft) to this book. We appreciate your recognition of this effort and accomplishment.

Teaching Features

This volume distinguishes itself on the market in many ways. One key feature is the book's well-written and comprehensive part openers, which add cohesion to the section and to the whole book. The themes of the book are very clearly presented in these section openers.

The author has also greatly enhanced the book by adding extensive pedagogy. This is quite strong and well developed. Each chapter has an introduction, a conclusion, references, glossary terms, questions for critical thought, annotated further readings, and annotated related websites.

The art program is equally extensive. There are many figures, tables, and boxed inserts per chapter, as well as case studies and lived experiences throughout.

PART I

DEFINING AND MEASURING POVERTY IN CANADA

PART I PROVIDES AN OVERVIEW OF THE CONCEPT OF POVERTY, ITS importance in terms of the modern welfare state, and various means of defining and then measuring its incidence. The four chapters in this section place the incidence and experience of poverty in Canada within the context of two important theoretical concepts that help make sense of the experience of poverty in Canada: social inequality and social exclusion.

Chapter 1, "Poverty and the Modern Welfare State," provides a theoretical perspective on poverty and its relationship to public policy based on analysis of the modern welfare state. After providing some key definitions of poverty, it places the incidence of poverty within a public policy perspective. It discusses how the dominant understandings of poverty and its causes reflect both the political and economic structures of society and its prevailing attitudes toward people living in poverty. Together these factors inform governments' general approach to welfare provision. Nations differ in how they distribute resources, and these differing political economies determine how poverty and related issues are addressed. Focus is on how poverty is understood in the neo-liberal and neo-conservative paradigms, the Marxist and social democratic views, and the continental-European conservative tradition that finds its manifestation in Canada in the "red Tory" approach to governance.

Chapter 2, "Canadian Perspectives on Poverty," provides an historical overview of how Canadian policy-makers have understood the phenomenon of poverty. It then describes the various approaches to defining and measuring poverty in Canada and elsewhere. The concept of deprivation and associated indices of deprivation are provided. Work done in the United Kingdom is especially insightful. These approaches to defining and measuring poverty include the concept of absolute poverty, which is related to the development of the Market Basket Measure in Canada, and relative poverty, which informs Statistics Canada's low income cut-offs and low income measure. Various international approaches are also presented, the most important of which is the less-than-50%-of-median-income poverty indicator. Canadian poverty statistics based upon these measures are presented. An explanation is offered as to why concepts such as social inequality and social exclusion are important means of understanding the significance of these statistics.

Chapter 3, "Who Is Poor in Canada?", provides details on the incidence of poverty in Canada and identifies particularly vulnerable groups: Aboriginal populations, women, single parents, people of colour, people with disabilities, recent immigrants to Canada, and those with less education. These groups' experiences of poverty are placed within the context of public policy decisions made by federal, provincial and territorial, and local jurisdictions. These decisions occur in the areas of income guarantees, labour and employment policies, and provision of housing, education, and child care, among others. Identities that are at risk for experiencing poverty in Canada (based on class, gender, race, disability status, etc.) are not necessarily at risk of experiencing poverty in other nations that allocate resources differently.

Chapter 4, "Making Sense of Poverty: Social Inequality and Social Exclusion," places the incidence and experience of poverty in Canada within two important conceptual frameworks. The framework of *social inequality* considers how societal structures, personal identities, and current historical context lead to differing opportunities and life chances for Canadians. Particularly important are theories and analyses suggested by the work of Karl Marx and Max Weber. The conceptual framework of *social exclusion* explains how many Canadians are denied the opportunity to participate in important aspects of Canadian life. These concepts of social inequality and social exclusion provide insights into how Canadian political, economic, and social structures and processes lead these specific groups to experience poverty.

Chapter One

Poverty and the Modern Welfare State

No society can surely be flourishing and happy, of which the far greater part of the members are poor and miserable.—Adam Smith

Learning Objectives

At the conclusion of this chapter, the reader will:

- understand why poverty is a threat to Canadians' health and quality of life;
- have a sense of the meaning of living in poverty in Canada;
- be able to place the incidence of poverty in Canada within a public policy perspective;
- be able to relate the incidence and effects of poverty to various forms of the modern welfare state; and
- understand various perspectives that account for the incidence of poverty in a wealthy developed nation such as Canada.

Introduction

Canadians have traditionally considered their nation to be among the most humane and caring on the planet. Compared to the public policies of their American neighbour to the south, Canadians consider their public policies concerning the provision of health care and social services and other supports to citizens to be responsive, fair, and equitable. These supports to citizens constitute what has come to be known as the modern welfare state. Yet, Canada has one of the highest poverty rates for individuals and families among wealthy developed nations (Organisation for Economic Co-operation and Development [OECD], 2008). In reality, Canada's approach to public policy in a wide range of spheres—including public policy concerning the prevention of poverty—is quite undeveloped as compared to most European nations (OECD, 2009). And poverty is the strongest determinant of health (World Health Organization [WHO], 2008). Poverty is also the strongest determinant of a variety of other indicators of societal well-being, such as literacy levels, crime and safety, social cohesion and community solidarity, as well as general well-being (Judge and Paterson, 2002); these latter indicators are often described as measuring the quality of life.

Box 1.1: Frederich Engels on Poverty

All conceivable evils are heaped upon the poor.... They are given damp dwellings, cellar dens that are not waterproof from below or garrets that leak from above.... They are supplied bad, tattered, or rotten clothing, adulterated and indigestible food. They are exposed to the most exciting changes of mental condition, the most violent vibrations between hope and fear.... They are deprived of all enjoyments except sexual indulgence and drunkenness and are worked every day to the point of complete exhaustion of their mental and physical energies....

Source: Engels, F. (1845/1987). *The condition of the working class in England* (p. 129). New York: Penguin Classics.

This volume is about poverty in Canada and its effects upon health and quality of life. It applies a critical social science approach that aims to uncover the economic, political, and ideological forces that shape social conditions such as the extent of poverty. By understanding these forces, action can then be taken to change these conditions. More specifically, it considers poverty as resulting from governmental decisions that determine the organization and distribution of economic and social resources among the population. And these governmental decisions are shaped by both domestic and international politics and economics.

In this introductory chapter, arguments are advanced as to why the existence of poverty must be a major concern to Canadians. These arguments are based on the effects poverty has upon Canadians' individual and collective health as well as their quality of life. Combined, these outcomes influence Canada's ability to respond to the economic and social demands of a post-industrial and globalized economy.

Various definitions of poverty and frameworks are presented that assist in understanding why the incidence of poverty—with its related threats to health and quality of life—is so high in Canada as compared to many other wealthy developed nations. This sets the stage for introducing the general themes of this volume that are developed in subsequent chapters.

Why Is the Incidence and Experience of Poverty Important?

Among Canadians, the term *poverty* usually conjures up images of people living in dilapidated shacks who experience profound malnutrition and other forms of material deprivation that lead to illness and premature death. Such images accurately portray the incidence and experience of poverty for much of the world's population. And such poverty is indeed the cause of profoundly high levels of disease and illness, premature death, and general misery and unhappiness, in addition to political and social unrest, in the developing world (Leon and Walt, 2001).

In wealthy developed nations such as Canada, poverty is best understood as the experience of material and social deprivation that prevents individuals and communities, and even entire societies, from reaching their full human and societal potential (Townsend, 1993). This is the case since living under conditions of material and social deprivation limits participation in a wide range of cultural, economic, educational, political, and other societal activities normally expected in a wealthy developed nation. While not as obviously devastating to individual and community health and quality of life as the experience of poverty in the developing world, exclusion from these activities has important health consequences and implications for Canadians' quality of life (Guildford, 2000).

There are numerous reasons why having large numbers of Canadians experiencing the material and social deprivation and social exclusion associated with poverty should be of concern. These include developmental, economic, ethical, legal, health, safety, and spiritual concerns, among others.

Developmental concerns centre on Canadians failing to reach their full cognitive and emotional potentials as human beings. In these early years of the 21st century, human capacity for growth, achievement, creativity, and problem solving appears to be almost boundless. However, the attainment of such human heights is difficult for most people living in poverty and possibly impossible for many. Living in poverty is especially problematic for families with children (Esping-Andersen, 2002).

Economic concerns relate to the inability of Canadians to develop the skills that are necessary to cope in a rapidly changing economic environment. The demands of a rapidly evolving economic environment require the citizenry to adjust to rapidly changing occupational requirements (see Box 1.2). Living under conditions of material and social deprivation makes the accumulation of the cognitive and social skills necessary for such adaptation difficult. From an *ethical* perspective, Canadians share a belief that all members of society should have an opportunity to lead rich, fulfilling lives and that no one should face barriers that make such goals difficult or even impossible to obtain (Corak, 2005). As will be documented in the chapters to follow, poverty is a profound barrier to such opportunity.

Legally, the Canadian Constitution, including the Charter of Rights and Freedoms, and numerous international covenants to which Canada is a signatory require that Canadians be provided with the opportunities and supports required to live fulfilling lives free of fear, deprivation, and exclusion. By these legal criteria, Canada falls far short of meeting these legal requirements (see Box 1.3). Numerous reports have documented some of the failings of Canada in this regard.

Health concerns focus on poverty as a primary cause of disease, illness, and shortened life expectancy. For example, Canadians who live in the poorest 20% of urban neighbourhoods in Canada have significantly shorter life expectancies than other Canadians (Wilkins, 2007) (see Figure 1.1). Living in poverty is an especially important threat to the health of children since it has both immediate and long-lasting effects upon health.

Box 1.2: Poverty, Children, and the Modern Welfare State: Toward a Preventive Strategy

There is one basic finding that overshadows all others, namely that remedial policies for adults are a poor (and costly) substitute for interventions in childhood. Since a person's job and career prospects depend increasingly on his or her cognitive abilities, this is where it all begins. Activating or retraining adults is profitable and realistic if these same adults already come with a sufficient ability to learn. Households with limited resources can probably never be eradicated entirely, but their relative proportion can be minimized and this is our single greatest policy challenge. With this aim in mind, what does the scientific evidence tell us?

First and foremost, it all begins in early childhood. At this point, three factors are of crucial importance: health, income poverty, and "developmental priming mechanisms" such as reading to children, social stimuli, and guidance. Families with limited resources are likely to fall short on all three counts. A strong welfare state in the conventional sense can avert the first two factors, but if cognitive stimulation is key, we must rethink policy. We cannot pass laws that force parents to read to their children, but we can compensate. One option is to ensure that parents of small children are given the possibility of low-stress employment and adequate time with their children. A second, perhaps more effective option, is to promote universal, high-quality day care.

Source: Esping-Andersen, G. (2002). A child centred social investment strategy. In G. Esping-Andersen (Ed.), *Why we need a new welfare state* (p. 19). New York: Oxford University Press.

Promoting health and preventing disease is a long-established goal of health policy in Canada and essential to the sustainability of the health care system.

In relation to *safety*, it is well established that the incidence and experience of poverty is the primary cause of crime in communities (National Crime Prevention Program, 2003). The presence of poverty profoundly affects what Canadians normally think of as their quality of life.

Public Policy and Poverty

The term *social policy* is usually used to refer to issues that have direct relevance to social welfare, such as social assistance, child and family policy, and housing policy, but the argument expressed in this volume is that the incidence and experience of poverty is shaped by a broader range of public policy issues that include labour and employment, revenue, and tax policies, among others.

Box 1.3: United Nations Condemns Canada's Treatment of People in Poverty

UN Lashes out at Canada for Failure to End Poverty
Helen Branswell

LONDON—A United Nations committee issued a damning report Friday on Canada's treatment of the poor, single mothers and natives.

The UN Committee on Economic, Social and Cultural Rights issued a blistering attack on Canada's record over the last five years, saying the country has not ensured Canadians enjoy economic and social rights guaranteed by a UN covenant to which Ottawa is a signatory.

The committee's report painted a picture of a country that isn't taking care of citizens living at the low end of the economic spectrum, highlighting "crisis" levels of homelessness, skyrocketing usage of food banks, deep cuts to welfare rates and inadequate funding for battered women's shelters.

"The committee is gravely concerned that such a wealthy country as Canada has allowed the problem of homelessness and inadequate housing to grow to such proportions that the mayors of Canada's 10 largest cities have now declared homelessness a national disaster," said the report, released Friday in Geneva.

It placed particular emphasis on the living conditions of many First Nations communities.

"To me, this gives a black eye to Canada from a respected United Nations body," said Bill Namagoose, executive director of the Grand Council of the Cree, which made a presentation to the committee.

"Canada goes around the world saying that it's a champion of human rights.... I think he [Prime Minister Jean Chrétien] has to begin to address the situation in his backyard, also."

The committee was highly critical of the federal government for effectively shelving the report of the Royal Commission on Aboriginal Peoples.

"We are concerned about the high disparity between aboriginal people and the majority of Canadians, in terms of inadequate housing, high unemployment rate, the high rate of suicide and the lack of safe and adequate drinking water and the dispossession of their lands," committee chairwoman Virginia Dandan said at a news conference Friday.

The committee made 21 recommendations—calling the need for low-income housing to be treated as "a national emergency"—in a report that emphasized 26 areas of "principal" concern.

It called for national standards for welfare, reform of the Employment Insurance program so more workers are covered and more money from all levels of government to combat women's poverty and poverty among children.

"It's obviously one of the most scathing critiques of an affluent country that's ever been released by a UN human-rights body," said Bruce Porter, a spokesman for Charter Committee on Poverty Issues, one of several social-advocacy groups which made presentations to the UN committee.

Foreign Affairs Minister Lloyd Axworthy was cautious about responding, saying he hadn't read the report.

But he suggested some of the figures the committee relied on were from 1995, "so they don't take into account many of the initiatives that have been taken by this government." But non-governmental organizations like Porter's and Ontario's Low Income Families Together briefed the committee extensively on the current situation in Canada, so it was aware of new initiatives such as the National Child Benefit.

It just wasn't impressed that while Ottawa has instituted a program to help children in poor families, all but two provincial governments claw back the benefits.

As one of the 137 signatories to the UN covenant on economic, social and cultural rights, Canada must report to the committee every five years on progress it is making ensuring it lives up to the commitments in the document.

The covenant states citizens have the right to work and form labour unions, the right to adequate living conditions and the highest attainable standards of physical and mental health.

Concerned those promises aren't being met, the committee asked Canada for answers to 81 additional questions. Last week, a Canadian delegation spent two days before the committee to address those concerns.

But the officials offered vague generalities, while the committee sought specifics on questions like why the poverty rate among single mothers has risen during the last five years, a time of economic growth, or why such a wealthy country has so many homeless people.

The repeated use of such strong language as "gravely," "deeply" and "greatly concerned" and "perturbed" in a UN report on Canada will not please the federal government, which regularly boasts Canada has topped the UN's list of best countries to live in for the last five years.

But it was music to organizations that have been trying to challenge the government's social-policy record.

"I'm very pleased to see that they essentially hauled our government on the carpet," said Josephine Grey of Low Income Families Together.

"(But) what really matters is what happens now, what comes out of it."

Source: Branswell, H. (1998, December 5). UN lashes out at Canada for failure to end poverty. *Times–Colonist* (Victoria), p. E10.

Figure 1.1: Life Expectancy of Males and Females by Income Quintile of Neighbourhood, Urban Canada, 2001

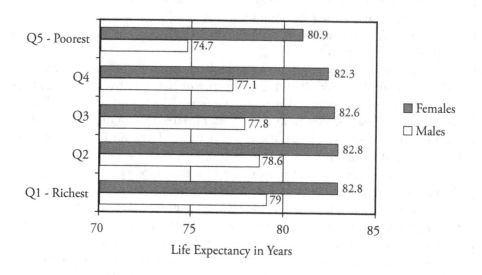

Source: Wilkins, R. (2007). *Mortality by neighbourhood income in urban Canada from 1971 to 2001.* HAMG Seminar, and special compilations. Ottawa: Statistics Canada, Health Analysis and Measurement Group (HAMG).

These public policy activities are courses of action or inaction taken by public authorities—usually governments—to address a given problem or set of problems (Briggs, 1961). Governments constantly make decisions about a wide range of issues, such as national defence and the organization and delivery of health, social, and other services. The decisions that are the special concern of this volume concern those that determine how economic and social resources are distributed among the population. Governments influence this distribution by establishing taxation levels, the nature and quality of benefits—whether these benefits are universal or targeted—and how employment agreements are negotiated. Governments are also responsible for establishing housing policies, maintaining transportation systems, enacting labour regulations and laws, and providing training related to employment and education.

The degree and depth of poverty within Canada's provinces and territories and local municipalities are strongly influenced by these public policies (Bryant, 2010). An increasing body of scholarship reveals that governmental decisions concerning how to allocate and distribute resources within the population of a jurisdiction are the primary determinants of poverty rates within a jurisdiction (Brady, 2003). Why is it that a wealthy developed nation such as Canada has 15% of its children living in poverty while far less wealthy nations such as Denmark and Finland have less than 3.0% of their children living in such conditions (OECD, 2008)?

Figure 1.2: Child Poverty in Wealthy Nations, Mid-2000s

Percentage of Children Living in Relative Poverty Defined as Households with <50% of the National Median Household Income

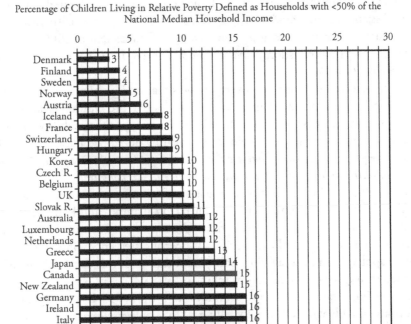

Source: Adapted from Organisation for Economic Co-operation and Development. (2008). *Growing unequal: Income distribution and poverty in OECD nations* (Table 5.2, p. 138). Paris: OECD.

It is argued in this volume that these differences are a result of public policy decisions that directly influence the incidence and lived experience of those living in poverty. These public policy decisions affect the availability of supports to children and families, benefits for those experiencing disability and unemployment, the amount of taxation and revenue available for programs, wages and employment security and benefits, and the distribution of other economic and social resources within the population. The incidence and experience of poverty have direct effects on the health of individuals, communities, and societies, and on a variety of indicators of quality of life.

Understanding and Explaining Poverty

How a phenomenon such as poverty is understood and explained profoundly influences our beliefs concerning poverty's causes and effects, and whether and how poverty should be addressed. Poverty can be defined in various ways. In one view—and this is the view normally associated with poverty in the developing world—poverty occurs when an individual or community is lacking the basic necessities of life (United Nations, 1995). These necessities include food, clothing, and shelter, among others. There are those who feel that such a definition also applies to poverty in Canada (Sarlo, 2000). Of course this raises the contentious question: *What are the basic necessities of life in a modern developed nation such as Canada?*

A more accepted view is that poverty is the situation in which individuals and communities lack access to the resources and amenities that are typically available to members of a society (Townsend, 1993). In this view, poverty is the inability to take advantage of all of the opportunities provided by a wealthy developed nation such as Canada. This view begs the question: *What are the resources and amenities required for individuals and communities to be healthy and reach their full human potential?*

Deciding upon which definition to use is very important. Use of the first benchmark finds there to be virtually no poverty in Canada (Williamson and Reutter, 1999). However, applying the second benchmark finds Canada to have one of the highest rates of poverty among wealthy developed nations. On what criteria does one decide which definition to apply? What are the public policy implications of this decision? These issues are examined throughout the chapters to follow.

Another important issue is how to understand the causes of poverty. Does poverty result from individual or community failings? Do people come to live in poverty because they lack education, have low motivation, adopt deviant lifestyles, or live in situations where they receive little community support? Or do people come to live in poverty as a result of public policies that create unjust and inequitable distribution of economic and social resources? In the first two explanations, the blame for experiencing poverty is attributed to characteristics of individuals and communities. In the last, poverty is seen as resulting from public policy decisions over which individuals and communities living in poverty have very little control.

Stemming from these questions are differences in how to respond to the incidence of poverty. Is the incidence of poverty—and the associated effects upon health and quality of life—primarily an issue to be dealt with through interventions with individuals and communities? Or is the problem of poverty—and the means of alleviating it—primarily political and economic issues to be addressed by policy-makers? If the answer is the latter, then there must be inquiry into how governments come to develop policies that create poverty. And central to this inquiry is identifying the various political and economic forces that influence governments to take these courses of action.

Explaining Poverty

The discussion of poverty in wealthy developed nations such as Canada has a strong moral undertone. More specifically, the distinction is sometimes made between the deserving and undeserving poor. The *deserving poor* are those whose poverty is seen as resulting from events outside of their control (Lister, 2004). These events may include acute or chronic illness, accidents, or the presence of a disability. The *undeserving poor* are those whose poverty is believed to result from some combination of sloth, moral turpitude, or other personal failings. The evidence in support of this distinction is lacking but this has not stopped governments and the public from making it.

In theory, making this distinction should result in more generous assistance and benefits being targeted to the "deserving" (i.e., sick, injured, or those with disabilities), rather than the "undeserving" (i.e., unemployed or low waged) poor. In reality, however, the benefits provided on the basis of this distinction tend to be rather similar in most nations. And in Canada, the benefits provided under both rubrics are very modest, placing recipients well below the poverty line (OECD, 2009).

These different ways of thinking about poverty represent what are termed *discourses*. Put simply, a discourse is the manner in which a society chooses to make sense of a phenomenon. The notion of discourse, however, also includes the idea that some frameworks of understanding are more easily acceptable at a given point in history because of how they fit with the dominant politics and economic processes of a society.

The view that poverty results from personal failings as well as the alternative view that poverty results from societal factors are both examples of discourses. There are three specific discourses that, while developed to consider the concept of social exclusion (see Chapter 4), have clear relevance to the understanding of poverty. These are the moral underclass (MUD), social integrationist (SID), and redistributionist (RED) (Levitas, 2005).

The MUD discourse essentially views poverty as reflecting the motivational and moral failings of those who are poor. Poverty is seen as a cultural phenomenon whereby people living in poverty come to be so by virtue of their lacking skills and adopting deviant habits, lifestyles, and attitudes. Related to this discourse is concern about overly generous welfare and other program benefits creating dependency, thereby reducing motivation to join the workforce. Levitas (2005) sees a gendered discourse as well: as a result of these personal failings, males are seen as becoming delinquents and criminals, whereas females are seen as becoming unwed mothers.

The RED discourse views poverty as resulting from the systematic exclusion of individuals from the economic and social resources required for participation in society. Much of this results from the operation of the market as a primary arbiter and distributor of resources within a society. Problems of poverty do not result from individual failings but from the failure of society to meet the economic and social needs of its citizens. It fails to do so by providing meagre benefits, lack of employment and educational opportunities, and low wages. The responses to poverty should be based on issues of extending citizenship rights by providing all citizens with what is necessary for a fulfilling existence.

The SID discourse is about including people living in poverty by engaging them in the workforce. The SID discourse need not be limited to issues of paid employment and can include other means of inclusion. However, Levitas argues that the usual direction involves active involvement in the market, while citizenship rights and entitlement to benefits are de-emphasized.

Box 1.4: Various Discourses on Poverty

The MUD (Moral Underclass) Discourse:

- asserts that the underclass or socially excluded are culturally distinct from the "mainstream";
- focuses on the behaviours of the poor rather than the structure of society;
- holds that benefits are bad for those who receive them, as they encourage dependency;
- is gendered: asserts that idle men become criminals and women become single mothers;
- does not acknowledge unpaid work;
- views dependency on the state as a problem, but does not view personal economic dependency—especially of women and children on men—as a problem.

The RED (Redistributionist) Discourse:

- views poverty as a primary cause of social exclusion;
- asserts that poverty can be reduced through benefit increases;
- places a value on unpaid work;
- includes a critique of inequality and moves beyond minimalist models of inclusion by addressing social, political, and economic citizenship;
- focuses on the processes that create inequality;
- implies radical reductions of inequalities and a redistribution of power and resources.

The SID (Social Integrationist) Discourse:

- has a narrow focus on paid work;
- does not ask why people not working are consigned to poverty;
- obscures issues of inequality among paid workers;
- has little focus on women and their receipt of lower pay than men, ignoring gender and class issues;
- does not illuminate inequality between owners of productive capacity and the bulk of the population;
- ignores unpaid work, implying acceptance of increases in women's total workload;
- undermines the legitimacy of non-participation in paid work.

Source: Adapted from Levitas, R. (2005). *The inclusive society: Social exclusion and new labour* (2nd ed.). Basingstoke, UK: Palgrave.

These discourses were developed for application to the British scene but have clear implications for understanding the public policy debate over poverty in Canada. The MUD discourse is the dominant explanatory discourse for understanding Canadian policy approaches toward social assistance, minimum wage, and employment insurance–eligibility requirements. It represents an implicit—and frequently explicit—view that it is necessary to make living on government benefits so unpleasant as to motivate individuals to join the workforce. At the very minimum, the approach makes living conditions extremely difficult for those who must rely on such benefits, and by doing so, threatens individual and community health. In its most extreme manifestation, it results in blatant "poor bashing" by which people who are living in poverty become subject to stigmatization and ridicule, thereby adding psychological and social insult to the injury of material deprivation (Swanson, 2001).

The SID discourse as outlined by Levitas sees its manifestation in the creation of efforts to include the non-working in—some say coerce into—the paid labour force. The public policy examples of this in Canada have generally been punitive in nature. These include workfare programs whose application appears to have more in common with the MUD rather than SID discourse. Alternatively, the SID discourse in Canada has also involved a variety of attempts by non-governmental agencies to ameliorate the most egregious conditions of social exclusion that result from inequitable distribution of economic and other material resources (Guildford, 2000).

The question of the extent to which such SID efforts can counteract the political and economic forces that drive increasing income and wealth inequality constitutes the heart of the RED or redistributionist discourse. In this approach, the primary problem is one of unequal distribution of wealth and power, thereby driving the incidence of poverty. These discourses are presented as pure types, but in practice they may be mixed. But they do accurately portray the various means by which Canadians and their policy-makers have come to understand the causes and effects of poverty (see Table 1.1).

According to Levitas, the discourses can be simply stated. In the MUD discourse, the problem is that people living in poverty have no morals. In SID, the problem is that people living in poverty have no jobs. In RED, the problem is that people living in poverty have no money. In this volume, the primary approach applied to understanding the incidence and consequences of poverty is the RED discourse. It views the source of poverty as being the unfair distribution of resources that are driven by inequalities in power and influence. The solutions advanced are primarily political and economic and involve action by social movements to influence governments through advocacy and involvement in electoral politics.

Related to the MUD, SID, and RED discourses are other discourses with application to the Canadian scene.

The *neo-liberal discourse* reflects a re-embrace of free-market ideology that first began to manifest in the mid-1970s. It helps to explain some recent changes in how governments address poverty. This represents a contrast to a communal view, whereby the government or state intervenes in the operation of the market economy to provide

Table 1.1: Examples of MUD, RED, and SID Discourses in Canada

Moral Underclass	Redistributionist	Social Integrationist
Extremely low levels of social assistance benefits across Canada	Hands-Off Campaign to end clawback of the National Child Benefit to social assistance recipients	Vibrant Communities Initiative
Reduction of eligibility for employment insurance in Canada	Growing Gap Report and similar initiatives from the Centre for Social Justice	Laidlaw Foundation Inclusion Initiative
Poor-bashing by Canadian governments and media	Numerous reports and statements from the National Council of Welfare	Workfare Initiatives across Canada*

* Note that many punitive elements associated with these initiatives can easily be placed within the MUD discourse.

benefits and supports associated with the welfare state (Coburn, 2000). The most obvious examples of the neo-liberal discourse are the political and economic regimes associated with Ronald Reagan in the USA, Margaret Thatcher in the UK, and Jean Chrétien in Canada.

Canada saw a dramatic restructuring of federal public policy during the Chrétien era of the 1990s. The Canadian government withdrew its involvement and funding from policy areas such as housing, dramatically changed the manner and amount of its monetary transfers to the provinces, and reshaped policy in favour of business and trade (Langille, 2009). The result was a dramatic reduction in program spending by the federal and provincial governments during the 1990s (Scarth, 2004). Not surprisingly, the period saw virtually no reduction in the extent of poverty in Canada, and many argue that the neo-liberal approach served to make the lives of people living in poverty even more difficult than was already the case (Coburn, 2010).

There has been a slight reversal of this trend in recent years with the federal government increasing spending in some areas such as housing, child care, and benefits to low-income families. Some provinces have raised social assistance rates and minimum wages (National Council of Welfare, 2010). These actions however, have been more than offset by growing income and wealth inequalities, with the result that little dent was made in poverty rates. The role of government investment in social infrastructure and support of Canadians through cash and other benefits is examined in the following chapters.

Neo-conservatism, like neo-liberalism, reflects a commitment to the role of the market as arbiter of resource distribution, but adds a moral tone to its policy approach toward poverty by attributing blame to those who are poor (Jeffrey, 1999). The best examples of this in Canada have been the Klein government in Alberta, the Harris government in Ontario, and the Campbell government in British Columbia. Under these regimes, people living in poverty are implicitly—and frequently explicitly—seen as responsible for their own sad state of affairs (Swanson, 2001). It should be noted that while these provincial governments explicitly blame poor people for their situation, many other Canadian governments have similar, though more hidden, attitudes toward people living in poverty. These attitudes are illustrated by their very stingy social assistance benefits and refusal to raise minimum wages to a level that allows for health and well-being.

People who live in poverty in these neo-conservative jurisdictions frequently report feeling ostracized and treated with disrespect by governmental authorities and agencies (Swanson, 2001). In addition to being asked to survive on clearly inadequate social assistance benefits or minimum wages, people in poverty must also cope with others laying blame for their situation on them. The issue of poor-bashing and who benefits from this is examined in later chapters.

The *Marxist*—and the related *social democratic*—discourse exists in opposition to the neo-liberal and neo-conservative discourses. It argues that the existence of poverty serves a variety of purposes for the wealthy and for corporations who dominate the economy. Since poverty results from the unequal distribution of economic resources within the population, every dollar not provided to individuals at the lower end of the socio-economic ladder is an additional dollar for those at the top (Wright, 1994). The individuals at the top do all they can to influence governments to maintain high levels of poverty since they profit from this. For the corporate sector, the presence of large pools of unemployed and poorly paid workers depresses wages, maximizes profits, and creates a split between members of the working class who are employed and those who are not.

The *feminist* critique focuses on why women are more vulnerable to living in poverty. It argues that there has been a feminization of poverty in developed nations such as Canada (Davies, McMullin, Avison, and Cassidy, 2001). This process reflects the operations of patriarchy in the society, whereby wealth, power, and prestige are made less available to women. Women become susceptible to poverty because the economic system takes no account of their bearing the greatest responsibility for child-rearing. This responsibility limits women's engagement in the workforce, making them less eligible for benefits. Social assistance rates take little account of the costs of raising children, such that being a female lone parent is strongly related to living in poverty.

The *racialization of poverty* discourse explains why people of colour are more susceptible to living in poverty. It sees people of colour as being especially susceptible to social inequality and the processes of social exclusion (Galabuzi, 2005). For example, people of colour in Canada are twice as likely to be living in poverty than other Canadians. This results from processes of discrimination and racism that are heightened by competition within the economic system and the greater concentration of wealth and power among the economic elites of society.

The Welfare State Typology

Another important theme developed throughout this volume is that the form welfare states take in capitalist societies profoundly influences the incidence of poverty. Nations systematically differ in how they approach the provision of supports and security across the lifespan (Esping-Andersen, 1990, 1999). These different forms of the welfare state influence the incidence of poverty, its health-and-quality-of-life-related effects, and public policy responses to poverty. The form of the welfare state influences—and is in itself influenced by—citizens' values and attitudes. Three forms of the modern welfare state have been identified: liberal, conservative, and social democratic (Bambra, 2009).

Canada, Ireland, the UK, and the USA are identified as *liberal welfare states*. With an emphasis on liberty, these nations rely upon the market to distribute goods and resources within the population (Saint-Arnaud and Bernard, 2003). Labour unions are weak, and only a minority of workers are covered by collective employment agreements. Associated with this is rather modest spending on social programs and reliance upon means-tested assistance rather than the provision of universal benefits for all. Means testing refers to benefits being primarily geared to low-income groups.

Social assistance is limited by traditional work-ethic attitudes that tend to stigmatize the needy and attribute failure to individual, rather than societal, failures. This reflects an implicit—and frequently explicit—view that people are poor due to their own failings. This individualistic approach fails to acknowledge the structural causes of poverty, such as public policies that skew the distribution of economic and other resources.

Conservative welfare states such as France, Germany, Belgium, and the Netherlands offer generous benefits and provide these based on employment status with emphasis on male primary breadwinners. Only a minority of workers belong to labour unions, but interestingly, a large majority of workers are covered by collective employment agreements. This represents a societal commitment to solidarity and the promotion of social cohesion. There is rather less explicit effort to support women in their complex employment and caregiver roles. The vast majority of benefits are earnings-related and contributory rather than universal entitlements as is the case with social democratic nations. It is assumed that the family will play an important role in supporting citizens.

Social democratic welfare states such as Sweden, Denmark, Norway, and Finland emphasize the role of the state in securing citizen rights. Emphasis is placed upon reducing inequality. Labour unions are strong, and a large majority of workers are covered by collective employment agreements. These nations have strong universal entitlement programs and strive to achieve full employment. Income and wealth inequalities are minimized by strong redistributive programs that involve progressive income taxes and generous health, social, and other benefits. Employment security and training are well resourced. Families are supported by state benefits when difficulties arise. Strong supports such as parental benefits and leave, child care, and equity-oriented labour and employment policies are provided for women.

Navarro and Shi drew upon Esping-Andersen's insights to relate welfare state type to a variety of indicators that included poverty rates and health status (Navarro and

Shi, 2002). Social democratic regimes show the lowest levels of poverty, less income inequality, and the best health; Liberal regimes show the highest levels of poverty and inequality, and the poorest health; Conservative regimes are in the mid-range. How does a nation come to belong to one of these groups? How can a nation—given its characteristics—come to adopt policies that will reduce poverty and associated health-and-quality-of-life effects? And how do these decisions explain the differences seen between individuals living in poverty and those who are not? These issues inform much of the content of this volume.

Social Determinants of Health: Linking Policy Decisions to Poverty, Health, and Quality of Life

Another theme running throughout this volume is that public policy determines the incidence and experience of poverty within a nation. Public policy does this by shaping the material and social conditions to which individuals and communities are exposed. Poverty represents a situation whereby these material and social conditions are so deprived as to threaten health and the quality of life. The mediating mechanisms between public policy decisions and the incidence and experience of poverty are the social determinants of health (Raphael, 2009b).

Social determinants of health are the economic and social conditions that shape the health of individuals, communities, and jurisdictions as a whole. Canadian researchers have outlined 14 of these: Aboriginal status, disability status, early life, education, employment and working conditions, food security, health services, housing, income and income distribution, race, social exclusion, social safety net, and unemployment and employment insecurity (Raphael, 2009a). Social determinants such as Aboriginal status, disability status, gender, and race do not by themselves lead to differing outcomes in living conditions. Rather, having this identity interacts with the way society is organized to produce conditions of vulnerability that make living in poverty more likely. In essence, social determinants of health are concerned with the quantity and quality of resources society makes available to its members.

For those living in poverty, the quality of their exposure to other determinants is compromised. For example, early life is an important social determinant of health that is compromised by the experience of living in poverty. Public policies that would either reduce the incidence of poverty among families with children or help remedy poverty's most egregious effects would be adequate minimum wages and higher social assistance benefits. Making regulated quality child care available along with other family services would help ameliorate the effects of poverty on children and families.

Employment and working conditions are another important social determinant of health. People living in poverty are more likely to have lower paying and more insecure employment. Public policies that would improve employment and working conditions, thereby reducing the incidence of poverty as well as its effects on health and quality of life, would include an active labour policy involving greater training and job creation to prevent poverty. It would also include enhanced regulation and enforcement of safety measures to help ameliorate poverty's effects. Support for collective employment bargaining and increasing worker control in the workplace would both reduce the incidence of poverty and also help ameliorate its effects.

Similar public policy action is possible in the case of other social determinants of health that are closely linked to living in poverty, such as education (e.g., increase support for literacy training, increase public spending on education, and reduce post-secondary tuition); food security (e.g., improve income supports, reduce poverty through job creation, improve food policy, and provide affordable housing); health services (e.g., increase public spending, promote access, and integrate services); and housing (e.g., improve income supports, provide affordable housing, institute controls on rental costs, and provide social housing).

This would also be the case in regard to income and income distribution (e.g., institute fair taxation policy, raise minimum wages, increase social assistance benefits, and provide family supports); social exclusion (e.g., enforce anti-discrimination laws, improve English-as-a-Second-Language education, enhance job training, and approve foreign credentials); social safety net (e.g., spend on a wide range of welfare state areas); and unemployment (e.g., promote active labour policy, improve unemployment benefits, and strengthen employment security through labour legislation).

Such policy actions are important since the quality of the social determinants of health determines the health status and quality of life of individuals, communities, and the nation as a whole. Social determinants of health shape the extent to which individuals, their communities, and the societal collective are provided with the physical, social, and personal resources to identify and achieve aspirations, satisfy needs, and cope with the environment. Poverty leads to a situation where exposures to various social determinants of health are so problematic as to result in a clustering of disadvantage. This clustering of disadvantage has particular effects upon the health and quality of life of children. Figure 1.3 shows that children living in poverty are especially likely to show poor functional health as measured by testing on eight basic attributes: vision, hearing, speech, mobility, dexterity, cognition, emotion, and pain and discomfort (Ross and Roberts, 1999).

The relationships among public policy, social determinants of health, the incidence and experience of poverty, and health and quality of life are iterative in that changes in one segment of the sequence influence both preceding and consequent ones. However, key social determinants of health such as income, unemployment and employment security, and the social safety net are the primary determinants of the incidence of poverty. Therefore, the primary approach taken in this volume is that of a directional sequence, as follows:

Public Policy → Social Determinants of Health → Incidence of Poverty → Health and QOL

Yet, once an individual experiences poverty, the quality of other social determinants of health, such as housing and food security, are compromised. And these difficulties are

Figure 1.3: Annual Family Income and Percentage of Children with Lower Functional Health, Canada, Includes Only Two-Parent Families, 1994–1995

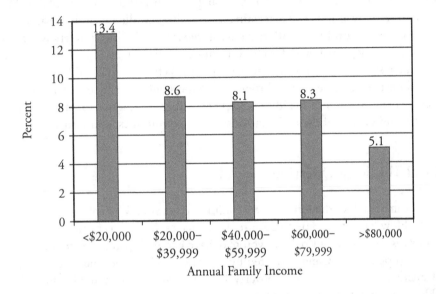

Source: From Ross, D.P., and Roberts, P. (1999). *Income and child well-being: A new perspective on the poverty debate* (p. 24). Ottawa: Canadian Council on Social Development. Prepared by the Canadian Council on Social Development using the National Longitudinal Survey of Children and Youth, 1994–1995.

compounded by poorly developed public policy that fails to adequately respond to the accumulation of deprivation. Public policy both creates poverty and also provides means of ameliorating its most egregious aspects. Therefore a more nuanced model would be as follows:

Public Policy → SDOH → Incidence of Poverty → SDOH → Public Policy → Health and QOL

Conclusions

In this volume, a critical social science approach that identifies the political and economic forces that create and maintain poverty is taken. The approach draws upon elements of sociological and political theory with emphasis upon the insights provided by the field of political economy. One of the most important contributions from the field of political economy is that the welfare state takes different forms in different nations. Canada's form of liberal welfare state is similar to that of Ireland, the United Kingdom, and the USA. It is very different from that seen in the Scandinavian countries and continental Europe. The political economy of Canada's welfare state shapes the incidence of poverty and its subsequent effects upon health and quality of life by setting the parameters within which public policy operates to influence resource production and distribution, thereby influencing the incidence of poverty.

The incidence and experience of poverty shapes the health and quality of life of Canadians. Poverty is an important determinant of health and illness, and a variety of non-medical outcomes subsumed within the term *quality of life*. Since poverty is the experience of material deprivation and exclusion from Canadian life, it leads to the inability to acquire the resources that allow participation in the activities expected from living in an advanced developed society. It is through these mechanisms that the quality of numerous social determinants of health are weakened, thereby leading to various threats to the health and quality of life of Canadians, their communities, and Canada as a whole.

Critical Thinking Questions

1. What images does the term *poverty* conjure up for you? What about *poverty in Canada*? How have you come to acquire these images? What has formed the content of your discussions about poverty you may have had with parents or friends?
2. How is poverty in Canada treated by the media? How does media coverage shape Canadians' understanding of poverty, its causes, and what should be done about it?
3. How has poverty been treated by courses or classes you may have undertaken?
4. How has what you have read in this chapter concerning poverty in Canada been consistent or inconsistent with the understanding you had prior to reading it?
5. Think about recent federal, provincial, and municipal election campaigns. Which party or parties have raised poverty as an election issue? Why do you think this has been the case? Which party do you think would make the greatest effort to address poverty? Why?

Recommended Readings

Blaxter, M. (2010). *Health* (2nd ed.). Cambridge, UK: Polity Press.
   This volume considers the key debates surrounding the concept of health today. It discusses how health is defined, constructed, experienced, and acted out in contemporary developed societies, drawing on a range of empirical data and theoretical approaches from a variety of nations. It considers conceptual models of the relationship of health to the structure of society, from inequality in health to the ideas of social capital, the risk society, and theories of evolutionary biology.
Bryant, T., Raphael, D., and Rioux, M. (2010). *Staying alive: Critical perspectives on health, illness, and health care* (2nd ed.). Toronto: Canadian Scholars' Press Inc.
   This book provides a range of approaches for understanding health issues. In addition to traditional health sciences and sociological approaches, this new book also provides the human rights and political economy perspectives on health. It focuses on these issues in Canada and the United States within an international context.

Esping-Andersen, G. (2002). *Why we need a new welfare state*. New York: Oxford University Press.

> Contributors argue that welfare states need to consider issues of social inclusion and justice. The volume focuses on four social domains: the aged and the transition to retirement; welfare issues related to changes in working life; risks and needs that arise in households, especially in families with young children; and the challenges of creating gender equality.

Lister, R. (2004). *Poverty*. Cambridge, UK: Polity Press.

> This book explores the meaning and experience of poverty in the contemporary world. It draws on thinking in the field of international development and real-life accounts to emphasize aspects of poverty such as powerlessness, lack of voice, loss of dignity and respect. In so doing, the book embraces the relational, cultural, and symbolic as well as material dimensions of poverty and makes important links between poverty and other concepts such as well-being, capabilities, social divisions and exclusion, agency, and citizenship.

Raphael, D. (2009). *Social determinants of health: Canadian perspectives* (2nd ed.). Toronto: Canadian Scholars' Press Inc.

> This collection summarizes how socio-economic factors affect the health of Canadians. It surveys the current state of the social determinants of health across Canada, and it provides an analysis of how these determinants affect Canadians' health. It has an explicit focus on public policy approaches to promoting health by improving the quality of these social determinants of health.

Relevant Websites

Campaign 2000—www.campaign2000.ca

> This website is an excellent source of child-centred information on federal and provincial budgets, political debates, and demographic reports. The campaign began shortly after the all-party motion to end child poverty by the year 2000 was passed by Parliament in 1989. Campaign 2000 represents a group of NGOs and associated researchers who see public policy as a means to ensure that no Canadian child is raised in poverty.

Luxembourg Income Study—www.lisproject.org/publications/wpapers.html

> The Luxembourg Income Study provide working papers on a range of issues related to income and other indicators. Data on Canada and other developed nations are used to produce these excellent papers that bear directly on poverty and how public policy shapes its incidence. All of the working papers can be downloaded from this site.

Organisation for Economic Co-operation and Development—www.oecd.org/home

> This site provides a wealth of reports, publications, and statistics about every aspect of society in modern developed states. Many of its contents are free or available electronically through your local university's library.

PovNet—www.povnet.org

> PovNet is an Internet site for advocates, people on welfare, and community groups and individuals involved in anti-poverty work. It provides up-to-date information about welfare and housing laws and resources in British Columbia and Canada. PovNet links to current anti-poverty issues and also provides links to other anti-poverty organizations and resources in Canada and internationally.

The Townsend Centre for International Poverty Research—www.bris.ac.uk/poverty/

> The Centre was launched on July 1, 1999, at the University of Bristol. It is dedicated to multidisciplinary research on poverty in both the developed and developing world.

Glossary Terms

Critical social science attempts to uncover the societal institutions that shape social conditions. By coming to understand the way that these institutions oppress people, action can be taken to change these forces. Critical social science also aims to fuse theory and action in order to bring about changes in the conditions that affect our lives (Seiler, n.d.).

Health is usually defined as the absence of disease. When used in this manner it is best described as *health status*. The World Health Organization (WHO) has a broader definition: the ability to have and reach goals, meet personal needs, and cope with everyday life. The WHO argues that health requires the following prerequisites: peace, shelter, education, food, income, a sound environment, and social justice. These definitions are primarily focused on the individual, while quality of life is usually focused on the larger community and society.

Political economy perspective is explicitly concerned with the political and economic structures that shape the distribution of power and resources within the population. It is also specifically focused on understanding how the creation and distribution of resources influence the health and quality of life of individuals and communities. This perspective has a strong commitment to identifying how political and economic structures can be changed to promote health and well-being.

Poverty is the condition whereby individuals, families, and groups lack the resources to obtain the type of diet, participate in the activities, and have the living conditions and amenities that are customary, or at least widely encouraged or approved of, in the society to which they belong. Poverty can be considered in terms of absolute poverty, whereby individual and families do not have enough resources to keep "body and soul together," or relative poverty, whereby they do not have the ability to participate in common activities of daily living (Gordon and Townsend, 2000).

Public policy is a course of action or inaction chosen by public authorities to address a given problem or interrelated set of problems. Policy is a course of action that is anchored in a set of values regarding appropriate public goals and a set of beliefs about the best way of achieving those goals. The idea of public policy assumes that an issue is no longer a private affair (Wolf, 2005).

Quality of life is a holistic construct that views individual and community human well-being in relation to immediate and more distant environments. It looks at both broad societal indicators and the lived experience of people. Concretely, quality of life is the extent to which individuals and communities are able to enjoy the important possibilities of life. Their ability to do so is influenced by public policies that develop and maintain a vibrant local economy; protect and enhance the natural and built environment; offer opportunities for the attainment of personal goals, hopes, and aspirations; promote a fair and equitable sharing of common resources; enable residents to meet their basic needs; and support social interaction and the inclusion of all residents in community life.

Welfare state is a nation in which organized power is used to modify the play of market forces in at least three directions: first, by guaranteeing individuals and families a minimum income irrespective of the market value of their work or property; second, by narrowing the extent of insecurity by enabling individuals and families to meet certain social contingencies (e.g., sickness, old age, and unemployment) that lead otherwise to individual and family crises; and third, by ensuring that all citizens without distinction of status or class are offered the best standards available in relation to a certain agreed range of social services (Briggs, 1961).

References

Bambra, C. (2009). Welfare state regimes and the political economy of health. *Humanity and Society, 33*(1&2), 99–117.

Brady, D. (2003). The politics of poverty: Left political institutions, the welfare state, and poverty. *Social Forces, 82*, 557–588.

Briggs, A. (1961). The welfare state in historical perspective. *European Journal of Sociology, 2*, 251–259.

Bryant, T. (2010). Politics, public policy, and health inequalities. In T. Bryant, D. Raphael, and M. Rioux (Eds.), *Staying alive: Critical perspectives on health, illness, and health care* (2nd ed., pp. 239–263). Toronto: Canadian Scholars' Press Inc.

Coburn, D. (2000). Income inequality, social cohesion, and the health status of populations: The role of neo-liberalism. *Social Science and Medicine, 51*(1), 135–146.

Coburn, D. (2010). Health and health care: A political economy perspective. In T. Bryant, D. Raphael, and M. Rioux (Eds.), *Staying alive: Critical perspectives on health, illness, and health care* (2nd ed., pp. 65–92). Toronto: Canadian Scholars' Press Inc.

Corak, M. (2005). Equality of opportunity and inequality across the generations: Challenges ahead. *Policy Options, 26*(3), 78–83.

Davies, L., McMullin, J., Avison, W., and Cassidy, G. (2001). *Social policy, gender inequality, and poverty.* Ottawa: Status of Women Canada.

Esping-Andersen, G. (1990). *The three worlds of welfare capitalism.* Princeton, NJ: Princeton University Press.

Esping-Andersen, G. (1999). *Social foundations of post-industrial economies*. New York: Oxford University Press.

Esping-Andersen, G. (2002). A child-centred social investment strategy. In G. Esping-Andersen (Ed.), *Why we need a new welfare state* (pp. 26–67). New York: Oxford University Press.

Galabuzi, G. E. (2005). *Canada's economic apartheid: The social exclusion of racialized groups in the new century*. Toronto: Canadian Scholars' Press Inc.

Gordon, D., and Townsend, P. (Eds.). (2000). *Breadline Europe: The measurement of poverty*. Bristol, UK: The Policy Press.

Guildford, J. (2000). *Making the case for social and economic inclusion*. Halifax: Population and Public Health Branch Atlantic Region, Health Canada.

Jeffrey, B. (1999). *Hard right turn: The new face of neo-conservatism in Canada*. Toronto: Harper Collins.

Judge, K., and Paterson, I. (2002). *Treasury working paper: Poverty, income inequality, and health*. Wellington, NZ: Government of New Zealand.

Langille, D. (2009). Follow the money: How business and politics shape our health. In D. Raphael (Ed.), *Social determinants of health: Canadian perspectives* (2nd ed., pp. 305–317). Toronto: Canadian Scholars' Press Inc.

Leon, D., and Walt, G. (Eds.). (2001). *Poverty, inequality, and health: An international perspective*. Oxford, UK: Oxford University Press.

Levitas, R. (2005). *The inclusive society: Social exclusion and new labour* (2nd ed.). Basingstoke, UK: Palgrave.

Lister, R. (2004). *Poverty*. Cambridge, UK: Polity Press.

National Council of Welfare. (2010). *Welfare incomes, 2009*. Ottawa: National Council of Welfare.

National Crime Prevention Program. (2003). *Factsheet: Crime prevention through social development*. Ottawa: National Crime Prevention Program.

Navarro, V., and Shi, L. (2002). The political context of social inequalities and health. In V. Navarro (Ed.), *The political economy of social inequalities: Consequences for health and quality of life* (pp. 403–418). Amityville, NY: Baywood.

Organisation for Economic Co-operation and Development. (2008). *Growing unequal? Income distribution and poverty in OECD countries*. Paris: OECD.

Organisation for Economic Co-operation and Development. (2009). *Society at a glance: OECD social indicators* (2009 ed.). Paris: OECD.

Raphael, D. (2009a). Social determinants of health: An overview of key issues and themes. In D.Raphael (Ed.), *Social determinants of health: Canadian perspectives* (2nd ed., pp. 2–19). Toronto: Canadian Scholars' Press Inc.

Raphael, D. (Ed.). (2009b). *Social determinants of health: Canadian perspectives* (2nd ed.).Toronto: Canadian Scholars' Press Inc.

Ross, D. P., and Roberts, P. (1999). *Income and child well-being: A new perspective on the poverty debate*. Ottawa: Canadian Council on Social Development.

Saint-Arnaud, S., and Bernard, P. (2003). Convergence or resilience? A hierarchical cluster analysis of the welfare regimes in advanced countries." *Current Sociology, 51*(5), 499–527.

Sarlo, C. (2000). Social assistance and poverty. *Fraser Forum, 2002*, 7–8.

Scarth, T. (Ed.). (2004). *Hell and high water: An assessment of Paul Martin's record and implications for the future.* Ottawa: Canadian Centre for Policy Alternatives.

Seiler, R. (n.d.). Human communication in the critical theory tradition. Retrieved January 20, 2011 from http://people.ucalgary.ca/~rseiler/critical.htm

Swanson, J. (2001). *Poor-bashing: The politics of exclusion.* Toronto: Between the Lines Press.

Townsend, P. (1993). *The international analysis of poverty.* Milton Keynes: Harvester Wheatsheaf.

United Nations. (1995). *Commitments of the UN World Summit on Social Development.* Copenhagen: United Nations.

Wilkins, R. (2007). *Mortality by neighbourhood income in urban Canada from 1971 to 2001.* Ottawa: Statistics Canada, Health Analysis and Measurement Group.

Williamson, D., and Reutter, L. (1999). Measuring poverty: Implications for the health of Canadians. *Health Promotion International, 14*(4), 355–364.

Wolf, R. (2005). *What is public policy?* Queen's University. Retrieved January 31, 2010 from www.ginsler.com/html/toolbox.htp

World Health Organization. (2008). *Closing the gap in a generation: Health equity through action on the social determinants of health.* Geneva: WHO.

Wright, E. O. (1994). The class analysis of poverty. In E. O. Wright (Ed.), *Interrogating inequality* (pp. 23–50). New York: Verso.

Chapter Two

Canadian Perspectives on Poverty

It would be nice if the poor were to get even half of the money that is spent in studying them.—Bill Vaughan

Learning Objectives

At the conclusion of this chapter, the reader will:

- understand how concepts of poverty are shaped by societal values and attitudes;
- be able to explain how different academic disciplines view poverty as a problem;
- have a historical perspective on how poverty in Canada has typically been viewed;
- be able to describe various means of defining and measuring the incidence of poverty;
- be able to identify current rates of poverty in Canada and explain how these differ by the measure applied; and
- understand how the incidence of poverty is related to income and wealth inequality.

Introduction

In this chapter, various means of defining poverty and measuring its incidence in Canada are presented. How Canadians and Canadian policy-makers understand the phenomenon of poverty has a profound influence upon its measured incidence, how people living in poverty experience it, and societal and governmental–policy responses to its presence. While there is strong evidence of the structural roots of poverty in wealthy developed nations, societal values and attitudes frequently attribute poverty to personal failings such as lack of ambition, sloth, or failure to attain educational credentials. When this is the case, poverty is seen as "just deserts" for these personal failings. If living in poverty is unpleasant, the reasoning goes, it should motivate individuals to somehow escape it. Poverty's unpleasantness also serves as a potent reminder to others of the costly returns of personal failure. This exemplifies the MUD or moral underclass poverty discourse presented in Chapter 1.

The SID (social integrationist) and RED (redistributionist) discourses view poverty as something that happens to people. For the most part, the argument goes, people experiencing poverty are victims of a society that either fails to include them in a range of activities (SID) or keeps them from receiving their fair share of society's resources (RED). In both views, people come to experience the material and social deprivation associated with poverty. These understandings influence how poverty is defined and measured by governments and other organizations. These understandings of poverty—and the measurements associated with them—also shape societal responses to its presence.

Adherents to the MUD discourse are likely to define poverty in a narrow, absolutist manner that appears more appropriate to the developing world than to a wealthy developed nation such as Canada. Poverty for them is the lack of basic necessities of shelter, food, and clothing (Sarlo, 2006). In contrast, SID and RED adherents prefer a relative approach where poverty is defined as individuals being denied the opportunities to participate in activities expected of citizens in a wealthy developed nation (Ross, Scott, and Smith, 2000).

The link between the discourses and defining approaches is such that absolute approaches produce very low poverty rates, making the explanation of poverty's presence more amenable to individualist and moral failure explanations. If the poverty rate is only one in 30, it is easier to blame individuals for getting themselves into their situation than to consider broader societal factors. In contrast, the relative approach produces much higher Canadian poverty rates (one in six), which makes it more difficult to blame individuals for their situation, thereby suggesting broader issues—i.e., society's inequitable distribution of economic resources and employment opportunities among its members—as a more useful explanation for the incidence of poverty.

As compared to elsewhere, there has been rather less attention given by Canadian policy-makers and researchers to defining poverty. In addition, it is of particular note that none of the measures developed and applied by the federal government—and these are the ones primarily used in Canada—are identified as poverty measures. Instead they are called measures of low income (Fellegi, 1997) (see Box 2.1). One reason for this reluctance to so label this situation arises from the normative, or prescriptive, aspect of the word poverty. The term *poverty* carries with it an implication and a moral imperative that something should be done about it (Piachaud, 1981). The term *low income*, in contrast, lacks this moral imperative. In actual practice, the various definitions of low income in use in Canada—and the figures of incidence of low income (rather high) and depth of low income (rather deep) obtained through their use—are similar to each other and to figures obtained from use of internationally agreed-upon measures of poverty (Human Resources Development Canada, 2003; National Anti-poverty Organization, 2004).

An Historical Context and Statistical Trends for Understanding Poverty in Canada

Morel provides a scholarly, and Swanson a more popular, review of poverty policy in Canada (Morel, 2002; Swanson, 2001). In Canada, a pre-industrial model of economic

Box 2.1: Statement by Statistics Canada on LICOs, Low Income, and Poverty

Recently the news media have provided increasing coverage of Statistics Canada's low income cut-offs and their relationship to the measurement of poverty. At the heart of the debate is the use of the low income cut-offs as poverty lines, even though Statistics Canada has clearly stated, since their publication began over 25 years ago, that they are not. The high profile recently given to this issue has presented Statistics Canada with a welcome opportunity to restate its position on these issues.

Many individuals and organizations both in Canada and abroad understandably want to know how many people and families live in "poverty," and how these levels change. Reflecting this need, different groups have at different times developed various measures which purported to divide the population into those who were poor and those who were not.

In spite of these efforts, there is still no internationally-accepted definition of poverty—unlike measures such as employment, unemployment, gross domestic product, consumer prices, international trade and so on. This is not surprising, perhaps, given the absence of an international consensus on what poverty is and how it should be measured. Such consensus preceded the development of all other international standards.

The lack of an internationally-accepted definition has also reflected indecision as to whether an international standard definition should allow comparisons of well-being across countries compared to some international norm, or whether poverty lines should be established according to the norms within each country.

The proposed poverty lines have included, among others, relative measures (you are poor if your means are small compared to others in your population) and absolute measures (you are poor if you lack the means to buy a specified basket of goods and services designated as essential). Both approaches involve judgmental and, hence, ultimately arbitrary choices.

In the case of the relative approach, the fundamental decision is what fraction of the overall average or median income constitutes poverty. Is it one-half, one-third, or some other proportion? In the case of the absolute approach, the number of individual judgements required to arrive at a poverty line is far larger. Before anyone can calculate the minimum income needed to purchase the "necessities" of life, they must decide what constitutes a "necessity" in food, clothing, shelter and a multitude of other purchases, from transportation to reading material.

The underlying difficulty is due to the fact that poverty is intrinsically a question of social consensus, at a given point in time and in the context of a given country. Someone acceptably well off in terms of the standards in a developing country might well be considered desperately poor in Canada. And even within the same country, the outlook changes over time. A standard of living considered as acceptable in the previous century might well be viewed with abhorrence today.

It is through the political process that democratic societies achieve social consensus in domains that are intrinsically judgmental. The exercise of such value judgements is certainly not the proper role of Canada's national statistical agency which prides itself on its objectivity, and whose credibility depends on the exercise of that objectivity.

In Canada, the Federal/Provincial/Territorial Working Group on Social Development Research and Information was established to create a method of defining and measuring poverty. This group, created by Human Resources Development Canada and social services ministers in the various jurisdictions, has proposed a preliminary market basket measure of poverty—a basket of market-priced goods and services. The poverty line would be based on the income needed to purchase the items in the basket.

Once governments establish a definition, Statistics Canada will endeavour to estimate the number of people who are poor according to that definition. Certainly that is a task in line with its mandate and its objective approach. In the meantime, Statistics Canada does not and cannot measure the level of "poverty" in Canada.

For many years, Statistics Canada has published a set of measures called the low income cut-offs. We regularly and consistently emphasize that these are quite different from measures of poverty. They reflect a well-defined methodology which identifies those who are substantially worse off than the average. Of course, being significantly worse off than the average does not necessarily mean that one is poor.

Nevertheless, in the absence of an accepted definition of poverty, these statistics have been used by many analysts to study the characteristics of the relatively worst off families in Canada. These measures have enabled us to report important trends, such as the changing composition of this group over time. For example, 20 to 30 years ago the elderly were by far the largest group within the "low income" category, while more recently lone-parent families headed by women have grown in significance.

Many people both inside and outside government have found these and other insights to be useful. As a result, when Statistics Canada carried out a wide-ranging public consultation a decade ago, we were almost unanimously urged to continue to publish our low income analyses. Furthermore, in the absence of a generally accepted alternative methodology, the majority of those consulted urged us to continue to use our present definitions.

In the absence of politically-sanctioned social consensus on who should be regarded as "poor," some people and groups have been using the Statistics Canada low-income lines as a de facto definition of poverty. As long as that represents their own considered opinion of how poverty should be defined in Canada, we have no quarrel with them: all of us are free to have our own views. But they certainly do not represent Statistics Canada's views about how poverty should be defined.

Source: Fellegi, I. P., Chief Statistician of Canada, Statistics Canada, On Poverty and Low Income, 13F0027XIE1999001, April 1999; http://www.statcan.gc.ca/bsolc/olc-cel/olc-cel?catno=13F0027XIE &lang=eng

and social organization was in place until 1900. The extended family was responsible—under penalty of law—for providing for family members who might be in need. In New France, a royal decree outlawed begging. And after the English victory over the French in Quebec, houses of correction that served to punish vagrancy were established. Morel (2002) provides the following excerpt from Bellemare:

> At first, society adopted a punitive attitude towards economic dependents and especially towards those who were able-bodied. The latter were placed in confinement or in workhouses to acquire the work habit. In the nineteenth century and throughout the first half of the twentieth century, every individual was responsible for ensuring his own economic independence. (p. 105)

The organization of social assistance—and the associated attitudes toward people living in poverty—was a legacy of late 16th-century England and France traditions. English Poor Law was taken up in Nova Scotia and New Brunswick, but Upper Canada did not adopt it. With the rise of 19th-century liberalism, poverty was seen as a failure of the individual to cope with the requirements of the economic and social systems. Providing relief to the "able-bodied" would lead to sloth and laziness in those who received it. Since the British North America Act of 1867 made no mention of income security, poverty policy came to be a provincial responsibility.

During the early 20th century, municipalities provided assistance to the able-bodied and jobless. It was only when recessions and depressions swelled the ranks of the unemployed that higher levels of government stepped in. Direct aid to the unemployed came about as a result of the Employment Coordination Act of 1918. In 1920, the federal government introduced an unemployment assistance program. The assistance provided, however, had to be repaid.

By 1933, almost 15% of Canadians were receiving some form of assistance. Yet the view prevailed that generous assistance led to poverty and social unrest. In 1935, Member of Parliament Henri Bourassa stated:

> The effect of our whole so-called social legislation is to debase the social spirit of our people, to create a fast growing class of beggars, loafers and crooked men, who expect the state to give them a living and who are endeavouring to avoid any individual or collective effort to help save their own situation. (Morel, 2002, p. 21)

However, more mature understandings prevailed and, in 1940, federal unemployment insurance was established. In 1956, according to Morel (2002), the federal unemployment assistance program came to see recognition of an "entitlement to assistance." And it was in 1966 as part of Prime Minister Lester Pearson's "War on Poverty" that the Canada Assistance Plan (CAP) was introduced. These were its dominant features (Morel, 2002):

- CAP had the federal government help finance social assistance costs of the provinces;

Box 2.2: Poverty and Deservingness in Canada

At various times in the history of social assistance in Ontario, much emphasis has been made of the connection between receiving assistance and "deservingness." Did you know that the idea of work in exchange for social assistance actually originated in Elizabethan England?

In 1601, the British Parliament passed the Elizabethan Poor Law. It assigned the care of the poor to the smallest unit of government, namely local parishes. In 1834, Parliament passed the Poor Law Amendment Act, also known as the New Poor Law.

The New Poor Law distinguished between "undeserving" and "deserving" poor and between "indoor" and "outdoor" relief. The undeserving poor were those considered capable of working. They were subjected to "indoor" relief. This meant that they were forced into a workhouse where they worked in exchange for meagre food and shelter.

The deserving poor included seniors, orphans, the sick and the disabled. Because they were unable to work, they were sometimes offered "outdoor" relief, i.e. they were given money directly, although very often they, too, had to rely on the workhouse.

The British exported the English poor law model to the new world. Nova Scotia enacted a poor law in 1763, as did New Brunswick in 1786. However, when the British introduced the main body of English civil law to the new-established province of Upper Canada (Ontario) in 1791, it neglected to include a poor law. While there was no formal system of public responsibility for the poor in Upper Canada, the social and moral norms entrenched by the British poor laws had firmly taken root.

At that time in Upper Canada, most people lived primarily in small, rural communities. They were more self-sufficient than they are today. Small, family farms enabled them to produce most of their own food. They obtained other goods through barter. In emergencies, neighbours helped each other. However, it was a very different story for people who had neither family nor friends. They had to rely on whatever charity existed locally. Assistance offered by charitable organizations was usually very meagre and administered in a harsh and humiliating manner. Having to turn to charity for help was deemed shameful. Poverty was considered a personal failure, the result of a weakness of character.

Well into the 19th century, Ontario had no regular system of poor relief or income maintenance other than county jails that served as catch-all institutions for diverse categories of people. The homeless and the destitute, the insane and the elderly, under the pretext of vagrancy, were all housed together with criminals. As the population of the province increased, the need for institutional care, particularly in the urban areas, became more critical.

The provincial government adopted a resolution to force Ontario counties to establish houses of refuge. The inmates of these establishments had to work in exchange for their subsistence. For example, in the 1880s, the House of Industry in Toronto required inmates to saw wood. By 1915, each applicant for relief was required to break a crate of rocks weighing 650 pounds.

Even during the unprecedented unemployment of the Great Depression, the concept of "deserving" versus "undeserving" poor persisted. Until 1934, all single, able-bodied men were required to work in exchange for assistance. Because of the high number of unemployed, particularly in the cities, local authorities often sent poor city-dwellers to work on farms in return for assistance. In 1934, the require-ment to work in exchange for assistance was extended to able-bodied, married men. The attitude was firmly entrenched at the federal level as well. In October 1932, at the end of the third year of the Depression, Prime Minister Bennett sanctioned the creation of a nationwide system of work camps for single, able-bodied, unemployed men. In return for shelter, three meals a day, work clothes, medical care, and 20 cents a day, the men worked 44 hours a week clearing bush, building roads, plant-ing trees and constructing public buildings.

Source: From Ontario Ministry of Community and Social Service (2003). *Stories from Our Past.*

- CAP had no maximum on the allowable costs that were incurred;
- CAP required the provinces to provide assistance to those in need;
- CAP banned the introduction of workfare in Canada.

At the same time, there was a relaxation of rules for gaining unemployment insur-ance, which benefited women and youth in particular. However, all of this began to reverse during the 1990s. Federal increases in CAP contributions to the wealthiest prov-inces—BC, Alberta, and Ontario—were capped at 5% in 1990. As a result, budget cuts in social assistance were made by the provinces during the 1990s, and in 1995, the CAP program was ended and replaced by the Canada Health and Social Transfer. The result of this was to lump social welfare spending in with health and post-secondary school spending. National standards of social assistance were also eliminated, and the CAP pro-hibition of workfare programs ended. Many argue that these changes ended the right to social assistance in Canada. In addition, new restrictive eligibility rules regarding receipt of unemployment insurance benefits profoundly reduced the number of Canadians eli-gible for these benefits.

The result of all of this was movement away, during the 1980s and especially the 1990s, from a strong social safety net and reductions in the amounts of assistance avail-able to Canadians. Social assistance provided as a percentage of median incomes declined in all provinces, and in some provinces, there was an absolute decline in assistance levels. The value of the minimum wage also declined in relation to average wages and in actual value in dollars, adjusted for inflation over these periods of time.

While all of this was happening, there was a shift toward harsher governmental practices and societal attitudes in regard to Canadians living in poverty. These shifts in practices and attitudes are taken up in later chapters that focus on the lived experience of poverty and the politics of poverty.

Poverty Rates in Canada Remain Stable over Two Decades

Poverty rates from 1984 to the present are available in Canada (Statistics Canada, 2010). The most striking aspect of these data is that there has generally been little change in rates over two decades. Interestingly, there had been improvement from 2004—when the first edition of this volume was published—to 2008 (see Figure 2.1). But these 2008 data do not take into account the impact of the global economic crisis, which has certainly raised poverty rates across Canada. This qualifier should be kept in mind as you review these figures.

Rates for unattached Canadians and for children living in female-led families over these two decades are very high, and overall rates for Canadians and for children—even with the improvements seen from 2004 to 2007—are high in international comparison.

The overall poverty rate of 18.7% in 1984 dropped to 13.6% by 2008. The rate for children declined from 21.1% in 1984 to 14.2% in 2008. Canadian seniors' rates declined from 30% to 13.1% over the period. The change in older Canadians' rates had much to do with reform of the pension system and increases in benefits as a result of public pressure.

Figure 2.1: Canadian Poverty Rates over Time, 1984–2008

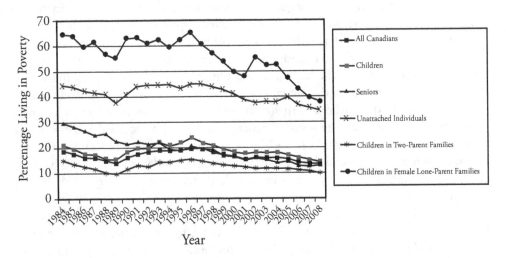

Source: "Canadian Poverty Rates Over Time, 1984-2008", adaptation from Statistics Canada CANSIM database, *http://cansim2.statcan.gc.ca*, Tables 202-2802, 202-2803, 202-2804, extracted in 2010.

The rate for unattached Canadians declined from 44.6% to 34.9%. And poverty rates for children in two-parent families declined from 15.1% to 10% in 2008, as did rates for children in female-led households—from 64.9% to a still very high 38.1%. The ebb and flow in rates is related primarily to growth and declines in the economy. The exception to this is the rates for older Canadians, which show a consistent decline over time.

As mentioned, lurking behind some of these improvements is the known threat of the economic recession, which began in 2008 and ran through 2009 and, some say, 2010. The 2008 figures represent the results of continuing growth in the economy. Historically, however, it is during recessions that people living in poverty rapidly lose much ground that is only very gradually made up (Curry-Stevens, 2009).

Validating the Study and Measurement of Poverty in Canada

Why should there be concern about poverty? While the presence of poverty is unacceptable in itself, it becomes more of a concern—and may attract more attention from policy-makers and the public—when it creates additional problems of one kind or another. Whether these are concrete problems such as increased illness, school failure, or crime, or problems of a more abstract nature, such as lack of civic participation, lower voter turnout, or declining economic productivity, an accompanying values component always contributes to the assessment of problem urgency.

In the United States, for example, poverty rates are very high, and it is apparent that these high rates contribute to very poor health status and very high crime rates as compared to other wealthy developed nations (Raphael, 2003b). Yet Americans generally do not see their high poverty rates and their consequences as urgent public policy issues. The belief in individual responsibility and the presence of powerful economic and political forces that favour the continuing accumulation of wealth among a minority of rich Americans trump concern with poverty and its effects upon health and quality of life.

Various societal sectors have identified problems that result from the presence of poverty. The medical profession considers poverty to be a concern since it threatens the immediate maintenance of the biological and physiological integrity of an individual. Poverty threatens the day-to-day functioning of bodily systems and organs. Therefore, attention is paid to those who lack shelter or are homeless, experience hunger and malnutrition, or have to make do with inadequate clothing. The medical profession also identifies immediate threats to life and limb such as poor water and sanitation. The explosion of homelessness and the use of food banks in Canada since the 1980s has been the focus of some medical researchers in Canada (Cheung and Hwang, 2004; Hwang and Bugeja, 2000).

Public health focuses upon the maintenance of biological and physiological integrity but does so within a longer time perspective. Poverty becomes a concern because material and social deprivation—in comparison to the situation of the average Canadian—has been shown to lead to a greater incidence of diseases and health conditions, or, more immediately, to the adoption of a variety of risk behaviours such as lack of adequate diet, physical inactivity, and excessive alcohol and tobacco use (Canadian Public Health Association, 1996).

While the public health agency of Canada continues to highlight the presence of poverty as a public health issue, provincial and local public health units—with some exceptions—have generally hesitated to educate the public about poverty as a public health issue (Raphael, 2003a). Some excellent examples of public health activity are available (Raphael, 2010).

The human development aspects of poverty have been the focus of the social development and social welfare sectors in Canada (Ross and Roberts, 1999). Poverty is a situation that makes the achievement of human potential difficult if not impossible to achieve. Drawing from psychologically oriented writers such as Abraham Maslow and Carl Rogers, and social development theorists such as Amarta Sen, the United Way and other community-based agencies have a continuing concern about the impact of poverty upon the human qualities of creativity, altruism, personal control, and life satisfaction (United Way of Greater Toronto, 2004; United Way of Ottawa, 2003; United Way of Winnipeg, 2003). Such problems have community and societal implications in addition to the implications for the individual.

Others have stressed how democracy and civil society are threatened by the presence of poverty (Rioux, 2010). The presence of poverty conflicts with the notion of the fair and equitable society. Section 7 of the Canadian Constitution's Charter of Rights and Freedoms, which guarantees that "everyone has the right to life, liberty and security of the person and the right not to be deprived thereof except in accordance with the principles of fundamental justice," is clearly violated by the experience of living in poverty (Government of Canada, 1982). Another Canadian example of this viewpoint is Pierre Trudeau's vision of the "just society": the promotion of equality of opportunity, support for the most disadvantaged, and provision of social security and equalization payments for those regions in most need (Trudeau, 1993). The experience of poverty makes achievement of these visions difficult.

Increasingly, the legal profession has taken up a human rights analysis of poverty (Chunn and Gavigan, 2004). Here, the argument is that living under conditions of poverty violates basic principles of justice to which Canada has committed itself through the signing of various international agreements. These agreements include the *Universal Declaration of Human Rights*, the *International Agreement on Social Development*, and the *Covenant to Eliminate All Forms of Discrimination against Women*, among others (Rioux, 2010). From this perspective, poverty is a concern because it represents conditions under which human beings are denied basic human rights of happiness, health, and well-being. Documentation of such violations in Canada is repeatedly made available to numerous international bodies.

Economics and political science disciplines are concerned with poverty because its existence leads to poor economic performance in the former case, and a weakening of democracy and democratic participation in the latter (Jackson, 2000). Living under conditions of material and social deprivation are clear threats to productivity, civil society, and the creation and maintenance of a responsive and vibrant democracy. Numerous economists have commented on the societal effects of a large number of Canadians living under conditions of material and social deprivation (Brooks, 2000; Stanford, 1999).

Finally, the faith community in Canada has raised theological concerns about the existence of poverty amid wealth and affluence (Swift, Balmer, and Dineen, 2010). It is not surprising that many faith communities of Canada view the existence of poverty as contrary to the basic visions and tenets of their faiths. The existence of poverty amid affluence in Canada is not God's Way. Certainly, there are additional perspectives from criminology, psychology, sociology, and other disciplines that reinforce the conclusion that poverty is not a phenomenon policy-makers should strive to increase. Clearly, the presence of poverty should be an important concern to Canadian policy-makers and the Canadian public.

From a practical standpoint, these approaches suggest various means of defining and measuring poverty. If the problems identified above appear only when individuals experience absolute poverty that immediately threatens life and limb, then justification is seen for using a narrow definition of poverty. If, however, these problems are apparent when individuals experience poverty as defined by a relative approach, use of a broader definition is justified. To preview the content that follows in later chapters, the evidence concerning the detrimental effects of poverty upon health and quality of life strongly suggests the value of adopting a relative approach toward defining and measuring poverty in Canada (Williamson and Reutter, 1999).

Defining and Measuring Poverty

In contrast to European efforts to first carefully define, and then to develop, appropriate measuring instruments of poverty, Canadian efforts at defining poverty have been limited.[1] Nevertheless, the implicit assumptions behind the various measures of low income used in Canada are clearly consistent with relative rather than absolute assumptions about the definition and measurement of poverty. For this reason, the findings from Canadian applications of low-income measures reported in this chapter are seen as indicating the incidence and depth of poverty—not low income—a convention applied throughout this volume.

Debates exist on how to define and measure poverty in Canada, though these issues are less contentious in Canada than in the USA. The World Summit on Social Development (United Nations, 1995) provides definitions of both absolute and overall poverty.

Absolute poverty is a condition characterized by severe deprivation of basic human needs, including food, safe drinking water, sanitation facilities, health, shelter, education, and information. It depends not only on income, but also on access to social services. Overall poverty has various manifestations, including lack of income and productive resources sufficient to ensure sustainable livelihoods, hunger and malnutrition; ill health; limited or lack of access to education and other basic services; increased morbidity and mortality from illness; homelessness and inadequate housing; unsafe environments; and social discrimination and exclusion. It is also characterized by a lack of participation in decision-making and in civil, social, and cultural life. It occurs in all countries: as mass poverty in many developing nations, pockets of poverty amid wealth in developed nations, loss of livelihood as a result of economic recession ... the poverty of low-wage workers, and the utter destitution of people who fall outside family support systems, social institutions and safety nets. (p. 57)

Absolute poverty is the stuff of poverty in developing nations. Overall poverty is about exclusion from activities expected in a wealthy developed nation and is almost synonymous with the concept of relative poverty. Researchers in the UK have drawn upon the World Summit's work to operationalize these definitions.[2] Their work is especially relevant to ongoing Canadian debates concerning the nature and measurement of poverty in a wealthy developed nation.

These UK researchers use the term *absolute poverty* to refer to living conditions in which individuals lack the basic necessities of life to "keep body and soul together." (Gordon, 2000, p. 75) Absolute poverty is related to health because of immediate conditions of severe deprivation. The researchers define the term *overall poverty* as not having those things that society thinks are basic necessities. It means not being able to do the things that most people take for granted (either because one can't afford to participate in usual activities or because one is discriminated against in other ways). What constitutes overall poverty will vary between different societies and at different points in time.

Overall poverty is related to health because people who are systematically excluded from the opportunities that are open to others come to show a wide variety of health problems as compared to those who can participate. Overall poverty as used by these UK researchers is very similar—if not identical to—the concept of relative poverty. Townsend gave the most widely used definition of overall or relative poverty in 1993, and Smeeding and Rainwater (2003) provide a recent restatement of the argument (see Box 2.3).

Relative poverty has proven to be very useful for understanding the meaning of poverty in wealthy developed nations and provides the conceptual underpinnings of much of the Canadian work in this area. In addition, the international use of relative poverty indicators also represents a commitment to this concept. Work in the UK illustrates what these absolute and overall—or relative—approaches actually mean in terms of individuals' living conditions.

Absolute Poverty

UK researchers have created a working definition of absolute poverty:

Absolute poverty means being so poor that you are deprived of basic human needs. In order to avoid absolute poverty, you need enough money to cover all of these things: adequate diet, housing costs/rents, heating costs, clothing, water rates, and prescription costs. (Gordon 2000, p. 76)

Box 2.3: The Meaning of Poverty in Wealthy Industrialized Nations

Individuals, families and groups in the population can be said to be in poverty when they lack the resources to obtain the type of diet, participate in the activities and have the living conditions and amenities which are customary, or at least widely encouraged, or approved, in the societies to which they belong. They are, in effect, excluded from ordinary living patterns, customs and activities.

Source: Townsend, P. (1993). *The international analysis of poverty* (p. 36). Milton Keynes: Harvester Wheatsheaf.

The argument is that objectively people cannot carry out the roles, participate in the activities, or maintain the social relations that are definitive of mainstream members of society if their resources (over some period of time) fall short of a "certain minimum." In such a situation, inadequacy of resources precipitates a lower-class style of life that is reactive to the inability to live the life identified with the standard package.

Source: Rainwater, L., and Smeeding, T. M. (2003). *Poor kids in a rich country: America's children in comparative perspective* (p. 147). New York: Russell Sage Foundation.

They based this definition on conceptual grounds but then validated it by investigating the extent to which various items were considered by people as being necessities. A representative sample of UK respondents identified the items necessary to avoid absolute poverty among adults and children (Gordon, 2000). Table 2.1 shows these items.

Overall or Relative Poverty

The working definition of overall poverty used by these UK researchers is as follows:

> In order to avoid overall poverty, you need enough money not only to cover basic human needs, but also enough money to ensure that you are able to live in a safe environment, have a social life in your local area, feel part of your community, carry out your duties/activities in the family and neighbourhood and meet the essential costs of transport. (Gordon 2000, p. 77)

Their investigation of indicators of this state revealed a great deal of consensus (Gordon, 2000). Table 2.2 shows these items.

These UK researchers also inquired of people how much money a week, after tax, was necessary to keep their household out of these situations of absolute and overall poverty.

Table 2.1: Items Identified as Necessary in the UK to Avoid Absolute Poverty (% Agreement)

Adults—Material Requirements	Children—Material Requirements
Beds and bedding for everyone (95%)	A warm, weatherproof coat (96%)
Heating to warm living areas (94%)	Bed and bedding for him/herself (96%)
Damp-free areas (93%)	New, properly fitting shoes (95%)
Two meals a day (91%)	Fresh fruit or vegetables daily (94%)
All medicines prescribed by a doctor (90%)	Three meals a day (92%)
Refrigerator (89%)	Books of his/her own (90%)
Fresh fruit and vegetables daily (86%)	All of the school uniform required (89%)
A warm, weatherproof coat (85%)	Enough bedrooms for every child over 10 (77%)
Meat/fish every other day (79%)	Meat/fish twice a week (77%)
Dictionary (53%)	

Adults—Social Requirements	Children—Social Requirements
Visits to friends/family (84%)	Celebrations of special occasions (92%)
Visiting friends/family in hospital (84%)	
Attending weddings, funerals, and other such occasions (80%)	

Source: Gordon, D. (2000). Measuring absolute and overall poverty. In D. Gordon and P. Townsend (Eds.), *Breadline Europe: The measurement of poverty* (p. 66). Bristol, UK: The Policy Press.

They then estimated the proportion of citizens in the UK that were living in such conditions. Little if any work like this has been done in Canada, although statistics on homelessness and food bank use (examined later) provide some rough estimates of the situation of absolute poverty in Canada, and statistics obtained through commonly applied Canadian measures of low income provide estimates of overall or relative poverty. An Ontario Deprivation Index has been developed that describes some of the conditions associated with living in poverty (Matern, Menelson, and Oliphant, 2009) (see below).

Canadian Definitions of Poverty

In Canada, the assumptions underlying the definitions of poverty are frequently implicit rather than explicitly stated. Indeed, as noted, the various measures used in Canada are not even called measures of poverty by Statistics Canada but rather indicators of low

Table 2.2: Items Identified as Necessary in the UK to Avoid Overall Poverty (% Agreement)

Adults—Material Requirements	Children—Material Requirements
Replace or repair broken electrical goods (85%)	Toys, dolls, etc. (83%)
Enough money to keep home in decent state of decoration (82%)	At least seven pairs of pants (85%)
Contents insurance (79%)	Educational games (84%)
Telephone (71%)	Visit school for sports days, etc. (81%)
Appropriate clothes for job interviews (69%)	At least four pairs of trousers (76%)
Carpets in living room and bedroom (67%)	Collect children from school (75%)
A small amount of money to spend on yourself (67%)	A carpet in the bedroom (75%)
TV (56%)	At least four jumpers (74%)
Roast joint once a week (56%)	A garden to play in (71%)
Replace worn-out furniture (54%)	Construction toys (67%)
An outfit to wear for social or family occasions (51%)	A bicycle (59%)

Adults—Social Requirements	Children—Social Requirements
Celebrations on special occasions (83%)	A hobby or leisure activity (89%)
A hobby or leisure activity (78%)	Going on a school trip (75%)
Friends or family round for a snack (64%)	Swimming (71%)
Presents for family or friends once a year (56%)	A holiday away from home (66%)
A holiday away from home (55%)	Having friends around for tea (56%)

Source: Gordon, D. (2000). Measuring absolute and overall poverty. In D. Gordon and P. Townsend (Eds.), *Breadline Europe: The measurement of poverty* (p. 68). Bristol, UK: The Policy Press.

income (see Box 2.1). However, many organizations and associations use these low-income indicators as measures of poverty, and this is the convention followed here.

Usually, the definitions of poverty that shape these Canadian measures need to be gleaned from the measurement methods applied since these approaches do not include explicit definitions of the constructs of low income or poverty. There are three primary measures of poverty in Canada: the low income cut-off or LICO, the low income measure, and the Market Basket Measure (see Box 2.4).

Box 2.4: Calculating Canadian Poverty Measures

LICOs

LICO is an income threshold below which an individual or family will likely devote a larger share of its income to the necessities of food, shelter, and clothing than an average individual or family would. According to the most recent base for LICOs, the 1992 Family Expenditures Survey, the average individual spent 30% of his or her pre-tax income on food, shelter, and clothing. The calculation of a LICO would identify the income level at which an individual would spend 50% of his or her pre-tax income food, shelter, and clothing in 1992 (i.e., 30% plus the 20 percentage point margin). This process is carried out for seven family sizes and five community sizes and results in a table of 35 cut-offs. This operation is done twice: once for pre-tax cut-offs, once for after-tax cut-offs.

Low Income Rate and Low Income Gap

To determine whether a person (or family) is in low income, the appropriate LICO (given the family size and community size) is compared to the income of the person's economic family. If the economic family income is below the cut-off, all individuals in that family are considered to be in low income. In other words, "persons in low income" should be interpreted as persons who are part of low income families, including persons living alone whose income is below the cut-off. Similarly, "children in low income" means "children who are living in low income families." Overall, the low income rate for persons can then be calculated as the number of persons in low income divided by the total population. The same can be done for families and various subgroups of the population; for example, low income rates by age, sex, province, or family types.

After having determined that an individual/family is in low income, the depth of their low income can be analysed by using the amount that the family income falls short of the relevant low income cut-off. For example, a family with an income of $15,000 and a low income cut-off of $20,000 would have a low income gap of $5,000. In percentage terms this gap would be 25%. The average gap for a given population, whether expressed in dollar or percentage terms, is the average of these values as calculated for each unit.

LIM (Low Income Measure)

For the purpose of making international comparisons, the LIM is the most commonly used low income measure. The use of the low income measure (LIM) was suggested in 1989 in a discussion paper written by Wolfson, Evans, and the OECD11, which discussed their concerns about the LICOs. In simple terms, the LIM is a fixed percentage (50%) of median adjusted family income, where "adjusted" indicates that family needs are taken into account. Adjustment for family sizes reflects the fact that a family's needs increase as the number of members increases. Most would agree that a family of five has greater needs than a family of two. Similarly, the LIM allows for the fact that it costs more to feed a family of five adults than a family of two adults and three children.

The LIMs are calculated three times; using market income, before-tax income, and after-tax income. They do not require updating using an inflation index because they are calculated using an annual survey of family income. For years prior to 1996, they were calculated by Statistics Canada using the Survey of Consumer Finances. From 1996 onward, they are calculated using the Survey of Labour and Income Dynamics (SLID). Unlike the low income cut-offs, which are derived from an expenditure survey and then compared to an income survey, the LIMs are both derived and applied using a single income survey.

The Market Basket Measure—an Additional Tool

The MBM complements the two traditional low-income measures and fills an important gap by being more sensitive to differences in living and household costs across Canada. However, it is neither a measure of basic needs, nor does it replace existing measures.

The MBM provides a new perspective on low income as it is based on a specific transparent basket of goods and services. The cost of purchasing this basket of goods and services has been determined for 48 different geographical areas in the 10 provinces.

The "basket" on which the MBM is based includes five types of expenditures for a reference family of two adults and two children: food, clothing and footwear, shelter, transportation (public transit or a used vehicle), and other household needs (e.g., school supplies, furniture, newspapers/magazines, recreation and family entertainment, personal care products, a telephone, etc.).

Developing the content of the MBM was a complex and rigorous process that involved substantial consultations nationally and in several provinces. Government departments, academic experts, non-governmental organizations, and advisory bodies to Statistics Canada all contributed to developing the measure.

Statistics Canada, on Human Resources Development Canada's behalf, began collecting data on the cost of goods and services in the basket in 2000 to calculate thresholds for the 48 geographical areas referenced. The work was completed in late 2002. Additional analysis and evaluation was then required to compare the cost of the basket to the disposable income available to households to purchase the goods and services contained in the basket, and to prepare the first report on the MBM, including a detailed methodological section.

Sources: Adapted from Statistics Canada. (2006). *Low income cut-offs for 2005 and low income measures for 2004.* Retrieved March 11, 2011 from www.statcan.ca/english/research/75F0002MIE/75 F0002MIE2006004.pdf and Human Resources and Development Canada. (2003). *Market Basket Measure Report now available.* Retrieved March 11, 2011 from www.hrsdc.gc.ca/eng/cs/comm/ news/2003/030527.shtml

Statistics Canada Low Income Cut-offs (LICOs)

The LICOs are the primary source of poverty rates in Canada. The LICOs origi-nated in a 1968 report by the Economic Council of Canada that presented a pov-erty approach developed by J. Podoluk at Statistics Canada (Ross, Scott, and Smith, 2000). A Statistics Canada survey had found that the average family in Canada in 1959 spent about 50% of its income on three necessities: food, clothing, and shelter. Statistics Canada decided that a family that spent 20% more than that or 70% of their income on these three areas were living in "straitened" or difficult circumstances. This standard of 70% being spent on basics has been adjusted. Since Canadians now spend, on average, 34.7% on these three necessities, the LICOs are now calculated on the basis of 54.7%: those Canadians now spending more than 54.7% of their pre-tax income on these necessities are said to be living in "straitened circumstances" or below the low-income cut-offs.

How does Statistics Canada calculate the LICO and the number of Canadians fall-ing below these LICOs? Statistics Canada periodically conducts a Family Expenditure Survey that estimates the amount that an average family spends on food, clothing, and shelter. They then calculate the value that would reflect this expenditure if it constituted more than 54.7% of a family's total income. This value becomes the LICO, and the number of Canadians whose income is at or below this value is the number of individu-als living in poverty. These values are adjusted for family size and for the population of the city or municipality. The most recent pre-tax LICOS are presented in Table 2.3.

Table 2.3: Before-Tax LICOs for 2009

| | Community Size | | | | |
| | Rural Areas | Urban Areas | | | |
		Less than 30,000	30,000 to 99,999	100,000 to 499,999	500,000 and over
1 person	15,302	17,409	19,026	19,144	22,229
2 persons	19,050	21,672	23,685	23,832	27,674
3 persons	23,419	26,643	29,118	29,299	34,022
4 persons	28,435	32,349	35,354	35,573	41,307
5 persons	32,250	36,690	40,097	40,345	46,850
6 persons	36,374	41.380	45,223	45,504	52.838
7 or more persons	40,496	46,071	50,359	50,661	58,827

Source: Adapted from Statistics Canada, Low Income Lines, 2008-2009, Income Research Paper Series, 75F0002MIE2010005, June 2010; http://www.statcan.gc.ca/bsolc/olc-cel/olc-cel?catno=75F0002MIE&lang=eng#formatdisp

Statistics Canada has begun to calculate a set of after-tax LICOs. The reasoning here is that after-tax figures actually reflect the amount of money that individuals have to spend after taxes redistribute some income. Using these figures, Statistics Canada has determined that the average Canadian family spends 43.6% of its after-tax income on food, clothing, and shelter. Therefore any family spending more than 63.6% of after-tax income on food, clothing, and shelter is living in "straitened circumstances." Raising this bar from 54.7% of pre-tax income to 63.6% of after-tax income reduces the poverty rate in Canada by about 4–5%.

There is a lively debate concerning which LICO is most appropriate (deGroot-Maggetti, 2002). The Canadian Council on Social Development (CCSD) argues for continued use of the pre-tax measures (Ross et al., 2000). They point out that while the after-tax measures take into account federal and provincial income taxes, these taxes constitute only 38% of government revenues. If Statistics Canada is going to adjust for taxes, the CCSD argues, it should include those revenue sources that contribute the other 62% of revenue, such as provincial sales taxes, EI and CPP premiums, the GST, and property taxes. Poverty figures obtained might look very different if these calculations were included.

Another reason for continued use of the pre-tax LICOs is that they appear to more accurately reflect the perceptions of Canadians concerning the income needed to avoid poverty. Data from Gallup polls indicate that these perceptions accurately mirror the figures generated by the pre-tax LICOs (see Figure 2.2). A third reason for continued use of the pre-tax approach is the concern of anti-poverty advocates that the government generated the post-tax measure to artificially reduce poverty rates rather than act upon the causes of poverty. The fourth reason is that the figures generated by the pre-tax LICOs more closely approximate the poverty rates that are provided by international organizations such as the United Nations and the Organisation for Economic Co-operation and Development using an approach similar to Statistics Canada's low income measure (LIM) (see below). Many groups concerned with poverty in Canada continue to use the pre-tax LICOs in their work, and this is the approach taken in this volume.

Statistics Canada Low Income Measure (LIM)

The LIM adopts a purely relative approach to poverty based simply on a family attaining less than one-half of the median gross income of Canadian families. The LIM adjusts for family size and for whether the household members are children or adults. It does not adjust for community size. Using this measure as compared to the pre-tax LICO usually reduces the overall low income rate in Canada by about 2–3% but the effects are not uniform across regions and family types. It should be noted that the LIM is very similar to the international measure of poverty that is commonly applied in analyses of poverty in wealthy developed nations but is not widely applied in Canada.

Figure 2.2: Relationship of Canadians' Views on Getting by with Income Levels Associated with LICOs

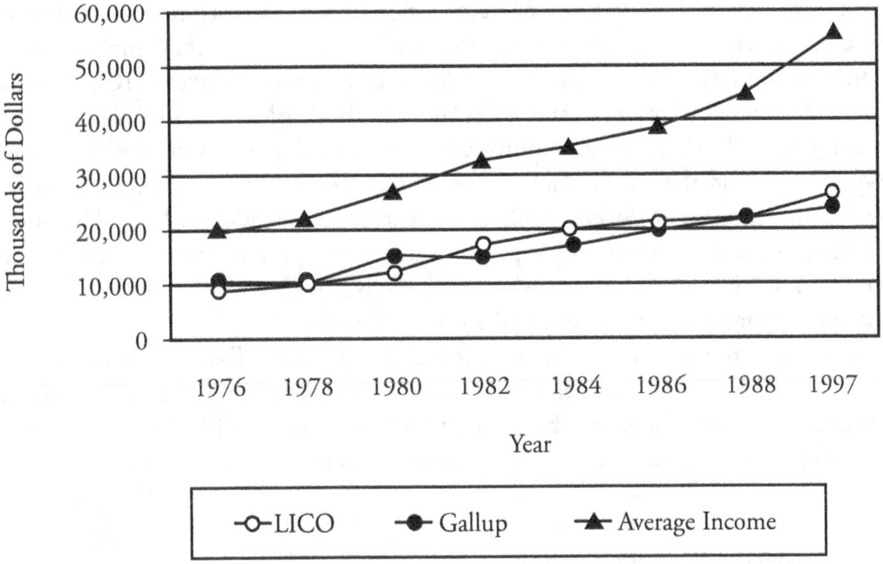

Source: From *The Canadian Fact Book on Poverty 2000* (p.31), by D. P. Ross, K. Scott, and P. Smith, 2000. Ottawa: Canadian Council on Social Development.

The Statistics Canada Market Basket Measure (MBM)

The MBM is a result of a federal/provincial/territorial initiative that attempted to deal with the criticisms that the LICOs and LIM were based on statistical abstractions rather than a concrete analysis of the living conditions of Canadians (Human Resources Development Canada, 2003). The approach was to construct a market basket of necessities for a four-member family, consisting of two adults and two children. In the introduction to the report, great pains were taken to show that this was an absolutist measure of poverty rather than a relative one. Having said this, the approach did *not* take a basic-needs approach that would limit the definition of experiencing poverty to profound material deprivation.

The criterion for food was based on Agriculture Canada's Nutritious Food Basket, which was priced for 18 urban centres across Canada. For clothing, the figures used were 75% of the amount budgeted for by the Social Planning Council of Metropolitan Toronto in 1991, and subsequently updated for cost changes. The shelter standard for the four-member family was an estimate for a three-bedroom apartment that was provided by the Canada Mortgage and Housing Corporation for all locations in Canada with populations exceeding 10,000. Other essentials—such as personal care, household needs, furniture, a telephone, public transportation, reading materials, recreation, entertainment, and school supplies—were allocated an amount equal to 60% of the sum for food and clothing.

A large number of organizations and associations were concerned that the MBM would reduce the poverty rate in Canada by as much as 33%. In reality, the figures obtained by this method are very similar to the levels of low income obtained by the LICOs. As shown in Table 2.4, the 2007 poverty rates calculated by the MBM, pre- and post-tax LICOs, and the after-tax LIM are roughly comparable. Of particular note is the similarity between pre-tax LICOs and the after-tax low income measure. The LIM is comparable to many international measures of poverty applied by organizations such as the United Nations and the Organisation for Economic Co-operation and Development. The one set of anomalies is related to the situation of seniors, where the pre-tax LICOs and after-tax LICOs produce higher poverty rates in comparison to the other measures.

Indeed, as a result of the rather lengthy and expensive MBM exercise—which has now just been repeated—and the similarity of the results obtained with other more established measures, there may be a need to refocus upon the LICOs—or perhaps the LIM—to provide the standard for ascertaining levels of poverty in Canada.

Fraser Institute Poverty Lines

This free-enterprise advocacy organization publishes poverty lines based on work by economist Christopher Sarlo (2001). He considers a person to be living in poverty "if he lacks any item required to maintain long-term physical well-being" (p. 11). Sarlo constructs a market basket of necessities for a four-member family, consisting of two adults and two children. The market basket includes shelter, food, clothing, hygiene, health care, transportation, and a phone. Any spending for social amenities is excluded. The basket appears to meet the most basic needs of an individual, showing little if any appreciation of the exclusionary effects of material and social deprivation. These calculations have the effect of reducing Canada's poverty rates by about 75% as compared to the pre-tax LICOs. The Fraser Institute poverty lines are not used by any other organization. It has been suggested that, "for those who want a basic Third-World measure of poverty, one that will do little more than provide for the short-term physical survival of a family, these lines are representative" (Ross et al., 2000, p. 26).

Depth of Poverty or Low-Income Gap

The depth of poverty refers to the average extent to which a group or groups of low-income Canadians' income falls below the established poverty lines. If a LICO is set at $15,000 and a family has an income of $12,000, then the depth of poverty is $3,000 or 20% ($3,000 short of the LICO of $15,000). This measure is particularly useful for determining the degree of material and social deprivation that a family or individual may be expe-

Table 2.4: Comparability of Various Measures of Low Income: Market Basket Measure, Low Income Cut-offs, and Low Income Measure for Various Groups, 2007

Group	MBM*	LICO-IAT	LICO-IBT	LIM-IAT
All Canadians	10.1	9.2	13.6	12.5
Children under 18 years of age	11.9	9.5	14.9	15.0
Those 65 years and over	2.6	4.8	12.5	10.4
Males	10.0	9.0	12.6	11.6
Females	10.2	9.4	14.5	13.3
All families	13.3	13.3	13.6	10.0
Children in two-parent families	6.7	5.1	10.6	10.2
Children in female lone-parent families	28.7	23.6	39.8	42.9
Unattached males	25.5	27.4	32.9	23.7
Unattached females	23.1	27.5	38.5	29.3

* MBM: Market Basket Measure
 LICO-IAT: post-income tax Low Income Cut-off
 LICO-IBT: pre-income tax Low Income Cut-off
 LIM-IAT: post-income tax Low Income Measure

Sources: Hatfield, M., Pyper, W., and Gustajtis, B. (2010). *First comprehensive review of the Market Basket Measure of Low Income.* Ottawa: Human Resources Development Canada; Statistics Canada. (2010). CANSIM tables. Ottawa: Statistics Canada.

riencing. Table 2.5 presents the depth of poverty calculated by the four most widely used measures of poverty in Canada for the year 2007. The magnitude of depth of poverty is quite high, with values of around 30% for all persons living in poverty, and of over 40% for unattached males. The depth of poverty for older Canadians is not as severe.

International Approaches

Virtually all researchers and agencies concerned with comparative analyses of poverty across wealthy developed nations use the indicator of less than half the median disposable income as a measure of poverty. This is the case for the United Nations Human

Table 2.5: Depth of Low Income for Various Groups in Canada, Calculated by Applying Various Measures: Market Basket Measure, Low Income Cut-offs, and Low Income Measure, 2007

Group	MBM	LICO-IAT	LICO-IBT	LIM-IAT
All Canadians	.326	.329	.320	.300
Under 18 years of age	.260	.262	.270	.260
65 and over	.258	.167	.160	.140
Males	.345	.347	.340	.310
Females	.309	.311	.300	.280
All families	.371	.368	.270	.270
Children in two-parent families with children	.232	.229	.240	.22
Children in female lone-parent families	.301	.307	.320	.300
Unattached males	.441	.429	.450	.410
Unattached females	.293	.368	.360	.320

Sources: Hatfield, M., Pyper, W., and Gustajtis, B. (2010). *First comprehensive review of the Market Basket Measure of Low Income.* Ottawa: Human Resources Development Canada; Statistics Canada. (2010). CANSIM tables. Ottawa: Statistics Canada.

Development Reports and UNICEF's Innocenti Research Centre, which focuses on child poverty (Innocenti Research Centre, 2000, 2005; United Nations Development Program, 2001). The Organisation for Economic Co-operation and Development (OECD) also applies this approach, as does the definitive research that comes from the Luxembourg Income Study (Rainwater and Smeeding, 2003; OECD, 2008). Low pay—a related concept—is commonly defined in these international approaches as being less than 66% of the median wage of a typical production worker (OECD, 2008).

The Innocenti Research Centre reports on child poverty also apply a measure of absolute poverty that is based on the USA poverty line (Innocenti Research Centre, 2000). This line is set so low as to constitute a clear indicator of absolute deprivation. It is useful for comparing how segments of one nation compare with another. For example, the bottom 20% of children in the United States have incomes that are noticeably lower than those of children in most other developed nations, even though the USA is a significantly wealthier nation overall (Rainwater and Smeeding, 2003). Later chapters consider these comparative issues in some detail.

Canadians' Views on Income Levels Associated with Poverty

Little is known about Canadians' views concerning what is needed to avoid either absolute or overall poverty. But what evidence is available indicates that Canadians' views are similar to those provided by currently used measures of poverty. *The Canadian Fact Book on Poverty* points out that since 1976, the Gallup Poll has been asking: "Generally speaking, what do you think is the least amount of money a family of four needs each week to get along in this community?" (Ross et al., 2000, p. 30). In 1996, the figure was $500 per week or $26,000 per year. If the results from these series of questions are plotted against the pre-tax LICOs, a remarkable consistency of results is obtained (see Figure 2.2). This provides strong evidence that the rates of poverty obtained by the pre-tax LICOs are consistent with the understandings held by most Canadians.

Deprivation Indices

Deprivation indices are measures that attempt to operationalize the material and social deprivation characteristic of living in poverty (Shaw et al., 2007). These have been used primarily to generate area-level indicators of deprivation. For example, the Townsend Index of Deprivation measured the percentage of (a) unemployed in an area, and (b) car ownership, home ownership, and overcrowding. The Jarman Underprivileged Area Score consists of indicators of (a) unemployment, (b) overcrowding, (c) lone seniors, (d) single parents, (e) those born in the "New Commonwealth," (f) children under aged five, (g) low social class, and (h) one-year migrants. These and other similar measures (see Shaw et al., 2007) are used primarily to plan and allocate resource and service allocations by governments and other institutions.

Measures of individual deprivation have been developed and include items such as those used to describe absolute and overall poverty in the UK (see Tables 2.1 and 2.2). An Ontario Deprivation Index has been developed and includes these 10 items:

1. Do you eat fresh fruit and vegetables every day?
2. Are you able to get dental care if needed?
3. Do you eat meat, fish or a vegetarian equivalent at least every other day?
4. Are you able to replace or repair broken or damaged appliances such as a vacuum or a toaster?
5. Do you have appropriate clothes for job interviews?
6. Are you able to get around your community, either by having a car or by taking the bus or an equivalent mode of transportation?
7. Are you able to have friends or family over for a meal at least once a month?
8. Is your house or apartment free of pests, such as cockroaches?
9. Are you able to buy some small gifts for family or friends at least once a year?
10. Do you have a hobby or leisure activity? (Matern et al., 2009).

These individually based measurement tools are certainly useful for identifying some of the situations associated with poverty, but it is not clear whether they will add anything to the public policy debate concerned with reducing the incidence of poverty. Considering the plethora of measures of poverty that are available and the clear moral imperative of reducing these rather higher rates, efforts spent on producing individual deprivation indices could better be directed elsewhere.

Relationship of Poverty to Income and Wealth Inequality

It should not be surprising that the incidence and depth of poverty within a nation is related to degree of income and wealth inequality. Nations that tolerate wide differences in income and wealth usually exhibit a basket of public policies that make the incidence of poverty more likely (Coburn, 2010). These policies include relatively lower taxation rates on the wealthy, a smaller proportion of public spending on social programs and social infrastructure, modest universal entitlements, and less commitment to full employment and gender equity (Navarro et al., 2004).

Part of the relationship between poverty and inequality is a reflection of the way by which poverty is measured in international studies. If poverty is defined as receiving less than 50% of the median income of a population, greater inequality will generally be related to greater incidence of poverty. However, most of the differences in poverty rates—and certainly the depth of poverty within a jurisdiction—are due to unequal jurisdictions placing greater reliance upon the marketplace as the arbiter of how economic resources should be distributed within the population (Esping-Andersen, 1999). As discussed in later chapters, these public policies—and associated higher rates of poverty and income and wealth inequality—are more characteristic of what are called liberal political economies. And Canada is identified as being within this category.

A variety of measures of inequality are available. These measures can be applied to consider distributions of income, wealth, education, or other resources within a jurisdiction. The most common measures are the Gini, Theil, and the Robin Hood indices (Kawachi and Kennedy, 1997; Morissette, Zhang, and Drolet, 2002; Myles, Picot, and Pyper, 2000). (See Glossary of Terms at the end of this chapter.) The Gini coefficient is the most popular, and its values range from .00 to 1.00. A value of .00 indicates perfect equality across the population. A value of 1.00 indicates that all resources are accumulated by one person. Another commonly used measure is the proportion of income received by the lower half of the population. Frequently, the income or wealth of the bottom 10% (or 20%) of the population can be compared to the top 10% (or 20%) of the population.

In international perspective, Canada's degree of income and wealth inequality is near the high end of wealthy developed nations. What exactly does income and wealth inequality look like in Canada today? Data from 2005–2006 provided by Statistics Canada and the Luxembourg Income Study shows that the average disposable income of the bottom 10% of Canadian families with children was $22,315, and for the next 10%, was $36,199 (Phipps and Butron, 2010) (see Figure 2.3). In contrast, the top 10% of Canadian families had average incomes of $175,400, and the next 10% earned on average $110,016.

In terms of wealth, differences among Canadians are striking (Curry-Stevens, 2009). In 2005 the poorest 10% of Canadian families had an average debt of –$9,600, and the next 10% had an average wealth of $10! The top 10% of Canadians had an average wealth of $1,194,000, and the next 10% had an average wealth of $413,750. The top 10% of Canadians controlled 58.2% of Canada's wealth in 2004 (Osberg, 2008). If the wealth of the next 10% of Canadians is added to that figure, this top 20% of Canadian families owned 75% of the total wealth of Canada. In contrast, the bottom 20% of Canadians possessed 0% of Canada's wealth. The importance of income and wealth inequality as mediators of the poverty and health relationship is examined in later chapters.

Figure 2.3: Average Disposable Income of Families with Children (2006) and Wealth of Canadian Families by Deciles (2005)

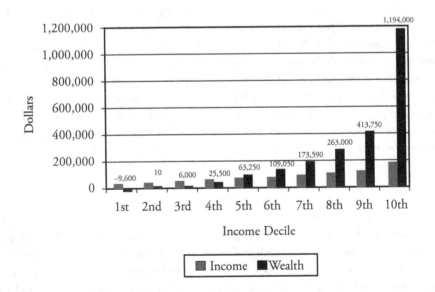

Sources: Curry-Stevens, A. (2009). When economic growth doesn't trickle down: The wage dimensions of income polarization. In D. Raphael (Ed.), *Social determinants of health: Canadian perspectives* (Fig. 3.6, p. 51). Toronto: Canadian Scholars' Press Inc.; Phipps, S., and Burton, P. (2010). *Families, time, and well-being in Canada*. Luxembourg Income Study (Working Paper No. 537). Syracuse, NY: Syracuse University.

Conclusions

Much of the theorizing about the meaning of poverty, its measurement, and its relation to material and social deprivation has been carried out by researchers working in the UK and other European nations. There has been relatively little Canadian effort expended on documenting how the definitions of poverty implied in Canadian measurements play out in people's lives. Compared to work done elsewhere, relatively little is known about the material possessions and situations of those identified as living below the LICOs, LIM, and MBM cut-offs.

The measures of low income developed by Statistics Canada are similar to poverty measures developed and applied in other nations. The Statistics Canada measures identify those living in poverty in Canada and provide ways of ascertaining both the incidence of poverty and poverty's association with a variety of health and quality of life indicators. These measures are consistent with the argument for adopting a relative approach to defining and measuring poverty. Poverty is about experiencing material and social deprivation that leads to the inability to participate in the activities assumed to be customary in a wealthy developed nation such as Canada. Adopting this position— as opposed to an absolute poverty definition—is especially important for developing appropriate policy responses. Williamson and Reutter (1999) argue that

> [T]he success of policy efforts by the health sector to improve the health of Canadians will be hampered if policy makers in the health sector allow themselves to be convinced that poverty is absolute in nature. If policy makers are committed to improving the health of Canadians, it is not good enough to reduce the proportion of Canadians living in poverty by simply redefining poverty as absolute and subsequently lowering the poverty lines. Instead, there is a need to develop a broad range of policies that effectively increase the proportion of Canadians who are able to meet their basic needs and participate meaningfully in society. Evidence about the relationship between income inequality and the health of populations, along with findings about the manner in which a variety of psychosocial factors influence health, leaves little doubt that relative conceptualizations and measurements of poverty ought to guide the development of policy. (p. 262)

Notes

1. See especially the 2006 volume *Poverty and Social Exclusion in Britain: The Millennium Survey*, C. Pantazis, D. Gordon, and R. Levitas (Eds.), Bristol, UK: The Policy Press, where significant attention has been expended on defining poverty, mapping its conceptual relationship to availability of economic resources and the experience of material and social deprivation, and developing measures of the same. The volume also includes findings of the relationship among these measures and the number of Britons experiencing various kinds of poverty, material and social deprivation, and social exclusion.

2. There is also a concept of "general poverty" where respondents are simply asked "What is the amount of money needed to keep you and their family out of poverty?" The values obtained

are more similar to the values obtained for "overall poverty" than "absolute poverty," suggesting that most Britons apply an "overall poverty" definition when thinking about the poverty experience.

Critical Thinking Questions

1. What has been your experience of being unable to participate in activities that others seem to be able to do? If this exclusion was continued over an extended period of time, would you consider yourself to be living in poverty?
2. What would be some of the indicators of absolute poverty in Canada? Do you normally observe individuals who would be considered as living in absolute poverty?
3. Which of the poverty measures discussed in this chapter make the most sense to you? Which would make the most sense to the Canadian public?
4. Why do you think the study of poverty is so undeveloped in Canada as compared to other nations?
5. What would be some of the reasons a free-enterprise organization such as the Fraser Institute would develop poverty indicators that show poverty to be virtually non-existent in Canada?

Recommended Readings

deGroot-Maggetti, G. (2002). *A measure of poverty in Canada: A guide to the debate about poverty lines.* Ottawa: Citizens for Public Justice. Online at http://action.web.ca/home/cpj/attach/A_measure_of_poverty.pdf

> An accessible overview of the different approaches to measuring poverty in Canada. The paper provides the policy implications of using particular measures as opposed to others.

Gordon, D., Levitas, R., and Pantazis, C. (2006). *Poverty and social exclusion in Britain: The Millennium Survey.* Bristol, UK: The Policy Press.

> This book is an authoritative study of the meaning and extent of poverty and social exclusion in Britain at the start of the 21st century. It charts the extent and nature of material and social deprivation and exclusion in Britain, measures the extent of social exclusion, and provides a clear conceptual understanding of poverty and social exclusion from both a British and international perspective.

Human Resources Development Canada. (2003). *Understanding the 2000 low income statistics based on the Market Basket Measure.* Ottawa: HRDC. Online at www.hrsdc.gc.ca/eng/cs/sp/sdc/pkrf/publications/research/2003-000151/page04.shtml

> This report provides the rationale, methodology, and findings from use of the MBM to estimate incidence of low income. Although the MBM was developed to provide a more concrete and accurate measure of low income, the rates of low income produced were remarkably similar to rates produced by measures already in use.

National Council of Welfare. (2004). *Income for living?* Ottawa: NCW. Online at www.ncwcnbes.net/documents/researchpublications/OtherPublications/2004Report-IncomeForLiving/ReportENG.htm

> This is the first report in which the NCW looked at the new Market Basket Measure poverty line. It compared the measure to four different levels of income: welfare, minimum wage, low wage, and average wage. The research showed that some Canadians working full-time live in poverty and cannot afford to pay average housing and child-care costs.

Williamson, D., and Reutter, L. (1999). Measuring poverty: Implications for the health of Canadians. *Health Promotion International, 14*(4), 355–364.

> This paper examines the implications that the conceptualization and measurement of poverty have for policies that aim to improve the health of Canadians. The manner in which poverty is conceptualized and measured has implications for the types, characteristics, and ultimately the success of policies that are developed to reduce poverty and its effect on health.

Relevant Websites

Canadian Council on Social Development (CCSD)—www.ccsd.ca

> The CCSD is a social policy and research organization focusing on social welfare and development issues of poverty, social inclusion, disability, cultural diversity, child well-being, employment, and housing. It provides statistics and reports on the state of poverty and income inequality in Canada and policy options for improving the health and well-being of Canadians.

Introspect Poverty Website—http://intraspec.ca/povertyCanada_news-and-reports.php

> This website provides up-to-date research, statistics, news, and resources on poverty, child poverty, and social policy in Canada, including national and provincial initiatives, local Ottawa services and charities, research and policy organizations, an abbreviated list of food banks by province, and additional resources.

National Council of Welfare (NCW)—www.ncwcnbes.net

> The NCW advises the Canadian government on matters related to social welfare and the needs of low-income Canadians. NCW publishes several reports each year on poverty and social policy issues. They provide critical analyses of measurement issues and how these instruments compare to the amount of monies provided to people who are on social assistance or to the working poor.

Statistics Canada—www.statcan.gc.ca/

> Statistics Canada produces a very wide variety of statistics concerning Canada's population, resources, economy, society, and culture. The Statistics Canada website provides access to reports, data tables, and its free ongoing magazine *The Daily*. In addition to conducting a Census every five years, there are about 350 active surveys on virtually all aspects of Canadian life.

Websites Concerned with Measures of Inequality
Intro Micro Measures of Distributional Inequality—http://tinyurl.com/zfmoj
MacArthur Research Network on SES and Health—www.macses.ucsf.edu/research/socialenviron/inequality.php
World Bank PovNet—http://tinyurl.com/ju3ex
 These three websites provide detailed information about measures of distributional inequality.

Glossary of Terms

Absolute poverty is a condition characterized by deprivation of basic human needs, including food, health, shelter, education, and information. In nations such as Canada it is strongly related to the availability of economic resources and the degree and quality of available social welfare services. While there has been much discussion and research into the defining and measuring of absolute poverty levels in many nations, this has not been the case in Canada. The USA poverty line is a measure of absolute poverty. In Canada, the Fraser Institute's poverty lines measure absolute poverty, but they are rarely used to do so. The best indicators of absolute poverty in Canada appear to be reports of hunger and food bank use, overcrowded housing and homelessness, and the inability to access required health services not covered by the health care system, dental care, and prescribed medicines. In Canada, social assistance levels are clearly set at or below levels associated with absolute poverty.

Income and wealth inequality refers to the extent to which economic resources are distributed unequally among members of a society. Regarding income, in a perfectly equal society each 10% of the population would receive 10% percent of overall income, and the bottom 10% would also receive 10% of overall income. Instead, what is more common is that the top 10% of the population gains much more than 10% of income, and the bottom 10% of the population gains much less than 10% of income. The same issue applies to wealth. In nations such as Canada, the top 10% possesses much more than 10% of the wealth, and the bottom 10% of the population much less than 10%. Income and wealth inequality are important as they are strongly associated with the incidence and depth of poverty within a nation. There are profound differences among nations in degrees of inequality and these differences result from public policies developed and implemented by governments.

Material and social deprivation—Deprivation is defined by Townsend as "a state of observable and demonstrable disadvantage relative to the local community or the wider society or nation to which the individual, family or group belongs" (Townsend, 1987, p. 125). Deprivation exists in two primary spheres: the material and the social. Material deprivation involves deprivation of the goods and conveniences that are part of modern life, while social deprivation refers to an inability to form relationships among individuals in the family, the workplace, and the community that are considered to be common within a society. In the UK, extensive effort has gone into defining what these aspects of life are. In Canada, material and social deprivation are inferred from individuals relating their experiences of being unable to participate in activities that seem on the surface to be eminently reasonable. Numerous studies indicate that living below the LICOs or other measures of low income in Canada are clearly related to the experience of material and social deprivation.

Measures of inequality are used to describe the degree to which a distribution of resources is not evenly provided across a population. The Gini coefficient measures the extent to which the distribution of income (or consumption) among individuals or households within a country deviates from a perfectly equal distribution. A Lorenz curve plots the cumulative percentages of total income received against the cumulative number of recipients, starting with the poorest individual or household. The Gini coefficient measures the area between the Lorenz curve and a hypothetical line of absolute equality, expressed as a percentage of the maximum area under the line. A value of .00 represents perfect equality, a value of 1.00, perfect inequality. The Robin Hood index is equivalent to the maximum vertical distance between the Lorenz curve and the line of equal incomes. The value of the index approximates the share of total income that has to be transferred from households above the mean to those below the mean to achieve equality in the distribution of incomes (see Relevant Websites).

Relative poverty (also known as *overall poverty*) is the situation in which individuals are unable to carry out or participate in the activities expected in a wealthy developed nation such as Canada. These deficits manifest themselves in a variety of spheres, including access to the food, clothing, and other amenities typical of most Canadians, involvement in occupational and leisure activities, and participation in decision making and in civil, social, and cultural life. The value of adopting a concept of relative poverty has been recognized by policy-makers, researchers, and citizen and community groups. Most measures of low income developed and applied in Canada assess the incidence and depth of relative poverty.

References

Bellemare, D. (1981). *La sécurité du revenu au Canada : une analyse économique de l'avènement de l'État-Providence, 1981* (Unpublished doctoral dissertation). McGill University, Montreal.

Brooks, N. (2000). *Taxation and citizenship.* Taxation and citizenship paper prepared for Breakfast on the Hill. Ottawa: Humanities and Social Sciences Federation of Canada. Retrieved March 15, 2011 from http://old.fedcan.ca/english/boh

Canadian Public Health Association. (1996). *Action statement for health promotion in Canada.* Retrieved March 15, 2011 from www.cpha.ca/en/programs/policy/action.arpx

Cheung, A., and Hwang, S. (2004). Risk of death among homeless women: A cohort study and review of the literature. *Canadian Medical Association Journal, 170*(8), 1243–1247.

Chunn, D. E., and Gavigan, A. M. (2004). Welfare law, welfare fraud, and the moral regulation of the never deserving poor. *Social and Legal Studies, 13*(2), 219–243.

Coburn, D. (2010). Health and health care: A political economy perspective. In T. Bryant, D. Raphael, and M. Rioux (Eds.), *Staying alive: Critical perspectives on health, illness, and health care* (2nd ed., pp. 65–92). Toronto: Canadian Scholars' Press Inc.

Curry-Stevens, A. (2009). When economic growth doesn't trickle down: The wage dimensions of income polarization. In D. Raphael (Ed.), *Social determinants of health: Canadian perspectives* (2nd. ed., pp. 41–60). Toronto: Canadian Scholars' Press Inc.

deGroot-Maggetti, G. (2002*). A measure of poverty in Canada: A guide to the debate about poverty lines.* Ottawa: Citizens for Public Justice. Retrieved December 2010 from http://action.web.ca/home/cpj/attach/A_measure_of_poverty.pdf

Esping-Andersen, G. (1999). *Social foundations of post-industrial economies.* New York: Oxford University Press.

Fellegi, I. P. (1997). *On poverty and low income.* Ottawa: Statistics Canada.

Gordon, D. (2000). Measuring absolute and overall poverty. In D. Gordon and P. Townsend (Eds.), *Breadline Europe: The measurement of poverty* (pp. 49–78) Bristol, UK: The Policy Press.

Gordon, D. (2006). The concept and measurement of poverty. In C. Pantazis, D. Gordon, and R. Levitas (Eds.), *Poverty and social exclusion in Britain: The millennium survey* (pp. 29–70). Bristol, UK: The Policy Press.

Government of Canada. (1982). Charter of Rights and Freedoms. Part I of the *Constitution Act.* Ottawa: Government of Canada.

Human Resources Development Canada. (2003). *Understanding the 2000 low income statistics based on the market basket measure.* Ottawa: Applied Research Branch Strategic Policy, HRDC.

Hwang, S., and Bugeja, A. (2000). Barriers to appropriate diabetes management among homeless people in Toronto. *Canadian Medical Association Journal, 163*(2), 161–165.

Innocenti Research Centre. (2000). *A league table of child poverty in rich nations.* Florence: Innocenti Research Centre.

Innocenti Research Centre. (2005). *Child poverty in rich nations, 2005* (Report Card No. 6). Florence: Innocenti Research Centre.

Jackson, A. (2000). *Why we don't have to choose between social justice and economic growth: The myth of the equity/efficiency trade-off.* Ottawa: Canadian Council on Social Development.

Kawachi, I., and Kennedy, B. P. (1997). The relationship of income inequality to mortality: Does the choice of indicator matter? *Social Science and Medicine, 45*(7), 1121–1127.

Matern, R., Menelson, M., and Oliphant, M. (2009). *Developing a deprivation index: The research process.* Toronto: The Daily Bread Food Bank and the Caledon Institute of Social Policy.

Morel, S. (2002). *The insertion model or the workfare model? The transformation of social assistance within Quebec and Canada.* Ottawa: Status of Women Canada.

Morissette, R., Zhang, X., and Drolet, M. (2002). *The evolution of wealth inequality in Canada, 1984–1999.* Retrieved October 2002 from Statistics Canada website: www.statcan.ca/english/research/11F0019MIE/11F0019MIE2002187.pdf

Myles, J., Picot, G., and Pyper, W. (2000). *Neighbourhood inequality in Canadian cities.* Statistics Canada, Business and Labour Market Analysis Division. Retrieved December 2010 from http://dsp-psd.pwgsc.gc.ca/Collection/CS11-0019-160E.pdf

National Anti-poverty Organization. (2004). *Market basket measure overview*. Ottawa: NAPO.

Navarro, V., Borrell, C., Benach, J., Muntaner, C., Quiroga, A., Rodrigues-Sanz, M., Verges, N., … Pasarin, M. I. (2004). The importance of the political and the social in explaining mortality differentials among the countries of the OECD, 1950–1998. In V. Navarro (Ed.), *The political and social contexts of health* (pp. 11–86). Amityville, NY: Baywood Press.

Organisation for Economic Co-operation and Development. (2008). *Growing unequal: Income distribution and poverty in OECD nations*. Paris: OECD.

Osberg, L. (2008). *A quarter century of economic inequality in Canada: 1981–2006*. Ottawa: Canadian Centre for Policy Alternatives.

Phipps, S., and Burton, P. (2010). *Families, time, and well-being in Canada*. Luxembourg Income Study (Working Paper No. 537). Syracuse, NY: Syracuse University.

Piachaud, D. (1981). Peter Townsend and the Holy Grail. *New Society*, 419–421.

Rainwater, L., and Smeeding, T. M. (2003). *Poor kids in a rich country: America's children in comparative perspective*. New York: Russell Sage Foundation.

Raphael, D. (2003a). Barriers to addressing the determinants of health: Public health units and poverty in Ontario, Canada. *Health Promotion International, 18*, 397–405.

Raphael, D. (2003b). A society in decline: The social, economic, and political determinants of health inequalities in the USA. In R. Hofrichter (Ed.), *Health and social justice: A reader on politics, ideology, and inequity in the distribution of disease* (pp. 59–88). San Francisco: Jossey Bass.

Raphael, D. (2010). *About Canada: Health and illness*. Halifax: Fernwood Publishers.

Rioux, M. (2010). The right to health: Human rights approaches to health. In T. Bryant, D. Raphael, and M. Rioux (Eds.), *Staying alive: Critical perspectives on health, illness, and health care* (2nd ed., pp. 93–120). Toronto: Canadian Scholars' Press Inc.

Ross, D. P., and Roberts, P. (1999). *Income and child well-being: A new perspective on the poverty debate*. Ottawa: Canadian Council on Social Development.

Ross, D. P., Scott, K., and Smith, P. (2000). *The Canadian fact book on poverty 2000*. Ottawa: Canadian Council on Social Development.

Sarlo, C. (2001, July 1). *Measuring poverty in Canada*. Retrieved October 2006 from Fraser Institute website: www.fraserinstitute.ca/shared/readmore.asp?sNav=pb&id=216

Sarlo, C. (2006). *Poverty in Canada: 2006 Update*. Vancouver: Fraser Institute.

Shaw, M., Galobardes, B., Lawlor, D., Lynch, J., Wheeler, B., and Davey Smith, G. (2007). *The handbook of inequality and socioeconomic position: Concepts and measures*. Bristol, UK: The Policy Press.

Stanford, J. (1999). *Economic freedom (for the rest of us)*. Ottawa: Canadian Centre for Policy Alternatives.

Statistics Canada. (2010). *Low income in Canada, pre-tax LICOs*. CANSIM tables. Ottawa: Statistics Canada.

Swanson, J. (2001). *Poor-bashing: The politics of exclusion*. Toronto: Between the Lines Press.

Swift, J., Balmer, B., and Dineen, M.(eds.) (2010). *Persistent poverty: Dispatches from the margins*. Toronto: Interfaith Social Assistance Reform Coalition.

Townsend, P. (1987). Deprivation. *Journal of Social Policy, 16*, 125–146.

Townsend, P. (1993). *The international analysis of poverty*. Milton Keynes: Harvester Wheatsheaf.

Trudeau, P. E. (1993). *Memoirs*. Toronto: McClelland & Stewart.

United Nations. (1995). *Commitments of the U.N. World Summit on Social Development*. Copenhagen: United Nations.

United Nations Development Program. (2001). *Human development report 2001: Making new technologies work for human development*. Geneva: United Nations Development Program.

United Way of Greater Toronto. (2004). *Poverty by postal code: The geography of neighbourhood poverty, 1981–2001*. Toronto: United Way of Greater Toronto.

United Way of Ottawa. (2003). *Environmental scan*. Ottawa: United Way of Ottawa.

United Way of Winnipeg. (2003). *2003 environmental scan and Winnipeg census data*. Winnipeg: United Way of Winnipeg.

Williamson, D. L., and Reutter, L. (1999). Defining and measuring poverty: Implications for the health of Canadians. *Health Promotion International, 14*(4), 355–364.

Chapter Three

Who Is Poor in Canada?

Where a great proportion of the people are suffered to languish in helpless misery,
that country must be ill policed, and wretchedly governed: a decent provision for
the poor is the true test of civilization.—Samuel Johnson

Learning Objectives

At the conclusion of this chapter, the reader will be able to:

- describe current levels of poverty across Canada, its provinces, and major urban areas;
- identify specific groups of Canadians especially vulnerable to poverty;
- explain the link between the experience of poverty and the presence of income and wealth inequality;
- understand the public policy mechanisms that put such individuals at risk for being poor;
- understand why risk factors for being poor in Canada are not necessarily risk factors in other countries; and
- provide some initial evidence on why the experience of poverty puts these individuals—and their communities—at risk for poor health and quality of life.

Introduction

Poverty levels are higher in Canada than most other wealthy developed nations (Organisation for Economic Co-operation and Development [OECD], 2008). This is because economic resources are distributed in such a way as to create larger numbers of people living on low incomes than is the case elsewhere. Additionally, there are a number of specific groups of Canadians that are at risk for experiencing poverty. These groups are Aboriginal Canadians, women, unattached adults, people of colour, recent immigrants to Canada, and persons with disabilities. Many of these individuals live in poverty because they work in low-wage occupations. For some groups of Canadians, poverty rates are strikingly high: female-led families, people with disabilities, and people receiving social assistance. These high rates result from public policy decisions on how to allocate economic resources. These decisions are shaped by political and economic forces that not only tolerate such levels but are complicit in their creation.

This chapter presents what is known about the incidence of poverty in Canada. Special attention is paid to those groups especially at risk. This information is provided at the national, provincial, and municipal levels. The primary measure used is the before-tax Statistics Canada *low income cut-offs* (LICOs). Another important set of statistics presented consists of measures of income and wealth inequality. Income and wealth inequality indicators provide a context for understanding the incidence and meaning of poverty. Incidence of poverty and degree of income and wealth inequality reflect common processes of resource distribution shaped by public policies. Statistics are also provided that show growing concentration of neighbourhood poverty in Canadian cities. Such concentrations of poverty have important health and quality-of-life implications.

These statistics are set in the context of public policy domains concerned with income and its distribution, employment security and working conditions, availability and quality of housing, and the organization and provision of social assistance. A neo-materialist explanation for the incidence of poverty and its relation to health and quality of life is applied: nations such as Canada with higher poverty rates distribute income and wealth less equally and invest less in social infrastructure (Lynch, Smith, Kaplan, and House, 2000). Group characteristics combine with public policy decisions to increase the risk of poverty and threaten the health and quality of life of individuals living in poverty.

Poverty Rates in Canada

There are many ways to organize and present poverty-related data. There are two especially important statistics that are used in this chapter. Poverty rate is the percentage of individuals whose income falls below the pre-tax LICOs (Ross, Scott, and Smith, 2000). Depth of poverty is the degree to which, on average, the income of these low-income individuals falls below pre-tax LICO lines. The most recent figures describe the situation in 2007–2008 and come from Statistics Canada's Survey of Labour Income Dynamics (Statistics Canada, 2010a). Canadian poverty rates are presented for all Canadians, families, children, and unattached non-elderly males and females. Provincial rates are examined for some key groups. The poverty rates for at-risk groups such as Aboriginal Canadians, people of colour, recent immigrants, and women help to illuminate their public policy antecedents. The situation of female-led families in Canada and of people receiving social assistance is especially problematic.

Canadian Poverty Statistics for Individuals, Families, and Children

In 2008, 13.6% of Canadians, 14.2% of children, and 13.1% of older Canadians were living in poverty. Among unattached non-elderly Canadians, 34.9% were living in poverty. And the figure for female lone-parent families was very high at 38.1%. Even among two-parent families, the child poverty rate was 10%. These figures are high in comparison to those of other wealthy developed nations. Figure 3.1 provides 2008 poverty rates for Canadians by age, gender, and family status.

When looking at age, Canadians over 65 years of age as a group had the lowest poverty rates, while Canadian children showed the highest. In many other wealthy developed nations, the poverty rates for children are usually lower than for the overall population (OECD, 2008; Smeeding, 2005). Canadian women have higher poverty rates than Canadian men, and this is especially the case among older Canadians and among unattached non-elderly Canadians. These issues are discussed in later sections of this chapter.

Figure 3.1 also shows that poverty rates differ among Canadians by family type and gender. Unattached individuals have much higher poverty rates than do people living in families. There is a consistent gender difference in that unattached women have especially high poverty rates, and women in families have slightly higher rates than do men in families. Even men in families show a poverty rate close to 10%. The reason for the differences in rates between men and women involve a variety of factors that are linked to women's attachment to the labour force, their wages and benefits, and their entitlement to benefits under the Employment Insurance Program (Jackson, 2010).

As noted, the percentage of children living in poverty in 2008 was 14.2%. Among two-parent families the rate was 10%, and among female lone-parent families the rate was 38.1%. Children in female lone-parent families have a 2 in 5 chance of living in poverty. The majority of children living in poverty, however, do not come from female lone-parent

Figure 3.1: Percentage of Canadians Living in Poverty by Age, Gender, and Family Situation, 2008

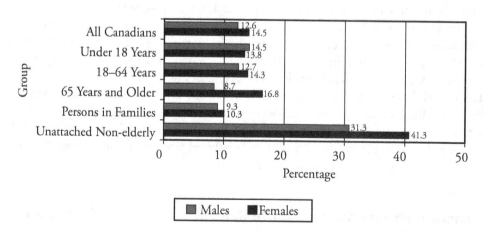

Source: "Percentages of Canadians living in Poverty by Age, Gender, and Family Situation, 2008," adapted from Statistics Canada CANSIM database, *http://cansim2.statcan.gc.ca*, Table 202-2802 extracted in 2010.

families, as this family type constitutes a relatively small group of overall Canadian families (Finnie and Sweetman, 2003). These figures do indicate, though, that female one-parent families are at very high risk for living in poverty. Such risk results, as previously mentioned, from a variety of employment and benefit issues related to women, and additional issues of low pay associated with unattached Canadians' involvement in the workforce. For children living in female lone-parent families, these gender and attachment-related factors come together to create significant risk for living in poverty.

To what extent are these figures consistent across Canada? Figure 3.2 shows the percentage of all Canadians, children, and individuals in female lone-parent families living in poverty by province. Overall poverty rates for Canadians are consistent across Canada. Generally, Alberta and Prince Edward Island have the lowest rates. Quebec has the highest overall, and Manitoba, the highest for children.

Some of the differences within regions that were apparent in 2004 are not seen for 2008. Differences among the Maritime provinces have lessened. Within the Prairies, Alberta has lower overall and child poverty rates than Manitoba and Saskatchewan, but similarly high female-led family rates.

Figure 3.2: Percentage of All Canadians, Children, and Individuals in Female Lone-Parent Families Living in Poverty, by Province, 2008

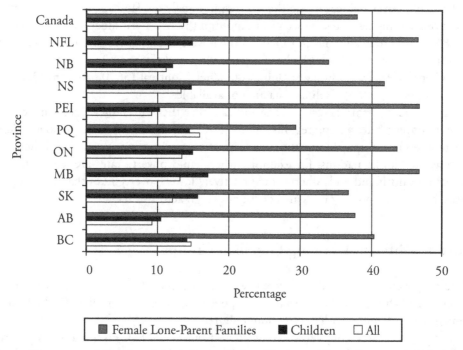

Source: "Percentages of Canadians living in Poverty by Age, Gender, and Family Situation, 2008," adapted from Statistics Canada CANSIM database, *http://cansim2.statcan.gc.ca*, Table 202-2802 extracted in 2010.

Concerning child poverty rates, Manitoba has the distinction of having the highest rates of children living in poverty, and Prince Edward Island and Alberta the lowest. Overall, the variation in child poverty rates among the provinces is generally narrow, with virtually all provinces showing rather high—and Alberta and PEI slightly lower—rates. The situation of female lone-parent families across Canada is especially problematic.

The lowest rates for these female lone-parent families are seen in Quebec, but in just about every other province, the poverty rates approach or exceed 40%. The figures for Newfoundland and Labrador, Manitoba, and Prince Edward Island are especially high.

Poverty rates for Census Metropolitan Areas, or CMAs, are also provided by Statistics Canada (Statistics Canada, 2010a). CMAs cover a much larger area than the cities proper and include areas that have a significant commuting association with the core cities. Overall poverty rates in 2008 are highest for Montreal (21.6%) and Vancouver (18%), and are lowest for Calgary (8.9%), Victoria (10.7%), and Edmonton (12%). The rates for other CMAs are midway between these values: Ottawa-Gatineau (15.1%), Toronto (15%), Winnipeg (14.2%), Halifax (13.5%), Saskatoon (12.4%), St. John's (13.2%), Regina, (11.7%), and Quebec City (10.4%).

Child poverty rates are highest in Montreal (21%), Regina (18.6%), St. John's (17.2%), Winnipeg (16.9%), Vancouver (16.2%), Edmonton (15.3%), and Ottawa-Gatineau (15.8%). The lowest rates, though still rather high, are seen in Quebec City (7.9%), Calgary (9.7%), Victoria (10.6%), and Halifax (10.9%). The rates for the other CMAs fall midway: Toronto (14.4%) and Saskatoon (14.8%).

For child poverty rates among those living in female-led families, there is very wide variation. The highest rates are seen in Edmonton (57.6%), Winnipeg (54.2%), Regina (53.8%), and Ottawa-Gatineau (53.1%). The lowest rates, though still rather high, are seen in Vancouver (22.7%), Quebec City (22.9%), and Calgary (24.1%).The rates for the other CMAs fall midway: St. John's (48.4%), Montreal (36.3), Toronto (32.1%), and Saskatoon (37.6%). Halifax data are not available.

These findings from across Canada indicate that there are rather significant differences in poverty rates among regions and major CMAs. However, there are no locations where rates are comparable to the very low rates seen in other national jurisdictions, such as the Nordic nations, for example, where child poverty rates are less than 5%. Prince Edward Island and Alberta show relatively lower poverty rates than other provinces, but overall, poverty rates are consistently high across Canada.

Poverty Differences among Canadian Groups

Data on poverty is reported in different ways. Sometimes the pre-tax LICOs are used; other times, after-tax LICOs. Sometimes poverty is reported for all individuals, and sometimes for families with and without children.

Campaign 2000 recently released tabulations from the 2006 Census that show poverty differences among social groups that are especially vulnerable to experiencing poverty (Campaign, 2010). In this case, pre-tax LICOs are used to generate child poverty rates (Figure 3.3).

Box 3.1: Things Are Not Getting Better

Why Poverty Is Worse Than It Was 30 Years Ago
Jean Swanson

Twenty-five years after working as a community organizer with the Downtown Eastside Residents' Association in Vancouver, I've come back to the community as a retired person, volunteering at the Carnegie Centre.

One good thing about being older is that you have actually experienced a little history. I believe there are some lessons for policy-makers in what I can remember about the Downtown Eastside.

Thirty years ago, as now, the Downtown Eastside was a poor neighbourhood. Then, as now, people with addictions were visible on the street. In those days alcohol was the drug used most often. Now it's other drugs.

But 30 years ago the stores along East Hastings Street weren't boarded up. We bought newspapers at Universal News. Residents could afford a few breakfasts a month at the Princess Cafe, a hot plate at Benmors, a coconut bun at the local bakery, a cheap shirt at Fields, a coffee at the Two Eagles Cafe.

Three decades ago, city hall planners weren't spending hours on end trying to figure out how to get richer people to move to the area to "revitalize" businesses.

Why are so many storefronts in the Downtown Eastside boarded up? Look no further than government policies for a big part of the answer. Low-income residents have lost a huge amount of purchasing power.

Thirty years ago, as now, most Downtown Eastside residents depended on low-wage work, pensions, unemployment insurance or welfare for their income. The purchasing power of three of those sources of income has declined drastically.

In fact, if we want to know how to quickly revive business in the Downtown Eastside, just restore the spending power of the current residents to 1975 levels. That would pump about $2 million a month into the cash registers of the community.

In 1975 the minimum wage in British Columbia was 122 per cent of the poverty line for a single person in a city. Today the $8 an hour minimum wage is only 78 per cent of the poverty line for a 37.5-hour week.

To look at it another way, a single person would have to make $12.51 an hour at a full-time, 37.5-hour-a-week job to have the same purchasing power as a minimum-wage worker had in 1975. A person who depends on today's $6 an hour so-called training wage will make only 58 per cent of today's poverty line with a full-time minimum-wage job.

Today, about 30 per cent of Downtown Eastside residents get their income from welfare, according to the city. Welfare for a single person whom the ministry considers employable is a maximum of $510 a month—$185 for support and $325 for shelter. In 1981, the support portion of welfare was $205. To have the same purchasing power as it had in 1982, the welfare support allowance would have to be $355.48 today. The current shelter portion of welfare is so low that most people have to use their food money for rent.

If the current welfare rate were raised to provide the same purchasing power as it did in 1989, there would be about $763,000 per month more purchasing power in the Downtown Eastside!

Before 1996, the federal Canada Assistance Plan made provinces provide welfare to people in dire need. In 1996, CAP was abolished. Today, numerous welfare rules and procedures effectively deny welfare to people in dire need. Two major studies have said that this is the main reason homelessness has doubled since 2002. Homeless people have virtually no purchasing power.

Can the Downtown Eastside be "revitalized" if provincial and federal policies create dire poverty and homelessness on the streets while city policies lure in people who can afford quarter-million-dollar condominiums?

In the book *The Impact of Inequality*, Richard Wilkinson, professor of social epidemiology at the University of Nottingham medical school, quotes study after study to show that great inequality destroys community, undermines democracy, fosters illness, makes learning difficult for poor students and increases despair, alienation and street crime.

The way to "revitalize" our community would be to restore purchasing power to the low-income residents who live here: Raise welfare rates, end the barriers to getting on welfare and boost the minimum wage.

Source: Swanson, J. (2006, February 21). Why poverty is worse than it was 30 years ago. *Vancouver Sun*, p. A11.

As shown, child (i.e., family with children) poverty rates are especially high for recent immigrants, all immigrants, those of Aboriginal identity, racialized groups, and those with a disability. As well, poverty rates were improving from 1996 to 2006, prior to the current economic recession.

Poverty rates for Aboriginal Canadians in general are higher in relation to overall Canadian rates. The Canadian 2000 Census revealed that 31.2% of Aboriginal Canadians living in families were living in poverty as compared to the overall Canadian rate of 12.9% (Jackson, 2010). Among unattached Aboriginal Canadians, the poverty rate was 55.9% as compared to the Canadian average of 38%. Data from 2005 using the after-tax LICOs showed a continuing double-digit difference in poverty rates between those of Aboriginal identity (21.7%) and non-Aboriginal Canadians (11.1%). Wilson and Macdonald (2010) provide further details of the 2006 average income gap of $8,000 between Canadians of Aboriginal identity ($18,962) and non-Aboriginal Canadians ($27,097).

In 1995, poverty rates for Canadians of colour were higher in every province than for other Canadians (Galabuzi, 2005). In Newfoundland and Labrador, the difference

Figure 3.3: Child Poverty Rates for Selected Social Groups in Canada: Children 0–14 Years, 1996–2006

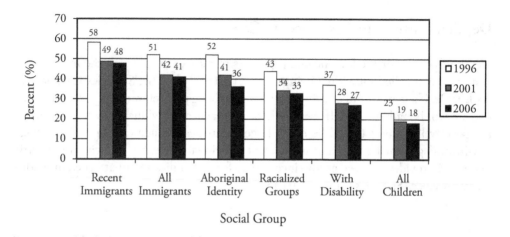

Source: "Child Poverty Rates for Selected Social Groups in Canada, Children 0-14 Years, 1996-2006," adapted from Statistics Canada, 2006, 2001 & 1996 Censuses through the Toronto Social Research and Community Data and Consortium (2006) and the Community Social Data Strategy (1996-2001), using LICO before-tax. Available on line at http://www.campaign2000.ca/reportCards/national/2010EnglishC2 000NationalReportCard.pdf

was relatively small, with 24.3% of Canadians of colour living in poverty as compared to 21.3% of other Canadians. But in the province of Quebec, the poverty rates for Canadians of colour was 52.2% as compared to 21.5% for other Canadians. This gap was apparent for every other province as well: in New Brunswick, 34% versus 20%; in Nova Scotia, 38% versus 19%; in Prince Edward Island, 28% versus 15%; in Ontario, 34% versus 15%; in Manitoba, 34% versus 11%; in Saskatchewan, 30% versus 18%; in Alberta, 35% versus 17%; and in British Columbia, 32% versus 18%.

What kind of trends do these figures represent? Figure 2.1 in the previous chapter provided poverty rates in Canada from 1984 to 2008 for all Canadians, children, seniors, unattached individuals, two-parent families, and female lone-parent families, based on before-tax LICOs. Given that the latest figures should be even higher than those of 2008, the most striking aspect of these figures is how little change they represent from rates seen in the 1980s. It is true that the rates for older Canadians significantly declined from 30% in 1984 to 13% in 2008. Much of this was the result of significant pension reforms and policy attention to the situation of older Canadians. Some improvement in rates was seen for unattached Canadians, two-parent families, and female lone-parent families. Rates for female-lone parent families and unattached individuals remained very high, however.

The improved 2008 figures follow a 10-year period of sustained growth in the Canadian economy. Historically, poverty rates decline during such periods and increase during periods of economic recession. Overall, however, these figures represent little change over the past two decades: the 2008 poverty rate for all Canadians of 14% can be expected to rise close to the 1984 rate of 19%.

Depth of Poverty or Low-Income Gap

Depth of poverty or the low-income gap refers to the extent to which the income of a family or unattached individual living in poverty falls below the Statistics Canada pre-tax LICOs. If a family or unattached individual is living just below the poverty line, then the gap will be rather small. If the family or unattached individual is living well below the poverty line, the gap will be much larger. Statistics Canada calculates the average low-income gap for families and unattached individuals identified as living in poverty. Figure 3.4 provides the average low-income gap for all families and unattached individuals by province (Statistics Canada, 2010b).

Figure 3.4: Average Low-Income Gap for All Families and Unattached Individuals for those Living in Poverty, by Province, 2007

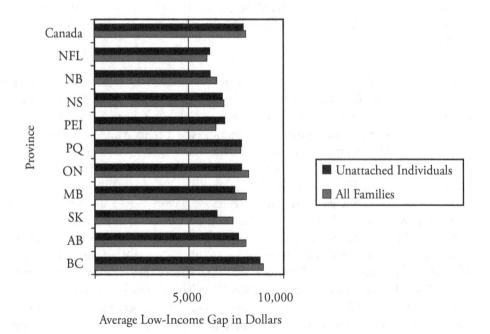

Source: "Average Low-Income Gap for All Families and Unattached Individuals for those Living in Poverty, by Province, 2007," adapted from Statistics Canada CANSIM database, *http://cansim2.statcan.gc.ca*, Table 202-2805 extracted in 2010.

In every province, families and unattached individuals living in poverty are, on average, living well below the poverty line. In Newfoundland and Labrador, this gap is the smallest but is still a staggering $6,100 for families and $6,300 for unattached individuals. The low-income gaps are higher in every other province, and especially high in British Columbia. This province has the second-highest poverty rates (see Figure 3.2) and the highest low-income gaps. In combination, these BC figures suggest that the "misery index" in British Columbia is the highest. These low-income gap figures indicate that poverty in Canada is not just a situation in which people fall just below poverty lines. Canadians living in poverty on average fall well below the poverty lines. This finding has profound implications for the health and quality of life of people living in poverty.

Earlier, it was suggested that poverty rates in Canada had shown little change over time. Have there been changes in the average low-income gap over this same period? Statistics Canada figures indicate that the average low-income gap for all Canadian families and unattached individuals from 1984 to 2008 remained remarkably constant over time. In 1984, the gap was $8,450 for families and $7,400 for unattached individuals. In 2008, the gap for families—in constant dollars—was reduced by $200 to $8,200, and it grew by $600 for unattached individuals to $8,000 (Statistics Canada, 2010b).

Relation to Income Trends

Poverty rates are very closely related to general income trends and the extent of income and wealth inequality. This is the case for a variety of reasons. The main reason is that income and wealth inequality represent resources being distributed unequally so as to benefit some at the expense of others. This usually means that well-off Canadians benefit most from a growing economy and that those near the bottom of the income distribution rather less so. If such is the case, individuals receiving less fall even further behind other Canadians in terms of being able to meet basic needs as assessed by the LICOs. Indirectly, a rising standard of living for some rather than all is associated with growth in living costs with those whose income and wealth are stagnating, being unable to keep pace. This either keeps the level of poverty at current levels or increases its incidence. Income and wealth inequality and the degree to which these indicators grow or shrink reflect public policy processes that shape resource allocation among Canadians.

Canadian Families and Children

In 2008, the median total income of all Canadian families was $54,800. For unattached non-elderly males it was $34,100, and for unattached non-elderly females, $25,900. For female lone-parent families, it was $37,900. The median means that half the group had incomes above and half had incomes below. Not surprisingly, unattached males and females have very low income (Statistics Canada, 2010c).

To what extent do these 2008 figures represent a trend over time? Figure 3.5 provides median income data for Canadian families and unattached individuals, from 1995 to 2008. Median income for all families increased by $7,600 over this period. Income for non-elderly unattached males was up but the increase was less for unattached non-elderly females. The median incomes for all Canadian families appear high. These numbers, in regard to families, may be deceiving, however. To what extent have these increases in income for families been consistent across the income range? Median income may simply be reflecting gains by the most well-off.

To address this issue, Statistics Canada reports total average income as a function of income quintile (Statistics Canada, 2010d). This simply means that families are placed into one of five equal groups ranked from lowest income to top income. Figure 3.6 presents these data for all family units in Canada from 1995 to 2008.

Figure 3.6 provides striking evidence that the gains in median income reported from 1995 to 2008 are predominantly acquired by one income group: the most well-off 20% of Canadian families. For those families in the top income quintile, average income grew from $128,000 to close to $170,000, an increase of over $40,000. In contrast, the average income of the bottom 20% of Canadian families grew by a mere $1,900 over that same period. Indeed, even the middle quintile of Canadian families saw their income grow by only about $7,500 over this 10-year period.

Figure 3.5: Median Total Income for All Families, Unattached Individuals, and Female-Led Families, Canada, 1995–2008

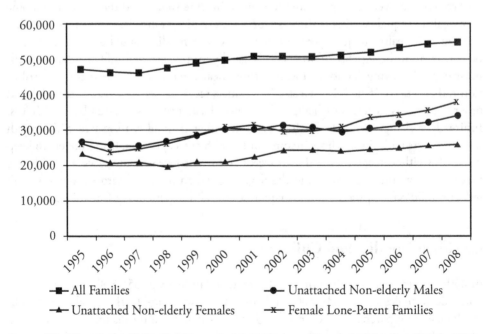

Source: "Total Income for All Families, Unattached Individuals, and Female-Led Families, Canada, 1995–2008," adapted from Statistics Canada CANSIM database, *http://cansim2.statcan.gc.ca*, Table 202-0403 extracted in 2010.

Figure 3.6: Total Average Income by Income Quintile, All Family Units, Canada, 1995–2008

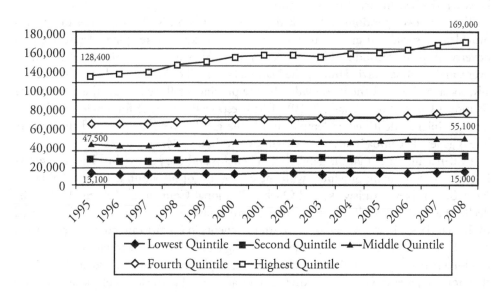

Source: "Total Income for All Families, Unattached Individuals, and Female-Led Families, Canada, 1995–2008," adapted from Statistics Canada CANSIM database, *http://cansim2.statcan.gc.ca*, Table 202-0701, extracted in 2010.

Similar findings are apparent when the income of non-elderly unattached Canadians is examined. The incomes of the top 20% of unattached Canadians rose by $17,000 from $68,800 in 1995 to $85,800 in 2008. The incomes of the bottom 20% of unattached Canadians, however, increased by only $1,300 from $7,500 in 1994 to $8,600 in 2008 (Statistics Canada, 2010c).

All of this reflects a growing degree of income—and wealth—inequality in Canada (see Figure 2.3 in the previous chapter). The finding that economic gains have been primarily accruing for the most well-off suggests that the growth in the economy has not been benefiting the Canadian population as a whole but rather those who are most well-off to begin with. Further evidence concerning the growth in income and wealth inequality, and an examination of the implications of such growth, follows analysis of why there are so many Canadian living in poverty and why specific groups are at higher risk of living in poverty.

Issues Driving the Incidence of Poverty

Four obvious issues drive the incidence of poverty in Canada. These are the level of social assistance benefits, the level of the minimum wage, the incidence of low-wage employment, and the differences in employment situations and wages of groups identified as being at risk for poverty. These issues arise throughout this volume. In this section, an overview of why these issues are important is presented.

Social Assistance

Issues associated with social assistance are examined in more detail in Chapter 7. Here, however, the benefit structure is examined.

There are two questions to be asked. The first question is: Are the levels of benefits provided by social assistance schedules adequate for keeping recipients from living in poverty? And the second is: Have the levels of social assistance benefits been declining over time? Analyses carried out by the National Council of Welfare indicate that, generally, social assistance benefits provided by the provinces fall well below the poverty line (National Council of Welfare, 2010). This is especially the case for single social assistance recipients identified as "employable." The gap between benefits and the poverty line is generally comparable across provinces (see Table 3.1).

Evidence indicates that the gap between benefits and the poverty line has been growing over time in many provinces with the exceptions of Newfoundland and Labrador, Nova Scotia, New Brunswick, and Quebec (National Council of Welfare, 2010). The decline has been especially great in Ontario, which saw social assistance benefits reduced by 22% in 1995. In real dollar values, current benefits in Ontario are now—as compared to 1992 in constant dollars—40% less for a single person considered employable, 20% less for a person with a disability, 12% less for a single parent with a child, and 29% less than for two parents with two children. It is clear, then, that the levels of social assistance benefits available to Canadians are so low as to make not living in poverty impossible.

Table 3.1: Total Welfare Income as a Percentage of the Poverty Line (After-tax LICOs) for Various Categories, by Province, 2009

Province	Single Employable	Person with a Disability	Lone Parent, One Child	Couple, Two Children
Newfoundland	62%	71%	102%	76%
Prince Edward Island	45%	59%	88%	83%
Nova Scotia	41%	59%	79%	71%
New Brunswick	24%	56%	85%	67%
Quebec	40%	59%	78%	65%
Ontario	41%	70%	77%	65%
Manitoba	37%	51%	66%	62%
Saskatchewan	56%	70%	95%	81%
Alberta	39%	51%	70%	63%
British Columbia	42%	62%	75%	61%

Source: Adapted from National Council of Welfare. (2010). *Welfare incomes: 2009* (Table 4, pp. A13–A14). Ottawa: National Council of Welfare.

Minimum Wages

In October 2010, minimum wages in Canada ranged from a high of $10.25 in Ontario to a low of $8.00 in British Columbia (About.com, 2010). In 2004, the National Council of Welfare calculated the extent to which 2000-level minimum wages allowed a full-time worker to approach or exceed the poverty lines based on the LICOs and the Market Basket Measure for the four largest provinces (National Council of Welfare, 2004) (see Table 3.2). For virtually every scenario presented, minimum wages fell below the LICOs level. However, for all cases in Quebec, and for half the cases in Ontario, minimum wages approached or exceeded the Market Basket Measure cut-off. This was not the case in Alberta or British Columbia, though, where earning the minimum wage meant living in poverty. There is little reason to think that current analyses would differ from these estimates.

Low Wages

Statistics Canada defines low-wage workers as those full-time workers earning less than $375 a week (Chung, 2004). A report tracked the proportion of Canadians in this situation from 1980 to 2000. The 2000 findings are presented in Table 3.3. In 2000, 16.3% of Canadian workers were identified as low-wage earners. The figure for any group identified in the table that is above that 16.3% figure represents a concentration of low-wage workers within that group. Of note is that groups identified as being at higher risk of living in poverty are more likely to be overrepresented among low-wage earners.

Twenty-one percent of Canadian women are low-wage earners, as compared to 12.1% of men. Being a recent or mid-immigrant is associated with greater likelihood of being a low-wage earner. And younger workers and those with less educational attainment are also more likely to be a low-wage earner. Finally, female lone parents are twice as likely to be low-wage earners than male lone parents. Findings from 1980 to 2000 (not tabled here) indicate an increasing concentration of low-wage workers among less educated males, younger workers, visible minority males, and immigrant males (Saunders, 2006).

Table 3.2: Minimum Wage Income as a Percentage of the Market Basket Measure and LICOs Poverty Lines for the Four Largest Provinces, 2000

Province	Single Employable		Person with a Disability		Single Parent, One Child		Couple, Two Children	
	MBM	LICO	MBM	LICO	MBM	LICO	MBM	LICO
Quebec	112%	83%	122%	90%	132%	112%	127%	97%
Ontario	92%	83%	100%	90%	92%	95%	100%	93%
Alberta	91%	73%	98%	78%	82%	75%	110%	91%
British Columbia	91%	84%	99%	91%	84%	88%	98%	93%

Source: Adapted from National Council of Welfare. (2004). *Income for living?* (pp. 16, 25, 35, 45). Ottawa: National Council of Welfare.

Box 3.2: Minimum Wages and Poverty in Canada

Summary: Bringing Minimum Wages above the Poverty Line

The vast majority of Canadians agree government should take action to reduce poverty and income inequality. A poll conducted by Environics Research for the Canadian Centre for Policy Alternatives indicates more than eight in 10 Canadians (85%) say if government took concrete action, poverty in Canada could be drastically reduced.

A similar proportion (88%) say that increasing the minimum wage to a level that will raise workers in full-time minimum wage jobs out of poverty is an effective way to reduce Canada's growing gap.

Advocacy for a higher minimum wage has been gaining momentum across the country, with many regional campaigns focusing on raising the minimum wage to $10. This study shows that raising the minimum wage to $10 an hour (in 2005 dollars) is do-able—in fact, it has been done in Canada in the past. The real (after-inflation) minimum wage in BC reached $10.15 per hour in 1976, and a number of other jurisdictions have had real minimum wages close to $10.

But recently that hasn't been the case. It has been common for provinces to allow several years to pass without a minimum wage increase, allowing inflation to erode the value of the real minimum wage over time.

Too often, politicians have been content to let the minimum wage languish until forced to act. To date, no government in Canada has been prepared to adopt a consistent approach to the determination of the minimum wage. Consequently, minimum wages in Canada have been influenced more by political than economic considerations. As a result, the real value of minimum wages in Canada has fluctuated.

Although minimum wage patterns vary from province to province, some general trends are evident from the data for all provinces:

- It's been a long time since the minimum wage hit its $10 peak. The minimum wage tended to increase, in real terms, from the beginning of our study period in 1968 until reaching a peak in the mid-to-late 1970s.
- After the late 1970s, the minimum wage dropped steadily, reaching a low point between 1984 and 1990 (depending on the province). Low-paid workers are overdue for a raise. While levels of education and experience have increased and GDP has grown, real wages remained stagnant from 1981 to 2004. Median wages (in 2001 dollars) have gone from $15.16 in 1981 to $15.33 in 2004, a mere 1.1% increase over 23 years. Wages are stagnant while workers are stepping up their work effort to help grow Canada's economy. A higher minimum wage is one of several steps toward a higher wage economy that acknowledges the contribution and value of Canadian workers.

Critics typically make three types of arguments against increasing minimum wages: there are so few people working at the minimum wage the problem is trivial; because most minimum wage earners are young people living at home, we shouldn't be worried about what they are paid; and, negative employment effects from increases in minimum wages are so substantial that higher minimum wages will actually hurt more than they will help.

This study debunks those myths.

Source: Murray, S., and Mackenzie, H. (2007). Summary of *Bringing minimum wages above the poverty line*. Retrieved March 11, 2011 from Canadian Centre for Policy Alternatives website: www.policyalternatives.ca/sites/default/files/uploads/publications/National_Office_Pubs/2007/minimum_wage_summary.pdf

Other Issues Resulting in Increased Risk of Living in Poverty

Aboriginal Canadians, people of colour, people with disabilities, recent immigrants, and women are at risk of living in poverty in large part due to the nature of their attachment to the workforce. In a nation such as Canada that provides modest social assistance benefits, income from paid employment is extremely important for keeping one out of poverty. Findings indicate that each of the groups mentioned above experiences greater incidence of unemployment and of part-time rather than full-time employment, and each receives lower wages than other Canadians (Jackson, 2010).

In addition to these differences in employment rates, there is now extensive evidence that working females receive less income from employment than working males, working visible minority Canadians receive less income from employment than Canadians of European descent, and working people with disabilities receive less income than working Canadians without disabilities. The situation of recent immigrants to Canada—many of whom are people of colour—is especially problematic. Extensive documentation of these income gaps is available in recent volumes by Galabuzi (2005) and Jackson (2010). Many have suggested a deepening of the racialization and feminization of poverty in Canada (Wallis and Kwok, 2008). An overview of groups at increased risk of poverty is provided here.

Aboriginal Canadians
Aboriginal Canadians are more likely to live in poverty, and this is related to a greater incidence of unemployment, unavailability of full-time employment, and lower income for both full-time and part-time employment (Galabuzi, 2005; Jackson, 2010; Smiley, 2009). The average income of Aboriginal Canadians in 2000 was $19,132, which is $10,000 less than the Canadian average of $29,769. The incidence of poverty of Aboriginal Canadians living in families was 31.2% (compared to 12.9% for all Canadians), and the percentage of unattached Aboriginal Canadians living in poverty was 55.9% (compared to 38% for all Canadians).

Table 3.3: Percentage of Wage Earners Who Are Low-Paid Workers, Canada, 2000

Characteristics	All	Men	Women
All Wage Earners	16.3	12.1	21.9
Education			
Less than High School	26.3	19.0	39.2
High School	20.7	15.6	27.0
Certificate	13.5	9.2	19.0
University	6.5	5.4	7.8
Age			
15–24	45.0	39.9	52.4
25–34	16.3	12.2	21.5
35–44	13.1	8.5	19.0
45–54	12.0	9.0	17.1
55–64	14.4	10.5	20.9
Immigrant Status			
Recent Immigrant	27.4	20.5	36.4
Mid-Immigrant	22.4	17.4	28.4
Old Immigrant	12.5	9.3	18.8
Canadian-Born	16.0	11.8	21.5
Visible Minority Status			
Visible Minority (VM)	21.2	17.2	26.0
Non-visible Minority	15.6	11.5	21.3
Canadian-Born VM	17.1	16.6	17.7
Canadian-Born Non-VM	16.0	11.8	21.6
Recent Immigrant VM	31.1	23.8	40.1
Recent Immigrant non-VM	18.7	13.0	26.8
Mid-Immigrant VM	24.7	19.7	30.7
Mid-Immigrant non-VM	16.8	12.3	22.8
Old-Immigrant VM	14.5	11.5	17.8
Old-Immigrant non-VM	11.4	8.0	16.1
Family Status			
Lone Mothers	23.3		23.3
Lone Fathers	10.7	10.7	
Unattached <40 Years of Age	25.3	22.2	30.7
Unattached 40+ Years of Age	17.2	13.5	22.5

Source: Adapted from Statistics Canada, Low-paid workers: How many live in low-income families? Perspectives on Labour and Income, 75-001-XIE2004110, Vol.5 No.10, October 2004; http://www.stat-can.gc.ca/bsolc/olc-cel/olc-cel?catno=75-001-XIE&lang=eng#formatdisp

Much of this has to do with the lower participation rate in the labour force (i.e., through employment or by looking for employment) of Aboriginal Canadians (61.4% versus 66.4% for Canada); the higher unemployment rate (19.1% versus 7.4% for Canada); the lower percentage of full-time workers (40.5% versus 53.9% for Canada); and the lower employment income for full-time workers ($33,416 versus $43,298 for Canada) and for part-time workers ($13,795 versus $19,207 for Canada).

Canadians of Colour

Canadians of colour are also more likely to be unemployed, have less full-time employment, and receive lower salaries than other Canadians (Galabuzi, 2005). Jackson (2010) reports that Canadians of colour as a group earned less in 2000 than Canadians in general ($27,149 versus $31,757). In addition, immigrants to Canada, many of whom are people of colour, are also likely to earn less than Canadians in general. Immigrants who arrived during the period of 1990 to 1994 earned on average $25,560, and immigrants who arrived from 1995 to 1999 earned $23,889 as compared to the Canadian average of $31,757.

Galabuzi (2005) adds that racialized groups in Canada in 1998 showed higher than average unemployment, with unemployment rates two to three times higher than non-racialized groups. These groups also experienced deepening levels of poverty, overrepresentation in lower paying and lower status jobs, differential access to housing, increasing racial and economic concentration in Canadian urban areas, and disproportionate contact with the criminal justice system (Ornstein, 2000; Pendakur, 2000; Reitz, 2001).

People with Disabilities

People with disabilities are less likely to be employed and, when they are employed, earn less than people without disabilities (Jackson, 2010). A full 52% of Canadians with disabilities are not in the labour force, forcing many of them to rely upon social assistance benefits. The low level of these benefits prevent living out of poverty.

In 2001, the average earnings of the 43% of people with disabilities who were employed were $32,385, whereas the average earnings of the 78.4% of people without a disability who were employed were $38,677.

Recent Immigrants to Canada

Statistics Canada has documented differences in income and employment status of recent and earlier immigrant to Canada (Picot, 2004). There is a consistent finding that the rate of low income among immigrants (particularly recent immigrants) has been rising since the 1990s while falling for people born in Canada. Picot attempted to identify the factors responsible for the deteriorating economic welfare of immigrants and found that the rise in low-income status affected immigrants in all education and age groups, including the university-educated (Picot, 2004). The study found that the economic returns to recent immigrants for their work experience and education were diminished in comparison to those of earlier immigrants. Considering that 75% of these recent immigrants were members of racialized groups, the hypothesis that racism and discrimination is responsible for these diminishing returns must be considered.

Box 3.3: Toronto Poverty Is Highly Racialized: York University Census Study

TORONTO, March 9, 2006—Poverty in Toronto is highly racialized, and the economic gap between members of European and non-European ethno-racial groups has been increasing over the last 30 years, a new study reveals.

All 20 of the poorest ethno-racial groups in the Toronto Census Metropolitan Area (CMA) are non-European, according to the study, Ethno-Racial Groups in Toronto, 1971–2001: A Demographic and Social Profile, released by the Institute for Social Research at York University. The 182-page report is based primarily on Statistics Canada's 2001 census, and compares those results with censuses of 1996, 1991, 1986, 1981, and 1971.

Extreme poverty is a daily reality for more than half of the members of the Bangladeshi, Somali, Afghan, and Ethiopian ethno-racial groups, the 2001 census reveals. Their family incomes fell below Statistics Canada's "low income cut-off"— the most commonly used standard for measuring poverty in Canada. Three groups faced poverty rates of between 40 and 50 per cent, and 14 other groups, five of them African and including Aboriginals, had poverty rates of between 30 and 40 per cent.

"Although every ethno-racial group experiences some poverty, many groups are facing extraordinary economic difficulty," says ISR Director Michael Ornstein, author of the report. "The magnitude of global differences in family income is not decreasing—quite the opposite."

Some groups face poverty levels that have remained about the same for 30 years. In 1971, Caribbean ethno-racial groups had 21.7 per cent of their members below the poverty line, compared to 25.2 per cent in 1981, 21 per cent in 1991, and 22.2 percent in 2001. These statistics alone only begin to describe the story. Ornstein notes that "because the low income cut-off figure does not account for Toronto's very high housing costs, these numbers, if anything, underestimate the extent of poverty."

"As the population from non-European groups in Canada has increased from about four per cent in 1971 to about 40 per cent in 2001, the racialization of poverty has increased," says Ornstein.

"In our highly individualistic society, we tend to think of poverty as the result of bad luck, such as someone losing a job, coping with a family breakup, or facing the challenges of immigrating or coming to Toronto from a small town. But this research reveals entire communities where the average income is very low and many, many people live in poverty," says Ornstein. "For groups with 20 or 25 per cent of people below the poverty line, we have to think in structural terms: about kids not completing high school, the low level of the minimum wage, the expense of good daycare, the problems of finding a job that uses their skills and credentials, the very high cost of housing and our governments' retreat from social housing over the last 20 years, and the effects of discrimination."

The census reveals that 40 per cent of African ethno-racial group members lived below the poverty line in 2001, compared to about 30 per cent of the members of the Arab and East Asian groups, and 20 per cent of the Aboriginal, South Asian, East Asian, Caribbean, and South and Central American groups. By comparison, only 10 per cent of European group members were below the poverty line, and for some European groups the figure was only about five per cent.

Substantial differences also exist in the economic situations of ethno-racial groups within larger global categories. For example, 53.1 per cent of Bangladeshis had incomes below the poverty line in 2001, compared to 36 per cent for the Pakistani group, about 33 per cent for Tamil and Sri Lankan groups, and 15 per cent for the Indian group. Among Torontonians who described themselves as having both South Asian and East Asian or South Asian and European ancestry, the poverty rate was about 12 per cent. (The average for the entire CMA population is 15 per cent below the poverty line.)

The research is based on the detailed information collected every five years from the randomly selected one-fifth of all Canadian households who receive the "long form" census questionnaire. In 2001, the CMA population of about 4.6 million was represented in a sample of approximately 800,000 census returns. The CMA is defined by Statistics Canada as the area in which patterns of commuting to work are centered on Toronto. The City of Toronto accounts for just over half of the CMA population, which also includes 23 surrounding municipalities, the largest of which are Brampton, Markham, Mississauga, Oakville and Vaughan.

For this research, the CMA population was divided into ethno-racial groups on the basis of the census question: "To which ethnic or cultural group(s) did your ancestors belong?" (emphasis original.) Most are individual nationalities, such as the British, Argentinian and Nigerian groups. Smaller groups were consolidated into residual categories, such as "other African," and there are also categories for persons with joint ancestry such as "South Asian and European." In total, the study covers 113 ethno-racial groups, subdivided into eight global regions, of which 78 are single nationalities. The report also provides detailed information on the demographic characteristics of ethno-racial groups, including their population growth since 1971, and their age composition, immigration language use, education, and employment.

The entire study is available in PDF format at http://www.isr.yorku.ca/home.html. Click on "Publications," then "Ethno-racial Report: Ethno-Racial Groups in Toronto."

Source: York University Media Services. (2006, March 9). *Ethno-racial report: Ethno-racial groups in Toronto* [Press release]. Retrieved March 11, 2011 from www.yorku.ca/mediar/archive/Release.php?Release=1060

Women

Women are more likely to be working part-time than men. In addition, women earn less than men, regardless of their occupation (Jackson, 2010). Among women working in management, for example, women earn on average $956 a week as compared to $1,261 earned by men. Even in occupations dominated by women, such as clerical jobs, women earn less than men ($518 a week compared to $605 a week). The earnings gap represents a number of issues. Women work fewer hours than men and their hourly wages are only 80% of the wages of men. Jackson (2010) points out that job fields that are more dominated by men tend to pay more, and even when women work in these fields, they tend to get paid less.

There are numerous reasons why women work fewer hours than men. A predominant reason concerns the lack of affordable and quality daycare, which forces family responsibilities onto women (Friendly, 2009). In 2001, women earned about two-thirds of the income of men. Even when women work full-time, their earnings equal only 72% of that earned by men (Jackson, 2010). And a study by Statistics Canada found that, even when controls for factors such as work experience and job-related responsibilities are applied, gender differences in wages between men and women remain. The report stated that "despite the long list of productivity-related factors, a substantial portion of the gender gap cannot be explained" (Drolet, 2001, abstract).

Rising Income and Wealth Inequality and the Concentration of Poverty

It was suggested earlier that the stagnating incomes and continuing high levels of poverty were occurring within a context of rising income and wealth inequality (Morissette, Zhang, and Drolet, 2002; Myles, Picot, and Pyper, 2000). As the economy has grown, the benefits of this growth have primarily been accruing for the most well-off Canadians. In contrast, the situation of the bottom 50% of Canadians has stagnated or declined. In addition to data showing that income gains have occurred primarily among the well-off, there is evidence that the number of people in the middle of the income distribution in Canada is levelling out, with numbers of Canadians increasing at both the top (rich) and bottom (poor) of the income distribution. Furthermore, inequalities in wealth have dramatically increased. The most recent data for 2006 shows an explosion of wealth at the top, while those at the bottom have actually lost ground in ownership of assets (Osberg, 2008). The bottom 20% of Canadians have no net assets, while the top 20% of Canadians own 75% of Canada's wealth.

As noted, Curry-Stevens (2009) shows that, in addition to the income gains going to the most well-off Canadians, the numbers of working poor and very well-off have increased while the number of middle-income people has declined. She also shows that low-income people suffer the greatest declines in income during recessions but make little of this up during economic recoveries. In contrast, the wealthy suffer relatively little during recessions but experience large growth in incomes during economic recoveries.

These analyses suggest that the current recession will see dramatic increases in the number of people living in poverty that will take a long period of time to reduce.

While poverty rates have remained constant, there is increasing concentration of poverty within urban neighbourhoods (Heisz and McLeod, 2004; Wilkins, 2007; Wilkins, Berthelot, and Ng, 2002). This concentration has a strong racial component to it, resulting in increasing racial segregation in Canadian cities and producing a situation that in other nations has been associated with urban decay and escalating social problems (Galabuzi, 2005).

Public Policy, Persisting Poverty, and Stagnating Incomes

Living in poverty results from a lack of financial resources. If analysis of the incidence of poverty is limited to looking at the wages individuals receive, then the incidence of poverty can be attributed to individual characteristics. People live in poverty because they are less educated. People live in poverty because they cannot work. And so on. But a public policy perspective asks what it is about a nation that leads to so many people being provided with so little economic supports that they live in poverty.

Canada's poverty rates are higher than most wealthy developed nations (OECD, 2008) because Canada has a greater degree of income inequality and a greater proportion of low-wage workers than most other wealthy developed nations (Picot and Myles, 2005). Within this context of greater poverty, the market sorts people such that those with less education, women, people with disabilities, people of colour, or immigrants become more likely to be included in those living in poverty. Yet in many other nations, being a woman, having a disability, being a person of colour, or being a recent immigrant is not as strongly related to living in poverty as is the case in Canada (Innocenti Research Centre, 2005). Much of this has to do with the levels of benefits provided to families, labour legislation and regulations in these other nations that promote economic security, and the making of public policies that assure that every citizen is able to achieve an acceptable standard of living.

In addition, changes in Canadian public policy have resulted in worsening housing situations, reductions in social assistance benefits in many provinces, and increasing food insecurity in many cities (Bryant, 2004; Food Banks Canada, 2010; McIntyre and Rondeau, 2009; Shapcott, 2009). All of these developments make the situation of people living in poverty more precarious than it already is.

Conclusions

A number of public policy domains contribute to the poverty situation in Canada. Social assistance provides benefits of last resort to Canadians unable to gain income in the labour market. These benefits in every province are well below the LICOs and in many cases have declined in relation to the poverty line. The situation is especially problematic for single individuals identified as "employable," a term that has a problematic meaning considering that the known unemployment rate in Canada has hovered around 6–9% over the past two decades. Many argue that the actual unemployment rate is around 12% or higher (Swartz, 2004). Eligibility for employment insurance has been drastically reduced, helping to keep wages down. Less than 50% of workers are now eligible for benefits (Black and Shillington, 2005). Low-paid employment is defined internationally as less than 66% of median income of a nation. Approximately 23% of Canadians are so defined—a figure that is very high in international comparison. Much of this can be traced to Canada's very low minimum wages (Battle, 2003).

The impact of low wages and benefits have been made worse by rising housing costs and shortages of affordable housing created by government withdrawal from the housing area (Shapcott, 2009) These decisions have led to a situation in which it appears that any Canadian who is not a well-educated male of European descent and without a disability is at increased risk of living in poverty. Why this may be the case constitutes the content of the next chapter.

Critical Thinking Questions

1. What does it say about Canadian society that so many groups appear to be at risk of experiencing poverty in Canada?
2. Do you think the risk of poverty is additive, such that the likelihood of someone being poor increases as a function of their being non-white + female + less educated? How would you test this hypothesis?
3. What do you think is the primary reason that members of the groups identified in this chapter are poor? Does it have to do with their characteristics, with how society is organized and managed, or with an interaction between both of these domains? Why?
4. What will be the future of Canada if nothing is done to address the higher poverty rates of the groups identified in this chapter? Can you predict that there will be different outcomes for different groups? What would these outcomes be? Why?
5. Do you know people who are experiencing poverty? Are they members of the groups identified in this chapter? Had you noticed this pattern before you read the material in this chapter?

Recommended Readings

Davies, L., McMullin, J. A., Avison, W., and Cassidy, G. (2001). *Social policy, gender inequality, and poverty.* Ottawa: Status of Women Canada. Online at http://dsp-psd.pwgsc.gc.ca/Collection/SW21-64-2000E.pdf

    In this report, quantitative and qualitative data are used to examine the factors and processes that influence poverty among women. Results indicate that mothers' choices about work and family shape, and are shaped by, broader gender arrangements that prioritize motherhood and marriage over economic independence.

Galabuzi, G. E. (2005). *Canada's economic apartheid: The social exclusion of racialized groups in the new century.* Toronto: Canadian Scholars' Press Inc.

> This book calls attention to the growing racialization of the gap between rich and poor, which is proceeding with minimal public and policy attention. This book challenges some common myths about the economic performance of Canada's racialized communities and points to the role of historical patterns of systemic racial discrimination as essential in understanding the persistent overrepresentation of racialized groups in low-paying occupations.

Jackson, A. (2010). *Work and labour in Canada: Critical issues* (2nd ed.). Toronto: Canadian Scholars' Press Inc.

> This book focuses on critical issues surrounding work and labour in Canada. It provides up-to-date data on the situation of people with disabilities, Canadians of colour, Aboriginal Canadians, women, and other groups at risk of living in poverty. It also places the Canadian employment scene in international perspective.

National Council of Welfare. (2004). *Income for living?* Ottawa: National Council of Welfare.

> This report looks at the income of people on welfare and the income of people with jobs. The study compares welfare incomes with the gross incomes and take-home incomes of full-time workers with minimum-wage jobs, jobs that pay $10 an hour, and jobs with average wages. *Income for Living* also looks at the impact of federal and provincial tax and benefit programs on these low-income and average-income people in Montreal, Toronto, Calgary, and Vancouver.

Policy Research Initiative. (2004). Poverty and exclusion: New perspectives, new approaches. *Horizons Magazine* [Special Issue], 7(2). Online at www.policyresearch. gc.ca/doclib/HOR_v7n2_200712_e.pdf

> Poverty rates in Canada stand little-improved from 20 years ago. This issue of *Horizons* contains several contributions that range from descriptions of how poverty has evolved and the groups affected to literature reviews and analytical pieces touching on tools and policies.

Wallis, M., and Kwok, S. (Eds.). (2008). *Daily struggles: The deepening racialization and feminization of poverty in Canada.* Toronto: Canadian Scholars' Press Inc.

> *Daily Struggles* offers a critical perspective on poverty by highlighting gender and race analyses simultaneously. This book connects human rights, political economy perspectives, and citizenship issues to other areas of social exclusion, such as class, sexuality, and disability.

Relevant Websites

Campaign 2000—www.campaign2000.ca

> Campaign 2000 is an advocacy group working to eliminate child poverty in Canada. The campaign began shortly after the all-party motion in the House of Commons was passed in 1989 to end child poverty by the year 2000.

Canada without Poverty—www.cwp-csp.ca

> Formerly the National Anti-poverty Organization, Canada without Poverty is a non-profit organization representing the millions of Canadians currently living in poverty. Its mandate is to eradicate poverty in this country. Its 19-member board is made up of people who currently live in poverty or have lived in poverty at some time in their lives, and its membership is made up of low-income individuals, organizations that provide direct and indirect services to the poor, and other concerned Canadians.

Canadian Council on Social Development (CCSD)—www.ccsd.ca

> The CCSD is a social policy and research organization focusing on social welfare and development issues such as poverty, social inclusion, disability, cultural diversity, child well-being, employment, and housing. It provides statistics and reports on the state of poverty and income inequality in Canada and policy options for improving the health and well-being of Canadians.

National Council on Welfare (NCW)—www.ncwcnbes.net

> The NCW advises the Canadian government on matters related to social welfare and the needs of low-income Canadians. NCW publishes several reports each year on poverty and social policy issues, presents submissions to Parliamentary Committees and Royal Commissions, and provides information on poverty and social policy.

Statistics Canada Analytic Studies Branch—www.tinyurl.com/m378c

> The papers in this series cover a wide variety of topics related to poverty. These include incidence rates, predictors of poverty, and various analyses that tease out various dimensions of poverty.

Glossary of Terms

Depth of poverty is also known as the low-income gap. It refers to the extent to which the income of a person or family living in poverty falls below the LICOs. In Canada, the average depth of poverty is very high. People living in poverty in Canada are not living just below the poverty lines; in many cases, they are living very far below these lines. The depth of poverty is especially great in Alberta, Ontario, and British Columbia.

Low-wage workers are those people living on incomes identified as significantly below the average-wage earnings. Statistics Canada defines a low-wage worker as earning less than $375 a week. Many advocacy groups define a low-wage worker as someone earning less than $10/hour. Internationally, a low-wage worker is defined as someone earning less than 66% of the median income. Canada's rate of low-wage workers (23%) is very high in international comparison.

Minimum wage is the lowest wage allowed within a jurisdiction. In Canada, this wage is set by each province. Unlike many other nations, Canada and its provinces do not have a statutory agency that is responsible for establishing a minimum livable wage for its citizens. In Canada, working full time on current levels of minimum wage is usually not enough to prevent someone from living in poverty. Canada's minimum wage levels are low in international comparison.

Poverty rates refer to the percentage of Canadians or a group of Canadians whose income is at levels below the LICOs. While Statistics Canada has been advocating use of the after-tax LICOs, most advocacy groups continue to use the pre-tax LICOs as a more valid and understandable indicator of the poverty line cut-offs.

Social assistance is also known as *welfare* and involves benefits of last resort. In Canada, one must have virtually no liquid assets to allow receipt of social assistance benefits. These levels are set so low as to put the ability to live on them in question. It is estimated that as many as 40% of people receiving such benefits are children. Despite numerous pleas and ongoing advocacy to improve the lives of those receiving social benefits, there is virtually no movement on the part of governments to significantly raise the levels of the benefits.

References

About.com (2010). Minimum wage in Canada. *Canada online.* Retrieved December 15, 2010, from http://canadaonline.about.com/od/labourstandards/a/minimum-wage-in-canada.htm

Battle, K. (2003). *Minimum wages in Canada: A statistical portrait with policy implications.* Ottawa: Caledon Institute.

Black, J., and Shillington, E. R. (2005). *Employment insurance: Research summary for the task force for modernizing income security for working age adults* (pp. 159–166). Toronto: Toronto City Summit Alliance.

Bryant, T. (2004). Housing as a social determinant of health. In D. Hulchanski and M. Shapcott (Eds.), *Policy options for an affordable rental housing strategy for Canada.* Toronto: Centre for Urban and Community Studies, University of Toronto.

Campaign 2000. (2010). 2010 *Report card on child and family poverty in Canada 1989–2010: Reduced poverty = better health for all.* Toronto: Campaign 2000.

Chung, L. (2004). Low-paid workers: How many live in low-income families? *Perspectives on Labour and Income, 16*(4), 23–32.

Curry-Stevens, A. (2009). When economic growth doesn't trickle down: the wage dimensions of income polarization. In D. Raphael (Ed.), *Social determinants of health: Canadian perspectives* (2nd ed., pp. 41–60). Toronto: Canadian Scholars' Press Inc.

Drolet, M. (2001). *The persistent gap: New evidence on the Canadian gender wage gap.* Ottawa: Analytic Studies Branch, Statistics Canada.

Finnie, R., and Sweetman, A. (2003). Poverty dynamics: Empirical evidence for Canada. *Canadian Journal of Economics, 36*(2), 291–325.

Food Banks Canada. (2010). *Hunger count 2009.* Toronto: Food Banks Canada.

Friendly, M. (2009). Early childhood education and care. In D. Raphael (Ed.), *Social determinants of health: Canadian perspectives* (2nd ed., pp. 128–142). Toronto: Canadian Scholars' Press Inc.

Galabuzi, G. E. (2005). *Canada's economic apartheid: The social exclusion of racialized groups in the new century.* Toronto: Canadian Scholars' Press Inc.

Heisz, A., and McLeod, L. (2004). *Low-income in census metropolitan areas, 1980–2000.* Ottawa: Statistics Canada.

Innocenti Research Centre. (2005). *Child poverty in rich nations, 2005* (Report Card No. 6). Florence: Innocenti Research Centre.

Jackson, A. (2010). *Work and labour in Canada: Critical issues* (2nd ed.). Toronto: Canadian Scholars' Press Inc.

Lynch, J. W., Smith, G. D., Kaplan, G. A., and House, J. S. (2000). Income inequality and mortality: Importance to health of individual income, psychosocial environment, or material conditions. *British Medical Journal, 320,* 1220–1224.

McIntyre, L., and Rondeau, K. (2009). Food insecurity in Canada. In D. Raphael (Ed.), *Social determinants of health: Canadian perspectives* (2nd ed., pp. 188–204). Toronto: Canadian Scholars' Press Inc.

Morissette, R., Zhang, X., and Drolet, M. (2002). *The evolution of wealth inequality in Canada, 1984–1999.* Retrieved December 15, 2010 from Statistics Canada website: www.statcan.ca/english/research/11F0019MIE/11F0019MIE2002187.pdf

Myles, J., Picot, G., and Pyper, W. (2000). *Neighbourhood inequality in Canadian cities.* Retrieved December 15, 2010 from Statistics Canada website: www.statcan.ca/english/research/11F00 19MIE/11F0019MIE2000160.pdf

National Council of Welfare. (2004). *Income for living?* Ottawa: National Council of Welfare.

National Council of Welfare. (2010). *Welfare incomes: 2008–2009.* Ottawa: National Council of Welfare.

Organisation for Economic Co-operation and Development. (2008). *Growing unequal? Income distribution and poverty in OECD countries.* Paris: OECD.

Ornstein, M. (2000). *Ethno-racial inequality in the city of Toronto: An analysis of the 1996 census.* Toronto: Access and Equity Unit, Strategic and Corporate Policy Division, Chief Administrator's Office.

Osberg, L. (2008). *A quarter century of economic inequality in Canada: 1981–2006.* Ottawa: Canadian Centre for Policy Alternatives.

Pendakur, R. (2000). *Immigrants and the labour force: Policy, regulation, and impact.* Montreal: McGill–Queen's University Press.

Picot, G. (2004). *The deteriorating economic welfare of immigrants and possible causes.* Ottawa: Statistics Canada.

Picot, G., and Myles, J. (2005). *Income inequality and low income in Canada: An international perspective.* Ottawa: Statistics Canada Analytic Studies Branch.

Reitz, J. G. (2001). Immigrant skill utilization in the Canadian labour market: Implications of human capital research. *Journal of International Migration and Integration, 2,* 347–378.

Ross, D. P., Scott, K., and Smith, P. (2000). *The Canadian fact book on poverty 2000.* Ottawa: Canadian Council on Social Development.

Saunders, R. (2006). *Low-paid workers in Saskatchewan.* Ottawa: Canadian Policy Research Networks.

Shapcott, M. (2009). Housing. In D. Raphael (Ed.), *Social determinants of health: Canadian perspectives* (2nd ed., pp. 221–234). Toronto: Canadian Scholars' Press Inc.

Smeeding, T. (2005). *Poor people in rich nations: The United States in comparative perspective.* Luxembourg Income Study (Working Paper No. 419). Syracuse, NY: Syracuse University.

Smiley, J. (2009). The health of Aboriginal people. In D. Raphael (Ed.), *Social determinants of health: Canadian perspectives* (2nd ed., pp. 280–301). Toronto: Canadian Scholars' Press Inc.

Statistics Canada. (2010a). *Low income in Canada, pre-tax LICOs*. CANSIM tables. Ottawa: Statistics Canada.

Statistics Canada. (2010b). *Low income gap in Canada, pre-tax LICOs*. CANSIM tables. Ottawa: Statistics Canada.

Statistics Canada. (2010c). *Total income by family type*. CANSIM tables. Ottawa: Statistics Canada.

Statistics Canada. (2010d). *Total income by quintile*. CANSIM tables. Ottawa: Statistics Canada.

Swartz, M. (2004, September 25). The REAL unemployment figure: It's much higher than we're led to believe. *Toronto Star*, p. D12.

Wallis, M., and Kwok, S. (Eds.). (2008). *Daily struggles: The deepening racialization and feminization of poverty in Canada*. Toronto: Canadian Scholars' Press Inc.

Wilkins, R. (2007). *Mortality by neighbourhood income in urban Canada from 1971 to 2001*. HAMG Seminar, and special compilations. Paper presented at the Statistics Canada, Health Analysis and Measurement Group, Ottawa.

Wilkins, R., Berthelot, J.-M., and Ng, E. (2002). Trends in mortality by neighbourhood income in urban Canada from 1971 to 1996. *Supplement to Health Reports, 13*,1–28.

Wilson, D., and Macdonald, D. (2010). *The income gap between Aboriginal peoples and the rest of Canada*. Ottawa: The Canadian Centre for Policy Alternatives.

Chapter Four

Making Sense of Poverty:
Social Inequality and Social Exclusion

*If the misery of the poor be caused not by the laws of nature, but by our institutions,
great is our sin.*—Charles Darwin

Learning Objectives

At the conclusion of this chapter, the reader will be able to:

- recognize the importance of theoretical frameworks for understanding phenomena such as poverty;
- describe how the concepts of social inequality and social exclusion explain the incidence of poverty in Canada;
- identify how the concepts of social inequality and social exclusion help to explain why particular groups of Canadians are at special risk of experiencing poverty; and
- outline how these theoretical frameworks can be applied to the Canadian scene to identify means of reducing and possibly eliminating the incidence of poverty.

Introduction

The presence of poverty among so many citizens of a wealthy developed nation such as Canada is not an inevitable aspect of modern life. Nor is it an inevitable result of economic globalization. It is also not inevitable that its incidence be concentrated among particular groups such as Aboriginal Canadians, working-class Canadians, females, recent immigrants to Canada, people of colour, lone-parent families, and people with disabilities. Theoretical frameworks exist to make sense of what it is about a society that creates poverty, to help identify those who are more likely to experience it, and to consider its effects upon the health and quality of life of those who experience it. These frameworks should also point the way toward actions and policies to reduce and potentially eliminate the incidence of poverty in Canadian society.

Two important areas of inquiry help to explain the economic and political structures that lead to so many individuals experiencing poverty (see Box 4.1). One of these—the study of social inequality—has a long tradition in sociology and continues to be an ongoing focus of sociologists and political scientists. *Social inequality* refers to long-lasting differences in power and resources among individuals or groups of people that influence the quality of their lives. The modern era of inquiry into social inequality began with Karl Marx (1818–1883) and his analysis of how economic resources are created and distributed among members of different social classes in capitalist societies. Social inequality was a central concern of another founder of sociology, Max Weber (1864–1920). Like Marx, Weber also outlined a key role for social class and economic structures, but added numerous ways by which power and influence are unequally distributed in society. These differences in power lead to a host of social inequalities, the most egregious of which is poverty. The explanatory frameworks created by these theorists continue to dominate current debates and examinations of social inequality and its sources. In contrast to Marx and Weber who saw social inequality as an important problem that requires strong responses, there are other schools of sociology—primarily structural functionalism—that see social inequality as a natural outcome of a society based on competition.

The second area of inquiry that helps explain the presence of various inequalities within the population and how these become translated into the experience of poverty, that of social exclusion, is of more recent origin. *Social exclusion* refers to the societal processes that lead to certain groups systematically being denied the opportunity to participate in commonly accepted activities of societal membership. Social exclusion

---

Box 4.1: Defining Social Inequality and Social Exclusion

Social Inequality
Social inequality can refer to any of the differences between people (or the socially defined positions they occupy) that are consequential for the lives they lead, most particularly for the rights or opportunities they exercise and the rewards or privileges they enjoy.

Source: From Grabb, E. (2006). *Theories of social inequality* (5th ed., p. 1). Toronto: Thomson Nelson.

Social Exclusion
Social exclusion is defined as a multi-dimensional process, in which various forms of exclusion are combined: participation in decision-making and political processes, access to employment and material resources, and integration into common cultural processes. When combined they create acute forms of exclusion that find a spatial representation in particular neighbourhoods.

Source: From Madanipour, A., Cars, G., Allen, J. (1998). *Social Exclusion in European Cities* (p.22). Oxford: Routledge.

emerged as a concern in Europe during the 1970s as increasing unemployment and growing income and wealth inequalities began to threaten societal stability. Unlike social inequality, which has been a mainstay concern of academic sociologists and political economists with little influence upon public policy-making, social exclusion emerged as a primary concern of the public policy community and then later became a focus of sociologists, political economists, and other academics.

Social inequality and social exclusion are both concerned with societal structures and how these contribute to differences in life experiences. While both concepts are concerned with how these inequalities come about and what can be done to reduce them, social inequality primarily focuses on how groups come to differ in access to a variety of economic and political resources, and social exclusion primarily focuses on outcomes of this differential access to resources. Both these areas of inquiry help explain the incidence of poverty in Canada and why particular groups are more likely to experience it than others.

The Importance of Theoretical Frameworks in Explaining Social Phenomena

Theoretical frameworks help us make sense out of what is going on in the world (Wilson, 1983d). Contrary to what we are usually taught about the world and how scientific inquiry takes place, "facts" do not simply exist in nature, ready to be plucked for analysis by physical and social scientists. In reality, there are endless numbers of objects, processes, and structures that exist in the world that are subject to a variety of possible interpretations. For example, visible light exists in a continuum of wavelengths that creates hundreds of different sensations to human eyes. To cope with this complexity, humans created a rather small number of colours, which, as a result of consensus, come to dominate our discussions of colour.

Similar conceptual frameworks exist to both describe and help explain phenomena and processes in every area of the natural sciences. Such frameworks direct attention to particular aspects of the world, provide means of understanding how the world works, and raise questions about areas of further inquiry. These frameworks are especially important when issues of the social—rather than physical—world are involved since these issues are usually complex, involve societal processes that are not easily observable, and are frequently contentious.

In the social sciences, there are also many ways to come to understand how the social world works. For many traditional social scientists, the primary approach is to focus upon the concrete and observable in order to identify consistent patterns between what are seen as causes and effects. This approach is best known as positivist social science (Wilson, 1983b). When considering issues such as the causes of poverty, its tendency is toward simplifying the phenomena to the observation and study of individual characteristics (e.g., lack of education, low motivation, single-parent status, etc.). Positivist science also involves application of experimental and other quantitative methodologies to the exclusion of examining the lived experience of people and analysis of broader societal structures and processes, such as the operation of the economic and political systems. There is also avoidance of what are called "normative" judgments, that is, outlining how the world *should* be instead of understanding how it is. The approach also takes little account of humans' abilities to interpret their world in various ways and to act upon these interpretations. Positivist social science therefore avoids analysis of the underlying structures and processes of society, finding these to be beyond its analytical and methodological tools. Box 4.2 summarizes the three main paradigms of inquiry in social science.

Two schools of thought have challenged positivist science. One school of thought is concerned with humans' interpretations and understandings of the world and goes by the names of idealism, constructivism, and interpretivism (Wilson, 1983a). Much of the material about the lived experience of poverty and how people understand it, as presented in Chapter 6, fits within this research paradigm. The second view is concerned with the identification and analysis of societal structures and processes and how these determine the distribution of economic, political, and social resources that exist in society, as well as the understandings that people have about these distributions. This school is variously known as realism, structuralism, or materialism and constitutes the primary approach taken in this chapter (Wilson, 1983c).

Realism's primary thesis is that the analysis of social life—including the incidence and effects of poverty—should not be limited to the concrete and observable nor be focused solely upon people's understandings of the world. Instead, it strives to identify how economic and political structures and processes interact with the existence of different classes, status groups, and associations in society to create differences in power and influence. Related to the concerns of this volume, the results of these differences in power are social inequalities, processes of social exclusion, and the presence of poverty.

How do we decide whether these differing methodological approaches are correct? Most social scientists avoid the term *correct* in favour of the term *useful*. A theorization can be assessed as being useful in terms of how the approach and findings from its application answer the following questions:

- Does the theorization explain the phenomena of interest?
- Does the theorization allow the making of predictions concerning the phenomena?
- Does the theorization point the way to further areas of fruitful inquiry?
- Does the theorization point the way to means of improving the situation?

In this chapter, the realist approach is applied in order to understand the incidence of poverty in Canada and its concentration within particular groups in Canadian society. This analysis should include the following (Wilson, 1983b):

- identification of the underlying structures and processes that lead to phenomena such as poverty;

Box 4.2: Paradigms of Understanding in the Social Sciences

Key Questions:
- Ontological: What is the nature of the knowable? Or what is the nature of reality?
- Epistemological: What is the nature of the relationship between the knower (the inquirer) and the known (or knowledge)?
- Methodological: How should the inquirer go about finding out this knowledge?

Positivist Approach
- There are no fundamental differences between natural and social science inquiries.
- The purpose of inquiry is to develop general principles and laws, and identify cause-and-effect relationships present in the world.
- Knowledge is advanced through observation of the observable and measurable.
- There is a distinction between facts and values; inquiry is value-free.
- There is a tendency to view phenomena at the individual level.
- There is an emphasis placed on experimental methods, surveys, and observations within a quantitative methodology.
- The focus is upon individual characteristics and how these interact with environmental events to create poverty.
- Key question: What are the correlates of poverty?

Idealist Approach
- Social reality is understood through meanings that individuals place on events.
- The purpose of inquiry is to identify multiple realities that exist.
- The individual is the active creator of the world.
- Reality results from the interaction of individuals with societal structures.
- If events are perceived as real, they are real in their consequences.
- Emphasis is placed on ethnographic methods, whereby the individual's understanding of the world is made explicit.
- There is a focus on the lived experiences of poverty and how these shape the individual's place and actions in the world.
- Key question: What is the lived experience of poverty?

Realist Approach
- Reality exists independent of individuals' constructions.
- Interpretations that individuals have of events are shaped by societal structures.
- Individuals are active creators of the world.

- The quest is for identifying underlying societal structures that influence events.
- There is a concern with people's understandings of events and how they are shaped by societal structures. There is also a particular interest in the idea of "false consciousness" by which individuals misunderstand how these events come to be.
- Emphasis is placed on a variety of methods used to identify the social structures that shape social phenomena and individuals' understandings of these phenomena.
- There is a focus on identification of the social structures that create poverty and individuals' understandings of its incidence, as well as identification of the means of promoting social change.
- Key question: Why are poverty rates in Canada so high as compared to other countries?

Source: Adapted from Wilson, J. (1983). *Social theory*. Englewood Cliffs: Prentice Hall and Lincoln, Y., and Guba, E. (1985). *Naturalistic Inquiry*. Newbury Park, CA: Sage.

- examination of the role that relations among classes, status groups, and associations play in creating patterns of poverty;
- placement of these relationships within the context of the economic and political system; and
- identification of how the societal structures and processes that create poverty both come about and can be changed.

C. Wright Mills provides a summary of the tasks social scientists should undertake in their efforts to identify the societal structures and processes that shape social life (see Box 4.3).

Social Inequality, Social Exclusion, and Poverty

The analysis of *social inequality* is primarily concerned with the organization of society and how societal structures and processes distribute power and resources in ways that create social inequalities (Grabb, 2006). These social inequalities exist in income and wealth, influence and power, and recognition, status, and prestige. People living in poverty have less of all of these resources than other Canadians. How do these social inequalities come about? Why are particular groups more likely to experience social inequality—and end up living in poverty—in today's Canada? The primary concepts that explain social inequality are social class, gender, and race. These frameworks relate

---

Box 4.3: C. Wright Mills on the Key Questions Facing Social Scientists

No social study that does not come back to the problems of biography, of history and of their intersections within a society has completed its intellectual journey. Whatever the specific problems of the classic social analysts, however limited or however broad the features of social reality they have examined, those who have been imaginatively aware of the promise of their work have consistently asked three sorts of questions:

1. What is the structure of this particular society as a whole? What are its essential components, and how are they related to one another? How does it differ from other varieties of social order? Within it, what is the meaning of any particular feature for its continuance and for its change?
2. Where does this society stand in human history? What are the mechanics by which it is changing? What is its place within and its meaning for the development of humanity as a whole? How does any particular feature we are examining affect, and how is it affected by, the historical period in which it moves? And this period—what are its essential features? How does it differ from other periods? What are its characteristic ways of history-making?
3. What varieties of men and women now prevail in this society and in this period? And what varieties are coming to prevail? In what ways are they selected and formed, liberated and repressed, made sensitive and blunted? What kinds of "human nature" are revealed in the conduct and character we observe in this society in this period? And what is the meaning for "human nature" of each and every feature of the society we are examining.

Source: Mills, C. W. (1959/1990). *The sociological imagination* (pp. 6–7). New York: Oxford University Press.

---

social inequalities back to the structures and processes of society and outline how these shape unequal access to economic, political, and social resources. Key to this analysis is the distribution of power within a modern capitalist society such as Canada.

The analysis of *social exclusion* is primarily concerned with the societal processes that lead to groups systematically being denied the opportunity to participate in commonly accepted activities associated with societal membership (Percy-Smith, 2000a). Poverty is seen as both an outcome of, and a contributor to, social exclusion. The concept of social exclusion shares many similarities with the concept of social inequality but is more explicit about sketching out the various means by which certain groups in Canada come to experience exclusion and poverty. This greater specificity has led to policy-makers and advocacy groups finding social exclusion to be a more attractive framework than social inequality for addressing numerous societal issues, including poverty. Whether this belief is valid remains to be seen. In any event, social exclusion—like social inequality—is especially likely among Aboriginals, working-class Canadians, women, new Canadians, racialized groups, and persons with disabilities (Galabuzi, 2005). Both concepts are relevant to understanding the health and quality-of-life outcomes associated with living in poverty.

Social Inequality

Social inequality is primarily concerned with identifying the societal structures and processes that lead to social inequality. Social structures—and the processes associated with them—have been defined in various ways. For many sociologists and other theorists, social structures are patterns of relations (or relationships) that are systematically associated with inequalities in wealth, power, and prestige. Karl Marx's view was that in capitalist economies, class represents the key social structure that shapes people's lives and creates social inequalities (Grabb, 2006). The key factor shaping social inequalities and the existence of poverty is the economic system and the relationship of owners to workers. Max Weber agreed with the importance of class and its interplay with the economic system but identified additional factors associated with social inequality in modern societies, such as status and parties (associations). Contemporary theorists continue to work with and extend these basic ideas.

Social structures can also refer to the organization of the state or government, agencies and organizations, and other societal institutions that shape human interactions. Governments develop and implement public policies that determine the distribution of wealth, power, and prestige within the population. Governments thus have the ability to create, maintain, or lessen social inequalities within the population. Governments at all levels—federal, provincial/territorial, and local—influence the incidence and effects of social inequality.

An important question is the extent to which state or government policy-making is independent of the operation of the economic system. One view is that the state is merely a reflection and a tool of the ruling economic elites that manage the economic system (Brooks and Miljan, 2003). Another view is that the state operates independently of these forces. And, of course, there is a midpoint view that, while the state is profoundly influenced by these economic elites, there is room for independent governmental action.

For other theorists, social structure simply refers to patterns of organization, relationships, or behaviours and attitudes that are relatively enduring. There is disagreement as to the source of these patterns and whether these patterns are problematic or simply reflect the organization of modern societies. Do these patterns result from the functioning of the economic system, from public policies made by the state, or from human nature? And once their sources are identified, do these patterns require remediation?

Class as a Determinant of Social Inequality: Marx and His Legacy

For Karl Marx, the history of humankind, especially in the modern era, is all about class, class relations, and class conflict (Marx and Engels, 1848). In the past, according to Marx, there was conflict between freeman and slave, lord and serf, patrician and plebeian. In the modern era, the rise of capitalism has created two classes: bourgeoisie and proletariat. In modern societies, the bourgeoisie represent those who control the economic system or, in the words of Marx, the means of production. The proletariat represents those who must sell their labour for wages. In order to exist, capitalism must create patterns of unequal relations, which Marx saw as very problematic, between these two classes. Social inequality, for Marx, is built into the nature of these relations.

Class relations are primarily exploitative relations. The bourgeoisie live off the labour of workers. The term *exploitation* refers to the idea that the owners who control the means of production profit from the surplus value of goods produced by workers. Surplus value—or profits—refers to the gap between what a worker earns for his or her labour and the actual value of the goods produced. In the view of Marx and others, the constant efforts to maximize profits by the bourgeoisie eventually leads to the living conditions of workers becoming so desperate as to foment socialist revolution. Marx terms the economic system and the relations it generates as the *base* of capitalist society.

Other adverse results of the exploitative relationship between owners and workers include the increasing alienation of workers from their labour and the growing gap between the material aspects of workers' lives and the lives of the owners of the means of production. As well, there is conflict between the need of the bourgeoisie to maximize profits by expropriating more and more surplus value from workers, and the requirement that workers be provided with enough wages to buy the products and services that the capitalist system produces.

Shouldn't workers' recognize these adverse effects? Yet, there are profound barriers to workers recognizing these problems and acting upon them. Marx uses the term *superstructure* to refer to two of these barriers. The first aspect of superstructure is the ideology that justifies the economic system that creates these social relations and the social inequalities that result. The ideology promulgated by system supporters is that people who control the means of production—and get wealthy in the process of doing so—have power because they are more motivated, intelligent, and creative than those who do not control the structures of the economy. Another justification for the status quo is the argument that the economic system creates wealth and well-being for all societal members, whether they are owners or workers.

The second aspect of superstructure is the structural embodiments of capitalist ideology. This may involve governmental actions such as laws, regulations, policies, and rules that maintain these class-related relations. For Marx, the state—and most political parties—were simply tools of the ruling economic interests, whose primary role was to justify and maintain the social relations necessary for operation of the economic system. In the modern era, structural embodiments of the superstructure also include a media that is dominated by these economic interests and the promotion of particular ideological approaches to social service provision and health promotion—that is, it is up to individuals to take care of their own health and well-being—or the importance of privatizing health and other services.

Social inequality is, therefore, built into class relationships. Poverty results as more and more of the resources of society are provided to the wealthy and powerful—to those who control the means of production. Indeed, as Marx is alleged to have said, "[t]he rich will do everything for the poor except get off their backs."

It has been argued that Marx's rather bleak view of the future of social inequality did not come to pass for numerous reasons (Grabb, 2006). First, the rise of the middle class showed that the Marxist view of only two classes was overly simplistic and assured that the polarization Marx visualized would not occur. Marx did recognize a class in the middle of bourgeoisie and workers—the petty bourgeoisie—but argued that it would eventually meld into the working class as objective living conditions worsened. Second, it is argued that the power of the bourgeoisie in modern society was managed by opposing forces, including the state. The rise of labour unions led to improved wages and working conditions, the implementation of social welfare policies ameliorated the worse excesses of unrestrained capitalism, and the tremendous wealth generated by capitalism improved living conditions of all classes within modern societies. Third, it is argued that workers considered their situation in modern capitalist societies and concluded that conditions would not improve within any other economic system. The fall of the Soviet state served to solidify this conclusion. The recent financial crisis that began in 2008, however, has led some to question the sustainability of the capitalist economic system as it is presently constituted (McCaskell, 2009; McNally, 2010).

Class, Status, and Party as Determinants of Social Inequality: Weber and His Legacy

Max Weber was also concerned about the role class played in creating social inequalities (Weber, 1968). Unlike Marx, he emphasized the stability of additional class groupings between the bourgeoisie and proletariat. Like Marx, Weber separated the bourgeoisie into the big capitalists—the bourgeoisie—and the petty bourgeoisie. Weber also separated the working class into those with more marketable skills—specialists, technicians, white-collar employees, and civil servants—and those who lacked these skills. Unlike Marx's view that the middle classes—the petty bourgeoisie and the skilled workers—would merge with the working classes, Weber believed that the skilled workers' grouping would increase in numbers and they would come to identify with the bourgeoisie rather than the proletariat workers.

The key distinction between Marx and Weber was Weber's identification of multiple bases of power differentials in society. In addition to class, Weber identified status and party as determinants of social inequality. For Weber, the politics of everyday life was essentially a struggle among individuals for power and influence. Class determined one's power and influence in the economic sphere of life. But status afforded one power and influence in the social-honour or prestige spheres of life. Both kinds of power were associated with access to greater material resources resulting in different *life chances*.

For Weber, class and status clearly overlapped. But status can come from sources other than class, such as educational credentials, race, gender, language, religion, and

Box: 4.4: The Experience of Social Inequality

Lise is twenty-seven. She was born in Ontario. She left university shortly after this interview.

Why am I poor? I'm caught in a capitalist society that still holds onto the view that everyone is responsible for their own well-being. I'm struggling to keep myself above water. Due to the lack of job opportunities in the city planning field, I decided to upgrade my qualifications by re-entering university. Yet summer full-time employment has not been sufficient to provide for meals, clothing, or transportation, never mind entertainment. Lack of funding from the government has put great restraints on my life. I am not able to live above a bare subsistence level. I do not feel like a worthwhile person, especially when living among fellow students who do not have to take a second thought about where their next meal comes from.

The university's preoccupation with profiteering has raised tuition and residence fees, thus prohibiting men and women from entering or returning to university in order to upgrade their skills to get out of unemployment.

To alleviate my immediate situation, I have applied for bursaries and student loans and searched for part-time employment, but I am at the mercy of someone else's decision. Beyond my personal capabilities, there is a wider community involvement that can affect not only myself but others. Government priorities need to be reoriented away from big business to the individual. Why should someone be discouraged from attending university just because they do not have the funds to carry on beyond paying for tuition and residence? Funding assistance should be carefully monitored so that the people who are in need receive the funds, not those who can milk the system for funds to support their Christmas tours to Hawaii or Europe.

My greatest fear is poverty. Being a woman in Canadian society puts me at great risk—single women, single parent women, divorced and elderly women genuinely live at levels lower than their male counterparts. All employment statistics indicate that in 1986 women can still look forward to earning a wage 60% of what a man will make in the same position. Attending university has been my source of advancement out of a poor situation—a situation I grew up in. I do not want to be preoccupied with budgeting my funds for the rest of this year or any year of my life.

Will I always be poor? Through sheer determination I will prevent poverty in my own experience as well as fight for all women to gain the rights we are entitled to, the same lifestyle any man can look forward to.

Source: Baxter, S. (1995). *No way to live: Poor women speak out* (p. 208). Vancouver: New Star Books.

place of residence. This status is not just associated with differences in prestige or honour but also with differences in access to economic, political, and social resources as well as influence. In a competitive society, these sources of status can be used to exclude others from obtaining these resources. Majority religious groups can exclude, discriminate against, or deny resources to non-members of these groups. People of one race can do this to those of other races. Men can exclude or deny opportunities to women. Educated people can discriminate or deny opportunities to the less educated. These concepts of status clearly interact with concepts of class to help explain social inequality. But they also appear to have an existence independent of purely economic issues related to class.

The final source of social inequality according to Weber is party. *Party* refers to voluntary associations that come together to pursue specific interests. These parties can be political parties but also include Canadian professional associations and organizations such as the National Action Committee on the Status of Women, the Canadian Chamber of Commerce, Friends of the CBC, Amnesty International, the Sierra Club, or a myriad of others.

Another important aspect of Weber's work is that of power. Power is the means by which one class or status group imposes its will on others. Power is a natural process in competitive societies when groups struggle for access to a wide range of economic, political, and social resources. A special case of power is that of domination, where regular patterns of inequality exist and are more or less accepted by the subordinate groups. Why would these groups do so? In the view of Weber, there are a variety of ways by which domination is accepted. These include three forms of legitimate domination: charismatic, legal, or traditional.

Charismatic legitimization of authority occurs when those who are dominated admire characteristics of those dominating them. *Legal legitimization* of authority involves acceptance of domination because subordinates believe that both the position of the authority and their own position is in fact legal according to law. *Traditional legitimization* of authority is when the right to be dominated is accepted, though this right may not exist in law. There are also various forms of domination that are not really legitimate. These include being dominated by force of habit, allowing domination because opportunities exist for personal advantage or profit, domination as an alternative to punishment or reprisal, or domination because no alternative appears possible.

The final relevant Weberian concept is that of bureaucracy and how states and agencies are administered. Weber was of the view that bureaucracies, or the organization of agencies—especially of the state apparatus—come to have a self-perpetuating character to them that institutionalizes social inequality. In addition to governments, social and service agencies, the media, schools, corporate and business organizations, the police, and the military are all capable of establishing bureaucratic structures that perpetuate social inequalities.

The initial source of power for these bureaucracies comes from the major economic and political institutions, such as the owners and controllers of the capitalist economy and the ruling elites dominated by groups of particular status. Bureaucracies serve as means by which these groups administer power. But these bureaucracies themselves come to have independent power and work to perpetuate their own positions of power and influence, as well as continuing to allow domination of some groups by others by setting up rules and resolutions that facilitate this domination. Weber called these bureaucracies the *means of administration.*

Key Issues within the Social Inequality Literature Relevant to Poverty in Canada

There are a number of issues related to social inequality that have direct relevance for understanding the incidence of poverty in Canada. These concern the role of the economic system, the role of the state and bureaucracies, the impact of class and status upon distribution of resources, and the distribution and application of power. All of these factors come together to shape how public policy in general, and poverty-related public policy in particular, are developed and applied in Canada (Grabb, 2006).

The Economic System

Social inequality and its most problematic outcome, poverty, are common to many different kinds of economic systems, but to what extent are these features both associated with and caused by specific modern forms of capitalist economies? Both Marx and Weber saw economic relations as the primary forces shaping social inequality. Neo-Marxist Erik Olin Wright (1994) argues that there are four common views about the cause of poverty in capitalist societies. The first two views, *poverty as a result of inherent individual characteristics* (e.g., genetics or low IQ) and *poverty as the by-product of contingent individual characteristics* (e.g., low motivation, poor work habits, and fatalism), place the cause of poverty within the individual. Such views neglect the role of societal structures—the economic and political organization of society—in both creating and maintaining poverty. These two views are common among many North Americans, though probably less so among Canadians than Americans.

There are also two views that place the cause of poverty within the economic system. The first view is that *poverty is a by-product of social causes,* and the second is that *poverty is a result of the inherent properties of the social system.* The by-product view holds poverty as a result of changes in the opportunities that are available—the opportunity structure—to disadvantaged people. Changing economic processes, as a result of economic globalization, lead to the decline of well-paying industrial jobs. As a result, there is lower demand for less-educated and less-skilled workers. The result is the creation of increasing numbers of people unsuited for the demands of a modern post-industrial economy.

The view of many social scientists and policy-makers who subscribe to this position is that "no one intended this calamity and no one really benefits from it, but it has the consequence of significantly deepening the problem of poverty" (Wright, 1994, p. 36.). Of course, this raises the question of why some modern changing capitalist economies have high levels of poverty while other modern changing economies do not.

The second system view is that social inequality—and its most obvious by-product, poverty—is built into the economic system. For capitalism to survive, it is argued, the value of workers' labour must be expropriated for the benefit of the owners of business. Wright (1994) argues:

> Poverty is not an accident; it is not a by-product. It is an inherent and crucial feature of a society whose economic structure is grounded in class and exploitation. The pivotal idea is that there are powerful and privileged actors who have an active interest in maintaining poverty. It is not just that poverty is an unfortunate consequence of their material interests, it is an essential condition for the realization of their interests. To put it bluntly, capitalists and other exploiting classes benefit from poverty. (p. 38)

Poverty is profitable in this view, because it suppresses wages, thereby increasing profits. It pits the employed against the unemployed, and makes the likelihood of working-class organization and action to respond to these issues less likely. Poverty also serves as a potent warning to those who are not poor of what awaits them if the employment offered them is not taken up. Such employment, however, may be low-waged, offer few benefits, and be of poor quality. Yet, such employment will be taken up because the alternative presented is the misery of poverty.

Wright argues that there are important political assertions that flow out of these differing views. The first view—poverty as a by-product—argues that the poverty-reduction task will be advanced by showing policy-makers that employment and training programs will serve to reduce poverty. Since no one really benefits from poverty, the argument goes, the task is one of educating and enlightening those in power about various solutions to poverty such as education and training programs. According to Wright, this view postulates that there may be some myopia among policy-makers and decision makers as to the causes of, and solutions for, poverty, but that they hold little if any malice toward people living in poverty.

In contrast, the class exploitation view of poverty argues that the reduction of poverty requires the defeat of powerful forces that benefit from poverty. These forces include policy-makers who are under the control of these poverty-supporting forces. As Wright (1994) explains,

> The persistence of extreme levels of poverty occurs not because powerful elites have mistaken ideas of what is in their interests and what would solve poverty, nor because they are short-sighted or unenlightened, but because they benefit from the existence of poverty and have unchallenged power. (p. 38)

Of course, this raises a question asked earlier: Why do some modern capitalist economies have high levels of poverty while other modern capitalist economies do not? For Wright and other Marxist-oriented writers, the answer is found in the strength of political forces that are able to challenge those who benefit from poverty. This leads to an examination of the role of the state.

The State

There are diverging views about the influence and power wielded by governments in wealthy industrialized nations with capitalist economies. The Marxist view is that the state—consisting of federal, provincial/territorial, and local governments—reflects the interests of the wealthy and powerful who own and therefore control the economy. Government officials—both elected and those high in the civil service—are beholden to these forces for a variety of reasons (Brooks and Miljan, 2003). The first is that government officials subscribe to the view that any government action that threatens the successful operation of the economy—continuing growth and expanding corporate profits—will threaten the economic health of the nation. Policies that threaten the interest of the owners of production will lead to credit ratings being lowered, investment capital flowing out of a nation, and the decline of the economy and its associated standard of living. No government, it is believed, can be elected under these conditions.

The second reason why the state is beholden to the owners of production forces is that the government officials and those high in the civil service come to share the beliefs, values, and attitudes of these economic elites. These beliefs include the perceived benefits of unrestrained capitalist economies, the need to control the influence and power of labour and its allies, and the motivational importance of poverty for keeping the population in line. If these beliefs are also common to those citizens who make a point of voting, then consistency with these beliefs assures future electoral success and employment for both elected officials and those in the higher levels of the civil service.

In opposition to the Marxist view of the subservient role of the state, the pluralist view is that government policy-making is based upon rational modes of policy analysis and planning (Brooks and Miljan, 2003). Governments make policy decisions, it is argued, based on the marketplace of ideas. New ideas compete with old ideas and, if judged as having reasonable chances of success, are adopted. This view begs the question: *Why is it that nations and jurisdictions differ so fundamentally in how the issue of poverty is understood and addressed?* All policy-makers around the globe are able to access the same body of research literature concerning the antecedents of poverty and the means of addressing it. There must be more to these decisions than competition of ideas in the marketplace of public policy.

The Impact of Class and Status

Perhaps the answer comes from which classes and status groups have influence within a society. For Marx, the influence of class was a profound determinant of advantage or disadvantage. For modern policy theorists, the relative power of different classes can be a primary determinant of influence in government decision making. If working-class organization is strong, then the interests of members of this class are more likely to be taken seriously. If working-class organization is weak, the opposite will result.

For Weber, too, class was important, but also important was membership in various status groups. Some of these status groups are defined by education and professional status, gender, and race. In Canada, other types of status can be added: immigrant status, Aboriginal status, disability status, or residential status. And also of key importance is what Weber called *party*—in other words, the various voluntary groups who try to gain influence with policy-makers.

Relatively little is known about the relative power possessed by various status groups in Canada. Much can be inferred, however, by looking at the broad shape of recent public policy in Canada. Current labour legislation clearly benefits the owners and managers of property and commerce, rather than those who labour in work settings. Medical doctors or physicians appear to have more influence, prestige, and power than nurses and other health professionals. The needs of suburban dwellers receive more attention from politicians than city dwellers. Changes in employment insurance make benefits less accessible to women than to men.

Home builders and homeowners receive greater governmental supports than do renters. The needs of people on social assistance clearly come second to the desires of members of the business sector and segments of the middle class that clamour for program reductions and reduced taxes. And, based on the continued existence of high levels of poverty, it can be concluded that the needs and concerns of people living in poverty must rank near the bottom of any hierarchy of influence (see Box 4.4).

Power

Influence is a result of power (Scott, 2001). Weber described power as the ability to impose views upon others. There are forms of both legitimate and illegitimate power. The power of those living in poverty appears to be virtually non-existent. As discussed above, their lack of power may be because the existence of poverty benefits those who have greater influence in shaping public policy. Their lack of power is related to their lack of status. And other groups that are more likely to live in poverty also have lower status and power in today's Canada, that is, Aboriginal Canadians, working-class Canadians, women, lone parents, people with disabilities, people with less education, and the sick and infirm. People are poor because they do not have the power to have their needs addressed. What poor people need is power. How they may be able to achieve this is a recurring theme in this volume.

Social Exclusion

Another concept key to understanding the existence and experience of poverty in today's Canada is social exclusion (Percy-Smith, 2000b). Social exclusion has been the focus of intensive public policy activity in Europe since the 1980s (Madanipour, Cars, and Allen, 1998). The impetus for this concern was increasing evidence that growing unemployment, as well as increasing income and wealth inequalities, were leading to a variety of social problems. In contrast to work on social inequality, which resides primarily in departments of sociology and political science at universities, social exclusion has a practical here-and-now feel about it. Of course, the fact that it is a concern of governments and authorities who are either in power or in positions of advantage suggests that its discourse may be primarily concerned with managing it as opposed to transforming the existing economic and political systems and other societal structures that create social exclusion in the first place.

According to Percy-Smith (2000a), definitions of social exclusion usually include some or all of these elements:

- A focus on disadvantage in social, economic, or political activity by individuals, households, spatial areas, or groups;
- An identification of the social, economic, and institutional processes by which this disadvantage comes about; and
- A consideration of the outcomes or consequences of exclusion for individuals, groups, or communities.

White (1998) identifies four key types of social exclusion. The first is social exclusion, which occurs as a result of legal sanction or other institutional mechanisms. This may involve laws preventing non-status residents or migrants from participating in a variety of societal activities. It may also include the result of systemic forms of discrimination that may be based on race, gender, ethnicity, or disability status, among other factors. The second form of social exclusion is the denial of social goods such as health care, education, housing, income, language services, or means of reducing discrimination. The third type of exclusion is called exclusion from social production. This involves a denial of the opportunity to participate and contribute to social and cultural activities. The fourth type is economic exclusion, whereby individuals cannot access economic resources and opportunities such as participation in paid work.

Burchardt, Le Grand, and Piacaud (1999) outline five dimensions of social exclusion. These concern consumption activities that are similar to common measures of poverty. Exclusion from savings activity involves lack of savings, lack of access to pensions, or lack of home ownership. Exclusion from production activity involves lack of paid work, lack of involvement in education or training, being retired, or having to look after a family. Exclusion from political activity is defined as lack of engagement in collective action to affect the wider environment. And exclusion from social activity is defined as the inability to interact with friends, family, or neighbours, or to identify with a cultural or other community group.

Percy-Smith (2000a) draws upon these two conceptualizations to produce an extensive list of dimensions of social exclusion. These dimensions, and some indicators of each, are provided in Table 4.1. The dimensions include economic, social, and political issues that are common to many conceptualizations of social exclusion. The neighbourhood, individual, spatial, and group dimensions provide some examples of how social exclusion manifests itself. Of course, such a typology begs the question: *What is driving the creation of exclusion in these dimensions and what can be done about them?*

Percy-Smith provides a signpost for identifying the contexts that create exclusion. Social exclusion is embedded within local and national contexts, as well as a broader frame of globalization with its associated structural changes in national and local economies. Parkinson (1998) argues that changes in the economic envi-

Table 4.1: Dimensions of Social Exclusion

Dimension	Indicators
Economic	Long-term unemployment Casualization and job insecurity Workless households Income poverty
Social	Breakdown of traditional households Unwanted teenage pregnancies Homelessness Crime Disaffected youth
Political	Disempowerment Lack of political rights Low registration of voters Low voter turnout Low levels of community activity Alienation/lack of confidence in political processes Social disturbance/disorder
Neighbourhood	Environmental degradation Decaying housing stock Withdrawal of local services Collapse of support networks
Individual	Mental and physical ill health Educational underachievement/low skills Loss of self-esteem/confidence
Spatial	Concentration/marginalization of vulnerable groups
Group	Concentration of above characteristics in particular groups: elderly, disabled, ethnic minorities

Source: Percy-Smith, J. (2000). Introduction: The contours of social exclusion. In J. Percy-Smith (Ed.), *Policy responses to social exclusion: Toward inclusion* (p. 9). Buckingham, UK: Open University Press.

ronment are creating more fragmented labour markets; creating various forms of precarious employment—including low-paid and service jobs rather than well-paid industrial jobs; and creating growing gaps in income between the wealthiest and poorest households. And, of course, how national, regional, and local governments understand these changes and respond to them will determine their influence and impact upon exclusion.

These national and local responses will reflect ideological values as to whether it is appropriate or useful for the state to interfere with the workings of the economy. It is no aberration that social exclusion as an area of public policy concern is well established in Europe—where welfare states are generally more developed—than in North America. As will be discussed, social exclusion—and a variant of social exclusion, social inclusion—has been the focus of some policy activity in Canada, but has not resulted in any systematic policy initiatives at any level of government to address the social exclusion of so many Canadians.

The portrayal of the drivers and mediators of social exclusion in Figure 4.1 reflects the general consensus among social exclusion theorists and policy analysts that the primary causes of social exclusion are structural rather than individual. People do not choose to be excluded. They may, however, be excluded because of personal characteristics. This recalls Wright's analysis of one explanation of poverty—or social exclusion, in the present case—as being a by-product of social causes. As such, public policy activity in Europe represents, at a minimum, the SID or social-integrationist discourse. In addition, some nations' policies have elements of a RED or redistributionist analysis (see Chapter 1). Social exclusion therefore can be seen as a difficulty with being integrated into society (SID). It can also be seen as reflecting basic problems with the distribution of economic resources within a nation (RED).

Figure 4.1: Social Exclusion in Context

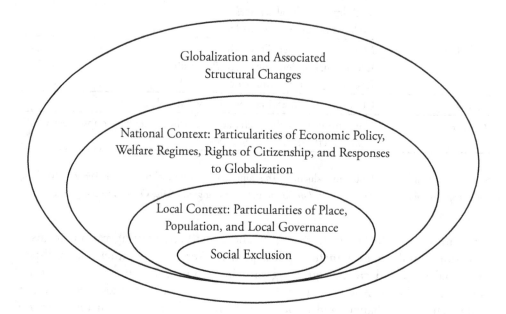

Source: Percy-Smith, J. (2000). Introduction: The contours of social exclusion. In J. Percy-Smith (Ed.), *Policy responses to social exclusion: Toward inclusion* (p. 5). Buckingham, UK: Open University Press.

Social Exclusion and Poverty

It should be recalled from Chapter 2 that exclusion from everyday activities was a key component of Townsend's concept of relative poverty. Poverty, according to the concept, is the lack of resources associated with the inability to participate in everyday activities. Townsend (1993) linked poverty to exclusion as follows:

> *Individuals, families and groups in the population can be said to be in poverty when they lack the resources to obtain the type of diet, participate in the activities and have the living conditions which are customary, or at least widely encouraged or approved, in the societies to which they belong. Their resources are so seriously below those commanded by the average individual or family that they are, in effect, excluded from ordinary living patterns, customs and activities. (p. 31)*

More recently, Rainwater and Smeeding (2003) have argued that:

> *Poverty in this view is a persistent shortfall of resources that results in a person not being able to act out mainstream social roles.... From this perspective, a social minimum is defined as a certain minimum of possessions in order for the family to meet cultural definitions of a family.... Nothing in this conception of poverty implies that this definition of poverty is merely subjective, or even that poverty is defined consensually. Rather, the argument is that objectively people cannot carry out the roles, participate in the activities, or maintain the social relations that are definitive of mainstream members of a society. (pp. 146–147)*

Social exclusion is both a cause of poverty and one of its results. A look at some proposed indicators of social exclusion draws attention to how poverty is integrally related to the concept of social exclusion. A sample representation of indicators for four dimensions is provided in Table 4.2.

Table 4.2: Key Dimensions of Social Exclusion

Dimension	Indicator
Consumption	Low income
Production	Not engaged in a socially valued activity
Political Engagement	Does not vote and not part of any campaigning organization
Social Interaction	Lacks emotional support

Source: Adapted from Burchardt, T., Le Grand, J., and Piacaud, D. (1999). Social exclusion in Britain 1991–1995. *Social Policy and Administration*, 33(3), 227–244.

The links between poverty and exclusion are especially likely within a laissez-faire or liberal economy, in which the marketplace shapes the distribution of economic, social, and political resources. The experience of poverty, associated as it is with material and social deprivation, will promote production exclusion by making the attainment of well-paying work less likely. The experience of poverty will also promote exclusion from political engagement, as the belief that one can control the world—especially its political aspects—is less likely as a result of poverty experiences. Exclusion from production—especially if it involves lack of paid work—will contribute to consumption exclusion or poverty.

The social-exclusion framework has led to a literal explosion of research, government statements and reports, and policy agreements in Europe. In the UK, a large-scale survey documented the extent of poverty and social exclusion and their relationship to each other within the population (Pantazis, Gordon, and Levitas, 2006). It was found that living in poverty—whether defined subjectively or objectively—strongly increased the likelihood of experiencing numerous forms of social exclusion. Especially affected was involvement in a variety of social activities. The collection of similar systematic sets of survey data in Canada is just beginning (Matern, Mendelson, and Oliphant, 2009).

Galabuzi's Synthesis of Social-Inequality and Social-Exclusion Concepts

Galabuzi (2005) points out that social exclusion describes both social structures and processes that lead to unequal outcomes among groups in society. Social exclusion arises from unequal access to the processes of production, wealth creation, and power. It involves denial of citizenship rights and alienation of both individuals and communities from this citizenship.

Based on White's (1998) framework, Galabuzi identifies the key elements of social exclusion as: exclusion from civil society involving political participation; exclusion from social goods, such as income, housing, and various services; exclusion from social production involving social and cultural activities; and exclusion from social consumption associated with normal forms of livelihood and economy. Other aspects of exclusion are involvement in the labour market, and economic and racial concentration in specific neighbourhoods.

In Canada, people of colour are especially susceptible to social exclusion because of increased oppression and marginalization of coloured communities, resulting from increasing socio-economic pressures related to economic globalization. Much of this has to do with the ascendance of neo-liberal-oriented public policy and its associated effects upon Canadian society. Commodification occurs when access to goods and services is subject to marketplace conditions rather than an entitlement provided by governments and agencies. Galabuzi (2005) explains that,

> [i]n the late 20th and early 21st centuries, social exclusion is a by-product of a form of unbridled accumulation whose processes commodify social relations, and validate and intensify inequality along racial and gender lines.... This intensification can be traced to the restruc-

Box 4.5: The Experience of Social Exclusion

Dana is a single mom with three children. She has a GAIN income and is thirty-one years old. She is a high school graduate, and has taken a mechanics course.

I am poor because I'm on welfare. My kids are being brought up poor. They can't do the things in sports that other kids do. I just haven't got the money.

If I work under the table cleaning other peoples' houses, welfare will find out and stop it out of my cheque. I would like to make some money to buy Christmas gifts for my kids, but what if welfare finds out—shit! I tried working but the kids started acting up and there just wasn't enough money to survive. I'm stuck. There is no way out—show me a way out of this mess.

More money would help. I need a job that pays at least $10 an hour. I would like more incentive programs, more real help. The social workers just don't understand. You really have to be stuck to know what it feels like.

Source: From Baxter, S. (1995). *No way to live: Poor women speak out* (p. 141). Vancouver: New Star Books.

Daphne is a white woman in her mid-thirties.

Why am I poor? That's an easy question to answer. I work for minimum wage and I can't save any money. I was turned down for a student loan. I have no way of buying medicine when I'm sick—I needed antibiotics but I had no money so I didn't get them.

What can be done? Free education. Free medicine. A much higher minimum wage. Make society realize that every human being is important and should be loved and cared for and nurtured. In our present society, everybody just climbs on top of each other, crushing the person below them.

Will I always be poor? I think I will be poor, but when I'm dead it won't matter, because you sure as hell can't take it with you. So rich and poor will be equal in death.

Source: From Baxter, S. (1995). *No way to live: Poor women speak out* (p. 92). Vancouver: New Star Books.

turing of the global and national economies, which emphasized commodification of public goods, demographic shifts leading to increased global South-North migrations, changes in work arrangements towards flexible deployments and intensification of labour through longer hours, work fragmentation, multiple jobs, and increasing non-standard forms of work. Not only have these developments intensified exploitation in the labour market, but they have also engendered urban spatial segregation processes, including the gendered and racialized spatial concentration of poverty. (p. 173)

A variety of trends lead to increasing social exclusion. As economic issues gain dominance over issues of community and societal well-being, governments increasingly withdraw from intervention in a wide range of public policy domains. These areas include employment and labour regulation, provision of goods and services, and provision of basic needs such as housing and shelter. The governments' withdrawal benefits those who own and control the major economic institutions. The members of classes and status groups most influenced by withdrawal of benefits and services have less influence and little power.

Economic conditions become more precarious and relationships among classes and status groups become more strained. Competition among groups becomes more intense, and class and status differences become heightened. Groups with less influence and power become subject to greater precariousness of employment, declining living conditions, and threatened health and quality of life. In Canada, these pressures and their effects are most apparent among recent immigrants and people of colour. Appropriately, Galabuzi's (2005) volume that documents these effects is entitled *Canada's Economic Apartheid: The Social Exclusion of Racialized Groups in the New Century.*

Galabuzi's analysis illuminates the basic problem addressed in this volume: How does public policy create conditions of poverty, thereby threatening the health and well-being of individuals, communities, and Canadian society? The social-inequality and social-exclusion literature directs attention to the societal structures that create these conditions. To what extent has this literature informed current policy activity in support of health and quality of life?

Social Inclusion and the Politics of Power

As noted, social inequality has a long tradition in sociology and political economy, and social exclusion has been the subject of intense activity in Europe since the 1980s. Interestingly, in Canada, these areas of inquiry have been renamed and transformed into what is termed *social inclusion*. Efforts to promote social inclusion are seen in a variety of community initiatives across Canada. These initiatives include the Laidlaw Foundation Social Inclusion Initiative, Vibrant Communities Canada, and activities by Health Canada's Atlantic Region Office (Born, 2008; Mitchell and Shillington, 2002).

Briefly, social inclusion represents an effort to take concepts that were developed within conflict models of society and reshape them into an approach reflective of a consensus model of society. Conflict models argue that within societies are a variety of competing interests that struggle to maintain influence and power and to increase access to economic, political, and social resources. Most writers of social exclusion stress that it results from inequitable and unjust allocations of resources. Social inclusion glosses over the sources of these social inequalities and focuses upon the means of reducing them by promoting inclusion.

Labonte (2009) identifies some of the problems associated with this approach, the most obvious concerning the question "How does one go about including individuals and groups into a set of structured social relationships that were responsible for exclud-ing them in the first place?" (p. 271). He also points out that uncritical application of a social-inclusion discourse can divert attention away from those who benefit from social exclusion, such as the employers who, through processes of discrimination, get to pay people of colour lower wages and thereby increase profit margins. Galabuzi (2005) has similar concerns about use of an uncritical social-inclusion discourse:

> In practice, social inclusion has emerged as a top-down policy framework used in a very par-tial way to respond to the extreme manifestations of a social exclusion that threatens social cohesion, while masking the structural causes of exclusion and so leaving them to reproduce alienation, powerlessness, and marginalization. Social exclusion draws from traditions that emphasize conflict in understanding society, and acknowledges the fact that society is strati-fied by hierarchies based on class, race, and gender. In contrast, social inclusion tends to de-emphasize the existence of hierarchies, preferring to assume the ideal of a level-playing field where inequalities can be erased by some state intervention to address instances of market failures without interrogating the inherent inequality of the market. (p. 175.)

Conclusions

Social inequality is about lack of power and how such lack of power is associated with an inability to access resources and opportunities. In its most troubling manifestation, social inequality is about living in poverty and experiencing the material and social deprivation associated with poverty. The result of having unequal access to resources and opportunities is social exclusion. Social exclusion is a process by which people are denied the opportunity to participate in civil society; are denied an acceptable supply of goods or services; are unable to contribute to society; and are unable to acquire the normal commodities expected of citizens.

All of these elements occur in tandem with the experience of material and social deprivation. Later chapters will show how the experience of social inequality and social exclusion is also associated with excessive psychosocial stress and with the adoption of health-threatening coping behaviours. Material and social deprivation, psychosocial stress, and adoption of unhealthy coping behaviours are primary determinants of health and quality of life.

The value of these concepts is that they recognize that social inequality and social exclusion happen to people as a result of economic, political, and social forces that shape governmental policy rather than as a result of the characteristics of individuals. Govern-ment policies are especially important in either increasing or decreasing the extent of social inequality and social exclusion within a society.

Grabb (2006) provides a synthesis of various approaches to social inequality that illuminates many of the issues related to the incidence and experience of poverty in Canada. The experience of poverty is about the workings of three key aspects of power. When there are high rates of poverty, the economic system is being managed in such

Figure 4.2: The Major Means of Power, Structures of Domination, and Bases for Social Inequality

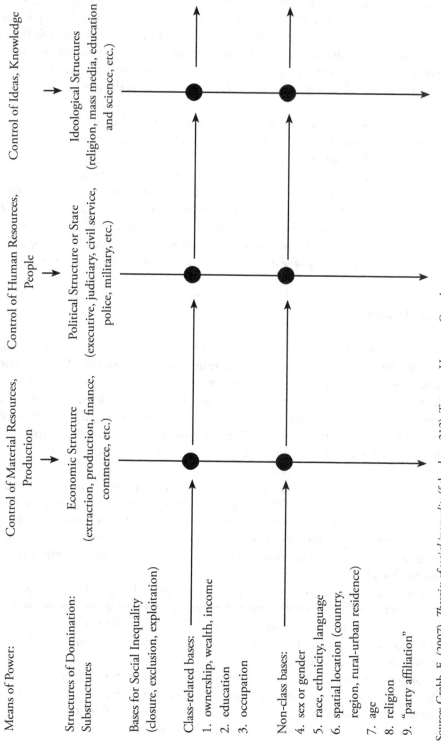

Source: Grabb, E. (2007). *Theories of social inequality* (5th ed., p. 212). Toronto: Harcourt Canada.

a manner that significant numbers of people are denied access to sufficient resources. Much of this is related to the role that class plays. And one's place in the class structure is shaped by one's wealth and income, education, and occupation. In the Canada of today, these economic processes extend beyond class to influence people's probability of living in poverty on the basis of non-class issues. Women, people of colour, New Canadians, Aboriginal Canadians, persons with disabilities, and rural residents are more likely to be poor than others. Ultimately, poverty is about the economics of a society and who receives resources and who does not.

The political structure reinforces these distinctions by enacting laws and regulations that codify these inequalities. Regardless of whether Canadian governments are or are not the handmaidens of economic interests, they clearly have not been acting seriously enough to reduce the incidence and effects of living in poverty. Governments have the opportunity to reduce the impact of class- and non-class-related attributes on the receipt of resources. The means by which they can do this is the enactment of a variety of public policies.

Finally, social inequalities are justified by the dominant ideas in society that seek to explain these inequalities. Whether it is through application of the MUD discourse and/or the imposition of stringent controls upon the receipt of social assistance and other benefits, the control of ideas is crucial for maintaining societal acceptance and/or tolerance of the social inequalities that exist in Canadian society and that result in high levels of poverty and, particularly, high levels of poverty among certain groups.

Social exclusion is the explication of what happens to people who lack power. The concept carefully maps out the wide range of areas of societal activities that become problematic for people who lack financial resources. In a society that does not commodify a great deal of services and activities, such lack of income is not as problematic. In a society such as Canada, social inequality leads to social exclusion in a clear and unambiguous manner. And all of these exclusion processes are associated with the experience of living in poverty.

The questions that these concepts force one to ask are as follows:

- Can poverty be understood as the result of social inequalities that reflect unjust and inequitable social structures?
- If so, how can these structures be changed?
- Can poverty be understood as both the cause and result of a process of social exclusion by which citizens are systematically excluded from participation in Canadian society?
- If so, what are the structures that promote this exclusion?

By considering these questions, it becomes apparent that social exclusion and social inequalities are inextricably linked.

Critical Thinking Questions

1. What are the key determinants of the distribution of power and resources, according to Marx and Weber?
2. What do you think are the determinants of the distribution of power and resources in Canada? Are your views consistent with those of Marx, Weber, both of them, or neither of them?
3. What are the areas of overlap between the concepts of social inequality and social exclusion? In what ways do they differ?
4. Do you think social inequality and social exclusion are increasing in Canada? On what do you base your opinion?
5. How can social inequality and social exclusion be reduced?
6. What are the consequences for Canada of not addressing social inequality and social exclusion?

Recommended Readings

Galabuzi, G. E. (2005). *Canada's economic apartheid: The social exclusion of racialized groups in the new century.* Toronto: Canadian Scholars' Press Inc.

This volume calls attention to the growing racialization of the gap between rich and poor, which is proceeding with minimal public and policy attention. Galabuzi points to the essential role of historical patterns of systemic racial discrimination in understanding the persistent overrepresentation of racialized groups in low-paying occupations.

Grabb, E. (2006). *Theories of social inequality: Classical and contemporary perspectives* (5th ed.). Toronto: Thomson Nelson.

This book reviews the theory and meaning of social inequality in nations such as Canada. In addition to the classic theorists Marx, Weber, and others, it updates developments in the field and provides an integrated analytical model that outlines the dimensions of social inequality today.

Hier, S. (2005). *Contemporary sociological thought: Themes and theories.* Toronto: Canadian Scholars' Press Inc.

This innovative new reader on contemporary sociological theory unites 21 influential European and American social theorists with 13 Canadian thinkers and writers to offer a strong Canadian interpretation of international theoretical currents, which include aspects of social inequality and social exclusion.

McMullin, J. (2008). *Understanding social inequality: Intersections of class, age, gender, ethnicity, and race in Canada* (2nd ed.). Toronto: Oxford University Press.

This book examines the factors that contribute to inequality in Canada. It provides a synthesis of research and theory on class, age, gender, and ethnicity or race. It also provides data related to all of these issues.

Mills, C. W. (1959). *The sociological imagination.* New York: Oxford University Press.

This classic text calls for a humanist sociology connecting the social, personal, and historical dimensions of people's lives. The sociological imagination for which Mills calls is a sociological vision, a way of looking at the world by which one can see links between the apparently private problems of the individual and important social issues.

Pantazis, C., Gorson, D., and Levitas, R. (2006). *Poverty and social exclusion in Britain: The millennium survey.* Bristol, UK: The Policy Press.

This UK survey reveals the meaning and extent of poverty and social exclusion in Britain. It provides thoughtful analysis of the meaning of poverty and social exclusion, and it points the way toward analysis and measurement of their extent in Canada.

Percy-Smith, J. (2000). *Policy responses to social exclusion: Towards inclusion.* Buckingham, UK: Open University Press.

This book examines current policy responses to social exclusion. It asks what is meant by social exclusion, what its dimensions are, how it is measured, and what the common threads are that run though contemporary policy.

Relevant Websites

Erik Olin Wright's Website—www.ssc.wisc.edu/~wright/

Erik Olin Wright is a professor of sociology at the University of Wisconsin—Madison. He is considered one of the leading neo-Marxist theorists and researchers. His website provides extensive bibliographies and many full-length articles, chapters, and interviews.

C. Wright Mills' Home Page—www.faculty.rsu.edu/~felwell/Theorists/Mills/

Outlined as a "site for undergraduates," this website is maintained by Frank W. Elwell of Rogers State University. Its contents includes an overview of the sociology of C. Wright Mills, Mills' major works, and a bibliography. It also has material on the "great" and modern social theorists, and a glossary of social science.

Dr. Elwell also maintains:

The Max Weber Website—www.faculty.rsu.edu/~felwell/Theorists/Weber/Whome.htm

Karl Marx's Sociology—www.faculty.rsu.edu/~felwell/Theorists/Marx/

Intute: Social Sciences—www.intute.ac.uk/socialsciences/

Intute: Social Sciences provides free access to high-quality resources on the Internet. Each resource has been evaluated and categorized by subject specialists based at UK universities.

Equity and Social Inequality in Canada, Metropolis Canada Website—www.tinyurl.com/m2b2t

This extensive annotated bibliography is part of the Metropolis Project. It is an international forum for comparative research and public policy development about population migration, cultural diversity, and the challenges of immigrant integration in cities in Canada and around the world.

Laidlaw Foundation Papers on Social Inclusion—www.laidlawfdn.org/working-paper-series-social-inclusion

This website presents a series of papers that cover a wide range of issues related to social inequality and social exclusion. See especially *Poverty, Inequality and Social Inclusion* by Andrew Mitchell and Richard Shillington.

Glossary of Terms

Class, in the Marxist sense, concerns the ownership of property and the power that goes with this. Class is determined by property, not by income or status. Since social classes are determined by distribution and consumption, class status reflects the production and power relations of classes.

Gender refers to the socially constructed roles, rights, responsibilities, possibilities, and limitations that, in a given society, are assigned to men and women—in other words, to what is considered "masculine" and "feminine" at a given time and in a given place.

Race is important in that it frequently serves as the basis for racism. *Racism* is a set of beliefs that asserts the natural superiority of one racial group over another, at the individual but also the institutional level. In one sense, racism refers to the belief that biology rather than culture is the primary determinant of group attitudes and actions. Racism goes beyond ideology; it involves discriminatory practices that protect and maintain the position of certain groups and sustain the inferior position of others.

Social structures are patterns of relations—or relationships—that are systematically associated with inequalities in wealth, power, and prestige. Marx's view was that in capitalist economies, the key factor shaping social inequalities and the existence of poverty is the economic system and the relationship of owners to workers. Max Weber agreed with the importance of class within the economic system but identified additional relationships associated with social inequality in modern societies, such as status and parties (associations).

References

Born, P. (Ed.). (2008). *Creating vibrant communities: How individuals and organizations from diverse sectors of society are coming together to reduce poverty in Canada.* Toronto: BPS Books.

Brooks, S., and Miljan, L. (2003). Theories of public policy. In S. Brooks and L. Miljan (Eds.), *Public policy in Canada: An introduction* (pp. 22–49). Toronto: Oxford University Press.

Burchardt, T., Le Grand, J., and Piacaud, D. (1999). Social exclusion in Britain 1991–1995. *Social Policy and Administration, 33*(3), 227–244.

Galabuzi, G. E. (2005). *Canada's economic apartheid: The social exclusion of racialized groups in the new century.* Toronto: Canadian Scholars' Press Inc.

Grabb, E. (2006). *Theories of social inequality* (5th ed.). Toronto: Harcourt Canada.

Labonte, R. (2009). Social inclusion/exclusion and health: Dancing the dialectic. In D. Raphael (Ed.), *Social determinants of health: Canadian perspectives* (2nd ed., pp. 269–279). Toronto: Canadian Scholars' Press Inc.

Madanipour, A., Cars, G., and Allen, J. (1998). *Social exclusion in European cities.* London: Jessica Kingsley.

Marx, K., and Engels, F. (1848). *The communist manifesto.* New York: Penguin Classics.

Matern, R., Mendelson, M., and Oliphant, M. (2009). *Developing a deprivation index: The research process.* Toronto: Daily bread Food Bank and the Caledon Institute of Social Policy.

McCaskell, T. (2009). *Neoliberalism as water balloon.* Retrieved March 10, 2011 from Vimeo website: http://vimeo.com/6803752

McNally, D. (2010). *Global slump: The economics and politics of crisis and resistance.* Oakland, CA: PM Press.

Mitchell, A., and Shillington, E. R. (2002). *Poverty, inequality, and social inclusion.* Toronto: Laidlaw Foundation Social Inclusion Series.

Pantazis, C., Gordon, D., and Levitas, R. (Eds.). (2006). *Poverty and social exclusion in Britain.* Bristol, UK: The Policy Press.

Parkinson, M. (1998). *Combating social exclusion: Lessons from area-based programmes in Europe.* Bristol, UK: The Policy Press.

Percy-Smith, J. (2000a). Introduction: The contours of social exclusion. In J. Percy-Smith (Ed.), *Policy responses to social exclusion: Toward inclusion?* (pp. 1–21). Buckingham, UK: Open University Press.

Percy-Smith, J. (Ed.). (2000b). *Policy responses to social exclusion: Towards inclusion?* Buckingham, UK: Open University Press.

Rainwater, L., and Smeeding, T. M. (2003). *Poor kids in a rich country: America's children in comparative perspective.* New York: Russell Sage Foundation.

Scott, J. (2001). *Power.* Cambridge, UK: Polity Press.

Townsend, P. (1993). *The international analysis of poverty.* Milton Keynes: Harvester Wheatsheaf.

Weber, M. (1968). *Economy and society: An outline of interpretive sociology.* New York: Bedminster Press.

White, P. (1998). Ideologies, social exclusion and spatial segregation in Paris. In S. Mursterd and W. Ostendorf (Eds.), *Urban degregation and the welfare state: Inequality and exclusion in western cities* (pp. 148–167). London, UK: Routledge.

Wilson, J. (1983a). Idealism. In *Social theory* (pp. 106–121). Englewood Cliffs, NJ: Prentice Hall.

Wilson, J. (1983b). Positivism. In *Social theory* (pp. 11–18). Englewood Cliffs, NJ: Prentice Hall.

Wilson, J. (1983c). Realism. In *Social theory* (pp. 166–175). Englewood Cliffs, NJ: Prentice Hall.

Wilson, J. (1983d). *Social theory.* Englewood Cliffs, NJ: Prentice Hall.

Wright, E. O. (1994). The class analysis of poverty. In E. O. Wright (Ed.), *Interrogating inequality* (pp. 32–50). New York: Verso.

Part II

The Experience of Poverty

PART II PROVIDES DETAILS CONCERNING THE EXPERIENCE OF POVERTY from the perspective of those who are living in poverty. The chapters focus on three key issues. How do people come to be poor in Canada? What is the lived experience of poverty? And, what are the experiences of those living in poverty with the social assistance and health care systems? These chapters provide a basis for understanding how living in poverty comes to have such profound effects upon health and quality of life.

Chapter 5, "Pathways to Poverty," reports on research of how people come to be poor in Canada. This research documents how changes in family and employment status come to force people into poverty. More specifically, breakups of relationships, incidence of illness and disability, and loss of employment are all potent predictors of poverty. These characteristics do not by themselves lead to living in poverty; these characteristics increase the likelihood of living in poverty because they interact with public policy approaches to resource distribution and provision of benefits. These characteristics and life situations are predictive of moving into poverty in Canada but are less important in other wealthy developed nations of the world.

Chapter 6, "The Lived Experience of Poverty," places a human face on the experience of poverty. This chapter provides details of the lived experience of poverty from ethnographic or qualitative studies of those living in poverty. These studies allow the voices of people who live in poverty to tell of their day-to-day struggles to survive and to describe how living in poverty affects their own and their families' health and quality of life. The stories of these individuals confirm that living in poverty is about material and social deprivation, exclusion from participation in a range of activities, and the experience of stigma and degradation. And these experiences are common to people living in poverty right across Canada.

Chapter 7, "Interactions with the Social Assistance and Health Care Systems," details the experiences of people living in poverty with the social assistance and health care systems. Canada's social assistance system is structured in such a manner as to make receipt of benefits difficult. In addition, the benefits provided fall far short of what is required to maintain an adequate standard of existence. Much of this has to do with the negative societal attitudes that exist toward those who are unable to obtain employment. In contrast, there is less stigma associated with use of the health care system by people living in poverty. People living in poverty have greater numbers of health problems and generally make greater use of the health care system. However, lack of economic resources restricts their access to many necessary health care services, even though Canada's health care system is supposed to provide universal access to services.

Chapter Five

Pathways to Poverty

Most of those dealing with social problems in the 1860s and 1870s failed to see
any link between the economic structure of London and the widespread poverty in
which most of the inhabitants of the East End lived. They tended to see the problem
in moral rather than in economic terms, believing that poverty was caused by the
thriftlessness and mendicant habits of the poor who had been demoralized by
the giving of indiscriminate charity.—Gillian Wagner

Learning Objectives

At the conclusion of this chapter, the reader will be able to:

- describe the life situations and specific life events that lead to poverty in Canada;
- understand why various indicators of disadvantage cluster with each other;
- explain how the experience of these situations and events combine with approaches to public policy to create the incidence and experience of poverty;
- identify examples of policy approaches that would weaken the link between specific life experiences and the experience of poverty; and
- place these poverty-producing life experiences in international perspective.

Introduction

This chapter reports the latest evidence of how people come to be poor in Canada. Many children are born into poverty because their parents live in poverty. Others come to be poor as their parents move into poverty. Some children living in poverty go on to experience poverty as adults. For these Canadians, adult poverty is a clear result of life-course trajectories that reflect material and social deprivation during childhood. Early-life trajectories lead to less accumulation of cognitive, social, educational, and health resources that combine with adult life events and opportunities to increase the likelihood of living in poverty. Childhood experiences of material and social deprivation and adult events and opportunities are related to Aboriginal status, social class, gender, immigrant status, race, level of education, disability status, and employment experiences.

For many adult Canadians, poverty results from life experiences that appear to have little relationship to prior life experiences. Debilitating illness, disability, breakup of a marriage or relationship, birth of children, or loss of employment can place one in poverty. Poverty also occurs for many who are fully engaged in the labour market but working at low-paid jobs. These adult situations and experiences, however, are more likely to occur among those already disadvantaged. The probability of experiencing poverty as an adult is shaped by previous life situations and the interaction of these trajectories with specific adult life events.

It is common among many professionals, the public, and the media to attribute the incidence of poverty solely to characteristics of the individual. In this view, people become poor—either inside or outside of the paid labour force—because they lack specific cognitive, social, or educational skills and resources. The importance of how a society chooses to distribute resources among the population is downplayed or ignored. Also ignored is how a society responds to the lack of these various personal skills or resources. Such analyses reflect what Mills and others have called psychologism—the attributing of cause to individual characteristics rather than social structures (see Box 5.1).

It is important to recognize that individual cognitive, social, and educational characteristics—associated with specific life trajectories and life experiences—by themselves do not lead to poverty. They lead to poverty because they exist within specific Canadian policy contexts that make poverty the likely outcome of their presence. These policy contexts reflect the strong market orientation of Canadian society that shapes the distribution of economic and social resources within the population. Being a female lone parent, for example, is strongly associated with living in poverty in Canada but not so in many other wealthy developed nations (Innocenti Research Centre, 2005). Being a full-time but low-waged worker is frequently related to living in poverty in Canada (Jackson, 2010). Being a full-time worker is not associated, however, with living in poverty in many other wealthy developed nations.

Box 5.1: Explaining Social Phenomena as Individual Phenomena

Psychologism refers to the attempt to explain social phenomena in terms of facts and theories about the make-up of individuals. Historically, as a doctrine, it rests upon an explicit metaphysical denial of the reality of social structure. At other times, its adherents may set forth a conception of structure which reduces it, so far as explanations are concerned, to a set of milieux. In a still more general way, and of more direct interest to our concern with the current research policies of social science, psychologism rests upon the idea that if we study a series of individuals and their milieux, the results of our studies in some way can be added up to knowledge of social structure.

Source: Mills, C. Wright (1959/2000). *The sociological imagination* (p. 67). New York: Oxford University Press.

Poverty and the Employment Market

Poverty is the experience of material and social deprivation that results from a lack of economic resources. In a market-dominated economy such as Canada, poverty is usually associated with low earnings or receipt of very low benefits for those unable to earn income in the employment market. For those engaged in the employment market, the marketplace stratifies individuals on the basis of social class, education, gender, race, disability status, and immigrant status, producing greater vulnerability to poverty for those at the bottom of the employment hierarchy. Being placed at the bottom of the employment market hierarchy is especially problematic because wages at these lower levels are frequently at poverty-perpetuating levels. Even for those whose wages are not at poverty levels, changes in family status can move them into poverty. Breakup of marriages or relationships, birth of children, or added expenses associated with parents' or children's illness or disability increase the probability of experiencing poverty, even if employment situations do not change.

Particularly problematic are life situations or events that make individuals unable to participate in the employment market. Lack of paid employment greatly increases the probability of experiencing poverty. Many working Canadian who lose their jobs—and this is especially the case during the 2008–2009 recession—are not eligible for employment insurance (Black and Shillington, 2005; Tremblay, 2009). Social assistance rates and disability benefits usually do not come close to lifting individuals out of poverty (National Council of Welfare, 2004, 2010). These realities reflect societal decisions regarding the allocation of resources among the population. Canadian policy responses to problematic life trajectories, life situations, and life events that increase economic and social vulnerability are generally undeveloped in comparison to policy responses in many other wealthy developed nations (Raphael and Bryant, 2004). Comparison of Canadian and other nations' approaches toward those who are economically vulnerable illuminates how these shape the pathways to poverty and societal responses to poverty once it occurs.

Life Situations, Life Events, and the Experience of Poverty

There are three primary sources that inform our understanding of how people come to be poor in Canada. The first is descriptive data that identifies the life situations associated with greater likelihood of experiencing poverty. For children, these life situations involve birth into families led by parents who are Aboriginal, lone-parent, especially female lone parent, are less educated, have a disability or debilitating illness, are of colour, and are recent immigrants to Canada (Campaign 2000, 2010). The risk of experiencing poverty as an adult is linked to these same characteristics. But there are also some additional ones: being female or being unattached (i.e., living by oneself) (Statistics Canada, 2010). The reason these adult characteristics come to be associated with poverty is that people with these characteristics possess fewer economic resources. Other important contributors to the experience of poverty that are directly related to economic assets include the increasing costs associated with meeting basic needs, such as housing and food (Bryant, 2009). For example, being a renter of housing is associated with increasingly greater proportions of income being allocated to shelter. In Canadian urban areas, increases in rental costs for low-income renters are far outstripping the renters' gains in income (Federation of Canadian Municipalities, 2008).

Not surprisingly, important predictors of poverty are lack of employment, low-paid work, and dependence on social assistance or disability benefits (Fleury and Fortin, 2004; Hatfield, 2004; National Council of Welfare, 2004, 2010). Additionally, being a lone parent or being unattached is related to poverty, as only one income source is available. This source of income may not be enough to reach the poverty line (Finnie and Sweetman, 2003).

The first kind of data that illuminates how people come to be poor involves analysis of the wage-earning and benefit-receiving characteristics of groups identified as being at high risk of poverty. Canadians who are of Aboriginal descent, are female, are lone parents, have less education, possess disabilities or debilitating illness, are of colour, or are recent immigrants to Canada have higher rates of poverty. These data illustrate how processes of social inequality and social exclusion lead to the experience of poverty.

The second kind of data that illuminate pathways to poverty comes from studies that follow Canadians over periods of time. These data identify the specific life events that lead one in and out of poverty over time. There are some excellent studies of these phenomena in Canada. These findings confirm that life events—such as the breakup of a relationship, job loss, or illness—lead to poverty. These life events place people in situations of greater economic vulnerability.

The third source of data is derived from individuals' accounts of their own experiences of poverty and their explanation of how they came to live in poverty. These data, which relate the experiences of people living in poverty, confirm much of the information collected from statistical surveys of the Canadian population. They also identify issues that are seldom explored in surveys and other studies of poverty in Canada.

Descriptive Data on Life Situations Associated with Poverty

In a study of which Canadians were living in poverty, Statistics Canada calculated 1996 poverty rates using the post-transfer, post-income tax low income cut-offs. It was found that 14.7% of Canadians under age 65 years were living in poverty (Hatfield, 2004). The groups with very high rates were unattached Canadians, Canadians with work-preventing disabilities, recent immigrants, lone parents, and Aboriginals living off-reserve. Statistics Canada also reported that many Canadians living in poverty did not come from these specific risk groups.

The poverty rates of these groups were measured at one point in time. An important question is whether their poverty experience is persistent. Statistics Canada examined Canadians' incomes over the periods of 1993–1998 and 1996–2001, and if their cumulative income fell short of the cut-offs over the extended time period, they were identified as being persistently poor (Hatfield, 2004). Using that definition, the percentage of Canadians aged 0–59 in 1996 who persistently experienced poverty was 8%, down from the single-time figure of 14.7%. Figure 5.1 shows the percentage of the members of five risk groups identified as falling within the one-time and persistent definitions of living in poverty.

While the persistent poverty rates are lower than the one-time rates, it is important to note that the one-time rates are consistent across time. What this means is that, in any given year, many people in the identified risk groups leave poverty but are replaced by others from these same risk groups. To illustrate, in 1996, 45.8% of lone parents were living in poverty. Many of these lone parents did not remain poor over the five-year period, but 21.8% of lone parents did. In 1997, the rate of poverty among lone parents was probably close if not identical to the 1996 rate, as other lone parents entered the poverty group, replacing those who left.

To identify some of the factors associated with these high poverty rates, Kaspsalis and Tourigny looked at 1998 data from Statistics Canada's *Survey of Labour and Income Dynamics* to see whether individuals had paid work over the course of the year (Hatfield, 2004). Results showed that involvement in the labour force significantly reduced poverty rates. For some groups, the reduction in poverty rates that resulted from being employed came close to the Canadian poverty average of 12%.

The poverty rates for Aboriginal people living off-reserve who had some paid work was much lower at 13%, compared to 43% for those without paid work. This was also the case for recent immigrants with some work (16% compared to 49%); unattached individuals aged 45–64 (12% compared to 70%); and lone parents (22% compared to 79%). These results suggest that involvement in the paid labour force is one way of

Figure 5.1: Percentage of Groups Experiencing Poverty in 1996 and Persistent Poverty from 1996–2001, Canada

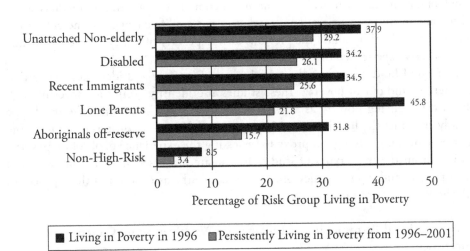

Source: Hatfield, M. (2004). Vulnerability of persistent low income. *Horizons, 7*(2),19–26.

avoiding poverty. It should be noted, though, that involvement with the labour force only reduced poverty rates to levels still above 10% and, for recent immigrants and lone parents, to levels above 15% and 20% respectively. These rates are very high in international comparison (Organisation for Economic Co-operation and Development, 2008).

One way, therefore, of avoiding poverty is to have steady paid labour. It was also suggested that moving from membership in a high-risk group—obviously not applicable for Aboriginals—was a way of avoiding poverty, as was drawing on a spouse for support, belonging to only one high-risk group, and graduating from high school. In actuality, the percentages of Canadians who remained in their respective risk group from 1996 to 2001 were rather high: unattached people, 71%; recent immigrants, 48%; lone parents, 41%; and people with a work-limiting disability, 20%. These individuals continue to be at risk of experiencing poverty. Asking them to change their status as a means of avoiding poverty is clearly not a viable public policy solution to their poverty.

The question can be raised: What is it about membership in these groups that makes attachment to the labour force problematic? And even if there is labour market involvement, poverty rates still continue to be high among these individuals. Much of this has to do with the points made earlier about life-course trajectories and how the labour market stratifies people on the basis of a variety of criteria and provides very low wages to those at the bottom of the stratification.

Longitudinal Studies of Poverty

Studies of situations and individuals' incomes over time identify specific life situations and events that lead people into and out of poverty. There are three kinds of longitudinal studies particularly relevant to the pathways-to-poverty question. The first kind of study looks at the extent to which status and income in one generation predicts status and income in the next generation. To what extent are life changes of one generation determined by the situation of the previous one? Is poverty of one generation predicted by the poverty experienced by the previous generation?

The second kind of study follows individuals over time and identifies events that lead them in and out of poverty. These studies also identify groups at especially high risk for experiencing poverty as a result of changes in life situations. The third type of study examines the life situations that move people into conditions of hunger. The experience of hunger is a good proxy for assessing the experience of absolute poverty. Findings from the three types of studies illuminate processes that lead one into and out of poverty and suggest policy options to reduce the association of these processes with the experience of poverty.

Intergenerational Transmission of Income and Wealth and Life-Course Trajectories

It is well established that parents' socio-economic position and associated assets such as income, wealth, and educational attainments shape their children's life-course trajectories. Children whose parents are of higher income and wealth are more likely to attain higher wealth and income themselves (Corak, 2004b). Children whose parents have attained higher educational credentials are more likely to show higher levels of cognitive functioning and educational achievement. These associations exist for a variety of reasons (Shaw, Dorling, Gordon, and Davey Smith, 1999). First, greater amounts of income and wealth provide children with greater exposure to material and social resources during childhood. Second, greater amounts of income and wealth reduce stress and anxiety experienced by parents, and they support child development by assuring better family environments. Third, greater amounts of income and wealth allow families to reside in neighbourhoods that provide more positive social and physical environments. These issues are examined in further detail in Part III of this volume.

There is some direct evidence of the intergenerational transmission of income in Canada. *Income elasticity* refers to the degree of earnings-advantage passed onto children as a function of their parents' incomes (Corak, 2004a). According to conventional wisdom, anyone has the chance to experience wealth or poverty regardless of their parents' backgrounds. In reality, this is a goal exceedingly difficult for people born into low-income situations to achieve. If there is complete advantage passed onto children—for example, an eight-fold gap in earnings among rich and poor adults is passed completely onto their children—then the elasticity coefficient obtained is 1.00. A coefficient of 0.50 would mean that half or a fourfold advantage of this eightfold gap would be passed on. If there is no advantage passed on, the figure would be 0.00.

The figures usually obtained for the USA and Britain are in the neighbourhood of 0.40, but may be as high as 0.60 (Corak, 2004b). Scandinavian nations tend to have lower values, near 0.20. A figure of 0.20 indicates that a 20% relative advantage—or disadvantage—is passed onto children as a function of parents' incomes.

Corak (2001) examined the income elasticity between five-year-averaged earnings of two-parent Canadian families in the late 1970s and early 1980s and their children's earnings as measured in 1998. Fathers passed on 26% of both their market income and earnings-advantage to their sons. Fathers passed on 23% of their advantage to their daughters' market income and 20% to their daughters' earnings. Values were similar (around 20%) for advantage passed on by combined parents' income to their male and female children.

Corak (2001) argues that the relationship between being of lower income status as a child and retaining that status as an adult is weak and presents little cause for concern. This conclusion can be queried. His report presents data showing that educational credentials of parents are becoming increasingly related to the university graduation of their children. In 1982, male university students came from a range of family backgrounds. Almost 30% (29.6%) of students came from a family in which the highest level of parents' education was less than secondary level; 31.8% came from a family in which the highest level of parents' education was secondary school; 10% had a parent who had attended college; and 28.7% had at least one parent with a university education. By 1995, only 14.8% of male university students came from a household with less-than-secondary-level parental education, and 41.1% had at least one parent with a university degree. For females, the proportion of university students' whose parents did not have a high-school education declined from 27.5% in 1982 to 15.9% in 1995, and the proportion of female university students whose parents had a university education increased from 28.6% in 1982 to 37.6% in 1995. The relationship between parents' education and their children attending university became stronger over this period.

There is also increasing evidence that living with very low incomes is predictive of numerous school-related indicators associated with eventual lower income status as adults. Willms (2002) provides data from the *National Longitudinal Study of Children and Youth* that show that very low family income is reliably related to lower receptive-vocabulary scores—an important indicator of school achievement and future success—of children. Almost 28% of children coming from families with very low income have low receptive-vocabulary scores, while only 8% of children whose families earned an income greater than $90,000 were so identified.

In addition, Willms (2002) reports that Canadian children whose family income is less than $25,000 have a 47% greater chance of experiencing cognitive difficulties in school; a 45% greater chance of behaviour problems in school; and a 41% greater chance of scoring high on an overall vulnerability index than other children. For each measure, around 10% of total variation of outcomes observed among Canadian children can be uniquely explained by the very low income-status measure. Generally, studies using school outcomes such as graduation rates find that low-income status accounts for 25% of total variation in outcomes.

Similar findings from numerous Canadian studies show a strong effect of income on later-life chances. The measures that are related to income include indicators of cognitive development and social development, such as school problems, psychiatric problems, and incidence of physical aggression (Ross and Roberts, 1999). In addition, there are literally hundreds of USA and UK studies that show similar findings: living in poverty increases the risk of numerous developmental problems associated with difficulties in adulthood (Keating and Hertzman, 1999).

Movement in and out of Poverty

When reviewing studies of movement in and out of poverty, it is important to query the measures chosen and why some measures are included and others are not. The following two studies show why this is important. In the first study, Finnie (2000a) examined factors related to movement into and out of poverty among Canadians 20 years or older based on tax-filing information for the period 1992–1996. Poverty was defined as existing in a family unit with less than 50% of median-adjusted (for family size) post-tax income. Table 5.1 provides average poverty rates for the 1992–1996 taxation years.

Attention should be paid to the meaning of the two different columns in the table. *Percentage in the group who are living in poverty* refers to the percentage of people in the family-status group that are living in poverty. *Percentage share of all Canadians living in poverty* refers to the overall contribution that those living in poverty in these groups make to the total number of people living in poverty. While overall poverty rates for male lone parents is 31.3%, the number of these family situations is few. As such, their contribution to the total number of people living in poverty is only 1.3%. Fifty-two percent of female lone parents are living in poverty, but they are also a relatively small group and make up only 15.4% of all Canadians living in poverty. The group that contributes the greatest number of people living in poverty is unattached females, amounting to almost one in five of people living in poverty in Canada. The other large contributing groups are attached females with children and unattached males.

These individuals were followed over time, and changes in family status were correlated with entrance into or out of poverty for both males and females. Entry rates are the percentage of people in a family status group who, as a result of a change in family status, enter the poverty group in a given year. Exit rates are the percentage of people living in poverty who, as a result of a change in family status, leave the poverty group in a given year. The data presented in Table 5.2 are annual rates averaged across 1992–1996.

The first thing to notice is that many Canadians living in poverty leave this situation in any given year. However, they are usually replaced in any given year. The figures to note are those that are exceptionally high in a year. Looking at the first group of Canadians who were unattached during the first year but then became lone parents in the second year, the data indicate that 16.2% of males who effected this transition moved into poverty. For females who were unattached and then became lone parents, the figure is much higher at 30%. The most striking findings are that movement into being a lone parent from any family status group is associated with movement into poverty and that

Table 5.1: Poverty Rates by Gender and Family Type, Averaged over 1992–1996, Canada

	% in the Group Who Are Living in Poverty	% Share of All Canadians Living in Poverty
Male		
Single	25.2	16.1
Attached with Children	10.9	13.7
Attached with No Children	8.2	10.4
Lone Parent	31.3	1.3
Female		
Single	23.1	19.9
Attached with Children	12.8	16.4
Attached with No Children	5.3	5.2
Lone Parent	52.4	15.4

Source: Finnie, R. (2000). *Low income (poverty) dynamics in Canada: Entry, exit, spell durations, and total time* (Table 1, p. 17). Ottawa: Applied Research Branch, Human Resources Development Canada.

this is especially the case for women. (See Table 5.2, where the corresponding results are presented in boldface.) Moving from being attached to being unattached is also associated with moving into poverty. This is especially the case for women who go from being attached with children to being unattached.

Table 5.2: Annual Rates of Entry into and Exit out of Poverty Averaged over 1992–1996 as a Function of First- and Second-Year Family Status and Gender

	Entry into Poverty		Exit from Poverty	
	Male	Female	Male	Female
Single (first year)				
Second Year Status:				
Single	6.1	4.8	18.7	18.8
Attached with Children	6.3	6.4	**50.1**	**64.5**
Attached with No Children	3.3	3.1	**63.6**	**74.9**
Lone Parent	16.2	**30.0**	20.5	12.3
Attached with Children (first year)				
Second Year Status:				
Single	12.1	22.6	36.3	33.7
Attached with Children	3.6	4.6	29.9	30.6
Attached with No Children	2.6	2.2	42.7	42.3
Lone Parent	17.1	**46.9**	25.2	13.0
Attached with No Children (first year)				
Second Year Status:				
Single	11.1	15.7	43.4	34.9
Attached with Children	5.3	5.4	30.0	34.2
Attached with No Children	2.6	2.0	34.4	38.9
Lone Parent	17.7	**47.9**	43.8	9.8
Lone Parent (first year)				
Second Year Status:				
Single	6.2	7.1	37.3	35.9
Attached with Children	8.4	6.2	**47.0**	**65.6**
Attached with No Children	-	-	67.6	75.4
Lone Parent	10.0	12.8	18.0	13.5

Source: Finnie, R. (2000). *Low income (poverty) dynamics in Canada: Entry, exit, spell durations, and total time* (Table 3, p. 22). Ottawa: Applied Research Branch, Human Resources Development Canada.

In terms of exit from poverty, numerous factors are associated with such movement. Especially noteworthy is moving from being unattached to being attached, either with or without children, and moving from being a lone parent to being attached, either with or without children (The corresponding results are presented in boldface in Table 5.2.) It should be noted that movement out of poverty is relatively common for all groups, whether experiencing transitions or not, except for being a lone parent and/or remaining a lone parent. This is the case for both males and females.

Finnie also found that duration of living in poverty predicted probability of exiting poverty. The longer one was living in poverty, the less likely it became that one would leave living in poverty the following year. For example, female lone parents aged 20–39 who remain female lone parents after one year of poverty have a 26.8% chance of leaving poverty the next year. After two years of living in poverty, their chances of leaving poverty the next year decreases to 16.1%. After three or four years of living in poverty, their chances of leaving poverty in the following year decline to 10.9%. This decline in likelihood of escaping poverty as a function of length in poverty is common across all gender, age, and family-type groups.

How persistent is poverty across groups? Finnie calculated the percentage of each group living in poverty that did not change its family status for either 0, 1, 2, 3, 4, or 5 years. Overall, 76.8% of Canadians were never poor, while 23.2% were living in poverty for at least some period of the five years studied. The groups at particular risk of ever living in poverty over the five-year period were single males (39.8%), lone-parent males (51.6%), single females (33.7%), and lone-parent females (68.9%). Of note is the percentage of each group that was living in poverty over the entire five-year period. Among single males, 16.4% remained in poverty over the period, as did 51.6% of lone-parent males, 33.7% of single females, and 36% of female lone parents.

While poverty rates and persistent poverty rates for single and lone-parent males and females are very high, an important question concerns how much these groups contribute to the total number of Canadians living in poverty. Female lone parents for example, have very high rates of poverty and persistent poverty, but what proportion do they constitute of the total number of persistent poor? Table 5.3 shows that among the never-poor, most of these Canadians are male and females either attached with children or attached without children. (Of the never-poor, 20.4% come from males attached with children, 21.4% from males attached without children, 19.9% from females attached with children, and 16.4% from females attached with no children.)

Among the total number of always-poor, lone-parent males account for less than 1% and lone-parent females account for 15.9%. These numbers are lower than the poverty rates seen among these groups because membership in these groups constitutes a relatively small proportion of the overall Canadian population. Therefore, their contribution to the overall number of poor Canadians is lower. Indeed, among the total number of always-poor, 19.2% come from attached males with or without children, and 17.1% from attached females with or without children. Finnie (2000b) points out:

Table 5.3: Percentage of Total Number of Canadians Either Never, Sometimes, or Always Living in Poverty Contributed by Each Family Situation, by Gender, 1992–1996

	Never in Poverty	Sometimes in Poverty	Always in Poverty	Overall % of Canadian Population
Male				
Single	5.8	10.3	**18.8**	7.4
Attached with Children	*20.4*	18.4	12.3	19.6
Attached with No Children	21.4	16.5	6.9	19.7
Lone Parent	0.2	0.5	0.9	0.3
Female				
Single	11.4	16.1	**27.4**	13.2
Attached with Children	*19.9*	23.0	14.4	20.1
Attached with No Children	*16.4*	7.8	2.7	14.1
Lone Parent	1.1	5.6	**15.9**	2.8

Italicized figures represent those groups contributing the most (>15%) to the overall "never living in poverty" population. **Bold figures** represent those groups contributing the most (>15%) to the overall "always living in poverty" population.

Source: Finnie, R. (2000). *Low income (poverty) dynamics in Canada: Entry, exit, spell durations, and total time* (Table 5d, p. 39). Ottawa: Applied Research Branch, Human Resources Development Canada.

> *While therefore, their high rates of chronic poverty might be good cause to direct policy measures at single mothers, even delivering this group from long-term poverty in its entirety would reduce the size of the overall always-poor population by only 16 percent, meaning that other groups would have to be helped in significant measure to diminish the number of long-run poor in any given year—by any truly substantial amount. (p. 39)*

Analyses of Poverty Transitions Using Additional Indicators

The next study examined comes from an unlikely source: The Federal Reserve Bank of San Francisco (Valletta, 2004). In this study, Canadian data, together with data from Germany, Great Britain, and the USA, were analyzed in terms of poverty dynamics. Valletta examined Canadian poverty dynamics for the 1993–1998 period by using tax-filing data. Both market income and disposable income (post-tax income) were examined. The two poverty lines used were those used in the Finnie study: less than 50% of the adjusted median family market income and less than 50% of the adjusted median family disposable income for Canadians.

Individuals included in the study were identified as living in poverty at least once and as living in poverty on average over the entire study period. In addition to looking at family status—two adults, children; single adult, children; two adults, no children; and single adult, no children—the study also looked at educational attainment of the family head, and numerous family and job-related events. The analyses carried out produced statistics that included risk ratios (the extent to which individuals experience greater risk of poverty as a result of a particular factor) and probability of entrance and exit from poverty (expressed as percentage of likelihood of entering or exiting poverty).

Figure 5.2 shows the relative risk of short- (at least once poor) and long-term (average-income poor) poverty among Canadians as a function of family type, educational attainment of family head, and family work attachment. The risk ratios use the proportion of the group experiencing poverty in relation to the entire population as a baseline. If a group constitutes 10% of the population and 20% of the group is living in poverty, then the group's risk is 2.0. As shown, families of lone parents have a 70% greater risk of being poor at least once and an almost 250% greater risk of being average-income poor. Also at greater risk are unattached adults with no children. The figure also shows that those with higher education have a lower risk of experiencing both kinds of poverty, while those with lower educational attainment have a higher risk. Finally, having no worker in the household during the first year of the study profoundly increases the risk of experiencing both types of poverty.

Figure 5.2: Relative Risks of Short- and Long-Term Poverty among Canadians as a Function of Family Type, Educational Attainment of Head of Household, and Family Work Attachment

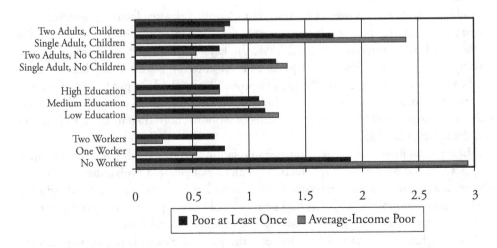

Source: Adapted from Statistics Canada, *The Ins and Outs of Poverty in Advanced Economies: Poverty Dynamics in Canada, Germany, Great Britain, and the United States*, Income Research Paper Series, 75F0002MIE2005001, p.24–26, January 2005; http://www.statcan.gc.ca/bsolc/olc-cel/olc-cel?lang=eng& catno=75F0002M2005001

Valletta showed how a number of events influence both entries and exits from poverty among Canadians (Valletta, 2004). He calculated the percentage of increased risk of an event being associated with moving into poverty in any given year. Similar to Finnie's findings, changes in family structure account for many changes. Not surprisingly, separation/divorce (10.4%) or a newly established family (14.6%) are predictors of increased risk of entry into poverty. Concerning exit from poverty, changes in family structure, including marriage (12.3%) or fewer members of family (5.2%), are associated with leaving poverty.

A major contribution of this study was its examination of how changes in employment status and time were related to entry and exit from poverty. Loss of a full-time job by the head of household was associated with a 82% greater chance of entering poverty. Similarly, fewer months at work for the family head was associated with a 72% greater chance of entering poverty, and a decline in earnings of 10% or more by the family head was associated with a 45% greater chance of entering poverty. Of note is that having a spouse lose full-time work was associated with a 33% greater chance of entering poverty, as was having the spouse having fewer months of work (40.2%) and having spousal earning declines by 10% or more (12.8%).

As for the relationship between exiting poverty and changes in employment, more full-time work for the head of the family was associated with a 79.5% greater chance of exiting poverty, as was more months of work, with a 75.4% greater chance of exiting poverty, and having earnings increased by 10% or more, with a 40.2% greater chance of exiting poverty. This held true for spousal increase in full-time work (36%), more months at work (35%), and increased earnings (35.5%). Overall, however, movement into poverty was primarily a result of changes in family structure (46.9%), fewer full-time workers (6.4%), largest decrease in earnings (27.3%), transfers (13.3%), or capital and other incomes (6.0%).

Valletta carried out an overall analysis that identified the key factors associated with leaving and entering poverty. By comparing the base entering poverty rate of 4.5% to the base leaving poverty rates of 32.4%, the key factors predicting movement into poverty were divorce (15% greater probability of entering poverty) and less work for the head of the household (10.2% greater probability). The best predictors of leaving poverty were more work for the household head (31.9%), more work for the spouse (22.5%), marriage (39.9%), and more hours of work for both the family head (31.9%) and the spouse (22.5%).

These probabilities should be examined in relation to the base rates of 4.5% for entry into poverty and 32.4% for exit. The best predictors of elevated probability of entering poverty are divorce (increasing risk fourfold), as well as less work for the head (tripling risk) or spouse (doubling risk). The best predictors of leaving poverty are getting married and having more full-time work (doubling exit probabilities for both).

Finally, what are the factors that increase the probabilities of being average-income poor for Canadians over the five-year study period? The best predictors are no workers in the family (adding an additional 15.4% chance of living in persistent poverty to the 9.1% baselines), being a single adult (adding a 6.8% probability), being single with children (adding 7.6%), being a child (adding 3.6%), and having low levels of education (2.8%).

Canada's Working Poor

More insights regarding pathways to poverty are provided in a study by Social Development Canada of Canada's working poor (Fleury and Fortin, 2004). In this study, a low-income (poor) worker was identified as a person whose work effort was high throughout the year but whose disposable family income fell below the Market Basket Measure of low income. In 2001, there were 653,000 low-income workers in Canada, and 1.5 million people directly affected by low income. More than one in three of these were children below the age of 18. These people represented more than 50% of all low-income people in Canada.

Among these low-income workers, 76% of them had worked more than 1,500 hours during the year. The average income of these workers was $12 per hour. In addition to being poor, these workers—and their families—also had significantly less access to work-related benefits than workers who did not have a low income in 2001. Only 17.9% of low-income workers had access to life or disability insurance, compared to 61.5% of other Canadian workers, and only 15.1% had an employer who offered a pension plan, compared to 48.7% of other Canadian workers. Dental plans were available to only 25.6% of low-income workers, compared to 74.6% of other workers, and only 26.6% of low-income workers had access to a health or medical plan, compared to 74.6% of other Canadian workers. Not surprisingly, the unionization rate was 10.8% for low-income workers, compared to 30.3% for other Canadian workers.

The study also looked at non-family-related factors that increased the probability that a worker would be living in low income. These factors were being self-employed (8.3%), being a recent immigrant (4.7%), not working full time (4.5%), working for a small firm (3.8%), being 18–24 years of age (3.6%), and living in a high-poverty area (3.5%).

Low-income workers in 1996 generally maintained connection with employment over the following period of time but at slightly lower levels than those who were not low-income in 1996. Nevertheless, while those who were working were likely to escape poverty at least once over the follow-up period, overall, almost half experienced persistent poverty, and this was the case even among those with high labour-market attachment. According to Fleury and Fortin (2004), "Although the working poor generally do not stay in a low-income situation for as long as other low-income persons, most of them experience a period of financial uncertainty that is more than temporary" (p. 55).

The events that led to low-income workers escaping poverty are of two kinds. Slightly more than half (53.5%) of low-income workers escaped poverty as a result of increases in their employment income. About one third (32.3%) did so as a result of changes in their family structure, and 14.2% as a result of changes in the employment income of other family members.

The authors conclude that about 50% of Canadians living in poverty have at least one person employed. While the work effort of these Canadians is significant, their working conditions are much less favourable than those without low family income. The primary circumstance responsible for their situation is having only one wage-earner. And while employment helps people move out of poverty, for most low-income workers, poverty is not a temporary situation.

Predictors of Food-Hunger Situations

The experience of hunger can be seen as reflecting the incidence of absolute poverty in Canada. McIntyre and colleagues used 1994 data from the National Population Health Survey to identify characteristics of Canadian families with children reporting hunger (McIntyre, Conner, and Warren, 2000). Families experiencing hunger at least once were more likely to show a number of characteristics associated with the experience of poverty. The factors associated with experiencing hunger at least once were having the primary caregiver experience poor health (thus increasing the risk of hunger 9.76 times more than those not experiencing poor health), being on social assistance (thus increasing the risk 9.2 times); main activity looking for work (being unemployed) (thus increasing the risk 7.44 times); having a child in fair or poor health (thus increasing the risk 5.2 times); and being of Aboriginal descent (thus increasing the risk 4.66 times).

McIntyre and Rondeau (2009) also used data from the National Population Health Survey to identify characteristics of those moving into situations of food hunger over time. In a sense, these analyses identified Canadians who were moving into situations of absolute material—and probably social—deprivation. Families that moved into hunger were those who had another mouth to feed (increased risk of 5.75 times), a father who experienced job loss (increased risk of 5.64 times), a mother in worsening health (3.45 times greater risk), or a child in worsening health (2.25 times greater risk). McIntyre reports that getting out of hunger depended upon only one change: the mother getting a full-time job, resulting in the family's income rising accordingly.

A similar analysis of who comes to live in poverty can be carried out based on data provided by Food Banks Canada (2010). In March of every year, the association carries out a Hunger Count survey. In addition to indicating the numbers of Canadians experiencing absolute food insecurity, the survey provides a number of descriptive characteristics concerning food bank users. The survey shows that users of food banks are likely to be single (37.8%); single parents (27.5%); two-parent households (23.4%); or couples with no children (11.3%). Their income situations are social assistance (50.5%); employment (11.4%); disability benefits (15.1%); no income (4.7%); pensions (6.6%); employment insurance (5.7%); or student loans (1.6%).

Stories of Entrance into Poverty

Researchers are increasingly interested in hearing about the experience of Canadians living in poverty. These experiences are important as they provide opportunities for those most affected by poverty to relate the impact it has on their lives and the lives of those they care about. In this section, people living in poverty provide their own insights on the pathways to poverty. Detailed presentation of the lived experience of poverty and its impacts on health forms the primary content of the next chapter in this volume.

Box 5.2: Public Policy Pathways to Poverty

A Mess Harper Could Easily Fix
Carol Goar

She, of all people, should have been prepared, Ann Evans says.

For eight years she worked as an employment counsellor, coaching clients on how to find work, helping them manage the financial and emotional stress of joblessness, listening to their heartbreaking stories.

But when she was laid off last fall, she learned two lessons that no placement worker could teach. One was how debilitating unemployment is. The other was how threadbare Canada's safety nets are.

"I'm out of work, living on $413 a week. There is no additional support for the medication that I have to take every day. I have a very modest two-bedroom bungalow in Scarborough that I am trying desperately to hang on to. I'm not sure that I will be able to."

Evans has no dependents [sic]. She'd be beside herself if she did.

She was hired in September 2004 by Job Skills, a non-profit agency in York Region funded by the federal government. Her position, co-ordinator of employment programs and services, fit perfectly with her qualifications and experience.

No one informed her at the time that she was filling in for an employee who was on maternity leave. When her contract came up for renewal in April 2005, she learned the truth. She was slated to leave in December.

The news came as a complete shock. But as a contract worker, Evans had no legal recourse.

With a raft of programs to manage, a nine-member staff to supervise and a job-finding club to run, she had no time to send out resumés or go to interviews. As her termination date approached, her health deteriorated. The depression she'd fought for years flared up. Her doctor increased her medication and told her to take early leave. Reluctantly, she did.

The first thing Evans discovered was that even if a person stops working for medical reasons, there is a two-week waiting period for EI benefits.

It took an additional five weeks for her claim to be processed. She didn't have much of a financial cushion because she'd only earned $38,000 a year as an employment counsellor. At one point, she had to ask her parents for help. "That's very humiliating at 40 years of age."

Since losing her job, she's done everything she taught others to do. She has applied for every opening posted on the Internet, sent her resumé to non-profit organizations, colleges and universities, followed up on tips from friends and acquaintances, explored training opportunities and looked into a career change.

But it is harder than Evans ever imagined. She has trouble scraping together money to get to interviews after paying the mortgage, insurance, hydro, gas, utilities and taxes. She can't afford to pay 25 per cent of the cost of the training, which the government requires. If she needed daycare, she'd be sunk.

She managed to find 11 days' work at the University of Toronto, preparing engineering students for job interviews. She reported it to Human Resources Canada and had her earnings deducted from her EI cheque before she'd even been paid.

In the past four months, Evans has had plenty of time to think about what is wrong with Canada's EI program.

The biggest problem is that benefit levels have been frozen for 10 years. The maximum weekly payment of $413 was set by long-retired employment minister Lloyd Axworthy three governments ago when he overhauled the system. The cost of living has gone up by 20.2 per cent since then.

There's no need for stinginess. The government has collected $48 billion more in EI premiums than it has paid out in benefits over the past decade.

The second problem—which doesn't apply to Evans—is that the majority of Canadians who lose their jobs (78% in Toronto) don't qualify for EI benefits. They either haven't accumulated enough hours of paid employment or they work in uninsured sectors of the economy.

At a time when casual and contract work is the norm for millions, the EI system offers them no protection.

The third problem is that job training—trumpeted by Ottawa as the solution to unemployment—is spotty and underfunded. Availability fluctuates with the budgetary cycle. People are pushed into programs for which they are totally unsuited. If their benefits run out midway through a course, they're on their own. "That, plus the 25 per cent upfront cost is a pretty strong deterrent," Evans says.

Her plight could be worse, she concedes. She has a supportive family and generous friends. She has access to public transportation. And she has a university education.

If she can't make the system work, Evans wonders, who can?

Cleaning up this mess would be a relatively simple task. Employment insurance falls entirely within federal jurisdiction, unlike most social programs. There is money in the fund. The deficiencies are glaringly obvious. And there is no question that Canada needs skilled workers.

Prime Minister Stephen Harper wouldn't face resistance from any of the opposition parties. He'd have the support of business. He might even make friends in some unlikely places.

Source: Goar, C. (2006, February 15). A mess Harper could easily fix. *Toronto Star*, p. A2.

Policies of Exclusion, Poverty, and Health

In *Policies of Exclusion, Poverty, and Health*, 21 women living in poverty in British Columbia related stories of their own lives (Ocean, 2005). Based on these stories and extensive interviews, the editor of the volume, who was also project director, concluded that the precursors of poverty for these women could be classified as either long- or short-term. Long-term precursors were an event or series of events during childhood in which the women reported abuse by family members or others. Short-term predictors of these women moving into poverty were changes in their family status that precipitated loss of income. The women also identified systematic discrimination toward them by numerous authorities as a result of their being women.

The editor concluded that childhood poverty and lack of literacy were *not* primary causes of their poverty. However, careful reading of the 22 women's stories suggests that in at least half the cases, childhood poverty was present and may have contributed to some of the traumatic situations that are described within the stories.

Realities of Parenting in Poverty

In *We Did It Together: Low-Income Mothers Working toward a Healthier Community*, 16 low-income women in Saskatoon met over an extended period of time to share their stories of living in poverty and to identify means of improving their communities and their lives (Green, 2000). As part of this effort, they identified the causes of their parenting in poverty and provided it in graphic form. Their work is presented in Figure 5.3.

Like the women in Ocean's work, these women reported that the pathways to their poverty usually began with growing up in unstable families. Unlike in Ocean, they identified childhood poverty as contributing to their experiencing numerous life problems that led to poverty. These living situations increased their likelihood of leaving school prematurely. As a result of this, secure work was not achievable. These women identified community factors that did nothing to change the trajectory they were set on as a result of their early-childhood and then later-adult experiences. Green (2001) provides nine women's stories that illustrate these pathways in *Telling It Like It Is*.

Public Policy, Clustering of Disadvantage, and the Experience of Poverty

If focus is limited to identification of individual and family characteristics associated with living in poverty, the solutions are focused on individuals. If education is related to higher waged employment—this argument goes—then increase education levels of Canadians. If employment is related to movement out of poverty, then ensure that everyone has a job.

The first problem with this analysis is that almost half of all people living in poverty *are* employed yet still do not earn wages that lift them out of poverty. Similarly, if the education levels of all Canadians were raised to the point that everyone possessed a university degree, there would still be people working in low-paying employment, single parents, people unable

Figure 5.3: Causes of Parenting in Poverty

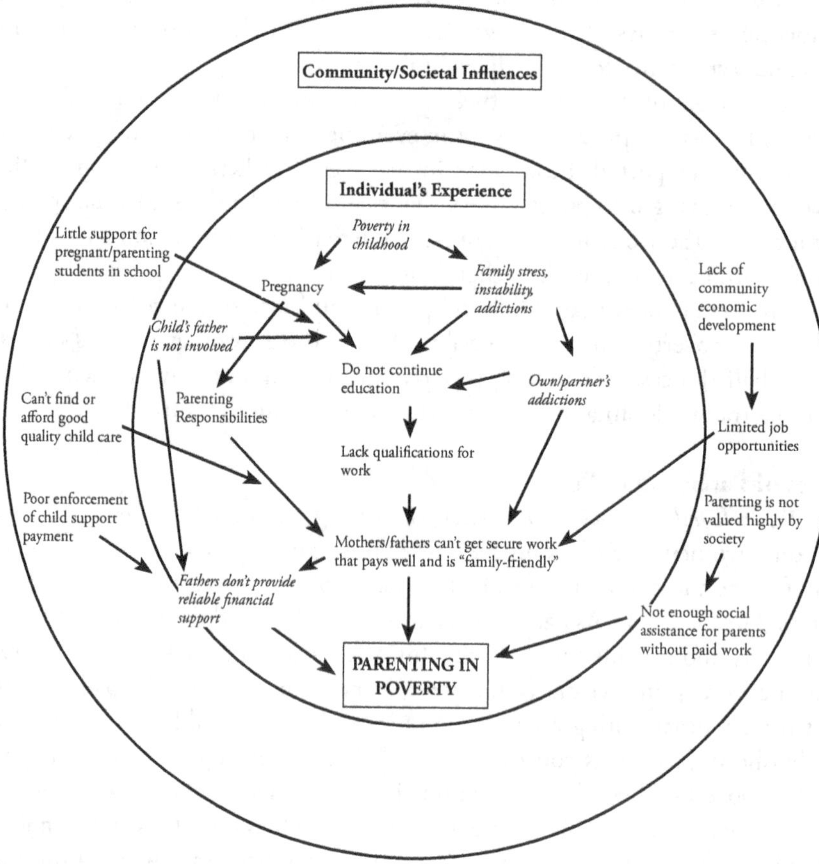

Source: From "We Did It Together": *Low Income Mothers Working Together Towards a Healthier Community* (p.31), by K. Green, 2000. Saskatoon: Prairie Women's Health Centre of Excellence.

Note: Italicized factors are those that did not apply to all participants.

to work because of disability or illness, and people unable to find employment. The very high poverty levels that exist in Canada—as compared to other wealthy developed nations—suggest that the primary causes of poverty are to be found in the public policy realm.

While public policy will be the focus of later chapters, three issues will be examined to illustrate how public policy interacts with life situations and life events to produce poverty. These issues are (a) the incidence of low-paid workers in Canada, (b) the gap between low-income earnings and low-end rental housing costs, and (c) very low social assistance rates and the clawback of the National Child Benefit in some Canadian provinces.

Low Income in Canada

Jackson (2010) provides data on the percentage of Canadian employed in low-paying employment (less than 66% of the average wage) as compared to Germany and Sweden.

Over one-third of Canadian women are considered low-wage earners, in comparison to 25% in Germany and only 8% in Sweden. Sixteen percent of Canadian men are low-waged, as compared to 7% in Germany and only 4% of Swedish men. Not surprisingly, poverty rates in Canada, Germany, and Sweden parallel these differences in the number of low-wage earners. These differences result from differences in minimum-wage levels, in policies related to job security and retraining, and in support for unionization among the workforce. These issues are examined in later chapters.

Low-Income Earnings and Low-End Rental Costs in Canadian Cities

A study by the Federation of Canadian Municipalities (2004) tracked changes from 1991 to 2001 in low-end incomes and low-end rental costs in Canadian cities. The study found that rental costs were far outstripping increases in incomes of low-wage earners. These developments can be traced to reductions in government spending on affordable housing, removal of rental controls in many jurisdictions, and the stagnating of incomes as a result of failures to increase minimum wages and protect job security (Shapcott, 2009). Of particular note was the federal government removing itself from the creation of affordable housing during the 1990s and similar actions by many provincial governments during this same period (Shapcott, 2009). Canada is the only developed nation without a national housing strategy (Bryant, 2009). Not surprisingly, there is a lack of affordable housing in Canadian cities, which is contributing to the incidence of poverty (Layton, 2008).

Social Assistance Rates and the Clawback of the National Child Benefit

Social assistance rates are consistently below levels needed to remove individuals and families from living in poverty. In many cases, these rates do not come even close to the poverty-leaving levels (National Council of Welfare, 2010). In addition, some provinces have refused to pass on the National Child Benefit provided by the federal government to families living on social assistance. Not surprisingly, the poverty rates of people on social assistance are remarkably high. And also not surprisingly, families and individuals on social assistance are most likely to experience hunger and are the primary users of food banks across Canada (McIntyre and Rondeau, 2009; McIntyre et al., 2000). Canada's social assistance rates are lower than those seen in most other wealthy developed nations.

Recapping: Group Membership and Poverty

Lone Parents

Lone parents are much more likely to have insufficient income than Canadian families in general. This is especially the case for female-led families. Much of this has to do with the high percentage of Canadian jobs that are low-paying, the lack of subsidized affordable child care, and the greater likelihood of these families being renters as opposed to homeowners. Low-end incomes have failed to keep pace with low-end rents in virtually every city in Canada. These factors combine with women's generally lower income to make their living conditions especially problematic.

People with Work-Limiting Disabilities

People with disabilities who are unable to work are more likely to be dependent on benefits rather than earned income (Rioux, 2010). Such benefits are very low in Canada and are not able to bring individuals close to the poverty lines in most cities (Fawcett, 2000).

Unattached Canadians, Aged 25–64

This group of Canadians are subject to many of the difficulties outlined for lone-parent families. Only one salary source is available and many Canadians' jobs are low paying. These factors combine to make being unattached a strong risk factor for living in poverty.

Recent Immigrants

In comparison to immigrants to Canada during earlier periods, recent immigrants are at a strikingly high risk for experiencing poverty. Recent immigrants are more likely to be unemployed and working at lower paying jobs than earlier immigrants and native-born Canadians. Galabuzi (2005) and Ornstein (2006) argue that these problems are a result of immigrants now being more likely to be people of colour than in the past. These authors suggest that recent immigrants are subject to discrimination that puts their life chances and their families' life chances at risk.

Aboriginal People Living Off-reserve

Aboriginal people living off-reserve are subject to numerous factors that make their living in poverty more likely. These include lower levels of education, greater incidence of a variety of health issues, and discrimination (Smiley, 2009).

People of Colour

Recent reports indicate that being a person of colour is a prime risk factor for living in poverty. Jackson points out that for every level of education, Canadians of colour earn less than other Canadians (Jackson, 2010). Indeed, this situation seems so striking as to suggest the growing presence of an economic apartheid (Ornstein, 2006; Galabuzi, 2005).

Women

Women experience a wide range of factors that increase their risk of living in poverty. These factors include earning less on average than men, having lower eligibility for employment benefits since family responsibilities interfere with full-time employment, and general discrimination in the workplace (Davies and McMullin, 2001; Day and Brodsky, 1999; Donner, 2002; Morris, 2000).

Finally, all of the above is especially relevant in light of the recession of 2008–2009 in which these vulnerable groups can be expected to be impacted the most by the job loss typical of such recessions (Yalnizyan, 2010) (see Box 5.3).

Box 5.3: The Problem of Poverty Post-recession

Every recession ushers in a rising tide of poverty. As jobless and underemployed people struggle to make ends meet, the nouveau poor swell the ranks of the déjà poor.

The most recent statistical update on incomes in Canada was released in June, telling us that in 2008, as the nation headed into a brutal recession, there were just over 3 million Canadians living in poverty in this country using the standard measure, Statistic Canada's after-tax low-income cut-off (LICO).

Statistics on annual income data come in two years after the fact and much has happened in this country since 2008. But if past recessions are any guide, between 750,000 and 1.8 million more Canadians will be counted as poor before recovery is complete. More than one in seven Canadians may have tumbled into poverty before this is over. Many of them will be working.

The greatest increase in poverty will be among working-age adults (18 to 64 years of age) and they will pull along hundreds of thousands of children who live with them. For the first time in decades, we may also see a sobering increase in the number of seniors coping with low income, a phenomenon which did not occur in previous recessions but has already reared its head in these new numbers.

Some will argue that this recession was brutal but short, and that Canada has been recovering faster than most other nations, so galloping poverty is not likely to be on the horizon. But Canadians entered this recession more exposed to the economic risks of joblessness than during any other recession since the Second World War, and the types of jobs created since last summer put recovery on shaky ground. Looking at the past tells us there is reason to worry, notwithstanding the signs of recovery in stock markets, GDP and profit margins. The recession of the 1980s marked an important increase in poverty but the rise and fall of poverty was relatively quick because, despite dramatic job losses, income support mechanisms were in place. The recession of the 1990s generated a much bigger escalation of poverty, both in magnitude and duration, because a protracted period of job loss ran into the scaling back of unemployment insurance and social assistance by federal and provincial governments.

As a consequence of that period, there was next to no cushion to soften the blow of the most shocking wave of job loss in our history during the opening six months of this recession, when almost half a million permanent and full-time jobs vanished. More than half of the jobless went without jobless benefits at the outset of the recession (43%) and despite modest reforms to the Employment Insurance Act—reforms which were introduced with sunset clauses, and scheduled to end soon—less than half of the unemployed remained without jobless benefits at the peak of the recession (48%). Dramatic reductions in asset limits for accessing welfare were put in the mid 1990s, designed to exclude any but the most destitute from income support. The legacy of this "tough love" has meant that many jobless middle class workers face economic free-fall and/or the prospect of grabbing any job, at any wage or hourly schedule, just to survive, often at incomes far inferior to what they had before.

Source: Yalnizyan, A. (2010). *The problem of poverty post-recession.* Ottawa: Canadian Centre for Policy Alternatives. Retrieved March 11, 2011 from http://tinyurl.com/2gxhhfo

Conclusions

There is clustering of advantage and disadvantage among Canadians. Individuals who are advantaged as children by way of income and wealth are more likely to achieve higher education levels, and better-paying and more secure employment. The availability of greater amounts of income and wealth also facilitate access to a variety of other commodities that shape health and quality of life, including quality child care, cultural and educational activities, leisure opportunities, and food and housing security (Bryant, 2009). These material living conditions shape psychological understandings of the world and promote a sense of control over one's life, feelings of self-efficacy, and a belief that the world is understandable. Those living in poverty are likely to experience the opposite living conditions and develop little sense of control, self-efficacy, or a belief that the world is understandable. These issues are taken up in Chapters 8 to 10.

Together, these positive or negative life experiences associated with advantage or disadvantage, and the psychological concomitants of experiencing these conditions, shape individuals' life trajectories over time. Material and social disadvantage associated with poverty contributes to lower educational achievement, and to employment that provides less compensation and security, which then contributes to continuing material and social disadvantage.

Similarly, policies that reduce the availability and affordability of housing and the amount of financial resources available to people affect resources available to Canadians. This is so since these policies—which produce low social assistance rates and minimum wages and lack of affordable housing—reduce the resources that can support other social determinants of health such as early life, food security, education, and recreation. These issues come together to have direct effects upon health and quality of life.

Critical Thinking Questions

1. What are some of the reasons why individual characteristics, rather than broader reasons, are frequently used to explain the incidence of poverty?
2. Why is being a single parent so strongly related to poverty in Canada and not so much in other nations?
3. How can the evidence about life transitions and their relationship to poverty inform public policy-making?

4. Do you think that most Canadians are aware that the percentages of low-wage work-ers differ so much between nations? If they were, what might be some of the results?
5. What role can governments play in reducing the impacts of life situations and tran-sitions upon the incidence of poverty?

Recommended Readings

Finnie, R. (2000). *Income (poverty) dynamics in Canada: Entry, exit, spell durations, and total time.* Ottawa: Applied Research Branch, Human Resources Development Canada. Online at http://tinyurl.com/2fhj6xw
> This study explores the dynamics of poverty in Canada over the 1992–1996 period, using the recently developed Longitudinal Administrative Databank. Relationships between changes in family status and poverty income are identified.

Green, K. (2001). *We did it together: Low income mothers working toward a healthier com-munity.* Saskatoon: Department of Community Health and Epidemiology, University of Saskatchewan. Online at www.pwhce.ca/pdf/didItTogether.pdf
> This report provides an example of how a group of women identify the pathways that led to their poverty. It also includes personal stories, and numerous policy rec-ommendations for reducing poverty and improving the health and quality of life of those living in poverty.

Jackson, A. (2010). *Employment and labour in Canada: Critical issues* (2nd ed.). Toronto: Canadian Scholars' Press Inc.
> This book focuses on issues surrounding work and labour in Canada. It provides up-to-date data on the situation of people with disabilities, Canadians of colour, Aboriginal Canadians, women, and other groups at risk for living in poverty. It also places the Canadian employment scene in international perspective.

Valletta, R. G. (2004). *The ins and outs of poverty in advanced economies: Poverty dynam-ics in Canada, Germany, Great Britain, and the United States.* San Francisco: Federal Reserve Bank of San Francisco. Online at www.tinyurl.com/r9smu. Also available as a Statistics Canada reprint at www.statcan.ca/english/research/75F0002MIE/75F0002 MIE2005001.pdf
> This paper compares poverty dynamics in four advanced industrial countries (Can-ada, Germany, the UK, and the USA) for overlapping six-year periods in the 1990s. Most poverty transitions, and the prevalence of chronic poverty, are associated with employment instability and family dissolution in all four countries.

Relevant Websites

Canadian Labour Congress (CLC)—www.clc-ctc.ca
> The Canadian Labour Congress is the national umbrella organization for 2.5 mil-lion unionized Canadian workers. The Social and Economic Issues sub-site con-tains many research papers on labour market issues (www.canadianlabour.ca/issues/

social-and-economic-issues). The site links to the websites of many unions in Canada and around the world.

International Labour Organization—www.ilo.org

The International Labour Organization is a United Nations organization that promotes "decent work." The site contains many research studies on labour and on working conditions around the world.

Luxembourg Income Study—www.lisproject.org/publications/wpapers.htm

The Luxembourg Income Studies provide working papers on a range of issues related to income and other indicators. Data on Canada and other developed nations are used to produce these excellent papers that bear directly on poverty and how public policy shapes its incidence. All of the working papers can be downloaded from this site.

Organisation for Economic Co-operation and Development—www.oecd.org/home

This site provides a wealth of reports, publications, and statistics about every aspect of society in modern developed states. Many of its contents are free or available electronically through your local university's library.

Statistics Canada Analytic Studies Branch—www.tinyurl.com/m378c

The papers in this series cover a variety of topics related to entrance into and out of poverty. They include incidence rates, predictors of poverty, and various analyses that tease out dimensions of poverty.

Glossary of Terms

Clustering of disadvantage refers to the phenomenon whereby people who are disadvantaged in one area, such as income, are also disadvantaged in other areas, such as housing, food security, and educational opportunities. Much of this clustering has to do with income being necessary to achieve various forms of security, such as housing and food security. Lack of income is also associated with living in communities where the amenities and services may be lacking as well.

Longitudinal study is a study where people are followed over time. In the case of living in poverty, longitudinal studies follow people over time and look at the life situations and events that lead them into and out of poverty.

Long-term versus *short-term poverty* refers to the duration of living in poverty. In Canada, most people living in poverty move in and out of the situation as a function of being employed, entering or leaving relationships, or changing demographics of the family. Long-term poverty can be defined as being poor over a five-year period.

Low-paid worker is defined in various ways. In Canada, a person can be considered a low-paid worker if they earn less than $10 an hour. Internationally, a low-paid or low-wage worker is a full-time worker who earns less than 66% of the average median wage.

Probability of changes in status refers to numerous ways of quantifying risk. Probability simply refers to the chance—out of 100—that a person will enter or leave a situation such as living in poverty. An increase of 50% means that a person has a one in two chance or, stated another way, out of 10 persons showing this risk factor, half will change status. Another way of expressing probability is through risk ratios or odds ratios. A probability is set against a standard value of 1.0. A person having twice the chance of changing status as compared to the comparison group will show a risk or odds ratio of 2.0. A person having a 50% greater chance will have a ratio of 1.50. A person having only a 50% chance of a situation change as compared to a comparison group will have a risk or odds ratio of 0.50.

References

Black, J., and Shillington, E. R. (2005). *Employment insurance: Research summary for the Task Force for Modernizing Income Security for Working Age Adults*. Toronto: Toronto City Summit Alliance.

Bryant, T. (2004). Housing as a social determinant of health. In D. Hulchanski and M. Shapcott (Eds.), *Policy options for an affordable rental housing strategy for Canada* (pp. 159–166). Toronto: Centre for Urban and Community Studies, University of Toronto.

Bryant, T. (2009). Housing and health: More than bricks and mortar. In D. Raphael (Ed.), *Social determinants of health: Canadian perspectives* (2nd ed., pp. 235–249). Toronto: Canadian Scholars' Press Inc.

Campaign 2000 (2010). 2010 *Report card on child and family poverty in Canada 1989–2010: Reduced poverty = better health for all*. Toronto: Campaign 2000.

Corak, M. (2001). *Are the kids all right: Intergenerational mobility and child well-being in Canada*. Ottawa: Statistics Canada Analytic Studies Branch.

Corak, M. (2004a). Generational income mobility in North America and Europe: An introduction. In M. Corak (Ed.), *Generational income mobility in North America and Europe: An introduction* (pp. 1–37). Cambridge, UK: Cambridge University Press.

Corak, M. (Ed.). (2004b). *Generational income mobility in North America and Europe*. Cambridge, UK: Cambridge University Press.

Davies, L., and McMullin, J. A. (2001). *Social policy, gender inequality, and poverty*. Ottawa: Status of Women Canada.

Day, S., and Brodsky, G. (1999). *Women's economic inequality and the Canadian Human Right's Act*. Ottawa: Status of Women Canada.

Donner, L. (2002). *Women, income, and health in Manitoba: An overview and ideas for action*. Winnipeg: Winnipeg Women's Health Clinic.

Fawcett, G. (2000). *Bringing down the barriers: The labour market and women with disabilities in Ontario*. Ottawa: Canadian Council on Social Development.

Federation of Canadian Municipalities. (2004). *Highlights report 2004: Quality of life in Canadian municipalities*. Ottawa: Federation of Canadian Municipalities.

Federation of Canadian Municipalities. (2008). *Trends and issues in affordable housing and homelessness*. Ottawa: Federation of Canadian Municipalities.

Finnie, R. (2000a). *The dynamics of poverty in Canada: What we know, what we can do* (C. D. Howe Institute Commentary 145). Toronto: C. D. Howe Institute.

Finnie, R. (2000b). *Low income (poverty) dynamics in Canada: Entry, exit, spell durations, and total time*. Ottawa: Applied Research Branch, Human Resources Development Canada.

Finnie, R., and Sweetman, A. (2003). Poverty dynamics: Empirical evidence for Canada. *Canadian Journal of Economics/Revue canadienne d'economique, 36*(2), 291–325.

Fleury, D., and Fortin, M. (2004). Canada's working poor. *Horizons, 7*(2), 51–57.

Food Banks Canada. (2010). *Hunger count 2009.* Toronto: Food Banks Canada.

Galabuzi, G. E. (2005). *Canada's economic apartheid: The social exclusion of racialized groups in the new century.* Toronto: Canadian Scholars' Press Inc.

Green, K. (2000). *"We did it together": Low income mothers working towards a healthier community.* Saskatoon: University of Saskatchewan.

Green, K. (2001). *Telling it like it is: Realities of parenting in poverty.* Winnipeg: Prairie Women's Health Centre of Excellence.

Hatfield, M. (2004). Vulnerability of persistent low income. *Horizons, 7*(2), 19–26.

Innocenti Research Centre. (2005). *Child poverty in rich nations, 2005* (Report Card No. 6). Florence: Innocenti Research Centre.

Jackson, A. (2010). *Work and labour in Canada: Critical issues* (2nd ed.). Toronto: Canadian Scholars' Press Inc.

Keating, D. P., and Hertzman, C. (Eds.). (1999). *Developmental health and the wealth of nations.* New York: Guilford Press.

Layton, J. (2008). *Homelessness: How to end the national crisis.* Toronto: Penguin Books Canada.

McIntyre, L., Conner, S., and Warren, J. (2000). Child hunger in Canada: Results of the 1994 National Longitudinal Survey of Children and Youth. *Canadian Medical Association Journal, 163*(8), 961–965.

McIntyre, L., and Rondeau, K. (2009). Food insecurity in Canada. In D. Raphael (Ed.), *Social determinants of health: Canadian perspectives* (2nd ed., pp. 188–204). Toronto: Canadian Scholars' Press Inc.

Morris, M. (2000, May 29). *Women, poverty and Canadian public policy in an era of globalization.* Paper presented at the International Colloquium: Globalization, Societies, Cultures Congress of the Social Sciences and Humanities, Edmonton, Canada.

National Council of Welfare. (2004). *Income for living?* Ottawa: National Council of Welfare.

National Council of Welfare. (2010). *Welfare incomes: 2008–2009.* Ottawa: National Council.

Ocean, C. (2005). *Policies of exclusion, poverty, and health.* Duncan, BC: WISE Society.

Organisation for Economic Co-operation and Development. (2008). *Growing unequal: Income distribution and poverty in OECD nations.* Paris: OECD.

Ornstein, M. (2006). *Ethno-racial groups in Toronto, 1971–2001: A demographic and social-economic profile.* Toronto: City of Toronto.

Raphael, D., and Bryant, T. (2004). The welfare state as a determinant of women's health: Support for women's quality of life in Canada and four comparison nations. *Health Policy, 68*, 63–79.

Rioux, M. (2010). The right to health—Human rights approaches to health. In T. Bryant, D. Raphael, and M. Rioux (Eds.), *Staying alive: Critical perspectives on health, illness, and health care* (2nd ed., pp. 93–120). Toronto: Canadian Scholars' Press Inc.

Ross, D. P., and Roberts, P. (1999). *Income and child well-being: A new perspective on the poverty debate.* Ottawa: Canadian Council on Social Development.

Shapcott, M. (2009). Housing. In D. Raphael (Ed.), *Social determinants of health: Canadian perspectives* (2nd ed., pp. 221–234). Toronto: Canadian Scholars' Press Inc.

Shaw, M., Dorling, D., Gordon, D., and Davey Smith, G. (1999). *The widening gap: Health inequalities and policy in Britain*. Bristol, UK: The Policy Press.

Smiley, J. (2009). The health of Aboriginal peoples. In D. Raphael (Ed.), *Social determinants of health: Canadian perspectives* (2nd ed., pp. 280–301). Toronto: Canadian Scholars' Press Inc.

Statistics Canada. (2010). Low-income in Canada CANSIM Tables. Ottawa: Statistics Canada.

Tremblay, D. G. (2009). Precarious work and the labour market. In D. Raphael (Ed.), *Social determinants of health: Canadian perspectives* (2nd ed., pp. 75–87). Toronto: Canadian Scholars' Press Inc.

Valletta, R. G. (2004). *The ins and outs of poverty in advanced economies: Poverty dynamics in Canada, Germany, Great Britain, and the United States*. San Francisco: Federal Reserve Bank of San Francisco.

Willms, J. D. (Ed.). (2002). *Vulnerable children: Findings from Canada's National Longitudinal Survey*. Edmonton: University of Alberta Press.

Yalnizyan, A. (2010). *The problem of poverty post-recession*. Ottawa: Canadian Centre for Policy Alternatives.

Chapter Six

The Lived Experience of Poverty

Poverty is like punishment for a crime you didn't commit.—Eli Khamarov

Learning Objectives

At the conclusion of this chapter, the reader will be able to:

- describe the limitations of applying traditional research approaches to further understanding of the experience of living in poverty;
- outline the importance of understanding the lived experience of poverty;
- understand the key components of ethnographic and qualitative research approaches;
- relate the common themes associated with the lived experience of poverty;
- begin to identify the pathways by which living in poverty affects health and quality of life; and
- present a framework for understanding how those living in poverty cope with the experiences of living in poverty.

Introduction

Focusing on the measurement of poverty and the statistical analysis of its incidence can make us forget that poverty is about real people living under real conditions of material and social deprivation. In this chapter, the human face of living in poverty is presented. Information from ethnographic and qualitative studies provides profound insights into the experience and effects of living in poverty. The experience of poverty is a personal experience but is also an experience that is embedded in interactions with families, neighbours, and others in the community. Such information reveals that the experience of poverty, its effects, and responses to it have both individual and interpersonal dimensions.

Experiential data are important for a variety of reasons. First, examining the experience of those living in poverty provides details concerning their material and social deprivation. These kinds of insights are not easily obtained by analysis of statistical data from large-scale surveys created by professional researchers. Second, examining the lived experience of poverty provides important evidence of the health-threatening and society-weakening effects of poverty. This evidence illuminates pathways that connect the poverty and health and quality-of-life relationships. Third, collecting, analyzing, and reporting on the lived experience of poverty provides a useful counterbalance to the power that academic researchers, government officials, policy-makers, the business sector, and others have to set—and potentially distort—the poverty-related public policy agenda. Those who set the public policy agenda usually have vested interests in maintaining the status quo; giving voice to those experiencing poverty makes questioning of the current state of affairs more likely. Fourth, reporting on the experience of those living in poverty, and giving them a voice in the process, facilitates their ability to organize themselves to form social movements that question the current state of affairs. It also supports existing social movements concerned with eliminating poverty in Canada.

The Importance of Understanding Lived Experience

Health research has been dominated by traditional positivist science (Bryant, Raphael, and Rioux, 2010). Put simply, this is the application of scientific methods developed largely in the physical and biological sciences to the study of health and social issues (Lincoln, 1994). Epidemiology is the clearest example of such an approach, but many important schools of psychology and sociology also apply this methodology (Park, 1993).

Traditional science is concerned with expanding knowledge by identifying cause-and-effect relationships among identifiable and measurable variables (Lincoln and Guba, 1985). Statistics is the primary tool used to describe and understand these relationships. Traditional science is reductionist; that is, it focuses on concrete and readily measurable variables at the expense of complexity and the whole (Wilson, 1983a). Scientific activity is seen as being value-free, with the scientist's role being that of discovering the "laws of nature." Traditional positivist science has been the target of much criticism concerning its relevance to understanding health and its determinants, to the processes of making public policy, and to providing responses to pressing social issues such as poverty, income and wealth inequality, and the marginalization of groups in societies. Since this model of science evolved from the physical and biological sciences, there is no role for human agency in the affairs of society. That is, the approach has difficulty in considering the role that human attitudes, values, and beliefs can play in developing and carrying out activities to change society.

For all of these reasons, there is a strong tendency of traditional researchers to reduce the study of poverty and its effects to the identification of associations between concrete and observable variables. A phenomenon such as poverty, and its causes and effects, is studied by relating individual characteristics (e.g., income level, education, coping mechanisms, etc.) to individual outcomes (e.g., health status, disease incidence, social adjustment, etc.). Analysis of the structural causes of poverty (e.g., distribution of resources, public policies that create poverty, political ideologies that drive public policy, etc.) and the complex effects of poverty (e.g., social exclusion, experience of stigma, internalization of blame, etc.) are uncommon among those working within this research paradigm.

Traditional approaches to the study of poverty and health have often not been concerned with understanding poverty, nor with improving the health and well-being of those living in poverty. They have been more concerned with documenting the variables that predict the incidence of poverty and identifying relationships between poverty and health. Once done, the research is considered to have been completed.

This research also rarely concerns itself with identifying and challenging existing power structures that create and maintain the policies that create poverty. The research is narrow and controlled by academics who are themselves part of the existing power structure. Ultimately, the research does little to reduce the incidence and effects of poverty. By being narrow and expert-driven, the research rarely considers societal factors that shape the experiences of people experiencing poverty.

Not all traditional research is guilty of these shortcomings. There is traditional research that can document the structural causes of poverty, identify its damaging effects upon individual and community health and quality of life, and be directed toward promoting positive policy change (Raphael and Bryant, 2002). It is just that there is relatively little of this kind of research within the traditional paradigm because its basic principles make such activities difficult. An alternative paradigm should focus upon the experience of people living in poverty, consider structural issues in addition to individual ones, and be more explicitly concerned with improving living conditions and creating a more equitable distribution of economic resources.

One such research approach is known as the constructivist, naturalistic, ethnographic, or qualitative tradition (Lincoln and Guba, 1985; Wilson, 1983b). Its focus is on the meanings and interpretations individuals give to their experiences and how these are embedded in their everyday lives. Also known as interactive knowledge, it strives to understand the connections among human beings, their experiences, and their relationship with social structures (Park, 1993). The methods used are those of participant observation, ethnographies, in-depth interviews, case studies, and analysis of life stories or narratives. The primary data used are people's own experiences, related in their own words. These words are then reviewed and themes, or key issues, are identified. The researcher takes these themes and places them into larger theoretical and conceptual frameworks that can help in understanding the experience of poverty (Guba, 1990).

There are numerous benefits that may accrue from using an alternative approach. These approaches provide voice (e.g., power, capacity, control, etc.) to individuals and communities experiencing poverty; increase theoretical and practical knowledge about the experience of poverty; identify immediate individual and community issues requiring action; and support community action to address the causes of poverty and to respond to its effects. The ultimate goal of these kinds of research activities is explicitly construed as effecting political and social change to reduce poverty (Bryant, Raphael, and Travers, 2007).

Poverty as Lived Experience

Relatively little research within this paradigm is done in Canada (Raphael et al., 2004). However, that which has been done is of high quality and provides profound insights into the experience of poverty and its effects upon health and quality of life. The research has also been useful in placing the experience of poverty within the current public policy environment in Canada. The focus in this chapter is on eight exemplary research projects, the primary concern of which was the examination of the lived experience of poverty. The findings from these eight studies are then assessed in terms of their validation of the premise that poverty is about the experience of material and social deprivation that comes about as the result of public policy decisions related to the distribution of resources within the population. The studies are also assessed as to the extent to which they help illuminate the pathways by which poverty comes to be related to health and quality-of-life issues.

Project 1—Feeling Poor: The Felt Experience of Low-Income Lone Mothers; and Welfare Babies: Poor Children's Experiences Informing Healthy Peer Relationships in Canada

These projects (McIntyre, Officer, and Robinson, 2003; Robinson, McIntyre, and Officer, 2005) gathered data on the lived experience of lone-parent mothers and their children as part of two larger studies in Atlantic Canada: Hungry Mothers of Barely Fed Children and Children's Feeding Programs. The larger studies examined the experience of hunger and food insecurity among low-income lone mothers and their children in the Maritime provinces. The Hungry Mothers study had three phases, each of which provided lived-experience data. In the first phase, 141 lone mothers completed a dietary intake questionnaire by telephone four times over the course of one month. The lived-experience data consisted of 345 comments that were offered by women as they completed the questionnaire. In the second phase of the study, the data came from face-to-face ethnographic interviews with 24 mothers that were part of the larger sample. The third data set consisted of the 250 comments provided by 33 participants who attended "returning-results" or feedback sessions upon the study's completion. The Children's Feeding Programs study consisted of nine case studies that involved participant observation, focus groups, and interviews with adults and children.

The data from these studies were carefully reviewed for comments that described social, emotional, physical, or psychological effects of poverty. These comments were then sorted into categories based on their similarities. These item categories were then each given an appropriate heading. This is the process normally known as thematic analysis in ethnographic or qualitative research. These themes were then reviewed and agreed upon by all the researchers to assure their validity. For mothers' experiences, 10 themes were identified: feeling deprived; feeling righteous; feeling the need for occupational choice; feeling better off than others; feeling the need to manage the appearance of poverty; feeling judged/degraded; feeling guilty; feeling isolated; feeling dependent; and feeling despondent. The following paragraphs provide examples of each theme. The original articles outlining the studies provide greater detail concerning the studies and more examples of comments associated with each theme (McIntyre et al., 2003; Robinson et al., 2005).

Feeling Deprived—The Experience of Material and Social Deprivation
- *"How are you going to get a boyfriend if you are wearing a garbage bag and rubber boots?"*
- *"Often run out of toilet paper, no shampoo for days, often no money for laundry soap, do without."* (p. 321)

Feeling Righteous—Coping by Gaining Meaning from the Situation
- *"We are poor and deal with it."*
- *"I tell my kids we are wealthy in love."* (p. 322)

Need for Occupational Choice—Feeling That One Has Little Control over One's Daily Activities
- *"I am forced to go out and work, or I am looked down upon. If you are at home, you are constantly nagged by social assistance."*
- *"If I work, they take my money away. What I make, they take. I have to do something. It makes me feel better."* (p. 322)

Better Off Than Others—Placing Oneself in Relation to Those Worse off
- *"I am poor but not as poor as her."*
- *"I can borrow money for food at times."* (p. 322)

Need to Manage the Appearance of Poverty—Coping with the Situation of Being Poor
- *"They are kids and shouldn't have to deal with that kind of worry or stress."*
- *"Mommy can't afford to give you nuggets this evening; we're on a budget."* (p. 323)

Judged/Degraded—Experiencing Negative Effect from Interactions with Others
- *"I mean like buying food off the reduced racks and buying food out of the carts that are all dented up and stuff—eating like a dog."*
- *"And then the taxi driver is looking at you, 'Ok not another charity case.'"* (p. 324)

Guilty—Feeling Responsible for the Situation of Poverty
- *"It's not the kids' fault, and its not really my fault, you know, but I still carry a lot of guilt."*
- *"I feel like I am trading their education for groceries, and I don't like it, and it is not a fair trade."* (p. 325)

Isolated—Cut off from Others in the Same Situation
- *"I thought I was the only one."*
- *"I didn't realize how many were suffering. We are all suffering, but we keep it at home."* (p. 326)

Dependent—Coming to Rely on Benefits in Order to Survive
- *"You get more dependent on government help and charities and less independent and less apt to get off the system or out of poverty."*
- *"Social-assistance recipients are easy prey."* (p. 325)

Despondent—Experiencing Despair and Hopelessness
- *"The worst feeling is having to say no to your children."*
- *"I am sick, mentally sick, with all the things going on." (p. 326)*

The authors note that the most pervasive comments were the negative emotions of feeling judged/degraded, guilty, isolated, and dependent. Nonetheless, the authors pointed out that these women were remarkably resilient and had adopted a variety of coping mechanisms to help them get by. They struggled to maintain some semblance of control over their lives in what appeared to be very difficult and very stressful circumstances.

Children's Experiences of Poverty

The primary source of data for children's experiences of poverty came from mothers (Robinson, McIntyre, and Officer, 2005). However, data from children and child-serving professionals such as teachers were also used. Seven themes were identified: feeling deprived, feeling like part of the "poor group," feeling embarrassed, feeling hurt, feeling picked on, feeling inadequate, and feeling responsible. The following paragraphs provide examples of each. Again, the previously mentioned articles outlining the studies provide greater detail and more examples of comments associated with each theme.

Feeling Deprived—The Experience of Material and Social Deprivation
- *"Can I join, can I join, can I join? No, you can't, no you can't. It's the food or you can join that club."*
- *"Daughter cries.... No one loves me.... She wants leather pants—but she can't have them and Christmas is coming." (p. 345)*

Feeling Like Part of the "Poor Group"—Recognizing That You Are Different from Others
- *"They know, though I think most of the kids can almost point out themselves. I mean they know at quite an early age the reality of their own situations."*
- *"Well Mommy, you know kids that take peanut butter and jam to school, they're called welfare babies. Well make sure you don't run out of lunches anymore." (p. 345)*

Feeling Embarrassed
- *"It lowers their self esteem if they don't have items to take to the bake sale."*
- *"I can't go on a school trip because Mommy couldn't afford it." (p. 346)*

Feeling Hurt—Experiencing Feelings of Shame
- *"You go to school and you see ... you know everything new or brand name ... like dripping with money, and here's my child going to the Salvation Army."*
- *"Kids are hurting inside." (p. 346)*

Feeling Picked on (by Students Who Are Not Poor about Participation in Feeding Programs)
- *"Children are taunted by statements such as 'Your mother can't afford to feed you.'"*
- *"You must be on welfare because you go there [a feeding program]." (p. 346)*

Feeling Inadequate—Being Treated as Inferior to Others

- *"You can't see if someone is hungry but you can see if they don't have the latest style in jeans and sneakers or whatever, there's a lot of peer pressure, even at a young age."*
- *"The teachers treat you differently if you are poor. You are bullied and put down more often." (p. 346)*

Feeling Responsible—Children Taking on Responsibility to Deal with Living in Poverty

- *"My son hides stuff that happens at school. He tries to make me feel good."*
- *"Mom, when I stop growing, will you buy me NIKE sneakers when you can?"*
- *"At supper the kids are tricking me into eating." (p. 346)*

The authors conclude that impoverished children suffer from a profound sense of not belonging, in addition to experiencing material and social deprivation. While schools and the community can play a role in supporting social relationships among poor children, the findings of the study suggest the need to prevent impoverishment among children within these families.

Project 2—Policies of Exclusion, Poverty, and Health: Stories from the Front

This project (Ocean, 2005) was developed with a twofold purpose: to collect stories from women living below Canada's poverty line and to provide a vehicle for those women to raise their concerns with the general public and policy-makers. The project was conceived and carried out by one of the storytellers living in poverty: Chrystal Ocean. She is also editor of the volume from which the results of the study are obtained.

There were three selection criteria for participation. First, the participant had to be female. Second, her household income had to be below the Statistics Canada low income cut-off. Third, she had to be living in the Cowichan Valley, an area on Vancouver Island with both small urban and rural communities. Stories were collected from 21 women. Fifteen of the stories were derived from transcripts of interviews with the women. The other six stories were written by the women themselves. All 21 stories are in the women's own words and were constructed from either a story written by the woman herself, a story that began as self-written but was completed by interview, a story constructed by the interviewer from the woman's own words, or a story that was based on the interview but was completed by the woman.

The volume *Policies of Exclusion, Poverty, and Health* also contains project reports that identify (a) predictors of poverty, primary effects of poverty, and secondary conditions and their effects; and (b) a set of recommendations (Ocean, 2005). The predictors of poverty identified in this study were presented in Chapter 5. In this chapter, the focus is on what the author calls the primary effects of the experience of poverty. The secondary conditions and effects focus on interactions with service providers, and are presented in Chapter 7.

Primary Effects: The Experience of Poverty

The discussion of the primary effects of poverty uses many examples that illustrate the lived experience of these women. Two major direct effects—or components—of the lived experience of poverty are the deterioration of emotional well-being and the deterioration of physical well-being.

Contained within the primary effect of deteriorating emotional well-being are themes of exhaustion, depression and despair, anger and frustration, stress, thoughts of death, challenges to self-esteem, and isolation. The following sections illustrate these themes with quotations from the women's stories.

Deterioration of Emotional Well-being

Exhaustion—Identified as Dominant Aspect of Women's Lives

- *"I'm so, so tired ... just enough to live, to be able to survive, to jockey all the things going on."*
- *"I'm exhausted ... I'm just exhausted, because the thought of waking up and trying to live through another day the way we have been is overwhelming." (p. 139)*

Depression and Despair—Common to over Half the Stories

- *"I live on a razor's edge. Right now, just maintaining work and maintaining my health takes everything. It takes everything I've got."*
- *"In a project like this, how many women are ... so tired—and I don't mean sick and tired—I mean almost exhausted to death and hopeless to death from trying to struggle through one more day." (p. 140)*

Anger and Frustration—Most Are Angry and Frustrated

- *"How can a nation that has the capabilities, resources, and command of technology that we do blatantly discriminate and hold women hostage through poverty? To me it's an obvious intent to keep us here. This way the status quo is preserved."*
- *"I don't like not having a little bit of money in my pocket. I used to feel guilty for that. Everybody else likes to have a little bit of money in their pocket. Shouldn't I? Am I not allowed that?" (p. 140)*

Stress—Most Get No relief from Stress

- *"Receiving public financial assistance makes me feel worthless. We are allowed to earn $400 a month. Anything over that, watch out; your Disability Benefits (DB) go. That's why I'm scared to go full-time, I may not be able to get DB again."*
- *"Sometimes I stop eating to insure there is food for my son. He notices and fears I will die."*
- *"How can a child trust this environment? How frightening this must be for him. How does he trust in a parent that cannot give him food. I have seen the confusion cause him anger and he strikes out at me." (p. 140)*

Thoughts of Death—For Many, a Daily Fact of Life

- *"I got so tired of being poor. I found it so stressful that I wanted to die."*

- *"If I didn't have these children and if I didn't have an ex-husband that the thought of him ever getting custody of them would kill me, I probably would have ended my life long ago. There's a point where you can't just keep doing it. It costs too much to live." (p. 140)*

Challenges to Self-Esteem—Difficult under Society's Onslaught
- *"You're a case file, you're 'the client.' You're never 'this person.' Nobody would ever say to their supervisor: 'This person needs help' ... so you cease to be."*
- *"One person stands on one side of a counter 'qualifying' another person who stands on the other side of the counter." (p. 141)*

Isolation—Lack of Money Creates Isolation and Marginalization
- *"Poverty keeps people away. I don't have a car or a phone. I can't entertain."*
- *"The isolation is comparative to solitary confinement. I can't afford a babysitter. I can't afford the bus ... and I won't walk at night." (p. 141)*

Deterioration of Physical Well-being
The following analysis is provided by the report's editor, who is also a storyteller:

"Low energy is caused by a number of factors, including lack of nutritious food, the requirements for maintaining emotional stability and the requirements for maintaining the physical endurance to keep moving."

Emotional demands reduce energy: *Those of us struggling daily with suicidal thoughts talk of the energy needed to fight the temptation to give in.*

Physical demands reduce energy: *All of us are stressed and most are malnourished, which makes our energy stores low. Most of us walk everywhere, since we haven't a vehicle and cannot afford transit fare.*

Weight: Some of us have gained weight from being on the "Welfare diet." Three make the connection between weight gain and diabetes: That many carbohydrates turn you into a blimp."

A few of us are underweight because we don't eat enough. We see ourselves with only two choices: eat a high-carb diet or eat much less, but at least some nutritious food: "Welfare puts you on such a diet you can't afford fresh fruits or vegetables, all carbohydrates." (p. 142)

Project 3—Left out: Low Income and Social Exclusion in Toronto and Edmonton

This project (Stewart, Reutter, Veenstra, Love, and Raphael, 2003, 2004) was a three-part study. The first phase examined the lived experience of low-income people in four neighbourhoods in Toronto and four neighbourhoods in Edmonton. The second phase consisted of surveys of citizens in each neighbourhood about their understandings of poverty, of how poverty comes about, and of the health effects of living in poverty. The third phase was an inquiry into public policy responses to the findings of the first two phases of the study. More specifically, the project was concerned with the concepts and lived experiences of social exclusion/inclusion and isolation/belonging, particularly among low-income people.

The findings presented here are from Phase I of the study and are focused on the lived experience of exclusion and isolation by low-income people. Thirty low-income individuals were interviewed in Toronto and 29 in Edmonton. Furthermore, three group interviews with 19 low-income people were held in Toronto, and three with 16 low-income people were held in Edmonton. Individual interviews were conducted using a semi-structured schedule.

The topics of study were a sense of belonging, support received and provided, participation in societal activities, effects of income on exclusion/inclusion and belonging/isolation, perceptions of causes of poverty, and identifying recommendations for promoting inclusion of those living on low incomes.

Experiences of Social Exclusion and Social Isolation

The project identified numerous ways that people on low income are both included in society and develop a sense of belonging. Overall, however, higher income people were reliably more likely to be involved than lower income people in leisure activities, physical activities, social activities, family activities, civic activities, cultural activities, work activities, religious activities, and volunteer activities.

The social activities in which low-income people reported not being involved were going out to restaurants, holding dinner parties, attending events with friends, inviting friends over, going out on dates, attending dances, going out for coffee, and buying gifts. There were a variety of themes that emerged from the examination of low-income participants' depictions of their activities and their sense of belonging.

Experience of Social Exclusion

Social exclusion describes the theme of being systematically excluded from being involved in a range of activities.

- "It feels we're still outcasts because we don't have money to give to the church and we can't afford to come in to some of their—they have certain things that they do on certain days, and we can't be involved because we don't have the money. But we try to get around that as much as we can." (Stewart et al., 2003, p. 17)
- "Because of the constraints of time and also the need to have finances to live on, I've not been able to do some of the community activities that I would like to, such as learning bridge or making use of whatever facilities are available there." (Stewart et al., 2003, p. 32)
- "I don't feel like I'm part of anything really. I know the church is great, but that's just the church. Outside of the church, we're basically nothing. We're just at home, and it gets really frustrating." (Stewart et al., 2004, p. 6)
- "I feel like an outcast from my family.... Well I don't get invited to a lot of family things.... Well they just don't invite me if there's a special family affair—then I'm not involved." (Stewart et al., 2004, p. 7)

- "I find it hard sometimes to go to the outside things because ... I feel like people might be judging me because I'm on assistance or low income or whatever. Sometimes I feel like they can tell just by looking at me." (Stewart et al., 2004, p. 9)
- "And when I have no money to go out for coffee or anything I isolate myself because friends are always saying 'oh come on out, don't worry about it I'll pay for it.' But I don't feel comfortable with that on a regular basis, once in a while that's okay." (Stewart et al., 2004, p. 9)

Identifying the Processes/Practices of Social Exclusion and Social Isolation

- Low-income people identified numerous factors that contributed to their exclusion and isolation. These included government and agency actions, prejudice and discrimination, inaccessibility to amenities, bureaucracy/red tape of agencies, undemocratic structures, lack of opportunity, and lack of community safety.
- "The social service system is set up to keep you reliant on them forever... I don't think its set up to get people independent, to get people to work, to get people feeling good about themselves, to have self respect and ... dignity... and ... the things you need to ... make some kind of life for yourself." (Stewart et al., 2003, p. 34).
- "They don't understand why I'm not working... I've got a few things wrong with me where I can't work so you're damned if you do, you're damned if you don't. If I get a job and I can't complete the task or I can't get there all the time because of my arthritis, then you're fired. And with arthritis I can't work all the time and social assistance expects me to walk around looking for jobs. And if you let them know you can't look for a job you're off the roll." (Stewart et al., 2004, p. 12).
- "There are road blocks in the system to allow these individuals to better themselves. I mean look at welfare. They're only allowed to earn so much money and then the money comes off your cheque. So you're in the welfare trap—you're in the system trap." (Stewart et al., 2003, p. 41)

The Specific Experience of Stigma Associated with Low Income

Low-income people gave specific examples of how other people think of them.

- "[They think] we're bums and we're trying to scam off the system."
- "There are so many prejudices against the poor. Stereotypical thinking, labelling of people." (Stewart et al., 2004, p. 10)
- "They kind of associate that you are less capable of doing well and achieving ... certain goals in your life. They associate you as having been less educated. You know you're a stereotype. It makes me sick.... I always have a bad feeling in my stomach like when I consider this so I try to block this out as much as I can and try to go on. But it's unhealthy. That can be more damaging because it chips away at your self-esteem and then our illness is connected to that, so

it wipes out everything. And you just end up being sick again." (Stewart et al., 2004, p. 12)

- "I think they think they're lazy, they don't want to help themselves. I think that they think that they made a choice to live like that. And that they probably are a burden on taxpayers such as themselves." (Stewart et al., 2004, p. 9)

The Specific Effects of Poverty

The low-income people in the study identified three key areas of concern: budgeting, housing, and bureaucracy and rules. Budgeting was seen as restrictive and stressful, consuming time and energy, requiring rolling bill payment and a focus on paying for housing and food. Nevertheless, hardly any money was available for clothing, and there was a constant concern about paying for dentists, laundry, toiletries, transportation, repayment of debts, and bank fees.

Regarding housing, obtaining first and last month's rent is difficult, and it's extremely difficult to find an affordable apartment, to live with others, or to obtain subsidized housing. Bureaucracy and rules make it difficult to acquire assistive devices necessary for daily living. There are ever-changing caseworkers, many of whom treat you as a criminal or suspect. In addition, the clawback rules reduce income and opportunities for increasing income, and there is always pressure to work or volunteer. All of these difficulties contribute to the constant experience of stress and its associated health effects.

The Specific Experience of Material Deprivation

Low-income participants in the study spoke eloquently of how difficult living conditions were if you are poor.

- "It's very difficult to work, take care of your children, and put food on the table when you're constantly fighting to pay rent and put food on the table and pay the bills. I mean it's almost impossible to keep up." (Stewart et al., 2003, p. 41)
- "My kids love fresh broccoli, fresh cauliflower—but we did without that for most of the three years we went through this retraining and finding a job process.... When fresh fruit ... and even canned fruit ... turns out just to be a treat, there's something wrong." (Stewart et al., 2003, p. 41)
- "It's a struggle all the time. I put all the bills there and I think ... which one are we going to pay this time?... I think we tend to not eat as well ... there seems to be more junk food coming into the house. I guess ...'we can't afford a lot but, boy, we can afford a bag of chips.'" (Stewart et al., 2004, p. 11)

The Daily Experience of Stress

Low-income participants also spoke of the daily experience of stress and constant worrying.

- "I just don't feel like I can enjoy myself really.... And do the things that regular people do to enjoy themselves ... I'm on Social Assistance... Even though I know I'm capable of doing a lot more. I'm just kind of stuck right now, being a single parent. But I am doing some training and upgrading to better my life. It makes you feel really, I don't know, I've been in this situation for quite some time, and it's just—it almost feels impossible to get out of." (Stewart et al., 2003, p. 42)

- "You're constantly watching virtually nickels and dimes, because you have your next bills in line.... The welfare amounts are not enough to live on.... So you're scrambling to make payments, and you're at a terrible disadvantage to begin with ... it's a constant scramble for th[e] ... poor to make ends meet." (Stewart et al., 2003, p. 41)

- "I've grown so accustomed to living this way that it's I never bother putting myself through it, you know anymore, you know. I've maybe grown numb from it really." (Stewart et al., 2003, p. 42)

- "When you're not meeting the mortgage every month ... having to pay the mortgage one month but then the utilities don't get paid—then you pay the utilities and the mortgage doesn't get paid. It's nerve-wracking. It is so stressful that then you find yourself—my husband had a real hard time not biting at us ... then it's starting to put the family itself in danger." (Stewart et al., 2004, p. 12)

Experiencing Judgmental Attitudes on a Continual Basis

In addition to deprivation, stress, and worry, low-income participants spoke of having to experience constant judging of themselves and their families by others.

- "Before I got sick I was making $40,000 a year. I went from that to UI sick leave to welfare in the space of, you know, 6 months. I've really noticed a difference—like I still have a hard time budgeting even though it's been 3 years.... Sometimes there's a feeling in me that— ... bearing in mind that I do have this chronic depression thing so there are some self-esteem issues there—I almost feel demeaned." (Stewart et al., 2004, p. 12)

- "I feel like they judge the kids, you know, like saying sometimes 'don't play with them,' you know. Maybe it's because they feel like, um, because somebody's on low income that they don't have much of an education, so their kids wouldn't be educated and they'd be dropouts and, you know, rejects, like troublemakers and stuff." (Stewart et al., 2004, p. 9)

- "You know, sometimes when I'm looking for work or I went to the doctor sometimes, they said 'oh, you are ... well you have the social [insurance card] ... or you are on assistance?' And then you feel little." (Stewart et al., 2004, p. 9)

- "I think some people see you doing what's perceived as sort of a menial task or whatever then they sort of they look down on it ... so various perceptions of what the hourly wage is being, but it's not very high. Some of the people have been extremely nice but other people are sort of, you know, like, you can sense that there's a sense of superiority that you're doing this. And you're doing this because of a necessity or whatever and it's not a very good job." (Stewart et al., 2004, p. 9)

While there are many activities that low-income people in this study identified as assisting them in being included and in belonging to their communities, the overwhelming sense is that low-income people are excluded from many activities. Low-income people report frequent experiences of material and social deprivation. Importantly, the experience of material and social deprivation and the exclusion and isolation that are associated with it are reported as being stressful. These stress-related experiences are identified as having clear health-related effects.

Project 4—Telling It Like It Is: Realities of Parenting in Poverty

This project (Green, 2001) brought together 15 low-income mothers whose children were of preschool age. They were identified through programs such as collective kitchens and parenting groups. The purpose of the project was to move beyond coping with their difficult living conditions and toward changing these conditions. Once the women identified that poverty was at the root of all their issues, they learned more about poverty and discussed their own stories and experiences. The project report consists of 15 stories that illustrate the challenges these women face living in poverty. The introduction to the stories gives an overview of the problems mothers living in poverty face.

> *Parenting is a hard job, as anyone who has raised a child knows. To make it even harder, try parenting in poverty! On top of the usual challenges of parenthood, like not having enough sleep, temper tantrums, and sibling rivalry, parents in poverty have a lot of other worries, like*

> - *How to get enough food.*
> - *Finding affordable housing that is free from hazards and in good shape.*
> - *For many of the families that don't own cars, getting themselves and their children to the places they need to go—especially during the winter.*
> - *Having enough money left after paying for housing, food, and transportation to buy the other things that growing children need (let alone their own needs). (Green, 2001, p. 1)*

The report then presents 15 stories of parenting in poverty. What follows are representative excerpts from these stories.

Tracey is a stay-at-home mother of two children whose husband has a full-time minimum wage job.

> *"We fit into the category of 'working poor.' We do not live from paycheque to paycheque—we live from payday to three days after payday, at best. Neither my friends nor my extended family fit into this category, nor do they realize that I do, thus I am constantly struggling to keep up the façade that I am financially okay. The truth is, I'm not. I'm poor. It is degrading and depressing.... I constantly worry about how I'm going to pay the bills, or what I'm going to do if one of our kids get sick and the prescription isn't covered, or what if there is a field trip at school and I don't have the extra money to send my child.... They say that money doesn't buy happiness. But it sure alleviates some of the stress that comes with being poor." (p. 3)*

Naomi is a First Nations woman. She is a single mother of four children, aged two to fifteen. They live in a rented townhouse in a middle-class neighbourhood. Her income consists of social assistance and the Saskatchewan Child Benefit.

"I've been in poverty from even before I was conceived—my mother and her mother before her.... It is the day before cheque day and I am exhausted thinking about how to get around with my kids, what bills to pay and what bills have to wait, how much food I can buy tomorrow and what we really need and what we can do without for now. One child needs shoes and the little one needs milk. There is always something one of them needs....

I get so angry at the way people look at people who are in poverty or on welfare, like they're all on drugs and drinking; they're bums, they should be put in a corner of the world and left there.... When I used to watch the Brady Bunch and stuff I used to think: Oh my God, I wish I had a home like that. Is that the way it's supposed to be? ... I know where I am in my life. I have fought to get out of that grave that was dug for me, even before I was born." (pp. 13–17)

Leeanne lives with her husband and their three children in a house they are buying through a local housing program. She works as a cook, and her husband, unable to work, receives workers' compensation benefits and stays at home with the children.

"I have money to help make sure all the bills are paid, and get things done in the yard and inside the house. And I can finally afford to give my kids an allowance every two weeks, which is nice—as long as they do their chores.... My husband and I rarely go out together. When we do, we swap baby-sitting with friends to save money. That's about the only way we can do it.... I think I've done pretty well with my life. We might not have a lot of money, or brand new furniture, but I've got three beautiful children, and they have a roof over their heads, food in the cupboard, clothes on their back, and parents that love them. It would be nice to have more, but if I don't, I don't." (pp. 18–21)

The report provides a series of recommendations, provided by the project's participants, for changes in the community. These recommendations are presented in Box 6.1.

Project 5—Living the Effects of Public Policy: The Gender and Racial Effects of Poverty

This project (Neysmith, Bezanson, and O'Connell, 2005) considered the effects of public policy on 40 families living in Ontario by eliciting their concerns and priorities through interviews. Each family was interviewed four times over the course of the three-year project. The authors analyzed the content of these interviews in terms of the changes that were taking place in Ontario as part of the Conservative government's Common Sense Revolution. The families interviewed represented a range of income levels. One chapter was specifically focused on the poverty experience of five of these families. Excerpts from these interviews follow.

Box 6.1: Desired Community Changes Outlined by Low-Income Mothers Working Together toward a Healthier Community

- An end to poverty, through better training programs and access to jobs, a higher minimum wage, and higher social assistance rates.
- An end to poor-bashing, recognizing that people's worth is not equal to their income, education, or the kind of clothes they wear, and that poverty is caused by many things beyond a person's control.
- More value placed on parenting, meaning better education and support for parents, more chances for respite, and adequate income for those who choose to stay home with their children.
- High-quality, affordable child care that meets parents' standards, including care by a relative.
- Safe and affordable housing.
- Access to basic shops and services, including affordable, healthy food (even for those without cars).
- Better programs for preventing and treating addictions of all kinds.
- Ongoing support for organizations and groups working to make their communities a healthier place.
- Better training and staffing in social service, health care, and other agencies, to ensure that all clients are treated with respect, fairness, and dignity, and given consistent, complete information.
- More control over what happens in our communities and the services and programs that are offered.
- Greater respect for each other, freedom from violence and discrimination.
- People taking responsibility for their community and working together to improve it. A sense of belonging and caring, people watching out for each other.
- A physical environment that is safe and attractive—including parks and playgrounds, streets, and buildings.

Source: From "We Did It Together," *Telling it Like it is: The Reality of Parenting in Poverty* (p.40), by K. Green and participants, 2001. Saskatoon: Prairie Women's Health Centre of Excellence.

Veronica, a sole-support mother of two children, ages three and six:

Lack of money is my number one concern. I never know from one month to the next if the hydro's going to be on, or the water, for that matter. And it's not even a matter of, you know, "Hey Mr. Harris, give me some more money on welfare." If there was more reliable day care, if there were more places in the work force that tolerated children, you know, that had day care. It's not as accessible as it once was. Any of these things would help. (pp. 75–76)

Anne, a sole-support mother with four boys ranging from infancy to eight years of age:

> I live literally cheque to cheque and once the money is gone, there's no more money. If they hadn't cut back our cheques, we'd be in better shape. I don't want handouts. If they allowed you to have maybe $150 more a month, we could get by....
>
> I used to be able to get certain medications covered on my health card and now I can't. I have to pay for these medications. And my kids have chronic asthma so that's a constant expense for me. The waiting lists are phenomenal for appointments [with medical specialists and social workers] because of the cutbacks. There used to be five intake workers. Now there's only one. So if your crisis isn't as bad as the next person's crisis, you're on a waiting list. They say, "I'm sorry, there's a waiting list due to social cutbacks." Everybody says it. (pp. 88–89)

Jenny, a sole-support mother with three young children:

> I feel isolated. I have the sense that there's a lot of things that I cannot do because of my financial situation. Like we can't go to church every Sunday. I would like to but I'm thinking that I don't have any clothes to wear there. My kids don't have any clothes. Are we going to show up in our grungy clothes to church?
>
> They have popcorn orders for 25 cents a day and they have to bring it the week before. 25 cents isn't a whole lot of money but when you have zero, zero, zero, that's money one day a month and it's just another thing. There's pizza day, hot dog day, popcorn day, book day, and they miss out on all of them. I don't have the money. They say "You're mean" and I say, "Hon that's not the way it is. If I had the money I'd buy you a big movie popcorn vending machine to have it in the house all the time." (pp. 82–84)

The authors' analysis places these stories in a context in which welfare changes are putting women, especially mothers, into situations in which they are forced to take on the worst jobs available, and they are introducing a constant state of emergency crisis management (Neysmith et al., 2005). These women are also faced with complete lack of child care and other means of supporting their children's development. Welfare regulations serve to "police motherhood" and to "punish sole-support mothers while continuing to demand they bear all responsibility for raising children, running households, and participating in the labour market" (p. 92).

Project 6—Poverty and Mental Illness in Ontario

This project (Wilton, 2003, 2004) was concerned with the effects of poverty on people with serious mental illness in the city of Hamilton, Ontario. The author examined the lived experiences of 22 people who had been diagnosed as having a serious mental illness. Fourteen of the 22 were male, and all participants lived in residential-care rental accommodations. Their experiences were considered in light of policy changes that had taken place in Ontario in the health care and social assistance domains.

Two questions guided the study: To what extent have recent developments in the policy and provision of mental health care and social assistance recognized and addressed the poverty experienced by people with serious mental illness? In what ways does poverty impact on the multiple life domains of social relations, family, leisure, and self-esteem? The first question can be easily answered. Welfare restructuring had led to a significant real decline in the value of income supports available to these individuals over the past decade.

Numerous themes emerged from these interviews. These concerned the meeting of basic needs, problems with family and friendships, access to leisure activities, and stigma. As well, exclusion as a result of their perceived poor appearance (a perception projected onto others) was especially important to these men and women. These themes—together with illustrative quotations from study participants—are presented below.

Meeting Basic Needs
The primary issue that emerged from interviews with participants was meeting basic needs. Some illustrative statements follow:

- I guess you just have to accept it and go on. You budget out your money at the beginning of the month and figure out how much you can spend every day, and when I see something that I'd like, well, you know that you just can't have it. I buy cheaper things with the clothing. I limit myself to a couple of coffees per week. I don't go to [the cinema] or anything like that and I watch a lot of television. (Wilton, 2004, p. 32)
- You've got to stretch that $112 out for the whole month and that's not easy to do because you've got four weeks, so you figure $25 a week and that's not a lot. [Int: How long does it last?] About two weeks, about that.... (Wilton, 2003, p. 145)
- Sometimes I go for a walk downtown, just to get some fresh air, and I might have the money, but I don't allow myself to even buy a coffee because it adds up over 30 days ... if you have one coffee a day. (Wilton, 2003, p. 147)
- My eight dollars goes with me taking a bus and going to [the coffee shop] for a coffee. I do that, and anxiety I can deal with by going to [the coffee shop], getting a coffee. (Wilton, 2003, p. 147)

Difficulties Maintaining Family Relations
Participants reported that their living conditions made maintaining family relationships very difficult.

- I can't even buy my grandchildren things for Christmas or anything like that. You just send them a lousy card. You feel torn apart. (Wilton, 2004, p. 33)
- I like to go for coffees with my friends, but I don't have the money for it. You know, I can't even go visit my sisters because I can't go out with them. I can't ask them to pay for my coffees or whatever because I don't want to feel like a bum all the time. (Wilton, 2004, p. 33)

- What it does is it takes away your... Like I've got daughters and it takes away your accessibility to see them. You try to make excuses because you don't have the money. You really don't. If you go out and spend fifteen, twenty bucks, you're in big trouble. (Wilton, 2003, p. 149)

Problems with Friendships
Living conditions also made developing and maintaining friendships difficult.

- I haven't gone to a movie in so long. I can't remember when. My girlfriend works, but she doesn't make a heck of a lot of money so I don't want to lean on her. I don't want to keep bringing up the problem of money. (Wilton, 2004, p. 34)
- It really cuts in to your social life. Like if I meet a girl or something, I couldn't afford to take her to dinner, or even if we went Dutch treat I'd have a hard time budgeting. The best I could do is take her out for a coffee, but if things progressed along. (Wilton, 2004, p. 34)
- If I had a bit more money, I'd be freer to get involved in relationships, be able to go out for an evening, maybe go down to a hamburger stand, and you don't have to back away and slide off into the corner. (Wilton, 2003, p. 150)

Lack of Leisure Opportunities
Not surprisingly, it is difficult to manage leisure opportunities.

- What I'd like to do is to go out to supper, not expensive places, but just to go out for a hamburger or something like that, just once a month or once every two months even.... I don't go now because I can't afford it. (Wilton, 2004, p. 34)
- Once you buy your clothes and your personal stuff, it really doesn't leave you that much money because if you want to go to a movie or something, you know, treat yourself to something, sometimes you can't. [Int: How do you feel about that?] Sometimes it makes you, you know, angry. (Wilton, 2004, p. 34)
- I like to go to [name] restaurant for a coffee or something. I was barred there for using too many of the creamers. They like you to buy a meal, but you can't do what other people do. You want to, even at a lower level. (Wilton, 2004, p. 34)

Lack of Self-Esteem and Experience of Stigma
Similar to findings from other studies of people living in poverty, participants reported a variety of negative interpersonal experiences.

- NO, you got nothing to go out with. Look, if you want to buy a jacket or something like that, a decent jacket could be fifty or a hundred, and it's wintertime. In the summer you might be able to just go in a shirt but ... that's basically it, but I mean you've got to get clothes that match the pants right, and the Salvation Army is kind of a joke. It's old man's clothes. YOU LOOK STUPID!

- You don't fit in. You've got to go [out] dressed like this, and that's what you got. You're conscious of what you look like. You automatically look like a bum. If I didn't have the [wheelchair] I'd automatically just blend in as a bum.
- It makes me feel kind of down because you can't go places. (Wilton, 2004, p. 35)
- It's more than someone on the street is getting, but it's not enough to live on. It gives me a headache sometimes. It can stress you out sometimes, just money. (Wilton, 2004, p. 35)
- You have to depend on other people, and who wants to depend on other people all the time. Sure, it's nice but it's like begging. It's the same thing. (Wilton, 2004, p. 35)
- It comes back to feeling better about yourself ... go to a store and buy a new pair of jeans rather than a second- or third-hand pair that's sitting in Amity. You don't know who it was that wore them last, and maybe they're not exactly your size, a shade too tight or a shade too short. You just feel like you're living on handouts all the time. (Wilton, 2003, p. 150)
- Usually if I see something I'd like I say: 'no, I can't have that it's too expensive.' You have to have a sense of value about things. On the one hand it makes me feel pretty good because I have money in my pocket, but in another sense I feel like a second-class citizen because I'm not having what other people are having. (Wilton, 2003, p. 150)

Perception of Poor Appearance Projected onto Others
There is specific concern about appearance and the reactions of others. (Wilton, 2003, p. 151)

- It's degrading and you start feeling really bad about yourself.
- Bad, it makes you feel bad.
- Not very equal, I mean, I want a decent pair of shoes ... I just want to scream.
- It kinda makes me feel like a bum on the street ... a very low class part of society. Sometimes I feel like people are saying: 'that guy's a bum' because of the way I dress.
- You're in a house like this where it's hot all the time. You're sweating all the time. Don't take long for body odour to build up. You may not be dirty but you're sweating and you still smell. Deodorant costs money. All these things cost money.

Spatial Location as an Aspect of Exclusion
The study also looked at spatial aspects of poverty.

- It's not important, but it would be nice to go see a movie once in a while just to get out and away from the house. You feel very caged in. It gets very closed in. (Wilton, 2003, p. 147)
- You stay out of the malls where they sell good clothes because you're just tormenting yourself. Why waste your time walking through the mall if you can't go in any of the shops. (Wilton, 2003, p. 148)

- You know, you look at something and you kinda feel 'I might as well get out of the store because I can't buy' so I mostly just walk through the mall and be on my way. (Wilton, 2003, p. 148)

The author concludes:

All experienced chronic poverty and most were unable to meet basic monthly needs. Poverty was also shown to have a deleterious impact on other areas of tenants' lives. Lack of income worked against contact with family members and constrained individuals in their efforts to build social and intimate relations. In addition, poverty contributed to a diminution of self-esteem and an exacerbation of social stigma among participants. (Wilton, 2004, p. 36)

Project 7—Persistent Poverty: Voices from the Margins

The Interfaith Social Assistance Reform Coalition comprises the major faith groups that are concerned with having governments create public policies that will reduce the burdens faced by Ontarians living in poverty. For years now it has been carrying out social audits of people in Ontario living in poverty. Its recent report was based on the work of several hundred volunteers who heard from thousands of people regarding poverty and its effects upon their lives and communities (Swift, Balmer, and Dineen, 2010).

In this report, focus was on issues of insecure and low-paying employment, accessing social assistance and disability payments, housing and housing insecurity, food insecurity and hunger, poverty and health, poverty's effects on families, and rural poverty. People's experiences were interspersed with commentaries by authorities on these issues. Five of these themes are examined here.

Insecure and Low-Paying Employment

One section of the report focuses on the role that insecure and low-paying employment plays in pushing people into poverty. Carl, in his late fifties, used to be a manager in an auto-parts company but lost his job during the 2008 economic downturn. He comments:

- I always had a good job, lived in nice places. I am frugal, but after paying rent, clothes, haircuts… I never dreamed of using a food bank. (p. 23)
- I need an economy where jobs actually exist for my qualifications. I need a social culture that values the skills of a man with my experience and will hire someone my age. (p. 23)

Other comments from interviewees included the following:

- My husband is working hard, and I enjoy being a stay-at-home mom. His job pays so little, minimum wage. Everything is going up. Hard work is not paying off. Up and down every month (p. 24).

Box 6.2: Melody's Story: They Don't Give It to You Because They Think You Deserve It

Melody says…

When you're on social assistance, it's demeaning. They don't give you the money because they think you deserve it, they give it to you because you're destitute, you've gotten nothing else so they have to give it to you. You're not awarded the money because you're going to do good things with this. You're given the money because if we don't you're going to die and it looks bad on our country's wealth to have all these people dying of hunger—although even with social assistance kids are still hungry.

They have you fill out all these demeaning forms and ask you every detail of your life. And then look at you and go ok, you're poor enough to be here. Good. Now that you're poor enough to be there, you need to work even harder for your money. Being on social assistance I don't have enough money to make sure my kids have everything they need. I have to split up the months and where I buy things. My kids do have clothes and food and stuff but if I didn't have other people who'd give me clothes, other people who would help support me, I don't think I could make it. All the furniture in my house was given to me. Maybe there's some plastic chairs that I bought for $2 at a second-hand shop but that's about the closest I've got to purchasing my own furniture. Everything that I have has been given to me because I just cannot pay for it myself. I'm not complaining. I'm really grateful that I have people that I can say this is what I need or they notice I have a need and they give it to me. But I find it a little bit embarrassing at times because I'm not able to say I own this or this is mine.

It's hard to get fruit and vegetables for my kids because they're a little bit pricier. I always have to make sure to buy in season because that's the cheapest but that's not always cheap enough. Sometimes it would be cheaper to buy the packaged peanut butter and crackers instead of buying real peanut butter or a bunch of bananas. It's really frustrating because children need to eat healthy foods to be part of society, just for their natural development and for their brains to grow, for them to be alert in school and to do the things that they need to do. And they can't. The food that I'm able to buy has lost its nutritional value. Foods that have nutritional values are usually 20 cents more expensive. Especially in the inner-city. I'm lucky to live in a suburb but if I lived in the inner-city it would be even more harder because everything is more expensive. Especially fruit and vegetables.

Another part that I find very frustrating is my kids feel that they cannot participate whether in the economy or whatever because they know we don't have the money for it… My kids are in soccer and they know they're sponsored and they're playing with some kids that are not sponsored. They'll overhear the parents ask me, "How are you paying for your kids to go play soccer?" Because they know I'm a single-mom and I've talked about being in university. I'll tell them, "My children are sponsored." When I say that, there's a change, there's a look. My kids pick up on that, and they ask me, "How come they stop talking to you?" I tell them well … they're sitting on the other side of the field.

But I know those other parents are thinking, "My tax dollars are paying for that." I feel like saying yeah but my kids are playing soccer and one day their tax dollars may pay for your kids or your grandkids. It comes back, it comes around. I also feel like saying, you know when money's spent like that it's not going into a big void where you're never going to see those dollars again. This is your tax dollars at work. You should be pleased that my kid is now equal to your child! But that would be a whole other topic.

It's always that feeling of because it's given to you it's not worthy. That bothers me and that's something I'm really working on changing. I think it is very important to explain to people but it's also very frustrating to have to.

Source: Women & the Economy, a Project of UN Platform for Action Committee. (2005). *They don't give it to you because they think you deserve it.* Manitoba: UNPAC. Retrieved March 11, 2011 from www.unpac.ca/economy/melody_sa.html

- Minimum-wage jobs are a problem in the system as you make too much to get a subsidy (for child care), but not enough to live half-decent (p. 24).
- It's hard to find a job when you're fifty-seven and there are lots of young people who are applying for the same thing. There are also people who are willing to work for less than minimum wage, and that undercuts others who really need that wage (p. 24).

Accessing Social Assistance and Disability Payments

Interviewees commented on how difficult it is to gain access to necessary resources through Ontario Works (OW) or the Ontario Disability Support Program (ODSP).

- The OW application process was the most degrading thing I have ever experienced. Even talking with the caseworker over the phone creates fear and panic. They speak to me in such an accusatory attitude, with allegations of fraudulent behaviour. (p. 43)
- It takes whatever dignity that you have and it dissolves it. (p. 43)

Food Insecurity and Hunger

It has been well noted that the assistance available on OW or ODSP or even minimum-wage employment is not adequate to provide an acceptable diet. This is especially important when people are ill.

- First priority is children, adults come second. If I have to eat bread and butter so my kids can eat better, that is what I have to do. (p. 76)
- We don't even get enough to have a healthy diet, which contributes to heart disease, health costs, obesity. But that's okay because we are stupid poor people. I'm being facetious. (p. 76)
- If my husband and I want our kids to eat healthy, I have to give up my heart medication, stomach medication, and migraine medication, and I do it because our kids come first. (p. 80)

Poverty and Health

Not surprisingly, participants drew the strong links between their precarious lives and their poor health.

- We go without so our children do not have to. My little girl has tummy aches, probably stress-related. My little boy is such a good little boy. Sunday afternoon, he was raking leaves. He knows if he plants a seed, something will grow and we will have something good to eat, some good vegetables. (p. 109)
- I'm in constant stress—fear of where my next rent money and food money are going to come from. (p. 94)
- I wear a hat constantly because I'm getting bald spots because of stress.

Poverty's Effects on Families

An analysis was made of how the stresses associated with living in poverty affects their families.

- My husband blows up because of his frustration. (p. 109)
- I try to teach my children control when it comes to food and to save some for tomorrow. We are getting used to accepting that this is the way life is. I try not to let my children cry. I wait until they go to bed and then I cry by myself in the bedroom. (p. 110)
- Last year when we got our Christmas hamper, my son was volunteering to help give out hampers to other people. On the way home he says, 'Mommy, I'm so glad we're not poor.' And I thought, 'I'm doing a good job at fooling you.'" (p. 110)

In a commentary about this project and its findings, Terence Finlay, retired Anglican Archbishop of Toronto, concludes:

> How long, O Lord? How long before our politicians listen? Four poverty audits have taken place since 1986. But we still desperately lack affordable housing. More families still use food banks. Sole-support mothers still must plead for relief from mandatory school fees. People with mental illness still wander our streets. This is scandalous in a rich place like Ontario. I encourage people to read Persistent Poverty and take action. Show that we still care for one another. (Swift, Balmer, and Dineen, 2010, back cover)

Project 8—Poverty and Living with Type 2 Diabetes

In this project 60 people with type 2 diabetes who were living in poverty were interviewed about their day-to-day lives and how they were managing their disease (Pilkington et al., 2010). The researchers were motivated to carry out this study in light of findings that death rates from diabetes have been increasing at an alarming rate in low-income neighbourhoods across Canada (Wilkins, 2007).

Participants were recruited from three community health centres and a community-based agency that provides health programs to homeless and under-housed individuals in Toronto, the largest city in Canada. Purposive sampling was conducted with the assistance of staff members to identify participants who represented the diversity of their clientele with respect to gender, race/ethnicity, and medical status.

Inclusion criteria were: (a) a diagnosis of type 2 diabetes, and (b) low-income status as defined by living below the Statistics Canada Low Income Cut-offs. Fifteen participants were recruited from each of the four centres, for a total of 60. The researchers identified an overarching theme of resilient struggle for survival amid hardship, and three sub-themes: balancing competing priorities, making the best of it, and using knowledge and bodily knowing in diabetes self-management.

Resilient Struggle for Survival amid Hardship

The researchers report that participants "described a daily struggle to survive in the face of multiple challenges presented by having to manage not only their diabetes, but also the various hardships that arise when living on a low income" (Pilkington et al., p. 122). Participants had difficulty obtaining basic necessities and were forced to work in low-quality, insecure jobs. Many were living in substandard housing and some were even homeless. In addition, many had pre-existing medical conditions, and since many were recent immigrants whose first language was not English, they also experienced cultural adjustment and language issues. One 56-year-old married woman commented:

> *Life has changed a lot because, for example, my mood is not the same. Sometimes I feel so worried because, if something happens to me, what's going to happen to my kids? As well, I've been facing high blood pressure and I never had problem like this.... I work at night, office cleaning. I arrive home around 11:30 PM, I fall to sleep between 3:00 and 4:00 AM, wake up at 10:30 AM. Then I make breakfast. I start cleaning and cooking. Then I have lunch and I set up little things at the house and then I have to leave for work; and that's every single day.... Now my sugar levels are always higher [rather] than lower ... and it makes me feel worried, because I don't want to have problems with my vision or anything like that ... I don't [test my blood] every day; 3 days a week, because the strips are very expensive.... Sometimes I don't take the medicine every day, because the medicine is expensive and my husband is not working, and because it is not the only medicine that I have to take, so I try to make it last. Sometimes, it seems to be easy to manage, but it's not when you have too many problems. (p. 122)*

Balancing Competing Priorities

Participants described a "constant juggling act required to survive" with low incomes but multiple priorities, such as buying the right foods, medication for their diabetes, or meeting the rent. One 42-year-old married woman stated:

> *I look which [food] is cheaper because my money is very small, so after giving rent, I just have little bit money.... Sometimes after the 20th [of the month] my money finished. It's very tight. And I just—a high amount I give for rent, because if I give it later, the money will be finished. So then I buy rice, because it's the main food, and some protein and eggs.... But when I eat [cheap rice] my sugar is going up.... Sometimes I borrow money because I have to be conscious about my health.... Sometimes my daughter's school, they want money for [things]. Then I don't have money. How can I give? And I feel very sad ... I try to manage. I use my daughter's child benefit. And sometimes I don't buy. Yeah, last month my money was finished, but I don't have any food at my home and I didn't buy. I didn't eat. And sometimes I need shoes, but I don't buy the shoes because I have to pay for food which is my basic need. (p. 122)*

Making the Best of It

This theme was about how participants "drew on support and resources from various sources—including friends and family, health services, and community and social services—in order to make the best of their difficult circumstances" (p. 122).

> *I see the nurse once and we talk about anything and everything ... they are good doctors and nurses. They are very attentive to us. Everybody here is very kind and understanding. (p. 123)*

Using Knowledge and Bodily Knowing in Diabetes

This theme was concerned with how "participants adapted medical and experiential knowledge about diabetes to their individual social circumstances in order to manage their diabetes as well as they could given their situation" (p. 123). A 38-year-old single male stated:

> *I went to see the diabetic nurse and a dietician and I have [an] endocrinologist. The main thing they tell me: "Cut the carbohydrates. Don't eat rice or potatoes." But it's hard to do without rice, because we [ethnic group] generally eat rice every day.... Sometimes I feel I don't want to eat, but with the [oral antihyperglycemic] tablets, I have to eat ... I have to take my blood sugar level every time in the morning and at bedtime, and I should not skip meals, and I have to be careful about what I am eating, and I can't eat the foods like before.... Sometimes I skip meals, but it makes me dizzy. I don't like that. Breakfast I don't feel like eating sometimes. I don't know why. Maybe the medication I am taking.... But my endocrinologist, she asked [me] to take insulin at night because my morning blood sugar level is high. But I said, "No. I do exercise. I take care of my meals. So please don't start that now. We can start next time; maybe you take my blood test and after we can decide." (p. 124)*

The findings of this study suggest that, while living in poverty is problematic, it becomes even more so when one is experiencing a serious life-threatening chronic disease such as type 2 diabetes. The situation of Canadians with type 2 diabetes being forced to live on economic resources that are so far below the poverty line as to preclude the acquisition of a diet or medication necessary to prevent the most severe health outcomes of this disease seems almost unbelievable. The situation described here is a reflection of public policies that do little to support people living in poverty even when they are experiencing a life-threatening disease. Since this study only looked at one disease, it is likely that the situation is similar for those low-income people experiencing other life-threatening diseases, such as cardiovascular disease, HIV/AIDS, and others.

Analysis: The Experience of Poverty

There is remarkable similarity of experience among people living in poverty. This is the case whether information is elicited from those residing in Atlantic Canada, Ontario, the Prairies, or British Columbia. The focus here is on five areas: the experience of material and social deprivation, the experience of stress, the experience of stigma and degradation, and poverty's impact upon health, and quality of life.

Experience of Material and Social Deprivation

The experience of poverty is the experience of deprivation. The stories of Canadians living in poverty show remarkable congruence with the theoretical concepts outlined by Townsend (1993) and Gordon (2006) in their discussions about the meaning and measurement of poverty (see Chapter 2). The results of these studies show clear evidence that people living in poverty are unable to participate in the activities expected of people living in a wealthy developed country.

The experience of deprivation has elements of both absolute and relative deprivation. For many people living in poverty, meeting basic individual and familial needs of housing, food, and clothing is an ongoing concern. Additionally, living in poverty makes participation in a range of everyday activities extremely problematic. This inability to meet basic needs and participate in everyday activities is a source of constant stress and worry.

The Experience of Stress

Constant worry and self-consciousness about day-to-day activities are common experiences of those living in poverty. Stress is a result of being unable to meet material and social needs. Stress is also a response to the experience of stigma, and the judgmental and devaluing attitudes of others. For mothers, the burden of stress is especially high. They must deal not only with the stress generated by their own experiences of deprivation but must also concern themselves with the effects that living in poverty have on their children.

The Experience of Stigma and Degradation

In addition to the burdens of living with material and social deprivation—and the stresses associated with these—people living in poverty must deal with the reality that others frequently blame them for their own situation. The belief that poverty is a result of moral failure on the part of those experiencing it can become internalized as feelings of guilt, shame, and failure. The experience of stigma adds to the profound issues that people in poverty must live with. The fact that many children experience stigma and must deal with its effects is especially disturbing. The issue of blaming victims for their own problems associated with "poor-bashing" is further examined in Chapter 11.

Poverty's Impact upon Health and Quality of Life

People living in poverty are also able to identify the personal and societal factors that both lead to poverty and shape their poverty-related experiences. Many of the participants clearly associate their experiences of living in poverty with poor health and quality of life. Both physical and emotional health are seen as being compromised by the material and social deprivation, exclusion, and stress and worries typical of those living in poverty. As will be demonstrated in later chapters, these experiences are consistent with research findings that link the experience of poverty with greater incidence of poor health and a wide range of other indicators of quality of life.

Conclusions

The findings presented here are straightforward. People living in poverty experience material and social deprivation, stress, stigma, and degradation by others. These experiences are clearly seen as threats to health and quality of life. What is astounding is that people living in poverty are able to cope with these burdens. Lister (2004) argues that people living in poverty act upon their situations, and these actions can be seen as falling into two dimensions: the personal versus the political dimension and the everyday versus the strategic dimension (see Figure 6.1).

For many people living in poverty, the stresses and hardships associated with poverty simply allow one to "get by." Many of the stories provided show how all-consuming getting by while living in poverty can be. Others may be able to plan ahead to "get out." Clearly, many people living in poverty strive to do that under exceedingly difficult circumstances. We should do whatever we can in the form of programs and supports to assist people in doing so, but the barriers that so many people living in poverty face in escaping it makes this an unlikely solution to the poverty problem. The solutions are to be found in changing the societal structures that create and maintain poverty.

People living in poverty can also move beyond the personal to enter the political/citizenship arena. Much of the work presented here originated in the efforts of people living in poverty to come together to raise and address issues of living in poverty. This involves

Box 6.3: Trying to Get off Welfare Is as Hard as Trying to Get on

The author of this story lives in the West Central area of Winnipeg. She says:

I am a single mother of six receiving $400 every two weeks, and allowed $387 for rent, $400 at the most, not including utilities.

Two and a half months ago, I applied at a training facility for computers and was denied because I was pregnant. I was told to come back after I had my baby. I went back to this training facility after I had the baby and got accepted but was told I needed my welfare worker's approval. Denied. I couldn't take the program.

I was denied by my worker because I have children under the age of 6 and was told I needed to stay home with them. I had child care arrangements worked out for the training program, and also for a job, if it happened.

I wanted to take a computer program so I could find a job to support my family better.

I was told welfare gives money for special needs or extra special needs and money for a bus pass. Not true. I can't get help for furniture or a washer and dryer or clothing. I can't get a bus pass unless I'm in school, working or for medical purposes only. I was told by my worker that my Family Allowance is to be used for these needs.

So, recently I went and bought a dryer and winter gear for four of my children, and you know how expensive that is. Well, I informed my worker what I used the Child Tax Benefit for and he got on my case. He told me that there are places I could've gone for free winter stuff. But you know how kids are—they want new clothing. They don't want to look poor or feel ashamed and embarrassed by wearing used clothing.

The bus passes I could really use, because it's hard travelling from place to place, especially with little ones. I go shopping to find the best deals and it's hard when you're restricted to certain shops that are within walking distance.

My daughters were also denied bus passes for school. The reason is that they don't live in the right area or should be going to school somewhere else. So my daughters have to walk over 10 blocks to get to school.

By the time I'm able to go out and get training and work I'll be in my 40s. The older I get, the harder it's going to be to get into the workforce.

I get put down because I'm on welfare and made to feel trapped and worthless because I can't get off welfare. It's a heartache and tears don't help. Help!

What can I do when I'm trapped between a rock and a hard place?

Source: Women & the Economy, a Project of UN Platform for Action Committee. (2005). *Trying to get off welfare is as hard as trying to get on.* Manitoba: UNPAC. Retrieved March 11, 2011 from http://www.unpac.ca/economy/anon.html

Figure 6.1: Forms of Agency Exercised by People Living in Poverty

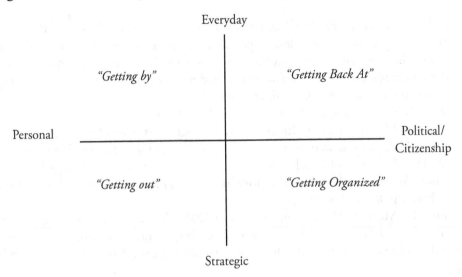

Source: Lister, R. (2004). *Poverty* (p. 130). Cambridge, UK: Polity Press.

"getting organized." In many cases, this may not be possible, and forms of resistance may develop. It may be that, for some, the means of coping is one of "getting back at." This may involve the circumventing of rules to ensure one's survival as well as that of close others. The issue of how people living in poverty can address the causes of poverty and identify how to reduce, if not eliminate, poverty is a recurring theme in the chapters that follow.

Critical Thinking Questions

1. What are some of the reasons that lived experience may not be considered valid "scientific" data by researchers and policy-makers?
2. Why is it that the experiences of people living in poverty are not better known or publicized?
3. How do you account for the remarkable similarity of themes that characterize the lived experience of people in poverty?
4. What could be done by the research and other communities to publicize the plight of people living in poverty?
5. Why do you think that the situation of people living in poverty seems to get so little attention from health researchers?

Recommended Readings

Baxter, S. (2002). *No way to live: Poor women speak out*. Vancouver: New Star Books.
This book presents a collection of personal stories as told to the author. The 50 women interviewed are very diverse but relate very similar experiences. The book also contains stories from a social worker and a welfare advocate, texts of speeches from activists, and useful facts, figures, and charts.

Green, K. (2001). *Telling it like it is: The realities of parenting in poverty*. Saskatoon: Department of Community Health and Epidemiology, University of Saskatchewan.
This publication was an outcome of a research project funded by the Prairie Women's Health Centre of Excellence. An associated report, *We Did it Together: Low Income Mothers Working toward a Healthier Community*, is available online at www.pwhce.ca/pdf/didItTogether.pdf

Laughlin, L., McPhee, D., and Pompeo, M. (2004). *Women's perspectives on poverty: Photos and stories by women on low-income in Calgary*. Calgary: Institute for Gender Research, University of Calgary. Online at www.ucalgary.ca/gender/WAFI%20Report2.pdf
The goal of this project was to produce materials to advocate for women-centred policy alternatives to achieve fair income levels for all people in Calgary and Alberta. Photovoice combines a participatory approach to photography with social action. Women who participated in planning and implementing the project were university- and community-based researchers, many of whom were living on low incomes.

Neysmith, S., Bezanson, K., and O'Connell, A, (2005). *Telling tales: Living the effects of public policy*. Halifax: Fernwood.
This report places the lived experiences of 40 families in Ontario in the context of policy changes undertaken during the Common Sense Revolution of the Mike Harris Conservative government. One chapter focuses specifically on the experiences of families living in poverty, but all chapters address issues of income insecurity, health and well-being, and quality of life.

Ocean, C. (2005). *Policies of exclusion, poverty, and health: Stories from the front*. Duncan, BC: WISE Society.
Arising from a project initiated and directed by a woman living in poverty, this volume contains numerous stories from women living in poverty, analyses of the causes and outcomes of living in poverty, and recommendations from the women themselves for action.

Reid, C. (2004). *The wounds of exclusion: Poverty, women's health, and social justice*. Edmonton: Qualitative Institute Press.
Based on the doctoral dissertation of Colleen Reid, this volume won an award for an outstanding qualitative study. The work covers a wide range of topics, with emphasis on health and social justice. It puts all of this work within a framework of participatory feminist research to enact change.

Swift, J., Balmer, B., and Dineen, M. (2010). *Persistent poverty: Voices from the margins*. Toronto: Between the Lines Press.

The publisher states: "The Interfaith Social Assistance Reform Coalition's latest social audit exposed a tattered social assistance system run by volunteers desperately struggling to fill the gaps. There can be no papering over the savage inequalities and suffering exposed in this compelling look at life from the margins."

Relevant Websites

Canada Without Poverty (CWP)—www.cwp-csp.ca
CWP is the national voice for and of people living in poverty. The website contains numerous reports, press releases, and analyses of poverty and its impact, with emphasis on the voice of people living in poverty.
Centre for Critical Qualitative Health Research—www.ccqhr.utoronto.ca/
The Centre for Critical Qualitative Health Research (CQ) is a teaching and research hub at the University of Toronto. CQ is a resource for qualitative researchers in the broader health research community at the University of Toronto, its affiliated research institutes, and in other research settings in Canada and internationally.
International Institute for Qualitative Methodology (IIQM)—www.uofaweb.ualberta.ca/iiqm/
IIQM is an interdisciplinary institute, under the auspices of the Faculty of Nursing at the University of Alberta. Its primary goal is facilitating the development of qualitative research methods across a wide variety of academic disciplines.
Prairie Women's Health Centre of Excellence—www.pwhce.ca
The Prairie Women's Health Centre of Excellence is one of the Centres of Excellence for Women's Health supported by the Women's Health Contribution Program, through the Bureau of Women's Health and Gender Analysis of Health Canada. The centres are dedicated to improving the health status of Canadian women by supporting policy-oriented and community-based research on, and analysis of, the social and other determinants of women's health.
Women and the Economy, UN Platform for Action Committee—http://unpac.ca/economy
UNPAC grew out of the 1995 United Nations Fourth World Conference on Women in Beijing and is devoted to demystifying the economy and women's place in it. The site offers links to major projects on women's economic inequality, women and globalization, women's economic contributions, and personal stories of women.

Glossary of Terms

Ethnographies are detailed explorations of people's lived experiences. Originally developed in the field of anthropology, ethnographies are now widely used in sociology and increasingly so in health studies. The methods applied can include long, open-ended interviews and detailed observations that are part of the method known as participant observation.

Lived experience is a form of knowledge that results from seeing the world through the eyes of those being studied. This is important, since individuals' constructions and understandings of events are crucial to understanding their impacts upon people and how these understandings shape their responses. Lived experience is different from both traditional positivist science and critical analysis in that people's understandings of their lived experiences are seen as valid regardless of whether these understandings are "accurate" using other benchmarks of indicators.

Naturalistic inquiry is a term popularized by Lincoln and Guba (1985) to refer to an approach that emphasizes people's understanding of the world. This form of inquiry is seen as profoundly superior to traditional approaches to knowledge generation that are based on natural science approaches. This is especially the case when people's behaviour is the focus of inquiry.

Stigma refers to the experiencing of shame and exclusion as a result of certain characteristics. Link and Phelan (2001) argue that it occurs through a four-step process. First, people distinguish and label human differences. Second, dominant attitudes link these labelled persons to undesirable characteristics or negative stereotypes. Third, labelled persons are distinguished as "other," to create separation of "us" from "them." Fourth, labelled persons come to experience loss of status and discrimination that create unequal outcomes. Differences in social, economic, and political power allow some to identify others as different, create these stereotypes, and allow for disapproval, rejection, exclusion, and discrimination.

Thematic analysis is the taking of raw data such as interview transcripts, notes from detailed observations, or written documents and identifying the themes that run through these data. For these themes to be seen as meaningful, they should recur in the different sets of data that are obtained from different people, places, or documents. The trustworthiness and transferability of the themes that are obtained can be assessed using methods that are similar to the traditional methods of assessing reliability and validity of data.

References

Bryant, T., Raphael, D., and Rioux, M. (2010). Researching health: Knowledge paradigms, methodologies, and methods. In T. Bryant, D. Raphael, and M. Rioux (Eds.), *Staying alive: Critical perspectives on health, illness, and health care* (2nd ed., pp. 121–140). Toronto: Canadian Scholars' Press Inc.

Bryant, T., Raphael, D., and Travers, R. (2007). Identifying and strengthening the structural roots of urban health: Participatory policy research and the urban health agenda. *Promotion and Education, 14*(1), 6–11.

Gordon, D. (2006). The concept and measurement of poverty. In C. Pantazis, D. Gordon, and R. Levitas (Eds.), *Poverty and social exclusion in Britain: The millennium survey* (pp. 29–70). Bristol, UK: The Policy Press.

Green, K. (2001). *Telling it like it is: The realities of parenting in poverty.* Saskatoon: Department of Community Health and Epidemiology, University of Saskatchewan.

Guba, E. (Ed.). (1990). *The paradigm dialog*. Newbury Park, CA: Sage.

Lincoln, Y. (1994). Sympathetic connections between qualitative research methods and health research. *Qualitative Health Research, 2*, 375–391.

Lincoln, Y., and Guba, E. (1985). *Naturalist inquiry*. Newbury Park, CA: Sage.

Link, B., and Phelan, J. (2001). Conceptualizing stigma. *Annual Review of Sociology, 27*(1), 363–385.

Lister, R. (2004). *Poverty*. Cambridge, UK: The Polity Press.

McIntyre, L., Officer, S., and Robinson, L. M. (2003). Feeling poor: The felt experience of low-income lone mothers. *Affilia, 18*(3), 316–331.

Neysmith, S., Bezanson, K., and O'Connell, A. (2005). *Telling tales: Living the effects of public policy*. Halifax: Fernwood Publishing.

Ocean, C. (2005). *Policies of exclusion, poverty, and health*. Duncan, BC: WISE Society.

Park, P. (1993). What is participatory research? A theoretical and methodological perspective. In P. Park, M. Brydon-Miller, B. Hall, and T. Jackson (Eds.), *Voices of change: Participatory research in the United States and Canada* (pp. 1–9). Toronto: OISE Press.

Pilkington, F. B., Daiski, I., Bryant, T., Dinca-Panaitescu, M., Dinca-Panaitescu, S., and Raphael. D. (2010). The experience of living with diabetes for low income Canadians. *Canadian Journal of Diabetes, 34*(2), 119–126.

Raphael, D., and Bryant, T. (2002). The limitations of population health as a model for a new public health. *Health Promotion International, 17*(2), 189–199.

Raphael, D., Macdonald, J., Labonte, R., Colman, R., Hayward, K., and Torgerson, R. (2004). Researching income and income distribution as a determinant of health in Canada: Gaps between theoretical knowledge, research practice, and policy implementation. *Health Policy, 72*, 217–232.

Robinson, L. M., McIntyre, L., and Officer, S. (2005). Welfare babies: Poor children's experiences informing healthy peer relationships in Canada. *Health Promotion International, 20*(4), 342–350.

Stewart, M., Reutter, L., Veenstra, G., Love, R., and Raphael, D. (2003). *Left out: Perspectives on social exclusion and social isolation in low-income populations: Final report*. Edmonton: University of Alberta.

Stewart, M., Reutter, L., Veenstra, G., Love, R., and Raphael, D. (2004). *Left out: Perspectives on social exclusion and social isolation in low-income populations: Public report*. Edmonton: University of Alberta.

Swift, J., Balmer, B., and Dineen, M. (2010). *Persistent poverty: Voices from the margins*. Toronto: Between the Lines Press.

Townsend, P. (1993). *The international analysis of poverty*. Milton Keynes: Harvester Wheatsheaf.

Wilkins, R. (2007). Mortality by neighbourhood income in urban Canada from 1971–2001. HAMG Seminar, and special compilations. Paper presented at the Statistics Canada, Health Analysis and Measurement Group, Ottawa.

Wilson, J. (1983a). Positivism. In J. Wilson (Ed.), *Social theory* (pp. 11–18). Englewood Cliffs, NJ: Prentice Hall.

Wilson, J. (1983b). Idealism. In J. Wilson (Ed.), *Social theory* (pp. 106–121). Englewood Cliffs, NJ: Prentice Hall.

Wilton, R. D. (2003). Poverty and mental health: A qualitative study of residential facility tenants. *Community Mental Health Journal, 39* (2), 139–156.

Wilton, R. D. (2004). Putting policy into practice? Poverty and people with serious mental illness. *Social Science & Medicine, 58*(1), 25–39.

Chapter Seven

Interactions with the Social Assistance
and Health Care Systems

Poverty does not produce unhappiness: it produces degradation.—George Bernard Shaw

Learning Objectives

At the conclusion of this chapter, the reader will be able to:

- document the extent of interaction of people living in poverty with the social assistance and health care systems;
- identify the unmet social service and health care needs of people living in poverty;
- describe the perceptions and experiences of people living in poverty with these systems;
- describe the effects of these interactions upon the health and quality of life of people living in poverty; and
- outline means of improving the quality of these interactions with the social assistance and health care sectors.

Introduction

The difficult material and social living conditions experienced by people living in poverty make interactions with a variety of service sectors much more likely. People living in poverty are more likely to access the employment insurance system. And many people living in poverty rely upon the benefits provided by the social assistance system. This is especially the case for people who are unable to participate in the labour force. These groups include people on social assistance, people with disabilities, and people who are unable to find work. These people must—by necessity—interact with social assistance and social service agencies. People living in poverty may also interact more with a range of services that are provided within Canadian communities. These include recreation centres, community health centres, community centres, and other voluntary organizations such as settlement houses, seniors' centres, youth services, and other community-based organizations. Interactions with the education system are also included within these domains.

Similarly, the experience of material and social deprivation makes it more likely that people living in poverty will experience greater incidence of disease and illness.

Chapters 8 to 10 document that this is indeed the case: people living in poverty have greater incidences of a wide range of health and health-related problems than those not living in poverty. By virtue of their greater incidence of health-related problems, interactions with the health care system should be more common than those not living in poverty. This chapter considers what is known about the quantity and quality of the interactions with the social service and health care sectors of people living in poverty. Of particular interest are the perceptions people living in poverty have about the quality of these interactions. The extent to which these interactions are shaped by the general Canadian approach to service provision—both social services and health care services—for people living in poverty is examined. The focus here is on income-related benefits and supports. While the purpose of the chapter is not to provide an in-depth presentation of the social services and health care systems, sufficient detail is provided to provide a context for understanding how people living in poverty interact with these service systems. Implications of these findings for the health and quality of life of individuals and communities experiencing poverty are examined, and means of improving the quality of these interactions are explored.

Income-Related Benefits in Canada

Canada's approach to the provision of income-related social benefits and services is typical of other liberal welfare states such as the USA, the UK, and Ireland (Organisation for Economic Co-operation and Development [OECD], 2009). In comparison to many European nations, benefits are less generous and are usually targeted to those in need, as opposed to being available on a universal basis (Esping-Andersen, 1999; Saint-Arnaud and Bernard, 2003). Social assistance or welfare is seen as providing benefits of last resort to individuals and families whose resources are inadequate to meet their needs and who have exhausted other avenues of support.

Employment insurance is available to people who are without employment and who meet the eligibility requirements. Recent changes to eligibility, however, have significantly reduced the percentage of Canadians who are eligible for such payments (Tremblay, 2009). Black and Shillington (2005) report that only 40% of Canadians are eligible to receive benefits and this figure drops as low as 30% in urban areas such as Toronto.

Social assistance or welfare is provided to people who have no employment income and very few assets. It is accepted that benefits in Canada provided under social assistance programs do not provide for much more than basic subsistence (OECD, 1999). This is the case even though many of those who rely on social assistance are children whose health and well-being are especially susceptible to the ill effects of living under conditions of material and social deprivation.

Many provinces have reduced benefits and reduced eligibility for social assistance (National Council of Welfare, 2010). Additionally, the imposition of "workfare" in many provinces has made a life even more difficult for many social assistance recipients.

There is increasing evidence that social assistance and social welfare benefits do little to maintain or improve the health and quality of life of people who must rely on these resources. The National Council of Welfare (2005a) stated:

> We have carried out extensive research on the welfare system, welfare incomes and welfare reform. It is our view that welfare policy in Canada has suffered serious neglect and is an utter disaster. Canada's "helping hand" is not working and people who must live on welfare are being left behind. (p. 1)

The Organisation for Economic Co-operation and Development (OECD) carried out a national case study of social assistance in Canada by focusing on approaches in four provinces: Alberta, New Brunswick, Ontario, and Saskatchewan (1999). The OECD pointed out that Canada is among the most affluent nations in the world. The report notes that public spending increased during the 1980s and peaked at 20% of gross domestic product (GDP) in 1993. Public spending has been falling ever since, though more recent data show a slight rise in the last few years. Indeed, during the 1990s, reduction in general government spending in Canada was so substantial that Canada's reductions were the highest among developed nations outside of Greece and Poland. Canada's social assistance programs are seen as barely providing more than bare subsistence (OECD, 1999).

The Canada Assistance Plan and the Canada Health and Social Transfer

The federal government is responsible for employment insurance, but social assistance and health are the responsibilities of the provinces. Funding for these provincial responsibilities is provided in part from the federal government through the Canada Health and Social Transfer (CHST). The CHST replaced the Canada Assistance Plan (CAP) with severe consequences for the provision of social assistance. Day and Brodsky (1998) argue that

> CAP provided that Canadians have a right to social assistance when in need, a right to an amount of social assistance that takes into account basic requirements, and a right to appeal when assistance is denied. Provinces were required to honour these conditions in order to qualify under CAP for 50:50 cost-sharing with the federal government of social assistance and important social services.
>
> In place of CAP, the Budget Implementation Act (BIA) (1995) creates the CHST, a new vehicle for transferring federal funds to the provinces. The BIA eliminates the conditions formerly attached to social assistance spending. It removes the separate designation of funds for social assistance, combines those funds with block funds for health and post-secondary education, and permits the provinces to spend the funds in any way they wish. It continues the general trend of reducing federal contributions to social programs. By doing so, it increases the

likelihood that the federal government will not be able to maintain national standards for any of Canada's social programs, not only because of its reduced spending, but because of the demands of the provinces for control over the programs that they are increasingly responsible for funding. (p. 1)

The primary change then, was that CAP provided separate envelopes for federal support of social welfare, post-secondary education, and health spending, but the CHST lumped all of these envelopes within a single block grant. This has been associated with decreasing spending on social welfare to the benefit of health care spending. Very recently, the CHST was separated into a Canada Social Transfer and Canadian Health Transfer. The effect of this upon social programs such as social assistance and benefits continues to be minimal, keeping most recipients well below the poverty line (National Council of Welfare, 2010).

Employment Insurance

All employed Canadian workers pay into the Employment Insurance (EI) Program, which is operated by the federal government. After a two-week waiting period, the rate of weekly benefits is 55% of weekly insurable earnings, which is set at an annual high of $43,200. This means that benefits can be as high as 55% of $43,200 or $23,764 a year or $457 per week (Service Canada, 2010). However, workers may not be eligible to receive benefits if they

- voluntarily left employment without just cause;
- were dismissed for misconduct; or
- are unemployed because they are directly participating in a labour dispute (strike, lockout, or other type of dispute) (Service Canada, 2010).

Requirements for receiving employment insurance vary from location to location. The benefit is payable for a period between 14 and 45 weeks after a two-week waiting period. Profound changes have taken place in eligibility for EI, and EI coverage has fallen across Canada from 80% of workers in 1990 to just over 40% in 2004 (Black and Shillington, 2005). This means that at any given time, less than half of employed workers who have paid into the EI program are eligible for benefits if their employment terminates (see Box 7.1).

Social Assistance or Welfare

Social assistance or welfare programs are the responsibility of provinces and territories in Canada. Social assistance programs across Canada distinguish among recipients along a number of dimensions. There are benefits for those who are deemed to be unable to

Box 7.1: Weakening of the Social Safety Net in Canada

Ontarians Can No Longer Count on Employment Insurance to Provide Temporary Income between Jobs: Toronto and Ottawa Have Lowest Coverage in Canada

The Task Force for Modernizing Income Security for Working Age Adults released its review of Employment Insurance (EI) today, revealing that EI no longer fulfils its role of providing temporary income to most unemployed Canadians who are between jobs.

The inadequacy of EI is most pronounced in Ontario's large cities. The report discloses that Ottawa and Toronto have the lowest levels of coverage in the country with only one in five unemployed workers in those cities receiving any EI benefits.

"EI is irrelevant for the majority of unemployed in Ontario's cities, including Toronto," says Susan Pigott, CEO of St Christopher House and Co-Chair of the Task Force. "The result is that those folks fall straight through what should be the first layer of our social safety net, and many do not stop falling until they land on social assistance. There needs to be a new approach."

Highlights of the MISSWA report include:

- EI coverage has fallen across Canada to just over 40% of the unemployed in 2004, from 80% in 1990.
- The precipitous decline in EI coverage was the result of changes in EI combined with changes in the labour market. More self-employed and more people in "non-standard" jobs such as temporary and contract work can't get EI.
- Cities like Toronto with high immigration levels and high rates of temporary and contract employment have fared the worst in coverage.
- The unemployed across Ontario have always had lower coverage than the rest of Canada and the gap has grown over the past twelve years.
- While Toronto would be expected to be a net contributor to EI given its lower unemployment rate, the gap in coverage has seen a huge gap in contributions versus benefits—Toronto now contributes 19% of EI funds and receives only 10% of EI benefits.

"Toronto's very low EI coverage relative to other regions with similar unemployment rates is primarily the result of high immigration levels," say study authors Jill Black and Richard Shillington. "Many unemployed immigrants face much tougher rules to qualify for EI creating a penalty for those cities like Toronto where immigration has been so important to labour force growth."

David Pecaut, Chair of the Toronto City Summit Alliance and Co-chair of the Task Force, says, "Poor EI coverage in our large cities like Toronto shows that the Canadian social safety net needs fundamental reform. This is both a social and an economic imperative as cities like Toronto could face fiscal disaster in the next recession as the unemployed fall through the safety net and land on provincially and municipally funded social assistance."

Source: Black, J. and Shillington, R. (2005, October 6). *Ontarians can no longer count on Employment Insurance to provide temporary income between jobs* [Press release]. Employment Insurance: Research Summary for the Task Force for Modernizing Income Security for Working Age Adults. Toronto: The Greater Toronto Civil Action Alliance (formerly the Toronto City Summit Alliance). Retrieved March 11, 2011 from http://tinyurl.com/s3vjh

participate in paid work and benefits for those deemed able to participate in paid work (National Council of Welfare, 2010). These benefits are very low. The Organisation for Economic Co-operation and Development (1999) notes, "Everywhere the basic social assistance payment is not intended to cover much more than immediate basic needs for housing, clothing, food, and recurring household expenses" (p. 42). This has not changed since this 1999 conclusion. This analysis merely states the obvious. The National Council of Welfare has long argued that social assistance benefits fall far short of providing recipients with resources to assure the necessities of life (National Council of Welfare, 2010).

In Canada, the OECD notes, the basic principle is that social assistance should not exceed the income of employed low-income workers. It is intended "*not* to give a reasonable standard of living" (OECD, 1999, p. 43). In Switzerland, as an alternative example, "[t]he CSIAS guidelines … define a basic payment rate sufficient to 'guarantee the beneficiary an existence which respects human dignity' and to 'give beneficiaries the possibility of actively participating in social life'" (p. 43).

There are assets tests in Canada that are strict in comparison with other OECD nations. Possession of liquid financial assets such as savings and private pension plans preclude receipt of social assistance. These assets must be spent prior to benefits being received. In essence, one must almost be destitute before assistance can be provided (National Council of Welfare, 2010).

The OECD points out that the 1990s saw reductions in benefits and/or restriction of eligibility for benefits across Canada. In 1992, Saskatchewan sharply reduced benefits to those deemed to be "fully employable." In 1993, Alberta cut benefit rates and New Brunswick restricted access to benefits. In 1995, Ontario cut benefits by 21.6%. The introduction of mandatory "workfare" requirements in many localities made receipt of benefits dependent upon looking for and/or finding paid employment or gaining participation as unpaid volunteers in various settings.

The National Council of Welfare (2005b) summarizes how eligibility for social assistance benefits is assessed. The person must be between 18 and 65. Students can qualify in some provinces/territories if they meet certain stringent requirements. Parents must try and secure any court-ordered support. Strikers are usually not eligible. Immigrants must go to their sponsors for support. Applicants must meet a means test. The assets of the applicant and of his or her household are compared to budgetary levels set by the government. The Council argues that these requirements are usually set way too low.

Applicants' liquid and fixed assets are examined by the welfare system. In most provinces, a principal residence and furniture are excluded, as is the value of a car. If applicants' assets are above these levels, the person is not eligible for assistance. Income from

Table 7.1: Liquid Assets Allowable for Receipt of Social Assistance or Welfare

	Single Person Considered Employable	Single Person with a Disability	Lone Parent, One Child	Couple, Two Children
Newfoundland and Labrador	$500	$3,000	$1,500	$1,500
Prince Edward Island	$50 to $200	$900	$50 to $1,200	$50 to $1,800
Nova Scotia	$500	$500	$1,000	$1,000
New Brunswick	$1,000	$3,000	$2,000	$2,000
Quebec	Applicants: $862 Recipients: $1,500	Applicants: $862 Recipients: $2,500	Applicants: $1,232 Recipients: $2,870	Applicants: $1,757 Recipients: $2,975
Ontario	$572	$5,000	$1,550	$2,130
Manitoba	$4,000	$4,000	$8,000	$16,000
Saskatchewan	$1,500	$1,500	$3,000	$4,000
Alberta	$583	$1,530	$1,062	$1,533
British Columbia	Applicants: $150 Recipients: $1,500	$3,000	Applicants: $250 Recipients: $2,500	Applicants: $250 Recipients: $2,500
Yukon	$500	$1,500	$1,000	$1,600
Northwest Territories	$300	$5,000	$380	$560
Nunavut	$0	$5,000	$0	$0

Source: National Council of Welfare. (2010). *Welfare incomes: 2009* (Table 6.1). Ottawa: National Council of Welfare.

sources such as employment, pensions, and EI will exclude receipt of benefits. The Child Tax Benefit, but not the supplement, is considered exempt. All non-exempt income is subtracted from the total needs of the household's resources. Table 7.1 summarizes levels of liquid assets that can be retained in Canada.

These are very strict criteria for support by international standards. A 2004 report prepared for the Ontario Minister of Community and Social Servi███████inted out that there are 800 rules and regulations that need to be applied to calcu██████ntarians are eligible for social assistance and how much they are entitled to each month (Matthews, 2004). According to the report,

> Many of those rules are punitive and designed not to support people, but rather to keep them out of the system. Because there are so many rules, they are expensive to administer and often applied inconsistently from one caseworker to another, even within the same office. Further, the rules are so complicated that they are virtually impossible to communicate to clients, and it takes years to train a caseworker. (p. 25)

In its analysis of Canada's social assistance system, the OECD (1999) outlines two opposite poles of benefit administration that result from elected officials exercising their power to determine the procedures that professional staff should follow. These are described as follows:

- *One is that benefits are a right; that potential claimants should be informed of their rights and encouraged to apply; that claimants should be treated as customers of a service; and that the role of the administration should be to process claims as quickly and accurately as possible.*
- *The other approach is that social assistance is not unrequited (the claimant has to do something in return for benefit receipt). Benefit availability is contingent on tight eligibility criteria and can be accessed only when all other sources have been exploited. Clients need not be informed of any "right"—if they really need help they will apply. Claimants should be discouraged to the greatest extent possible, as the benefit is still fulfilling its role as a safety net even if potential claimants chose to avoid the administrative hassle by seeking other means of support. Claimants are not customers; they are people who have thrown themselves at the mercy of the taxpayer, and the taxpayer has every right to expect that every possible check for eligibility is undertaken, however long that may take. (p. 72)*

The first scenario is that benefit claimants' requests are considered legitimate and expedited. The second scenario is the opposite. Alberta is seen as an exemplar of the second scenario. And Ontario is seen as not being far behind: "An extended amount of time is spent on intake, challenging and checking every detail of a claim in detail so that no-one receives a cent more than she is entitled to" (OECD, 1999, p. 74).

In Ontario, a variety of restrictive regulations were initiated as part of the Common Sense Revolution of the Mike Harris Conservative government. Included among these were various rules that assumed that any male and female sharing a dwelling were in a common-law relationship and subject to having benefits rescinded. This "spouse in the house rule" was deemed to be unconstitutional. Another change was that people attending post-secondary educational institutions were no longer eligible to receive social assistance benefits. Ontario also instituted a lifetime ban on receiving benefits if one is convicted of "welfare fraud." These two regulations came together to produce at least one well-known tragic outcome (see Box 7.2).

The restrictive approach to social assistance is less intense in New Brunswick and Saskatchewan where much processing of claims takes place over the telephone and where cross-referencing of records is done to expedite claim processing (OECD, 1999). In every province, however, there has been intense emphasis on fraud control. Welfare fraud hotlines take anonymous calls, and while provinces report that these procedures have proved worthwhile, others argue that the actual amount of welfare fraud is minimal. Any fraud that does occur results from the desperation experienced by people unable to live on the benefits provided (Chunn and Gavigan, 2004; Mosher, Evans, Morrow, Boulding, and VanderPlaats, 2004). The politics driving this emphasis on curbing welfare fraud are considered in Chapter 11.

Interactions with the Social Assistance Sector

There are a few studies that focus on the experiences of people who interact with the social assistance sector. The findings of these studies are consistent with a wealth of anecdotal information that has accumulated: people who receive social assistance are likely to feel hassled, degraded, and stigmatized by the social assistance system. The gap between what authorities state these programs are designed to accomplish and their actual effects upon those who participate in these programs is great.

Canada West Foundation (CWF) Study of Albertans Receiving Social Assistance

A CWF study examined the experiences of Albertans who had been on social assistance during the 1960s (Elton, Sieppert, Azmier, and Roach, 1997). Alberta's system was significantly reorganized, with the primary result being a close to 80% reduction in the number of people receiving social assistance. CWF was able to contact 769 people who had left the system. While some of the comments are positive, many are extremely negative.

> *Welfare really made a big difference. To get that when I did, as I was out of options, and it gave me time to get my life together. I had to get the pieces together and get on. Being on social services gave me a chance to do that.*
>
> *This has not been easy going on welfare, but the character and the goodness of the people— I think they care. Personally I think they are really neat people. Paperwork is the big staler.*
>
> *I was often treated as a statistic, number or nobody. I found I had to make an effort to make these people see me as a person of quality and worth.*

Box 7.2: The Case of Kimberly Rogers

Let's Keep Fighting System for Kim Rogers' Sake
Michele Landsberg

We thought we knew her.

All of us had labels summing up Kimberly Rogers' life: welfare cheat, loser, unwed mother-to-be. Suicide. We never heard her own voice or saw her eyes. We all—even the compassionate—had unspoken subtitles to the silent movie of her life, projected fuzzily to us in news stories: Guilty of welfare fraud. Sentenced to six months house arrest in a tiny Sudbury apartment. Then, on Aug. 9, 2001, found dead after a sizzling heat wave sent temperatures in her prison soaring to more than 40C.

But a more touchingly rounded picture of Kim Rogers began to emerge for those who actually attended the inquest into her death.

"Amazingly, you could see attitudes shifting," recalled Jacquie Chic, a lawyer for the Income Security Advocacy Centre in Toronto, who was there. "The jury and even her estranged family weren't sympathetic at first. They seemed to believe the government was right to force welfare rates so low. But as they heard the evidence of how cruel the system is, you could see the shock on their faces."

A working-class woman who struggled all her life against poverty, Kim fled an abusive relationship in Toronto to move home to Sudbury and start fresh.

"To me, she was a hero," Chic said. "She graduated from social services at Cambrian College with high praise for her work with handicapped children."

But how dumb a policy is this: You can't live on Ontario student loans, and yet you're a criminal if you get welfare at the same time. Kim was pregnant—and she needed welfare because, battling ill health, she couldn't work. In Ontario, while inflation leaped 15 per cent and rents by 26 per cent, welfare rates remained frozen for seven years at $520 a month for a single person.

When Kim pleaded guilty to having received $13,000 of welfare over three years, Judge Greg Rodgers ordered her into house arrest, with three hours a week to go out to shop. Shop? She had no income. Her welfare was automatically cut off. The judge was very righteous in denouncing her. "Welfare is there for people who need it," he said, "not for people who ... want things and who want money."

Right. Kim wanted "things" like food to eat while she prepared to give birth to a much-wanted child.

Bravely, although she dreaded the humiliation of public scrutiny and contempt, Kim launched a court Charter challenge of her six-month welfare ban. She told the court about running out of food, with no local agencies able to provide more. She was depressed, sleepless, frightened about her baby's future. I was heartstruck by a handwritten list of desired foods—yogurt, crackers, fresh veggies—that Kim Rogers gave her welfare worker. She titled it "foods I like." And she was so diffident, so self-denigrating, that she put the "I" in quotation marks, as though she had no right to use the first person pronoun.

Judge Gloria Epstein of the Superior Court heard her and denounced the welfare ban as "adversely affecting not only the mother and child, but also the public—its dignity, its human rights commitments and its health care resources."

But even after her welfare was ordered restored, Kim had only $18 left a month after rent and the student loan claw-back. Penned up in her stifling apartment, she was terrified to go outside, even into the backyard, lest authorities punish her by seizing her infant once it was born. (The eight-month fetus, a girl, died with Kim.)

What kind of people harden their hearts so brutishly that it seems a splendid idea to let people starve and despair in the midst of plenty?

The Ontario Tories don't stint themselves. And they don't exercise "zero tolerance" for their own self-indulgent spending. In their first six years in pig heaven, Tory MPPs charged the public purse for lavish steak dinners, fancy hotels, movies, trips to Las Vegas—$2 million total in expenses. One minister was sent to the back benches. Not exactly starvation and death.

Most Ontarians aren't as withered of conscience as their elected members. The Kim Rogers jury, sobered and saddened by the evidence, asked Ontario to raise welfare rates and end the cruelty of "zero tolerance." So far, 15 cities have echoed the demand.

Social Services Minister Brenda Elliott, a former teacher and entrepreneur, was unmoved. She instantly retorted that "zero tolerance" and the lifetime welfare ban "work" and will not be changed.

Ms Elliot has a strange cabinet record. As environment minister, she boasted of taking chauffeured limos instead of the bus for brief trips to the Legislature. She went to the Walkerton inquiry and refused to take responsibility for those deadly decisions in her ministry. ("We're a team.") She hangs tough on refusing treatment for autistic children over the age of 6.

She is especially contemptuous on the subject of Kim Rogers' lonely, anguished death. The minister says she is very satisfied that the "numbers on welfare continue to drop."

Let's put the screws to these callous MPPs even before the coming election. Join the campaign to phone the compassion-challenged minister at 416-325-5225 and insist that she raise the welfare rates to a living level.

This activism will be the only decent farewell we can offer to Kim Rogers.

Source: Landsberg. M. (2003, January 25). Let's keep fighting system for Kim Rogers' sake. *Toronto Star*, p. K01.

It's very frustrating for single moms trying to juggle the kids and the job. How can you get ahead when social services takes everything extra that you get? They even take away child support payments. You need things for your child, and they take away the money.

I was never happy when I was on welfare. I went through hell. I was treated like hell. Honest people get treated like garbage and the people that rip them off are never checked up on.

Nobody wants to go on welfare. It's a humiliating process no matter how much social welfare wants to help. (p. 7)

Overall, the study found that over 60% of study participants rated their interactions with Alberta authorities negatively. Indeed, there have been so many concerns about the treatment of social assistance claimants in Alberta that a lawsuit against the government was instituted. It claimed damages against the government for its shoddy treatment of people. A court ruled in favour of the complainants, and the Alberta government was required to pay out over $100 million (see Box 7.3).

Only about half (53.3%) of study participants left social assistance as a result of finding employment. And about 16% were transferred to other benefit programs. An important finding concerns the situation of those who have left social assistance. The Canada West Foundation study found that many of these former social assistance clients remain in extremely precarious living situations. Over two-thirds (68.2%) reported not having enough money to meet their food and shelter requirements at least once since leaving the program. And more than four in five who returned to the program (83.9%) reported not having these basic resources. The study's conclusions follow:

- Those who have left welfare are, as a group, better off financially and psychologically than those that are back on welfare.
- The findings show that many former welfare recipients are engaged in a daily struggle to achieve self-sufficiency.
- The multiple and complex nature of the personal problems and circumstances that lead people to seek welfare reinforces the need for continual improvements and adaptations in the delivery of social assistance. (p. 8)

The Wounds of Exclusion: Interactions with Social Assistance

Reid (2004) studied the interactions of women with the social assistance system in British Columbia as part of a major study of women's lived experience of poverty. Reid interviewed 20 women, 12 of whom provided a second interview. Reid summarized her findings as follows:

In the interviews and research team meetings, the women spoke at length about their encounters with the welfare office, social workers, and financial aid workers. The women said they were belittled, abused and treated as files numbers, and "non-persons." The women described their workers as snarky, rude, high and mighty, snooty, discriminating, and low-level threatening. (p. 135)

Box 7.3: Alberta Provincial Lawsuit Settled

EDMONTON (CP)—The Klein government has quietly agreed to spend more than $100 million to settle a class-action lawsuit over its treatment of severely handicapped, widowed, and poor Albertans. The settlement, believed to be the first in Alberta's history, was approved by the Alberta Court of Queen's Bench last month.

The settlement, which could affect as many as 30,000 Albertans, stems from decades of what the lawsuit claimed was the illegal and abusive bureaucratic treatment of people using social programs.

Donald Fifield, a truck driver who has been on the provincial Assured Income for the Severely Handicapped program, or AISH, since suffering a devastating leg injury in 1983, said his family was forced to eat porcupine to survive after the province mistakenly docked his allowance.

"We ate porcupine meat and did all kinds of stuff trying to keep alive because we couldn't afford nothing else," he said. "This goes back a long ways and there's been a lot of hurt." Fifield, now 64, and another man filed the suit in September 2004, just before the last provincial election.

They challenged policies that arbitrarily docked them for overpayments caused by administrative errors and denied them full compensation when they were underpaid.

The Fifields were docked allowance for failing to report Donald's wife, Carol, had found a temporary minimum-wage job.

Officials later discovered when they reviewed the file they had been notified. They also cut the family off assistance and made the Fifields send back their entire December cheque one year because they earned $58 too much to qualify.

Their lawyer, Phillip Tinkler, said it was ironic that after passing the Class Proceedings Act, the provincial government was its first target.

Gwen Vanderdeen-Paschke of Alberta Human Resources says the province disputes the allegations, but decided it was in the best interests of Albertans to settle.

"We decided it was better to enter into a settlement that does provide some fair and reasonable terms for people who come forward than expending all those resources on defending our position," she said.

Fifield, in a wheelchair since his leg was amputated nine years ago, is thrilled the case is settled. "We're helping a lot of people. That's what makes us feel the best," he said. "We were worried that if we lost the case we might lose our house."

Liberal Leader Kevin Taft called the government treatment of settlement plaintiffs "a profound and enduring betrayal of widows, of the severely handicapped, of the most vulnerable members of society."

Taft called on Premier Ralph Klein to apologize and said the government should investigate how the problems continued undetected for so long.

Since some of the funds paid to benefit recipients were federal monies transferred to the province for income support programs, Taft also suggested more accountability for transfer payments may be in order.

Source: (2006, January 16). Alberta Settles Lawsuit Launched by Disadvantaged, *The Guelph Mercury*, A5.

Social workers were seen as young and inexperienced with no appreciation of the life situations of their clients. One client stated: "These welfare workers, they're just these younger pups right out of school, and you can tell they're reading right out of their textbook, they don't know a thing about real life" (p. 136). The workers that were seen as sensitive and caring were seen as likely to burn out and leave.

Women reported that the attitudes of workers were judgmental and threatening and acted as if they assumed that clients were not capable of taking care of themselves. This general distrust led to careful surveillance of clients' activities and constant questioning of their claims and situation. Some specific comments from women were:

> It's low-level threatening is what it is. And if you go into any of the offices it tells you how you are supposed to be treated and how you're supposed to treat the person ... lack of integrity comes into it for a lot of these workers. (pp. 136–137)
>
> I hate having them [welfare workers] go up my ass with a microscope. That's kind of a rude way to put it, but that's how I feel. I feel like I'm under a microscope all the time. (p. 137)
>
> They [the social workers] never say "how would it be to be in their shoes, how would it be to be in her pain, in her depression?" They never do that. They never return phone calls, it's not possible to make appointments. (p. 137)
>
> If you go in and ask if you can get a food voucher, "well, why didn't you judge your money better?" And they give you such an attitude. And it's just so hard. And there's no privacy in that place at all. You and everyone in the world can hear you. But you know all that plays on you. I get this big knot in my stomach. (p. 138)
>
> The one thing I think that's missing there under "experiences of welfare" is the fact that you're treated as a liar when you walk through the door.

An important issue—related to the inability to make appointments—was that clients would have to line up outside the office in order to see their workers. Women commented:

> You have to stand out there and line up, there's no such thing as an appointment, so it doesn't matter what the weather is, what your health is, you stand in that line and they only take the first so many and the rest come back tomorrow. (p. 137)
>
> They start lining up about 6:30 in the morning on welfare day and the people walking by you—you can just see their faces. They're like "look at all those bums." (p. 137)

Finally, there is the issue of information. Women consistently reported being unable to find out what benefits, training, and other opportunities were available to them.

> They don't tell you benefits, they don't tell you how it works, they don't tell you about your healthcare ... they don't offer information, you have to extract it from them like, it's like doing a root canal or something. They don't explain all of it, they don't tell you your rights. (p. 137)
>
> Like it seems like when you do start asking all they do is get snotty with you and you get the run around and all you're trying to do is better yourself. You want to go back to school or you want to find out what's available to you to better yourself. And it's just crazy. (p. 137)
>
> They want you to get off welfare, but once you do get ahead, they penalize you. (p. 138)

Other Studies of Social Assistance

An extensive study by Wallace, Klein, and Reitsma-Street (2006) analyzed the structure of the social assistance system in British Columbia and the experiences of people within the system. It concluded that unreasonable barriers are preventing people in real need from accessing benefits of last resort (see Box 7.4.).

Box 7.4: Restructuring of BC's Social Assistance System

- British Columbia's welfare application system is not working—it discourages, delays and denies people who need help. The process of seeking income assistance has become so restrictive, and so complicated to navigate, that it is systematically excluding from assistance many of the very people most in need of help.
- The government's narrative about more people leaving welfare for work is not supported by the evidence. Data shows that the recent drop in the caseload is not the result of more people leaving welfare. Rather, fewer people are entering the system and accessing assistance. Simply put, the caseload reduction is mainly a front-door story.
- In the first year after the new welfare legislation was introduced in April 2002, the number of applicants who began to receive welfare benefits dropped by 40%, from an average of 8,234 entries (or "starts") per month to just 4,914 starts per month. The number of welfare "exits" also fell, but only slightly, from 8,388 to 7,631 per month.
- The acceptance rate for those who apply for welfare has dropped dramatically. In June 2001, 90% of people who began an application for welfare were successful in gaining income assistance. By September 2004, only 51% of those who sought welfare were granted assistance.
- The application system is now so complicated that many people need help from an advocate to successfully navigate the process.
- Many people are being "diverted" to homelessness, charities and increased hardship. The Ministry claims that people are being "diverted to employment"; however, the evidence shows that many are not.
- In some cases, denying people assistance reduces their ability to be self-sufficient. Lack of assistance forces some people to focus their time and resources on meeting basic shelter and food needs rather than looking for work. Without a permanent residence, a phone line, access to transportation or appropriate clothing, searching for work is difficult if not impossible.

Source: Wallace, B., Klein, S., and Reitsma-Street, M. (2006). *Denied assistance: Closing the front door on welfare in BC.* Vancouver: Canadian Centre for Policy Alternatives. Retrieved March 11, 2011 from http://tinyurl.com/h8jzm

In Ontario, Neysmith and colleagues examined the effects of recent policy changes—including welfare policy—on the lives of 50 families (Neysmith, Bezanson, and O'Connell, 2005). With specific regard to families receiving social assistance, the study identified how bureaucratic control made the receipt of social assistance very difficult. Much of this is related to the general attitude toward welfare common to administrative systems in Canada. The following comments were representative:

> [My welfare worker] wanted a letter of explanation from my son's doctor. She wanted medical records proving that my son was sick. I drew the line, and I almost went back with my ex. I was this close [holding her thumb and index finger close together] because I thought, with his income and me working part-time, I could tell [my worker] to go to hell. But I'm trapped. That's not an option either. It's either deal with this abusive woman or deal with a previous partner and I'm stuck in the middle. And I just find she's been very militant since this whole concept of Ontario Works came in play—very, very militant. (p. 79)
>
> I had a nice relationship with my worker where I lived before. I moved here and I don't know what happened. They want a doctor's letter; I take the doctor's letter to show them I need treatment. I need to see the doctor often. Welfare said they want another letter, my doctor sent them [another one]. Now my doctor is tired of them and doesn't send nothing. [Welfare also] wanted a school letter, every day I have to go to school. They wanted an income tax return letter or they would kick my baby out of day care. I went to school to register, they said they need last year's attendance. Where am I going to get last year's attendance? They ask for so much. They need an excuse to kick you off. No, they're not supporting me. They do not listen to me. (p. 87)
>
> Somebody reported to the Mother's Allowance hotline that my husband was living here. I flipped. I was in the hospital! I have four children that I could not take care of! Yes, he was here, but normally he isn't here at all. He was staying here to care for his children for the three days that I was sick in the hospital! He doesn't even pay support. It took me two years to get away from him. Did they think I'm just going to let him move back in here? (p. 90)

And similar findings are seen in the examination of British Columbia's social assistance program (Wallace et al., 2006). The report provides many instances of people being treated in a degrading and humiliating manner:

> I'm not saying they should be coddling people, but I mean, people need to be civil, you know what I mean? ... People think they're worthless because they're treated that way. They won't think that trying for anything else is even worth their time, because you know, who's gonna give them a chance? You know, half of this attitude really is the government. If they could treat people like they're human beings maybe people could start acting like that, you know. (p. 43)
>
> Before it was not as dehumanizing as it is now. Now you just know you have no rights. Actually, [I] did notice something on TV the other day about the relief camps they had during the Depression and apparently once someone was there they didn't even have a vote. You just became a non-person. And I almost feel they would be quite happy if they could do that. (p. 43)

Proposals to Improve the Welfare System

The National Council of Welfare (NCW) prepared a brief based on a Welfare-to-Work Roundtable held in 2002 in Ottawa (National Council of Welfare, 2003). The NCW argued for the system to be made simpler to understand and easier for people to use to get the right benefits and services in order to get on with improving their lives. The NCW specifically recommended:

- ending the clawback of federal child benefits,
- providing basic maternity support for all mothers and newborns,
- building a national child care program for all families,
- developing training and bridging programs for new and re-entrants into the labour market,
- allowing welfare recipients to maintain and develop assets,
- enabling lone parents with student loans to continue to receive welfare, at least until the amount of child benefits reaches the actual cost of raising a child, and
- providing supplements to low-income lone parents who can't fully benefit from tax credits available to higher earning lone parents. (p. 18)

More recently, the National Council of Welfare pointed out how the current system requires applicants to be destitute (see Table 7.1) and makes it almost impossible to escape poverty (National Council on Welfare, 2010) (see Box 7.5). They noted that, in some cases, allowable asset levels have increased but the situation remains rather bleak:

> *Most welfare incomes remain far below any socially accepted measure of adequacy. In 2009, most individuals and families applying for welfare had to be nearly destitute before they could receive welfare. When we looked at how asset levels have changed over the past twenty years, we found that many have not changed at all and some have actually gone down, either through policy decision or erosion from inflation. In a few cases, however, there have been significant increases and this, we think, is a more forward-looking and cost effective approach. Asset stripping not only impoverishes people before they qualify for welfare, but it also limits their ability to climb the welfare wall to get out of the welfare trap. Allowing people to retain some financial cushion can prevent major upheaval and enable the search for employment or the upgrading of skills necessary to move forward in their lives. (p. v)*

Health Care in Canada

Canada's health care system entitles all Canadians, regardless of income, status, or any other grouping, to health care services. While close to 30% of all health care expenditures in Canada come from private sources, Canadians rightly view their nation as providing health care to people based on the basis of need, not wealth. The key question to be asked is whether people living in poverty are having their health care needs met.

Box 7.5: Report on Welfare System in Canada

Welfare Design Outdated, Counterproductive

OTTAWA, ONTARIO, December 13, 2010—A new report from the National Council of Welfare (NCW) shows that welfare can be harder to get today than 20 years ago. This means more people were forced into destitution to qualify for welfare in 2009, when the recession's casualties were mounting.

Canadians cannot receive welfare if their liquid assets, such as cash, money in bank accounts or even retirement savings, are over the limit set for their particular circumstances. The NCW report, *Welfare Incomes 2009*, illustrates many cases where these asset limits have eroded, whether by inflation or design. The limit can be as low as $50.

NCW Chairperson John Rook explained there is great variability across provinces, territories and individual situations, "but in general the combination of low asset limits, low earnings exemptions and low welfare rates—far below the poverty line—creates the perfect trap, especially for single people. The absence of shock absorbers and springs that help people help themselves is completely counterproductive."

Getting a job is not the answer it should be. In some Canadian jurisdictions, there are no earnings exemptions at all and welfare benefits are reduced dollar-for-dollar by the amount earned. In such cases, people on welfare are left financially worse off once work-related costs, such as transportation, are taken into account.

Rook said the NCW does not just want to see people exit welfare, but to escape poverty and to thrive.

Don Drummond, former Chief Economist of the TD Bank, commenting on the report, said "Canada's welfare system is a box with a tight lid. Those in need must essentially first become destitute before they qualify for temporary assistance. But the record shows once you become destitute you tend to stay in that state. You have no means to absorb setbacks in income or unexpected costs. You can't afford to move to where jobs might be or upgrade your skills."

For those who do exit welfare, their finances do not necessarily improve because they lose welfare-related support, such as housing, health and dental care. The loss of this support can mean a major setback for these people, said Rook, and it is a large part of the disincentive barrier called "the welfare wall." The report says more effective approaches can achieve better results and points to examples of innovation and potential. Manitoba's new liquid asset policy of allowing $4000 per person, up to $16,000 for families, makes it a leader. Lone parents in some other provinces get welfare rates that at least reach the poverty line. Raising asset and earnings limits, bringing rates up and making regular adjustments for inflation can be a part of the solution, but alone are not enough.

"To solve the problems of social assistance, we must literally think—and act—outside the box," said Rook, "in this case, outside the welfare system." He indicated federal child benefits provide a source of stable income for families with children and play an important role in reducing welfare use and preventing poverty. *Welfare Incomes 2009* focuses on the newer Working Income Tax Benefit (WITB), which also operates outside the welfare system. It is available to welfare recipients with earnings and thus helps work pay. The WITB goes in the right direction, according to the report, but the amounts need to be increased to help welfare recipients, particularly singles, avoid or overcome the "welfare wall."

The report calls for a comprehensive approach to both income support and the provision of appropriate services geared to income level rather than welfare status. The Council is encouraged by poverty reduction strategies that take this approach and is confident these kinds of investments will pay off for all Canadians.

The National Council of Welfare is an independent body established to advise the federal government on issues related to poverty and social development.

Source: National Council of Welfare. (2010, December 13). *Welfare design outdated, counterproductive: More effective solutions exist says new National Council of Welfare report* [Press release]. Retrieved March 11, 2011 from http://tinyurl.com/268hm4x

Numerous studies have addressed this issue and some have particularly focused on the role that income plays in access to health care services. Also of importance is the nature of the interactions of people living in poverty with the health care sectors and the identification of means by which these interactions could be improved. Another important question is whether the quality of these interactions appears to be as negative as the ones with the social assistance sector that were reported by people living in poverty.

Health Status and Use of the Health Care System

It would be expected that people of lower income—especially those living in poverty—would make greater use of the health care system. Living in poverty is associated with generally poorer health. And findings indicate that this is indeed the case. The Canada/United States Survey of Health included a representative sample of Canadians and provides insights into these health and health care issues (Sanmartin and Ng, 2004).

The 3,505 Canadians sampled in this study were divided, upon the basis of household income, into five quintiles. The participants were then asked to rate their health as either excellent, very good, good, fair, or poor. The participants also reported the presence of a severe mobility problem and any unmet health care needs. Figure 7.1 shows the percentage of respondents, by income quintile, providing a fair or poor response, a mobility restriction, and unmet health care needs. Findings are consistent with numerous other studies that show that income level is a strong predictor of reported health status. Canadians within the lowest income quintile reported the greatest likelihood of fair or poor health, of having a severe motor mobility, and of having an unmet health care need. This survey did not assess frequency and type of health services used, but other Canadian studies have addressed this issue.

The Canadian Institute for Health Information (CIHI) examined differences in hospitalization rates for ambulatory care-sensitive conditions (ACSC) and mental illness among Canadians living in differing socio-economic neighbourhoods in 33 Census Metropolitan Areas (CMAs) across Canada (CIHI, 2010a). ACSC were defined as those conditions for which hospitalization could be potentially avoided had the person received adequate primary health care. These conditions included epilepsy, chronic obstructive pulmonary disease, asthma, heart failure and pulmonary edema, hypertension, angina, and diabetes.

Socio-economic status was ascertained by application of the Quebec Deprivation Index, which operationizes socio-economic status (SES) at the area level. It combines social measures (percentage of single-parent families, percentage of persons living alone, percentage of persons separated, widowed, or divorced) and material measures (percentage without high-school graduation, percentage employed, and average income) to assign neighbourhoods to one of five groups, from most deprived to least deprived. Hospital admission rates are then compared among these groups. In essence, this measure groups' neighbourhoods from the very poor to the very wealthy.

Figure 7.1: Percentage of Canadians Indicating Various Health Care Problems by Household Income Quintile, 2002/2003

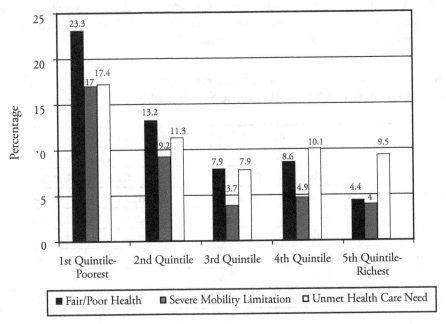

Source: Adapted from Statistics Canada, Joint Canada/United States Survey of Health: Findings and Public Use Microdata File, 82M0022XIE2003001, Table A.7, June 2004; http://www.statcan.gc.ca/bsolc/olc-cel/olc-cel?catno=82M0022X&lang=eng

Table 7.2 provides findings concerning hospitalization rates per 100,000 population for the 33 CMAs combined as a function of SES group. As can be seen, hospitalization rates are strikingly higher for those identified as living in the most deprived 20% of neighbourhoods. Differences among socio-economic groups are generally greater for men than for women. The report comments that differences associated with socio-economic status—that is, the differences between the wealthiest group and all others—accounts for an estimated 33–40% of hospitalization rates.

It is estimated that the costs of these excess rates associated with socio-economic status for ACSC is approximately $89 million for men and $71 million for women. The excess costs for mental illness hospitalization associated with socio-economic status are approximately $123 million for men and $125 million for women. Of particular note is that the greatest differences among socio-economic groups are between the lowest—or poorest—group and the next one up. This is consistent with other research that shows that adverse health effects associated with lower income and other measures of deprivation are especially concentrated among Canadians living in poverty (Auger and Alix, 2009; Wilkins et al., 2002; Wilkins, 2007).

The Canadian Institute for Health Information (2010b) also carried out an extensive analysis of income-related health inequalities in regard to admission for heart attacks in communities of at least 50,000 population across Canada. They categorized neighbourhoods using percentage of persons falling below the Statistics Canada low income cut-offs to create five quintiles from the least affluent to the most affluent, and then reported on hospitalization rates for heart attacks. Table 7.3 shows that income quintile was also related to a number of other indicators, such as unemployment rate, home ownership, recent immigrants, and others. It also shows wide differences in hospitalization for heart attacks among neighbourhoods of differing income levels.

Table 7.2: Age-Standardized Hospitalization Rates for 33 Census Metropolitan Areas by Socio-economic Status, 2006

	Age-Standardized Hospitalization Rates			
	ACSC		Mental Illness	
	Rate per 100,000		Rate per 100,000	
SES Group	Males	Females	Males	Females
1–Highest	208	150	256	260
2	261	193	299	304
3–Middle	302	223	348	360
4	368	276	424	419
5–Lowest	507	405	636	611

Source: Canadian Institute for Health Information. (2010). *Hospitalization disparities by socio-economic status for males and females* (Appendix C, p. 15). Ottawa: CIHI.

Table 7.3: Characteristics of Residents and Hospitalization Rates for Heart Attacks by Affluence of Neighbourhood, Canada, 2006

Measure	Q1 Poorest	Q2	Q3	Q4	Q5 Richest
Resident Characteristics					
Low Income Rate (%)	31.9	17.7	11.7	8.4	6.3
Unemployment Rate (%)	9.9	6.9	5.8	5.2	4.7
Housing Owned (%)	40.4	63.6	75.6	82.6	85.9
Post-secondary Graduates (%)	50.6	55.0	59.3	63.6	71.1
Aboriginal Population (%)	7.8	3.3	2.6	2.4	1.9
Recent Immigrants (%)	7.3	3.9	2.8	2.1	1.8
Lone-Parent Families (%)	25.0	18.3	14.8	21.1	9.4
Living Alone (%)	16.2	12.5	9.5	7.8	6.9
Hospitalization Rates/100,000 for Acute Myocardial Infarctions (Heart Attacks) 2008–2009					
Males	361	329	315	300	267
Females	168	148	138	130	113

Source: Canadian Institute for Health Information. (2010). *Health indicators 2010* (Table 1, p. 2; Figure 2, p. 11). Ottawa: CIHI.

Roos and Mustard (1997) carried out a very extensive study of health care utilization among 600,000 residents of Winnipeg that assessed whether primary care and specialist services were equally likely to be accessed by Canadians of different incomes. Enumeration areas of approximately 700 people were classified, based on median income, into one of five income quintiles. Table 7.4 shows that income quintiles were also related to a number of other indicators such as female-led households, unemployment rate, and educational level.

Table 7.4 also shows a wide range of health indicators and how these are related to income quintile. These indicators include age-standardized death rates, life expectancy, and death rates from specific diseases. For virtually every indicator, health is worse among the lowest-quintile population. Not surprisingly, the study also found that hospital use indicators (numbers of people hospitalized, number of discharges, and hospital days) were strongly related to income quintile, with the rates highest for the lowest income areas. On average, the number of people hospitalized per 1,000 residents was 102 in the poorest quintile, compared to 65 in the richest quintile. Similarly, the average number of days spent in hospital (not tabled) for the poorest quintile per 1,000 residents was 937 days for the poorest quintile and 500 for the richest. But an important question is whether

Table 7.4: Characteristics of Residents, Health Indicators, and Physician Contact Rates by Relative Affluence of Neighbourhood, Winnipeg, 1992

Measure	Q1 Poorest	Q2	Q3	Q4	Q5[d] Richest	Ratio[e]
Resident characteristics						
Mean household income ($)	18,607	25,719	31,050	37,942	53,777	2.9
Female-headed household (%)	31	16	13	6	4	7.8
HS graduates aged 25–34 (%)	63	65	71	75	82	1.3
Unemployed aged 45–54 (%)	10	7	5	4	3	3.3
Treaty status Aboriginals (%)	7	2	1	0	0	3.3
Age-standardized death rates						
Males	13.7	10.2	8.7	7.8	6.2*	2.2
Females	9.4	8.0	7.3	6.7	6.6*	1.4
Ages 0–74	6.7	4.5	3.9	3.1	2.7*	3.4
Life expectancy[a]						
Males	65.3	70.5	72.8	74.3	76.6	1.2
Females	74.4	77.8	79.5	80.0	82.1	1.1
Deaths by type of disease						
Chronic diseases[b]	4.0	3.1	2.9	2.5	2.3*	1.7
All cancers	2.9	2.3	2.2	1.9	1.8*	1.6
All injuries[c]	0.8	0.5	0.4	0.3	0.2*	4.0
Mean visits per resident to:						
All physicians	5.8	5.2	5.0	4.8	4.7*	1.2
General practitioner	4.2	3.6	3.4	3.3	3.0*	1.4
Specialist						
Referred	0.2	0.2	0.2	0.2	0.2	1.0
Unreferred	1.4	1.4	1.4	1.3	1.5	0.9
Percent with 1 or more contact with:						
Any physician	84.0	85.0	85.2	84.6	85.0	1.0
General practitioner	76.2	65.6	75.6	75.0	73.1	1.0
Specialist						
Referred	18.0	17.9	18.0	18.0	18.0	1.0
Unreferred	36.5	37.9	37.7	37.4	40.3	0.9

[a]Life expectancy is based on five years of mortality data from 1989–1993.
[b]Chronic diseases: deaths from ischemic heart disease, diabetes, asthma, hypertension, vascular complications, and emphysema.
[c]All injuries: deaths from motor vehicles, falls, vehicular non-traffic, drowning, poisonings, fire and flames, and suicide.
[d]From chi square test of linear trends in rates across income groups, * p<.001.
[e]Ratio = Q1/Q5: Q1 = Poorest; Q5 = wealthiest.

Source: Adapted from Roos, N. P., and Mustard, C. A. (1997). Variation in health care use by socioeconomic status in Winnipeg, Canada: Does the system work well? Yes and no (Tables 1, 2, 6; pp. 94, 95, 100). *Milbank Quarterly, 75*(1), 89–111.

this clearly higher health need among lower income people is translated into greater use of primary care and specialist services. If health care is provided on the basis of need, it would be expected that greater contact would be seen for lower income people. As shown in Table 7.4, lower income residents were more likely to see physicians, including general practitioners. But they were not more likely to see or be referred to specialists than those living in the wealthiest quintile of neighbourhoods.

These findings concerning seeing specialists have been replicated by others. Dunlop and colleagues looked at national data from the National Population Health Survey (Dunlop, Coyte, and McIsaac, 2000). They found that need of health care—itself related to income—was related to greater use of physician services. These services included both primary care and specialist care. However, when analyses specifically looked at type of physician, it was found that while those in the lowest income quintile were more likely to access general practitioners, they were less likely to have visited a specialist than wealthier Canadians. These and other findings point to clear problems with universal access to specialist care among lower income Canadians. The reasons for these findings have not been identified.

Finally, an extensive international study examined a very wide range of general and cost-related access and medical bill problems among Canadians classified as below average, average, and above average in income (Schoen and Doty, 2004). The findings were that 20% of Canadians with below-average income found it difficult to see a specialist as needed, while only 14% of Canadians with above-average income had this problem. Canadians with below-average income were also more likely to have to wait more than five days or more to see a doctor (27% of these Canadians) than above-average income Canadians (20% of these Canadians). There was a variety of other physician-related issues identified by the study. Especially important were differences for cost-related access problems between Canadians of above-average, average, and below-average income.

In analyses that controlled for a wide range of factors such as age, education, minority status, and residential location, below-average-income Canadians were—as compared to above-average-income Canadians—50% less likely to see a specialist when needed, 50% more likely to find it difficult to get care on weekends or evenings, and 40% more likely to wait five days or more for an appointment with a physician. There were no reliable differences between average-income Canadians and above-average income Canadians on these measures.

However, differences were seen for average-income Canadians as well as below-average-income Canadians for cost-related measures. Compared to above-average-income Canadians, lower-average-income Canadians were three times more likely to not fill a prescription due to cost, three times more likely to have a medical problem but not be able to see a doctor due to cost, and 60% more likely to not get a needed test or treatment. Even average-income Canadians were almost twice as likely to not get a prescription filled, and 60% more likely to not see a dentist when needed due to cost, as compared to above-average-income Canadians. Average-income Canadians were also twice as likely to have problems paying medical bills than above-average-income Canadians.

On more specific measures of patient-doctor interaction, such as being treated with respect and dignity, having health concerns taken seriously, having enough time with the physician, and receiving good information, there were no differences among Canadians with higher-than-average income, average income, and below-average income.

Dental Care

Additionally, this same international study found that below-average-income Canadians were four times more likely to report a dental problem but not see a dentist due to cost, and over four times more likely to have problems paying medical bills than above-average-income Canadians.

Studies that have looked at dental care find a strong relationship between income and use of dental services. Income is related to seeing a dentist. The lower one's income, the less likely they will have seen a dentist (Millar and Locker, 1999). This relationship holds for both those insured and not insured (see Figure 7.2), though Millar and Locker found that just about all low-income Canadians were not insured. They also found that the lowest-

Figure 7.2: Percentage of Canadian Population Aged 15 or Older Who Visited a Dentist by Dental Insurance Status and Household Income, 1979–1997

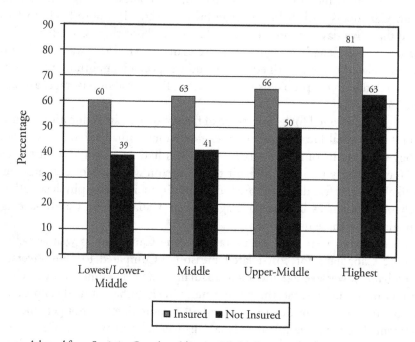

Source: Adapted from Statistics Canada publication Health Reports, Catalogue 82-003, Volume 11, Number 1, Release Date: August 18, 1999, p.59, URL:http://www.statcan.ca/bsolc/english/bsolc?catno=82-003-X&CHROPG=1#issue1999001

income-quartile group of Canadians were more likely to have fillings and extractions than wealthier groups, but were less likely to come in for cleaning and insured checkups.

A more recent study examined dental issues between Canadians identified as being of lower, average, or higher income (Health Canada, 2010). Middle income was defined as an income of $30,000 to $59,000 for a family of one or two persons; $40,000 to $79,000 for a family of three or four persons, and $60,000 to $79,000 for a family of five or more. Families with less that these figures were classified as lower income and those families with more were classified as higher income.

Figure 7.3 shows the percentage of lower, middle-, and higher income Canadians having private or public dental insurance. As shown, almost 50% of lower income Canadians did not have any dental insurance. Among higher income Canadians this figure was only 20%.

The Health Canada (2010) study also found a strong relationship between reporting poor or fair oral health and income. Almost three times as many low-income Canadians between the ages of 20 and 60 report problems as compared to higher income Canadians. As well, lower income is related to greater incidence of persistent oral pain, avoiding dental professionals because of costs, and declining recommended dental treatments (Figures 7.4 and 7.5).

Figure 7.3: Percentage of Lower, Middle, and Higher Income Canadians Having Public or Private Dental Insurance, 2007–2009

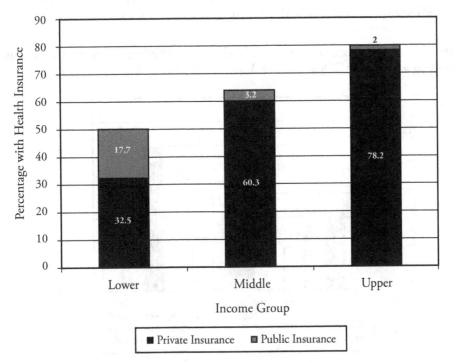

Source: Health Canada. (2010). *Report on the findings of the oral health component of the Canadian Health Measures Survey* (Table 2, p. 70). Ottawa: Health Canada.

Figure 7.4: Percentage of Lower, Middle, and Higher Income Canadians at Differing Ages Reporting Poor Oral Health, 2007–2009

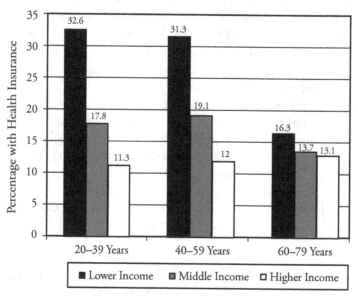

Source: Health Canada. (2010). *Report on the findings of the oral health component of the Canadian Health Measures Survey* (Table 3, p. 71). Ottawa: Health Canada.

Figure 7.5: Percentage of Lower, Middle, and Higher Income Canadians Reporting a Variety of Oral Health Issues, 2007–2009

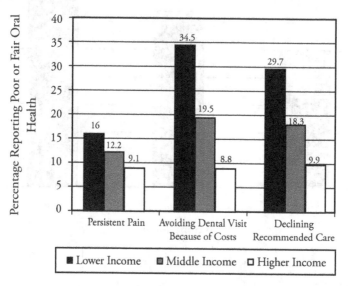

Source: Health Canada. (2010). *Report on the findings of the oral health component of the Canadian Health Measures Survey* (Table 5, p. 73; Table 11, pp. 12, 79, 80). Ottawa: Health Canada.

Lived Experiences of Receiving Health Care

Little detail is known about the actual lived experiences of people living in poverty with the health care system. As part of a larger ethnographic study of women living in poverty, Reid (2004) found about half of women reported interactions to be generally negative. Reid identified two key issues. The first was that these women did not have resources to access the "extras" that keep one well. Here are two such examples:

> I don't have the income so I can't take part in physiotherapy and do the exercises. Because I don't have the money I can't do all the things I would need to get myself in that healthy state of mind and every thing ... I feel I'm limited to the resources I can get to because of money. (p. 139)
>
> This month I had to go off my supplements because I had to pay for other things. So I'm feeling it ... the supplements are very expensive. They're good quality and they're what I need. But it was a choice this month to not feel very good. (p. 140)

The other issue was that about half the women felt they were not being treated fairly by the health care system. As the following quotations highlight, they felt they were not treated as well as those with more financial resources.

> Because we have no money, they don't keep us long. They are like, "next." But if you're rich you have a private room then you can stay longer, the nurses treat you better, everybody treats you better. (p. 141)
>
> I went to Pearl Vision, and I said that I was on low-income disability, and what was the price range for my glasses, and he just pointed his finger over, and said "the welfare glasses are over there." (p. 141)

However, the primary concern of the women was not being able to afford aspects of health care that were not covered by the system. The reports of unsatisfactory interaction with health care providers are not consistent with the international study reported earlier (Schoen and Doty, 2004), but it should be noted that the Commonwealth study did not specifically identify the responses of people living in poverty.

Conclusions

Many people living in poverty are forced to interact with the social assistance system. The benefits they receive from this system are not at a level that allows for experiences consistent with what is expected to keep citizens living well and healthy within a developed nation like Canada. In addition, the social assistance system is frequently organized in such a way as to make receipt of assistance difficult at best, and degrading and humiliating at worst. Additionally, governments have been putting forward the idea that people receiving social assistance are somehow undeserving of these benefits and of respect from others.

In contrast, interactions with the health care system seem to be relatively free of such problems. People living in poverty make greater use of the hospital system and are as likely to have access to primary care—with some exceptions—as people who are not living in poverty. They are, however, less likely to be referred to specialist care. The reasons for this have not been sufficiently investigated. In general, findings presented in this chapter indicate that social assistance is a process characterized by stigma, personal humiliation, and attitudes unworthy of a modern developed nation. In contrast, the organization and provision of services in the health care system are generally free of these issues. There are serious concerns, however, related to the ability of people living in poverty to access medicines and additional required services. These problems appear to be especially relevant to issues of dental care.

Critical Thinking Questions

1. What do you think are some of the effects of having so many working Canadians ineligible to receive employment insurance? Are you willing to support and pay into a system that will not be available to you if you need it?
2. Why do you think the benefits provided by the social assistance system are so meagre? Do you think that providing people with so little to live on motivates them to achieve employment or makes their lives so difficult as to make gaining employment even more difficult?
3. Why do you think that people living in poverty are less likely to be seen by health care specialists? What could be done to improve this situation?
4. Why do you think that people accessing the social assistance system are looked down upon, while users of the health care system are not?
5. How does having fewer people eligible for employment insurance and receiving extremely low benefits affect the operation of the job market and the quality of jobs? What are the effects on job quality of having large numbers of people desperate to gain any source of income, however meagre?

Recommended Readings

Matthews, D. (2004). *Review of employment assistance programs in Ontario Works and Ontario Disability Support Program.* Toronto: Ministry of Community and Social Services. Online at http://tinyurl.com/34o7f42

> This report was prepared for Ontario's Minister of Community and Social Services upon election of the Liberal government. It presents a series of recommendations based on extensive consultations with service providers and users of social assistance across the province. It outlines a picture of an unresponsive system whose primary purpose is one of preventing people from receiving social assistance rather than supporting them in their periods of difficulty.

Mosher, S. (2005). *Walking on eggshells: The experience of abused women with social assistance in Ontario.* Final report of research findings from the Woman and Abuse Welfare Research Project. Online at http://tinyurl.com/2xhjb

This report was prepared for the Law Commission of Ontario and provides a very disturbing picture of the difficulties women who have suffered abuse experience with the social assistance system in Ontario. Using the words of women themselves, and backed up by extensive legal and critical analyses, the picture emerges of women who, already having been abused, are submitted to another round of institutional abuse as they attempt to receive social assistance.

Organisation for Economic Co-operation and Development. (1999). *The battle against exclusion: Social assistance in Canada and Switzerland.* Paris: OECD.

This is one of a series of extensive analyses of social assistance practices in developed nations. In this volume, Canada and Switzerland are the focus. Canada's approach is seen as basically one of begrudging the provision of supports to people in need of social assistance. Benefits are very low, and numerous roadblocks to receiving benefits exist.

Schoen, C., Blendon, R., DesRoches, C. M., and Osborn, R. (2002). *Comparison of health care system views and experiences in five nations: Findings from the Commonwealth Fund 2001 International Health Policy Survey.* New York: Commonwealth Fund.

This report provides extensive analyses of citizens' views about their access to and satisfaction with their health care systems. The picture emerges in Canada of low-income people being unable to access health care services that entail any degree of costs. The findings are consistent with Canadian studies concerning the impact of poverty on the ability to access health care services.

Swanson, J. (2001). *Poor-bashing: The politics of exclusion.* Toronto: Between the Lines Press.

Jean Swanson has for decades been a service provider and volunteer with anti-poverty organizations in British Columbia and elsewhere. In this volume she documents how Canadians living in poverty—and especially those receiving social assistance—are subjected to exclusion and vilification by elected officials of all political stripes, by the media, and, increasingly, by the public. Her analysis looks at which sectors of society benefit from bashing people living in poverty and outlines various means by which poor-bashing can be countered.

Wallace, B., Klein, S., and Reitsma-Street, M. (2006). *Denied assistance: Closing the door on welfare in BC.* Vancouver: Canadian Centre for Policy Alternatives. Online at http://tinyurl.com/h8jzm

This report documents how the Campbell government in British Columbia has made the receipt of social assistance more and more difficult for people already living in very difficult situations. The barriers include unreasonable criteria for receipt of benefits and lengthy waiting periods during which people have no means of support. The result has been a dramatic reduction in the number of people receiving benefits. This has occurred in tandem with increasing economic and social inequalities that are making the lives of people living in poverty even more precarious.

Relevant Websites

Canadian Institute for Health Information (CIHI)—www.cihi.ca
The Canadian Institute for Health Information provides information about health status and the health care system in Canada. CIHI attempts to support the effective delivery of health services and raise awareness among Canadians of the factors that contribute to good health.

Canadian Social Research Links—www.canadiansocialresearch.net/welfare.htm
This website has links to just about every aspect of social policy and welfare in Canada. On his personal web page, founder Gilles Séguin states: "I launched Canadian Social Research Links, on my own time and on my own dime, so that I could share my collection of web links with colleagues in the social research community, whether in government, the non-governmental sector or academia."

Disabled Women's Network Ontario (DAWN)—http://dawn.thot.net
DAWN Ontario is a feminist, cross-disability organization working toward access, equity, and full participation of women with disabilities. This offers up-to-date information concerning poverty and activism.

National Council of Welfare (NCW)—www.ncwcnbes.net
The NCW website contains reports, fact sheets, and press releases that describe social assistance programs across the provinces and the gap between expectations and realities in the system. Over the years, these reports have become increasingly critical of governmental approaches to social assistance.

PovNet—www.povnet.org
PovNet is an Internet site for advocates, people on welfare, and community groups and individuals involved in anti-poverty work. It provides up-to-date information about welfare and housing laws and resources in British Columbia and Canada. PovNet links to current anti-poverty issues and provides links to other anti-poverty organizations and resources in Canada and internationally.

Statistics Canada Health Reports—www.statcan.ca/english/ads/82-003-XPE/
Health Reports is a peer-reviewed quarterly journal of accurate health data and superior analyses in one convenient source. Available in both print and PDF formats, each issue contains at least three articles detailing vital, current topics in health and health care. You may need to access this site through your university's library.

Glossary of Terms

Poor bashing is a process by which people living in poverty are not only blamed for their own problems but are assumed to have any number of such negative characteristics as sloth, dishonesty, and immorality. It is manifested in very low social assistance rates, severe restrictions and surveillance, and negative government and media coverage. Poor-bashing seems to increase as objective living conditions of the most vulnerable declines.

Social assistance or *welfare* is a program that provides benefits of last resort in Canada. To qualify for social assistance one must be almost destitute. Applications for social assistance are onerous and difficult, and treatment of people on social assistance tends to be harsh and punitive.

Specialist health care refers to health care provided by physicians not considered to be general practitioners. In most provinces access to specialist care occurs through the recommendation of the general practitioner or primary care physician. Specialists include dermatologists, cardiologists, neurologists, and so forth.

Surveillance is a term used to refer to institutions exerting undue control over receivers of assistance or benefits. In the case of recipients of social assistance, it can involve intrusive questioning, unannounced inspections of premises, and general intrusion into personal affairs.

Unmet health care needs are needs that are not met by the health care system. These can occur through lack of access to care covered under Canada's health care system because of doctor shortages, scheduling issues, or other barriers. It can also result when services are not covered under the system, such as rehabilitation, medicines, or other de-listed services.

Welfare fraud occurs when receivers of social assistance are not entitled to benefits and are aware of this. In recent years welfare fraud has been blown up into an issue out of all proportion to its actual incidence. In addition, many argue that to survive on the benefits that are provided, the acceptance of benefits that one may not be entitled to is not fraud, but is actually a survival technique.

References

Auger, N., and Alix, C. (2009). Income and health in Canada. In D. Raphael (Ed.), *Social determinants of health: Canadian perspectives* (2nd ed., pp. 61–74). Toronto: Canadian Scholars' Press Inc.

Black, J., and Shillington, E. R. (2005). *Employment insurance: Research summary for the Task Force for Modernizing Income Security for Working Age Adults.* Toronto: Toronto City Summit Alliance.

Canadian Institute for Health Information. (2010a). *Hospitalization disparities by socio-economic status for males and females* (Appendix C, p. 15). Ottawa: CIHI.

Canadian Institute for Health Information. (2010b). *Health indicators 2010.* Ottawa: CIHI.

Chunn, D. E., and Gavigan, A. M. (2004). Welfare law, welfare fraud, and the moral regulation of the never deserving poor. *Social and Legal Studies, 13*(2), 219–243.

Day, S., and Brodsky, G. (1998). *Women and the equality deficit: The impact of restructuring Canada's social programs.* Ottawa: Status of Women Canada.

Dunlop, S., Coyte, P. C., and McIsaac, W. (2000). Socio-economic status and the utilisation of physicians' services: Results from the Canadian National Population Health Survey. *Social Science and Medicine, 51*(1), 123–133.

Elton, D., Sieppert, J., Azmier, J., and Roach, R. (1997). *Where are they now?* Calgary: Canada West Foundation.

Esping-Andersen, G. (1999). *Social foundations of post-industrial economies.* New York: Oxford University Press.

Health Canada. (2010). *Report on the findings of the oral health component of the Canadian Health Measures Survey.* Ottawa: Health Canada.

Matthews, D. (2004). *Review of employment assistance programs in Ontario Works and Ontario Disability Support Program.* Toronto: Ministry of Community and Social Services.

Millar, W., and Locker, D. (1999). Dental insurance and use of dental services. *Health Reports, 11*(1), 55–67.

Mosher, J., Evans, P., Morrow, E., Boulding, J., and VanderPlaats, N. (2004). *Walking on eggshells: Abused women's experiences of Ontario's welfare system.* Toronto: York University.

National Council of Welfare. (2003). *Summary report of the NCW's Welfare-to-Work roundtable.* Ottawa: National Council of Welfare.

National Council of Welfare. (2005a). *From poverty to prosperity. Presentation to the Standing Committee on Finance for the 2005 pre-budget consultations.* Ottawa: National Council of Welfare.

National Council of Welfare. (2005b). *Welfare incomes: 2004.* Ottawa: National Council of Welfare.

National Council of Welfare. (2010). *Welfare incomes: 2009.* Ottawa: National Council of Welfare.

Neysmith, S., Bezanson, K., and O'Connell, A. (2005). *Telling tales: Living the effects of public policy.* Halifax: Fernwood Publishing.

Organisation for Economic Co-operation and Development. (1999). *The battle against exclusion: Social assistance in Canada and Switzerland.* Paris: OECD.

Organisation for Economic Co-operation and Development. (2009). *Society at a glance: OECD social indicators* (2009 ed.). Paris: OECD.

Reid, C. (2004). *The wounds of exclusion: Poverty, women's health, and social justice.* Edmonton: Qualitative Institute Press.

Roos, N. P., and Mustard, C. A. (1997). Variation in health care use by socioeconomic status in Winnipeg, Canada: Does the system work well? Yes and no. *Milbank Quarterly, 75*(1), 89–111.

Saint-Arnaud, S., and Bernard, P. (2003). Convergence or resilience? A hierarchial cluster analysis of the welfare regimes in advanced countries. *Current Sociology, 51*(5), 499–527.

Sanmartin, C., and Ng, E. (2004). *Joint Canada/United States survey of health, 2002–03.* Ottawa: Statistics Canada.

Schoen, C., and Doty, M. M. (2004). Inequities in access to medical care in five countries: Findings from the 2001 Commonwealth Fund international health policy study. *Health Policy, 67,* 309–322.

Service Canada. (2010). *Employment insurance regular benefits.* Retrieved March 31, 2011 from www.servicecanada.gc.ca/eng/ei/types/regular.shtml#eligible

Tremblay, D. G. (2009). Precarious work and the labour market. In D. Raphael (Ed.), *Social determinants of health: Canadian perspectives* (2nd ed., pp. 75–87). Toronto: Canadian Scholars' Press Inc.

Wallace, B., Klein, S., and Reitsma-Street, M. (2006). *Denied assistance: Closing the front door on welfare in BC.* Vancouver: Canadian Centre for Policy Alternatives.

Wilkins, R., Berthclot, J.-M., and Ng, E. (2002). Trends in mortality by neighbourhood income in urban Canada from 1971–1996. *Supplement to Health Reports, 13,* 1–28.

Wilkins, R. (2007). *Mortality by neighbourhood income in urban Canada from 1971–2001.* Statistics Canada Health Analysis Group. Ottawa: Statistics Canada.

Part III

Poverty, Health, and Quality of Life

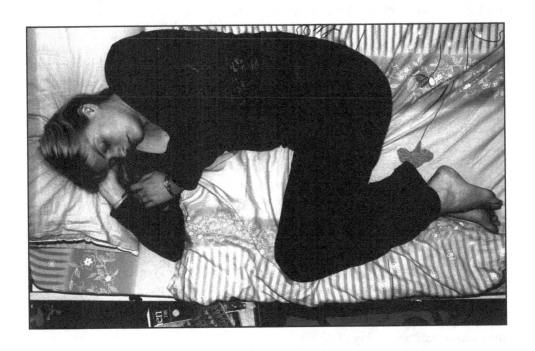

PART III PROVIDES DETAILS CONCERNING THE HEALTH AND QUALITY-of-life effects of living in poverty. These effects occur at the individual, community, and societal levels. That they are so profound suggests that the presence of high levels of poverty in Canada pose the greatest threat to the health and quality of life of Canadians.

Chapter 8, "Poverty and Health," reviews the emerging literature on the effects of material and social deprivation associated with poverty on the development of a wide range of diseases. The incidence and death from heart disease, diabetes, and mental illness are strongly related to whether one lives in poverty. The effects on health of the living conditions associated with living in poverty are far more important than the bio-medical and lifestyle risk factors that command the primary attention of policy-makers, the media, and the public. The reasons for the overemphasis on lifestyle issues such as diet, physical activity, and tobacco use are explored, and means of drawing attention to the poverty and health relationship are identified.

Chapter 9, "Poverty and Health: Mechanisms and Pathways," discusses the latest research that considers how the experience of poverty leads to poor health among individuals, communities, and entire jurisdictions. It considers a variety of models that examine how living conditions come to "get under the skin" to shape health. These include what are called materialist, psychosocial comparison, and neo-materialist approaches. How poverty comes to influence health is also considered by applying models of the physiological and psychological processes that occur as a result of living in poverty. To understand how poverty comes about and comes to influence health, models of political economy that consider the distribution of resources among the population and the forces that shape that distribution are also presented.

Chapter 10, "Poverty and Quality of Life," expands the discussion of the health effects of poverty into non-medical areas that consider individual, family, community, and even societal well-being. Living in poverty is seen as influencing a wide range of developmental, psychological, and community indicators of quality of life. These findings are supplemented by various indicators provided by non-governmental organizations such as the Federation of Canadian Municipalities, United Ways across Canada, and the Conference Board of Canada. Of particular interest is how the experience of living in poverty is associated with the incidence of crime, social breakdown, and other indicators of adverse quality of life.

Chapter Eight

Poverty and Health

In the prospect of poverty there is nothing but gloom and melancholy.—Samuel Johnson

Learning Objectives

At the conclusion of this chapter, the reader will be able to:

- describe the different means by which the poverty and health relationship is documented;
- provide details concerning the health status of people living in poverty;
- explain how poverty affects the health of children in the present and in later life;
- identify how risk factor approaches divert attention away from the health-threatening living conditions experienced by those living in poverty;
- explain why poverty and health issues receive such scant attention by policy-makers, health professionals, and the media; and
- identify means by which this neglect could be rectified.

Introduction

The poverty and poor-health relationship is one of the most robust associations known to the health and social sciences. But does living in poverty *cause* poor health? Perhaps living in poverty *results* from poor health. Maybe both living in poverty and experiencing poor health reflect a common origin, such as poor genes or unhealthy habits. In this chapter, conclusive evidence is presented that poverty—and the material and social deprivation associated with it—is a primary cause of poor health among Canadians. The evidence for this assertion comes from hundreds of studies in Canada and elsewhere that have employed a wide range of methods.

Studies show that the living conditions experienced by those living in poverty are associated with a very wide range of health indicators. Poverty is a strong predictor of life expectancy and an individual's perceptions of their health. Poverty predicts the incidence of, and death from, a staggeringly wide range of diseases. Poverty also predicts incidence of and death from injuries, levels of health literacy, and use of health services. And experiencing poverty during childhood is not just a good predictor of poor health in childhood, but also a good predictor of health problems during adulthood.

Despite this accumulated evidence, relatively little attention is given to poverty and the living conditions associated with poverty as an important health issue by elected representatives, health care and public health officials, and the media. Instead, focus is usually on the risk behaviours people living in poverty engage in, such as physical inactivity, poor diet, and tobacco and alcohol use. There is an assumption that addressing these behaviours would ameliorate the primary health-threatening aspects of poverty. This focus is common despite evidence indicating that these risk behaviours play a relatively small role in shaping the poor health outcomes that people living in poverty experience.

In this chapter, the evidence concerning the poverty and health relationship is reviewed. Focus is upon the health of Canadians living in poverty. Data on the health of groups known to have a higher incidence of poverty—such as Aboriginal peoples, people of colour, women, and recent immigrants—are also presented. The conclusion reached is that the living conditions associated with poverty—rather than the risk behaviours of people living in poverty—are the primary cause of poor health among these Canadians. The reasons for the neglect by policy-makers and the media of living in poverty as a primary cause of poor health are explored, and actions to rectify this neglect are presented.

Identifying Poverty as a Cause of Poor Health

There are many ways to show that a factor such as living in poverty is a cause of poor health status. First, the terms *poverty* and *health status* have to be defined. Canadian researchers usually examine individuals' levels of income and identify those at the bottom 20% of the distribution, or some similar variant, as living on low incomes or living in poverty. Some researchers identify those living below the low income cut-offs as living in poverty (Raphael et al., 2005).

Health status is usually measured by self-reported health status or the presence of a disease or affliction. Morbidity rates refer to the incidence (new cases of a disease or affliction in a year) or prevalence (the number of total cases) of a group reported each year. Mortality rates refer to death rates for specific diseases and are also commonly used. Mortality rates involve calculating the death rates or proportion of a population of a group that succumbs to a disease or affliction in a given year. In all these calculations, the age of the study group is taken into account to compensate for the increased morbidity and mortality rates experienced by people of advancing age.

The simplest way to examine the relationship between poverty and health is to identify a group of people—either individuals or families living in poverty—and compare their scores on a number of health indicators to the scores of a group of people not living in poverty. The differences observed are then subjected to a statistical test to ascertain whether these differences occurred by chance. If these differences have not occurred by chance, then they could be attributed to the experience of one group living in poverty and the other group not living in poverty.

A variant of this approach is to look at a large group of people and identify the income of each person or family and their scores on a number of health measures. A statistical measure of association is then calculated to show the relationship between income and health status. These income and health scores can be plotted against each other. Those whose income is at the lower end of the income distribution are identified as living in poverty, and their health status scores are examined.

These kinds of studies collect data at a single point in time and are called cross-sectional studies. These are correlational studies in that they can show an association between poverty and health at one point in time, but cannot be relied upon by themselves to demonstrate causation between poverty and health status; that is, to conclusively demonstrate that living in poverty causes poor health.[1] Most studies of health status in Canada are these kinds of studies (Raphael et al., 2005).

The kind of study more able to show that living in poverty causes poor health status is called a longitudinal or panel study. In this kind of study, information is collected on individuals over a period of time. By collecting and analyzing a variety of kinds of data at differing points of time, it can be determined which factor precedes the other. If living in poverty is the cause of poor health status, then it would be expected that deterioration in health would be seen after the onset of living in poverty. Similarly, if conditions of material and social deprivation are the cause of both immediate and future poor health status, it would be expected that experiencing poverty as a child would predict not only poor health status during childhood but also poor health status in adulthood.

A third kind of study can illuminate how living in poverty causes poor health. This is called an ethnographic or qualitative study. In this type of study, there is an attempt to understand the lived experiences of people in order to identify the means by which living in poverty leads to poor health. People talk about their own lives and how living in poverty affects their health and well-being. Evidence is validated by hearing the same themes in the stories obtained from other people in similar circumstances; by researchers documenting their own observations of the poverty experience; and by the plausibility of the information provided by the respondents. Chapter 6 in this volume provides this kind of data.

Virtually every Canadian or other study that includes indicators of poverty and health status finds poverty to be strongly associated with poor health status (Raphael et al., 2003). The longitudinal studies that allow causation to be inferred find the experiences associated with living in poverty to be a primary cause of poor health status in children, youth, adults, and older individuals (Benzeval and Judge, 2001; Davey Smith, 2003; Davey Smith and Gordon, 2000; Kuh and Ben-Shilmo, 1997). To date, the most persuasive longitudinal studies documenting poverty as the cause of poor health status have been done outside Canada. There are few longitudinal studies of poverty and health in Canada. But every study done within Canada finds poverty to be a reliable and strong predictor of poor health status, however defined (Canadian Population Health Initiative, 2004; Phipps, 2002).

An overview of 252 Canadian studies describes how researchers apply various methodologies to define income, poverty, and health and demonstrate the association among these measures (Raphael et al., 2003; Raphael et al., 2005). In this chapter, the emphasis is on traditional epidemiological studies that utilize quantitative measures to document the poverty and health-status relationship. The studies presented here are primarily cross-sectional—with some longitudinal surveys—that analyze how the experience of poverty predicts scores on health status indicators such as life expectancy, morbidity, and mortality rates associated with various diseases, and individuals' reports of their own health status.

Poverty and Its Relationship to Health

Living in poverty is an especially important determinant of health. Living in poverty also serves as a marker of specific experiences with many social determinants of health (Shaw, Dorling, Gordon, and Smith, 1999).[2] In addition to serving as an indicator of the experience of material and social deprivation, living in poverty is a determinant of the quality of early life (Browne, 2004); education (Ungerleider, Burns, and Cartwright, 2009); employment and working conditions (Jackson, 2009; Tremblay, 2009); and food security (McIntyre and Rondeau, 2009). Living in poverty is also a determinant of the quality of housing (Bryant, 2009); of the need for a social safety net (Armstrong, 2009); of social exclusion (Galabuzi, 2009); and of unemployment and employment insecurity across the life span (Tremblay, 2009).

Income is the best predictor of just about every health indicator that describes Canadians (Auger and Alix, 2009). While income is related to health indicators across all levels of income, from very poor to very wealthy, it appears that income exerts its greatest effects upon those living in poverty (Graham, 2004; Lynch, Kaplan, and Salonen, 1997; Ross and Roberts, 1999; Wilkins, Berthelot, and Ng, 2002; Wilkins, Houle, Berthelot, and Ross, 2000). That is, the gap in health outcomes between people living in poverty and those on the step above on the income ladder is greater than the health differences on the other rungs of the ladder. Children's health is especially vulnerable to conditions of living in poverty (Raphael, 2010). Chronic diseases such as coronary heart disease and type 2 diabetes are strongly related to living in poverty, as is the incidence of respiratory disease, lung cancer, and some other cancers (Davey Smith, 2003; Raphael, Anstice, and Raine, 2003; Raphael and Farrell, 2002).

Life Expectancy and Premature Mortality in Urban Canada

The most definitive work in Canada on income and health is done by Wilkins and colleagues (Wilkins et al., 2002; Wilkins, 2007) at Statistics Canada, who study mortality from various diseases among residents in urban Canada. Data on Canadians' income is not routinely collected at time of death, so these researchers examine the relationship between income, age, and cause of death by drawing upon the deceased's census tract to estimate their income. First, urban neighbourhoods are placed in one of five quintiles based on the number of people living below Statistics Canada's low income cut-offs (which correlates very well with average income) as provided by the Canadian Census. The first quintile therefore includes the areas where the average income is the highest; the fifth quintile includes those where the average income is the lowest. Analyses reveal that in 2001, 5.5% of people living in the first quintile, 10.1% of those in the second quintile, 15.3% of those in the third quintile, 22.1% of those in the fourth quintile, and 35.4% of those in the fifth quintile were living in poverty, as defined by Canada's low income cut-offs.

Then, based on information available from hospital records, life expectancies and infant mortality rates for the areas within each income quintile are calculated. The relationships among premature years of life lost prior to age 75, cause of death, and the income level of the neighbourhood in which the deceased lived is assessed. There may be error in these analyses that relate income to mortality based on residential area, since some people living in poverty live in well-off neighbourhoods and vice versa. Essentially, these analyses are *conservative* estimates of the relationship between income level and mortality rates. The income and health relationship is probably stronger than indicated by Wilkins' and colleagues' data.

In 2001, life expectancy differed widely among urban neighbourhoods of varying incomes. Lower life expectancy was especially likely among the fifth or lowest income quintile of neighbourhoods. Among males in this lowest income quintile, life expectancy of 74.7 years was 2.4 years shorter than the next quintile group, and 4.3 years shorter than males in the wealthiest quintile group (see Figure 1.1 in Chapter 1). Females living in the lowest income quintile had a life expectancy of 80.9 years, which was 1.4 years less that those in the next group, and 1.9 years shorter than the wealthiest income quintile.

A particularly interesting finding was that the gap in life expectancy between men and women is 6.2 years in the fifth, or poorest, income quintile group. It is less so in the fourth (5.2 years) and third income quintile (4.8 years), even less in the second income quintile (4.2 years) and least in the wealthiest income quintile (3.9 years). Income interacts with gender to predict life expectancy. Poverty seems to be a much stronger threat to life expectancy for men than for women.

These differences in life expectancy reflect findings that Canadians living within the poorest 20% of urban neighbourhoods die earlier than other Canadians from a wide range of diseases, such as cardiovascular disease, cancer, diabetes, and respiratory diseases, among others (Wilkins et al., 2002; Wilkins, 2007). Table 8.1 provides specific findings of income-related differences in mortality.

As shown in Table 8.1, the burden of ill health is concentrated in the lowest income quintile of neighbourhoods in urban Canada. For just about every cause of death, the poorest neighbourhoods fare much worse than the others. Table 8.1 shows death rates by quintile for various causes, with Q1 being the richest quintile, and Q5, the poorest. RR shows the ratio of premature years lost between the Q1 and Q5 quintiles. RD shows how many years are lost between the Q1 and Q5 quintiles. Excess figures show how many years are lost between the richest quintile and all others, and the final column shows the percentage of all premature years of life lost that can be attributed to differences between the richest and the other quintiles.

The "% Excess" column provides an indicator of which afflictions are particularly related to poverty and/or income inequalities. While overall there is a 10% excess for all causes of mortality related to income differences, excess deaths from afflictions that are

Table 8.1: Age-Standardized Mortality Rates per 100,000 Population, for Both Sexes and for Males and Females for Selected Causes of Death by Neighbourhood Income Quintile, Urban Canada, 2001

Cause of Death	Q1	Q2	Q3	Q4	Q5	RR[1]	RD[2]	Excess[3]	% Excess[4]
				Both Sexes					
All Causes	417.2	426.8	447.8	466.2	551.8	1.32	134.7	46.0	9.9
Circulatory Diseases	128.4	130.1	135.1	140.6	168.5	1.31	40.2	12.5	8.9
Diabetes	10.7	13.3	13.7	15.9	19.5	1.82	8.8	4.1	27.5
Homicide	.9	1.2	1.2	1.8	2.5	2.89	1.7	0.7	44.1
Ill-Defined Conditions	5.1	5.2	6.1	7.5	10.7	2.11	5.6	1.8	26.5
Infectious Diseases	5.1	6.3	6.7	8.8	12.6	2.48	7.5	2.8	35.9
Injury and Poisoning	26.9	27.3	28.7	30.8	43.0	1.60	16.1	4.7	14.0
Neoplasms	143.7	148.4	151.8	155.8	170.0	1.18	26.3	10.4	6.7
Perinatal Conditions	4.1	3.4	4.5	4.7	5.6	1.36	1.5	0.4	9.5
Suicide	7.5	9.2	9.6	11.2	14.2	1.91	6.8	3.0	28.6
				Males					
All Causes	514.6	536.6	574.1	605.5	724.5	1.41	209.8	78.4	13.2
Circulatory Diseases	164.4	172.4	181.5	189.5	228.1	1.39	63.7	23.3	12.4
Diabetes	13.2	15.4	16.5	21.2	24.6	1.86	11.4	5.1	27.8
Homicide	1.4	1.7	1.6	2.7	4.1	3.0	2.7	1.0	42.3
Ill-Defined Conditions	6.3	6.6	7.8	10.0	13.8	2.20	7.5	2.7	29.9
Infectious Diseases	5.9	8.1	9.0	11.5	18.1	3.08	12.2	4.7	44.3
Injury and Poisoning	39.3	40.6	42.2	45.1	63.6	1.62	24.3	7.4	15.9
Neoplasms	171.4	179.4	190.1	195.8	217.5	1.27	46.2	19.5	10.2
Perinatal Conditions	4.5	3.7	5.3	5.5	6.3	1.42	1.9	0.7	13.3
Suicide	12.3	15.2	15.0	16.9	21.8	1.78	9.6	4.1	25.2

| Cause of Death | Females | | | | | | | | |
	Q1	Q2	Q3	Q4	Q5	RR[1]	RD[2]	Excess[3]	% Excess[4]
All Causes	349.4	349.5	357.4	365.2	421.9	1.21	72.6	20.1	5.4
Circulatory Diseases	102.9	100.6	102.2	105.5	124.6	1.21	21.7	4.6	4.3
Diabetes	8.9	11.8	11.6	11.9	15.7	1.77	6.8	3.2	26.7
Homicide	0.4	0.8	0.8	0.9	1.0	2.36	0.6	0.4	46.5
Ill-Defined Conditions	3.9	3.8	4.7	5.3	7.9	2.01	4.0	1.1	22.5
Infectious Diseases	4.4	4.8	5.0	6.4	7.6	1.72	3.2	1.2	22.1
Injury and Poisoning	15.4	15.0	16.4	17.8	24.1	1.57	8.7	2.4	13.3
Neoplasms	127.1	129.4	126.5	128.6	136.6	1.07	9.5	2.7	2.1
Perinatal Conditions	3.7	3.0	3.7	3.9	4.8	1.30	1.1	0.2	4.1
Suicide	3.1	3.5	4.6	5.9	7.0	2.27	3.9	1.7	35.8

1 Inter-quintile rate ratio (Q5/Q1). This is the difference in mortality rates between the poorest to richest neighbourhoods.

2 Inter-quintile rate difference (Q5–Q1). This is the difference in mortality rates between the poorest and richest neighbourhoods.

3 Population-attributable risk (Total–Q1). This is the difference in mortality rates associated with income differences between the richest neighbourhoods and all others.

4 Population-attributable risk percentage [100 × (Total − Q1)/Total]. This is the percentage of mortality rates associated with differences between the rates of the richest neighbourhoods and all others.

Source: Adapted from Statistics Canada, Mortality by neighbourhood income in urban Canada from 1971 to 1996, Health Reports – Supplement, 82-003-SIE2002001, Vol. 13, July 2002; http://www.statcan. gc.ca/bsolc/olc-cel/olc-cel?catno=82-003-SIE&lang=eng

particularly related to income differences are diabetes, homicide, ill-defined conditions, infectious diseases, and suicides.

The overall effect of income differences on premature years of life lost (prior to age 75) in urban Canada was calculated (Wilkins, 2007). In 2001, 20.4% of years of life lost for all causes prior to age 75 in Canada could be attributed to income differences. This figure is obtained by using the mortality rates in the wealthiest or first quintile of neighbourhoods as a baseline and considering all deaths above that rate to be excess related to income differences. The magnitude of income effects (20.4%) approaches or exceeds that associated with the major killers such as cancers (32.6%) and heart disease (16.5%).

Excess in mortality associated with income manifests itself in a wide range of diseases. Wilkins and colleagues took the excess years of life lost associated with income differences and examined which diseases these were associated with. They found that 25.2% of this income-related excess manifests itself in circulatory disorders, 17.0% in deaths from injuries, and 13.8% with cancers.

Related Studies of Income and Health

The data for infant mortality and low birth-weight rates showed similar trends (see Figure 8.1). The gap between the lowest income quintile and the next quintile was the largest for infant mortality and low birth-weight rates. The infant mortality rate and low birth-weight rates are 40% higher in the poorest income quintile than in the richest quintile area.

An Ontario study reinforces the finding of the strong effect of income upon health status. In this study, self-reported health status as well as an objective measure of func-

Figure 8.1: Infant Mortality (per 1,000), 2001 and Low Birth-Weight Rates (per 100), 1996 by Income Quintile of Neighbourhood, Urban Canada

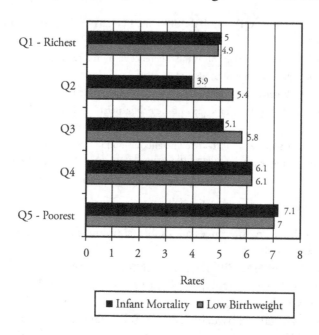

Source: Adapted from Wilkins, R. (2007). *Mortality by neighbourhood income in urban Canada from 1971 to 2001*. Ottawa: Statistics Canada, Health Analysis and Measurement Group and Wilkins, R., Houle, C. Berthelot, J.M., & Ross, D.P. (2000). The changing health status of Canada's children, ISUMA, 1(2), p. 61.

tional health (e.g., vision, sight, mobility, pain, etc.) was examined in relation to both personal and area variables (Xi, McDowell, Nair, and Spasoff, 2005). Findings indicate that individual level of income was a primary determinant of both self-reported and functional health (see Figure 8.2). Self-reported health is exactly that: a person rates his or her health as excellent, very good, good, fair, or poor. Functional health is an objective measure of motor, sensory, and pain-related health.

The analysis showed that being of low income gave an individual an almost 4 times greater risk of reporting fair or poor health than high-income individuals. An individual of low income also had a 2.5 times greater risk of having poor scores on the health utilities index. These low-income effects were much stronger than the effects of no regular exercise, smoking, and having less education. Income-related health inequalities such as these are generally higher in Canada than would be expected from income-distribution and health

Figure 8.2: Odds Ratios for Risk Factors Associated with Self-Rated Fair or Poor Health, and Low Scores (<50 percentile) on the Health Utilities Index (HUI), Ontario

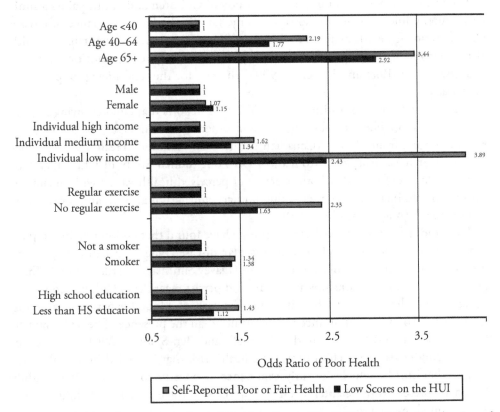

Source: Adapted from "Income Inequality and Health in Ontario," by G. Xi et al., 2005, *Canadian Journal of Public Health*, 96, p.209–210.

data derived from other nations (Humphries and van Doorslaer, 2000). This may have to do with Canada's generally less-developed social safety net and general approach to economic and social provision, compared to other wealthy industrialized nations.

Poverty and the Health of Children

Living in poverty has important health consequences for children and for their health as adults (Canadian Institute on Children's Health, 2000; Raphael, 2010). As noted earlier, the infant mortality rates of those living in the poorest 20% of Canadian urban areas is 40% higher than the wealthiest 20% of Canadians as is the low-birth weight (Wilkins et al., 2000; Wilkins, 2007). Low birth weight (weight <2500 grams) is a very important measure of health status, as it is consistently related to the experience of chronic disease such as heart disease and type 2 diabetes in adulthood (Raphael et al., 2003; Raphael and Farrell, 2002). Wilkins reports that the low birth-weight rates range from 4.9% in the wealthiest urban areas to 7.0% percent in the poorest quintile of urban neighbourhoods in Canada (Wilkins et al., 2000).

Data from the National Longitudinal Study of Children and Youth paints a similar picture. Children from the lowest income families had a 13% chance of having poor functional health as measured by a composite measure of eight basic health attributes: vision, hearing, speech, mobility, dexterity, cognition, emotion, and pain and discomfort (Ross and Roberts, 1999). The rate for the wealthiest group of children was only 5%.

Indeed, the Canadian Institute for Child Health reports that children living in poverty are the most likely to have asthma and other chronic diseases, visit emergency rooms, and die from injuries (Canadian Institute on Children's Health, 2000). Quebecois researchers, using data from the 1998 Longitudinal Study of Child Development in Québec, found that both overall and perceived health varied with income in five-month-old infants, even after taking into account health at birth and other socio-demographics (Auger and Alix, 2009).

Longitudinal studies carried out in Europe have found that children living in poverty are more likely to develop cardiovascular disease, type 2 diabetes, respiratory problems, and some forms of cancer as adults (Davey Smith and Gordon, 2000). These poverty and health relationships are robust and persist regardless of adult income status as adults. These same findings indicate that early childhood experiences of living in poverty are of more importance to later health than the presence of behavioural risk factors in adulthood (Davey Smith, Grunnell, and Ben-Shlomo, 2001). In essence, experiencing poverty as a child provides a health risk that is carried into adulthood. The mechanisms by which the early experience of poverty comes to influence adult health are presented in Chapter 9. Other correlates of the experience of child poverty are presented in Chapter 10.

Chronic Disease and Poverty: Cardiovascular Disease and Type 2 Diabetes

Findings from an examination of the precursors of the incidence and death from cardiovascular disease and type 2, or adult-onset, diabetes further illustrate the poverty and health association. Wilkins et al. (2002) found cardiovascular disease to have the greatest association with the experience of poverty. Many Canadian and other studies report similar findings (Raphael, 2002). A Canadian study examined the relationship between income and deaths due to hypertensive and rheumatic heart disease, among others (Wood, Sallar, Schechter, and Hogg, 1999). Men in the lowest income group in British Columbia had a death rate from hypertensive disease of 2.3/100,000, compared to 0.8/100,000 for the highest income group: a ratio of almost 3:1. For rheumatic heart disease, the comparative figures were 1.2/100,000 and 0.9/100,000—a ratio of 1.3:1, indicating a 30% greater risk of death for low-income men. The authors state:

> For almost every cause of death examined, the rate of mortality was higher in individuals of lower social and socioeconomic classes than individuals of the upper social and economic classes. This trend was most noticeable in deaths due to hypertensive heart disease, tuberculosis, asthma, and pneumonia and bronchitis. (Wood et al., 1999, p. 1755)

A study in Manitoba found death rates from ischemic heart disease to be 43% higher in the lowest income quintile as compared with the highest (Roos and Mustard, 1997). And one very detailed study looked at the relationship of median income of neighbourhood and the incidence of, and survival from, acute myocardial infarction (heart attack) among 51,000 Ontario patients admitted to hospital from 1994–1997 (Alter, Naylor, Austin, and Tu, 1999). Ontario neighbourhoods were categorized into five quintiles as a function of median income. Anyone who had suffered a heart attack within the previous year was excluded, as were those less than 20 or more than 105 years of age. The number of heart attack admissions for the wealthiest quintile of Ontario neighbourhoods was 4,614. For the next quintile, the number was 8,090 and for the middle quintile, 11,837. However, the number of admissions for the fourth, or second-poorest, quintile was 13,935, and for the poorest quintile, 13,115. One-year survival rates were higher for those in the wealthier neighbourhoods (82%) as compared to those in the poorest areas (76.4%).

This same study also found—consistent with findings presented in Chapter 7—pronounced differences in access to specialized cardiac services as a function of the income status of patients. Those patients who were from more well-off neighbourhoods had greater rates of coronary angiography and shorter waiting times for catheterization. These findings were not a function of severity of illness, the speciality of the attending physician, or the characteristics of the hospital, but rather the income level of the patient. This finding of differential treatment of people as a function of their income level is common (Williamson and Fast, 1998).

As noted, numerous longitudinal studies (usually European) document how low income precedes the incidence of, and death from, cardiovascular disease. In Canada, there is very limited data that considers in detail how low income leads to the incidence of cardiovascular disease. The 1996/1997 National Population Health Survey found that those with heart disease had almost a two times greater chance of living in poverty than those Canadians without heart disease, but these individuals were also more likely to not be working, making a causative inference of low income leading to incidence of heart disease difficult. But data from the 1998/1999 National Population Health Survey provides evidence in support of the poverty-causes-poor health hypothesis (Chen, 1999).

Middle-aged Canadians were identified who reported a decline in their health status from 1994–1995 to 1998–1999. Being in the lowest and the lower-middle income groups was associated with an 80% greater chance of reporting a decline in health over that period. In addition, being in the upper-middle and highest income group was associated with twice the chance of reporting an improvement in health status. While disease can lead to lower income, carefully designed studies such as those described above clearly indicate that low income—or poverty—serves as a predictor of disease (Davey Smith, Ben-Shlomo, and Lynch, 2002; Raphael, 2002).

Diabetes

Diabetes mellitus is a common chronic disease that affects over 2 million Canadians (Hux, Booth, and Laupacis, 2002). All forms of diabetes are characterized by the presence of high blood glucose (hyperglycemia) due to defective insulin secretion, insulin action, or both. During an acute episode, coma and even death may result from blood sugar that is very high or very low, due to medication overdoses. Chronic hyperglycemia may lead to serious complications including damage to the heart, kidneys, eyes, nerves, and blood vessels. The treatment for diabetes rests on blood glucose (glycemic) control, to be achieved with diet, exercise, and medications—the "three pillars" of the diabetes management regimen.

Diabetes mellitus is classified into three main types: type 1 or juvenile diabetes, gestational diabetes, and type 2 or mature-onset diabetes. Juvenile diabetes usually develops during childhood, and its onset is generally acute. It occurs when the pancreas fails to produce insulin, often as a result of autoimmune damage. Gestational diabetes is a temporary condition of glucose intolerance during pregnancy and is often a precursor of type 2 diabetes later in life. Type 2 diabetes usually develops during adulthood, although age of incidence is decreasing, and results from predominant insulin resistance with relative insulin deficiency, to a predominant secretory defect with insulin resistance. Onset can be insidious, as insulin secretion may decline gradually. Type 2 affects approximately 90% of Canadians diagnosed with diabetes.

An examination of the distribution of diabetes in the population reveals a disproportionate burden among low-income—including Aboriginal—Canadians (Hux et al., 2002; Young, Reading, Elias, and O'Neil, 2000). Data from the Institute for Clinical

Evaluation Sciences indicate that, in Ontario, the prevalence rate for diabetes is four times greater among women in low-income communities than among those living in high-income communities (Hux et al., 2002). The rate for males in low-income communities is 40% higher, and among lower-middle-income communities, 50% higher than in well-off communities, still very significant figures. Cross-Canadian data indicates that the prevalence of diabetes mellitus among Canadians aged 45–64 years with household incomes of $10,000–29,999 is twice (6%) that of those living in households with incomes of $60,000 or more (3%).

Wilkins (2007) provides striking evidence of how increases in mortality rates from diabetes among Canadians since the mid-1980s have been especially great among Canadians living in urban low-income communities (see Figures 8.3a and 8.3b). Wilkins and colleagues (2002) describe earlier findings—which have since grown worse—regarding diabetes mortality in urban Canada as follows:

> For diabetes among males, mortality rates for most quintiles decreased from 1971 to 1986, but then increased from 1986 to 1996. Because the increases in the latter period were especially large for the poorest quintiles, the inter-quintile rate differences widened from 1986 to 1996. For diabetes among females, mortality rates for all quintiles declined from 1971 to 1986 and then changed little from 1986 to 1996, except for the poorest quintile, in which rates increased rapidly. Therefore, the inter-quintile rate difference was considerably greater in 1996 than it had been in 1986. The trends with respect to the overall rates and socio-economic disparities in diabetes mortality are disquieting and deserve further study. (p. 19)

A recent analysis provides striking evidence of how the incidence of diabetes is related to living in poverty but also how this relationship is also related to visible minority status. Figures 8.4a, 8.4b, and 8.4c depict the incidence of diabetes, depth of poverty, and proportion of residents who are visible minorities for the City of Toronto. They are almost identical. What this indicates is that poverty is clearly related to diabetes and that those most likely to be poor *and* have diabetes are members of visible minority groups. Dinca-Panaitescua and colleagues provide evidence that poverty is not only strongly related to the presence of type 2 diabetes but is also a precursor to its onset (Dinca-Panaitescua et al., in press, 2010).

Suicide

Suicide rates are strikingly higher for Canadians living within the poorest urban income-quintile areas (Wilkins, 2007). In 2001, the age-standardized death rate for males in the poorest income quintile was 21.8 per 100,000, compared to 12.3 per 100,000 for the richest income quintile. Suicide rate for the poorest quintile of females was 7 per 100,000, compared to 3.1 per 100,000 for females in the richest quintile.

Similar figures are seen for the prevalence of major depression in Canada, where low-income individuals have a rate of 8.5% compared to the 3.7% rate for higher income

Figure 8.3a: Diabetes Mortality, Urban Canada, Males 1971–2001

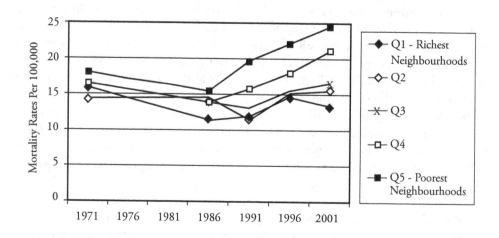

Source: R. Wilkins, "Mortality by neighbourhood income in urban Canada from 1971 to 2001," from the Health Analysis Measurement Group (HAMG), HAMG Seminar and special compilations (Ottawa: Statistics Canada).

Figure 8.3b: Diabetes Mortality, Urban Canada, 1971–2001, Females

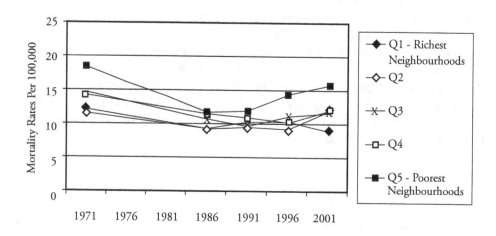

Source: R. Wilkins, "Mortality by neighbourhood income in urban Canada from 1971 to 2001," from the Health Analysis Measurement Group (HAMG), HAMG Seminar and special compilations (Ottawa: Statistics Canada).

Figure 8.4a: Where Diabetes Hits Hardest

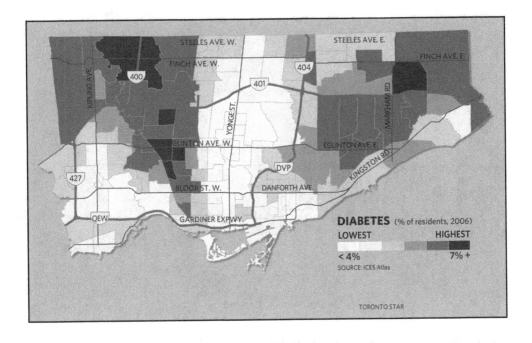

Figure 8.4b: Visible Minorities

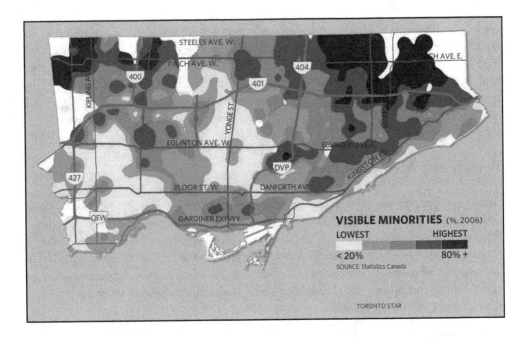

Figure 8.4c: Poverty in the City

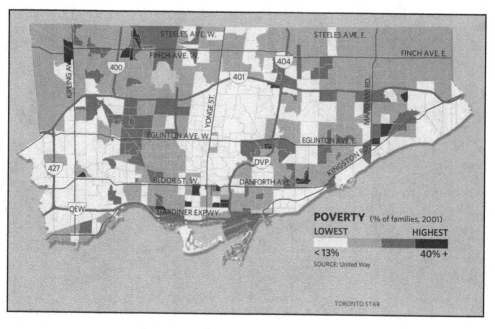

Source: *Toronto Star*, www.thestar.com/staticcontent/772097 (reproduced with permission) using data from the United Way of Greater Toronto (2004) (poverty), Institute for Clinical Evaluation Sciences (Glazier et al., 2007) (diabetes), and Statistics Canada (Charron, 2009) (visible minorities).

Canadians (Patten et al., 2006). Another study found that prevalence of depression in 25 major Canadian cities was higher among low-income males (10.8%) and females (17%) than among middle- and high-income males (6.5%) and females (11.0%) (Smith, Matheson, Moineddin, and Glazier, 2007). A report from Health Canada concludes: "Low income is an important risk factor for becoming psychologically distressed, and stressors account for part of this increased risk" (Orpana, Lemyre, and Gravel, 2009, abstract).

Poverty and Aboriginal Health

Aboriginal peoples are more likely to be living in poverty (Wilson and MacDonald, 2010), and they also show greater incidence of a range of afflictions and premature death from a variety of causes (Health Canada First Nations and Inuit Health Branch, 2003; Smiley, 2009). These greater incidences result from poverty and the poor quality of any number of social determinants of health (e.g., housing, food security, employment and working conditions, social exclusion, etc.), and reflect a history of exclusion from Canadian society (Smiley, 2009).

There is a large gap in mortality between the Aboriginal and the general Canadian population. In 1996–1997, mortality rates among First Nations and Inuit people were almost 1.5 times higher than the national rate (Shah, 2004). During this same period, infant mortality rates among First Nations people were close to 3.5 times the national rates. Neonatal death rates were double the general Canadian rates, and post-neonatal mortality rates were almost four times higher.

Furthermore, off-reserve Aboriginal people rate their health status lower than the overall Canadian population (Tjepkema, 2002). For every age group between 25 and 64, the proportions of Aboriginal people reporting fair or poor health is double that of the total population. The effect is more pronounced among Aboriginal women. For example, 41% of Aboriginal women aged 55–64 reported fair or poor health, compared with 19% of women in the same age group in the total Canadian population. Among those aged 65 and over, 45% of Aboriginal women reported fair or poor health, compared with 29% in the total female population. Poor economic and social conditions are responsible for these differences in health.

Health Inequalities Related to Gender

According to Health Canada (2002), average life expectancy at birth in 1999 was 79.0 years. Women had an average life expectancy of 81.7 years while men averaged 76.3. Women's apparent health advantage is not as obvious as it appears (Pederson, Raphael, and Johnson, 2010). Women report more frequent long-term disability and chronic conditions than men (DesMeules, Turner, and Cho, 2003). Ruiz and Verbrugge (1997) argue that the higher mortality rate and lower life expectancy of men compared to women can be misinterpreted to imply that women enjoy superior health, but this ignores the higher prevalence of chronic conditions in women, particularly in later life. Additionally, differences in men and women's health may be lessening. There may be a narrowing of the gender health gap in industrialized countries, which is due to men increasing their life expectancy.

Health Inequalities Related to Race and Immigrant Status

Recent immigrants to Canada and people of colour are especially at risk for experiencing poverty (Galabuzi, 2005). Literature has now emerged that shows inequalities in health exist between Canadians of European and non-European descent, between white Canadians and Canadians of colour, and between recent and non-recent immigrants. Cross-sectional and longitudinal data from the National Population Health Survey (Ng et al., 2004) provides compelling evidence that the health of immigrants to Canada—especially non-European or non-white immigrants—shows deterioration over time as compared to Canadian-born residents and European immigrants. Newbold and Danforth (1993) found immigrants to Canada were more likely to rate their health as poor or fair than non-immigrants and that this was especially the case for those who have been in Canada for longer periods of time.

To illustrate, a recent longitudinal analysis of National Population Health Survey data (Ng, Wilkins, Gendron, and Berthelot, 2004) categorized respondents into four groups: recent (10 years or less) European immigrants; recent non-European immigrants; long-term (more than 10 years) European immigrants; and long-term non-European immigrants. The likelihood that individuals reported a transition from good, very good, or excellent health to either fair or poor health over time in Canada was then examined.

As compared to the Canadian-born population, recent non-European immigrants were twice as likely to report a deterioration in health from 1993–1994 to 2002–2003. Long-term non-European immigrants were also more likely to report such health deterioration. There was no effect reported for either of the two European immigrant groups. Recent non-European immigrants were 50% more likely to become frequent visitors to doctors than the Canadian-born population. For each of these analyses, the health inequalities were related to various social determinants of health, such as income, employment, and degree of social exclusion.

Health Inequalities Related to Geographic Location

It is well established that where one lives is an important factor in health inequalities. Canadians living in Eastern Canada report generally poorer health than do Central Canadians, and Western Canadians show the best health status (Statistics Canada, 2001). Canadians living in rural areas show poorer health than do urban dwellers (Mitura and Bollman, 2003, 2004).

Statistics Canada recently examined the predictors of life expectancy, disability-free life expectancy, and the presence of fair or poor health among residents of 136 regions across Canada (Shields and Tremblay, 2002). The health predictors included socio-demographic factors (i.e., percentage of Aboriginal population, percentage of visible minority population, unemployment rate, population size, percentage of population aged 65 or over, average income, and average number of years of schooling). Other health predictors were rates of daily smoking, obesity, infrequent exercise, heavy drinking, high stress, and depression.

Behavioural factors were weak predictors of health status as compared to socio-demographic measures. While obesity rate predicted 1% of the variation and smoking rate 8% of the variation among communities in life expectancy, socio-demographic factors predicted 56% of variation in life expectancy. In terms of reports of fair or poor health, obesity predicted 10%, and smoking rate predicted 4% of variation among communities. But socio-demographic factors predicted 25% of the differences among communities.

This study also found that having less than secondary-school education increased the risk of reporting fair or poor health by 44%; that being a daily smoker increased the risk by 53%; and that being obese did so by 74% (Tremblay, Ross, and Berthelot,

2002). But being in the lowest income group increased the risk of reporting fair or poor health by more than 307%. And being of lower middle income did so by 238%. Even middle-income people had a 53% greater risk of fair or poor health as compared to the highest income group.

Poverty and HIV/AIDS

A recent review examined the relationship of income and poverty to HIV/AIDS (Spigelman, 2002). It was pointed out that there is little research that directly addresses the relationship but that findings seem to be very suggestive of such a link. People with low incomes are more likely "to be at risk of HIV infection, to have HIV/AIDS, to progress from HIV to AIDS and to succumb to AIDS more quickly." This conclusion was based on studies from the USA that show that low-income women in California had an HIV prevalence rate four times more than all women. A Health Canada–funded study found that gay men with incomes less than the poverty line were twice as likely as more affluent gay men to die within 10 years of contracting HIV. Another study found that those engaging in high-risk behaviours had lower incomes and were younger than non-risk takers. Young gay men with less than a high-school education were nearly twice as likely to be risk-takers. (See Box 8.1.)

Material and Social Deprivation and the Clustering of Disadvantage

The fact that living in poverty is associated with poor health is not in dispute. While the exact mechanisms by which disease results from poverty remain a focus of research, current evidence is converging around three main ways: the experience of material and social deprivation during early life and adulthood; the experience of excessive psycho-social stress; and the adoption of health-threatening behaviours. These mechanisms are presented in Chapter 9.

But also related to the poverty and health relationship is the clustering of disease and disadvantage. That is, living in poverty is associated with a wide range of health-threatening factors. Living in poverty leads to poor health because of the overall effects of poor life situations. UK researchers have argued that "[h]ealth inequalities are produced by the clustering of disadvantage—in opportunity, material circumstances, and behaviours related to health—across people's lives" (Shaw et al., 1999, p. 65).

Data from the Ministry of Health in Quebec illustrates this clustering of diseases (Auger and Alix, 2009). First, Auger and Alix collated health data from provincial vital statistics, registries, and surveys and analyzed these data on the basis of census tract classified into quintiles of area deprivation. As shown in Figure 8.5, strong relationships of health status with area income were seen. The lowest income quintile consistently had poorer measures of health. These measures included death from cancers, circulatory disease, respiratory disease, and injuries.

Box 8.1: Poverty Contributes to HIV/AIDS and HIV/AIDS Contributes to Poverty

Disclaimer:

Please note that the media release entitled "Poverty contributes to HIV/AIDS and HIV/AIDS contributes to Poverty" is dating back to October 15, 2004. The statistics written in this release have changed. Please refer to the Canadian AIDS Society website (http://www.cdnaids.ca) for a more up-to-date view on CAS' work and HIV/AIDS statistics in Canada.

October 17, International Day for the Eradication of Poverty

OTTAWA, ON, October 15, 2004—In 1987 the International Day for the Eradication of Poverty was born when thousands of people gathered at the Human Rights Plaza in Paris, France. The day, October 17, was formally recognized by the United Nations General Assembly in 1992. This year's Canadian theme is, "Together, We Go Further," which aims to bring together people from different walks of life to express our shared commitment to end poverty and to honour the efforts and accomplishments of those who struggle with poverty daily. The Canadian AIDS Society (CAS) is encouraging people to come together in the same spirit as those who gathered at the Human Rights Plaza in France and make it known that the HIV epidemic in Canada is also an epidemic of poverty. The marginalization of people living with and vulnerable to HIV that is associated with poverty is unacceptable, and it is time that governments of all levels took action to eliminate poverty. Policies that force people into poverty make people more vulnerable to HIV and significantly reduce the quality of life of people living with HIV.

In January of 2004, CAS began a 27-month project that will identify a strategy to combat the lack of comprehensive and accessible information about federal and provincial income security, employment support and health benefits for people living with HIV. The Income Security Project through partnerships and research will generate and disseminate information about current programs and benefits to people living with HIV/AIDS, community-based AIDS organizations, other anti-poverty and disability organizations, and to program administrators and policy makers.

It is estimated that approximately 56,000 Canadians are living with HIV/AIDS. Last year alone there were up to 5,000 new infections in Canada. Income insecurity and poverty play a key role in HIV transmission and progression. "For people living with HIV/AIDS, living in poverty means that they have more difficulty accessing the services that they need. Having medication doesn't mean much if someone has to worry about where their next meal will come from or doesn't have a safe place to call home," said Gail Flintoft, Chair of the Canadian AIDS Society Board of Directors. "People need to take notice of the consequences of poverty, and lobby for change. There is no cure for HIV/AIDS, but it is preventable, and it is time that poverty prevention is integrated into the AIDS movement."

To mark this International Day for the Eradication of Poverty, CAS as part of the Income Security Project is releasing its position statement on poverty and HIV/AIDS, as well as promoting a community inventory that will continue to be updated. In the near future, we will also release a set of fact sheets. The fact sheets illustrate three trends that are happening in Canada—living in poverty is a determinant of health that increases vulnerability to HIV, once diagnosed, people living with HIV are at risk of drifting into poverty, and living in poverty can speed up the progression of HIV. "We hope that this information will encourage dialogue among those living with HIV/AIDS, community-based AIDS organizations, anti-poverty and disability groups, policy makers, researchers and the medical community. Programs must be reformed to meet the real needs of those people they were created to help," said Paul Lapierre, Executive Director. "These fact sheets are only the beginning of our work to raise awareness about HIV and poverty. The AIDS community is joining the anti-poverty movement, because poverty has a serious, detrimental impact on individual and public health."

The Canadian AIDS Society is committed to advocating for increasing economic security for people living with HIV/AIDS, and other economically marginalized groups. CAS will continue to seek out partnerships with other community groups and individuals to increase awareness around the devastating impacts of poverty, and work within the community-based AIDS movement to support the innovative work that is occurring at the community level and lobby for minimum standards that ensure that the needs of all Canadians are met.

The Canadian AIDS Society is a coalition of 120 community-based AIDS organizations across Canada. The CAS mandate is to speak as a national voice and act as a forum for a community-based response to HIV infection, as well as to advocate for persons so affected.

Source: Canadian AIDS Society. (2004, October 15). *Poverty contributes to HIV/AIDS and HIV/AIDS contributes to poverty* [press release]. Retrieved March 11, 2011 from www.cdnaids.ca/web/pressreleases.nsf/cl/cas-news-0136

Another study illustrates the clustering of disadvantage, health outcomes, and various social indicators in Montreal. This study linked health data sets to the population census via the local community health centre (CLSC) that serviced the district. This was done by linking the census data to the 29 CLSC districts in Montreal, and these were grouped into six administrative sub-regions. These are West, West-Central, North, South-West, East-Central, and East. Morbidity and mortality were calculated for both CLSC districts and geographic sub-regions. Table 8.2 also shows how these health and social indicators are linked. It is clear that the South-West, East-Central, and East are the areas with the greatest health and social issues.

Figure 8.5: Standardized Mortality Ratio for All Deaths and for Four Leading Causes of Death, by Level of Material Deprivation in the Neighbourhood, Quebec, 2000

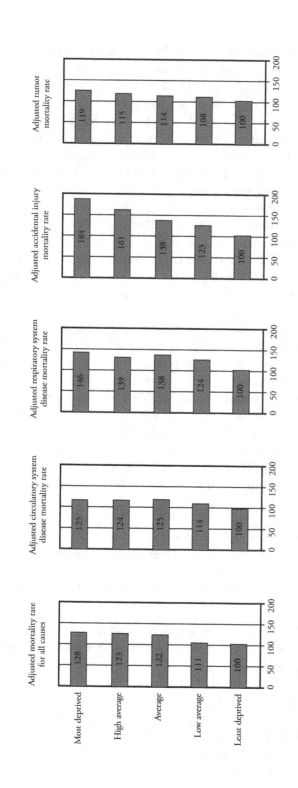

Sources: Minister of Health and Social Services. *Death registry, Québec, 2000–2004*: and Statistics Canada. *2001 Census, population counts.* Ottawa: Statistics Canada.

Table 8.2 shows that the South-West and East-Central areas are relatively poor and the West and West-Central areas are the most well-off. In the poorest—and worst health—areas, a majority of children under five years were under the low income cut-off. There were greater proportions of single-parent families and social assistance recipients. The two poorest areas reported the lowest neighbourhood quality of life and least neighbourhood safety.

Lessard and colleagues (2002) also report that the suicide rate was significantly higher in the East-Central area as compared to the West (i.e., the suicide mortality rate per 100,000 inhabitants was 23 versus 9). The pregnancy rate among adolescents was also much higher in poorer neighbourhoods (42.2 versus 16.1 per 1,000 persons 14–17 years of age).

Table 8.2: Life Expectancy and Mortality Rates for Four Leading Causes of Death and Various Social Indicators, Montreal Sub-regions, 1994–1998

Health Indicators	West	West-Central	North	South-West	East-Central	East
Life Expectancy						
Males	77.2	75.9	77.4	73.1	70.7	73.8
Females	82.1	82.0	82.6	79.5	79.4	80.4
Mortality Rates per 100,000						
Tumours	230	237	216	295	296	266
Respiratory	71	67	65	100	93	89
Circulatory	290	307	267	369	371	349
Accidental Injury	22	21	20	22	30	23
Social Indicators (% of Residents) Receiving Social Assistance	4.5	9.6	15.7	17.4	18.1	14.5
Single-parent families	16	24	30	35	36	32
Children under 5 living under low income cut-off	22	42	53	50	58	46
Percentage of residents who believe neighbourhood does not have good quality of life	8.2	8.9	13.3	18.3	23.0	14.1
Percentage of residents who do not consider neighbourhood to be safe	5.6	7.3	7.7	10.8	17.1	9.8

Source: Lessard, R., Roy, D., Choinière, R., Lévesque, J., and Perron, S. (2002). *Urban health: A vital factor in Montreal's development* (p. 47). Montreal: Direction de la santé publique.

A Toronto report looked at three key indicators of children's health and well-being as a function of average neighbourhood income: singleton low birth weight, readiness to learn at age of school entry, and teen pregnancy rate (McKeown et al., 2008). These are well-established indicators of both childhood and adult health status, and general well-being. Table 8.3 provides the demographics and health outcomes found in these neighbourhoods and demonstrates how the clustering of disadvantage is associated with a range of adverse health outcomes.

Explaining the Poverty and Health Relationship

In developed nations such as Canada, there are two primary explanations that have been applied to explain the existence of health inequalities in general and the poor health of people living in poverty in particular (Townsend, Davidson, and Whitehead, 1992). The cultural/behavioural explanation is that individuals' behavioural choices (e.g., tobacco and alcohol use, diet, physical activity, etc.) are responsible for their developing and dying from a variety of diseases. The materialist/structuralist explanation emphasizes the mate-rial conditions under which people live their lives (Lantz et al., 1998; Raphael, 2006;

Table 8.3: Key Demographic Characteristics and Various Health Outcomes of Differing Income Quintiles within Toronto, 2006

	Quintile by Income				
	Q5— Poorest	Q4	Q3	Q2	Q1— Richest
Demographic Characteristics					
Population	507,965	481,700	512,510	484,740	508,710
% Living Below LICO	40.9	29.5	23.5	18.1	10.5
Average Household Income (after tax)	$43,480	$49,822	$56,143	$63,660	$94,381
% Unemployed, 15 yrs +	10.4	8.4	7.4	6.8	5.3
Health Outcomes					
Low Birth Weight/100	6.3	5.7	5.6	5.5	4.5
Lack of Readiness to Learn (%)	34	28	28.9	24.9	19.5
Teen Pregnancy Rates/1,000	41.9	35.5	31.9	24.3	15.9

Source: McKeown, D., MacCon, K., Day, N., Fleiszer, P., Scott, F., and Wolfe, S. (2008). *The unequal city: Income and health inequalities in Toronto* (Table 1, p. 7). Toronto: Toronto Public Health.

Roux, Merkin, and Arnett, 2001). These conditions include availability of resources to access the amenities of life, working conditions, and quality of available food and housing, among others (Raphael, 2009). Access to health-enhancing conditions is also related to general approaches to governance (Ross et al., 2000). Evidence clearly favours the materialist explanation of the sources of health inequalities and the exceptionally poor health of people living in poverty (Acheson, 1998; Gordon, Shaw, Dorling, and Davey Smith, 1999; Raphael, in 2010; Shaw et al., 1999; Townsend et al., 1992).

Jurisdictions differ profoundly to the extent that the health of people living in poverty is a cause of concern requiring action (Bryant, 2006). A review examined how 13 developed nations address health inequalities. England, Wales, Scotland, Northern Ireland, Ireland, New Zealand, and Sweden have undertaken systematic governmental efforts to identify the existence and magnitude of health inequalities—which include focus on the health of those living in poverty—and their sources (Crombie, Irvine, Elliott, and Wallace, 2005). In contrast, Canadian efforts to establish how poverty and income inequality influence health are limited to reports by the non-governmental Canadian Population Health Initiative and research programs by the Canadian Institute for Health Research (Canadian Population Health Initiative, 2004; Phipps, 2002; Ross, 2002; Ross, 2004). Outside of governmental attention to Aboriginal health, the extent of Canadian activity directed toward the issue of people living in poverty is minimal (Statistics Canada, 2004).

Health promotion and population health discourses in Canada, for the most part, do not focus explicitly on the health of people living in poverty (Raphael, 2000).[3] Compared to developments in Europe, reducing health inequalities in Canada takes a back seat to policy statements about improving social and physical environments (Health Canada, 2001). There has been no defining Canadian versions of the United Kingdom's "Black Report" (Black and Smith, 1992) or *Independent Inquiry into Health Inequalities* (Acheson, 1998) focused on health inequalities and the health of people living in poverty.

The concern with improving environments is common to many statements by federal and provincial governmental and public health agencies about addressing the determinants of health (Raphael, 2000). A broad environmental approach can be positive, as attention is directed—and participation from these sectors, invited—to a range of determinants of health such as income, housing, employment, and food security rather than solely on documenting relationships between health outcomes and these issues. The negative aspect of such an approach is that living conditions experienced by the most vulnerable Canadians, those living in poverty, may not receive the attention they deserve.

Improving the health of people living in poverty and the conditions that spawn poverty gives way to a general emphasis on "health promotion" and "population health" that directs resources to those Canadians who may not be living in poverty and whose health is not particularly problematic. This point is somewhat academic, as in practice, most health promotion action (with some notable exceptions, such as that seen in the Montreal Regional Health Authority and scattered health units across Canada) is focused on modifying individual risk behaviours, with little attention being given to the broader issues identified in government and public health documents (Raphael, 2000). There is little evidence that statements about the health role played by environments are being converted into efforts to improve these environments (Raphael, 2001).

Addressing the Poverty and Health Relationship

Despite Canada's reputation as a leader in health promotion and population health, the media and elected, health care, and public health officials do not usually see poverty as a health issue. Instead, the health problems of people living in poverty are usually seen as reflecting their own risk behaviours. This is the case even though evidence indicates that poverty is a much stronger determinant of health than these behaviours.

As one example, a report from Statistics Canada devoted most of its content to documenting how health behaviours (e.g., smoking, exercise, weight, etc.) and psychosocial variables (e.g., stress and depression) helped explain differences in health status among health regions (Shields and Tremblay, 2002). This was done even though data from the same study showed that self-reported income—with the health of people of lower income being especially poor—was far and away the best explanation for these regional differences in health outcomes (Tremblay et al., 2002).

This emphasis is also puzzling given that poverty has been identified as a key determinant of health in many federal and provincial statements (Government of British Columbia, 2000; Government of Ontario, 1994; Hamilton and Bhatti, 1996; Health Canada, 1998). Similarly, Canadian Public Health Association (CPHA) policy statements stress the importance of the societal determinants of health, including poverty (Canadian Public Health Association, 1993, 1996, 1997, 2000).[4] (See Box 8.2.)

Yet, despite the best continuing efforts of Health Canada and CPHA document writers to promote the importance of poverty as a health issue, Canadian focus remains on behavioural change. There are some very important issues raised by this focus. First, evidence indicates that these behavioural risk factors play a rather small role in understanding the poor health of people living in poverty (Lantz et al., 1998). Second, focusing on behaviours rather than life situations leads to "victim blaming," whereby disadvantaged people are blamed for their own health problems, a concern raised in Canada over 20 years ago (Labonte and Penfold, 1981). Third, emphasis on risk behaviours fails to address the underlying issues of why disadvantaged people adopt these behaviours (Benzeval, Judge, and Whitehead, 1995). Fourth, these approaches are generally unsuccessful in developing effective interventions for behaviour change in disadvantaged groups (Jarvis and Wardle, 1999). Fifth, and perhaps most important, an emphasis on behavioural risks diverts attention from poverty, including its causes, its health effects, and the need for societal action to reduce and eliminate it (Raphael, 2003). Labonte (1994) states:

> *The argument was simple. The health of oppressed people (poor, women, persons from minority cultures, workers, and others) was determined at least as much, if not more, by structural conditions (poverty hazards, powerlessness, pollution, and so on) than by personal lifestyles. Moreover personal lifestyles were not freely determined by individual choice, but existed within social and cultural structures that conditioned and constrained behaviour. Behavioural health education, social marketing, or wellness approaches to health promotion fostered victim blaming by assuming that individuals were entirely responsible for their choices and behaviour. They also blamed the victim indirectly by ignoring the structural*

Box 8.2: Canadian Public Health Association Resolution on Poverty and Health

Reducing Poverty and Its Negative Effects on Health

WHEREAS 20% of Canadian children, 15% of Canadians in families, and more than one-third (36%) of unattached Canadians all lived in poverty* in 1997 (the most recent year for which data are available) despite economic growth, declining unemployment rates, and Canada's number one human development ranking among all countries in the world since the early 1990s,

WHEREAS poverty, whether conceptualized and measured as absolute or relative in nature, negatively affects the health of individuals, communities, and society as a whole,

WHEREAS the most effective way to reduce the negative health consequences of poverty is, first and foremost, to reduce the rate and depth of poverty in Canada, and also to reduce economic burden and barriers to health experienced by people in poverty,

WHEREAS poverty is a complex phenomenon that is rooted in a network of social, economic, and political factors and conditions, some of which include changing labour market conditions as well as social assistance benefits and minimum wages that are insufficient to meet basic needs and allow meaningful participation in society,

WHEREAS it is highly improbable that poverty and the economic burden and barriers to health experienced by people in poverty will decline in the absence of social and economic policies and programs that specifically aim to reduce the rate and depth of poverty and aim to reduce the economic burden and barriers to health experienced by people in poverty,

WHEREAS the federal, provincial, and territorial governments in Canada have implemented some policies and programs that aim to reduce the negative health consequences of poverty (e.g., pre- and post-natal and early intervention programs) and aim to reduce the economic burden (e.g., child tax benefit) and barriers to health (e.g., comprehensive health benefits for children in working poor families) experienced by some people in poverty, but Canada does not have a comprehensive coordinated network of social and economic policies and programs, the specific purposes of which are to reduce the rate and depth of poverty and to reduce the economic burden and barriers to health experienced by people in poverty, and

WHEREAS the Canadian Public Health Association (CPHA) has gone on record acknowledging the negative health consequences of social and economic inequities such as poverty, acknowledging its commitment to reducing such inequities, and purporting the responsibility of public health professionals to the reduction of health inequities,

THEREFORE BE IT RESOLVED THAT the Canadian Public Health Association (CPHA) reconfirm its commitment to the reduction of social and economic inequities by working in partnership with health, social, and anti-poverty organizations and coalitions (e.g., Canadian Council on Social Development, Canadian Centre for Policy Alternatives, Canadian Nurses Association, National Anti-Poverty Organization, Campaign 2000, Child and Family Canada) to influence the federal, provincial, and territorial governments to develop and implement a comprehensive coordinated network of policies and programs that aim to reduce the rate and depth of poverty and aim to reduce economic burden and barriers to health experienced by people in poverty,

AND FURTHER BE IT RESOLVED THAT CPHA develop and implement a social marketing campaign to educate and promote dialogue with the public about the persistence of poverty in the midst of economic growth and declining unemployment rates; the negative effects that poverty has on the health of individuals, families, communities, and society as a whole; and solutions/strategies for reducing poverty and its negative health consequences.

*Poverty is defined here as the relative deprivation of income that is necessary to meet basic needs and a standard of living that is consistent with the norms of the society within which one lives.

Source: Canadian Public Health Association. (2000). *Reducing poverty and its negative effects on health* (2000 CPHA Resolution No. 2). Retrieved March 11, 2011 from www.cpha.ca/uploads/resolutions/2000_e.pdf

determinants of health, those causes that are embedded within economic, class- and gender-based patterns of social relationships. (p. 79)

Why is there this blind spot? Health care and public health officials downplay poverty because raising it may be seen as threatening to their relationship with governments who provide their status and funding. The denial of poverty as an important health issue is consistent with the ascendance of governmental commitments to neo-liberalism and neo-conservative ideologies that position societal issues, including health and health promotion, as individual issues beyond the concern of governments and their institutions (Nettleton, 1997). While even centre-left governments are prone to lifestyle approaches (NDP-led province Manitoba has healthy lifestyles initiatives), more conservative governments can promote these approaches at the same time as they weaken the societal structures that affect population health far more profoundly (Raphael, 2006).

There are instances in Canada where poverty has been raised as a health issue by health authorities. The Public Health Agency of Canada has established a National Coordinating Centre for the Determinants of Health in the Maritime Region, which is hosted by St. Francis Xavier University in Antigonish, Nova Scotia. Poverty has been raised as a key health issue by local public health units in Alberta (e.g., Chinook, Edmonton, and Calgary); Ontario (e.g., Peterborough, Waterloo, Sudbury, and Perth); British Columbia (Interior Health); and Quebec (e.g., Montreal). At a recent meeting of the Ontario Public Health Association, delegates voted to urge the Provincial Medical Officer of Health to incorporate poverty and other determinants of health as issues to be included in the mandatory guidelines for public health practice. This view was endorsed by the association that represents provincial health officers. There may be other examples of such activity (Sudbury Health Unit and Alder Group, 2006).

In contrast, the poverty and health issue has been taken up enthusiastically by various non-health sectors that are concerned with social development, welfare, and societal well-being. These organizations include the charitable sectors, especially the United Way across Canada (United Way of Greater Toronto, 2004; United Way of Greater Toronto and Canadian Council on Social Development, 2002; United Way of Ottawa, 2003; United Way of Winnipeg, 2003), religious and faith organizations concerned with poverty (Swift, Balmer, and Dineen, 2010), and various anti-poverty organizations such as Canada Without Poverty, Campaign 2000, and the Income Advocacy Resource Centre. To date, however, these activities have had little if any impact on having elected officials at the federal and provincial levels address poverty as a health issue. Such analyses have also failed to inform recommendations concerning the prevention of chronic diseases (see Box 8.3)

Conclusions

Poverty is associated with a wide range of health issues. These relationships are so strong as to suggest that poverty is the primary determinant of health, however defined. Poverty is an especially important issue for children, as it not only threatens their health and well-being in childhood but carries health risks that can manifest during adulthood. Despite these findings, and numerous governmental and health-association documents and reports acknowledging these findings, there is little if any action being directed toward raising poverty as an important health issue.

In contrast to other nations where research and policy concern with poverty and health has a long-standing history, such as the UK, few Canadian researchers explicitly focus on the health of people living in poverty (Raphael et al., 2005). And when these researchers do focus on the health of those living in poverty, many are likely to attribute differences in health to behavioural risk factors such as tobacco use, physical activity,

Box 8.3: Poverty and Health

Poverty a Leading Cause of Type 2 Diabetes, Studies Say
Andrea Janus

For years, Canadians have heard that obesity, a lack of physical activity and a family history are the top risk factors for developing Type 2 diabetes.

But new Canadian research says that, in fact, it is living in poverty that can double or even triple the likelihood of developing the disease.

"What we know about Type 2 diabetes is not only are low-income and poor people more likely to get it, but they're also the ones that, once they get it, are much more likely to suffer complications," Prof. Dennis Raphael, one of the researchers, told CTV.ca in a telephone interview.

"And the complications from Type 2 diabetes when they're bad are really bad, whether it's amputations, or blindness, or cardiovascular disease."

Researchers from York University analyzed two sets of data: the Canadian Community Health Survey (CCHS) and the National Population Health Survey (NPHS) for a study published in the journal *Health Policy*.

The first set of data showed that for men, being in the lowest-income category (earning less than $15,000 per year), doubles the risk of developing Type 2 diabetes compared to being in one of the highest-income brackets (earning more than $80,000 per year). The risk remains the same when other risk factors are taken into account, such as education, body mass index and physical activity levels.

The findings are even more striking for women in the lowest-income category. For them, the risk of developing Type 2 diabetes is more than triple the risk of women in the highest-income category. When education, body mass index and physical activity levels are taken into account, the risk is still well more than double. Results from the NPHS analysis are just as striking. Researchers found that living in poverty in the two years prior to diagnosis increased the risk of developing Type 2 diabetes by 24 per cent, a risk not changed when factoring in weight or physical activity. Living in poverty at any time increased the risk by 26 per cent.

Generally speaking, subjects who lived more often in poverty during the 12-year study period had a 41 per cent greater chance of developing the disease. When obesity and physical activity levels were taken into account, the risk remained very high, at 36 per cent.

The studies are consistent with other findings that link living conditions—what they call the social determinants of health—with Type 2 diabetes, as well as other ailments.

Raphael, a professor of health policy and management at York, said conventional wisdom about Type 2 diabetes would suggest that once obesity, lack of physical activity and other lifestyle risk factors were taken into account, diabetes incidence rates would even out between lower- and higher-income groups.

While weight, a sedentary lifestyle and other health problems are still key risk factors, the findings suggest that health-care workers who specialize in diabetes should be paying closer attention to the socio-economic conditions that can lead to them.

"When you're in a situation where 15 per cent of kids and their families are living in poverty, and people are worried from day-to-day about their jobs and homelessness, and immigrants are not being provided with what they need to be healthy, and the evidence that suggests these are all things that contribute to the onset of Type 2 diabetes, there has to be more of a balance in how we understand the causes of illness," Raphael said.

But what is it exactly about living in poverty that contributes to type 2 diabetes?

The studies point to living conditions that put low-income adults and children at risk for myriad diseases, not just diabetes. First of all, there is the chronic stress of low-income living that can adversely affect health. The strain of being short on money and living in inadequate housing, or not having any housing at all, can spike levels of cortisol, a hormone released when the body is under stress. While cortisol helps the body deal with stress, constantly elevated levels can cause a wide range of negative side effects, such as high blood sugar levels or high blood pressure.

Residents of lower-income neighbourhoods also often find it difficult to access fresh, healthy foods and programs that promote physical activity, both of which are key to managing stress, controlling weight and, therefore, preventing disease.

Raphael also points to previous research, which suggests adverse circumstances in early childhood, from low birth weight to deprivation as a youngster, raise a child's risk of developing a number of conditions, from respiratory and cardiovascular diseases to diabetes.

"So we're basically talking about systematic stress over time, lack of control that eventually leads to higher cortisol levels, among other things. Cortisol and other stuff literally messes up the ability of the body to use the insulin that's available. And it's not well understood," Raphael said.

Poor More Likely to Suffer Complications

For another part of their study, the researchers interviewed 60 diabetes patients who reside in low-income Toronto neighbourhoods. What they learned is that the very conditions that contribute to diabetes also make it extremely difficult to manage the disease, meaning low-income patients are suffering from some of the most debilitating side effects.

Raphael and his team found that insufficient income, inadequate or insecure housing and food insecurity were key barriers to managing the disease. According to their interviews, 72 per cent of patients said they lacked the financial resources to follow the kind of diet needed to keep their diabetes in check.

Many said they had to choose between paying rent or feeding their children and managing their disease.

Raphael said his team's findings show that tackling broader issues of poverty—lack of employment or under employment, housing, food security and health coverage—are key to managing diabetes, and other ailments.

"The primary thing is basically for the government, with other sectors of society, to manage the economy in the service of all," he said.

Source: Adapted from Janus, A. (2010, November 21). Poverty a leading cause of Type 2 diabetes, studies say. CTV.ca News. Retrieved March 11, 2011.

and diet. Nevertheless, there is a body of Canadian work that looks to understand the health of people living in poverty as reflecting societal structures and processes. There is research that focuses on the political economy of health inequalities, and how changes in economic structures and processes associated with increasing economic globalization and the adoption of neo-liberal public policies create and maintain high poverty levels in Canada (Coburn, 2000, 2004, 2010; Teeple, 2000).

There is increasing interest in poverty as a health issue by various non-health sectors. Considering the increasing concern with the sustainability of the health care system, it would be expected that the incidence of poverty, and its profound effects on health, would be taken more seriously (Romanow, 2002). To date, this has not generally been the case. However, the importance of the poverty and health issue, and the increasing evidence of the effects of poverty upon health and quality of life, suggest some hope for the future.

Notes

1. The fact that these cross-sectional studies cannot demonstrate causality has not stopped traditional risk factor researchers from using such studies in such a way as to assume causality. This is especially the case when factors identified by Sarah Nettleton (1997) as the "holy trinity of risk," that is, diet, physical activity, and tobacco use, are identified as being responsible for the onset of disease and illness.

2. Many argue that income is a poor proxy for measuring social class, which is a much more profound indicator of socio-economic position. Unlike the situation in the United Kingdom, there is very little data available on the social class position of Canadian study participants. What data are available on social class and health are consistent with the income and health data reported here. See McMullins and Davies' (2010) recent analysis of the role social class plays in health in developed nations such as Canada.

3. A most recent example of the unwillingness of policy-makers to address health inequalities is seen in the newly minted Public Health Goals for Canada (Public Health Agency of Canada, 2005). While any number of consultation session participants outlined reducing inequalities in health and the sources of these health inequalities as primary concerns, the document contains only one oblique reference to health inequalities: "A strong system for health and social well-being responds to disparities in health status and offers timely, appropriate care."

4. Despite the passing of a resolution calling for CPHA action on the poverty and health relationship in 2000, follow-up revealed that the CPHA had done little if anything to implement it.

Critical Thinking Questions

1. What findings concerning the poverty and health relationship were particularly surprising to you? How do these findings contrast with your previous understandings of the causes of disease?

2. What findings in this chapter were consistent with information provided in Chapter 6, "The Lived Experience of Poverty"? How so?
3. Why do you think that poverty is generally not seen as a health issue by health care and public health officials?
4. Do you think that Canadian elected officials are unaware of these findings relating poverty to health or simply do not care? What leads you to this conclusion?
5. Who benefits from not having poverty seen as a health issue? How do they benefit?
6. What can be done to raise public awareness of the poverty and health relationship?

Recommended Readings

Auger, N., and Alix, C. (2009). Income and health in Canada. In D. Raphael (Ed.), *Social determinants of health: Canadian perspectives* (2nd ed., pp. 61–74). Toronto: Canadian Scholars' Press Inc.

> Nathalie Auger and Carolyne Alix provide an overview of what is known about the relationship between income (especially poverty) and health. They provide different ways of measuring income and how these measures can be related to health. Their review provides conclusive evidence that income (especially poverty) is a key determinant of health.

Bryant, T., Daiski, D., Lines, E., Dinca-Panaitescu, S., Dinca-Panaitescu, M., Pilkington, B., and Raphael, D. (2010). *Type 2 diabetes: Poverty, priorities, and policy—the social determinants of its incidence and management.* Toronto: School of Health Policy and Management. Online at http://tinyurl.com/ycysb9l

> This report by a York University team of researchers from the School of Health Policy and Management and the School of Nursing examines the contribution of socio-economic factors to the incidence and management of type 2 diabetes among people living in poverty.

Canadian Population Health Initiative. (2008). *Reducing gaps in health: A focus on socio-economic status in urban Canada.* Ottawa: CPHI.

> This report provides a broad overview of the links between socio-economic status and health in 15 Canadian census metropolitan areas (CMAs), while exploring socio-economic patterns and gradients within those CMAs and across urban Canada.

Davey Smith, G. (Ed.). (2003). *Inequalities in health: Life course perspectives.* Bristol, UK: The Policy Press.

> This is an extensive collection of papers that document the strong relationships between poverty and health at different stages of the life course. Of particular note is that material and social deprivation in childhood is a strong predictor of the incidence of a wide range of disease in adulthood, independent of a person's life situation as an adult.

Lightman, E., Mitchell, A., and Wilson, B. (2008). *Poverty is making us sick: A comprehensive survey of income and health in Canada.* Toronto: The Wellesley Institute. Online at http://tinyurl.com/36z9wov

The authors use Canadian Community Health Survey data to paint a comprehensive picture of how poverty is related to the incidence of a wide range of diseases and afflictions.

Raphael, D. (2010). The health of Canada's children. *Paediatrics and Child Health, 15*(1–4). Online at http://tinyurl.com/37rfhrr

This four-part series on children's health in Canada was published in the journal *Paediatrics and Child Health* from January to April, 2010.

Relevant Websites

Canadian Population Health Initiative—http://tinyurl.com/39e38d9

The Canadian Population Health Initiative (CPHI) aims to expand the public's knowledge of population health. CPHI's mission is to: (a) foster a better understanding of factors that affect the health of individuals and communities; and (b) contribute to the development of policies that reduce inequities and improve the health and well-being of Canadians.

Canadian Public Health Association—www.cpha.ca/en/programs/policy.aspx

The Canadian Public Health Association has issued numerous policy statements and documents about the impact of adverse living conditions—including poverty—on health.

2009 AOHC Conference Report—www.aohc.org/index.php?ci_id=3296&la_id=1

This website details the outcomes of the 2009 Association of Ontario Health Centres annual conference *At the Intersection of Poverty and Health*. The conference was designed to refocus and re-ignite energies across the sector to continue and enhance work on poverty, and to consider a higher goal to eradicate and not just reduce poverty, and not just for children, but for all Ontarians.

Unnatural Causes: Is Inequality Making Us Sick?—www.unnaturalcauses.org/

California Newsreel undertook a project of providing a documentary series that would serve as the basis for establishing a new public health in the US. The website provides details about the documentary and provides numerous resources to build awareness of, and support for, a broader approach to addressing poverty and its health effects.

World Health Organisation Commission on the Social Determinants of Health—www.who.int/social_determinants/en/

Responding to increasing concern about persisting and widening inequities, WHO established the Commission on Social Determinants of Health (CSDH) in 2005 to provide advice on how to reduce them. The Commission's final report was launched in August 2008, and contained three overarching recommendations: (1) improve daily living conditions; (2) tackle the inequitable distribution of power, money, and resources; and (3) measure and understand the problem and assess the impact of action.

Glossary of Terms

Incidence refers to the number of new cases of a disease or illness that occur during a given time period. Thus, the incidence of a heart attack will typically be given as a proportion of the population that experience this event over a given year. These rates are standardized so that they take into account the age of a population to ensure that differing rates are not simply a result of one population having a larger number of older citizens as compared to another.

Life expectancy is the number of years that a person can expect to live upon being born. It is usually seen as being one of the best indicators of the overall health of a population.

Morbidity refers to the incidence and prevalence of a disease or illness. It is an epidemiological term that simply refers to the amount of sickness in a society.

Mortality refers to death from a disease or illness. Mortality rates are usually given as a percentage of proportion of a population during a given time period. These rates can be adjusted for the age of the population to allow for comparisons between groups.

Premature years of life lost (PYLL) refers to the total number of years lost to disease, illness, or injuries of a population in relation to a specified age. If the age standard is set as 75 years of age, all years lost to disease or injury are counted as PYLL. If someone dies at age 65, then there are 10 years of PYLL. If the person dies at age 10, then there are 65 years of PYLL. PYLL provides an overall indicator of the cost to human life of a particular affliction.

Prevalence refers to the percentage or proportion of a population suffering from an illness or disease at a given point in time. It takes into account both new cases and continuing cases. Prevalence rates of different groups can be standardized to take into account differences in age distributions between groups.

Variance refers to the degree that the value of an indicator is dispersed around the mean of that indicator. For example, if one looks at the life expectancies of a group of people, some will live longer lives and some will live shorter lives. The aim of research is to explain this variation around the mean. If a variable is related to whether some people live longer and some shorter lives, the question is asked: *How much of the variance around that mean does the variable explain?* If a variable is a perfect predictor of the outcome, it explains 100% of the variance in the outcome. If a variable is a poor predictor of the outcome, it explains only a little of the variance in the outcome measure.

References

Acheson, D. (1998). *Independent inquiry into inequalities in health*. London, UK: Stationary Office.

Alter, D. A., Naylor, C. D., Austin, P., and Tu, J. (1999). Effects of socioeconomic status on access to invasive cardiac procedures and on mortality after acute myocardial infarction. *New England Journal of Medicine, 341*(18), 1360–1367.

Armstrong, P. (2009). Public policy, gender, and health. In D. Raphael (Ed.), *Social determinants of health: Canadian perspectives* (2nd ed., pp. 350–361). Toronto: Canadian Scholars' Press Inc.

Auger, N., and Alix, C. (2009). Income and health in Canada. In D. Raphael (Ed.), *Social determinants of health: Canadian perspectives* (2nd ed., pp. 61–74). Toronto: Canadian Scholars' Press Inc.

Benzeval, M., and Judge, K. (2001). Income and health: The time dimension. *Social Science and Medicine, 52*(9), 1371–1390.

Benzeval, M., Judge, K., and Whitehead, M. (1995). *Tackling inequalities in health: An agenda for action*. London, UK: Kings' Fund.

Black, D., and Smith, C. (1992). The Black Report. In P. Townsend, N. Davidson, and M. Whitehead (Eds.), *Inequalities in health: The Black Report and the health divide* (pp. 44–218). New York: Penguin.

Browne, G. (2004). Early childhood education and health. In D. Raphael (Ed.), *Social determinants of health: Canadian perspectives* (pp. 125–138). Toronto: Canadian Scholars' Press Inc.

Bryant, T. (2009). Housing and health: More than bricks and mortar. In D. Raphael (Ed.), *Social determinants of health: Canadian perspectives* (2nd ed., pp. 235–249). Toronto: Canadian Scholars' Press Inc.

Bryant, T. (2010). Politics, public policy, and health inequalities. In T. Bryant, D. Raphael, and M. Rioux (Eds.), *Staying alive: Critical perspectives on health, illness, and health care* (2nd ed., pp. 239–263). Toronto: Canadian Scholars' Press Inc.

Canadian Institute for Children's Health. (200). *The health of Canada' children: ACICH profile* (3rd ed). Ottawa: Canadian Institute for Children's Health.

Canadian Population Health Initiative. (2004). *Improving the health of Canadians*. Ottawa: Canadian Population Health Initiative.

Canadian Public Health Association. (1993). *Inequities in health*. Ottawa: Canadian Public Health Association.

Canadian Public Health Association. (1996). *The health impacts of unemployment*. Ottawa: Canadian Public Health Association.

Canadian Public Health Association. (1997). *Health impacts of social and economic conditions: Implications for public policy*. Ottawa: Canadian Public Health Association.

Canadian Public Health Association. (2000). *Reducing poverty and its negative effects on health: Resolution passed at the 2000 CPHA Annual Meeting* [Position paper]. Retrieved October 31, 2006, from www.cpha.ca/english/policy/resolu/2000s/2000/page2.htm

Charron, M. (2009). *Neighbourhood characteristics and the distribution of police-reported crime in the city of Toronto*. Ottawa: Statistics Canada.

Chen, J. J. (1999). Health in mid-life. *Health Reports, 11*(3), 35–46.

Coburn, D. (2000). Income inequality, social cohesion, and the health status of populations: The role of neo-liberalism. *Social Science and Medicine, 51*(1), 135–146.

Coburn, D. (2004). Beyond the income inequality hypothesis: Globalization, neo-liberalism, and health inequalities. *Social Science and Medicine, 58*(1), 41–56.

Coburn, D. (2010). Health and health care: A political economy perspective. In T. Bryant, D. Raphael, and M. Rioux (Eds.), *Staying alive: Critical perspectives on health, illness, and health care* (2nd ed., pp. 65–92). Toronto: Canadian Scholars' Press Inc.

Crombie, I., Irvine, L., Elliott, L., and Wallace, H. (2005). *Policies to reduce inequalities in health in 13 developed countries.* Dundee, UK: University of Dundee.

Davey Smith, G. (Ed.). (2003). *Inequalities in health: Life course perspectives.* Bristol, UK: The Policy Press.

Davey Smith, G., Ben-Shlomo, Y., and Lynch, J. (2002). Life course approaches to inequalities in coronary heart disease risk. In S. A. Stansfeld (Ed.), *Stress and the heart: psychosocial pathways to coronary heart disease* (pp. 20–49). London, UK: BMJ Books.

Davey Smith, G., and Gordon, D. (2000). Poverty across the life-course and health. In C. Pantazis and D. Gordon (Eds.), *Tackling inequalities: Where are we now and what can be done?* (pp. 141–158). Bristol, UK: The Policy Press.

Davey Smith, G., Grunnell, D., and Ben-Shlomo, Y. (2001). Life-course approaches to socio-economic differentials in cause-specific adult mortality. In D. Leon and G. Walt (Eds.), *Poverty, inequality, and health: An international perspective* (pp. 88–124). New York: Oxford University Press.

DesMeules, M., Turner, L., and Cho, R. (2003). Morbidity experiences and disability among Canadian women. In *Women's health surveillance report: A multi-dimensional look at the health of Canadian women.* Ottawa: Health Canada, Canadian Population Health Initiative.

Dinca-Panaitescua, S., Dinca-Panaitescu, M., Bryant, T., Daiski, I. Pilkington, B., and Raphael, D. (2010). The dynamics of the relationship between poverty experience and type 2 diabetes: Longitudinal results. Toronto: School of Health Policy and Management.

Dinca-Panaitescua, S., Dinca-Panaitescu, M., Bryant, T., Daiski, I., Pilkington, B., and Raphael, D. (in press). Diabetes prevalence and income: Results of the Canadian Community Health Survey. *Health Policy.*

Galabuzi, G. E. (2005). *Canada's economic apartheid: The social exclusion of racialized groups in the new century.* Toronto: Canadian Scholars' Press Inc.

Galabuzi, G. E. (2009). Social exclusion. In D. Raphael (Ed.), *Social determinants of health: Canadian perspectives* (2nd ed., pp. 252–268). Toronto: Canadian Scholars' Press Inc.

Glazier, R. H., Booth, G. L., Gozdyra, P., Creatore, M. I., and Tynan, M. (2007). *Neighbourhood environments and resources for healthy living—A focus on diabetes in Toronto: ICES Atlas.* Toronto: Institute for Clinical Evaluative Sciences.

Gordon, D., Shaw, M., Dorling., D., and Davey Smith, G. (1999). *Inequalities in health: The evidence presented to the independent inquiry into inequalities in health.* Bristol, UK: The Policy Press.

Government of British Columbia. (2000). *A Report on the health of British Columbians.* Victoria: Government of British Columbia.

Government of Ontario. (1994). *Wealth and health, health and wealth.* Toronto: Government of Ontario, Queen's Printer for Ontario.

Graham, H. (2004). Tackling health inequalities in health in England: Remedying health disadvantages, narrowing health gaps, or reducing health gradients? *Journal of Social Policy, 33,* 115–131.

Hamilton, N., and Bhatti, T. (1996). *Population health promotion: An integrated model of population health and health promotion.* Retrieved October 2006 from Health Canada website: www.hc-sc.gc.ca/hppb/phdd/php/php.htm

Health Canada. (1998). *Taking action on population health: A position paper for health promotion and programs branch staff.* Retrieved October 2006 from www.hc-sc.gc.ca/hppb/phdd/pdf/tad_e.pdf

Health Canada. (2001). *The population health template: Key elements and actions that define a population health approach.* Retrieved October 2006 from www.hc-sc.gc.ca/hppb/phdd/pdf/discussion_paper.pdf

Health Canada. (2002). *Healthy Canadians: A federal report on comparable health indicators 2002.* Ottawa: Health Canada.

Health Canada, First Nations and Inuit Health Branch. (2003). *A statistical profile on the health of First Nations in Canada.* Ottawa: Health Canada, First Nations and Inuit Health Branch.

Humphries, K., and van Doorslaer, E. (2000). Income related health inequality in Canada. *Social Science and Medicine, 50*(5), 663–671.

Hux, J., Booth, G., and Laupacis, A. (2002, September 18). *The ICES practice atlas: Diabetes in Ontario* [Report]. Retrieved October 2006 from Institute for Clinical Evaluative Sciences website: www.ices.on.ca/

Jackson, A. (2009). The unhealthy Canadian workplace. In D. Raphael (Ed.), *Social determinants of health: Canadian perspectives* (2nd ed., pp. 99–113). Toronto: Canadian Scholars' Press Inc.

Jarvis, M. J., and Wardle, J. (2003). Social patterning of individual health behaviours: The case of cigarette smoking. In M. G. Marmot and R. G. Wilkinson (Eds.), *Social determinants of health* (2nd ed., pp. 224–237). Oxford, UK: Oxford University Press.

Kuh, D., and Ben-Shilmo, Y. (Eds.). (1997). *A life course approach to chronic disease epidemiology.* Oxford, UK: Oxford University Press.

Labonte, R. (1994). Death of a program: Birth of a metaphor. In I. Rootman, A. Pederson, and M. O'Neill (Eds.), *Health promotion in Canada: Provincial, national, and international perspectives* (pp. 72–90). Toronto: Saunders.

Labonte, R., and Pinfold, S. (1981). Canadian perspectives in health promotion: A critique. *Health Education, 19*(3–4), 4–9.

Lantz, P. M., House, J. S., Lepkowski, J. M., Williams, D. R., Mero, R. P., and Chen, J. J. (1998). Socioeconomic factors, health behaviors, and mortality. *Journal of the American Medical Association, 279*(21), 1703–1708.

Lessard, R., Roy, D., Choinière, R., Lévesque, J., and Perron, S. (2002). *Urban health: A vital factor in Montreal's development..* Retrieved October 2006 from Direction de la santé publique de Montréal website: www.santepub-mtl.qc.ca/Publication/autres/annualreport2002.html

Lynch, J., Kaplan, G., and Salonen, J. (1997). Why do poor people behave poorly? Variation in adult health behaviours and psychosocial characteristics by stages of the socioeconomic lifecourse. *Social Science and Medicine, 44*(6), 809–819.

McIntyre, L., and Rondeau, K. (2009). Food insecurity in Canada. In D. Raphael (Ed.), *Social determinants of health: Canadian perspectives* (2nd ed., pp. 188–204). Toronto: Canadian Scholars' Press Inc.

McKeown, D., MacCon, K., Day, N., Fleiszer, P., Scott, F., and Wolfe, S. (2008). *The unequal city: Income and health inequalities in Toronto.* Toronto: Toronto Public Health.

McMullin, J., and Davies, L. (2010). Social class and health inequalities. In T. Bryant, D. Raphael, and M. Rioux (Eds.), *Staying alive: Critical perspectives on health, illness, and health care* (2nd ed., pp. 181–204). Toronto: Canadian Scholars' Press Inc.

Mitura, V., and Bollman, R. D. (2003). *The health of rural Canadians: A rural–urban comparison of health indicators.* Ottawa: Statistics Canada.

Mitura, V., and Bollman, R. D. (2004). *Health status and behaviours of Canada's youth: A rural–urban comparison.* Ottawa: Statistics Canada.

Nettleton, S. (1997). Surveillance, health promotion and the formation of a risk identity. In M. Sidell, L. Jones, J., Katz, A. Peberdy (Eds.), *Debates and dilemmas in promoting health* (pp. 314–324). London, UK: Open University Press.

Orpana, H. M., Lemyre, L., and Gravel, R. (2009). Income and psychological distress: The role of the social environment. *Health Reports, 20*(1), 21–28.

Patten, S. B., Wang, J. L., Williams, J. V., Currie, S., Beck, C. A., Maxwell, C. J., and El-Guebaly, N. (2006). Descriptive epidemiology of major depression in Canada. *Canadian Journal of Psychiatry, 51*(2), 84–86.

Pederson, A., Raphael, D., and Johnson, E. (2009). Gender, race, and health inequalities. In T. Bryant, D. Raphael, and M. Rioux (Eds.), *Staying alive: Critical perspectives on health, illness, and health care* (2nd ed., pp. 205–238). Toronto: Canadian Scholars' Press Inc.

Phipps, S. (2002). *The impact of poverty on health.* Ottawa: Canadian Population Health Initiative.

Public Health Agency of Canada. (2005). *Public health goals for Canada.* Retrieved October 2006 from www.healthycanadians.ca/NEW-1-eng.html

Raphael, D. (2000). Health inequalities in Canada: Current discourses and implications for public health action. *Critical Public Health, 10*(2), 193–216.

Raphael, D. (2001). Canadian policy statements on income and health: Sound and fury—signifying nothing. *Canadian Review of Social Policy, 48*, 121–127.

Raphael, D. (2002). *Social justice is good for our hearts: Why societal factors—not lifestyles—are major causes of heart disease in Canada and elsewhere.* Centre for Social Justice Foundation for Research and Education. Retrieved October 2006 from www.socialjustice.org/pubs/justiceHearts.pdf

Raphael, D. (2003). Barriers to addressing the determinants of health: Public health units and poverty in Ontario, Canada. *Health Promotion International, 18*(4), 397–405.

Raphael, D. (2006). Social determinants of health: Present status, unresolved questions, and future directions. *International Journal of Health Services, 36*(4), 651–677.

Raphael, D. (Ed.). (2009). *Social determinants of health: Canadian perspectives* (2nd ed.). Toronto: Canadian Scholars' Press Inc.

Raphael, D. (2010). The health of Canada's children. *Paediatrics and Child Health, 15*(1–4).

Raphael, D., Anstice, S., and Raine, K. (2003). The social determinants of the incidence and management of Type II Diabetes Mellitus: Are we prepared to rethink our questions and redirect our research activities? *Leadership in Health Services, 16*(3), 10–20.

Raphael, D., Colman, R., Labonte, R., MacDonald, J., Torgeson, R., and Hayward, K. (2003). *Income, health, and disease in Canada: Current state of knowledge, information gaps, and areas of needed inquiry.* Toronto: York University School of Health Policy and Management. Retrieved October 2006 from www.atkinson.yorku.ca/draphael

Raphael, D., and Farrell, E. S. (2002). Beyond medicine and lifestyle: Addressing the societal determinants of cardiovascular disease in North America. *Leadership in Health Services, 15*(4), 1–5.

Raphael, D., Macdonald, J., Labonte, R., Colman, R., Hayward, K., and Torgerson, R. (2005). Researching income and income distribution as a determinant of health in Canada: Gaps between theoretical knowledge, research practice, and policy implementation. *Health Policy, 72,* 217–232.

Romanow, R. J. (2002). *Building on values: The future of health care in Canada.* Saskatoon: Commission on the Future of Health Care in Canada.

Roos, N. P., and Mustard, C. A. (1997). Variation in health care use by socioeconomic status in Winnipeg, Canada: Does the system work well? Yes and no. *Milbank Quarterly, 75*(1), 89–111.

Ross, D. P. (2002). *Policy approaches to address the impact of poverty.* Ottawa: Canadian Population Health Initiative.

Ross, D. P., and Roberts, P. (1999). *Income and child well-being: A new perspective on the poverty debate.* Ottawa: Canadian Council on Social Development.

Ross, D. P., Roberts, P., and Scott, K. (2000). Family income and child well-being. *ISUMA, 1*(2), 51–54.

Ross, N., Wolfson, M., Dunn, J., Berthelot, J. M., Kaplan, G., and Lynch, J. (2000). Relation between income inequality and mortality in Canada and in the United States: Cross sectional assessment using census data and vital statistics. *British Medical Journal, 320*(7239), 898–902.

Roux, A., Merkin, S., and Arnett, D. (2001). Neighbourhood of residence and incidence of coronary heart disease. *New England Journal of Medicine, 345*(2), 99–106.

Ruiz, M. T., and Verbrugge, L. M. (1997). A two-way view of gender bias in medicine. *Journal of Epidemiology and Community Health 51,* 106–109.

Shah, C. (2004). Aboriginal health. In D. Raphael (Ed.), *Social determinants of health: Canadian perspectives* (pp. 267–280). Toronto: Canadian Scholars' Press Inc.

Shaw, M., Dorling, D., Gordon, D., and Davey Smith, G. (1999). *The widening gap: Health inequalities and policy in Britain.* Bristol, UK: The Policy Press.

Shields, M., and Tremblay, S. (2002). The health of Canada's communities. *Supplement to Health Reports, 13,* 1–25.

Smiley, J. (2009). Aboriginal health. In D. Raphael (Ed.), *Social determinants of health: Canadian perspective* (2nd ed., pp. 280–301). Toronto: Canadian Scholars' Press Inc.

Smith K., Matheson, F., Moineddin, R., and Glazier, R. (2007). Gender, income, and immigration differences in depression in Canadian urban centres. *Canadian Journal of Public Health, 98*(2), 149–153.

Spigelman, M. (2002). *HIV/AIDS and health determinants: Lessons for coordinating policy and action.* Ottawa: Ministerial Council on HIV/AIDS.

Statistics Canada. (2001). Health reports: How healthy are Canadians? Annual report. *Health Reports, 12*(3), 1–58.

Statistics Canada. (2004). *2001 Aboriginal profile: Highlights for cities in Canada.* Ottawa: Statistics Canada.

Sudbury Health Unit and Alder Group. (2006). *Determinants of health: Developing an action plan for public health.* Sudbury: The Sudbury and District Health Unit.

Swift, J., Balmer, B., and Dineen, M. (2010). *Persistent poverty: Voices from the margins*. Toronto: Between the Lines Press.

Teeple, G. (2000). *Globalization and the decline of social reform: Into the twenty-first century*. Aurora, ON: Garamond Press.

Tjepkema, M. (2002). The health of the off-reserve Aboriginal population. *Supplement to Health Reports, 13*, 1–17.

Townsend, P., Davidson, N., and Whitehead, M. (Eds.). (1992). *Inequalities in health: The Black Report and the health divide*. New York: Penguin.

Tremblay, D. G. (2009). Precarious work and the labour market. In D. Raphael (Ed.), *Social determinants of health: Canadian perspectives* (2nd ed., pp. 75–87). Toronto: Canadian Scholars' Press Inc.

Tremblay, S., Ross, N. A., and Berthelot, J.-M. (2002). Regional socio-economic context and health. *Supplement to Health Reports, 13*, 1–12.

Ungerleider, C., Burns, T., and Cartwright, F. (2009). The state and quality of Canadian public elementary and secondary education. In D. Raphael (Ed.), *Social determinants of health: Canadian perspectives* (2nd ed., pp. 156–169). Toronto: Canadian Scholars' Press Inc.

United Way of Greater Toronto. (2004). *Poverty by postal code: The geography of neighbourhood poverty, 1981–2001*. Toronto: United Way of Greater Toronto.

United Way of Greater Toronto, and Canadian Council on Social Development. (2002). *A decade of decline: Poverty and income inequality in the city of Toronto in the 1990s*. Toronto: Canadian Council on Social Development and United Way of Greater Toronto.

United Way of Ottawa. (2003). *Environmental scan*. Ottawa: United Way of Ottawa.

United Way of Winnipeg. (2003). *2003 environmental scan and Winnipeg census data*. Winnipeg: United Way of Winnipeg.

Wilkins, R. (2007). Mortality by neighbourhood income in urban Canada from 1971 to 2001. HAMG Seminar, and special compilations. Ottawa: Statistics Canada, Health Analysis and Measurement Group.

Wilkins, R., Berthelot, J.-M., and Ng, E. (2002). Trends in mortality by neighbourhood income in urban Canada from 1971 to 1996. *Supplement to Health Reports, 13*, 1–28.

Wilkins, R., Houle, C., Berthelot, J.-M., and Ross, D. P. (2000). The changing health status of Canada's children. *ISUMA, 1*(2), 57–63.

Williamson, D., and Fast, J. (1998). Poverty and medical treatment: When public policy compromises accessibility. *Canadian Journal of Public Policy, 89*(2), 120–124.

Wilson, D., and Macdonald, D. (2010). *The income gap between Aboriginal peoples and the rest of Canada*. Ottawa: The Canadian Centre for Policy Alternatives.

Wood, E., Sallar, A., Schechter, M., and Hogg, R. (1999). Social inequalities in male mortality amenable to medical intervention in British Columbia. *Social Science and Medicine, 49*(12), 1751–1758.

Xi, G., McDowell, I., Nair, R., and Spasoff, R. (2005). Income inequality and health in Ontario: A multilevel analysis. *Canadian Journal of Public Health, 96*(3), 206–211.

Young, K. T., Reading, J., Elias, B., and O'Neil, J. (2000). Type II diabetes mellitus in Canada's First Nations: Status of an epidemic in progress. *Canadian Medical Association Journal, 163*(5), 561–566.

Chapter Nine

Poverty and Health: Mechanisms and Pathways

Poverty is the worst form of violence.— Mohandas Gandhi

Learning Objectives

At the conclusion of this chapter, the reader will be able to:

- discuss various frameworks by which poverty comes to influence health;
- describe the shortcomings of individually oriented approaches to understanding the poverty and health relationship;
- identify the benefits of looking at broader, structurally oriented approaches to understanding the poverty and health relationship;
- extend the analysis of the poverty and health relationship to analysis of the political and economic forces that shape the distribution of wealth and power within a society; and
- explain the role that economic globalization plays in the poverty and health relationship.

Introduction

There is little dispute that the experience of poverty is a primary cause of disease and illness. Study after study finds that the experience of living under conditions of material and social deprivation is the best predictor of health outcomes, and its effects on health swamp the influence of behavioural risk factors such as diet, physical activity, and even tobacco use.

In this chapter, three types of frameworks that explain how the experience of poverty leads to health outcomes are presented. First, there are very narrow frameworks that limit attention to behavioural risk factors, such as physical activity, diet, and tobacco and alcohol use and how these come to influence health. These approaches to the experience of poverty focus on identifying those individuals whose health-threatening behaviours are worthy of attention by behavioural health promoters. These approaches usually say nothing about how the material and social deprivation experienced by people living in poverty directly affects their health and shapes their adoption of these health-threatening behaviours. These narrow models certainly do not emphasize actions to reduce the incidence of poverty among Canadians.

Second, and of much greater value, are broader frameworks that consider how the experience of material and social deprivation associated with living in poverty both directly and indirectly influence health. These frameworks identify the immediate and more distant societal structures that shape the poverty experience and show how the experience of poverty leads to health problems. More detailed biological and psychological frameworks consider how this experience of poverty comes to influence bodily systems and sets the stage for present and future disease. These biological and psychological approaches consider how people's bodies respond to the experience of material and social deprivation and help explain how the experience of living in poverty "gets under the skin" to determine health.

Third, there are frameworks that examine how political and economic forces determine the distribution of economic and social resources, creating the experience of living in poverty. These frameworks show how high rates of poverty represent societal approaches to societal organization and resource provision. These frameworks also include the role economic globalization can play in producing high levels of poverty and shaping how society responds to the needs of people living in poverty. Included within these broader frameworks are analyses of the pathways and mechanisms by which gender, race, and status lead to the experience of poverty and then shape its contribution to health. Despite these advances in knowledge, however, there is still an inordinate amount of attention paid by researchers, health workers, and the media to individualistic approaches focused on individual risk behaviours. Numerous reasons are advanced in this chapter as to why this might be the case.

Individual Approaches

An individual perspective limits its analysis of the health risks associated with living in poverty to individual biomedical and behavioural risk factors for disease (Raphael et al., 2005). For biomedical indicators, this is associated with screening for physiological and medical risk factors such as hypertension, excess weight, cholesterol, and high blood glucose levels, among others (Labonte, 1993). The appropriate responses to these threats are some form of mandated behavioural regime or treatment with drugs. In the case of behavioural risk factors such as lack of physical activity, type of diet, and use of alcohol and tobacco, the response is to exhort the individual to carry out a series of changes in their behaviour.

These individual perspectives carry the assumption that these biomedical and behavioural factors are primary contributors to the health conditions experienced by people living in poverty (Nettleton, 1997). While these risk factors may contribute to disease, this is little evidence to assign them a primary role in explaining how the poverty and health relationship comes about. Indeed, evidence has accumulated that biomedical and behavioural factors play a relatively minor role—as compared to life circumstances—in predicting life expectancy, cardiovascular disease and stroke, type 2 diabetes, respiratory disease, and stomach cancer among other afflictions (Davey Smith and Gordon, 2000; Johnson et al., 2003; Lawlor, Ebrahim, and Smith, 2002). Additionally, there is an assumption that these risk factors can be modified—with resultant improvements in health—either by medical interventions or by "healthy choices" on the part of the person living in poverty (Fitzpatrick, 2001).

There is also little evidence in support of the healthy choices assumption. Biomedical and behavioural risk factors are heavily structured by the material and social living conditions people experience (Jarvis and Wardle, 2006; Shaw, Dorling, Gordon, and Davey Smith, 1999). And there is little evidence of success for behavioural interventions applied to vulnerable populations such as those living in poverty (O'Loughlin, Paradis, Gray-Donald, and Renaud, 1999). Finally, the focus on biomedical and behavioural risk factors puts forth a particular ideological view concerning the sources of health inequalities in general, and the living situations and health status of people living in poverty in particular. Travers (1996) argues:

> *Individualism assumes that the current social system provides sufficient and equal opportunity for individuals to move within the social system according to their abilities. Within this ideological construct, poverty results from the individual's failure to seize the opportunity or to work sufficiently hard within the current social structure; it is not a reflection of inadequacies and inequities within that social order. (p. 551)*

Despite their clear inadequacy for explaining the means by which people living in poverty come to experience poor health status, individualist approaches dominate public understandings, health care and public health discourses and messaging, and governmental policy to health promotion and population health (Canadian Population Health Initiative, 2004; Raphael, 2000). Why this is so is considered following the presentation of more relevant and useful frameworks that explain the pathways and mechanisms by which poverty comes to be so strongly related to health.

Poverty as Material and Social Deprivation

In earlier chapters, poverty was defined as the situation where economic resources are so limited as to constitute a situation of material and social deprivation that is associated with an inability to participate in activities normally expected of members of a wealthy developed nation. It was also argued that poverty represents a situation that results from the organization of society and from how a society distributes economic and social resources. And in Chapter 8, it was demonstrated that the health status of people living in poverty is profoundly influenced by these processes. Brunner and Marmot (2006) provide a broad descriptive model that outlines how the organization of society shapes health. While the model contains no explicit recognition of the experience of poverty, it can guide examination of the mechanisms and pathways by which poverty comes to determine health. The model links social structure to health and disease via material, psychosocial, and behavioural pathways. Genetics, early life, and cultural factors are further important influences upon population health. Their model is presented in Figure 9.1.

Figure 9.1: Social Determinants of Health

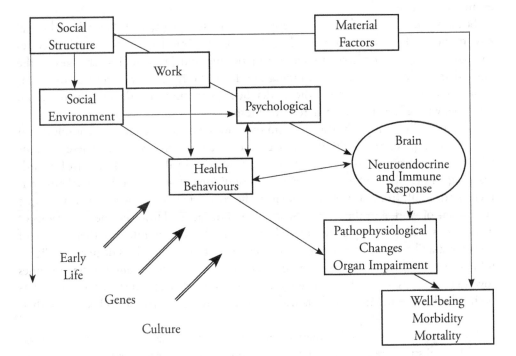

Source: Brunner, E., and Marmot, M. G. (2006). Social organization, stress, and health. In M. G. Marmot and R. G. Wilkinson (Eds.), *Social determinants of health* (Figure 2.2, p. 9). Oxford: Oxford University Press.

Are material and social deprivation—the primary components of the definition of poverty applied in this volume—considered in Brunner and Marmot's model? Not exactly. In their model, "[m]aterial circumstances are related to health directly, and via the social and work environment" (Brunner and Marmot, 2006, p. 8). Social structure is provided as a catch-all for the organization of society and how it distributes both access to and actual material and social resources. Though not elucidated by their model, the concepts of class, status, and party that define social inequality (see Chapter 4) shape both the organization of the social structure and how it distributes access to resources. Additionally, the components of social exclusion (as presented in Chapter 4) map out these dimensions: legal exclusion; exclusion from social goods such as income, housing, and various services; exclusion from social production involving social and cultural activities; and exclusion from social consumption associated with normal forms of livelihood and economy. All these issues come together to increase risks to health for people living in poverty.

The model shows a direct link between social structure and health status (i.e., well-being, morbidity, and mortality) that reflects the impact of material factors. Material factors are the concrete living conditions that include both positive exposures to health-enhancing events and situations as well as exposures to negative, health-threatening events and situations.

Social structure itself shapes a variety of key environments, such as work and social environments. These environments then shape psychological and behavioural processes that come to influence nervous-system functioning and physiological changes in the body that can lead to disease and premature death. Early life, genes, and culture contribute to processes at all levels of the model. Social structure has a direct influence upon early life, with effects that carry across the lifespan.

Like many linear models, this diagram does not take into account the complexity of the relationships among health determinants and the relationships of these determinants with health outcomes. All of these factors are iterative in that each has both forward-reaching and feedback effects. For example, conditions of work and the social environment both result from, as well as influence, the social structure. Social structure shapes conditions of work and the quality of social environments. However, the conditions of work and wages that people are exposed to then feeds back to influence their degree of power and ability to determine aspects of the social structure, such as degree of political influence, responsiveness of governments to needs and aspirations, and societal attitudes toward the groups to which they belong. Low-waged workers, for instance, will have less political influence and governments will be less responsive to their needs because of their lower class and status.

Similarly, neighbourhoods experiencing high crime rates as a result of the organization of social structure and its distribution of resources may develop adverse reputations that limit their ability to influence societal and governmental responsiveness and attitudes toward their community. Such feedback may further marginalize and stigmatize the community in question, although it would be hoped that responses would be more positive. And all of these specific environments have direct effects upon health through material factor pathways.

Psychological factors and health behaviours also feed back to affect the quality of work and social environments as well as the social structure itself. Stress-producing circumstances associated with living in poverty may create unpleasant work and social environments that make coping and managing even more difficult. One way to think about this is to consider that all the factors in Figure 9.1 are interrelated. In relation to the experience of poverty, Table 9.1 outlines pathways by which poverty shapes the quality of a variety of health determinants and is itself shaped by the quality of these same health determinants. The experience of poverty is related to health through its being both an influence upon and the result of its association with various health determinants.

As shown in Table 9.1, for every health determinant, the experience of poverty creates adverse conditions for health. In the following sections, four models that fill in some of the underlying processes outlined in Figure 9.1 are presented: the materialist, neo-materialist, life-course, and social comparison models. Within these four broad models, more specific accounts of pathways mediating the poverty and health phenomena are presented.

Table 9.1: How the Experience of Poverty Contributes to—and Results from—the Adverse Quality of Various Determinants of Health

Health Determinant	Role Played in the Poverty and Health Relationship
Social Structure	Determines the availability of material and social resources available to the population, and the organization and quality of work and social environments. Poverty results from a failure of the social structure to provide individuals with the resources necessary to avoid material and social deprivation, thereby leading to health and other problems.
Work Environment	Shapes work dimensions that promote health and well-being. Also determines the amount of money that results from work, quality of benefits, and degree of security. The experience of poverty both leads to differing experiences of workplace quality, and is a result of workplaces not providing resources to meet material and social needs.
Social Environment	Degree of social support and quality of social interactions influenced by availability of material resources and conditions of everyday life. Poverty makes availability of these supports less likely. Poverty also weakens quality of immediate social environment due to clustering of disadvantaged individuals within specific spatial areas.
Psychological	Experience of control, reward, and status result from differing family, social, and work environments. Experience of stress related to ability to meet basic needs, experiencing of stigma, and exclusion shapes adoption of coping mechanisms. Poverty creates adverse experiences and these experiences in turn make transcending poverty more difficult.
Health Behaviours	Represent means of coping with effects of material and social deprivation associated with poor-quality environments. When chosen as a response to the experience of poverty, these have the potential to further threaten health, making escape from poverty less likely.
Brain	Stress and auto-immune systems weakened by accumulated adverse experiences associated with material and social deprivation, lack of control and adequate rewards, and chronic experience of fight or flight reaction. Adverse health makes escape from poverty less likely.
Pathophysiological Changes	Disease resulting from organ impairment results from adverse experiences associated with poverty. Degree of economic resources interacts with availability of health and social services to contribute to degree of health impairment.
Health Status	Onset of disease and illness interacts with economic and societal supports available to shape progression of illness as well as social, work, and other environments. Conditions of poverty make positive outcomes less likely.

Materialist Explanations for the Poverty and Health Relationship

The materialist framework sees the objective living conditions of people living in poverty as explaining the poverty and health relationship (Bartley, 2003). The materialist approach is concerned with how objective living conditions associated with poverty come to shape health. According to the materialist argument as outlined by Benzeval and colleagues, there are three key mechanisms that link poverty to health: (a) experience of adverse living conditions; (b) experience of excessive stress; and (c) adoption of health-threatening coping behaviours (Benzeval, Judge, and Whitehead, 1995). All of these mechanisms reflect experience with the concrete living conditions associated with poverty. The first part of the *materialist* argument is that individuals living in poverty experience exposures to positive and negative living conditions over their lives that differ profoundly from those not in living in poverty. These different exposures accumulate to produce adult health outcomes (Shaw et al., 1999).

For people living in poverty, exposures to living situations and events are especially likely to be negative. Socio-economic position in general and poverty in particular are powerful predictors of health, as they are indicators of material advantage or disadvantage over the lifespan (Lynch and Kaplan, 2000). These material conditions of life include childhood deprivation related to lack of nourishment and poor housing, and adult issues of unemployment, occupational hazards, lack of resources to acquire health and social services, among others (Shaw et al., 1999). Material conditions of life determine health by influencing the quality of individual development, family life and interaction, and community environments (Brooks-Gunn, Duncan, and Britto, 1998). And the material conditions of life associated with poverty lead to greater likelihood of physical problems (infections, malnutrition, chronic disease, and injuries); developmental problems (delayed or impaired cognitive, personality, and social development); educational problems (learning disabilities, poor learning, early school leaving), and social problems (socialization, preparation for work and family life) (Davey Smith and Gordon, 2000; Hertzman, 1998, 1999a; Hertzman and Frank, 2006; Roberts, Smith, and Nason, 2001; Ross and Roberts, 1999).

While people living in poverty show the greatest effects of material and social deprivation, there are also graded effects, whereby lower-middle-class people are more affected than middle-class people who are more affected than upper-middle-class people, and so on (Benzeval, Dilnot, Judge, and Taylor, 2001; Graham, 2001). Some have argued that evidence of this graded effect suggests that psychological rather than material living conditions shape health outcomes; that is, people's position in the social hierarchy affects their feelings of worth and their health (Marmot, 2004; Wilkinson, 2001; Wilkinson and Pickett, 2009). However, materialists counter by arguing that findings of steeped differences among social classes and income groups occurs because

> [t]he social structure is characterized by a finely graded scale of advantage and disadvantage, with individuals differing in terms of the length and level of their exposure to a particular factor and in terms of the number of factors to which they are exposed. (Shaw et al., p. 102)

And the primary and most severe disadvantage is centred on people living in poverty.

Within a materialist framework, Benzeval and colleagues (2001) develop the concepts of income potential and health capital to explicate some of the features of the poverty and health relationship:

> Income potential *is the accumulation of abilities, skills and educational experiences in childhood that are important determinants of adult employability and income capacity. Education is seen as the key mediator in this association, being strongly influenced by family circumstances in childhood and a central determinant of an individual's income in adulthood.*

> Health capital *is the accumulation of health resources, both physical and psychosocial, inherited and acquired during the early stages of life which determine current health and future health potential. (p. 97)*

In their model, childhood circumstances are a result of their parents' characteristics, their objective living conditions, and other aspects of their social environments. These all contribute to their immediate health status and their potential to acquire income in adulthood. As adults, both the experiences of childhood and adult situations then go on to influence health as adults (see Figure 9.2).

A more detailed rendering of the influence of material factors upon health is provided by van de Mheen, Stronks, and Mackenbach (1998). In their model, childhood socio-economic circumstances (a) are explicitly related to childhood health; (b) set a trajectory that, if left unchanged, will continue to accumulate socio-economic advantage or disadvantage over time; and (c) have both direct influence upon adult health and an indirect effect upon adult health through mediating processes of personality and health

Figure 9.2: Income and Health: A Life Course Perspective

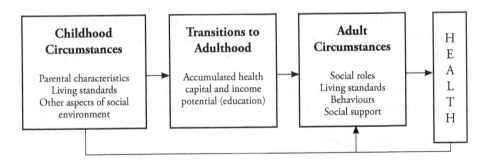

Source: Benzeval, M., Dilnot, A., Judge, K., and Taylor, J. (2001). Income and health over the lifecourse: Evidence and policy implications. In H. Graham (Ed.), *Understanding health inequalities* (Figure 6.1, p. 98). Buckingham, UK: Open University Press.

behaviours. These mediating processes include a psychological sense of personal control and efficacy, and the adoption of health-threatening behaviours such as tobacco use, diet, and alcohol use (see Figure 9.3).

There are also selection processes by which unhealthy adults fall into a spiral of lowering socio-economic conditions. This model certainly seems plausible for Canada. The results from van de Mheen and colleagues' study of Dutch citizens and many other similar studies support the usefulness of understanding the role that the material and social deprivation associated with living in poverty plays in explaining health outcomes.

Figure 9.3: Living Conditions, Socio-economic Inequalities, and Children's Health

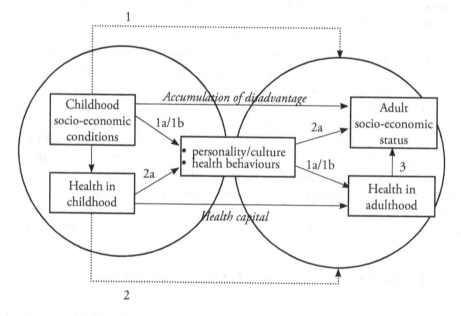

1   Contribution of childhood socio-economic conditions to socio-economic health inequalities in adult life
1a   Independent effect of childhood socio-economic conditions on adult health
1b   Independent effect of childhood socio-economic conditions on adult health through health behaviours and personality/cultural factors
2   Contribution of childhood health to socio-economic health inequalities in adult life
2a   Contribution of childhood health to socio-economic health inequalities in adult life through selection on health in childhood
3   Selection on health in adult life

Source: van de Mheen, H., Stronks, K., and Mackenbach, J. 1998. A lifecourse perspective on socioeconomic inequalities in health (Figure 1, p. 194). In M. Bartley, D. Blane, and G. Davey Smith (Eds.)., *The sociology of health inequalities*. Oxford, UK: Blackwell Publishers.

The second component of the materialist model is that the living conditions associated with living in poverty produces health-threatening stress. The human fight-or-flight reaction evolved as a means of dealing with sudden and dangerous threats in the environment (Brunner and Marmot, 2006). The body responds to these immediate threats by either fighting or fleeing. Such a response involves a variety of bodily systems: the sympathetic and parasympathetic nervous systems, the neuroendocrine system, and the metabolic system. If, however, the reaction is chronically elicited as a response to continual threats of insecure income, housing, and food, among others, it takes its toll on health.

Chronic elicitation of the fight-or-flight reaction can weaken the immune system and disrupt the neuroendocrine and metabolic systems (Brunner and Marmot, 2006; Lupien, King, Meaney, and McEwan, 2001). And evidence from surveys and explorations of the lived experience of poverty indicate that living in poverty makes such stress especially likely (Allison, Adlaf, Ialomiteanu, and Rehm, 1999; Avison, 1997; Cohen, Kaplan, and Salonen, 1999; Davey Smith, Ben-Shlomo, and Lynch, 2002; Stewart et al., 1996). Indeed, there is accumulating evidence that individuals who experience difficult living circumstances associated with living in poverty come to have maladaptive responses to stress, weakened immunity to infections and disease, and greater likelihood of metabolic disorders (Davey Smith et al., 2002; Lupien et al., 2001; Sapolsky, 1992; Wamala, Lynch, and Horsten, 1999). (See Figure 9.4.)

Figure 9.4: The Psychobiological Stress Response

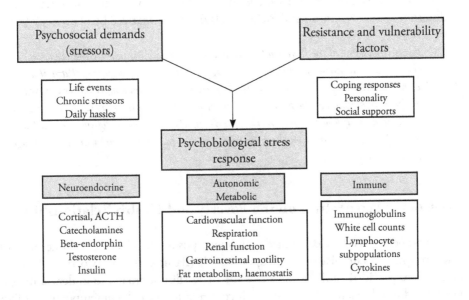

Source: Steptoe, A. (1998). Psychophysiological bases of disease (pp. 39-78). In *Comprehensive Clinical Psychology*, Volume 8: Health Psychology, Johnston, D.W. and Johnston, M. Eds., New York: Elsevier Science.

A specific model of how chronic elicitation of the fight-or-flight reaction can come to shape two key chronic diseases—cardiovascular disease, and type 2 or insulin-resistant diabetes—is provided by Brunner and Marmot (2006). They clearly specify how the social environment can have a direct stress-related effect upon the circulatory and metabolic systems leading to cardiovascular disease and type 2 diabetes. Brunner and Marmot also show how stress responses can promote health-threatening behaviours such as tobacco use, lack of physical activity, and increased fat and sugar intake, all of which further contribute to the incidence of these two diseases. Nevertheless, approaches to cardiovascular disease and type 2 or insulin-resistant diabetes are dominated by lifestyle approaches to risk and prevention despite the accumulating evidence in support of a broader, social determinants–oriented approach (Raphael, Anstice, and Raine, 2003; Raphael and Farrell, 2002).

The third component of the materialist model is that material deprivation and the stress associated with it lead to the adoption of health-threatening behaviours as coping responses. Numerous Canadian studies show that people living in poverty are more likely to participate in what are termed risk-related behaviours (Health Canada, 1999; Pomerleau, Pederson, Østbye, Speechley, and Speechley, 1997; Potvin, Richard, and Edwards, 2000; Williamson, 2000). Individuals who experience the deprived material and social conditions associated with living in poverty are more likely to take up tobacco, use alcohol, have poor diets, and engage in less physical activity. The materialist explanation, however, views these behaviours as a reflection of life circumstances (Bartley, 2003; Shaw et al., 1999; Shaw et al., 2006). Similarly, the adoption of carbohydrate-dense diets and subsequent weight gain are seen as means of coping with difficult circumstances (Wilkinson, 1996; Wilkinson and Pickett, 2009). As summarized by Shaw et al. (1999):

> We also see that some of the factors which contribute to health inequalities—such as smoking and inadequate diet—are themselves strongly influenced by the unequal distribution of income, wealth and life chances in general. These factors do not simply reflect the lack of knowledge or fecklessness of the poorer members of society. If we are to tackle inequalities in health we need an approach which deals with the fundamental causes of such inequalities, not one which focuses mainly on those processes which mediate between social disadvantage and poor health. (p. 105)

Life-Course Perspectives on the Poverty and Health Relationship

Life-course perspectives are concerned with how exposures to adverse economic and social conditions have a cumulative effect upon health (Bartley, 2003). Two such life-course models were provided earlier to illustrate the materialist approach to understanding the poverty and health relationship. While it is common to research contemporaneous living situations as contributors to health, it is important not to neglect the accumulated effects upon health of experiences across the lifespan. This is especially important when considering how living in poverty influences health. In Canada, the lack of longitudinal studies of health can reinforce a focus on the immediate health effects of living in poverty (Raphael et al., 2005). However, research from elsewhere provides evidence of the importance of these cumulative effects (Davey Smith et al., 2002; Davey Smith and Gordon, 2000; Davey Smith, Hart, Blane, Gillis, and Hawthorne, 1997; Lynch, Kaplan, and Salonen, 1997; Power, Bartley, Davey Smith, and Blane, 1996).

Hertzman (2000a) outlines three types of health effects that have relevance for a life-course perspective. *Latent effects* are biologic or developmental early life experiences that influence health later in life. These biologic or developmental factors that impact at sensitive periods in human development have a lifelong effect, regardless of later circumstances. Some of these effects may occur prior to birth and are related to the quality of nutrients received, incidence of infections and mothers' use of tobacco, all of which affect availability of oxygen to organs. These latent effects may come to affect blood clotting and cholesterol metabolism, and lead to coronary heart disease and type 2 diabetes in later life.

During infancy, latent effects upon health may result from malnutrition and infections. Malnutrition may affect health, cognitive development, and educational attainment during childhood and later life. Infections such as colds, earaches, and respiratory problems can provide long-term developmental risk and increase problems with airway and respiratory function.

All of these latent effects are more common among people living in poverty. As well, there is a greater incidence of low birth-weight, which is a reliable predictor of incidence of cardiovascular disease and adult-onset diabetes in later life (Barker, Forsen, Uutela, Osmond, and Eriksson, 2001; Bartley, Power, Blane, Davey, and Shipley, 1994; Davey Smith et al., 2002; Forssas, Gissler, Sihvonen, and Hemminki, 1999). Exposure to poor environmental conditions as a child can lead to later respiratory problems as an adult. Experience of nutritional deprivation during childhood has a variety of lasting health effects (Forsen, Eriksson, Tuomilehto, Osmond, and Barker, 1999; James, Nelson, Ralph, and Leather, 1997; Sarlio-Lahteenkorva and Lahelma, 2001).

Pathway effects are experiences that set individuals onto trajectories that influence health, well-being, and competence over the life course. Children living in poverty are more likely to enter school with delayed vocabulary (Willms, 1997, 2002). This then sets them upon a path that leads to lower educational expectations and achievement, poorer employment prospects, less accumulation of financial resources, and greater likelihood of illness and disease across the lifespan (Ronson and Rootman, 2009). Material and social deprivation associated with poor-quality neighbourhoods, schools, and housing also sets children living in poverty on paths that do not support health and well-being across the lifespan (Hertzman, 1998, 1999b, 2000b; Hertzman and Frank, 2006; Hertzman and Power, 2003). Early life may be a particularly critical or sensitive period in itself or it may serve as a marker indicating down which path a person is headed. In either event, early life establishes a pathway that leads to the accumulation of exposures to either positive or negative health producing effects.

Cumulative effects represent the accumulation of advantages or disadvantages over time (Hertzman and Frank, 2006; Hertzman and Power, 2003). These involve a combination of latent and pathways effects. Children living in poverty begin to accumulate these disadvantages, and if they continue to live in poverty, these disadvantages further accumulate. If they escape poverty, accumulation of disadvantage stops, but the previously accumulated disadvantage continues with them into adulthood producing greater likelihood of adverse health outcomes.

The effects of the accumulation of positive or negative health effects over time are multi-faceted and involve individual, family, and community factors. This is especially the case for diseases such as cardiovascular disease, type 2 diabetes, respiratory disease, and some cancers. Adopting a life-course perspective directs attention to how the experience of living in poverty influences health at every level of development—early childhood, childhood, adolescence, and adulthood. As noted, much of the specific evidence for life-course effects comes from studies from outside Canada, but increasing availability of data from Canadian studies that follow people over time should confirm the robust findings of the accumulative adverse health effects of living in poverty (Dooley and Curtis, 1998; Ross, Roberts, and Scott, 1998).

The notion of latent, pathway, and cumulative effects helps to explain much of the empirical findings concerning the impact of living in poverty upon child and adult health. In the end, however, the implications for policy are probably the same, whichever effects, latent, pathway, or cumulative is most influential in shaping health: reduce poverty and ensure that people currently living in poverty do not experience material and social deprivation.

Neo-materialist Explanations for the Poverty and Health Relationship

The neo-materialist argument, like the materialist approach, is concerned with how health outcomes come to be associated with exposures to positive and negative living conditions over the lifespan, but extends the analysis to consider how these threatening living conditions come about (Bartley, 2003; Lynch, Smith, Kaplan, and House, 2000). In this analysis, focus is on how a society allocates resources among the population. Generally, nations with higher poverty rates are less likely to distribute income and wealth equitably and are lower spenders on social infrastructure that includes education and libraries, social services, public health coverage, and supports for the unemployed and those with disabilities. The effects of these meagre public expenditures go on to magnify the health-related effects associated with living in poverty. Not surprisingly, such unequal jurisdictions frequently show poorer population health profiles.

Canada has a smaller proportion of people living in poverty, a smaller gap between rich and poor, and spends relatively more on public infrastructure in some key areas than the USA (Ross et al., 2000). Not surprisingly, Canadians generally enjoy better health than Americans as measured by infant mortality rates, life expectancy, and incidence of, and mortality from, a range of diseases, as well as childhood injuries (Innocenti Research Centre, 2000, 2001; Jackson, 2002; Organisation for Economic Co-operation and Development, 2009). But Canada does not do as well as Sweden, where distribution of resources is much more equalitarian, poverty rates are very low, and health indicators are among the best in the world. And as noted in Chapter 8, the profound health-status differences that exist between Canadians living in poverty and those who do not reflect both the extent of poverty in Canada (neo-materialist view) and the health-related effects of living in poverty (materialist view).

The neo-materialist view directs attention to both the effects of living conditions associated with poverty on individuals' health (materialist view) and the societal factors that determine the quality of these living conditions (neo-materialist). How a society decides to distribute resources among citizens is especially important.

Social Comparison Explanations for the Poverty and Health Relationship

In the research literature, the social comparison approach is usually presented as a competing explanation to the materialist framework (Bartley, 2003). In this model, material and social conditions of life are downplayed in favour of the view that individual placement in the social hierarchy and social distance explain differences in health status (Raphael, 2003). Rather than focus on the effects of material and social deprivation associated with poverty, the argument here is that the health status of people living in poverty in developed nations is shaped by citizens' interpretations of their standings in the social hierarchy (Kawachi and Kennedy, 2002). There are two mechanisms by which this occurs.

At the individual level, the perception and experience of personal status in unequal societies lead to stress and poor health for those living in poverty. Comparing their status, possessions, and other life circumstances to others, individuals experience feelings of shame, worthlessness, and envy that have psychobiological effects upon health. These comparisons lead to attempts to alleviate such feelings through overspending, taking on additional employment that threatens health, and adopting health-threatening coping behaviours such as overeating and use of alcohol and tobacco (Kawachi and Kennedy, 2002). Figure 9.5 illustrates this process.

At the communal level, the widening and strengthening of hierarchy weakens social cohesion. Individuals become more distrusting and suspicious of others, thereby weakening support for communal structures such as public education, health, and social programs. An exaggerated desire for tax reductions on the part of the public weakens public infrastructure.

This model can be criticized on various grounds. First, it neglects the profound and concrete effects of material and social deprivation on health, especially among people living in poverty (Lynch et al., 2000). Second, it depoliticizes issues of societal organization and distribution of economic and other resources among the population, obscuring the sources of poverty and the political, economic, and social forces that maintain it (Muntaner, 2004). Third, it reduces the health-related effects of poverty to psychological processes of maladaptive coping on the part of people living in poverty (Shaw et al., 1999).

Some of the processes described by the social comparison model may help to explain how living under conditions of material and social deprivation contributes to health. Comparing oneself to others and seeing oneself come up short can clearly contribute to

Figure 9.5: Summary of Possible Relationships between Social Comparisons, Other Psychological Factors, Deprivation, and Health

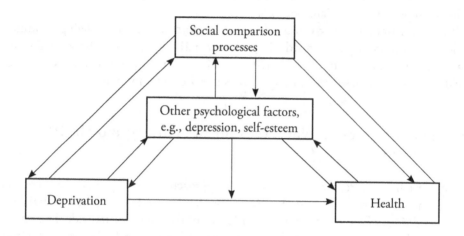

Source: Graham, E., MacLeod, M., Johnston, D., Dibben, C., Morgan, I., and Briscoe, S. (2000). Individual deprivation, neighbourhood, and recovery from illness. In H. Graham (Ed.), *Understanding health inequalities* (Figure 11.1, p. 177). Buckingham, UK: Open University Press.

poor health. But the source of these comparisons lies not with individual interpretations of these shortcomings, but rather in the societal structures and processes that create such inequalities. In addition, the perception of coming up short may not originate with individuals who are living in poverty but rather with the attitudes and views that exist among societal members who are not poor. And these attitudes and views may be shaped by the same forces that create the societal process that create and maintain poverty, serving therefore to justify its existence.

Tarlov (1996) attempted an integration of the materialist and social comparison approaches. In this model, both the experience of differences in the material and social conditions of life and the interpretations of these differences contribute to health. People living in poverty experience inequity, limited opportunity, employment instability, and social segregation. These all lead to the experience of material and social deprivation. In addition, people living in poverty observe social inequality. People living in poverty see that their housing, education, social acceptance, employment, and income are inferior to others. These observations of inequality produce stress that reflects the dissonance between expectations and realities. These stress reactions lead to a variety of health-threatening biological reactions related to lipid disorders and the creation of atherosclerotic plaque formation in the circulatory system.

Social comparison processes appear to be especially relevant to the experiences of people living in poverty. But the sources of these interpretations must be seen as embedded in the material and social conditions of life associated with poverty.

Societal Structures and the Experience of Material and Social Deprivation and Psychosocial Stress

There are still some missing pieces to the materialist and neo-materialist models. These are the specific mechanisms by which the experience of poverty and its health effects are shaped by immediate and more distant features of the environment. Raphael and colleagues use the term *horizontal structures* to refer to the more immediate societal structures with which people living in poverty interact (Raphael et al., 2005). They then consider how these interactions come to produce health effects. More distant societal structures that influence the incidence of and the experience of living in poverty are called *vertical structures* (Raphael et al., 2005). Understanding the experience of poverty and its health effects involves both kinds of structures.

Some horizontal structures with which people living in poverty interact are the health and social services within a community; the availability and quality of housing; the educational, employment, and recreational opportunities available; and other material and social resources to be found within a community. There are extensive literatures that detail how the organization of these horizontal structures shapes the experience of poverty. For example, people living in poverty are more likely to experience inadequate housing (Bryant, 2009; Shaw, 2001), less adequate educational opportunities and schools (Willms, 1999, 2001), more precarious work and poorer working conditions (Jackson, 2009; Tremblay, 2009), and less safe and cohesive neighbourhoods (Bédard, 1996; Hatfield, 1997). Some of these issues are taken up in Chapter 10.

Vertical structures represent the political, economic, and social forces that determine how income and other resources are distributed to individuals. Focus on opportunities for employment and training, distribution of income and social benefits, and social welfare and tax policies within a jurisdiction constitutes such an analysis (Raphael, 2009). Jurisdictions make decisions that not only create or maintain poverty, but shape the quality of the horizontal structures with which people living in poverty must interact. The analysis of some of these vertical structures is taken up in Chapter 11.

Gender, Race, and Disability-Related Pathways That Mediate the Poverty and Health Relationship

In addition to the materialist, life-course, neo-materialist life-course, and social comparison approaches to understanding how poverty influences health, specific pathways and mechanisms related to gender, race, and disability have been outlined. The following sections consider these pathways and mechanisms.

Gender
Gender is an important pathway mediating the poverty and health relationship. Women are more likely than men to be living in poverty in Canada. This is the case because, for the most part, women are responsible for raising children and caring for the health

needs of families (Armstrong, 2009). As a result, women are less likely to be working full time and are less likely to be eligible for employment insurance benefits (Jackson, 2010; Tremblay, 2009).

Women are also more likely to be employed in lower paying occupations and experience discrimination in the workplace. In addition, just about every public policy decision that weakens the provision of economic and social security—such as failure to raise minimum wages or social assistance benefits, reducing access to public health services, limiting the availability of affordable housing or government-supported quality child care, and introducing restrictive workfare requirements—disproportionately affects women more than men (Armstrong, 1996). Excellent analyses of how gender can inform an analysis of the pathways mediating poverty and health in Canada are available (Armstrong, Lippman, and Sky, 1997; Davies, McMullin, Avison, and Cassidy, 2001; Hadley, 2001; Lochhead and Scott, 2000; Pahlke, Lord, and Christiansen-Ruffman, 2001; Rosenberg and Wilson, 2000; Townson, 2000; Travers, 1996).

Race

Race is also becoming an important pathway mediating the poverty-and-health relationship. The poverty situation of Aboriginal Canadians is well established (Lee, 2000; MacMillan, MacMillan, Offord, and Dingle, 1996; Smiley, 2009). Other people of colour in Canada earn less income, are more likely to be unemployed, and experience more precarious employment than other Canadians (Galabuzi, 2005; Jackson, 2010). This all comes together to produce higher rates of poverty for people of colour in Canada. The situation of recent immigrants of colour in Canada is especially problematic. Attempts to explain these differences as being a function of educational and employment experience differences have generally been unsuccessful (Hou and Picot, 2003; Picot, 2004).

Galabuzi (2005) suggests that processes of discrimination and exclusion are interacting with greater employment pressures and the increasing precariousness of employment associated with increasing economic globalization. The result is the increasing concentration of poverty among specific neighbourhoods of colour and increasing evidence of adverse health and social effects upon individuals and communities (Hou and Picot, 2003; United Way of Greater Toronto, 2004).

Newbold and Danforth (1993) found that immigrants to Canada were more likely to rate their health as poor or fair than non-immigrants, and that this was especially the case for those who had been in Canada for longer periods of time. Ng, Wilkins, Gendron, and Berthelot (2004) found that, compared to the Canadian-born population, recent non-European immigrants were twice as likely to report a deterioration in health from 1993–1994 to 2002–2003.

Disability

People with disabilities are profoundly disadvantaged in a variety of areas related to poverty (Fawcett, 2000; Lee, 2000). These include employment opportunities, wages, and receipt of benefits (Jackson, 2010). Canadian public policy toward people with disabilities is underdeveloped in relation to other nations, a topic taken up in Chapter 12.

Political and Economic Pathways

Political and economic pathways are analyses specifically concerned with how political decisions shape the distribution of economic and social resources. This area is becoming increasingly important with growing economic globalization and its impact upon the distribution of economic and social resources and political decision making. This is a very underdeveloped area in the Canadian health sciences literature. A recent review found increasing attention being directed to this area by a few Canadian researchers (Raphael et al., 2005). Particularly important are works by both Coburn and Lynch (Coburn, 2000, 2004; Lynch, 2000).

In a 2000 paper, Coburn argued that neo-liberalism as a governing ideology was a useful explanatory device for explaining the incidence of poverty and growing inequality in nations such as Canada, the USA, and the UK. He suggested that emphasis upon the marketplace as the arbiter of distribution of resources would be associated with higher rate of poverty, weakened social infrastructure, and declining health and quality of life.

Lynch (2000) responded to Coburn's article and provided a model that outlines some of the key issues. Of particular importance to consideration of the poverty-and-health relationship is the component of his model concerned with people living in poverty, euphemistically termed "Individual income for those at the bottom of the social hierarchy" in Figure 9.6.

Figure 9.6: A Neo-material Interpretation of Income Inequality and Health

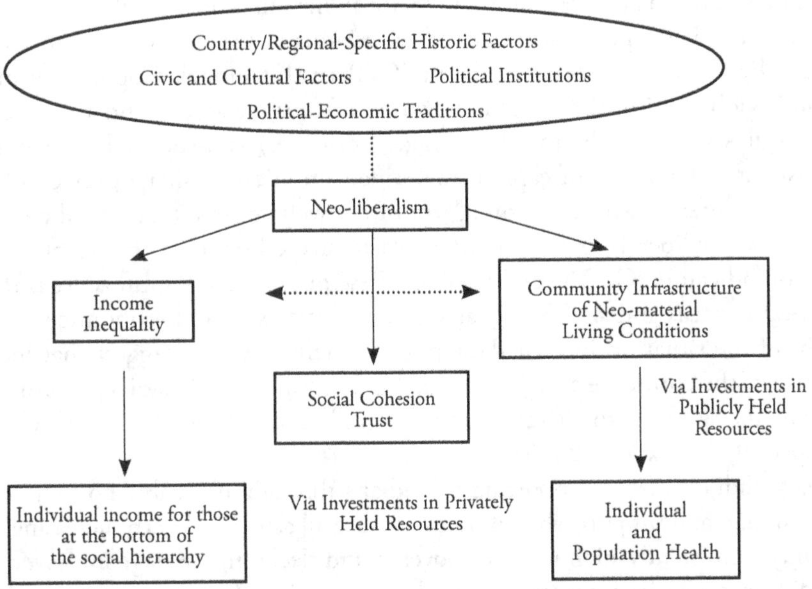

Source: Lynch, J. (2000). Income inequality and health: Expanding the debate (Figure 1, p. 1003). *Social Science and Medicine*, 51, 1001–1005.

In Lynch's model, the situation of people living in poverty—*individual income for those at the bottom of the social hierarchy*—represents the result of a series of processes. Income inequality reflects decisions by societies to allocate resources inequitably. This process results in poverty for many as a direct result of providing low wages and limited benefits to those in need. At the same time, there is limited investment in community infrastructure. These limited commitments affect the health of both people living in poverty and those who are not. It may be that these limited investments especially impact the health and well-being of people living in poverty. The important addition of the Lynch model is placing the degree of income inequality and incidence of poverty as resulting from the adoption of neo-liberal ideology and public policy approaches to resource organization and distribution.

As noted earlier, neo-liberalism is the belief that the marketplace should be the arbiter of how economic and other resources are organized and distributed. It suggests a limited role for government in a wide range of areas. Neo-liberal-oriented governments are more likely to countenance the presence of poverty as they take limited action to control growing income inequality and impoverishment of citizens at the bottom of the social hierarchy. Their withdrawal from provision of a variety of services also magnifies the impact of poverty on health.

For Lynch (2000), whether a nation chooses to go along this path is related to a number of factors such as history, traditions, institutions, and organization of civic society and culture. Political and economic traditions are probably key to understanding the degree of income inequality and poverty within a nation. These traditions and the other components near the top of Lynch's model probably also influence how a nation's government responds to another important factor in health: economic globalization.

A more explicitly political model of these processes with relevance to Canada is provided by Coburn (2004). (See Figure 9.7.) In this model, Coburn outlines how economic globalization (implemented through free-trade agreements that allow business to quickly move jobs to where wages are lower) is associated with both neo-liberalism and the power of capital (investment monies) to shape public policy (A). These forces interact with a nation's form of the welfare state (i.e., social democratic, conservative, or liberal) and the market (B) to shape how these forces play out in a variety of indicators (C). The end result of these public policy approaches is the quality of health status and well-being, as well as a nation's overall economic wealth (D). In light of the situation in Canada, Coburn's analysis would suggest that increasing influence of the corporate elite in Canada has been driving Canadian governments to withdraw the supports to citizens that historically formed the Canadian welfare state (see especially McCaskell, 2009).

This withdrawal from supporting Canadians through affordable housing, employment training, and support when jobs are lost are all associated with increasing income inequality, consistently high levels of poverty, and declining or stagnant governmental expenditures on social infrastructure such as education, housing, transportation, etc. The result should be stagnating or declining levels of health and well-being. As seen in later chapters, there is evidence to suggest that this may indeed be happening in Canada.

Figure 9.7: Globalization, Welfare States, and Population Health

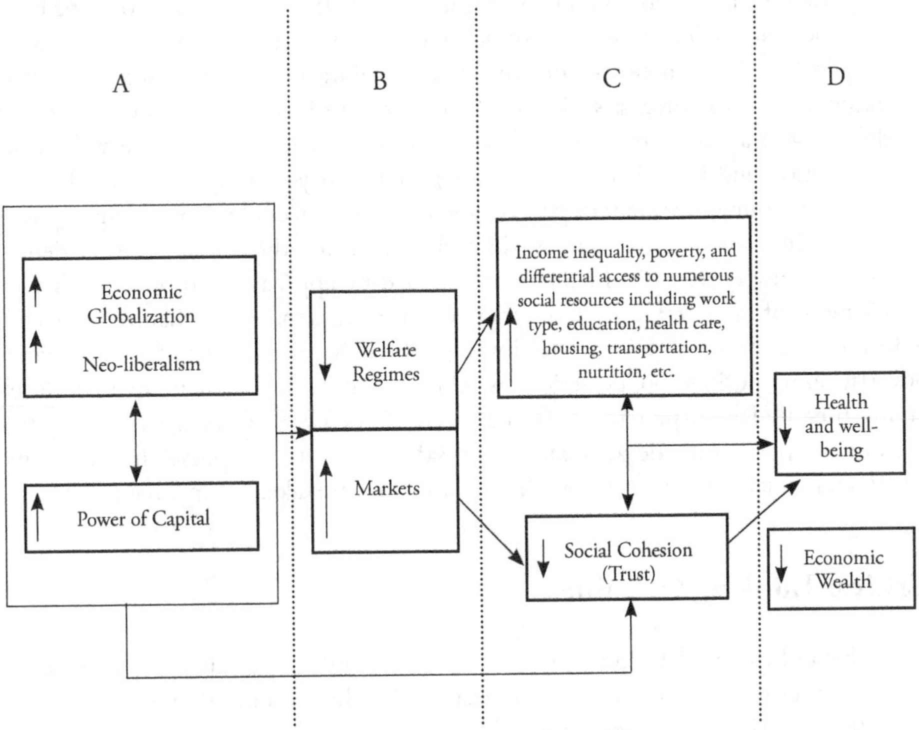

Source: Coburn, D. (2004). Beyond the income inequality hypothesis: Globalization, neo-liberalism, and health inequalities (Figure 2, p. 44). *Social Science and Medicine, 58*, 41–56.

Conclusions

Materialist explanations for the poverty and health relationship are that people living in poverty have systematically different material and social experiences than those not living in poverty. These differences in experiences shape their health. These include greater exposures to material and social conditions of deprivation and fewer exposures to health-enhancing situations and experiences. Neo-materialist explanations focus on the extent to which societies provide limited resources to the population, thereby both creating poverty and magnifying the health-related effects of experiencing poverty. Social comparison theories state that individual compare themselves to each other, and if they find themselves lacking, they experience feelings of stress, envy, and jealousy that threaten their health. This view downplays the importance of material and social deprivation.

There are also other models that concern themselves with the specific features of immediate and distant environments that shape health, especially for those living in poverty. Gender, race, and disability status interacts with environments to shape health. Finally, there are political and economic models that attempt to place public policy-making in broader frameworks of economic distribution that are influenced by globalization and other forces associated with the power of capital or wealth. These latter models suggest a strong role for understanding the broad nature of the welfare state in each nation and how this nature shapes public policy-making. These public policy activities determine the extent of poverty and the experiences of people living in poverty.

Explicit in some of these frameworks and implicit in others is that the incidence of poverty and responses to its incidence are shaped by approaches to public policy. The implications of these frameworks are that governments should do whatever they can to reduce the incidence of poverty and improve the living conditions of people living in poverty. Some positive policy actions would be to provide adequate income, develop family-friendly labour policies, implement active employment policies involving training and supports, provide adequate social safety nets, and improve the provision of health and social services to citizens. These key issues are taken up in Chapters 11 to 14.

Critical Thinking Questions

1. Which of the models do you think are most useful for explaining how the experience of poverty comes to influence health? On what grounds do you say this?
2. What experiences have you personally experienced or observed in others of material and social deprivation? Did these experiences have obvious health or health-related effects?
3. Have you ever had any experiences in which you compared yourself to others and felt bad about it? Do you think that having these negative responses over an extended period of time could make you ill?
4. Which models do you think would be most useful for informing policy-makers and the general public as to the importance of addressing poverty for improving health?
5. Why do you think these models are rarely, if ever, mentioned in the media? What can be done to rectify this?

Recommended Readings

Bartley, M. (2003). *Health inequality: An introduction to concepts, theories, and methods.* Cambridge, UK: Polity Press.

> Large differences in life expectancy exist between the most privileged and the most disadvantaged social groups in industrial societies. This book assists in understanding the four most widely accepted theories of what lies behind inequalities in health: the behavioural, psychosocial, material, and life-course approaches.

Brunner, E., and Marmot, M. G. (2006). Social organization, stress, and health. In M. G. Marmot and R. G. Wilkinson (Eds.), *Social determinants of health* (2nd ed., pp. 6–30). Oxford, UK: Oxford University Press.

This chapter contains details of how social structure and its correlates such as material resources, stress, and health behaviours get under the skin to determine health. The chapter also details how various bodily systems are profoundly affected by the experience of stress associated with living conditions.

Coburn, D. (2004). Beyond the income inequality hypothesis: Globalization, neo-liberalism, and health inequalities. *Social Science and Medicine, 58,* 41–56.

Coburn provides a synthesis of political-economy concepts to help explain the high poverty rates and increasing inequality seen in today's Canada. He outlines a key role for globalization and the increasing influence of neo-liberalism as a governing ideology in shaping the experiences of Canadian in general and people living in poverty in Canada in particular.

Graham, H. (2007). *Unequal lives: Health and socioeconomic inequalities.* Maidenhead, UK: Open University Press.

Unequal Lives provides an evidence-based introduction to social and health inequalities. It brings together research from social epidemiology, sociology, and social policy to guide the reader to an understanding of why people's lives and people's health remain so unequal, even in rich societies where there is more than enough for all.

Keating, D. P., and Hertzman, C. (Eds.). (1999). *Developmental health and the wealth of nations.* New York: Guilford Press.

This book provides contributions that explore the psychological and developmental processes by which health inequalities come about. Concern about economic inequality and poverty as a source of health and other outcomes is evident throughout the volume.

Raphael, D., Colman, R., Labonte, R., MacDonald, J., Torgeson, R., and Hayward, K. (2003). *Income, health, and disease in Canada: Current state of knowledge, information gaps, and areas of needed inquiry.* Toronto: York University. Online at www.atkinson.yorku.ca/draphael

This report provides a systematic overview of how income is conceptualized as a variable in health research in Canada. It contains detailed descriptions of various approaches to conceptualizing income and poverty and how these studies measure their effects upon health, and it provides a critique of gaps in research.

Shaw, M., Dorling, D., Gordon, D., and Davey Smith, G. (1999). *The widening gap: Health inequalities and policy in Britain.* Bristol, UK: The Policy Press.

In this excellent volume, the authors identified the 15 "worst health" and 13 "best health" constituencies in Britain and examine area differences on a wide range of health and socio-economic indicators. Their analysis takes place within a lifespan perspective whereby health differences are seen as resulting from an accumulation of material disadvantages that reflect widely differing economic and social life circumstances.

Relevant Websites

Canadian Centre for Policy Alternatives Growing Gap Project—www.policyalterna-tives.ca/projects/growing-gap/about
>The Growing Gap project takes an in-depth and sustained look at one of the biggest challenges of our time: worsening income and wealth inequality in Canada. A team of economists and researchers has been tracking household income, wealth, spend-ing, and credit data, unearthing a troubling phenomenon.

Canadian Population Health Initiative (CPHI)—www.cihi.ca/CIHI-ext-portal/inter-net/EN/Home/home/cihi000001
>The CPHI's role is to expand the public's knowledge of population health. It works with partners across the country to: (a) generate new knowledge about the factors affecting the health of different groups of Canadians; (b) analyze evidence about the effectiveness of policy initiatives and provide a range of policy options based on best evidence; and (c) bring researchers, policy-makers and health practitioners together to move the most current population research findings into policy and practice.

Canadian Public Health Association Policy Statements—www.cpha.ca/english/policy/pstatem/polstate.htm
>This website contains numerous CPHA statements about poverty, income, and other social determinants of health.

Prairie Women's Health Centre of Excellence—www.pwhce.ca/research.htm
>The Prairie Women's Health Centre of Excellence works with the community to conduct new research specific to women in Manitoba and Saskatchewan, and with colleagues across the country. Its current focus areas are: Aboriginal women's health issues; women, poverty and health; health of women living in rural, remote, and northern communities; and gender in health planning.

Research from the National Longitudinal Survey of Children and Youth (NLSCY)—www.statcan.ca/english/rdc/rdcprojectsnlscy.htm
>This website provides details concerning the many studies and reports being carried out within this project.

The Policy Press—www.policypress.org.uk/
>The Policy Press is the specialist publisher in the UK of social and public policy books, reports, journals, and guides. As a not-for-profit organization aiming to improve social conditions, it is committed to publishing titles that will have an impact on research, teaching, policy, and practice. Many of its volumes are con-cerned with poverty, its effects upon health, and means of reducing its incidence.

Glossary of Terms

Globalization is the process of rapid economic integration between countries. It has been driven by the increasing liberalization of international trade and foreign direct investment, and by freer capital flows. The process manifests itself mainly through an intensification of activities in the following areas: international trade in goods and services; capital flows; the role of multinational enterprises; the reorganization of production networks on an international scale; and the adoption of new technology, including information technology (International Labour Organisation, 1999).

Neo-liberalism refers to the dominance of markets and the market model. It has the following tenets: (1) markets are the best and most efficient allocators of resources in production and distribution; (2) societies are composed of autonomous individuals (producers and consumers) motivated chiefly or entirely by material or economic considerations; and (3) competition is the major market vehicle for innovations. The essence of neo-liberalism, in its pure form, is a more-or-less thoroughgoing adherence, in rhetoric if not in practice, to the virtues of a market economy, and, by extension, a market-oriented society (Coburn, 2000).

Pathways are about how poverty comes to influence health.

- *Biological pathways* specify the physiological mechanisms by which living conditions determine health and the incidence of illness. These pathways focus on material insults to the body and the processes by psychosocial stress disrupts bodily systems.

- *Materialist analyses* are about how poverty leads to differential exposures to health-damaging or health-enhancing elements in living and working conditions, both positive and negative aspects of the world.

- *Psychosocial pathways* are the explanations related to either (a) the experience of belonging to a particular social class or (b) the experiences of stress of living associated with living in poverty and how these come to be related to health.

- *Behavioural/cultural* explanations are about how health-related behaviours are associated with poverty and come to influence health.

- *Gender analyses* focus on the role gender plays in mediating the poverty and health relationship. Of particular interest are the social structures that disadvantage women in the workplace.

- *Political economic analysis* is concerned with the political, economic, and social forces that shape the incidence of poverty and the societal structures that mediate the poverty and health relationship.

References

Allison, K., Adlaf, E., Ialomiteanu, A., and Rehm, J. (1999). Predictors of health risk behaviours among young adults: Analysis of the national population health survey. *Canadian Journal of Public Health, 90*(2), 85–89.

Armstrong, P. (1996). Unravelling the safety net: Transformations in health care and their impact on women. In J. Brodie (Ed.), *Women and Canadian public policy*. Toronto: Harcourt Brace.

Armstrong, P. (2009). Public policy, gender, and health. In D. Raphael (Ed.), *Social determinants of health: Canadian perspectives* (2nd ed., pp. 350–361). Toronto: Canadian Scholars' Press, Inc.

Armstrong, P., Lippman, A., and Sky, L. (1997, July 5). *Women's health, social change, and policy development.* Paper presented at "Gender and Health: From Research to Policy," the Fifth National Health Promotion Research Conference, Halifax, Nova Scotia.

Avison, W. (1997). Single motherhood and mental health: Implications for primary prevention. *Canadian Medical Association Journal, 156*(5), 661–663.

Barker, D., Forsen, T., Uutela, A., Osmond, C., and Eriksson, J. (2001). Size at birth and resilience to effects of poor living conditions in adult life: Longitudinal study. *British Medical Journal—Clinical Research, 323*(7324), 1273–1276.

Bartley, M. (2003). *Understanding health inequalities.* Oxford, UK: Polity Press.

Bartley, M., Power, C., Blane, D., Davey, G., and Shipley, M. (1994). *Birthweight and later socioeconomic disadvantages: Evidence from the 1958 British cohort study.* Toronto: Canadian Institute for Advanced Research.

Bédard, M. (1996). *The economic and social costs of unemployment.* Retrieved December 2010 from Human Resources Development Canada website: www.hrsdc.gc.ca/eng/cs/sp/sdc/pkrf/publications/bulletins/1996-000027/1996-000027E.pdf

Benzeval, M., Dilnot, A., Judge, K., and Taylor, J. (2001). Income and health over the lifecourse: Evidence and policy implications. In H. Graham (Ed.), *Understanding health inequalities* (pp. 96–112). Buckingham, UK: Open University Press.

Benzeval, M., Judge, K., and Whitehead, M. (1995). *Tackling inequalities in health: An agenda for action.* London: Kings' Fund.

Brooks-Gunn, J., Duncan, G. J., and Britto, P. R. (1998). Are SES gradients for children similar to those for adults? Achievement and health of children in the United States. In D. P. Keating and C. Hertzman (Eds.), *Developmental health and the wealth of nations: Social, biological, and educational dynamics* (pp. 94–124). New York: Guilford Press.

Brunner, E., and Marmot, M. G. (2006). Social organization, stress, and health. In M. G. Marmot and R. G. Wilkinson (Eds.), *Social determinants of health* (2nd ed., pp. 17–43). Oxford, UK: Oxford University Press.

Bryant, T. (2009). Housing and health: More than bricks and mortar. In D. Raphael (Ed.), *Social determinants of health: Canadian perspectives* (2nd ed., pp. 235–249). Toronto: Canadian Scholars' Press Inc.

Canadian Population Health Initiative. (2004). *Select highlights on public views of the determinants of health.* Ottawa: CPHI.

Coburn, D. (2000). Income inequality, social cohesion, and the health status of populations: The role of neo-liberalism. *Social Science and Medicine, 51*(1), 135–146.

Coburn, D. (2004). Beyond the income inequality hypothesis: Globalization, neo-liberalism, and health inequalities. *Social Science and Medicine, 58*, 41–56.

Cohen, S., Kaplan, G., and Salonen, J. (1999). The role of psychological characteristics in the relation between socioeconomic status and perceived health. *Journal of Applied Social Psychology, 29*(3), 445–468.

Davey Smith, G. (Ed.). (2003). *Inequalities in health: Life course perspectives.* Bristol, UK: The Policy Press.

Davey Smith, G., Ben-Shlomo, Y., and Lynch, J. (2002). Life course approaches to inequalities in coronary heart disease risk. In S. A. Stansfeld and M. Marmot (Eds.), *Stress and the heart: Psychosocial pathways to coronary heart disease* (pp. 20–49). London, UK: BMJ Books.

Davey Smith, G., and Gordon, D. (2000). Poverty across the life-course and health. In C. Pantazis and D. Gordon (Eds.), *Tackling inequalities: Where are we now and what can be done?* (pp. 141–158). Bristol, UK: The Policy Press.

Davey Smith, G., Hart, C., Blane, D., Gillis, C., and Hawthorne, V. (1997). Lifetime socioeconomic position and mortality: Prospective observational study. *British Medical Journal, 314*(7080), 547–552.

Davies, L., McMullin, J. A., Avison, W., and Cassidy, G. (2001). *Social policy, gender inequality, and poverty.* Ottawa: Status of Women Canada.

Dooley, M., and Curtis, L. (1998). *Child health and family socioeconomic status in the Canadian National Longitudinal Survey of Children and Youth.* Hamilton, ON, and Halifax, NS: McMaster University Canadian International Labour Network and Dalhousie University.

Fawcett, G. (2000). *Bringing down the barriers: The labour market and woman with disabilities in Ontario.* Ottawa: Canadian Council on Social Development.

Fitzpatrick, M. (2001). *The tyranny of health: Doctors and the regulation of lifestyle.* London, UK: Routledge.

Forsen, T., Eriksson, J. G., Tuomilehto, J., Osmond, C., and Barker, D. J. P. (1999). Growth in utero and during childhood among women who develop coronary heart disease: Longitudinal study. *British Medical Journal—Clinical Research, 319* (7222), 1403–1407.

Forssas, E., Gissler, M., Sihvonen, M., and Hemminki, E. (1999). Maternal predictors of perinatal mortality: The role of birthweight. *International Journal of Epidemiology, 28*(3), 475–478.

Galabuzi, G. E. (2005). *Canada's economic apartheid: The social exclusion of racialized groups in the new century.* Toronto: Canadian Scholars' Press Inc.

Graham, H. (Ed.). (2001). *Understanding health inequalities.* Buckingham, UK: Open University Press.

Hadley, K. (2001, June). *And we still ain't satisfied: Gender inequality in Canada, a status report for 2001.* Centre for Social Justice, Foundation for Research and Education and National Action Committee on the Status of Women. Retrieved October 2006 from www.socialjustice.org/pubs/womequal.pdf

Hatfield, M. (1997). *Concentrations of poverty and distressed neighbourhoods in Canada.* Retrieved December 2010 from Human Resources Development Canada website: www.hrsdc.gc.ca/eng/cs/sp/sdc/pkrf/publications/1997-002563/page00.shtml

Health Canada. (1999). *Toward a healthy future: Second report on the health of Canadians.* Retrieved December, 2010, from Public Health Agency of Canada website: www.phac-aspc.gc.ca/ph-sp/report-rapport/toward/pdf/toward_a_healthy_english.PDF

Hertzman, C. (1998). The case for child development as a determinant of health. *Canadian Journal of Public Health, 89*(Suppl 1), S14–S19.

Hertzman, C. (1999a). The biological embedding of early experience and its effects on health in adulthood. *Annals of the New York Academy of Sciences, 896,* 85–95.

Hertzman, C. (1999b). Population health and human development. In D. P. Keating and C. Hertzman (Eds.), *Developmental health and the wealth of nations: Social, biological, and educational dynamics* (pp. 21–40). New York: Guilford Press.

Hertzman, C. (2000a). The case for an early childhood development strategy. *ISUMA, 1, 2.*

Hertzman, C. (2000b). The socioeconomic, psychosocial, and developmental environment. In S. J (Ed.), *Improving population health in industrialized nations* (pp. 87–104). London: Office of Health Economics.

Hertzman, C., and Frank, J. (2006). Biological pathways linking the social environment, development, and health. In J. Heymann, C. Hertzman, M. Barer, and R. G. Evans (Eds.), *Healthier societies: From analysis to action* (pp. 35–57). Toronto: Oxford University Press.

Hertzman, C., and Power, C. (2003). Health and human development: Understandings from life-course research. *Developmental Neuropsychology, 24*, (2–3), 719–744.

Hou, F., and Picot, G. (2003). *Visible minority neighbourhood enclaves and labour market outcomes of immigrants*. Ottawa: Analytic Studies Branch, Statistics Canada.

Innocenti Research Centre. (2000). *A league table of child poverty in rich nations*. Florence: Innocenti Research Centre.

Innocenti Research Centre. (2001). *A league table of child deaths by injury in rich nations*. Florence: Innocenti Research Centre.

International Labour Organisation. (1999). *Country studies on the social impact of globalization: Final report*. Geneva: International Labour Organisation.

Jackson, A. (2002). *Canada beats USA—but loses gold to Sweden*. Retrieved October 2006 from Canadian Council on Social Development website: www.ccsd.ca/pubs/2002/olympic/indicators.htm

Jackson, A. (2009). The unhealthy Canadian workplace. In D. Raphael (Ed.), *Social determinants of health: Canadian perspectives* (2nd ed., pp. 99–113). Toronto: Canadian Scholars' Press Inc.

Jackson, A. (2010). *Work and labour in Canada: Critical issues* (2nd ed.). Toronto: Canadian Scholars' Press Inc.

James, P. T., Nelson, M., Ralph, A., and Leather, S. (1997). Socioeconomic determinants of health: The contribution of nutrition to inequalities in health. *British Medical Journal, 314*(7093), 1545–1548.

Jarvis, M. J., and Wardle, J. (2006). Social patterning of individual health behaviours: The case of cigarette smoking. In M. G. Marmot and R. G. Wilkinson (Eds.), *Social determinants of health* (2nd ed., pp. 224–237). Oxford, UK: Oxford University Press.

Johnson, A. A., El-Khorazaty, M. N., Hatcher, B. J., Wingrove, B. K., Milligan, R., Harris, C., and Richards, L. (2003). Determinants of late prenatal care initiation by African American women in Washington, DC. *Maternal and Child Health Journal, 7*(2), 103–114.

Kawachi, I., and Kennedy, B. (2002). *The health of nations: Why inequality is harmful to your health*. New York: New Press.

Labonte, R. (1993). *Health promotion and empowerment: Practice frameworks*. Toronto: Centre for Health Promotion and ParticipAction.

Lawlor, D., Ebrahim, S., and Davey Smith, G. (2002). Socioeconomic position in childhood and adulthood and insulin resistance: Cross sectional survey using data from British women's heart and health study. *British Medical Journal, 325*(12), 805–807.

Lee, K. (2000, April 17). *Urban poverty in Canada: A statistical profile*. Retrieved December 2010 from Canadian Council on Social Development website: www.ccsd.ca/pubs/2000/up/

Lochhead, C., and Scott, K. (2000). *The dynamics of women's poverty in Canada*. Status of Women Canada. Retrieved December 2010 from http://vanieropac.vaniercollege.qc.ca:81/GOVdocs/2007/Lochhead.pdf

Lupien, S., King, E., Meaney, M., and McEwan, B. (2001). Can poverty get under your skin? Basal cortisol levels and cognitive function in children from low and high socioeconomic status. *Development and Psychopathology, 13*(3), 653–676.

Lynch, J. (2000). Income inequality and health: expanding the debate. *Social Science and Medicine, 51*(7), 1001–1005.

Lynch, J., and Kaplan, G. A. (2000). Socioeconomic position. In L. F. Berkman and I. Kawachi (Eds.), *Social epidemiology* (pp. 13–35). New York: Oxford University Press.

Lynch, J., Kaplan, G., and Salonen, J. (1997). Why do poor people behave poorly? Variation in adult health behaviours and psychosocial characteristics by stages of the socioeconomic lifecourse. *Social Science and Medicine, 44*(6), 809–819.

Lynch, J. W., Davey Smith, G., Kaplan, G. A., and House, J. S. (2000). Income inequality and mortality: Importance to health of individual income, psychosocial environment, or material conditions. *British Medical Journal, 320*, 1220–1224.

MacMillan, H. L., MacMillan, A. B., Offord, D. R. D., and Dingle, J. L. (1996). Aboriginal health. *Canadian Medical Association Journal, 155*(11), 1569–1578.

Marmot, M. (2004). *Status syndrome: How your social standing directly affects your health and life expectancy*. London, UK: Bloomsbury.

Marmot, M., and Wilkinson, R. (Eds.). (2006). *Social determinants of health* (2nd ed.). Oxford, UK: Oxford University Press.

McCaskell, T. (2009). *Neoliberalism as a water balloon*. Retrieved March 10, 2011 from http://vimeo.com/6803752

Muntaner, C. (2004). Commentary: Social capital, social class, and the slow progress of psychosocial epidemiology. *International Journal of Epidemiology, 33*(4), 1–7.

Nettleton, S. (1997). Surveillance, health promotion and the formation of a risk identity. In M. Sidell, L. Jones, J. Katz, and A. Peberdy (Eds.), *Debates and dilemmas in promoting health* (pp. 314–324). London, UK: Open University Press.

Newbold, K. B., and Danforth, J. (2003). Health status and Canada's immigrant population. *Social Science and Medicine, 57*, 1981–1995.

Ng, E., Wilkins, K. Gendron, F., and Berthelot, J. M. (2004). Dynamics of immigrant health in Canada: Evidence from the National Population Health Survey. Ottawa: Statistics Canada.

O'Loughlin, J. L., Paradis, G., Gray-Donald, K., and Renaud, L. (1999). The impact of a community-based heart disease prevention program in a low income, inner city neighbourhood. *American Journal of Public Health, 89*(12), 1819–1826.

Organisation for Economic Co-operation and Development. (2009). *Health at a glance: OECD indicators 2009*. Paris: OECD.

Pahlke, A., Lord, S., and Christiansen-Ruffman, L. (2001). *Women's health and wellbeing in six Nova Scotia fishing communities*. Retrieved December 2010 from Centre of Excellence for Women's Health website: www.cewh-cesf.ca/PDF/acewh/fishing-communities.pdf

Picot, G. (2004). *The deteriorating economic welfare of immigrants and possible causes*. Ottawa: Statistics Canada.

Pomerleau, J., Pederson, L. L., Østbye, T., Speechley, M., and Speechley, K. N. (1997). Health behaviours and socio-economic status in Ontario, Canada. *European Journal of Epidemiology, 13*(6), 613–622.

Potvin, L., Richard, L., and Edwards, A. (2000). Knowledge of cardiovascular disease risk factors among the Canadian population: Relationships with indicators of socioeconomic status. *Canadian Medical Association Journal, 162*, S5–S12.

Power, C., Bartley, M., Davey Smith, G., and Blane, D. (1996). Transmission of social and biological risk across the lifecourse. In D. Blane, E. Brunner, and R. Wilkinson (Eds.), *Health and social organization* (pp. 188–203). London: Routledge.

Raphael, D. (2000). Health inequalities in Canada: Current discourses and implications for public health action. *Critical Public Health, 10*(2), 193–216.

Raphael, D. (2003). A society in decline: The social, economic, and political determinants of health inequalities in the USA. In R. Hofrichter (Ed.), *Health and social justice: A reader on politics, ideology, and inequity in the distribution of disease* (pp. 59–88). San Francisco: Jossey Bass.

Raphael, D. (2009). Introduction to the social determinants of health. In D. Raphael (Ed.), *Social determinants of health: Canadian perspectives* (2nd ed., pp. 2–19). Toronto: Canadian Scholars' Press Inc.

Raphael, D., Anstice, S., and Raine, K. (2003). The social determinants of the incidence and management of Type II Diabetes Mellitus: Are we prepared to rethink our questions and redirect our research activities? *Leadership in Health Services, 16*, 10–20.

Raphael, D., and Farrell, E. S. (2002). Addressing cardiovascular disease in North America: Shifting the paradigm. *Harvard Health Policy Review, 3*(2), 18–28.

Raphael, D., Macdonald, J., Labonte, R., Colman, R., Hayward, K., and Torgerson, R. (2005). Researching income and income distribution as a determinant of health in Canada: Gaps between theoretical knowledge, research practice, and policy implementation. *Health Policy, 72*, 217–232.

Roberts, P., Smith, P., and Nason, H. (2001). Children and familial economic welfare: The effect of income on child development. Applied Research Branch, Human Resources Development Canada. Retrieved October 2006 from ww.hrdc-drhc.gc.ca/sp-ps/arb-dgra/publications/research/2001docs/W-01-1-11/IW-01-1-11e.pdf

Ronson, B., and Rootman, I. (2009). Literacy and health literacy: New understandings about their impact on health. In D. Raphael (Ed.), *Social determinants of health: Canadian perspectives* (2nd ed., pp. 170–186). Toronto: Canadian Scholars' Press Inc.

Rosenberg, M. W., and Wilson, K. (2000). Gender, poverty and location: How much difference do they make in the geography of health inequalities? *Social Science and Medicine, 51*(2), 275–287.

Ross, D. P., and Roberts, P. (1999). *Income and child well-being: A new perspective on the poverty debate*. Ottawa: Canadian Council on Social Development.

Ross, D. P., Roberts, P. A., and Scott, K. (1998). *Variations in child development outcomes among children living in lone-parent families*. Retrieved December 2010 from Human Resources Development Canada website: www.hrsdc.gc.ca/eng/cs/sp/sdc/pkrf/publications/research/1998-001325/1998-001325.pdf

Ross, N., Wolfson, M., Dunn, J., Berthelot, J. M., Kaplan, G., and Lynch, J. (2000). Relation between income inequality and mortality in Canada and in the United States: Cross sectional assessment using census data and vital statistics. *British Medical Journal, 320*(7239), 898–902.

Sapolsky, R. M. (1992). *Stress, the aging brain, and mechanisms of neuron death*. Cambridge, MA: MIT Press.

Sarlio-Lahteenkorva, S., and Lahelma, E. (2001). Food insecurity is associated with past and present economic disadvantage and body mass index. *The Journal of Nutrition, 131*(11), 2880–2884.

Shaw, M. (2001). Health and housing: A lasting relationship. *Journal of Epidemiology and Community Health, 55*, 291–296.

Shaw, M., Dorling, D., and Davey Smith, G. (2006). Poverty, social exclusion, and minorities. In M. G. Marmot and R. G. Wilkinson (Eds.), *Social determinants of health* (pp. 196–223). Oxford, UK: Oxford University Press.

Shaw, M., Dorling, D., Gordon, D., and Davey Smith, G. (1999). *The widening gap: Health inequalities and policy in Britain*. Bristol, UK: The Policy Press.

Smiley, J. (2009). The health of aboriginal people. In D. Raphael (Ed.), *Social determinants of health: Canadian perspectives* (2nd ed., pp. 280-301). Toronto: Canadian Scholars' Press Inc.

Stewart, M., Brosky, G., Gillis, A., Jackson, S., Johnston, G., Kirkland, S., Leigh, G., Pawliw-Fry, B., Persaud, V., and Rootman, I. (1996). Disadvantaged women and smoking. *Canadian Journal of Public Health, 87*(4), 257–260.

Tarlov, A. (1996). Social determinants of health: The sociobiological translation. In D. Blane, E. Brunner, and R. Wilkinson (Eds.), *Health and social organization: Towards a health policy for the 21st century* (pp. 71–93). London, UK: Routledge.

Townson, M. (2000). *A report card on women and poverty*. Ottawa: Canadian Centre for Policy Alternatives.

Travers, K. D. (1996). The social organization of nutritional inequities. *Social Science and Medicine, 43*(4), 543–553.

Tremblay, D. G. (2009). Unemployment and the labour market. In D. Raphael (Ed.), *Social determinants of health: Canadian perspectives* (2nd ed., pp. 75–87). Toronto: Canadian Scholars' Press Inc.

United Way of Greater Toronto. (2004). *Poverty by postal code: The geography of neighbourhood poverty, 1981–2001*. Toronto: United Way of Greater Toronto.

van de Mheen, H., Stronks, K., and Mackenbach, J. (1998). A lifecourse perspective on socio-economic inequalities in health. In M. Bartley, D. Blane, and G. Davey Smith (Eds.), *The sociology of health inequalities* (pp. 193–216). Oxford, UK: Blackwell Publishers.

Wamala, S., Lynch, J., and Horsten, M. (1999). Education and the metabolic syndrome in women. *Diabetes Care, 22*(12), 1999–2003.

Wilkinson, R. G. (1996). *Unhealthy societies: The afflictions of inequality*. New York: Routledge.

Wilkinson, R. G. (2001). *Mind the gap: Hierarchies, health, and human evolution*. London, UK: Weidenfeld and Nicolson.

Wilkinson, R. G., and Pickett, K. (2009). *The spirit level: Why greater equality makes societies stronger*. New York: Bloomsbury Publishing.

Williamson, D. (2000). Health behaviours and health: Evidence that the relationship is not conditional on income adequacy. *Social Science and Medicine, 51*(12), 1741–1754.

Willms, J. D. (1997). Literacy skills and social class gradients. *Policy Options, 18*(6), 22–26.

Willms, J. D. (1999). Quality and inequality in children's literacy: The effects of families, schools, and communities. In D. P. Keating and C. Hertzman (Eds.), *Developmental health and the wealth of nations: Social, biological, and educational dynamics* (pp. 72–93). New York: Guilford Press.

Willms, J. D. (2001). Three hypotheses about community effects on social outcomes. *ISUMA, 2*(1), 53–62.

Willms, J. D. (Ed.). (2002). *Vulnerable children: Findings from Canada's National Longitudinal Survey.* Edmonton: University of Alberta Press.

Chapter Ten

Poverty and Quality of Life

The mother of revolution and crime is poverty.—Aristotle

Learning Objectives

At the conclusion of this chapter, the reader will be able to:

- define quality of life as it refers to both individuals, communities, and entire nations;
- explain how poverty influences a wide range of aspects of quality of life;
- outline the pathways by which poverty is associated with greater incidence of crime;
- explore how community resources support people who are living in poverty; and
- understand how public policy solutions to poverty also offer solutions to a range of social problems.

Introduction

The effects of living in poverty on health are profound. But also of importance are poverty's effects upon the quality of life of individuals, communities, and the nation. Living in poverty influences individual issues of personal well-being, interpersonal relations, and growth and development. As examples, the experience of poverty has been shown to influence one's level of literacy, educational achievement, and personal adjustment. Living in poverty also influences family life and peer relations, and shapes aspects of community quality of life, such as community belonging and isolation, social inclusion and exclusion, social cohesion and integration, and crime and safety. And at a jurisdictional level, there is evidence that the levels of poverty within a society can influence economic growth and labour productivity. These indicators of quality of life are in themselves important and are also closely related to individuals' physical and mental health.

In Canada, numerous non-governmental agencies and professional associations, such as the United Way of Canada and the Federation of Canadian Municipalities, have spearheaded efforts to recognize and address the links between poverty and quality of life. Social development, social justice, and faith groups have also highlighted the corrosive effects upon society of having many of its citizens living in poverty. These efforts are supported by recent reports by the Conference Board of Canada and other business-associated organizations. Outside of documents and resolutions emanating from the Canadian Public Health Association, and the efforts of a handful of public health units and health-related associations across Canada, the health care and public health sectors have generally been quiet on these issues. This may be changing, however, as public health agencies and organizations find it increasingly difficult to ignore the corrosive effects upon society of many of its citizens living in poverty (Health Council of Canada, 2010).

Of particular importance to quality of life is evidence that increasing income and wealth inequality—an important contributor to the incidence of poverty—is an important predictor of the incidence of crime within neighbourhoods, cities, and larger jurisdictions (Wilkinson and Pickett, 2009). While the mechanisms by which income and wealth inequality come to threaten quality of life remain a subject of debate, the evidence concerning the effects of increasing income and wealth inequality and continuing high levels of poverty are persuasive and require attention by policy-makers.

Defining Quality of Life

Quality of life is about defining and assessing the degree to which "the good life" has been achieved (Raphael, 2010). There is a strong normative aspect within most quality-of-life frameworks, since quality of life is outlined as a goal worth striving for rather than simply being a subject of reflection and inquiry (Michalski, 2001). There are numerous frameworks for considering quality of life that share a concern with identifying—and moving toward—what seems intuitively obvious: providing citizens, communities, and society with the opportunity to achieve their full human potential. Practically, quality of life refers to a range of phenomena that, by moving beyond traditional indicators of physical and mental health and illness, map out the essentials of human existence (Raphael and Bryant, 2004). In this chapter, a variety of quality-of-life approaches and research studies are drawn upon to illustrate that living in poverty threatens the quality of life of individuals, communities, and society.

Lindstrom's (1992) model of quality of life provides an overview of the domains of quality of life that should be considered within an inquiry of the relationship between poverty and quality of life. His model considers four spheres. The *personal sphere* includes physical, mental, and spiritual resources. The *interpersonal sphere* includes family structure and function, intimate friends, and extended social networks. The *external sphere* includes aspects of work, income, and housing. The *global sphere* includes the societal macro environment, specific cultural aspects, and human rights and social welfare policies. These four domains clearly resonate with many of the poverty-related issues considered within this volume.

Lindstrom's model suggests that inquiry into the effects of living in poverty should examine the quality of life of individuals, how individuals interact with others, the institutions and agencies with which individuals must interact, and the political and economic structures that both shape these various interactions and the quality of life of individuals.

Raphael, Renwick, and Rootman (1997) drew upon this model and others to develop a Canadian approach to considering quality of life. The model has been applied to defining and assessing the quality of life of individuals (Raphael, 1996; Raphael et al., 1997); communities (Raphael, Renwick, Brown, Phillips et al., 2001; Raphael, Renwick, Brown, Steinmetz et al., 2001); and the extent to which Canadian society is supporting citizen quality of life (Bryant et al., 2004; Raphael, Brown et al., 2001). Findings from these inquiries reinforce the importance of addressing poverty as a quality-of-life issue.

Being, Belonging, and Becoming: The Quality of Life of People Living in Poverty

The model developed by Raphael and colleagues (1997) defined quality of life as "[t]he degree to which a person enjoys the important possibilities of his/her life" (p. 120). Based on an extensive literature review, and numerous and ongoing consultations with community members, service professionals, and authorities in the field, three broad domains of human functioning were outlined: *being, belonging,* and *becoming*. These domains and subsequent sub-domains are outlined as essential components of human existence. Ongoing testing of this assumption with a very wide range of individuals, groups, and service sector professionals repeatedly confirms the validity of this assumption.

Being reflects "who one is." *Physical being* encompasses physical health, personal hygiene, nutrition, exercise, grooming, clothing, and general physical appearance. *Psychological being* includes psychological health and adjustment, cognitions, feelings, and evaluations concerning the self such as self-esteem, self-concept, and self-control. *Spiritual being* refers to personal values, personal standards of conduct, and spiritual beliefs.

Belonging concerns one's fit with one's environment. *Physical belonging* describes connections with the physical environments of home, workplace, neighbourhood, school, and community. *Social belonging* includes links with social environments and involves acceptance by intimate others, family, friends, co-workers, and neighbourhood and community. *Community belonging* represents access to resources such as adequate income, health and social services, employment, educational and recreational programs, and community events and activities.

Becoming refers to the purposeful activities one carries out to achieve personal goals, hopes, and aspirations. *Practical becoming* describes day-to-day activities such as domestic activities, paid work, school or volunteer activities, and seeing to health or social needs. *Leisure becoming* includes activities that promote relaxation and stress reduction. *Growth becoming* activities promote the maintenance or improvement of knowledge and skills and adapting to change.

The analysis of how living in poverty influences quality of life draws from a variety of sources concerned with the lives of people living in poverty. The first source constitutes surveys such as the National Longitudinal Study of Children and Youth, the Canadian Population Health Survey, other Statistics Canada surveys, and numerous research studies. Using traditional research methods and quantitative analyses, these surveys and supports examine indicators of functioning and well-being among Canadians identified as living in poverty.

The second source of insights into the quality of life of people living in poverty comes from a series of studies on community quality of life and social exclusion carried out in Toronto and Edmonton. One set of studies explicitly examined the components of, and support for, quality of life in two low-income Toronto communities (Raphael, Renwick, Brown, Phillips et al., 2001; Raphael, Renwick, Brown, Steinmetz et al., 2001). These studies not only identified how community features can either support or threaten quality of life, but also identified how people living in poverty cope and manage. Another study examined the use of health and social services by low-income community members in Toronto and Edmonton (Williamson et al., 2006). This study identified how a variety of community resources and agencies support the quality of life of people living in poverty. Yet another study examined processes of social exclusion and isolation, as well as social belonging, of low-income people in Toronto and Edmonton (Reutter et al., 2005, 2006). In this study, features of neighbourhoods were identified that allow people living in poverty to avoid exclusion and isolation from their family, friends, and neighbours.

The third source of insights into the quality of life of people living in poverty is evidence from qualitative studies of the lived experience of people living in poverty. Information from some of these studies has already been presented in Chapters 6 and 7. Those studies clearly illustrate how living in poverty threatens the quality of life of people living in poverty.

Being: Physical, Psychological, and Spiritual

Chapters 8 and 9 document the profound effects of living in poverty upon physical and mental health and identified the pathways and mechanisms by which poverty shapes health. Numerous studies show that living in poverty profoundly affects just about every aspect of human functioning. In this section, focus is upon the functioning of children and their families.

Data from Canada's National Longitudinal Survey of Children and Youth provides evidence that children living in poverty are more likely to have a range of emotional or behavioural, educational, or social problems (Ross and Roberts, 1999). This is especially the case for very poor children.

Willms (2002) provides a model that helps to explain how living in poverty affects children and their families. In this model, socio-economic status—of which poverty is the most problematic—has a direct impact on children's outcomes. This pathway is concerned with the effect of material and social deprivation upon children's physical, mental, and social development.

Living in poverty also influences children's outcomes through what is called the *opportunity structure*. Within neighbourhoods high in poverty, opportunities for personal and social support are fewer, and children are exposed to daycare and schools of lesser quality. Living in poverty also affects children's outcomes because it shapes *family*

Figure 10.1: Percentage of Children with Various Problems as a Function of Family Income, Canada, 1994–1996

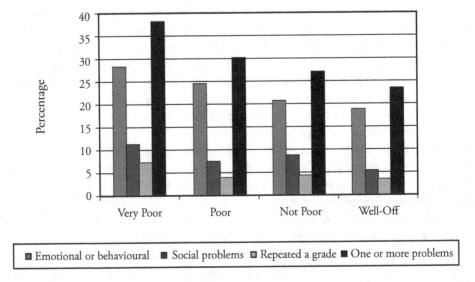

The Health of Canada's Children: A CICH Profile, 3rd edition (Table 7-31, p. 195). Ottawa: Canadian Institute of Child Health, 2000.

resources. Families that are living in poverty are more likely to have personal problems, difficulties in parenting, and greater incidence of mental distress. These are all results of the material and social deprivation associated with living in poverty. These opportunities and family resources go on to contribute to children's outcomes.

Findings from the National Longitudinal Study of Children and Youth show that children who live in poverty have poorer cognitive and behavioural outcomes (Willms, 2002). Canadian children living in poverty have close to a 50% greater chance of experiencing cognitive difficulties in school; a 45% greater chance of behaviour problems in school; and a 41% greater chance of scoring high on an overall vulnerability index (Willms, 2002). For each measure, around 10% of total variation observed among all Canadian children can be uniquely explained by the very low income status measure. Generally, living in poverty explains about 25% of the variation among children in whether they graduate from high school or not. Findings from Willms' study also support the opportunity structure component of his model: children living in poverty are likely to have families with fewer resources and live in communities that offer fewer opportunities.

Brooks-Gunn, Duncan, and Britto (1999) provide a similar model to explain their findings that living in poverty directly influences children's verbal ability and behaviours. In addition, living in poverty has direct negative effects upon the mental health and well-being of parents. These adverse effects upon mental health contribute to more difficult parenting. In turn, these mental health issues and the parenting behaviour associated with them all contribute to children's outcomes.

It is easy when considering these kinds of models to fall into the trap of deciding that intervention is required at intermediate levels of the causal chain, thereby ignoring the sources of children's difficulties. The source of child and family problems is the experience of material and social deprivation as a result of living in poverty. It is extremely common for policy-makers and service providers to either (a) assume that since nothing can be done to reduce poverty, efforts should be put into parenting programs, psychological counselling activities, and other ways to break the link between poverty and children's problems; or (b) simply blame parents who are living in poverty for their children's problems and design programs to cure these parents of their inadequacies.

In either case, the effect is to ignore the primary cause of these child and family problems and in all probability enact programs that will do little to improve children's and their families' lives. Since most models of the poverty and quality-of-life relationship posit a direct link between living in poverty and negative child outcomes, attempts to improve parenting skills and treat mental health issues will likely do little good. The most egregious example of this reasoning involves the Canadian provinces that withhold or claw back the federal National Child Benefit from families on social assistance and then allocate these funds for programming (National Council of Welfare, 2004). Monies intended for families on social assistance is taken from them and invested in programs to make them better parents! The clawback of the benefit creates the problem, and the monies taken are used in an attempt to remedy it. These models suggest that these funds would be better utilized by giving them directly to those for whom they were intended.

Another set of data provides evidence of the psychological effects of living in poverty. The National Population Health Survey (Health Canada, 1999) has a series of questions that determine whether the respondent has a sense that events in the world are (a) meaningful and (b) controllable. These perceptions have been shown to be powerful predictors of health and well-being (Antonovsky, 1987). Forty-seven percent of Canadians whose incomes are in the lower one-third of income earners have scores indicating that life is not meaningful as compared to only 26% of higher income earners (Health Canada, 1999). In addition, 26% of lower income earners believe that life is not controllable as compared to only 12% of higher income earners.

These perceptions of meaninglessness and lack of control are related to health and indicators of quality of life because they reflect accumulated experiences of success and failure in life as well as the ability of individuals to act upon their environment. A sense of efficacy allows for full participation in educational, recreational, and other opportunities, should they arise, to promote personal development and the development of those around them. Having little sense of control over a difficult-to-understand world promotes learned helplessness—a sense of futility in living—that leads to increased stress and anxiety and the taking up of coping behaviours potentially dangerous to health, such as tobacco and alcohol use (Lynch, Kaplan, and Salonen, 1997). Further evidence concerning the corrosive effects of living in poverty upon human functioning and development are plentiful (Ross and Roberts, 1999).

Belonging: Physical, Social, and Community

The second component of the quality-of-life approach is the individual's connections with others. Statistics Canada carried out an extensive analysis of Canadians' sense of and actual involvement with aspects of their nation, province, and communities as part of its 2003 General Social Survey on Social Engagement (Schellenberg, 2004). Of particular interest is whether Canadians who live in poverty are less likely to both feel and be connected with various societal institutions.

Canadians were asked: "How would you describe your sense of belonging to Canada (your province, your local community)?" (Schellenberg, 2004, p. 5). The findings indicated that there was little difference among Canadians of different income groups in their sense of belonging to Canada. Among the lowest income group (household income <$20,000), 13.5% said their sense of belonging to Canada was somewhat or very weak, as compared to 11.7% of the wealthiest group (household income >$80,000. For the provincial and local question, differences were greater. Among the lowest income group, 25.8% expressed a weak sense of belonging to the province and 38.7% did so for the community. This was in contrast to the wealthiest Canadians, of whom 23% expressed a weak sense of belonging to the province, and 32.2%, a weak sense of belonging to their local community. These differences, however, are not of a particularly high magnitude.

Confidence in Selected Public Institutions

Some interesting differences emerge among income groups when Canadians are asked about their confidence in a variety of public institutions (see Table 10.1). Canadians living in the lowest income group are much less likely to express a "great deal" or "quite a lot" of confidence in the police, education system, and justice system than other Canadians. They are, however, more likely to express confidence in the welfare system and federal Parliament than other Canadians. Even so, a majority of Canadians in the lowest income group express little confidence in both these institutions.

General Perceptions of Trust

More profound differences emerge when issues of trust and belief in others are assessed (Schellenberg, 2004). Responses to two questions reveal people in the lowest income group are less trusting of others. Only 43.3% of Canadians in the lowest income group felt that people can be trusted. The figure for the wealthiest group was 66.1%. In addition, 53.4% of the lowest income group felt that "[o]ne cannot be too careful in dealing with people" (p. 9). Only 32.5% of the wealthiest group felt this way.

A similar question inquired into whether it would be "very" or "somewhat likely" that a wallet or purse containing $200 would be returned if found by someone who lived close by. Only 33.1% of people living in the lowest income group felt this would be "very" likely. The response for the wealthiest group of Canadian was 53.1%.

Table 10.1: Percentage of Canadians Expressing a Great Deal or Quite a Lot of Confidence in Selected Public Institutions as a Function of Household Income

Household Income	Police	Health Care System	Education System	Welfare System	Federal Parliament	Justice System
Less than $20,000	78.2	65.2	65.7	46.4	44.6	53.5
$20,000 to $39,999	83.2	65.1	70.1	43.8	41.4	57.8
$40,000 to $59,999	86.5	66.6	72.2	42.2	44.2	60.6
$60,000 to $79,999	87.7	67.6	72.4	40.1	41.9	59.4
$80,000 or more	89.3	70.4	69.5	38.6	42.9	64.2

Source: Statistics Canada, 2003 General Social Survey on Social Engagement, Cycle 17: An Overview of Findings, 89-598-XIE2003001, July 2004; http://www.statcan.gc.ca/bsolc/olc-cel/olc-cel?catno=89-598-X&chropg=1&lang=eng

Political Involvement

Generally, Canadians are rather uninvolved with political activities. But Canadians who were in the lowest income group were the least likely to be involved in a range of political activities than those with greater economic resources (Schellenberg, 2004). For example, 22% of Canadians in the lowest income group have searched for information on an issue as compared to 34.8% of the wealthiest group of Canadians. The figures for other activities for the lowest and highest income group were: (a) contacted newspaper or politician (11.9% vs. 17.8%); (b) signed petition (25.4% vs. 37.4%); (c) boycotted/chose product for ethical reason (17.5% vs. 32.7%); (d) attended a public meeting (11.7% vs. 29%); and (e) participated in a march or demonstration (6.1% vs. 6.8%).

Use of the Internet for Personal Communication

Finally, Canadians were asked whether they had used the Internet to communicate with friends and family during the previous month (Schellenberg, 2004). Canadians in the lowest income group were less likely to have done so for friends (36.3%) and relatives (30.8%) than the wealthiest group of Canadians (62.8% and 54.6% respectively).

Becoming: Practical, Leisure, and Growth

The study entitled *The Left out: Perspectives on Social Exclusion and Social Isolation in Low-Income Populations* examined aspects of belonging and participation among residents in Toronto and Edmonton (Stewart, Reutter, Veenstra, Love, and Raphael, 2003, 2004).

Ethnographic interviews were carried out with 30 low-income and 30 higher income people in Toronto, and 29 low-income and 30 higher income people in Edmonton. The purpose of the study was to assess the degree to which living in poverty influenced participation in activities as well as a sense of belonging. Interviews were coded for a variety of issues. These included geographic, institutional, and other shared interests such as ethno-racial or cultural identify.

Sense of Belonging

Generally, people living in poverty were less likely than those not living in poverty to indicate a sense of geographic belonging (63% vs. 75%); institutional belonging (47% vs. 87%); and shared interests (32% vs. 43%). Nineteen percent of people living in poverty indicated no sense of belonging to any aspect of their community as compared to only 5% of those not living in poverty.

Participation in Activities

People living in poverty were less likely to participate in a very wide range of activities than people not living in poverty (see Table 10.2.) These differences did not simply reflect a lack of interest in various activities. When asked about the activities they would like to participate in, but could not because of financial issues, people living in poverty mentioned a much wider range of activities than did people not living in poverty. The differences were especially great for social, family, and work activities.

And the lack of participation in these activities was not benign. The presence of aversive or unpleasant effects associated with this non-participation was greater for those living in poverty. These aversive effects of non-participation in desired activities were emotional (59% for those living in poverty vs. 30% for those not living in poverty); physical (29% vs. 8%); social (37% vs. 10%); and apathy/hopelessness (22% vs. 3%).

Community Quality of Life: Identifying the Structures That Support Quality of Life of People Living in Poverty

In these studies, community members in two Toronto low-income communities were asked about their communities and their quality of life (Raphael, Renwick, Brown, Phillips et al., 2001; Raphael, Renwick, Brown, Steinmetz et al., 2001). These neighbourhoods differed on some key dimensions. South Riverdale is a mixed-income downtown Toronto area that has a reputation for community activism and involvement. It has plentiful services and agencies, and its physical setting is integrated into surrounding areas. Many of its residents are of Chinese descent. It is represented by NDP elected officials.

Lawrence Heights is a more homogeneous income area whose subsidized housing is isolated from the surrounding committee. It is in a suburban area, has rather limited services, and has been represented for the most part by Liberal elected representatives. Many of its residents are of black descent.

Table 10.2: Percentage of Interviewees Living in Poverty (n = 59) and Not Living in Poverty (n = 60) Participating in Various Types of Activities, and Percentage Wishing to Participate in Activities but Unable to Do So Because of Financial Issues

Activities	% Participating in Activity		% Wishing to Participate but Unable to Do So	
	Living in Poverty	Not Living in Poverty	Living in Poverty	Not Living in Poverty
Leisure	52	65	29	7
Physical	30	43	34	27
Social	54	65	41	17
Family	25	47	27	8
Civic	25	40	12	5
Cultural	22	22	22	7
Work	34	43	34	10
Religious	10	23	5	2
Educational	25	25	17	7
Volunteer	42	62	15	8
Other Individual	10	22	12	0
External Household	17	28	8	2
Children-Centred	14	37	10	0

Source: Adapted from Stewart, M., Reutter, L., Veenstra, G., Love, R., and Raphael, D. (2008). *Leftout: Perspectives on social exclusion and social isolation in low-income populations: Final report.* Edmonton: University of Alberta.

Residents of South Riverdale and Lawrence Heights were asked four simple questions:

- What is it about your neighbourhood or community that makes life good for you and the people you care about?
- What is it about your neighbourhood or community that does not make life good for you and the people you care about?
- What is available in your community to help you when you have a problem or worry?
- What are some programs and services that could improve your quality of life and those you care about? (Raphael, Renwick, Brown, Steinmetz et al., 2001, p. 183).

Information from these group interviews was analyzed and some common themes emerged concerning community supports and threats to quality of life. Despite the geographical and social differences among these communities, responses were very similar. Residents in both areas saw crime and safety, cuts to services, and poverty and unemployment as key threats to community quality of life. In Lawrence Heights the residents added racism to their list of threats to the community's quality of life.

Residents of both communities saw access to amenities, community agencies and services, public transportation, churches, housing, and schools as supporting community quality of life. The community members were clearly aware of the effects upon community quality of life of the presence of poverty. Additionally, they were clearly able to express how cuts and reductions to services were interacting with the incidence of poverty to threaten quality of life. Some typical comments from the communities included (Raphael, Steinmetz, and Renwick, 1998):

> Due to the welfare cuts, people are short of money and don't have that much money to buy what they've got to buy.... [W]hen the Harris government took power, the first thing he went after was the poor. He went after social housing ... people now have nowhere to go. You see the growth of homelessness. People don't have families to go to, for example, people that come from abusive families.... Counselling for people with psychiatric problems, that's being threatened to be cut by the provincial government. People out there need help, they don't need cuts, and the more cuts that appear, the more anger that's going to keep growing out there.... People out there have trouble coping and when they have trouble coping they get out of control. (Raphael, Steinmetz, and Renwick, 1998, p. 15)
>
> There's a lot of unemployed people here. This is a real centre for unemployed people and when you get lots of people who are unemployed there's lots of frustration and there's going to be violence, and there's no question that without services that's going to increase. (Raphael, Steinmetz, and Renwick, 1998, p. 19)

These findings were reinforced by information obtained from service providers and elected representatives of the area (Raphael, Renwick, Brown, Phillips et al., 2001; Raphael, Renwick, Brown, Steinmetz et al., 2001). These findings indicate that government withdrawal from the provision of social and other health services was seen as threatening the health and quality of life of low-income individuals living within these communities (Raphael, Phillips, Renwick, and Sehdev, 2000).

The primary reason that government withdrawal from service provision was threatening the health and quality of life is found in the nature of how individuals within these communities coped with the experience of living in poverty. For many people living on low incomes, the community agencies and service organizations provided a means of subsistence and coping with problems (e.g., food banks, drop-in centres, literacy programs, etc.) but also provided a means of connecting with others within the community through activities and programs (e.g., community health centres, youth and seniors programs, etc.). The importance of these services and programs was reinforced by a study on use of these services, as described below.

Low-Income Consumers' Experiences with Health-Related Services

In this study, use of health-related services by Toronto and Edmonton residents living in poverty was examined through interviews and focus groups (Stewart et al., 2001; Williamson et al., 2006). Ninety-nine residents in Edmonton and 100 residents of Toronto who were living in poverty were individually interviewed about the services, supports, and programs they use to stay healthy and what they do when they require medical attention for illness or injury. These interviews were followed up with 14 focus groups involving 52 people living in poverty, 17 service providers and managers, 21 advocates, and 15 senior-level public servants. These interviews were submitted to thematic analyses.

Health care services used were private care physicians, community health centres, walk-in facilities, and emergency departments. Only a handful (n=12) of interviewees were able to access assistance from other health care professionals. Health care was sought for a variety of acute and chronic conditions. Of more interest was the finding that two of three participants reported that use of a wide range of community-based services was essential to their health. These included food and clothing banks, collective kitchens, and shelters. Other commonly used services were child and family support services, settlement and cultural services, libraries, religious and spiritual services, and a variety of psychosocial counselling and assistance agencies.

Ninety percent of interviewees indicate that lack of money was a primary reason for using these services. These services served to reduce isolation, help with the management of stress and anxiety, and ease the general burden of living in poverty. About half (51%) of interviewees indicated they did not know how they would cope without these supports. For example:

> I would have some very sick kids and I would be probably digging a hole under my house and hiding in it! It would be terrible. How do you cope if you don't have the things that you need?

> [The services] are very important. Life would be very difficult, very stressful, very lonely, very poor. ... (Williamson et al., 2006, p. 12)

Interviewees indicated that the primary factors influencing their use of these services were lack of income and quality of service. Two in three indicated that they could only use services that were either low cost or free. About 40% indicated that required services could not be obtained by them because of cost. These included physical therapy, counselling, dental care, and required medicines. Respondents indicated (one in five) that their children were not able to access recreation programs and activities because of cost.

About half of interviewees indicated that they were more likely to access services where providers were friendly, welcoming, empathic, and respectful. And 40% indicated that they had stopped using services because providers did not listen to them. Here are some of their explanations:

> I remember at one point I had gone into a drug store. I had to get a prescription filled, and the pharmacist ... said there was a two-dollar charge and I said "that's fine." He said "welfare case," and I heard it, and my daughter was standing right beside me.

You feel like you're begging to those people.… I always feel like I've got to beg for everything and you got to talk through windows with ten people standing there listening to everything you're talking about. (Williamson et al., 2006, p. 114)

Participants were asked to provide recommendations for improving (a) health-related policies, programs, and services for people living in poverty; and (b) the life circumstances of people living in poverty. These recommendations centred on having the same choices as wealthier Canadians regarding services and care. They wished to have access to vision care, dental care, and counselling, as well as prescription drugs. They also desired affordable recreational services and programs for lower income people.

These low-income individuals were somewhat at a loss to explicate a means of improving their lack of economic resources. This should not be surprising as their lives are a constant struggle to cope and make ends meet. The authors concluded that the findings indicated a need to increase access to health-related services, provide respectful and compassionate health-related services, and improve the socio-economic circumstances of Canadians living in poverty. The way to do this was to reform social assistance, increase minimum wages, and institute housing policies to provide accessible, affordable housing.

Social Indicators and Quality of Life

The experience of living in poverty shapes the quality of life. However, it is important to note that the lives of people living in poverty are shaped by the general quality of life of communities. The quality of life of people living in poverty and the quality of life of communities influence each other. One way of thinking about this is to imagine that a society with an excellent quality of life may very well have few people living in poverty. And a society that has few people living in poverty may very well have an excellent quality of life.

Such a hypothesis would be consistent with the neo-materialist analysis of poverty that argues that poverty—and its health and quality-of-life effects—results from a society's investment in social infrastructure and its commitment to equitable distribution of resources. It would be expected, therefore, that indicators of community quality of life would be both a result of the presence of poverty as well as one of its causes. And, indeed, evidence from Canada indicates that this may be the case.

The Federation of Canadian Municipalities (FCM) provides ongoing reports of various indicators of quality of life in Canadian cities. These performance ratings are integrally tied to the presence of poverty and the urban environments within which people living in poverty reside. And these performance ratings are, in large part, a result of governmental provision of benefits and supports as well as investments by governments in social infrastructure—an issue taken up in later chapters. The FCM indicators of community quality of life are complemented by reports by United Ways across Canada that direct attention to quality-of-life indicators as a means of assessing the impacts of

Canadian public policies (United Way of Greater Toronto and Canadian Council on Social Development, 2002; United Way of Ottawa, 2003; United Way of Winnipeg, 2003). And an essential component of these analyses is the presence of poverty and its meaning for the lives of those living in poverty. Similarly, the Canadian Policy Research Networks (CPRN) has developed a framework for considering quality of life (Michalski, 2001). CPRN has also provided reports cards that provide insights into various aspects of quality of life clearly relevant to considering the impact of living in poverty upon quality of life.

FCM Quality of Life Reporting System

The Federation of Canadian Municipalities (1999) developed and has been reporting on a Quality of Life Reporting System (QOLRS). The system consists of nine sets of indicators that are available for many cities:

- Demographic and background information
- Affordable appropriate housing
- Civic engagement
- Community and social infrastructure
- Education
- Local economy
- Personal and community growth
- Personal financial security
- Personal safety

The FCM has issued a number of reports that address important urban quality-of-life issues, many of which are strongly related to increasing poverty as a result of growing income and wealth inequalities. Some of these reports are sharply critical of governments' efforts to support quality of life in Canada cities by reducing poverty and income inequality. There has been increasing focus on Canadian governments' withdrawal from providing social infrastructure to reduce poverty and support citizens who may be living in poverty (see Box 10.1). The titles and excerpts from these reports that follow give a sense of their content and their tone, and provide a context to understand the continuing high incidence of poverty in Canada and the adverse conditions people living in poverty experience.

Special City Issues: Housing and Social Assistance

The 2004 FCM report notes that rental costs are a significant issue for people of lower incomes. FCM calculated the gap between the rises in lower-end rents and increases in lower-end incomes. Lower-end rental costs are far outstripping the incomes of lower-income people in just about every Canadian city. In some cases the gap between rising rents and rising incomes is as great as 60% (see Figure 10.3). Much of this is a result of the federal and provincial governments reducing their involvement in providing affordable housing.

Box 10.1: Decaying Situations in Canadian Cities

Mending Canada's Social Safety Net: The Role of Municipal Governments

The sixth theme report from the Federation of Canadian Municipalities' Quality of Life Reporting System (QOLRS) focuses on the growing municipal role in filling the holes in Canada's fraying social safety net.

The 24 QOLRS communities are home to more 17 million people, making up 54 per cent of Canada's population. As other Quality of Life theme reports since 2003 have shown, poverty and other inequalities persist among vulnerable groups in these communities.

This report looks at the growing need for municipal social services, a need made more urgent by the recent recession and the federal and provincial retreat from traditional social supports, which has shifted the burden to municipal governments.

The report introduces the concept of social infrastructure, the support system provided by municipal governments and made up of direct social services, such as affordable housing, emergency shelters and subsidized childcare, as well as public services like transit, recreation and libraries.

Together these municipal services help fill the gap left by shrinking federal and provincial social assistance programs. They form the social infrastructure that a growing number of people rely on to earn a living, raise their families, and cope with difficult times. Social infrastructure is particularly important to vulnerable people on limited incomes, especially during a recession.

The report finds that while the need for these services has increased, investments have not kept up.

Highlights

The report identifies a destructive dynamic in which poverty, most prevalent among certain growing vulnerable groups, combines with shrinking federal and provincial support for social services to increase demands on limited municipal resources. This dynamic creates an urban environment where substantial numbers of people are disadvantaged, despite generally positive (until recently) economic conditions.

The dynamic grows from the following trends:

- The persistence of poverty despite economic growth—While certain populations experienced relative improvements in their socio-economic situation (e.g., seniors, aboriginals, people with disabilities) during the five-year period of relative economic growth from 2001 to 2006, others were left even further behind (e.g., single mothers and families with young children, the working poor, immigrants, and social-assistance recipients).
- The erosion of traditional social-policy tools—Traditional social policy tools to combat poverty and unemployment eroded during the survey period. The federal role in national social programs has declined as seen in the prolonged shortage of funding for social housing, restrictions on Employment Insurance

(EI) eligibility, and the elimination of the Canada Assistance Plan (CAP). Concurrently, provincial downloading of social-service costs and responsibilities to municipalities and the not-for-profit sector has, in many cases, further exacerbated the situation, weakening municipal social infrastructure.

- The fraying social safety net—Tougher requirements for social assistance have contributed to the increase in working poor families and the incidence of homelessness. More restrictive eligibility rules for EI over the past 15 years will affect the increased numbers of QOLRS residents who are losing their jobs as a result of the recent recession. Once their EI is exhausted, many of these unemployed people will turn to welfare, which is administered and financed by municipal governments in many of the QOLRS communities.
- The municipal role in patching the social safety net—The report highlights a range of social infrastructure with strong municipal involvement, including social housing, emergency shelters, public transit, childcare, recreation, and libraries. Together, these facilities, programs and services help fill the gap left by shrinking federal and provincial social assistance. They form the social infrastructure that a growing number of people rely on to earn a living, raise their families, and cope with difficult times.
- The looming deficit in municipal social infrastructure—Cities have stepped in to fill holes in the social safety net left by federal and provincial governments as they retreat from funding social programs. Even with these investments, long waiting lists for services, increasing homelessness and a growing number of working-poor families suggest demand is outpacing the municipal capacity to respond.

Changing the dynamic described above requires tackling all of its components. The withdrawal of federal/provincial support for social programs and the lack of a commitment to sustained funding has forced more people in the QOLRS communities onto services supported by the municipal property tax base, which was intended to pay primarily for physical infrastructure.

The report supports FCM's call for continued federal contributions to cities in the form of the GST refund, the permanent Gas Tax Fund and the various infrastructure programs now in place. These help to free funds to meet the growing need for social services and other public services that support vulnerable groups, such as public transit, recreation and libraries, but they are not a long-term solution.

As Canada slowly recovers from the recent recession and governments contemplate balancing their budgets, this report makes clear the human cost of allowing the social safety net to fray. Municipal social infrastructure provides a second line of defence, catching the increasing number of people who slip through gaps in the traditional safety net. If this second line of defence should fail, the consequences for Canada's most vulnerable will be severe.

Source: Federation of Canadian Municipalities. (2010, March 4). *Mending Canada's social safety net: The role of municipal governments*. Retrieved December 2010 from www.fcm.ca//CMFiles/2010-03-22QoL%20bckgrnder_En_Final1JQX-3242010-5929.pdf

Box 10.2: Recent Reports from the Federation of Canadian Municipalities Highlight Key Quality of Life Issues

2010—*Mending Canada's Frayed Social Safety Net: The Role of Municipal Governments*
The report reveals a destructive dynamic in which poverty—aggravated by the growth of vulnerable groups—combines with shrinking federal and provincial support for social services to increase demands on limited municipal resources. This dynamic creates an urban environment where substantial numbers of people are disadvantaged, despite generally positive (until recently) economic conditions. (FCM, 2010)

2009—*Immigration and Diversity in Canadian Cities and Communities*
Recent immigrants are suffering from high rates of underemployment and poverty. This has significant implications for municipal governments, as they struggle to provide adequate affordable housing, emergency shelters, social assistance and public health services to newcomers. (FCM, 2009)

2008—*Trends and Issues in Affordable Housing and Homelessness*
The estimated 150,000 to 200,000 homeless people in Canada are the visible tip of a much larger population of financially marginal individuals and households that are at risk of ending up on the street. According to some estimates, some 700,000 households nation-wide are spending more than half of their income on shelter, leaving them at considerable risk of homelessness, with some 600,000 to 650,000 people, many of them children, living in inadequate or sub-standard housing. (FCM, 2008)

2004—*Incomes, Shelter, and Necessities*
This report points to the severe lack of affordable housing as a prime cause of economic hardship among children, single-parent families, and seniors living in the 20 QOLRS communities. The shortage of affordable housing is among the most pressing issues facing municipalities. It means too many people, particularly single-parent families, living in temporary shelter or crowed into sub-standard and sometimes unsafe housing. It also means more people living on the streets and straining the ability of social service agencies to help them. (FCM, 2004)

2003—*Falling Behind—Our Growing Income Gap*
The three cities in this study are very different. Saskatoon, Calgary, and Toronto are significantly different in their physical size, composition, economy, population size, and composition. Therefore, commonalities were initially difficult to identify. However, upon completion of the study, it is clear that the cities share a common challenge in terms of growing income disparities and their impact. This suggests that the income gap and income polarization is greater than an isolated big city problem. (FCM, 2003)

Figure 10.2: Difference between Changes in Low Incomes and Changes in Low-End Rents in Various Canadian Municipalities, 1991–2001

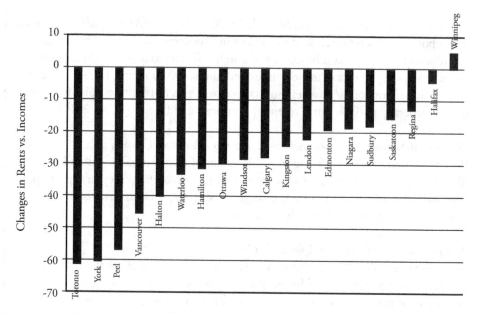

Source: From Highlights Report 2004. *Quality of Life in Canadian Municipalities* (Chart 27, p. 27), by the Federation of Canadian Municipalities, 2004. Ottawa: Federation of Canadian Municipalities.

The report also notes that families on social assistance are experiencing even greater difficulty in having their basic needs met. The ability of benefits to cover basic needs continues to decline.

These findings indicate that the presence of poverty is integrally tied up with societal decisions on how to distribute resources among the population. The FCM reports provide an ongoing portrait of how public policy decisions reflect a general orientation to resource provision that both influences the incidence of poverty as well as shapes its effects upon health and quality of life.

FCM Reports: Implications

The data in the FCM reports—and most others—document a growing gap in income among urban residents, an increasing lack of affordable housing, and an increasing gap between minimum wages, social assistance rates, and housing rental rates. The implications of these findings are profound in light of the growing evidence of poverty being related to adverse health outcomes.

The work of FCM has been supported and complemented by the United Way across Canada. In many cities, the United Way is using quality-of-life frameworks to consider the public policy decisions that are shaping city life. In Toronto, the United Way produced a number of groundbreaking studies that highlight how increasing evidence of

Box 10.3: Landlord Eviction of Tenants Increases

Eviction Bids Soar in Toronto
Naomi Carniola

Toronto landlords are seeking to evict tenants at a higher rate than ever before, and last year filed nearly 30,000 applications to kick people out of their homes, a tenants' group says.

The Federation of Metro Tenants' Associations said the 29,090 eviction applications filed by landlords here last year is a 10 per cent jump over the previous year, and the highest on record since Ontario implemented the Tenant Protection Act in 1998.

Across the province, more than half the tenants "were evicted without a hearing at the Ontario Rental Housing Tribunal," the association said in a statement.

No figures on actual evictions are available for Toronto.

The numbers put paid to the notion that "because vacancy rates are a little higher, things are fine for tenants," said Dan McIntyre, program co-ordinator for the federation, which yesterday released the numbers obtained from the Ontario Rental Housing Tribunal.

"The figures show people are unable to cope with high rents and the eviction process is too easy so people are losing their homes," McIntyre said.

Toronto Councillor Kyle Rae, whose downtown ward houses many people living on the edge, said he wasn't surprised by the numbers or the huge jump over last year.

Provincial legislation protecting tenants has become weak and ineffective, Rae argued, and provisions allowing landlords to jack up the rent before a new tenant moves in have put affordable housing in Toronto beyond the reach of the working poor.

"The City of Toronto has been calling on the province to scrap the Tenant Protection Act," he said, adding the Liberals, in the last provincial election, "ran on a platform to dismantle it."

Rae said the act fails to protect tenants while the city is trying "to ensure people at the lowest end of the economic scale get access to affordable housing—and that's no longer maintained because the Tenant Protection Act allows landlords to increase rents once a tenant leaves the unit.

"It's time for the province to act on its promise."

Housing expert Michael Shapcott, a policy analyst at the Wellesley Central Health Corp., an organization that supports research on issues of urban health, said he's not surprised by the data.

Tenants in Toronto have experienced consistent rent increases—often at double the rate of inflation, he said, while household income has remained the same or dropped.

"When you put those two trends together, it's no surprise more and more tenants are having difficulty paying their rent," said Shapcott.

"Many tenant households are able to hang in for a while. They take money out of their food budgets ... but after a while it all catches up."

The soaring eviction applications shocked Jennifer Ramsay, the advocacy and outreach co-ordinator for the Advocacy Centre for Tenants Ontario.

"An increase of 10.7 per cent is unprecedented in the whole time the (Ontario Rental Housing) tribunal has been operating," she said.

Housing Minister John Gerretsen could not be reached for comment, and Brad Butt, president and CEO of the landlord lobbying group, the Greater Toronto Apartment Association, was unavailable for comment.

But the act, seen by many as outmoded and ineffective, is on its way out, said Brad Duguid, Liberal MPP for Scarborough Centre and Gerretsen's parliamentary assistant.

Duguid said last week the long-awaited and much-delayed legislation to repeal the Tenant Protection Act is expected this spring.

Relief, if it comes, will be welcomed by tenants across the province. Figures released by the Metro tenants' association show Ontario's landlords filed 64,864 eviction applications in 2005, an increase of 8.7 per cent from the previous year—and the highest number since 1998.

The biggest jump in eviction applications occurred at the rental tribunal's Scarborough office, which recorded an increase of 14.1 per cent.

Source: Carniol, N. (2006, February 20). Eviction bids soar in Toronto. *Toronto Star*, p A1.

---

decaying social environments—including stagnating or increasing poverty levels and increasing income inequality—threaten the future of the city (United Way of Greater Toronto, 2004; United Way of Greater Toronto and Canadian Council on Social Development, 2002). In Winnipeg and Ottawa, the United Way is involved in activities that reinforce and extend the findings of the FCM reports.

Other Worrisome Signs

There is evidence that the incidence of poverty is becoming increasingly concentrated within specific neighbourhoods in Canadian cities (Wilkins, Berthelot, and Ng, 2002, Wilkins, 2007). This concentration has both economic and racial aspects (Frenette, Picot, and Sceviour, 2004; Hou and Picot, 2003). Economically, it is seen as reflective of the increasing polarization of income in Canadian cities by which individuals cannot continue to afford housing in more mixed-income areas. Wilkins and colleagues report that, in 1971, the poorest 20% of urban neighbourhoods in Canada had 31% of its residents living beneath Statistics Canada's low income cut-offs. By 2001, this had increased to 35%. Similarly, there were increases in concentration of people living in poverty in the second-poorest neighbourhoods as well: from 20% to 22%. In contrast, the proportion of people living in poverty in the wealthiest neighbourhoods declined from 8% to 5% over this period.

Galabuzi (2005) argues that such concentration of poverty has been associated with higher crime rates and increasing deterioration of quality of life in USA areas and neighbourhoods. There is evidence that this process of race-related concentration of lower income Canadians may have already begun in major Canadians cities (Hou and Picot, 2003; Myles, Picot, and Pyper, 2000). Figure 10.3 presents a model of how this process has been associated with poor quality-of-life outcomes in the USA.

Crime and Security

Freedom from crime and security is a primary component of citizens' views as to what constitutes quality of life (Canadian Council on Social Development, 2000; Schetagne, Jackson, and Harman, 2001). One of the most consistent findings to emerge in the literature is that poverty is a key determinant of whether one falls into a life of crime (Jamieson and Hart, 2003; National Crime Prevention Program, 2003). Additionally, there is an emerging literature that shows that income inequality is a primary determinant of a crime level in a jurisdiction. Indeed, the links between crime prevention and health promotion would appear to be so strong as to constitute justification for a common agenda to address both issues.

The linkages among poverty, crime, and health promotion are remarkably consistent. Poverty is a strong determinant of both crime and health (Standing Committee on

Figure 10.3: Impacts on Individuals and Neighbourhoods of Processes That Concentrate Disadvantage in Specific Areas

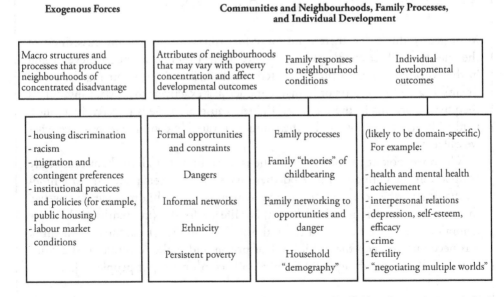

Source: *Neighbourhood Poverty: Volume 1, Context and Consequences for Children* (Figure A, p. xvii), by J. Brookes-Gunn, G. Duncan, and J. Aber (Eds.), New York: Russell Sage Foundation.

Justice and the Solicitor General, 1993). It has long been known that individuals who have experienced living in poverty are much more likely to become involved in criminal activities. This point has been repeatedly made in Canada by the National Council of Welfare (National Council of Welfare, 2001).

It has also become apparent that jurisdictions with higher levels of poverty—usually associated with greater levels of income and wealth inequality—also have higher levels of crime. International comparisons show that income inequality is related to both homicide and robbery rates among nations (Fajnzylber, Lederman, and Loayza, 2002). And it should not be surprising that income inequality is also related to homicide rates in the 50 states of the USA (Kaplan, Pamuk, Lynch, Cohen, and Balfour, 1996; Kennedy, Kawachi, and Prothrow-Stith, 1996).

It is less well known that homicide rates are also strongly related to income inequality among the 10 Canadian provinces (Daly, Wilson, and Vasdev, 2001). Provinces with higher levels of income inequality have reliably higher levels of homicide. The reason for this is simple. Living in poverty is associated with material and social deprivation, exclusion from a range of societal activities, and generally poorer physical, emotional, and social outcomes. It should not be surprising then that the incidence of poverty is related to a societal dysfunction such as crime. Indeed, the question that may be asked is: *Why are crime rates in Canada not higher than they are?*

The Caledon Institute outlines these risk factors for crime: child and family poverty, inconsistent and uncaring parenting, experiences of family violence, substance abuse, poor schooling, unemployment, and social exclusion (Jamieson and Hart,

---

Box 10.4: Clarence Darrow on the Causes of Crime

Most people think that there is no cause for crime, except the pure cussedness of the ones they call criminals. But as a matter of fact there is a cause for everything in this world and there is no way to remove the evil without removing the cause. There's a cause for all sorts of human conduct just exactly as there is a cause for all the physical actions in the universe. The real cause of crime is poverty, ignorance, hard luck, and generally youth. These almost invariably combine to produce what we call a crime.

When we look at the prisoners in the jails we find that all of them practically are poor, at least nine-tenths. And these have always been poor. At least nine-tenths began what they call a criminal career as mere children, eleven, twelve, thirteen. At a time in life when the ways of life are fixed. Nine-tenths of them are ignorant. They have never had the training that intelligent parents would think was necessary to keep their child out of prison and make him safe in the community. All of these things almost universally combine to put people in jail.

Source: Darrow, C. (1924). Online at www.youtube.com/watch?v=9mrvXtO4wsI

2003). The National Crime Prevention Program provides the following risk factors: poor or inadequate parenting, substance abuse, inappropriate peer association, poor academic achievement, and lack of training or employment (National Crime Prevention Program, 2003). The Standing Committee on Justice and the Solicitor General reported in 1993 that "[crime] is the outcome of the interaction of a constellation of factors that include: poverty, physical and sexual abuse, illiteracy, low self-esteem, inadequate housing, school failure, unemployment, inequality and dysfunctional families" (Standing Committee on Justice and the Solicitor General, 1993, p. 11).

A series of reports from Statistics Canada show a strong relationship of crime rates to poverty rates in Canadian cities (Statistics Canada, 2010). A summary report provides a table that shows whether a number of variables differ between high and low crime neighbourhoods in seven Canadian cities: Edmonton, Halifax, Montreal, Regina, Thunder Bay, Winnipeg, and Saskatoon (Savoie, 2008). For all 14 crime measures (violent and property crime across seven cities), median household income was significantly different between high and low crime neighbourhoods, with the high crime neighbourhoods having lower median incomes. Similarly, the proportion of neighbourhood populations that were low-income households also discriminated between high and low crime neighbourhoods for 13 crime measures, the only exception being property crime rates in Halifax. In every case, the higher the proportion of low-income population, the higher the crime rate.

Detailed analyses of the links between poverty and crime rates in Canadian cities are presented in a number of reports (Statistics Canada, 2010). A recent report graphically shows the strong relationship between the proportion of the population in a neighbourhood living on low incomes (i.e., in poverty) and local violent crime, sexual assault, and robbery rates in Toronto (Charron, 2009) (see Figures 10.4a, 10.4b, 10.4c, and 10.4d).

Crime levels have shown little movement in Canada over the past few decades, but the form crime is taking may be changing. In Toronto, there has been a rash of extremely violent murders committed among gang members using handguns. Analyses have suggested that these incidents may be the tip of an iceberg that resulted from a decade or more of increasing income inequality, stagnating or increasing poverty levels, and general deterioration in quality of life (see Box 10.5). Data from other nations indicate that nations that invest less in citizens produce poorer health outcomes, show lower quality of life, and have higher crime rates (Jackson, 2002). The extent to which continuing high levels of poverty will interact with increasing income and wealth inequality to raise crime levels in Canada remains an open question.

Figure 10.4a: Average Income of Neighbourhoods, City of Toronto, 2006

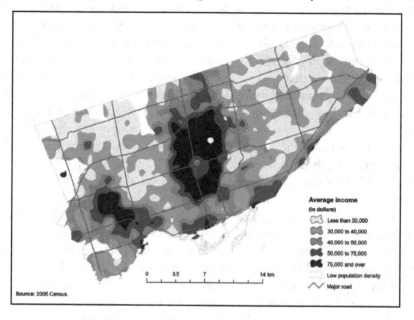

Figure 10.4b: Local Violent Crime Rates, City of Toronto, 2006

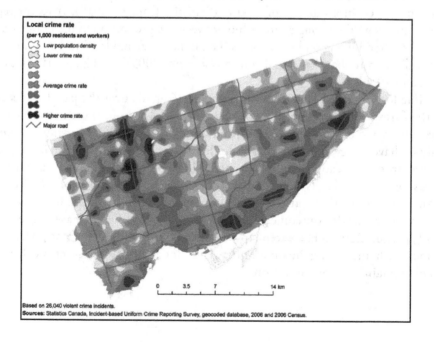

Figure 10.4c: Local Rates of Sexual Assault Incidents, City of Toronto, 2006

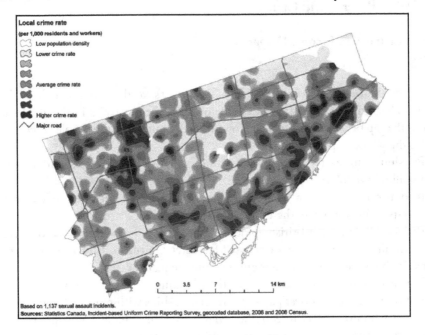

Figure 10.4d: Local Rates of Robbery Incidents, City of Toronto, 2006

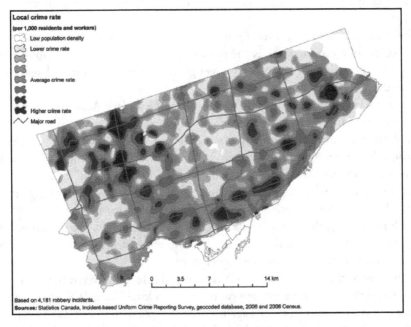

Source: Charron, M. (2009). *Neighbourhood characteristics and the distribution of police-reported crime in the city of Toronto* (Maps 3, 5, 8, and 13). Retrieved March 11, 2011 from Statistics Canada website: www. statcan.gc.ca/pub/85-561-m/2009018/maps-cartes-eng.htm

Box 10.5: Poverty and Crime

Guns, Crime, and Income Disparity
Leslie Scrivener

For anyone worried about violent crime in Toronto, it's worth looking at a United Way report called Poverty by Postal Code. One of the scariest statistics in the 2004 study reveals the gap between the people in Toronto with money and the people without.

It's the widest gap in Canada.

Put simply, for every $1 the poorest families in Toronto have to spend, the richest families have $27.

Income differences that big are troubling in themselves, but when linked to violence, especially homicide, there is even greater cause for alarm.

Richard Wilkinson, a British epidemiologist, says at least 40 international studies (including one on Canada done at McMaster University) show "a robust relationship" between homicide rates and income inequality.

But income inequality goes deeper than looking at who has more money—it roots around in the murkiest parts of our relationships with our neighbours.

People who live in very unequal societies trust each other less, hostility is higher and there is more discrimination against minorities and women, studies show.

Wilkinson, who is an expert in public health, first started looking at inequality to understand why some studies show that people are healthier in more egalitarian societies.

The social environment affects our health, he found, with stress, social status and a feeling of connectedness as the most important features in contributing to a feeling of well-being. That is to say, we feel good if we measure up well against our neighbours.

About social status, he writes in Annals of the New York Academy of Sciences, "We know ourselves partly through each other's eyes."

In short, we care about how others see us and we crave respect. "Remember the stomach-tightening feelings of shame and embarrassment, almost self-loathing, when we feel we have made ourselves look foolish in others' eyes?" he asks.

There's a great deal to suggest, he writes, "that the most frequent trigger to violence is disrespect, loss of face and people feeling looked down upon."

With more inequality, people will have fewer or worse jobs, lower incomes, and feel deprived of the clothes, the cars, and the houses—markers of status—that others have, and that elevate them to a higher status.

Vulnerable to the humiliation of relative—not absolute—poverty, they will be less willing to overlook incidents that appear to involve a loss of face, Wilkinson says.

This link is seen more in crimes against other people than in crimes against property, he adds in an interview from the U.K., where he is a professor at the University of Nottingham.

In the late 1990s, when Tony Blair's Labour government was keen to show that it was not coddling criminals, it launched a campaign that was tough on crime but also addressed the causes of crime. Violence rates went down a bit, said Wilkinson.

But for the most part in debates about violence in the U.K., research about the causes of crime and income disparities hardly comes into the discussion.

Last year there were 52 gun deaths in Toronto, nearly double the number in 2004.

Income inequality is only one part of the complex web of factors that lead to increased violent crime, and it has come up rarely, if at all, in the current federal election campaign.

Looking at other predictors—poverty, inadequate housing, school failure, fatherless children—it is reasonable to think that Toronto could see the murder rate continue to rise.

Add to this an unemployment rate among young blacks in Toronto almost double that of non-blacks and an expected boom in the number of teenagers—the teen population of Toronto is expected to grow by 21 per cent in the next five years. (In contrast, the number of children under 12 is expected to grow by only 6 per cent.) The number of teenagers is of interest because most violent crime is committed by young men in their late teens to their thirties.

In Boston, the same demographic increase in 15- to 19-year-olds has created a slight increase in gun crime, Rev. Eugene Rivers said when he visited the Star's editorial board last week.

Boston made a mistake when it cut programs that fund youth street workers, he says.

"We're paying for it now," says Rivers, who was one of the architects of a strategy that brought a downturn in crime in his city.

Through the late 1990s, the Conservative government of Mike Harris introduced cuts to education and social programs, which in turn led to the loss of 1,500 jobs at Toronto public schools—including social workers, child and youth workers, music teachers and lunch-room supervisors.

"Things started going to hell in Toronto in the early '90s," says Dennis Raphael, associate professor of health policy and management at York University and one of Canada's leading researchers on the links between living conditions and health.

"We're certainly not on top of this wave and coming down. If anything, thinking of the social policy environment, it's beginning," he says.

But violent crime rate in Toronto is still far lower than that of U.S. cities. In Baltimore, for example, a city of 600,000, the number of murders recently dropped to 270, and that's considered a victory of sorts.

These city-to-city comparisons are valid, says Scot Wortley, associate professor of criminology at the University of Toronto. Canada and the U.S. are similar societies, except for levels of crime and Canada's social welfare programs, public education and health care.

Crime won't fall merely by introducing get-tough-on-crime programs, says Wortley. Building more prisons, longer prison sentences—the sorts of things voters hear from politicians during an election campaign—alone will not reduce violence.

"By doing that you will not create social conditions to reduce crime," says Wortley. "Taking away social spending from the poor to imprison the poor, you'll create more crime."

Canadians need to ensure that they don't lose programs that help bridge income inequality, he says. "Along with crime-fighting initiatives, we should also try to identify and preserve those uniquely Canadian social institutions that have already contributed to our relatively low crime rate."

Toronto city leaders and clergy are trying to figure out what else, besides tougher laws, works to reduce crime, and how to measure that reduction.

City councillor Michael Thompson, who along with Toronto's black clergy raised $20,000 (U.S.) to bring Rivers to Toronto, says education is one way to bridge income inequality.

Other possibilities include job creation, more after-school recreation and sports, and involving clergy who know how to stretch the donations they receive.

Toronto Parks and Recreation department is the largest employer of youth in the city, says Brenda Librecz who heads the department. Some 10,000 kids are on the payroll. To involve more young people, the department recently dropped its minimum age for employment to 14.

But Wortley says there is little objective evaluation of what works and what doesn't work in municipal crime-prevention programs.

"Midnight basketball leagues occupy kids and they are less likely to get into trouble. But kids are more sophisticated than we give them credit for. They can tell the differences between window dressing and real opportunities such as job training, mentorship and strong education programs.

"If we can't provide real direction and support and hope, they are doomed for failure. They look around and see society is not fair. They don't believe the American or Canadian ideology that anyone can pick himself up by his bootstraps and succeed. They see the support that middle-class kids get."

From his vantage point, Wilkinson says, "Look at income distribution and pay attention to who is right at the bottom.... All this is about people feeling valued and needed."

Source: Scrivener, L. (2006, January 15). Guns, crime and income disparity. *Toronto Star*, p. D01.

Quality of Life as a Societal Phenomenon: Canadian Quality of Life in Comparative Perspective

There is increasing interest in comparative national analyses of quality of life and how the incidence of poverty—and associated quality-of-life outcomes—is related to a society's willingness to support its citizens in meeting their basic needs. Raphael and Bryant (2004) studied women's quality of life by examining various indicators of issues particularly germane to women in Canada, the USA, the UK, Denmark, and Britain. The USA and UK have very high poverty rates. Sweden and Denmark show very low rates of poverty, which is a result of governmental support of their citizens through various benefits and services.

Raphael and Bryant (2004) drew upon a model of quality of life developed by the Canadian Policy Research Networks (CPRN) (Michalski, 2001). CPRN identified—based on a broad consensus-building exercise—priority themes for considering quality of life. These themes, in order of importance, are political rights and general values, health (including health care), education, environment, social programs, personal well-being, community, economy and employment, and government. These themes were used to identify indicators from a variety of sources.

The indicators of relevance here were, in addition to poverty rates, support for early childhood education and child care, support for long-term home health care, and the security provided by replacement benefits associated with unemployment. Measures of income inequality and gender equity in government were also examined.

The findings were remarkably consistent in that Sweden and Denmark were more likely to provide supports and benefits to citizens across a very wide range of indicators. Poverty levels and income inequality were relatively low, and benefits and supports were high. Gender equity was greater. In contrast, the USA and the UK provided much more modest supports to citizens. Canada shared many characteristics with the USA and the UK, with some evidence of more generous benefits and supports. Raphael and Bryant concluded that nations such as Sweden and Denmark, which have very low poverty rates, also invested significantly more national resources into services and benefits, early childhood education and care, and support for seniors. It was concluded that low levels of poverty are more likely and high quality of life is significantly more probable when public policy approaches emphasize equitable distribution of resources.

These findings are reinforced by an analysis of a wide range of indicators of social development by Jackson (2002). In this analysis, Canada is compared to the USA—a nation with a very high level of poverty—and Sweden—a nation with a very low level of poverty—on a wide range of indices. As shown in Table 10.3, Sweden consistently emerges as supportive of individual and societal social development; the USA much less so. And Canada shows many similarities to the USA profile.

And finally, the Conference Board of Canada (2003, 2006, 2009) has provided numerous analyses of how investment in social infrastructure promotes general quality of life, including economic performance and competitiveness. Their analyses indicate that the social democratic nations of Sweden, Norway, Finland, and Denmark, which invest more in services and benefits, not only have lower poverty rates but also a superior quality of life. These issues are explored further in the following chapters.

Table 10.3: 25 Key Indicators of Social Development

Legend: | GOLD | SILVER | BRONZE |

	Canada	US	Sweden
INCOME AND POVERTY			
Income per person (%US)	79%	100%	70.2%
Poverty Rate	10.3%	17.0%	6.4%
Child Poverty Rate	15.5%	22.4%	2.6%
JOBS			
Employment Rate	71.1%	74.1%	74.2%
Unemployment Rate	6.8%	4.0%	5.9%
Working Long Hours	22.0%	26.0%	17.0%
Low Paid Jobs	20.9%	24.5%	5.3%
Earnings Gap	3.7	4.6	2.2
EMPLOYMENT SECURITY			
UI Benefits as % Earnings	28.0%	14.0%	29.0%
Job Supports	0.5 %	0.2%	1.9%
Unionized Rate	36.0%	18.0%	89.0%
SOCIAL SUPPORTS			
Health Care (Public Share)	69.6%	44.7%	83.8%
Tertiary Education (Public Share)	60.0%	51.0%	91.0%
Private Social Spending	4.5%	8.6%	3.0%
HEALTH			
Life Expectancy (Men)	75.3	72.5	75.9
Life Expectancy (Women)	81.3	79.2	81.3
Infant Mortality/100,000	5.5	7.2	3.5
CRIME			
Homicides per 100,000	1.8	5.5	N/A
Assault/Threat per 100,000	4.0	5.7	4.2
Prisoners per 100,000	118	546	71
EDUCATION			
Adults/Post Secondary Ed.	38.8%	34.9%	28.0%
High Literacy (% Adults)	25.1%	19.0%	35.5%
Low Literacy (% Adults)	42.9%	49.6%	25.1
Grade 12 Math Score	519	461	552
CIVIC PARTICIPATION			
Voter Turnout	56.2%	49.1%	83.2%

Source: Jackson, A. (2002). *Canada beats USA—but loses gold to Sweden.* Retrieved October 2006 from Canadian Council on Social Development website: www.ccsd.ca/pubs/2002/olympic/indicators.htm

Conclusions

Similar to findings showing the relationship between living in poverty and poor health, there is a strong relationship between living in poverty and quality of life. Living in poverty has profound effects upon personal functioning, connections with others, and the ability to reach significant personal goals. These adverse outcomes come about through the experience of material and social deprivation. Living in poverty is both a result of, and a contributor to, community quality of life. There are features of communities that support quality of life, and these features may be especially important for people who lack financial resources. The Federation of Canadian Municipalities is documenting these declines in community quality of life and placing these findings within a public policy perspective.

Crime is just one of the by-products of high rates of poverty and income inequality. Considering the material and social deprivation typical of the experience of living in poverty, findings of a strong association of poverty with crime should not be surprising. The links between poverty, crime, and health are increasingly being recognized. Evidence from other jurisdictions would suggest that Canadian society is at risk for increasing crime levels. While there is some evidence of more violent crime becoming common in Toronto, the future of crime rates in Canada remains an open question.

Quality of life provides a context for understanding how poverty comes about and how living in poverty is experienced, and for predicting its outcomes. Public policy decisions that do little to check growing income inequality, provide affordable housing, or ensure reasonable levels of benefits, supports, and services make the poverty experience more likely and once it occurs, more unpleasant. Considering all this evidence, it is a wonder that so little public policy attention is directed to addressing poverty. Why this is so is considered in the next chapter.

Critical Thinking Questions

1. Consider the information you obtain from the media, your academic courses, and your family and friends concerning what constitutes the "good life." How often are these features related to decisions that governments make about resource allocation and distribution?
2. What are the specific features of living in poverty that threaten a community's quality of life? How are these related to the experience of material and social deprivation?
3. What are the effects of having a wide range of professionals such as psychologists, sociologists, nurses, community developers, and others intervening in distressed communities to influence the outcomes of living in poverty rather than addressing the causes of poverty directly? Could these interventions be making the situation worse? How so?
4. What is your immediate response when you hear about a crime incident? How often do you think the public will support a "quick fix" rather than attempting to get at the roots of crime?

5. Why do you think policy-makers and government officials seem not to understand the effects of living in poverty upon all aspects of individual, community, and societal quality of life? What can be done about this?

Recommended Readings

Federation of Canadian Municipalities. (2008). *Trends and issues in affordable housing and homelessness.* Ottawa: FCM.
Federation of Canadian Municipalities. (2009). *Immigration and diversity in Canadian cities and communities.* Ottawa: FCM.
Federation of Canadian Municipalities. (2010). *Mending Canada's social safety net: The role of municipal governments.* Ottawa: FCM.

> These and other reports from FCM document the quality-of-life situation in Canadian cities and show how poverty and its effects interact with governmental policies to influence a wide range of aspects of quality of life. Online at www.fcm.ca

Michalski, J. H. (2001). *Asking citizens what matters for quality of life in Canada: Results of CPRN's public dialogue process.* Ottawa: Canadian Policy Research Networks. Online at http://cprn.org/doc.cfm?doc=90&l=en

> This report details an extensive process by which Canadians were asked about the components of quality of life and then asked to consider the state of quality of life across Canada. The Canadian Policy Research Networks has since shut down due to lack of funding.

Raphael, D. (Ed.). (2010). *Health promotion and quality of life in Canada: Essential readings.* Toronto: Canadian Scholars' Press Inc.

> Health and quality of life are vital indicators of societal functioning. The way a society distributes resources among its population reveals much about the society itself. This unique volume unites readings that explore the integral link between quality of life and public policy choices. It also provides an up-to-date analysis of the barriers facing those attempting to improve quality of life and health.

Wilkinson, R. G., and Pickett, K. (2009). *The spirit level: Why more equal societies almost always do better.* London, UK: Allen Lane.

> This work summarizes the wide range of societal characteristics that are affected by income inequality and the poverty that is associated with it.

Relevant Websites

Atkinson Foundation Canadian Index of Wellbeing (CIW)—www.ciw.ca/en/Home.aspx
> The CIW is a way of measuring well-being that goes beyond narrow economic measures such as the GDP. It provides insights into the quality of life of Canadians overall, and in specific areas that matter: our standard of living, our health, the quality of our environment, our education and skill levels, the way we use our time, the

vitality of our communities, our participation in the democratic process, and the state of our leisure and culture.

Canadian Centre for Policy Alternatives Growing Gap Project—www.policyalternatives.ca/projects/growing-gap/about

The Growing Gap project takes an in-depth and sustained look at one of the biggest challenges of our time: worsening income and wealth inequality in Canada. A team of economists and researchers have been tracking household income, wealth, spending and credit data, and unearthing a troubling phenomenon.

The Federation of Canadian Municipalities—www.fcm.ca

The FCM is carrying out ongoing documentation of the quality of life of Canadian municipalities. It does so by collecting a wide range of indicators that consider income, housing, service, health, and others and placing all of these findings within public policy frameworks.

The University of Toronto's Quality of Life Research Unit—www.utoronto.ca and www.utoronto.ca/seniors

This website provides a wealth of information concerning quality of life, its measurement, and findings from a range of studies. Of particular importance is the model of quality of life that was developed and how it has been applied among individuals (e.g., persons with disabilities, adolescents, seniors, etc.), communities, and jurisdictions.

United Way of Canada Websites across Canada

—www.unitedwaytoronto.com/

—www.unitedwayottawa.ca/

—www.unitedwaywinnipeg.mb.ca/

—www.unitedway.ca/splash/index.htm

The United Way has undertaken the task of reporting on quality of life in communities across Canada. Many of the reports focus on the effects of poverty and direct attention to government policies that are doing little to improve the situations. The sites presented here are provided as examples and do not include many other United Way branches across Canada that are also doing good work.

Glossary of Terms

Crime prevention through social development focuses on addressing the social and economic factors that may place individuals at risk to commit crime or be victimized by crime. Risk factors and root causes of crime include, but are not limited to: child abuse and neglect, family violence and bullying, school difficulties, illiteracy, Fetal Alcohol Spectrum Disorder, substance abuse, and lack of employment opportunities (Government of Alberta, 2006).

Human and social development refers to establishing conditions that will promote optimal development. These processes show strong associations with many social determinants of health such as education, food, housing, educational and recreational opportunities, and freedom from insecurity and crime.

Neighbourhood effects are health and quality-of-life effects that accrue up and above factors associated with the characteristics of the individuals who live there. These effects may show themselves in terms of educational achievement, crime, and health indicators, among others.

Quality of life is a holistic construct that views human health and well-being within the contexts of immediate and more distant environments. It combines elements of broad societal indicators with the actual lived experience of people.

Social indicators are statistics that—similar to the economic statistics of the national accounts—are intended to provide a basis for making concise, comprehensive, and balanced judgments about the conditions of major aspects of society. The Organisation for Economic Co-operation and Development defines a social indicator as a "direct and valid statistical measure which monitors levels and changes over time in a fundamental social concern."

Spatial concentration of disadvantage refers to the concentration of conditions of material and social deprivation within specific areas. These concentrations reflect processes of exclusion and inequality taking place in a society. In the USA, such concentration has been associated with a wide range of social illness including crime, lower educational achievement, and increasing alienation and anomie.

References

Antonovsky, A. (1987). *Unraveling the mystery of health: How people manage stress and stay well.* San Francisco: Jossey Bass.

Brooks-Gunn, J., Duncan, G. J., and Britto, P. R. (1999). Are SES gradients for children similar to those for adults? Achievement and health of children in the United States. In C. Hertzman (Ed.), *Developmental health and the wealth of nations: Social, biological, and educational dynamics* (pp. 94–124). New York: Guilford Press.

Bryant, T., Brown, I., Cogan, T., Dallaire, C., LaForest, S., McGowan, P., ... Young, J. (2004). What do Canadian seniors say supports their quality of life? Findings from a national participatory study. *Canadian Journal of Public Health, 95*(4), 299–303.

Canadian Council on Social Development. (2000). *The personal security index, 2000.* Retrieved October 2006 from www.ccsd.ca/pubs/2000/psi/psi.pdf

Charron, M. (2009). *Neighbourhood characteristics and the distribution of police-reported crime in the city of Toronto.* Retrieved March 11, 2011 from Statistics Canada website: www.statcan.gc.ca/pub/85-561-m/2009018/part-partie1-eng.htm

Conference Board of Canada. (2003). *Defining the Canadian advantage.* Ottawa: Conference Board of Canada.

Conference Board of Canada. (2006). *Performance and potential: The world and Canada.* Ottawa: Conference Board of Canada.

Conference Board of Canada. (2009). *How Canada performs 2009: A report card on Canada.* Ottawa: Conference Board of Canada.

Daly, M., Wilson, M., and Vasdev, S. (2001). Income inequality and homicide rates in Canada and the United States. *Canadian Journal of Criminology, 43*(2), 219–236.

Fajnzylber, P., Lederman, D., and Loayza, N. (2002). Inequality and violent crime. *Journal of Law and Economics, 45*(1), 1–40.

Federation of Canadian Municipalities. (1999). *Quality of life reporting system: Quality of life in Canadian communities*. Ottawa: Federation of Canadian Municipalities.

Federation of Canadian Municipalities. (2003). *Falling behind: Our growing income gap*. Ottawa: Federation of Canadian Municipalities.

Federation of Canadian Municipalities. (2004). *Income, shelter, and necessities*. Ottawa: Federation of Canadian Municipalities.

Federation of Canadian Municipalities. (2008). *Trends and issues in affordable housing and homelessness*. Ottawa: Federation of Canadian Municipalities.

Federation of Canadian Municipalities. (2009). *Immigration and diversity in Canadian cities and communities*. Ottawa: Federation of Canadian Municipalities.

Federation of Canadian Municipalities. (2010). *Mending Canada's social safety net: The role of municipal governments*. Ottawa: Federation of Canadian Municipalities.

Frenette, M., Picot, G., and Sceviour, R. (2004). *How long do people live in low-income neighbourhoods? Evidence for Toronto, Montreal, and Vancouver*. Ottawa: Analytic Studies Branch, Statistics Canada.

Galabuzi, G. E. (2005). *Canada's economic apartheid: The social exclusion of racialized groups in the new century*. Toronto: Canadian Scholars' Press Inc.

Government of Alberta (2006). Defining crime prevention. Solicitor General and public security. Retrieved March 11, 2011 from 222.solgen.gov.ab.ca/crime_prev/questions.aspx

Health Canada. (1999). The health status of Canadians. In *Towards a healthy future: Second report on the health of Canadians* (pp. 11–38). Ottawa: Health Canada.

Health Council of Canada. (2010). *Stepping it up: Moving the focus from health care in Canada to a healthier Canada*. Toronto: Health Council of Canada.

Hou, F., and Picot, G. (2003). *Visible minority neighbourhood enclaves and labour market outcomes of immigrants*. Ottawa: Analytic Studies Branch, Statistics Canada.

Jackson, A. (2002). *Canada beats USA—but loses gold to Sweden.*. Retrieved October 2006 from Canadian Council on Social Development website: www.ccsd.ca/pubs/2002/olympic/indicators.htm.

Jamieson, W., and Hart, L. (2003). *Compendium of promising crime prevention practices in Canada*. Ottawa: Caledon Institute.

Kaplan, G. A., Pamuk, E. R., Lynch, J. W., Cohen, R. D., and Balfour, J. L. (1996). Inequality in income and mortality in the United States: Analysis of mortality and potential pathways. *British Medical Journal, 312*(7037), 999–1003.

Kennedy, B. P., Kawachi, I., and Prothrow-Stith, D. (1996). Income distribution and mortality: Cross-sectional ecological study of the Robin Hood index in the United States. *British Medical Journal, 312*(7037), 1004–1007.

Lindstrom, B. (1992). *The essence of existence: On the quality of life of children in the Nordic countries*. Goteborg, Norway: Nordic School of Public Health.

Lynch, J., Kaplan, G., and Salonen, J. (1997). Why do poor people behave poorly? Variation in adult health behaviours and psychosocial characteristics by stages of the socioeconomic lifecourse. *Social Science and Medicine, 44*(6), 809–819.

Michalski, J. H. (2001). *Asking citizens what matters for quality of life in Canada: Results of CPRN's public dialogue process*. Ottawa: Canadian Policy Research Networks.

Myles, J., Picot, G., and Pyper, W. (2000). *Neighbourhood inequality in Canadian cities*. Statistics Canada, Business and Labour Market Analysis Division. Retrieved December 2010 from http://dsp-psd.pwgsc.gc.ca/Collection/CS11-0019-160E.pdf

National Council of Welfare. (2004). *Income for living?* Ottawa: National Council of Welfare.

National Crime Prevention Program. (2003). *Factsheet: Crime prevention through social development*. Ottawa: National Crime Prevention Program.

Raphael, D. (1996). Determinants of health of North-American adolescents: Evolving definitions, recent findings, and proposed research agenda. *Journal of Adolescent Health, 19*(1), 6–16.

Raphael, D. (Ed.). (2010). *Health promotion and quality of life in Canada: Essential readings*. Toronto: Canadian Scholars' Press Inc.

Raphael, D., Brown, I., Bryant, T., Wheeler, J., Herman, R., Houston, J., ... Weisbeck, F. (2001). How government policy decisions affect seniors' quality of life: Findings from a participatory policy study carried out in Toronto, Canada. *Canadian Journal of Public Health, 92*(3), 190–195.

Raphael, D., Brown, I., Renwick, R., Cava, M., Weir, N., and Heathcote, K. (1997). Measuring the quality of life of older persons: A model with implications for community and public health nursing. *International Journal of Nursing Studies, 34*(3), 231–239.

Raphael, D., Brown, I., Renwick, R., and Rootman, I. (1997). Quality of life: What are the implications for health promotion? *American Journal of Health Behavior, 21*(2), 118–128.

Raphael, D., and Bryant, T. (2004). The welfare state as a determinant of women's health: Support for women's quality of life in Canada and four comparison nations. *Health Policy, 68*(1), 63–79.

Raphael, D., Phillips, S., Renwick, R., and Sehdev, H. (2000). Government policies as a threat to public health: Findings from two community quality of life studies in Toronto. *Canadian Journal of Public Health, 91*(3), 181–187.

Raphael, D., Renwick, R., Brown, I., Phillips, S., Sehdev, H., and Steinmetz, B. (2001). Community quality of life in low income urban neighbourhoods: Findings from two contrasting communities in Toronto, Canada. *Journal of the Community Development Society, 32*(2), 310–333.

Raphael, D., Renwick, R., Brown, I., Steinmetz, B., Sehdev, H., and Phillips, S. (2001). Making the links between community structure and individual well-being: Community quality of life in Riverdale, Toronto, Canada. *Health and Place, 7*(3), 17–34.

Raphael, D., Steinmetz, B., and Renwick, R. (1998). *The people, places, and priorities of Riverdale: Write-ups of the group discussions and individual interviews*. Toronto: Department of Public Health Sciences.

Reutter, L., Veenstra, G., Stewart, M., Raphael, D., Love, R., Makwarimba, E., and McMurray, S. (2005). Lay understandings of the effects of poverty: A Canadian perspective. *Health and Social Care in the Community, 13*(6), 514–530.

Reutter, L., Veenstra, G., Stewart, M., Raphael, D., Love, R., Makwarimba, E., and McMurray, S. (2006). Public attributions for poverty in Canada. *Canadian Review of Sociology and Anthropology, 43*(1), 1–22.

Ross, D. P., and Roberts, P. (1999). *Income and child well-being: A new perspective on the poverty debate.* Ottawa: Canadian Council on Social Development.

Savoie, J. (2008). *Analysis of the spatial distribution of crime in Canada: Summary of major trends, 1999, 2001, 2003, and 2006.* Ottawa: Canadian Centre for Justice Statistics, Statistics Canada.

Schellenberg, G. (2004). *2003 General social survey on social engagement, cycle 17: An overview of findings.* Ottawa: Statistics Canada.

Schetagne, S., Jackson, A., and Harman, S. (2001). *Gaining ground: The personal security index 2001.* Retrieved December 2010 from Canadian Council on Social Development website: www.ccsd.ca/pubs/2001/psi2001/psi2001.pdf

Standing Committee on Justice and the Solicitor General. (1993). *Crime prevention in Canada: Toward a national strategy. Twelfth report of the Standing Committee on Justice and the Solicitor General.* Ottawa: Supply and Services Canada.

Statistics Canada. (2010). *Crime and justice research paper series.* Ottawa: Statistics Canada. Retrieved March 11, 2011 from http://tinyurl.com/27u9j6e

Stewart, M., Fast, J., Letourneau, N., Love, R., Raine, K., Raphael, D., ... Wilson, D. (2001). *Low-income consumers' perspectives on determinants of health services use.* Edmonton: University of Alberta.

Stewart, M., Reutter, L., Veenstra, G., Love, R., and Raphael, D. (2003). *Left out: Perspectives on social exclusion and social isolation in low-income populations: Final report.* Edmonton: University of Alberta.

Stewart, M., Reutter, L., Veenstra, G., Love, R., and Raphael, D. (2004). *Left out: Perspectives on social exclusion and social isolation in low-income populations: Public report.* Edmonton: University of Alberta.

United Way of Greater Toronto. (2004). *Poverty by postal code: The geography of neighbourhood poverty, 1981–2001.* Toronto: United Way of Greater Toronto.

United Way of Greater Toronto and Canadian Council on Social Development. (2002). *A decade of decline: Poverty and income inequality in the city of Toronto in the 1990s.* Toronto: Canadian Council on Social Development and United Way of Greater Toronto.

United Way of Ottawa. (2003). *Environmental scan.* Ottawa: United Way of Ottawa.

United Way of Winnipeg. (2003). *2003 environmental scan and Winnipeg census data.* Winnipeg: United Way of Winnipeg.

Wilkins, R. (2007). *Mortality by neighbourhood income in urban Canada from 1971 to 2001.* HAMG Seminar, and special compilations. Ottawa: Statistics Canada, Health Analysis and Measurement Group.

Wilkins, R., Berthelot, J.-M., and Ng, E. (2002). Trends in mortality by neighbourhood income in urban Canada from 1971 to 1996. *Supplement to Health Reports, 13,* 1–28.

Wilkinson, R. G., and Pickett, K. (2009). *The spirit level: Why greater equality makes societies stronger.* New York: Bloomsbury Publishing.

Williamson, D., Stewart, M., Hayward, K., Letourneau, N., Makwarimba, E., Masuda, J., ... Wilson, D. (2006). Low-income Canadians' experiences with health-related services: Implications for health care reform. *Health Policy, 76,* 106–121.

Willms, J. D. (Ed.). (2002). *Vulnerable children: Findings from Canada's National Longitudinal Survey.* Edmonton: University of Alberta Press.

PART IV

POLITICS, PUBLIC POLICY, AND POVERTY

PART IV PLACES THE INCIDENCE OF POVERTY FIRMLY WITHIN A public policy perspective. Poverty is seen as a result of public policy decisions that shape the distribution of resources among the population. Canadian public policy is compared to policy approaches elsewhere to identify how these processes operate in Canada to maintain high levels of poverty. Various means of addressing the continuing problem of poverty in Canada are considered and evaluated in terms of their likelihood of success.

Chapter 11, "The Politics of Poverty," provides a political analysis of poverty in Canada. It considers the politics of poverty as involving three processes. The first is a process by which the incidence of poverty is determined by political, economic, and social forces that influence elected governments to shape public policy in particular ways. The second is a process by which political parties committed to eliminating poverty come to win power. This process illustrates the role that left political parties and working-class organizations play in producing progressive welfare policies that reduce poverty. The third is how public attitudes and values interact with political activities to create policies that either support those living in poverty or make their situations more difficult. It explores the incidence of poor-bashing in Canada and shows who benefits from such attitudes.

Chapter 12, "Canadian Public Policy and Poverty in International Perspective," examines how dimensions of public policy determine the levels of poverty existing within a jurisdiction as well as the jurisdiction's responses to its incidence. These policy domains include public expenditures on supports and benefits to citizens as well as the extent of the social safety net. Canadian standings on various health indicators are contrasted with those of other wealthy developed nations and are found to be mediocre at best. The role that expenditures on health, seniors, the disabled, and families play in creating poverty is considered, as well as Canadian performance on providing income and social security through benefits and supports to citizens. Canada lags far behind many wealthy developed nations in expenditures that support its citizens. This lack of commitment to its citizens is a strong contributor to Canada's high poverty rates.

Chapter 13, "Anti-poverty Strategies and Programs," provides an overview of the strategies and programs that federal and provincial authorities have implemented to reduce poverty in Canada. Most of these appear to be incremental in nature and aim to bring individuals and families above the poverty line. They are certainly not concerned with structural change that would create a more equitable distribution of economic and other resources across the population. Not surprisingly, their success in poverty reduction has been modest. This chapter also provides details of recent anti-poverty reports from the Canadian Senate and House of Commons committees. The likelihood of the wide-ranging recommendations being implemented in the current political environment is considered. The chapter concludes by identifying some specific policies that would reduce the incidence of poverty in Canada, thereby improving Canadians' health and quality of life. There is a need for broader anti-poverty approaches that address the inequalities in power and influence in Canadian society that create poverty.

Chapter 14, "Poverty and the Future of the Canadian Welfare State," identifies ways of addressing poverty and the barriers to having these actions implemented. An analysis of how politics plays a key role in producing differing poverty rates is provided. The implications of this analysis for action to reduce poverty are examined and the barriers to action are identified. Specific actions that Canadians can take to reduce poverty are presented. It is suggested that the most effective way to accomplish poverty reduction is by increasing the influence of the left in Canadian policy-making and by making it easier for Canadians to unionize their workplace. Finally, evidence is presented of how—despite opinions to the contrary—poverty-reducing public policies are not a barrier to economic growth and productivity. Indeed, the nations with the lowest poverty rates are now leaders on a wide range of economic indicators.

Chapter Eleven

The Politics of Poverty

A man who sees another man on the street corner with only a stump for an arm will be so shocked the first time he'll give him sixpence. But the second time it'll only be a three penny bit. And if he sees him a third time, he'll have him cold-bloodedly handed over to the police.
—Bertolt Brecht

Learning Objectives

At the conclusion of this chapter, the reader will be able to:

- explain how poverty in Canada is a result of public policy decisions that shape the distribution of economic and other resources;
- give details of how these public policy decisions are shaped by economic and political forces and justified through various ideological discourses;
- describe how political parties come to hold power, thereby shaping public policy that influences the distribution of resources and the incidence of poverty;
- explain how public attitudes and values toward poverty both result from political and economic structures and then go on to contribute to the maintenance of these political and economic structures; and
- understand the concept of poor-bashing and explain how various groups benefit from such activities.

Introduction

This chapter examines the politics of poverty. The term *politics* is used to refer to three different processes. The first process is how the incidence of poverty within a society is determined by public policies that are shaped by political and economic forces and then justified through various discourses about poverty. Theories are available to both describe and explain how these forces shape public policy.

The second process to which the term *politics* refers is how political parties committed to reducing poverty come to win power. Political parties that favour poverty reduction have differing abilities to win elections, depending on the degree of party organization, the strength of supportive labour and other social movements, and the extent of public support for progressive public policies in general and poverty-reducing policies in particular. Also important is the organization and strength of those political and economic forces that oppose policies that promote equitable resource distribution that would reduce poverty.

The third process referred to by the term *politics* is how public attitudes toward those living in poverty are shaped. These attitudes come to influence the creation of policies that either support those living in poverty or make their situations more difficult. The phenomenon of poor-bashing in Canada is an example of how public attitudes toward the poor are shaped by societal sectors that benefit from the existence of poverty. The chapter concludes by considering how the groundwork can be established to enable citizens—including those living in poverty—to influence public policy as a means of reducing the incidence of poverty, thereby improving Canadians' health and quality of life.

Politics as the Political and Economic Forces and Justifying Discourses That Shape Policy-Making in Canada

Canada has one of the highest poverty rates among wealthy developed nations (Organisation for Economic Co-operation and Development [OECD], 2008). Much of this has to do with public policies that determine how the resources of the nation are to be distributed among the population. Various models of public policy have been developed in an attempt to explain how governments make public decisions. These are the pluralist, materialist, and public choice approaches (Brooks and Miljan, 2003). These models aim to make explicit the political and economic forces that shape the making of public policy.

The pluralist model of public policy-making is the model of governance that is taught in Canadian civics classes. In this view, public policy decisions result from governments and other policy-makers choosing directions based on the competition of ideas in the public arena (Brooks and Miljan, 2003). This competition of ideas is facilitated by various interest groups who lobby governments to accept their position. Pluralists recognize that there may not be a level playing field in these lobbying attempts, since political and economic elites have an upper hand. Nevertheless, the pluralist approach assumes that the governmental policy-making process is generally open, and those with the better ideas will come to see their views adopted by governments.

Pluralists assume, therefore, that Canadian policy-making is a generally democratic process. It is a rational process whereby the best ideas are put into practice. Individuals, communities, agencies, organized groups, labour, and business, all have a place at the policy-making table. Canadian governments strive to implement the Canadian constitutional principles of peace, order, and good government by implementing reasonable public policy.

The materialist model posits that governments in capitalist societies such as Canada enact policies that serve the interests of economic elites. These elites are the owners and managers of large corporations whose primary goals are to maximize profits, provide growing dividends to shareholders, and institute public policies that keep business costs down. These interests are also likely to lobby for minimal governmental intervention in business practices and to resist business regulation and progressive labour legislation. Lowering corporate and income taxes is also an important policy objective. Since taxes are required to fund governmental services, economic interests frequently call for reduction in program spending to allow tax decreases. Business interests generally oppose moves that enable workers to form unions that would see the realization of collective bargaining. Collective bargaining is related to the receipt of higher wages, stronger benefits, and increased employment security for union members.

These economic elites are able to influence governments through a variety of processes. First, they are able to influence government through their ability to shift investment capital from location to location. A government that institutes non-business friendly policies could see business and investment leaving the jurisdiction. Second, lending agencies whose interests are consistent with business can raise borrowing rates for debt-ridden jurisdictions that institute what they see as problematic policies. Third, the people who have the financial resources to consider running for the dominant political parties may either come from the business class and/or hold their values. These individuals can expect not only to receive financial support for their runs at political office, but also employment opportunities within these same sectors if they fail to be re-elected or upon their retirement from public office (see Box 11.1).

The public choice model focuses on the individual policy-maker and the process by which he or she develops and implements policies that maximize the benefits to society (Brooks and Miljan, 2003). In this model, the policy-maker looks out for society's interests (including his or her own) by balancing the concerns of a wide range of stakeholders that include business, labour, the needs of elected officials and senior civil servants, and the media, among others.

What then do these models have to say about policy approaches to poverty? First, a model should help explain why poverty rates in Canada have remained basically unchanged since 1984. Second, it should help explicate why some national jurisdictions have striven to reduce poverty, while others such as Canada have remained generally indifferent to its presence. Third, it should illuminate a means of influencing policy-makers to implement poverty-reducing policies. These issues are explored further following a review of how public policy directions in various sectors have shaped the incidence of poverty in Canada.

An Overview of Canadian Public Policy Related to Poverty

Throughout this volume, instances of government action—or inaction—on poverty and the factors that drive poverty have been highlighted. Income and wealth inequality is increasing, with Canadians at the top of the income distribution enjoying improving conditions and the situation of those at the bottom either stagnating or declining. Owners of housing are increasing their incomes while tenants' incomes are decreasing. Social assistance benefits and minimum wages are not sufficient to keep people from living in poverty. Indeed, the percentage of the poverty line reached by these benefits is

Box 11.1: The Politics of Policy-Making: Taking Care of Business

Martin Took Rides on Private Jets

Conflict commissioner clears him because planes were owned by "close personal friends"
Robert Fife, Ottawa Bureau Chief, CanWest News Service
Tuesday, December 2, 2003

OTTAWA—Paul Martin flew on private corporate jets of some of Canada's wealthiest businessmen for pleasure and business during his years as finance minister.

The trips were not publicly declared as required under federal conflict of interest rules.

Howard Wilson, the federal Ethics Counsellor, said yesterday that Mr. Martin, who becomes prime minister on Dec. 12, took five trips aboard corporate jets between 1995 and 2002, a time when he was making major decisions affecting corporate taxation and programs related to the business sector.

Mr. Martin flew to the Caribbean on holidays in 2002 on New Brunswick billionaire Wallace McCain's corporate jet. In 1995 and 1999, he joined Montreal multi-millionaire Lawrence Pathy on his company jet for a family vacation. Mr. Pathy is a former business partner of Mr. Martin's in Canada Steamship Lines.

As finance minister, Mr. Martin also flew in 2000 aboard the company jet of Power Corp. of Canada, run by Montreal billionaire Paul Desmarais, and in 2001 on corporate aircraft of Toronto-based Onex Corp., whose chairman Gerry Schwartz is a close friend.

"I have been provided with information that he had taken some flights. This is all official business and there was reimbursement made as was our practice at the time for the commercial costs," Mr. Wilson said.

Mr. Wilson said Mr. Martin had accepted free trips aboard the corporate jets for personal reasons but said he absolved him of any conflict of interest because the aircraft were owned by personal friends.

The Conflict of Interest Code forbids ministers from accepting gifts greater than $200 that are unrelated to their official duties, but allows for benefits from "close personal friends."

"He would give me a call—Mr. Martin directly—about a few things and our general approach was that ... if it is a personal friend, then we would not have any difficulties," he said.

Mr. McCain, who owns Maple Leaf Foods and is a principal shareholder in McCain Foods, was judged a close personal friend of Mr. Martin's, as was Mr. Pathy.

Mr. Wilson said he asked Mr. Martin to have Ottawa reimburse Mr. Desmarais and Mr. Schwartz for the trips because they involved some finance department business.

Mr. Martin also personally reimbursed Mr. Schwartz for accommodation at a B.C. fishing lodge they went to in 2001 and later flew back to Ottawa on the Onex plane.

"From my perspective, that was official business and so therefore our standard response was to have the office pay for the trip and they did," Mr. Wilson said. "I guess the lodging he was in was also reimbursed, but that was probably done by him personally."

The disclosure of Mr. Martin's use of corporate jets while he was finance minister came only after persistent inquiries by CanWest News Service. Mr. Wilson and Mr. Martin's officials had refused to say whether Mr. Martin used corporate aircraft during last month's furor over a series of ministers who flew on jets and holidayed for free at a fishing lodge owned by the billionaire Irving family of New Brunswick.

The Martin flights were never publicly disclosed on the list of ministerial gifts as required under the conflict code. The code states any gift over $200 requires a "public declaration that provides sufficient detail to identify the gift, hospitality or other benefit received, the donor and the circumstances."

The only gift Mr. Martin declared during his nine years as finance minister was an engraving of the Palacio Real in Madrid that he received in 1994 while attending an International Monetary Fund and World Bank meeting in Spain.

Mr. Wilson said Mr. Martin didn't have to publicly declare the Desmarais and Schwartz trips because he "discharged whatever obligation there might have been" by having taxpayers reimburse Power Corp. and Onex.

He added that the rule for public disclosure of gifts over $200 is often not applied, which was why Mr. Martin did not bother to declare the vacation flights with his corporate friends.

"If it's an invitation from a family member or a close personal friend, our practice has been not to have a public declaration of those," he said.

Scott Reid, a Martin spokesman, said Mr. Martin followed Mr. Wilson's instructions: "He was aware of all five trips and was content the rules were followed."

Last month it emerged that Industry Minister Allan Rock, Environment Minister David Anderson, Human Resources Minister Jane Stewart, Labour Minister Claudette Bradshaw and Dominic Leblanc, parliamentary secretary to Defence Minister Jim McCallum, accepted free flights or holidays at the Irving salmon lodge.

When the issue hit Parliament, Ms. Bradshaw, Mr. Anderson and Mr. Rock reimbursed the Irvings.

In most of the cases, Mr. Wilson found the Cabinet ministers either knew a member of the Irving family or were close to people who did, and therefore concluded they did not breach the rules.

Source: *Martin took rides on private jets.* Retrieved March 2011 from http://urbantoronto.ca/showthread.php?372-Martin-took-rides-on-private-jets

Mike Harris

On June 8, 1995 Mike Harris became the twenty-second Premier of Ontario following a landslide election victory. Four years later, the voters of Ontario re-elected
Mike Harris and his team—making him the first Ontario Premier in more than 30
years to form a second consecutive majority government. Prior to his election to
the Ontario Legislature in 1981, Mike Harris was a schoolteacher, a School Board
Trustee and Chair, and an entrepreneur in the Nipissing area.

After leaving office, Mr. Harris formed his own consulting firm. As president of
Steane Consulting Ltd., Mr. Harris serves as an advisor to several Canadian compa-
nies, including Cassels Brock and Blackwell LLP as Senior Business Advisor. Mr.
Harris also serves as a Director on several public boards including Magna
International Inc., Chartwell Seniors Housing REIT, Canaccord Financial,
FirstService Corporation, and Route 1.

Mr. Harris also serves as a Director on the Boards of the Tim Horton Children's
Foundation, the Mount Royal University Foundation. He is also a Senior Fellow
with the Fraser Institute, a leading Canadian economic, social research and education organization.

Source: Mike Harris, 2011.

declining. Employment insurance benefits are now unavailable to over half of Canadians
currently employed. Governments have purposefully chosen to withdraw from policy
areas that prevent poverty, such as the provision of social housing. Governments have
chosen not to strongly intervene in areas such as early childhood education and care.
Moves that have occurred, such as the National Child Benefit, are only tentative steps
toward poverty reduction (see Chapter 13).

Campaign 2000—a major child poverty advocacy group—outlines public policy as
key to poverty reduction (Freiler, Rothman, and Barata, 2004). The group points to
the following public policies as responsible for the maintenance of high poverty rates
in Canada:

- failure to increase minimum wages to keep up with living costs
- failure to provide adequate social assistance benefits to avoid poverty
- provincial clawing back of the federal Child Benefit from families on social
  assistance
- cutbacks in child care
- cancellation of new social housing and of rent control by some provincial governments

- decreased government spending on social assistance
- reduction of access to unemployment insurance by the federal government
- federal and provincial withdrawals from investments in housing
- cuts to the social safety net by federal and provincial governments.

In 2002, accumulating evidence that continuing high levels of poverty were contributing to a wide range of health problems and quality-of-life social ills among Canadians provided the stimulus for the organization of a Health Canada–funded national conference on the social determinants of health. The conference provided a forum for considering Canadian governments' actions in a wide range of areas that impact upon the incidence of poverty in Canada and its effects upon health and quality of life. As stated in the Toronto Charter that evolved from the conference:

> Evidence was also accumulating that a high level of poverty—an outcome of the growing gap between rich and poor—has profound societal effects as poor children are at higher risk for health and learning problems in childhood, adolescence, and later life, and are less likely to achieve their full potential as contributors to Canadian society. (Raphael, Bryant, and Curry-Stevens, 2004, p. 1)

A variety of policy domains were considered at the conference, and a key theme was that public policy was doing little if anything to address the factors that were creating and maintaining the high levels of poverty seen in Canada. An important recommendation with particular relevance for the issue of poverty was that

> [g]overnments at all levels should review their current economic, social, and service policies to consider the impacts of their policies upon these social determinants of health. Areas of special importance are the provision of adequate income and social assistance levels, provision of affordable housing, development of quality childcare arrangements, and enforcement of anti-discrimination laws and human rights codes. It is also important to increase support for the social infrastructure including public education, social and health services, and improvement of job security and working conditions. (Raphael et al., 2004, p. 273)

The conference produced a volume, since updated, that provides detail of the policy failures associated with a variety of areas closely related to the incidence and health and quality-of-life effects of poverty (Raphael, 2009). These areas included unemployment and employment issues, working conditions, food security, early childhood education and care, housing, and racism and discrimination. Three of these areas—income distribution, housing, and early child development—have recently been reviewed and are explored here to provide a flavour of how Canadian public policy is influencing the incidence and experience of poverty (Bryant, Raphael, Schrecker, and Labonte, in press).

Income Inequality and Poverty in Canada

Figure 11.1 shows that income inequality in Canada has increased since 1980, with the increase being especially great for market income (Statistics Canada, 2010). The reduction in the Gini coefficient that results from the effects of receiving other income such as social assistance and the distributional aspects of the tax system is significant but still well below the effects that occur in most other OECD nations (Rainwater and Smeeding, 2003; Organisation for Economic Co-operation and Development, 2008). Much of this has to do with governments shifting the tax burden from the wealthy to the middle class and poor and doing little to redistribute wealth from the rich to the poor.

Figure 2.1 in Chapter 2 showed that the percentage of Canadians living in poverty had changed little from 1984 to 2008. Canada is one of the few nations where child poverty rates were higher than overall poverty rates over the past two decades (OECD, 2008), and it should be noted that the improvement seen in poverty rates from 2004 to 2007 predated the economic crisis that began in 2008.

Housing Affordability

A significant aspect of poverty in Canada is its relation to affordable housing. Housing is an absolute necessity, and its affordability in Canada continues to be a crisis (Shapcott, 2009). According to the Canada Mortgage and Housing Corporation, "affordable housing costs less than 30% of before-tax household income. Shelter costs include the following: a) for renters, rent and any payments for electricity, fuel, water and other municipal services; and b) for owners, mortgage payments (principal and interest), property taxes, and any condominium fees, along with payments for electricity, fuel, water and other municipal services" (Canada Mortgage and Housing Corporation, 2009).

Figure 11.1: Gini Coefficient for Various Types of Income, Canada, 1980–2007

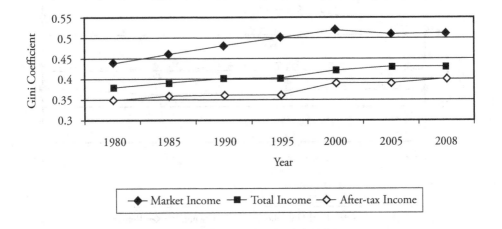

Source: Adapted from the Statistics Canada CANSIM database http://cansim2.statcan.gc.ca, Table 202-0705, extracted in 2010.

Many Canadian households experience housing affordability issues, and this number increased from 1991 to 2006 (Figure 11.2). This situation, associated with especially low levels of income and wealth, is particularly acute for Canadian renters in urban areas (Hulchanski, 2001, 2007). Indeed, the proportion of tenants spending more than 30% of their total income on rent is higher in Canadian cities than the Canadian average (43% in Vancouver, 42% in Toronto, and 36% in Montreal) (Statistics Canada, 2004). The proportion spending more than 50% of their income—putting them at risk of imminent homelessness—is also strikingly high (22% in Vancouver, 20% in Toronto, and 18% in Montreal). Increases in rental costs have far outpaced income increases among low-income renters in virtually all Canadian urban areas (Federation of Canadian Municipalities, 2004).

This housing situation is the result of the federal and some provincial governments withdrawing from investment in social housing during the 1990s. Also, some provincial governments abolished rent control, which had ensured an affordable private rental market. These changes have coincided with retrenchment in other social policy areas in Canada (Bryant, Raphael, Schrecker, and Labonte, in press).

Healthy Child Development

Childhood development is profoundly influenced by the presence of poverty. Positive conditions during childhood support child health but also have long-lasting effects on health during adulthood (Friendly, 2009). Regulated quality child care has an especially

Figure 11.2: Percentage of Canadian Households Spending >30% of Income on Shelter Costs, 1991–2006

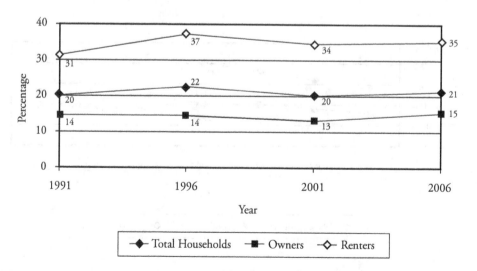

Source: Canada Mortgage and Housing Corporation. (2009). *Housing in Canada online*. Retrieved from http://cmhc.beyond2020.com/TableViewer/tableView.aspx?ReportId=3&IF_Language=eng

positive impact on children living in the worst socio-economic conditions. Outside of Quebec, the availability of regulated child care for Canadian families is 10–15% (Friendly, 2009). Recent analyses document how the amount of money allocated to regulated child care in each of the provinces of interest trails well behind allocations made in Quebec (Friendly, 2009). Overall, only 17% of Canadian families have access to affordable regulated child care.

In Chapter 12, Canadian public policy actions toward a variety of poverty-related domains are considered in international comparison. These analyses indicate that not only are Canadian poverty rates among the highest in modern developed nations, but the resources and services provided to Canadians are significantly less developed than those provided elsewhere. These findings reinforce the argument that poverty and its effects upon health and quality of life have not been a primary focus of Canadian policy-makers.

Models of Public Policy and Poverty Reduction

Why have poverty and its effects not been a primary focus of Canadian governments? The pluralist view would argue that governments are either (a) choosing to implement policies that seem most reasonable for the greatest common good, or (b) have not been provided with compelling arguments by interest groups concerned with reducing poverty. This is clearly not the case as advocacy groups have been outlining the costs of poverty for Canadian society for decades now. The pluralist model of policy-making would argue that anti-poverty advocates need to get organized and have their voices heard by policy-makers; that is, ongoing consciousness raising, advocacy, lobbying, and building coalitions should achieve policy change. This is clearly an inadequate explanation for policy inaction. What explanations do the other models suggest?

The materialist model of policy-making would argue that Canadian elected officials are primarily concerned with developing and implementing policies that defend the interests of economic elites. And there is indeed evidence that the already wealthy have done very well over the past two decades, even during the recent recession (Mackenzie, 2010). The concerns of members of other classes and groups—especially those living in poverty—attract rather less attention.

In this model, powerful players who have the ability to guide the economic and political systems are seen as creating the circumstances that, while benefiting them through increases in income and wealth, create high levels of poverty. In order to justify these shifts in economic resources, an ideological discourse is created. This discourse argues that those on top have earned the right to such exorbitant riches while those at the bottom are themselves responsible for their own sad state of affairs (see Chapter 4).

What is to be done? The materialist model suggests organizing the population to oppose and defeat the powerful interests that influence governments to maintain poverty. These defeats can occur in the workplace through greater union organizing and the promotion of class solidarity. These defeats can also occur in the electoral and parliamentary arenas, by the ascendance of working-class power.

The public choice model would suggest that it is not in the overall interests of Canadian policy-makers to address poverty. People living in poverty have little influence with policy-makers, since their concerns are not seen as being shared by most Canadians. And in any event, people living in poverty are less likely to vote. In contrast, those interests who benefit from poverty are highly organized and are able to exert influence upon policy-makers, thereby controlling the public policy agenda. Put simply, raising and addressing issues of poverty provides little benefit to governing parties. The public choice model argues that policy dynamics must change such that policy-makers who do not address poverty, along with their political masters, will experience electoral consequences. These issues are taken up in later chapters.

Politics as the Ability of Progressive Political Parties to Win Power

Given these realities, is there any reason to concern oneself with the political process? Is there any benefit to having political parties that are concerned with poverty reduction elected to office? All the major political parties in Canada—Bloc Québécois, Conservative, Green, Liberal, and NDP—assure the public of their commitment to reducing and eliminating poverty. Indeed, in 1989 every member of the House of Commons from every party supported a resolution promising to eliminate child poverty by the year 2000. Yet, the year 2000 has come and gone, and Canada's poverty rates remain stubbornly high and the depth of poverty remains unchanged. Indeed, Canada's poverty rate has been among the highest among developed nations since accurate measurement of its incidence began. Should those concerned with poverty reduction bother with politics then? The answer is "definitely yes."

Policy Platforms

By all rights, poverty reduction *should* be an important policy goal, but, as argued here, may not be a priority for any government of the day. Indeed, the rather limited action on poverty in general and child poverty in particular since 1989—during periods of federal Liberal and Conservative governments—illustrates this argument.

Canadian federal elections were held in 2006 and 2008. In the lead-up to the elections, the advocacy group Campaign 2000 gathered party responses to policy options to reduce child poverty. Tables 11.1 and 11.2 summarize these options and party positions. These party positions are important since governmental action is essential for reducing poverty to low levels. Despite the popular rhetoric of growing the economy as a means of reducing poverty, in no nation does the marketplace by itself come close to eliminating the incidence of poverty (Innocenti Research Centre, 2005).

Across 2006 and 2008, NDP positions are consistent with every policy option provided by Campaign 2000 except one minor one. The Conservative Party of Canada position was opposed to every policy option except one minor one. In 2006, these policy options include making resources available for poor families through higher child tax benefits and minimum wages, increasing funding for social housing, and providing

Table 11.1: Federal Party Positions for the 2006 Federal Election on Issues Identified by Campaign 2000 as Essential to Eliminating Child Poverty

Ranking: "Yes" indicates party position meets Campaign 2000 policy recommendation
"Partial" indicates party position partially meets Campaign 2000 policy recommendation
"No" indicates party makes no commitment that meets Campaign 2000 policy recommendation

ISSUE	CPC	LIBERAL	NDP	BLOC
Increase Canada Child Tax Benefit to $4,900/child by 2007 and end clawback from families on social assistance	No	No	Yes[a]	No
Commit to key principles (quality, universal, accessible and developmental programming) for child care system	No	Yes	Yes	No[b]
Introduce legislation to secure early learning and child care as permanent social program	No	No	Yes	No[b]
Increase federal funding for a national public system of Early Learning and Child Care	No[c]	Yes	Yes	Yes
Commit to increase social housing and increase funding by $2B/year	No	Partial	Yes	Yes
Raise the federal minimum wage to $10/hour	No	No[d]	Yes	No[b]
Restore eligibility for Employment Insurance	No	No	Yes	Yes
Increase funding for post-secondary education	No	Partial[e]	Partial[f]	Yes

Notes on rankings:
(a) NDP would increase CCTB to $4,200 by 2010. Their commitment achieves 86% of Campaign 2000's recommendation of $4,900 CCTB.
(b) Bloc positions reflect concern with Quebec rather than federal issues; hence negative responses to federal pan-Canadian issues.
(c) Conservatives are committing $1,200/year per child under six to families. This is an income transfer to families, not a child care program.
(d) The Liberal party commits to introducing a Working Income Tax Benefit that does recognize the challenges of the working poor and could supplement low-wage work to maximum of $1,000/year.
(e) The Liberal Party commits to paying up to $3,000 of first-year and graduating-year tuition fees for undergrad students.
(f) The NDP has committed to fully restoring transfers for post-secondary education, but not clear if this would lead to reduced tuition.

Source: Adapted from Campaign 2000. (2006). *Addressing child and family poverty in Canada: Where do the parties stand?* (p. 2). Toronto: Campaign 2000.

Table 11.2: Federal Party Positions for the 2008 Federal Election on Issues Identified by Campaign 2000 as Essential to Eliminating Child Poverty (only national parties included)

Ranking: "Yes" indicates party position meets Campaign 2000 policy recommendation
"Partial" indicates party position partially meets Campaign 2000 policy recommendation
"No" indicates party makes no commitment that meets Campaign 2000 policy recommendation

ISSUE	CPC	LIBERAL	NDP	GREEN
Establish specific targets and timetables for poverty reduction	No	No	Yes	Yes*
Increase Canada Child Tax Benefit or equivalent to $5,100/child per year	No	Yes	Yes	No
Establish a system of universally accessible early childhood education and care (ECEC)	No	Yes	Yes	Yes
Invest in a National Housing/Homelessness Strategy	No	Yes	Yes	Yes
Raise minimum wage to $10 per hour	No	No	Yes	Yes
Increase WITB to $2,400 per year for all employed adults	No	No**	Yes	No***
Restore eligibility for Employment Insurance	No	Yes	Yes	No****
Enhance maternity/parental leave	Yes	Yes	Yes	Yes
New Canadians: Steps to recognize foreign credentials	No	Yes	Yes	Yes
Establish a poverty reduction strategy for First Nations communities	No	Yes	Yes	Yes
For urban Aboriginal peoples	No	No	No	No
Establish a basic income for individuals with a disability	No	Yes+	Yes+	Yes
Improve access to both post-secondary education and training/skills upgrading	No	Yes	Yes	Yes

Notes on rankings:
*   Greens strongly support targets and timetables but not yet able to set them.
*   Liberals have stated they will enrich the WITB but amount has not been specified.
***   Greens have stated that the Guaranteed Liveable Income (GLI) will eliminate the need for the WITB and will alleviate many of the problems associated with the current EI program.
**** Greens appear to incorporate EI into GLI and, therefore, eliminate EI as it currently exists.
+   Liberals and NDP make proposals that contribute to a basic income for people with disabilities.
Other notes: Campaign 2000 has not received a response from the Conservative Party as of Sept. 29, 2008 and has obtained platform information from their website.

Source: Adapted from Campaign 2000. (2008). *Addressing child and family poverty in Canada: Where do the parties stand?* (p. 2). Retrieved March 11, 2011 from www.campaign2000.ca/resources/election/PartyGridSummarySept2008.pdf

a national system of early learning and child care. The Liberal Party position was supportive of the early learning and child care options and partially supportive of the social housing recommendation. The Bloc position was generally supportive of these recommendations, but its focus on Quebec led to negative positions on pan-Canadian issues.

The national child care issue is particularly relevant to remedying conditions of child deprivation and lack of employment activity. Child care programs along the lines proposed by Campaign 2000 are known to support childhood development, especially among the less advantaged; support parents in education, training, and employment; foster social cohesion; and support gender equity and equity for children with disabilities (Friendly, 2009). And it should be noted that, in 2007, close to 75% of Canadian women whose youngest child was from three to five years of age were active in the labour force and could make use of such a program if it were available.

The 2008 grid enlarged the number of policy areas, but the pattern remained the same. On poverty-reducing strategies identified by Campaign 2000, the NDP achieved the highest scores, and the Conservative Party the lowest. The scores of the Liberal and Green parties were lower than the NDP but much higher than the Conservatives.

What is the source of party differences? Do they result from careful cost–benefit analyses carried out by groups of experts in human development, health sciences, and economics? No. Party differences usually reflect values positions that form the basis of each party. The NDP positions, along with some positions of the current Liberal and Green parties, are consistent with social democratic principles of equality. The Conservative position is consistent with liberty. The Bloc presents a mix of social democratic and separatist tendencies. This analysis highlights the importance of the political in the policy process. And, not surprisingly, analyses reveal that child poverty rates—an aggregate indicator of a cluster of policy approaches—is primarily determined by the influence of the political "left" in governmental policy-making.

Among developed nations, left Cabinet share is the best predictor of child poverty rates. Rainwater and Smeeding (2003) found a striking relationship between left Cabinet share in national governments from 1946 to the 1990s and child poverty rates. Among 14 nations between 1946 and 1990, the presence of left political parties in national government was strongly related to the probability that a child would not experience poverty. The correlation was a very strong one. Sweden, for example, had a 32% left Cabinet share with any one child having 42–1 odds of escaping child poverty. Belgium had a 13% left Cabinet share with a child having 18–1 odds of escaping child poverty. Canada had 0% left Cabinet share, and a child had only 6–1 odds of escaping child poverty.

What exactly is left Cabinet share? This term refers to having members of a social democratic or left party involved in running government by being in Cabinet. Canada has never had a member of a left party in federal Cabinet. Canada has had, however, left influence during minority government situations. The welfare state institutions of Medicare and public pensions were established during periods of minority government rule in which the NDP held the balance of power. A recent analysis suggests that it has been during periods of minority party rule in Canada where especially progressive public policy has been implemented (Russell, 2008).

Figure 11.3: Odds in 14 Nations of Escaping Child Poverty, by Left Cabinet Share

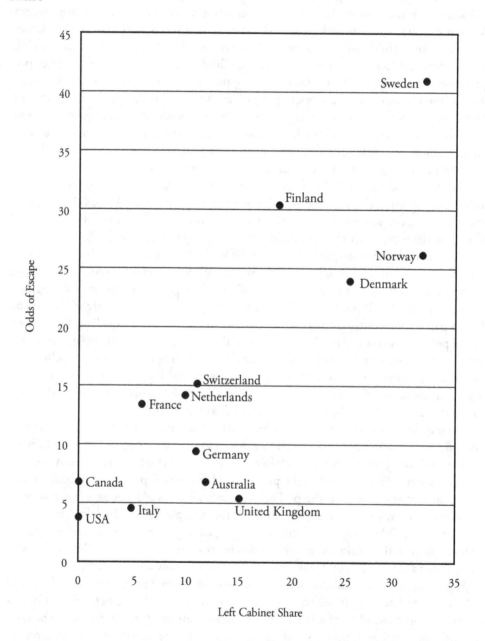

Source: Rainwater, L., and Smeeding, T. M. (2003). *Poor kids in a rich country: America's children in comparative perspective* (p. 71). New York: Russell Sage Foundation.

Further, Brady (2003) studied 16 Western democracies for the period of 1967 to 1997 and looked at the impact of left political institutions on a nation's poverty rate. The findings showed that the power of left political institutions have a powerful effect on poverty reduction. It does so through processes of high voter turnout and the backing of left parties that support the welfare state. In addition, the coordination of wage negotiation—a result of strong union density or membership—combines with welfare state policy to reduce poverty. Since the welfare state is an essential determinant of poverty, left political institutions are critical to understanding comparative historical variation in both the strength of welfare states and level of poverty among the population. Brady (2009) has since followed up with a volume exploring these findings.

During the federal Liberal minority government of 2005, the NDP held the balance of power. During the spring 2005 budget negotiations, the NDP offered its support to the Liberals in return for significant added spending for child care, social housing, and public transportation. This resulted in the suspension of planned tax reductions to the corporate sector and in additional social spending. This is an example of left influence upon poverty-related public policy. (The subsequent election of a minority Conservative government, however, saw the scuttling of these plans.)

Are there intrinsic aspects of the Canadian electoral system that minimize the influence of left parties and like-minded voters? Or is the limited influence of the NDP simply a reflection of the Canadian public having little sympathy for progressive public policy in general and poverty reduction in particular? The evidence points to the former explanation.

Proportional Representation, Left Influence, and Poverty

Canadians' understandings and attitudes toward poverty do not appear to be the primary barrier in the development of public policy to address poverty. Instead, the "first past the post" electoral system minimizes the influence of progressive political parties (see Box 11.2). In the first-past-the post system, a party has to come in first in order to win the local seat. In contrast, in the system called proportional representation, a party that garners only 20% of the votes in every district would receive 20% of the seats in the legislature.

As it turns out, nations that have proportional representation have more developed welfare states as well as lower poverty rates (see Figure 11.4). As noted, the influence of left political parties is important to the development of the welfare state and its maintenance in the post-industrial capitalist era. These parties are more likely to support redistribution of wealth and advocate for universal social and health programs. Esping-Andersen (1985) has argued that the imposition of proportional representation in the Nordic nations was integral to the development of their welfare states. Alesina and Glaeser (2004) provide an extended examination of how proportional representation enhanced the growth and influence of left political parties, thereby strengthening the welfare state. Such political systems enable more parties—particularly political parties that are pro-redistribution—to gain representation that contributes to the formation of more fragmented legislatures or minority governments. And proportional representation systems buffer welfare programs from spending cuts if governments of the day attempt to turn back the clock on progressive public policies.

Box 11.2: One-Minute True or False Democracy Quiz

1. Every vote is equal—it doesn't matter who you support or where you live.
False. Voters are not equal with first-past-the-post voting. For example, in the 2004 federal election, more than a half-million Green Party voters elected no one at all. Meanwhile, fewer than half-million Liberal voters in Atlantic Canada alone elected 22 Liberal MPs.

2. Election results are fair—what we say at the ballot box is what we get.
False. The current voting system routinely distorts results. A party winning 40 percent of the votes may get 60 percent of the seats. Another party winning 20 percent of the votes may get 10 percent of the seats or none at all.

3. A party must win a majority of votes to form a majority government.
False. In fact, since World War I, Canadians have had only four majority governments elected by a majority of voters. In 1993, the Liberals won a majority of seats with less than 39 percent of the votes.

4. Government is always formed by the party that wins the most votes.
False. In the 1990s, two provincial governments were formed by parties that came in second in the popular vote.

5. Voters who oppose the government are always represented by opposition parties.
False. Under the current voting system, the opposition almost always has fewer seats than deserved. In the 1987 New Brunswick election, not a single seat went to opposition parties that were supported by 40 percent of the voters.

6. Canada has more women in parliament than either Turkmenistan, Laos or Eritrea.
False. Canada has only 21% women in the House of Commons, far less than comparable Western democracies and many other countries using proportional voting systems.

7. Canada ranked 108th in the world in voter turnout in the 1990s.
False. It's even worse. Canada ranked 109th and turnout continues to decrease with record lows being set in the last two elections.

8. Most older European nations use 12th century voting systems, while Canada uses a modern voting system.
False. Most European countries moved to various types of proportional voting systems over the past 50 to 100 years. Canada, along with Britain and the US, remain the only major western democracies still using the antiquated first-past-the-post voting system.

Source: Fair Vote Canada. (2005). *Democracy quiz.* Retrieved March 11, 2011 from www.fairvote-canada.org/en/democracy_quiz

Figure 11.4: Degree of Proportional Representation and Extent of Transfers as Percentage of Gross Domestic Product

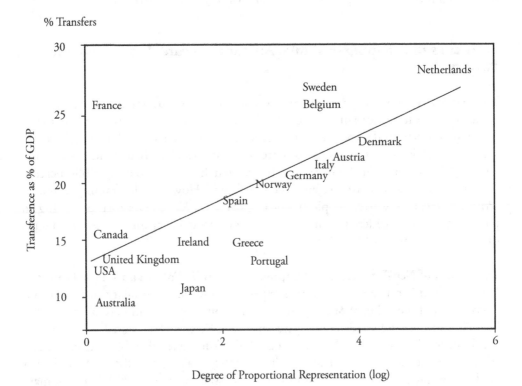

% Transfers

Transference as % of GDP

Degree of Proportional Representation (log)

Source: From Alesina, A., and Glaeser, E. L. (2004). *Fighting poverty in the US and Europe: A world of difference* (p. 86). Toronto: Oxford University Press.

Importantly, proportional representation is on the public policy agenda of both the federal and provincial governments. In many provinces, governments have initiated processes of electoral reform. To date, probably due to public misunderstanding, these initiatives have been defeated in Ontario and PEI and failed to reach a 60% required threshold in British Columbia. If proportional representation were to be implemented in Canada, this would provide a strong impetus for strengthening the welfare state and bringing in health-supportive public policies. In a sense, governments would be in a permanent minority government situation, a situation that has been associated with progressive public policy in Canada at both the federal and provincial levels.

Proportional representation is therefore important since it guarantees that left or progressive political parties and voters will always be able to influence government policy. In Canada it would mean that there would always be minority governments that would have to compromise to stay in power. Canada could become a nation with a more developed welfare state that would allocate a greater percentage of wealth on social spending and other programs, thereby helping to reduce poverty.

Politics as the Shaping of Public Attitudes toward Those Living in Poverty

To what extent do Canadians attribute the incidence of poverty to failures of society as opposed to failures of individuals? Are Canadians aware of the links between living in poverty and experiencing poor health and, if so, how do they explain these links? Related to these questions are the attitudes Canadians hold toward "the deserving poor" and the "undeserving poor," which are reflected in public perceptions regarding social assistance and "welfare fraud." However, the framing of public attitudes toward poverty, people living in poverty, and benefits to those living in poverty must be considered in the context of increasing governmental commitments to the ideology of neo-liberalism.

The Impact of Neo-Liberalism as Shaping Both Public Policy and Public Opinion

Neo-liberalism is a belief that the marketplace should be the primary institution for organizing and allocating resources and services among the population (Coburn, 2000). Neo-liberalism experienced a resurgence in the UK, the USA, and Canada during the Thatcher, Reagan, and Mulroney eras. Bashevkin argues that Blair, Clinton, and Chrétien accelerated the trend in neo-liberal policy-making and that they and their predecessors used welfare as a hot-button political issue (Bashevkin, 2002). The primary tenets of neo-liberalism, according to Coburn (2000), are as follows:

- Markets are the most efficient allocators of resources in production and distribution;
- Societies are composed of autonomous individuals (producers and consumers) motivated chiefly by material or economic considerations; and
- Competition is the major market vehicle for innovations.

In public policy domains related to health and social welfare, including poverty-related policy, neo-liberalism celebrates individual initiative rather than identifying and responding to collective needs. This is associated with governmental withdrawal from a wide range of policy areas such as housing provision, income security, and active labour policy, among others. Considering that Canada is already identified as a liberal political economy that allows the marketplace to exert undue influence on public policy, Canada is especially susceptible to neo-liberal ideology.

Teeple (2000) provides a well-developed analysis of the role neo-liberalism has played in the decline of Canada's welfare state. Neo-liberalism serves as a justification for increasing economic globalization and the concentration of wealth and power in the cause of increasing corporate profits. For Teeple, the unrestrained economic power of wealthy elites has eroded the post–World War II welfare state that supported redistribution of wealth and the provision of strong health and social services.

Coburn (2010) and Teeple (2000) describe a process of economic globalization in which the market determines political, social, and economic activity. The rise of neo-liberalism in liberal political economies (e.g., Thatcherism in the United Kingdom, Reaganism in the United States, and Mulroneyism in Canada) has created increased income inequalities and the weakening of social provision. Certainly, policies followed by liberal Finance Minister Paul Martin during the 1990s reflected both a neo-liberal approach and a distinct threat to the Canadian welfare state (Scarth, 2004).

How does this dominant discourse, that of celebrating governmental withdrawal from concern with the collective and celebration of the individual, justify continuing high levels of poverty? The answer is deceptively simple: Blame people living in poverty for their own situation. And then demonize them even worse by making their receipt of social assistance or other benefits an affront to society. Swanson (2001) calls this pattern of blaming and demonizing people living in poverty *poor-bashing*.

Poor-Bashing in Canada

The 1990s was a period of governmental withdrawal from action in support of the health and well-being of the vulnerable. Beginning with changes in Ottawa, program spending was so drastically reduced that federal and provincial public expenditure was at levels not seen since the late 1940s (Hulchanski, 2002). Minimum wages did not keep up with inflation, and many provinces reduced the level of benefits available to people living in poverty. Eligibility for unemployment insurance was also dramatically reduced, such that only 40% of currently employed Canadians are able to receive benefits if their employment ends (Black and Shillington, 2005). This is the situation even though the cited Canadian unemployment levels continue to be high in international comparison and the actual employment rate may be as much as twice as high as the official figure (Baker, 2009; Swartz, 2004).

Swanson (2001) documents how governmental statements and attitudes toward people living in poverty, accompanied by similar media bias, drastically changed during the 1990s from one of forbearance and tolerance to a "war of exclusion, prejudice, and hatred against the poor in Canada" (p. 3). Swanson documents how all governments in Canada, from the very conservative right to the left, took it upon themselves to either create or pander to increasingly negative attitudes and perceptions toward people living in poverty.

Goaded on by right-wing think-tanks such as the Fraser Institute and the C.D. Howe Institute, and national business organizations such as the Canadian Council of Chief Executives (previously known at the Business Council on National Issues), the problem of people living in poverty was not seen as resulting from material and social deprivation brought about by increasingly draconian public policies, but rather as the result of individual moral and personal shortcomings. Indeed, the 1990s saw Canada begin in earnest to adopt the MUD (moral underclass discourse) explanation for the presence of people

Box 11.3: Poor-Bashing

Interview with Jean Swanson, anti-poverty activist and author of *Poor-Bashing: The Politics of Exclusion*

JF: How would you define poor-bashing for those who may not be familiar with the term?

JS: Poor-bashing is when people who are poor are stereotyped, ignored, blamed, patronized, pitied, falsely accused of being drunk and having large families and not looking for work. Other ways are institutional, for example, low welfare rates is a type of poor-bashing. Having poverty in a world where it is possible to eliminate it is a type of poor-bashing.

JF: What do you say to people who argue that Canada is a rich country and people who are poor choose to live that way?

JS: There is a section in the book in which I ask that question to a single mother that I interviewed. She said "I didn't choose to be on welfare. Harris made choices that put me where I am." The latest wealth stats have just come out. They show the poorest half of Canada's population to have 6% of the wealth, and the richest half to have 94%. There is a general opinion that the way to get some of that 94% is to get an education and a job but it's not because there are laws that prevent people without money from getting into that 94%. There are laws that help the rich that don't help the poor. You have different choices available to you if you are rich than if you are poor.

JF: Is poor-bashing new or has it changed with increasing globalization?

JS: Poor-bashing has always existed—I trace it back 500 years in European society. With globalization, corporations are wanting the cheapest labour. They traditionally exploited women and people of colour (and especially women of colour), now the drive for globalization is very intense and they are wanting to expand the number of people they can legitimately exploit. This is where poor-bashing comes in—it is now applied to men and women of European background. Poor-bashing is a way of concealing who has the real power.

JF: Why hasn't there been much progress made against poverty?

JS: In the mid-1970s, corporations got together to push their agenda of privatization, deregulation, free trade, and cuts to social programs to increase profits. As this agenda was implemented by the federal and provincial governments, poverty increased. The corporations used their think tanks (for example the Fraser Institute and C.D. Howe) to push poor-bashing which blamed the poor for the poverty that the policies of the corporations and think tanks were creating. This was pushed by the media and politicians and had a big effect in increasing poor-bashing in the minds of people who weren't in power. Poor-bashing made the cuts to welfare and unemployment insurance seem legitimate.

JF: In *Poor-Bashing*, you devote an entire chapter to the language of poor-bashing. Why is language so important?

JS: Some words and phrases are inculcated into our consciousness and you can't use them without poor-bashing, without blaming the poor for poverty. For example, the word incentive. Incentive is a big one. When you talk about the incentive to work you stop talking about poverty and start talking about cheap labour and people don't realize this because we have been programmed. Another one is dependency, that people on employment insurance or welfare are dependent on the system. Dependency implies that people use welfare or unemployment insurance because they are lazy or childlike or personally flawed in some way. Why aren't corporations considered dependent on sweat shop labour?

JF: Who did you write *Poor-Bashing* for?

JS: For poor people who I hope will take the blame off themselves for poverty. And also for working people. There is such a great need for working people to unite with poor people, not blame them. Poverty and poor-bashing undermine the working conditions of working people. And also for people with a social conscience who are often taken in by language and the media—I hope it opens their eyes to become allies of the poor. I tried to write the book in plain language and I hope it will be a tool for people who want to end poor-bashing and who want to live in a fair and just society.

JF: What's wrong with the media's tendency to focus on the personal stories of individuals who are struggling with poverty—isn't it a good thing to tell these otherwise unknown stories?

JS: The media takes a lot of approaches to covering stories on poverty. Lies. Double standards—for example, playing up welfare fraud and playing down corporate fraud. "Poornography"—portraying people who are poor as sufferers—is part of the journalistic technique of "putting a face on the problem." The problem with this is that is doesn't politicize the problem, it doesn't point to the causes of poverty, and it doesn't point to a solution (often charity is offered as the answer).

JF: How is your book different in its approach to poverty?

JS: I have been involved with the anti-poverty movement for 25 years. I was the president of the National Anti-Poverty Organization for 2 years and I've worked with End Legislated Poverty for 15 years. I've made a lot of contacts in the anti-poverty movement. Travelling with the NAPO board allowed me to meet people from across Canada, from Newfoundland to Victoria. I interviewed 30 poor people and anti-poverty activists and incorporated their thinking about it and their analysis of it. This is new for a book on poverty. Other books on poverty do not talk about the why of it—why are people putting up with this?

JF: How does the book help people who are poor-bashed?

JS: The first thing about challenging poor-bashing that everyone I interviewed said is that you have to understand that you are not to blame. You have to understand the economic system causing poverty and how poverty is legislated. You have to learn about how there is enough wealth to end poverty and that people benefit from poor-bashing and poverty. Poverty is government policy and anybody that is bashed becomes cheaper in the labour market. You have to challenge self-bashing, as a form of racism or sexism (although different), and you have to challenge the language/myths/media/politicians that do it.

JF: Are there coalitions to be built among anti-poverty activists and other anti-oppression groups (racism, sexism, classism)?

JS: Ultimately we need to unite campaigns about poor-bashing with coalitions against racism. The most important thing in uniting with other anti-oppression groups is to say what's on their mind and to learn about other forms of oppression. We need a lot of listening but in the end we need to build a coalition.

JF: How do we end poverty in Canada and the world?

JS: One necessary step is to end the kind of thinking that puts people into groups like "the poor" or "those on welfare" to justify treating them badly and/or blame them for poverty. If we stop blaming poor or other oppressed people for poverty, we can expose the policies, laws, and economic system that force millions of people to compete against each other, driving down wages and creating more poverty.

JF: What do we have to do to put an end to poor-bashing?

JS: We have to think about poverty in a different paradigm—as something that is caused. Ending poor-bashing isn't just a matter of being nice. Ending poor-bashing means asking questions about the unequal distribution of wealth and income.

Jean Swanson has worked as an anti-poverty activist for twenty-five years. A former board member and president of the National Anti-Poverty Organization, Swanson co-chaired the B.C. Action Canada Network in its fight against the free trade deals. For the past fifteen years she has worked for the coalition End Legislated Poverty.

Source: From Between the Lines Press. (2001, March). Jean Swanson, anti-poverty activist and author of *Poor-bashing: The politics of exclusion* in conversation with Joanna Fine. Retrieved March 11, 2011 from www.btlbooks.com/Links/swanson_interview.htm

living in deepening poverty. For the most part, according to Swanson (2001), little has changed in the new millennium.

Typical of the era were the drastic reductions in levels of social assistance benefits in many provinces. This era also saw the clawback in many provinces of the National Child Benefit (NCB), a federal initiative developed to reduce child and family poverty in Canada. The NCB provides about $120 a month per child to families on social assistance. When instituted in 1997, provinces were allowed to claw back the benefit from these families. Though the federal government provides these monies, every province except Newfoundland and Labrador and New Brunswick went on to "recover" this benefit from families living in poverty.

Instead, many provinces allocated the monies to "programs" to assist the poor. The irony of this is that the programs designed to help families living in poverty are being funded from monies taken from their own pockets, perpetuating and deepening their health-threatening living conditions. The effect of this has been to make living conditions even more problematic for these Canadians. It has done nothing to alleviate problems of homelessness and housing insecurity, and hunger and food insecurity.

Also typical was the coming to the forefront of the issue of "welfare fraud" by elected politicians of the left and right (Swanson, 2001). The result was increasing intolerance of people living in poverty and an even greater resistance to having the material and social deprivation they experienced addressed.

The governmental, media, and public concern with welfare fraud reached a level that was completely out of proportion to its actual incidence (Chunn and Gavigan, 2004; Mosher and Hermer, 2005). Legal scholars have argued that this preoccupation has served to criminalize the receipt of social assistance such that the mere receipt of benefits makes one a likely suspect of deception and fraud (see Box 11.4).

Swanson (2001) outlines an even more sinister backdrop to this era of poor-bashing. The creation of workfare programs forced people living on social assistance to take any available employment, no matter how low paying or unpleasant. These programs serve to

Box 11.4: Welfare Fraud and Poor-Bashing

Welfare fraud is frequently characterized as pervasive, although if one considers actual instances of criminal convictions for fraud, the incidence is exceptionally low: convictions represented roughly 0.1% of the social assistance caseload in 2001–02, notwithstanding more than 38,000 investigations being undertaken. The notion that fraud is rampant has been used to support a wide array of mechanisms to detect and deter fraud. These include broad consents to the release of personal information, information-sharing agreements with a host of state and non-state entities, expanded powers for eligibility review officers, consolidated verification procedures (requiring the extensive and ongoing production and verification of documentation), provincial and local fraud control units, protocols negotiated with local police and crown attorneys, a toll-free welfare hotline, and for a period of time in Ontario, a lifetime ban on receipt of welfare if convicted of welfare fraud. Significantly, notwithstanding that an earlier government commissioned review of social assistance in Ontario concluded that adequate welfare benefits were the single most important measure to reduce fraud, the Conservative government of Mike Harris rejected this as an anti-fraud strategy, instead opting to reduce benefits by 21.6%.

Those who are in receipt of welfare benefits live within the web of surveillance created by these various measures to detect and deter fraud. They commonly report feeling distrusted and under suspicion not only in their interactions with the welfare system, but more broadly with neighbours, landlords, teachers, etc.—that is, with anyone who might take up the invitation of the government to aid in the fight against welfare fraud by calling the welfare fraud hotline. The two areas where fraud investigations are most commonly targeted are the failure to report income, and the failure to disclose that one is living with a spouse. Several important observations can be made regarding the policing of both income and intimate relationships. The rules regarding each are complex and often counter-intuitive and it is frequently difficult to discern when the reporting obligation arises. Secondly, behaviour which in any other context would never attract criminal investigation—in fact, behaviour which is frequently lauded—becomes the object of suspicion, interest, interrogation and potentially sanction: a regular meal at a friend's house; an evening out on a date or a visit to your home; or the payment of your hydro bill by your parents. Thirdly, both areas, but especially that of "spouses," impact most harshly upon women.

The normative character of the "crime" of welfare fraud is also revealed by the disparities that exist between welfare fraud regulation and other forms of economic misconduct. In almost every respect "tax evasion" and "employee standards violations" (in particular the failure of employers to pay wages owing) are viewed in a much less punitive and severe light in terms of the moral culpability attached to the conduct, the range of detection and enforcement tools utilized and the penalties that follow upon conviction. This disparity suggests a clear normative distinction at work, one that is aligned with neo-liberal values that views poor people as not deserving of support, but rather of intense scrutiny and inequitable treatment.

We are drawn to the conclusion that the receipt of social assistance itself has become criminalized through the category of welfare fraud. Simply being on social assistance results in one being positioned as a penal object in a climate of moral condemnation, surveillance, suspicion and penalty. This criminalization is particularly gendered in that the majority of people on social assistance are women, and the majority of them are single parents. And it is not only the intimate aspect of women's lives that is utilized as an area of control in social assistance regulation, but also the social sphere of everyday life as well. And despite a rhetoric of "community responsibility" in government discourse, it is the very people that might constitute a support network in the community—neighbours, family, boyfriends, landlords, school officials—that are either re-responsibilized as agents to snitch on any perceived "fraud," or are possibly complicit in rule breaking by being supportive, by for example, buying food for a mother and her child who have exhausted what is a completely inadequate benefit for that month. And the insidious character of this criminalization completely devalues women as mothers—that, for example, being a single parent surviving in poverty constitutes simply "sitting around" and "doing nothing." It is no wonder that being on social assistance has been characterized by an experience of fear, retribution and isolation—qualities that "cracking down" on welfare fraud intentionally generate.

Source: From Mosher, J., and Hermer, J. (2005). *Welfare fraud: The constitution of social assistance as crime* (pp. 7, 9). Paper prepared for the Law Commission of Canada. Retrieved March 11, 2011 from www.tinyurl.com/9b42b

---

create a desperate cadre of workers whose presence suppresses the wages of those not on social assistance. Low-wage jobs create even more poverty. Adding to these problems are provincial governments that require social assistance recipients to take on unpaid work previously held by paid workers. Such programs depress wages even further and create resentment among working-poor Canadians toward those even lower on the social hierarchy ladder. The situation may worsen as a result of the 2008 recession (see Box 11.5).

Public Understandings about the Causes of Poverty

Despite the general sense that poor-bashing has become more acceptable and certainly more visible in Canada society, a series of studies suggests that most Canadians have a more mature understanding of the causes of poverty and its effects upon health and quality of life. Reutter, Neufeld, and Harrison (1999) asked Albertans why living in poverty is associated with poor health. There are four hypotheses. The myth hypothesis is that there is no relationship between poverty and poor health. The drift hypothesis is that people move into poverty as a result of poor health. The behavioural

Box 11.5: Recessions and Attitudes toward the Poor

Scapegoating the Poor

There's an old African proverb that is becoming uncomfortably apt to apply to human behaviour in Canada: "As the waterhole gets smaller, the animals get meaner." In other words, as the food, water, and other basic resources dwindle, so does the willingness to share. The sense of community and cooperation is replaced by an ugly survival-of-the-fittest mentality.

A big difference, however, exists between what happens at a shrinking waterhole in Africa and what happens in Canada when jobs disappear, incomes fall or stagnate, and government services are cut back. The African waterhole gets smaller because there's a drought; it's a natural and unavoidable disaster. In Canadian society, however, the necessities of life for the weakest among us are being deliberately reduced or withheld.

Our welfare "waterhole" is being systematically siphoned away, its contents transferred from the pockets of the poor into the bank accounts and stock portfolios of the rich.

There is no shortage of money in Canada. Our GDP—the country's entire financial output—has doubled since the 1970s. Corporate executives and major investors still wallow in wealth, much of it coming from taxpayer-funded government bailouts. The big banks still post record profits. Our billionaires may have lost a few million in the financial meltdown, may even have to delay buying their next yacht or private jet, but they know their fortunes are secure and will continue to grow.

A barbaric maldistribution of income that leaves millions of their fellow citizens destitute doesn't bother them in the least. As long as the income needed to help the neediest is diverted to them instead, they will make sure their political lackeys block any proposed reforms.

In the past, picking on the weak and poor was not something that could be done with impunity. Prior to the onset of corporate globalization and neoliberalism, most people—even many of the rich themselves—would be shocked by today's obscenely inequitable distribution of income and the widespread misery it inflicts. Today, however, as food is snatched out of the mouths of hungry kids, many people shrug it off as an unavoidable (if regrettable) part of the capitalist system.

As for the commercial media, instead of exposing and deploring the plight of the hundreds of thousands mired in poverty, they either ignore them or maliciously search for and denounce the few people on welfare who are abusing the system. Although they are clearly the exceptions, they are depicted as typical "welfare bums," too lazy to work and content to live parasitically off the hard work of others.

It's regrettably easy to stir up this kind of antipathy against the underprivileged, or even against neighbours or co-workers who seem to be faring better in our jungle law economic system. Instead of calling for a fair income for everyone, the tendency for many is to keep striving to outdo their fellow citizens. It's one of the baser instincts fostered by a system that puts individual competitiveness above communal cooperation.

The human animals, it seems, also tend to get meaner as their economic water-hole gets smaller. They don't blame the bloated plutocrats who are greedily sucking up the largest share of the country's fluid assets. They turn their wrath instead on those who are competing with them more effectively, or even against the poor and disadvantaged who are resented for taking the welfare crumbs (or minimum wages) they allegedly don't deserve.

* * *

It's eerily reminiscent of a laboratory experiment I was reading about last year in which sadistic scientists provoked naturally peaceful mice to fight among themselves. This was done with an extended colony of mice that coexisted in harmony as long as they had enough to eat and drink. Gradually the scientists reduced their supply of food and water. They wanted to find out at what reduced level of sustenance the mice could be induced to "compete" for their dwindling rations.

Eventually, of course, growing hunger turned the biggest and strongest mice against the weaker ones. At first they simply nipped at them and drove them from the food and water containers. Then, as the food was drastically curtailed, the attacks became fiercer. The weakest mice eventually died, either from their wounds or starvation. A cooperative community of mice was deliberately converted into a war zone.

Like these lab mice, we Canadians have also been subjected to a contrived reduction of our collective means of livelihood. We've been forced to make do with fewer jobs, lower incomes, declining services.

Being somewhat more intelligent than mice, and not nearly as powerless, we don't have to react as they did. We can direct our anger against our corporate and political tormentors instead of lashing out at our less fortunate fellow citizens.

When we scapegoat the poor, the jobless, and the homeless among us, we are letting the corporate lab technicians trigger our most brutal and sub-human instincts. It's the worst possible reaction to Canada's growing unemployment and needlessly high poverty rates. Yes, our economic and social waterhole is getting smaller—but it is being deliberately and callously made smaller.

So far, too many of us have reacted selfishly. It's time we regained the caring and sharing virtues we prided ourselves on in the past. It's time to stop getting meaner and start getting kinder—and smarter.

Source: Finn, E. (2010, May 1). Scapegoating the poor: Let's start blaming the plutocrats, not their victims. *The Monitor*. Retrieved March 11, 2011 from Canadian Centre for Policy Alternatives website at: www.policyalternatives.ca/publications/monitor/scapegoating-poor

hypothesis is that poor health results from the unhealthy behaviours associated with being poor. The structural hypothesis is that living conditions associated with poverty are the cause of poor health.

As shown in Table 11.3, respondents held contradictory perceptions. While a majority agreed with the "drift" hypothesis, there was a split concerning the structural explanations, though a majority agreed people living in poverty have more stress. In a later study, Albertans were asked to provide the one best explanation for the poverty and health relationship from among: (a) There are no real links between poverty and health (myth); (b) People drift into poverty because of poor health (drift); (c) Poor people are unhealthy because of the circumstances in which they live (structural); and (d) Poor people are unhealthy because their behaviour makes them unhealthy (behavioural) (Reutter, Harrison, and Neufeld, 2002). The most common response was the structural explanation (68%), followed by the behavioural (17%), drift (6%), and myth (5%). Four percent expressed no opinion.

Table 11.3: Percentage of Albertans Providing Various Attributions for Why Poverty Is Related to Health (n = 1216)

Explanation		Agree	Neutral	Disagree
Myth	There is no real link between poverty and health.	15.6	9.2	75.2
Drift	People become poor after they get sick.	64.0	14.0	21.9
Behavioural	Poor people are unhealthy because they aren't motivated to look after their health.	34.9	13.7	51.5
	Poor people are unhealthy because they don't know the effects of harmful behaviours such as smoking.	26.8	9.3	63.9
.	Poor people are unhealthy because they lack the skills to manage their money.	31.9	14.0	54.1
Structural	Poor people are unhealthy because society creates barriers that reduce their opportunity for employment.	44.3	16.1	39.5
	Poor people are unhealthy because they live under more stressful conditions.	54.8	14.7	30.6
	Poor people are unhealthy because they get inadequate health care.	34.6	10.7	54.7

Source: Reutter, L., Neufeld, A., and Harrison, M. (1999). Public perceptions of the relationship between poverty and health (Table 1, p. 14). *Canadian Journal of Public Health*, 90(1), 13–18.

Another study examined Canadians' understanding of poverty and its causes and effects among residents of four communities in Edmonton and four communities in Toronto (Reutter et al., 2005, 2006). Respondents were asked to indicate their degree of agreement or disagreement to questions regarding the causes of poverty. The distribution of responses indicated that most people had a structural understanding as to its causes (see Table 11.4).

In addition, most respondents had a mature understanding of the links between poverty and health, and poverty and quality of life. Ninety-one percent felt there was a relationship between poverty and health. When asked to indicate agreement or disagree with statements specifying various pathways mediating the poverty and health relationship, 71% agreed that poor people have more stress in their lives, and 84% agreed that not having adequate shelter, food, or clothes is the main reason poor people have bad health. However, 76% also agreed that lifestyle choices such as smoking, poor diet, not getting any exercise, and so on are the main causes of bad health. Clearly, Canadians hold contradictory attitudes toward the causes of poor health among people living in poverty, but appear receptive to structural explanations as to the causes and effects of poverty.

Table 11.4: Percentage of Toronto and Edmonton Residents Providing Various Attributions As to the Causes of Poverty (n = 1671)

Item	Strongly Agree	Somewhat Agree	Neutral	Somewhat Disagree	Strongly Disagree
Government policies have caused some people to become poor.	29.9	43.5	0.3	19.0	7.3
Most people are poor because of unequal opportunities in our society.	19.1	40.0	0.6	25.4	15.0
Most people are poor because they grew up in a poor family.	9.6	46.7	0.2	26.6	16.9
Most people are poor because they are lazy.	8.0	17.1	0.5	29.3	45.1
Poverty is just part of modern progress and globalization.	8.8	29.2	1.0	27.2	33.8

Source: Reutter, L., et al. (2006). Public attributions for poverty in Canada. (Table 3, p. 9). *Canadian Review of Sociology and Anthropology*, 43(1), 1–22.

On a more discouraging note, examination of Canadians' general views toward the determinants of health suggests profound gaps in their understanding. The Canadian Population Health Initiative (2004) carried out a survey into the understanding of the importance of various determinants of health. Canadians were first asked the open-ended question: *If you had to identify the three most important factors that contribute to good health, what would they be?* Among the 1,200 respondents, 82% said diet or nutrition, 70% said physical activity, 13% said proper rest, and 12% said not smoking. When provided with a list of various health determinants and asked to indicate the importance of each, only 33% indicated that income played a strong or very strong role in health. And only 49% indicated that having employment had a strong impact on health. Lifestyle responses predominated (smoking, 80% agreement; eating habits, 72% agreement; being overweight or obese, 71% agreement; having stress, 68% agreement; and amount of exercise, 65% agreement). Interestingly, the quality of water, 64%, and the quality of air, 64%, were seen as having a strong impact, as was being exposed to second-hand smoke, at 61%.

Basic Attitudes toward Individual Responsibility

Canadians' attitudes toward poverty and health appear to be ambiguous. On the one hand, Canadians are receptive to structural arguments concerning the causes of poverty and the nature of the poverty and health relationship. On the other hand, structural explanations for the poor health of people do not seem to be uppermost in their minds.

This should not be surprising considering the constant messaging in Canada concerning the importance of individual responsibility for health and success. And there is indeed evidence that, at base, Canadian attitudes are more aligned with individualistic attributions for responsibility than more communal or structural ones.

Alesina and Glaeser (2004) reported that Canadian views toward the role that luck plays in determining income are more consistent with Americans' views than those of citizens who lived in well-developed welfare states with very low poverty rates. Canadians are more likely to attribute a lesser role for luck in determining income than citizens of most other nations (see Figure 11.5). Only about 35% of Canadians assign luck an important role. And these findings indicate that high welfare spending correlates strongly with the belief that poverty is society's fault. Among developed nations whose citizens are more likely to attribute poverty to societal causes, rather than individual flaws, welfare spending is higher. Educating the public about the societal causes of poverty would go a long way in strengthening support for the welfare state and reducing poverty in Canada and elsewhere.

Arts and Gelissen (2001) looked at national differences in citizen beliefs on issues involving social solidarity and justice. They asked whether governments should provide a job for everyone; provide health care for the sick; provide a decent standard of living for the elderly; reduce income differences; help students from low-income families; and provide decent housing for those who cannot afford it. Britons and Swedes scored the highest, and Americans scored the lowest. Canada's score was closer to the USA than to the UK and Sweden views, which were more supportive of government intervention in support of citizens.

And all of this is related to how people see themselves along the political spectrum. In the 1999–2002 World Values Survey and European Values Study, Canadians were asked

Figure 11.5: Belief That Luck Determines Income and Welfare Spending as a Percentage of Gross Domestic Product

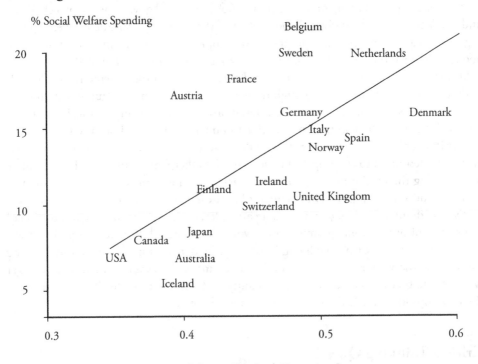

Source: Alesina, A., and Glaeser, E. L. *Fighting poverty in the US and Europe: A world of difference* (p. 187). Oxford: Oxford University Press.

to position themselves on the political spectrum (Inglehart, Basanez, Diez-Medrano, Halman, and Luijkx, 2004). In 2000, 21% of these Canadians considered themselves to be on the "left," 54% in the "centre," and 25% on the "right." Canada does not have proportional representation. If this were the case, then the 21% of Canadian voices on the left would have greater likelihood of having their voices heard. And such a system would probably increase the number of votes on the left. Voters would not feel their votes were being wasted if they resided in generally conservative areas where the chance of a left candidate gaining victory was slim.

Conclusions

A final study provides some evidence concerning future Canadian public support for action on poverty. As part of the Edmonton and Toronto survey discussed earlier

(Reutter et al., 2005, 2006), respondents were asked some questions concerning governments' role in addressing poverty. When asked who should take the *most* responsibility for supporting people living on low incomes, 66% indicated governments, 5% charities, and 28% friends and relatives. When asked if the money governments were spending on education and training programs for people with low incomes was too much, about right, or too little, 72% said too little, 25% about right, and only 4% too much. Additionally, 75% of respondents indicated agreement with the statement that "people with low incomes do not have enough money to participate in community activities."

These results, presented here, suggest that if provided with strong political leadership, a majority of Canadian would be receptive to policies that would both reduce poverty and assist people living in poverty. This could be accomplished by allocating greater governmental resources to training and education. Whether Canadians would be receptive to increasing the minimum wage and social assistance rates, providing more affordable housing, and supporting the enforcement of anti-discrimination laws remains unclear.

Even without a sea change in Canadian attitudes, it is apparent that the imposition of some form of proportional representation would in all probability increase policy attention to the situation of people living in poverty. Evidence from elsewhere offers strong support for the view that such electoral systems make the establishment of a stronger welfare state that is focused on issues of equity and fairness more likely. What some of these systems look like is the subject of the next chapter.

Critical Thinking Questions

1. Why do you think governments are doing so little to reduce poverty?
2. Do you vote? Have you ever thought that your vote could serve to reduce or increase the incidence of poverty? What could be done to communicate this message to others?
3. Do you recall hearing the issue of poverty being discussed during election campaigns? What are some of the reasons that politicians would choose to raise, or not raise, poverty as an election issue?
4. Have you ever participated in or witnessed poor-bashing? What was your reaction to it?
5. What are some of the arguments in favour of proportional representation? What are some reasons to be opposed to it?

Recommended Readings

Alesina, A., and Glaeser, E. L. (2004). *Fighting poverty in the US and Europe: A world of difference.* Toronto: Oxford University Press.

> The authors provide an analysis of how historical traditions and political and social structures explain differences between American and European approaches to fighting poverty. Their presentations include data from Canada in addition to the USA and Europe.

Brady, D. (2009). *Rich democracies, poor people: How politics explain poverty.* New York: Oxford University Press.

> Brady investigates why poverty is so entrenched in some affluent democracies whereas it is a solvable problem in others. Drawing on over 30 years of data from 18 countries, Brady argues that cross-national and historical variations in poverty are principally driven by differences in the generosity of the welfare state.

Bryant, T. (2010). Politics, public policy, and health inequalities. In T. Bryant, D. Raphael, and M. Rioux (Eds.), *Staying alive: Critical perspectives on health, illness, and health care* (2nd ed., pp. 239–263). Toronto: Canadian Scholars' Press Inc.

> Bryant shows how the quality of various social determinants of health is influenced by public policies created by governments. She traces the political, economic, and social influences that lead governments to take one public policy position rather than another. Political ideology and political and social organization are strong influences upon public policy, such that liberal nations such as Canada, the USA, and the UK are not as supportive of poverty reduction and health as those of social democratic nations.

Langille, D. (2009). Follow the money: How business and politics define our health. In D. Raphael (Ed.), *Social determinants of health: Canadian perspectives* (2nd ed., pp. 305–317). Toronto: Canadian Scholars' Press Inc.

> Langille offers an analysis of the political forces influencing the social determinants of health in Canada. The erosion of these determinants results from Canadian public policy being increasingly shaped to the needs of business. The ideology of neo-liberalism—driven by owners and managers of major transnational enterprises—wields an enormous influence over public policy with the main levers being macroeconomic policy that sets constraints on the role and scope of government.

Swanson, J. (2001). *Poor-bashing: The politics of exclusion.* Toronto: Between the Lines Press.

> The special language of poor-bashing disguises the real causes of poverty, hurts and excludes people who are poor, cheapens the labour of people who have jobs, and takes the pressure off the rich. Swanson, a 25-year veteran of anti-poverty work, exposes the ideology of poor-bashing in a clear, forceful style. She examines how media "poornography" operates when reporters cover poverty stories. She also reveals how government and corporate clients use poor-bashing focus groups. The book includes key chapters on the history of poor-bashing.

Relevant Websites

Canada without Poverty (CWP)—www.cwp-csp.ca

> CWP is a non-profit, non-partisan organization that represents the interests of low-income people in Canada. CWP works to eradicate poverty in Canada by ensuring the concerns of low-income people are reflected in federal policy and decision making; defending the human and economic rights of low-income people; and assisting local and regional organizations to bring low-income people into decision- and policy-making processes in their communities.

Canadian Centre for Policy Alternatives (CCPA)— www.policyalternatives.ca

> The CCPA is an independent, non-partisan research institute concerned with issues of social, economic, and environmental justice. Founded in 1980, the CCPA is one of Canada's leading progressive voices in public policy debates. See especially its Growing Gap project and search through CCPA publications using "inequality and poverty" as a key phrase.

Fair Vote Canada—www.fairvote.ca

> The purpose of Fair Vote Canada is to gain broad, multi-partisan support for a fair voting system based on the principles that all voters are equal, and that every vote must count. Fair Vote Canada believes that, in order to provide a fair and equal voice for every citizen, and to accurately reflect the will of the voters, our voting system should incorporate a process of proportional representation.

National Political Parties

Conservative Party of Canada—www.conservative.ca/

Green Party of Canada—www.greenparty.ca

Liberal Party of Canada—www.liberal.ca

New Democratic Party of Canada—www.ndp.ca

Ontario Coalition Against Poverty—www.ocap.ca

> OCAP is a direct-action anti-poverty organization based in Toronto. It mounts campaigns against regressive government policies as they affect poor and working people. In addition, it provides direct-action advocacy for individuals against eviction, termination of welfare benefits, and deportation. OCAP believes in the power of people to organize themselves.

Glossary of Terms

Advocacy is sometimes divided into two types: systemic and individual advocacy. Systemic advocacy, also referred to as social action, includes efforts aimed at changing legislation, policies, practices, opportunities, or attitudes. It is directed at making changes in the system that will affect the lives of a group of people. Individual advocacy includes efforts aimed at supporting, empowering, or acting on behalf of an individual. Sometimes viewed as "going to bat" for a person, individual advocacy helps where one feels that a person has not been treated as he or she should have been (Multiple Sclerosis Society of Canada, 2006).

Left political parties are political parties that support the redistribution of wealth by way of income support and publicly funded programs for individuals with disabilities, and families and individuals with low income. Strongly aligned with the labour movement, they also advocate for policies to support workers and other policy initiatives that reduce social and health inequalities in a population. The New Democrats in Canada, the Social Democrats in Sweden, and the Labour Party in the UK are considered left parties. The USA does not have a politically relevant left party.

Politics refers to how decisions about the organization of society and how it distributes resources are made. Politics is about power and influence, attitudes and values, and the means of shaping society. While politics is usually thought of in terms of what happens during electoral campaigns, politics is a constant ongoing exercise in influencing policy-makers to act in certain ways. Politics in liberal capitalist societies such as Canada are heavily influenced by wealthy economic interests.

Poor-bashing is the phenomena of attacking poor people. Such attacks take various forms and include attributing a variety of negative attitudinal and motivational characteristics to them, treating those who receive social assistance as criminals, and blaming people living in poverty for their own situation. Poor-bashing seems to increase as the objective living conditions that people living in poverty are subjected to worsen.

Proportional representation refers to a variety of systems used for electing a legislature in which the number of seats a party wins is more or less proportional to the percentage of popular votes cast. This is in contrast to the first-past-the-post approach where the party candidate with the most votes in each constituency wins the seat. Proportional representation is the norm in most European nations. It is seen as contributing to the influence of left parties on progressive legislation in many modern welfare states.

References

Alesina, A., and Glaeser, E. L. (2004). *Fighting poverty in the US and Europe: A world of difference.* Toronto: Oxford University Press.

Arts, W., and Gelissen, J. (2001). Welfare states, solidarity, and justice principles: Does the type really matter? *ACTA Sociologica, 44*(4), 283–299.

Baker, T. (2009, March 19). Hidden unemployment: The human cost of recession. *Toronto Star.* Retrieved March 11, 2011 from www.thestar.com/comment/article/604500.

Bashevkin, S. (2002). *Welfare hot buttons.* Toronto: University of Toronto Press.

Black, J., and Shillington, E. R. (2005). *Employment insurance: Research summary for the task force for modernizing income security for working age adults.* Toronto: Toronto City Summit Alliance.

Brady, D. (2003). The politics of poverty: Left political institutions, the welfare state, and poverty. *Social Forces, 82*(2), 557–588.

Brady, D. (2009). *Rich democracies, poor people: How politics explain poverty.* New York: Oxford University Press.

Brooks, S., and Miljan, L. (2003). Theories of public policy. In S. Brooks and L. Miljan (Eds.), *Public policy in Canada: An introduction* (pp. 22–49). Toronto: Oxford University Press.

Bryant, T., Raphael, D., Schrecker, T. and Labonte, R. (in press). Canada: A land of missed opportunities for addressing the social determinants of health. *Health Policy.*

Canada Mortgage and Housing Corporation. (2009). *Housing in Canada online.* March 11, 2011 from http://cmhc.beyond2020.com/TableViewer/tableView.aspx?ReportId=3&IF_Language=eng

Canadian Population Health Initiative. (2004). *Select highlights on public views of the determinants of health*. Ottawa: CPHI.

Chunn, D. E., and Gavigan, A. M. (2004). Welfare law, welfare fraud, and the moral regulation of the never deserving poor. *Social and Legal Studies, 13*(2), 219–243.

Coburn, D. (2000). Income inequality, social cohesion, and the health status of populations: The role of neo-liberalism. *Social Science and Medicine, 51*(1), 135–146.

Coburn, D. (2010). Health and health care: A political economy perspective. In T. Bryant, D. Raphael, and M. Rioux (Eds.), *Staying alive: Critical perspectives on health, illness, and health care* (2nd ed., pp. 65–92). Toronto: Canadian Scholars' Press Inc.

Esping-Andersen, G. (1985). *Politics against markets: The social democratic road to power.* Princeton, NJ: Princeton University Press.

Federation of Canadian Municipalities. (2004). *Highlights report 2004: Quality of life in Canadian municipalities*. Ottawa: Federation of Canadian Municipalities.

Freiler, C., Rothman, L., and Barata, P. (2004). Pathways to progress: Structural solutions to address child poverty. *Campaign 2000*. Retrieved October 2006 from Campaign 2000 website: www.campaign2000.ca/res/dis.html

Friendly, M. (2009). *About Canada: Childcare.* Halifax: Fernwood Publishers.

Hulchanski, D. (2001). *A tale of two Canada's: Homeowners getting richer, renters getting poorer.* Toronto: Centre for Urban and Community Studies, University of Toronto.

Hulchanski, D. J. (2002). *Can Canada afford to help cities, provide social housing, and end homelessness? Why are provincial governments doing so little?* Toronto: Centre for Urban and Community Studies, University of Toronto.

Hulchanski, D. (2007). *The three cities within Toronto: Income polarization among Toronto's neighbourhoods, 1970–2000.* Toronto: Centre for Urban and Community Studies, University of Toronto.

Inglehart, R., Basanez, M., Diez-Medrano, J., Halman, L., and Luijkx, R. (Eds.). (2004). *Human beliefs and values: A cross-cultural sourcebook based on the 1999–2002 values survey.* Delegacion Coyoacan: Siglo XXI Editores.

Innocenti Research Centre. (2005). *Child poverty in rich nations, 2005* (Report Card No. 6). Florence: Innocenti Research Centre.

Mackenzie, H. (2010). *Recession-proof: Canada's 100 best paid CEOs.* Ottawa: The Canadian Centre for Policy Alternatives.

Mosher, J., and Hermer, J. (2005). *Welfare fraud: The constitution of social assistance as crime.* Paper prepared for the Law Commission of Canada. Retrieved March 11, 2011 from www.tinyurl.com/9b42b

Multiple Sclerosis Society of Canada. (2006). *Advocacy.* Retrieved October 2006 from www.mscalgary.org/advocacy.htm

Organisation for Economic Co-operation and Development. (2008). *Growing unequal: Income distribution and poverty in OECD nations.* Paris: Organisation for Economic Co-operation and Development.

Rainwater, L., and Smeeding, T. (1995). *Doing poorly: The real income of American children in a comparative perspective* (Working Paper No. 127). Retrieved January 2011 from Luxembourg Income Study website: www.lisproject.org/publications/liswps/127.pdf

Rainwater, L., and Smeeding, T. M. (2003). *Poor kids in a rich country: America's children in comparative perspective*. New York: Russell Sage Foundation.

Raphael, D. (Ed.). (2009). *Social determinants of health: Canadian perspectives* (2nd ed.). Toronto: Canadian Scholars' Press Inc.

Raphael, D., Bryant, T., and Curry-Stevens, A. (2004). Toronto Charter outlines future health policy directions for Canada and elsewhere. *Health Promotion International, 19*(2), 269–273.

Reutter, L., Harrison, M. J., and Neufeld, A. (2002). Public support for poverty-related policies. *Canadian Journal of Public Health, 93*(4), 297–302.

Reutter, L., Neufeld, A., and Harrison, M. (1999). Public perceptions of the relationship between poverty and health. *Canadian Journal of Public Health, 90*(1), 13–18.

Reutter, L., Veenstra, G., Stewart, M., Raphael, D., Love, R., Makwarimba, E., and McMurray, S. (2005). Lay understandings of the effects of poverty: A Canadian perspective. *Health and Social Care in the Community, 13*(6), 514–530.

Reutter, L., Veenstra, G., Stewart, M., Raphael, D., Love, R., Makwarimba, E., and McMurray, S. (2006). Public attributions for poverty in Canada. *Canadian Review of Sociology and Anthropology, 43*(1), 1–22.

Russell, P. H. (2008). *Two cheers for minority government*. Toronto: Emond Montgomery Publications Limited.

Scarth, T. (Ed.). (2004). *Hell and high water: An assessment of Paul Martin's record and implications for the future*. Ottawa: Canadian Centre for Policy Alternatives.

Shapcott, M. (2009). Housing. In D. Raphael (Ed.), *Social determinants of health: Canadian Perspectives* (2nd ed., pp 221–234). Toronto: Canadian Scholars' Press Inc.

Statistics Canada. (2004). *Owner households and tenant households by major payments and gross rent as a percentage of 1995 household income, 1996 Census, Census Metropolitan Areas*. Ottawa: Statistics Canada.

Statistics Canada. (2010). *Gini coefficients of market, total and after-tax income, by economic family type*. CANSIM table 2020705. Ottawa: Statistics Canada.

Swanson, J. (2001). *Poor-bashing: The politics of exclusion*. Toronto: Between the Lines Press.

Swartz, M. (2004, September 25). The real jobless figures are higher than you might think. *Toronto Star*, p. D12.

Teeple, G. (2000). *Globalization and the decline of social reform: Into the twenty-first century*. Aurora, ON: Garamond Press.

Chapter Twelve

Canadian Public Policy and Poverty in International Perspective

When I feed the poor I am called a saint. When I ask why they are poor,
I am called a communist.—Archbishop Dom Helder Camara

Learning Objectives

At the conclusion of this chapter, the reader will be able to:

- place Canada's health performance in international perspective;
- provide a comparative analysis that considers how Canada's approach to public policy and resource allocation are linked to the incidence of poverty;
- explain why public policy approaches to resource allocations determine both the incidence and effects of poverty;
- apply Esping-Andersen's welfare-state typology to both understand and generate questions about a jurisdiction's approach to poverty and poverty-related issues; and
- describe potential lessons that can be learned from other nations' approaches toward poverty and poverty-related issues.

Introduction

This chapter examines Canadian public policy and its effects upon the incidence and effects of poverty in international perspective. Canadian standings on various health indicators, poverty rates, poverty-related indicators of quality of life, and public policy commitments to its citizens are compared with those of other wealthy developed countries. Canada does not do well in such comparisons. Canadian poverty rates are high, poverty-related indicators of health and quality of life are mid-range, and public policy commitments to support citizens are undeveloped as compared to most other wealthy developed nations.

Canadian public policy approaches to the provision of supports and benefits to citizens in a range of areas are examined in relation to these other nations. Some of the policy domains examined are early childhood education and care, family benefits, employment and labour policy, pensions, and the organization and generosity of disability, health care, social assistance, and unemployment benefits. Canada is identified as being firmly placed within the "liberal welfare state" camp along with the USA, the UK, and Ireland. These nations share relatively undeveloped welfare systems, foster individualist understandings as to the causes of poverty, and rely upon market-oriented approaches to public policy in general and poverty reduction policy in particular. The approaches of several European nations toward public policy in general and poverty reduction policy in particular are examined for their implications for the Canadian scene. The example of the UK is held out as an example where a nation with many similarities to Canada has adopted an aggressive approach to address the incidence of poverty and its effects upon health and quality of life. Unfortunately, the recent election of a conservative–liberal democratic coalition promises to curb these gains.

Canadian Health Statistics in Comparative Perspective

Before examining Canadian poverty rates and public policy in international perspective, Canadian standings on a number of health indicators in relation to other wealthy developed nations provide a context for these analyses. These data come from a variety of sources but the key ones are the Organisation for Economic Co-operation and Development (OECD), the Innocenti Research Centre, and the Luxembourg Income Study (LIS). The important indicators considered are those of population health of a nation: life expectancy, infant mortality rate, low birth-weight rate, childhood death by injury, childhood death by maltreatment, and teenage pregnancy rate. For every measure the rank of 1 is the best, with increasing rank indicating poorer relative performance.

Life Expectancy
The most recent data available for life expectancy at birth for OECD nations is from 2007 (OECD, 2009b). Life expectancy for Canadian males is 78.4 years, and for women, 83.0 years. Canada is now ranked 7th of 30 wealthy developed nations for life expectancy for men, and ranked 8th of 30 wealthy developed nations for women. Average life expectancy in Canada increased by 9.4 years from 1960 to 2007. This improvement is below the OECD average of 10.7 years.

Of note is the very low life expectancy ranking of the USA, 24th of 30 wealthy developed nations, where men's life expectancy is 75.4 years, and women's 80.7 years. Nations with greater male life expectancies than Canada are Japan (79.2 years); Switzerland (79.5); Australia (79.0); Italy (78.5); Iceland (79.4); and Sweden (78.9). For women, nations that exceed Canada are Japan (86.0 years); Switzerland)84.4); Australia (83.7); Italy (84.2); Iceland (82.9); Spain (84.3); and France (84.4).

Infant Mortality Rate
Infant mortality rates for the OECD countries are available for 2007 (OECD, 2009b). Infant mortality rate refers to the incidence of newborns dying during their first year of life. It is frequently seen as providing the single best indicator of overall population

health. Canada's 2007 rate of 5.0/1,000 gives it a rank of 24th of these 30 wealthy developed nations. Nations with the highest infant mortality rates are Turkey (20.7/1,000); Mexico (15.7); USA (6.7); Slovak Republic (6.1); Poland (6.0); and Hungary (5.9). Nations with exceptionally low rates are Luxembourg (1.8/1,000); Iceland (2.0); Sweden (2.5); Japan (2.6); and Finland (2.7).

Low Birth-Weight Rate

Low birth-weight rate is an important indicator of health because it is associated with a wide range of health problems across the lifespan. Low birth weight is usually defined as a newborn weighing less than 2500 grams. In 2007, Canada's low birth-weight rate was 6.1 per 100 newborns. This gives Canada a ranking of 10th of 30 wealthy developed nations. Nations with the highest rates are Turkey (11.3); Japan (9.7); Greece (9.0); USA (8.3); Hungary (8.2); and Belgium (7.9). Nations with the lowest rates are Iceland (3.8 per 100); Sweden (4.1); Finland (4.3); Luxembourg (4.5); Korea (4.7); and Ireland (5.0).

Childhood Death by Injury Rate

During the period of 1991–1995, 9.7 Canadian children per 100,000 died from injuries (Innocenti Research Centre, 2001a). Canada's rate gives it a ranking of 18th of these 26 wealthy developed nations. Nations with exceptionally low rates are Sweden (5.2); UK (6.1); Italy (6.1); and the Netherlands (6.6). Nations with very high rates are Korea (25.0); Mexico (19.8); Portugal (17.8); USA (14.1); New Zealand (13.7); and Poland (13.4).

Child Maltreatment Deaths

During the 1990s, the incidence of childhood death by maltreatment in Canada was 0.7 per 100,000 (Innocenti Research Centre, 2003). This gave Canada an overall ranking of 20th out of 27 wealthy developed nations. A slightly modified ranking that takes into account "undetermined intent" raises Canada's rate to 1.0 per 100,000 but improves its relative ranking to 16th of 27. Nations with very low childhood death from maltreatment—including undetermined intent—are Spain (0.1); Greece (0.2); Italy (0.2); Ireland (0.3); and Norway (0.3). Nations with relatively high rates are Portugal (3.7); Mexico (3.0); and USA (2.4).

Teenage Birth Rate

Teenage birth rate is usually seen as an indicator of social disorganization in wealthy developed nations (Innocenti Research Centre, 2001b). Women who experience teenage pregnancy are at risk for poor educational outcomes, and children born to such parents are at risk for a variety of health and social problems. Canada's teenage birth rate for 2005 of 13.2 births per 1,000 women ages 15–19 years gives it a rank of 18th of 30 wealthy developed nations. Nations that were very high are Mexico (65.9); USA (49.8;); Turkey (39.7); UK (24.8); New Zealand (23.4); Hungary (20.7); and the Slovak Republic (20.0). Nations that show very low rates are Japan (3.7); Korea (3.7); Switzerland (4.5); Netherlands (4.7); France (6.7); and Sweden and Italy (6.8).

In summary, Canada shows an unexceptional profile on a variety of health indicators. While doing relatively well on male and female life expectancy, with rankings of 7th and

8th respectively, the infant mortality rank of 24th is very problematic, as are the rankings for deaths from child injury (18th) and from child maltreatment (16th). Teenage pregnancy rates give Canada a very poor ranking of 19th among wealthy developed nations.

Canadian Poverty Rates in International Perspective

As argued in previous chapters, poverty is a profound threat to the health and quality of life of individuals, communities, and society as a whole. Where does Canada stand on this indicator of commitment to its citizenry? Three primary sources and related analyses are considered here. Overall poverty rates come from the 2009 edition of *Society at a Glance* (OECD, 2009b). Child poverty rates are provided by the OECD (2008) and the Innocenti Research Centre (2000). The more nuanced analyses on poverty rates over time for 11 nations, including Canada, come from a Luxembourg Income Study paper (Smeeding, 2005).

Overall National Poverty Rates

Internationally agreed-upon conventions define the rate of poverty as the number of individuals with a disposable income of less than 50% of the median income of the entire population. Canada's overall poverty rate for the mid-2000s was 12.0%, which is above the OECD average of 10.6% (OECD, 2008). Canada's relative rank in this important rating was 19th of 30 wealthy developed nations. Nations whose poverty rates are very low are the Nordic states of Denmark (5.3%); Sweden (5.3%); Norway (6.8%); and Finland (7.34%). Also included are the Netherlands (7.7%); Luxembourg (8.1%); Hungary (7.1%); and the Czech Republic (4.3%). Nations that do noticeably worse than Canada include Mexico (18.4%); USA (17.1%); Turkey (15.9%); and Ireland (15.4%).

Child Poverty—Relative and Absolute Rates

Society at a Glance (OECD, 2009b) provides data on child poverty in wealthy developed nations. Figure 1.2 in Chapter 1 showed relative child poverty rates for Canada and other wealthy developed nations during the late 1990s. Canada's relative child poverty rate of 15.1% gave it a ranking of 21st of 30 wealthy developed nations. Nations with exceptionally low child poverty rates were the Nordic nations (Denmark, 3%; Sweden and Finland, 4%; and Norway, 5%) and Austria (6%). Nations with exceptionally high rates were Turkey (25%); Mexico and Poland (22%); and the USA (21%).

In 2000 the Innocenti Research Centre calculated absolute child poverty rates for the mid-1990s by applying the USA poverty standard as translated into national currencies and adjusted for national purchasing power. The USA poverty standard is set very low and is usually seen as an indicator of very limited resources associated with serious material and social deprivation. Using this standard, Canada's rate of 9.5% placed it 7th of 19 nations for whom these data were available.

Former communist central European nations such as Poland (absolute poverty rate equals 93%); Hungary (91%); and the Czech Republic (83.1%) had very high absolute poverty rates but much lower relative poverty rates. Spain (42.8%); Italy (36.1%); the UK (29.1%); and Ireland (21.4%) had both relatively high absolute poverty rates and relative poverty rates. The USA absolute poverty rate was 13.9%.

While some nations have low relative poverty rates and high absolute poverty rates, it is of interest to direct attention to those nations that maintain both low absolute rates in addition to low relative rates. The Nordic nations had very low absolute poverty rates (Sweden, 5.3%; Norway, 3%; Denmark, 5.1%; and Finland, 6.9%), as well as Belgium (7.5%) and Luxembourg (1.2%), thereby maintaining their excellent rankings on both kinds of poverty indicators. These nations clearly provide children with the concrete resources sufficient to support health and quality of life and do so in a manner that avoids wide inequalities in the distribution of these resources that are seen in nations such as Canada.

More Detailed Analyses from the Luxembourg Income Study

How do the differing levels of poverty among nations come about? An analysis of data from the Luxembourg Income Study (LIS) provides insights into this process. The LIS provides income and demographic information on households in over 25 nations from 1967 to the present and provides ongoing analyses that are available through a series of working papers (see "Relevant Websites," this chapter.) Smeeding (2005) provides an analysis of available data on income and poverty and analyses of trends over time for 11 wealthy developed nations. These nations represent four Anglo-Saxon nations (Canada, Ireland, the UK, and the USA); four continental European nations (Austria, Belgium, Germany, and the Netherlands); one Southern European nation (Italy); and two Nordic nations (Finland and Sweden).

These analyses are useful because they highlight differences among liberal, conservative, and social democratic political economies. Examination of these differences illustrates how public policy serves to determine poverty rates. Table 12.1 details overall poverty rates, rates for children, rates for children with single parents, and rates for children in two-parent households for these 11 wealthy developed nations. Poverty rates are also provided for elders (seniors) and for adults or singles with no children. These poverty rates are based on the international convention of a poverty cut-off of less than 50% of median-adjusted disposable income for individuals.

Nations are listed from the highest rate (USA) to the lowest (Finland). When examining these data, it is useful to use the USA and UK as comparative benchmarks as nations traditionally associated with high poverty rates, and Finland and Sweden as nations traditionally associated with low poverty rates.

Canada's overall poverty rate of 11.4% places it in the middle of these 11 nations. Its rate is below that of the USA and the UK, but well above the Nordic nations of Finland and Sweden and above the continental nations as well. Canada's child poverty rate has traditionally been higher for children than for the overall population and this is also the case here, as it is for the USA and the UK. In contrast, in all other nations except for the Netherlands, poverty rates for children are lower than they are for the

Table 12.1: Relative Poverty Rates by Type of Household in 11 Wealthy Industrialized Nations, 1999, 2000

Nation	Overall	Households with Children (by Number of Parents)			Elders	Childless
		All Children	1 Parent	2 Parent		
USA	17.0	18.8	41.4	13.2	28.4	11.2
Ireland	15.0	15.0	45.8	10.8	48.3	13.1
UK	12.7	15.4	30.5	9.1	23.9	8.4
Canada	11.4	13.2	32.0	10.1	6.3	11.9
Germany	8.3	7.6	33.2	4.4	11.2	8.7
Belgium	8.0	6.0	21.8	4.3	17.2	5.9
Austria	7.7	6.4	17.9	5.1	17.4	7.0
Netherlands	7.3	9.0	30.7	7.6	2.0	6.4
Sweden	6.5	3.8	11.3	2.2	8.3	9.8
Finland	5.4	2.9	7.3	2.2	10.1	7.6
Overall Average	10.3	10.1	26.6	7.6	17.0	8.9

Source: Adapted from Smeeding, T. (2005). *Poor people in rich nations: The United States in comparative perspective. Luxembourg Income Study* (Working Paper No. 419, p. 30). Syracuse, NY: Syracuse University.

overall population. This is even the case for Finland and Sweden, which already had very low overall poverty rates.

The data provided for children living in one- and two-parent households highlight poverty rate differences among these nations. For Canadian children living in single-parent households, the poverty rate is a striking 32%, which is almost three times the rate for Swedish children living in this situation and over four times the rate for Finnish children in this situation. The situation for Canadian children, however, is not as bleak as for those living in single-parent families in Ireland and the USA. Yet, even for two-parent families, the poverty rate for Canadian children of 10.1% is close to five times the poverty rate of Swedish and Finnish children in comparable living arrangements.

Canadian elders fare much better. Canada's elder poverty rate of 6.3% is the second lowest among these nations, exceeded only by the strikingly low rate of 2% seen in the Netherlands. However, Canada's poverty rate for childless adults is very high at 11.9%, exceeding every nation except for Ireland. Canada's rate even exceeds the USA's poverty rate for this group.

How have Canada's rates changed over time? Smeeding (2005) compares overall poverty rates for each nation over a 23-year period from the base year of 1987 to 2000. In 1987, the relative poverty rate for Canada was 11.4%. For 2000, he provides two rates. The 2000 relative rate applies the same calculation to 2000 as that applied in 1987—the poverty line is less than 50% of the median disposable income for all residents. For Canada, the relative poverty rate in 2000 was identical to the figure seen in 1987, 11.4%.

The anchored rate refers to the percentage of Canadians in 2000 living below the poverty line, as it was calculated in 1987, and adjusted for increases in the cost of living since that time. In Canada, this figure is 11.0%. Using either measure therefore returns virtually the same 2000 rate. It is apparent that poverty rates in Canada have not changed from 1987 to 2000.

Analysis is then made of the effects on poverty rates of various government spending programs. Table 12.2 shows overall poverty rates at various levels of government intervention. Market income refers to income derived from gainful employment or investments and other private sources. Relying upon the market as the source of income provides overall poverty rates that are rather high across all nations. Canada's poverty rate based on market income would be 21.5%. Social insurance and taxes—referring to transfers such as child benefits and children's allowances and changes in distribution resulting from taxation—reduces Canada's poverty rate to 12.9%. Canada's poverty rate associated with the provision of a few more varied benefits—called social assistance by Smeeding—reduces the poverty rate a little bit more to 11.4%.

What is the calculated effect on poverty rates of these government programs? In Canada, social insurance programs reduce the poverty rate by 38.9%, and the overall disposable income poverty rate goes down by 46%. This seems quite hopeful but the overall reduction rate of 46% for Canada is well below the average rate of 60.9% for the nations included in this analysis. Indeed, Sweden reduces its poverty rate by 77.4% by such actions. Belgium, Germany, Austria, and Finland also reduce their overall poverty rate by at least 70% through government action. The USA reduces poverty by the smallest amount, 26.4%.

A summary indicator of how government intervention serves to reduce poverty is provided by the final column in Table 12.2. Canada expends 5.8% of Gross Domestic Product (GDP) on benefits and supports for non-elderly citizens. In contrast, Finland and Sweden spend over 10% of GDP on citizen benefits. The USA expends a miserly 2.3% of GDP in such expenditures. The importance of government expenditures in reducing poverty is illustrated by an analysis that reveals that non-elderly cash and near-cash (e.g., housing subsidies, active labour market subsidies, etc.) predicts 61% of the variation among these nations' non-elderly poverty rates. Nations that spend more money on these benefits have lower poverty rates. Nations that spend less have higher poverty rates.

Smeeding (2005) also shows that the percentage of low-paid workers is strongly related to the percentage of non-elderly citizens within a nation living in poverty. Canada has 23% of its workers identified as earning less than 65% of the median wage and a poverty rate of 12%. The USA has 25% of its workers earning low wages and has a poverty rate of 16%. In contrast, only 5% of Finnish and Swedish workers earn low wages and their poverty rates are 4.5% and 6% respectively. These variations in numbers of low-paid workers account for a strikingly high 85% of the variation among nations in

Table 12.2: The Anti-poverty Effect of Government Spending—Percent of All People Living in Poverty, 1999, 2000

Nation	Market Income	Social Insurance (and Taxes)	Social Assistance	Percent Poverty Reduction		OECD Social Expenditures on Non-elderly
				Social Assistance	Overall	
USA	23.1	19.3	17.0	16.5	26.4	2.3
Ireland	29.5	21.2	16.5	28.1	44.1	5.5
UK	31.1	23.5	12.4	24.4	60.1	7.1
Canada	21.1	12.9	11.4	38.9	46.0	5.8
Germany	28.1	10.6	8.3	62.3	70.5	7.3
Belgium	34.6	8.8	8.0	74.3	76.9	9.3
Austria	31.8	9.1	7.7	71.4	75.8	7.4
Netherlands	21.0	9.6	7.3	54.3	65.2	9.6
Sweden	28.8	11.7	6.5	59.4	77.4	11.6
Finland	17.8	11.4	5.4	36.0	69.7	10.9
Overall Average	27.0	13.8	10.3	47.2	60.9	7.4

Source: Adapted from Smeeding, T. (2005). *Poor people in rich nations: The United States in comparative perspective. Luxembourg Income Study* (Working Paper No. 419, p. 33). Syracuse, NY: Syracuse University.

the number of people living in poverty. In essence, the single best predictor of the number of people living in poverty in a nation is the number of people earning low wages.

What these findings suggest is that nations that spend less on citizens are more likely to have higher levels of poverty. The findings also indicate that nations that tolerate a high percentage of low-paid workers are also more likely to have higher poverty rates. The next sections explore the nature of these differences in governmental support of citizens through transfers and programs. The Canadian approach to these issues is examined within the context of the practices of other wealthy developed nations.

Societal Commitments to Citizens and Governmental Spending

An emerging literature is detailing how differences in poverty rates among developed nations result from systematic variations in approaches to public policy. One key indicator of public commitment to supporting citizens is percentage of Gross Domestic Product (GDP) transferred to citizens through programs, services, or cash benefits.

Nations may choose to transfer relatively small amounts and allow the marketplace to serve as the primary arbiter of how economic resources are distributed. Or a nation may choose to intervene to control the marketplace and make the primary decisions concerning these allocations of resources. As it turns out, the nations that transfer a greater proportion of resources are more likely to have lower poverty rates than those who transfer a smaller proportion of resources. (See Box 12.1.)

The Organisation for Economic Co-operation and Development regularly provides indicators of government operations, including provision of supports and services. An especially important indicator is extent of government transfers. Transfers refer to governments taking fiscal resources that are generated by the economy and distributing them to the population in the form of services and monetary supports; that is, as investments in social infrastructure. Such infrastructure includes education, employment training, social assistance or welfare payments, family supports, pensions, health and social services, and other benefits.

Among the developed nations of the OECD, the average public expenditure in 2005 was 20.6% of Gross Domestic Product (GDP) (OECD, 2010). There is a rather large variation among countries, with Denmark (spending 27.1% of GDP) and Sweden (spending 29.4%) being the highest public spenders. Canada ranks 26th of 30 wealthy developed nations and spends just 16.5% of GDP on public expenditures. The only nations that allocate a smaller percentage of GDP to public expenditures are Korea (6.9%); Mexico (7.4%); Turkey (13.7%) and the USA (15.9%).

Other wealthy developed nations that spend rather more—in addition to Denmark and Sweden—are France (29.2%); Germany (26.7%); Belgium (26.4%); Austria (27.2%); and Finland (26.1%). How do these differences in spending translate into specific policy areas? Figures 12.1a–12.1d show how Canada compares to a number of OECD nations in its transfer of resources to its citizenry, as indicated by percentage of GDP allocated to public expenditure on health, old age, incapacity-related benefits, and families.

Canada is among the highest spenders on public expenditure on health care and is exceeded only by Germany, France, Belgium, the USA, and New Zealand. The USA's high ranking on public spending is rather striking as much of its spending on health care is actually from private sources. Overall, the USA spends far and away the most monies on health care on a per capita basis when both public and private sources are taken into account (close to 16% of GDP) (Organisation for Economic Co-operation and Development, 2010).

It is in the other areas of benefits and supports to citizens that Canada reveals itself as a miserly public spender. Canada ranks near the bottom of nations in allocations to old-age-related spending, primarily pensions. Canada's spending of 3.8% of GDP gives it a rank of 26th of 30 wealthy developed nations. The only nations spending a smaller percentage of GDP on old age benefits are Ireland, Iceland, Korea, and Mexico. Italy, France, Austria, and Greece are among the highest spenders on older citizen benefits.

Canada ranks among the lowest spenders on incapacity or disability-related benefits and programs, allocating less than 1% of GDP. Its rank is 27th of 30 wealthy developed

Box 12.1: Taxes and Services

Cost of Cutting Taxes Not Worth the Savings
Elaine Power and Jamie Swift

Two of the major political parties in the upcoming election are promising tax cuts to "put more money in taxpayers' pockets."

"Great," we think. Who wouldn't want more money in their pockets, especially as the post-holiday credit-card bills arrive?

There are two important questions we need to consider before jumping to the conclusion that tax cuts are a good thing: a) will tax cuts really put more money in our pockets? and b) what are the costs of those tax cuts?

The first problem is that tax cuts at the federal level mean, in part, reduced income transfers to the provinces, which then download the problem to municipalities.

We've already lived through a decade of decreased federal funding to the provinces, compounded by provincial tax cuts and downloading of services. So Ontario's city governments must make tough decisions: Raise taxes. Cut services. Impose user fees for services that were once free. Or all of the above.

It's a new version of the old "trickle-down" theory of economics. Some people, especially the more affluent, may end up with more money because of Ottawa's tax cuts. But it is not a sure thing.

More important are the costs of tax cuts.

What doesn't get funded—or is inadequately funded—because "we can't afford it"? Tax cuts affect programs that Canadians value: education, health care, public health, the environment, income support programs, and so on. They erode "public goods" such as clean air and water that are impossible to produce for profit.

Tax cuts already have a proven track record: The Walkerton water disaster. An ongoing crisis in health-care funding. Aboriginals living in Third World conditions. Inadequate funding for education. A growing gap between the rich and the poor. Reduced help for marginalized groups like "high-risk" youth and victims of domestic abuse. One in six children living in poverty, and double that rate for Indian, immigrant and visible minority children. A deplorable lack of affordable housing.

The simple fact is that tax cuts undermine the government's ability to act. And this is exactly what the tax cutters intend. Tax cuts are an integral component of a particular ideological position, often called neo-liberalism, which argues—without supporting evidence—that the market can always provide goods and services better than government.

But can the market provide health care for all?

Evidence from the American experience suggests not. Can the market provide affordable housing for the alarming number of workers who do not earn a living wage? Evidence from the past 10 years of tax-cutting in Ottawa and Queen's Park, combined with a retreat from social housing programs, suggests not.

Downloading onto municipal governments also underpins the neo-liberal world-view. Our cities have the least fiscal capacity and are least able to regulate a market dominated by a small number of ever more powerful corporations.

Canadians are not overtaxed. The Organization for Economic Co-operation and Development ranks Canada among the lowest taxed industrialized nations: 21st among 30 industrialized nations, and fifth among the seven largest.

We wove our social safety net after World War II, when Canadians saw themselves as nation-builders. In the wake of the events of the 1930s and 1940s, we had a collective sense that no one should ever again have to suffer the humiliations of unemployment and poverty experienced during the Great Depression.

Canadians believed then—as we do now—that we could look after each other and work together to achieve whatever national goals we set for ourselves. We could build a better future for all Canadians. We still can.

Taxes are the price we pay for a decent, caring, and civilized society.

When a candidate promises you tax cuts, ask him or her what the real cost will be. Instead of gazing down at the bottom line, let's start asking ourselves what kind of Canada we want to build together. And let's demand that our politicians work for the public good.

Elaine Power teaches in Queen's School of Physical and Health Education and Jamie Swift teaches in Queen's School of Business.

Source: Power, E., and Swift, J. (2006, January 19). Cost of cutting taxes not worth the savings. *Toronto Star*, p. A17.

nations. The Nordic nations rank near the top. The only nations allocating a smaller percentage to incapacity or disability-related issues are Japan, Korea, and Turkey. And Canada ranks very poorly on family benefits, achieving a rank of 25th of 30 of these nations. Only Mexico, Japan, USA, Korea, and Turkey spend less on families.

Another way to slice up the expenditure pie is to consider spending on income supports to the working-age population and social services outside of health and pensions. Income support involves family benefits, wage subsidies, and child support paid by governments to help keep low-income individuals and families out of poverty. Social services include counselling, employment supports, and other community services.

Not surprisingly, Canada ranks relatively low on income supports to the working-aged population. Canada spends just 3.1% of Net National Income (a measure similar to the GDP) in income supports to the working-age population (ranked 24th of 30), and 3.0% on social services (excluding health) (ranked 10th of 30). Canada's spending on social services of 3.0% is relatively high among nations. But consider that Sweden spends 7.8% on income support and another 7.8% on social services, and Denmark spends 9.6% on income support and an additional 6.7% on social services. And these

Figure 12.1a: Public Expenditure on Health as % of GDP, 2007

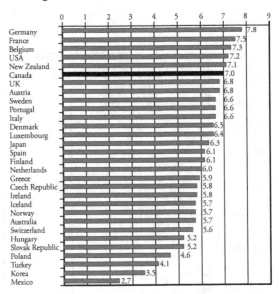

Source for Figures 12.1a–d: Organisation for Economic Co-operation and Development. (2010). *Social expenditure: Aggregated data. OECD Social Expenditure Statistics* (database). doi: 10.1787/data-00166-en

Figure 12.1b: Public Expenditure on Old Age as % of GDP, 2007

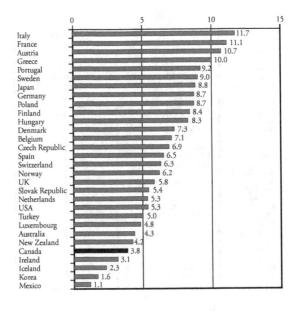

Figure 12.1c: Public Expenditure on Incapacity-Related Benefits as % of GDP, 2007

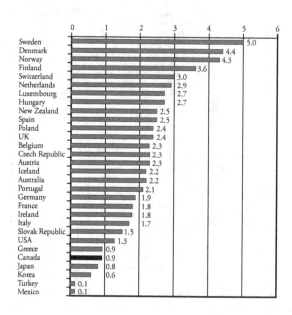

Figure 12.1d: Public Expenditure on Family Benefits as % of GDP, 2007

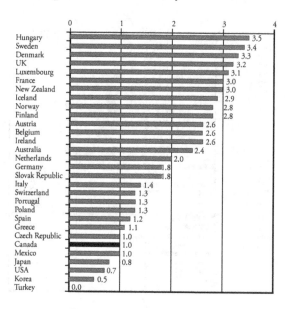

are the nations with very low poverty rates (Organisation for Economic Co-operation and Development, 2010).

Active Labour Market Program

Active labour policy refers to the extent that governments support training and other policies that foster employment and reduce unemployment. Canada allocates 0.3% GDP to such policies. This provides Canada with a ranking of 17th of 30 wealthy developed nations. The highest spenders are Belgium (1.2%); Denmark (1.3%); and Netherlands and Sweden (1.1%). The USA (0.1%) and Turkey, Iceland, and Mexico (0%) are the lowest spenders. These programs are also contributors to lower poverty rates (Organisation for Economic Co-operation and Development, 2010).

Public Policy and Poverty: Implications for Day-to-Day Life

How do these differing commitments to supporting citizens translate into differing conditions of day-to-day life? Only a few sets of issues can be examined here: resources available to the unemployed, level of social assistance benefits, level of minimum wages, and level of pension benefits.

Unemployment Benefits

Figure 12.2 shows the benefit replacement levels for unemployed individuals—as a percentage of the average production worker's salary—over a five-year period. For most Canadians, benefits that would be available over the five-year period would be Employment Insurance (EI), which would expire after about a year of benefits. At that point, if a family has liquid assets, these would need to be spent prior to receiving social assistance benefits (see Chapter 7). Therefore, for these non-destitute families, EI provides only 47% replacement income over this period. This ranks Canada 21st of 29 wealthy developed nations (for which data is available) in its generosity of benefits. One-year benefits are 70% of median income (up to an annual income of $40,000), but this would apply only to the minority of newly unemployed Canadians who would qualify for such benefits.

Social Assistance or Welfare

The OECD identifies social assistance and welfare support as "benefits of last resort." As discussed in earlier chapters, Canadian benefits in most cases do not come close to reaching Canada's low income cut-offs. How do these benefits compare to international agreed-upon standards of poverty? And how do these benefits compare to levels provided in other wealthy developed nations? Figures 12.3a and 12.3b provide data that address these questions. Poverty is identified using cut-offs associated with 50% of median income of families.

On average, Canadian social assistance benefits for a married couple with two children provide 33% of median average income. This places these benefits at 17% less than the <50% of median income indicator of poverty. As compared to the other wealthy

Figure 12.2: Average Net Replacement Rates over Short Term (1 year) and Long Term (5 years) of Unemployment for Persons Earning 67% and 100% of Average Earnings, 2006

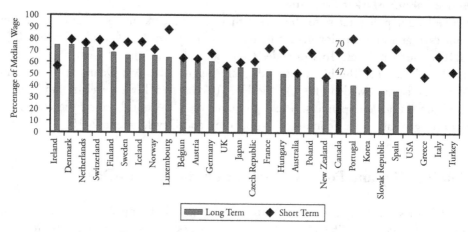

Source: Organisation for Economic Co-operation and Development. (2009). *Economic policy reforms: Going for growth* (Figure 4.2, p. 119). Paris: OECD.

developed nations for which these data are provided, Canada ranks 21st of 26 in providing these benefits of last resort.

Similar data are seen for benefits available to a lone parent with two children. The Canadian rates are 35% of the average median wage, 15% below the poverty line, and give Canada a rank of 19th of 26 nations.

Minimum Wages

As noted earlier, Smeeding (2005) identified the percentage of low-paid workers as the best predictor of the percentage of citizens living in poverty. How does Canada compare to other nations in having minimum wages that keep people out of poverty? Figure 12.4 provides data that address these questions.

For a Canadian lone-parent family with two children, the wages received places the family at 48% of the median household income. This is below the commonly accepted poverty cut-off of 50% of median income level. For a two-parent family with two children working full time at minimum wages, the level of 43% of the median income achieved also places the family below the poverty line. Canada's ranking for wages for a lone-parent working family is 9th of 15 wealthy modern developed nations for which data are available. For the two-parent working family, Canada is ranked 10th of 15 wealthy developed nations. In reality, Canada's performance is much worse than this as none of the Nordic nations (Sweden, Norway, Denmark, Finland, and Iceland) have statutory minimum wages. These are not seen as necessary by these countries since wages are set by collective agreements and governmental commissions at a level that keeps families out of poverty.

Figure 12.3a: Average Net Incomes Provided by Social Assistance as Percent of Median Equivalent Household Income, Married Couple with Two Children, 2005

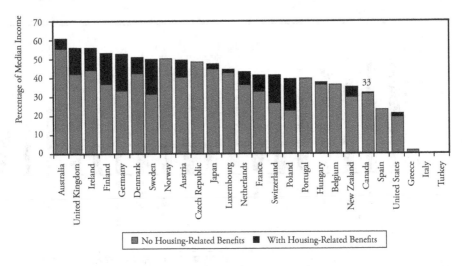

Source: Organisation for Economic Co-operation and Development. (2010). *Society at a glance, OECD social indicators* (Chart EQ41, p. 95). Paris: OECD.

Figure 12.3b: Average Net Incomes Provided by Social Assistance as Percent of Median Equivalent Household Income, Lone Parent with Two Children, 2005

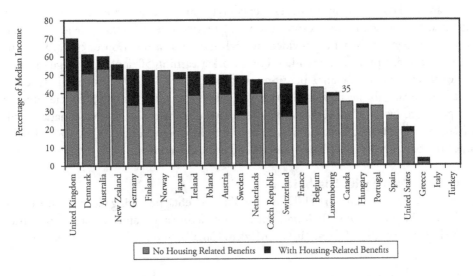

Source: Organisation for Economic Co-operation and Development. (2010). *Society at a glance, OECD social indicators* (Chart EQ41, p. 95). Paris: OECD.

Figure 12.4: Net Incomes at Statutory Minimum Wages, Lone Parent with Two Children and Couple with Two Children as Percentage of Median Household Income, 2005

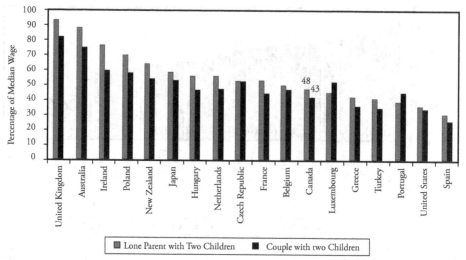

Source: Organisation for Economic Co-operation and Development. (2010). *Society at a glance, OECD social indicators* (Chart EQ42, p. 95). Paris: OECD.

Pensions

The Canada Pension Plan provides benefits to individuals upon retirement. The Organisation for Economic Co-operation and Development (2005) provides data on the value of pension benefits provided by each nation as a function of the gross earnings of an average production worker. For a worker earning 50% of an average production worker's income, Canada's pension provides a rate of 89% of these earnings. For a Canadian earning the average production worker's income, the rate is 57%. The rates for average-waged workers are very low by international comparison, giving Canada a rank of 22nd of 30 wealthy developed nations. For very low-paid workers, Canada achieves a somewhat better rank of 12th of 30 wealthy developed nations.

Support for People with Disabilities

Canada allocates less than 1% of GDP to disability benefits, providing Canada with a rank of 17th of 20 nations (OECD, 2003). Poland, the Netherlands, and the Nordic countries are the highest spenders. Korea, Turkey, Mexico, Canada, and the USA are the lowest.

Becoming Unemployed in Canada, Sweden, and Finland: A Tale of Three Nations

Consider the experience of becoming unemployed in Canada. Recent data indicates that only 40% of Canadians are eligible for received benefits (Black and Shillington, 2005). This is a result of very stringent eligibility requirements. If you are eligible for benefits, you receive them for at most a year. You are then required to dispose of virtually all of your liquid assets in order to receive social assistance. Availability of job training cannot be assumed (OECD, 1999).

In contrast, consider the situation in Finland and Sweden. In Finland, 90% of unemployed workers are eligible to receive earnings-related benefits for up to 500 working days or 100 weeks (OECD, 1998). Those who did not pay into a plan can receive a flat-rate benefit for a similar period. Following this rather lengthy period, all Finns are eligible for 180 working days of labour market support. After that, there is means-tested labour market support for an indefinite period. During all of this time, child allowances are universal and tax-free, and remain uninterrupted.

In Sweden, if you become unemployed, you have a 90% chance of being entitled to benefits by virtue of having paid into an insurance fund (OECD, 1998). You can receive benefits for 300 working days. If you are of the 10% who did not contribute, you are eligible to receive labour market assistance (training and income support) for 150 working days. After this time (300 or 150 days respectively), Swedes can apply for further support. At this time many enter job training, and if a job is not available upon completion of training, many re-qualify for unemployment insurance.

And consider what happens if a job does become available. In Finland and Sweden only 5% of jobs are considered low paying (Smeeding, 2005). In contrast, in Canada, 23% of jobs are so identified. These differences in approach in responding to issues of unemployment are mirrored in numerous other public policies for those with disabilities, on social assistance, or otherwise unable to participate in the paid labour force (OECD, 1998, 1999, 2003).

Making Sense of Variations in Government Support of Citizens

The presentation of profound national differences in poverty rates and degree of social provision has spawned much speculation about the nature of modern welfare states (Brady, 2009). The different poverty rates of modern developed nations clearly reflect different orientations to social provision. In a sense, these nations represent profoundly different manifestations of what is normally termed the welfare state. All wealthy developed nations have some form of welfare state.

In capitalist economies, the welfare state is defined as one that uses government, or state, power to modify the influence of market forces in at least three ways:

- by guaranteeing individuals and families a minimum income irrespective of the market value of their work or property;

- by narrowing the extent of insecurity by enabling individuals and families to meet certain social contingencies such as sickness, old age and unemployment, which lead otherwise to individual and family crises; and
- by ensuring that all citizens—without distinction of status or class—are offered the best standards available in relation to a certain agreed range of social services (Briggs, 1961).

What kind of welfare state does Canada have? Is it well developed or underdeveloped as compared to other modern developed nations? Study on the form that welfare states take reveals that Canada is seen—consistent with our findings presented above—as having a relatively weak welfare state, showing more similarities with the USA than with many European nations (Esping-Andersen, 1990, 1999, 2009).

It has been well documented that the Nordic nations of Denmark, Finland, Norway, and Sweden have very low poverty rates and much greater social provision in the forms of transfers and service than other nations. It has also been noticed that nations such as the USA, UK, Canada, and Ireland have traditionally had much higher poverty rates and less-developed welfare states. It is apparent that these Nordic countries have very different orientations toward social provision than these English-speaking nations. Sweden's welfare state, for example, is one of the oldest, with Sweden having begun building its programs in the 1920s (Burstrom, Diderichsen, Ostlin, and Ostergren, 2002). Many western countries, including Canada, the USA, and the UK, developed their welfare states in earnest after World War II (Teeple, 2000).

With the publication of *The Three Worlds of Welfare Capitalism* in 1990, Gosta Esping-Andersen (1990, 1999) identified three distinct clusters or welfare state regimes among wealthy developed nations that have generated much attention and research. Esping-Andersen's typology identified social democratic, liberal, and conservative welfare states that formed a continuum of government support to citizens. Saint Arnaud and Bernard (2005) added a fourth undeveloped conservative regime, which they term Latin. These range from high government intervention welfare systems in the social democratic countries to residual welfare systems in the liberal

Table 12.3: Examples of Members of Each Welfare State Regime

Liberal	Conservative	Social Democratic	Latin
Australia	Belgium	Denmark	Greece
Canada	France	Finland	Italy
Ireland	Germany	Norway	Portugal
UK	Netherlands	Sweden	Spain
USA	Switzerland		

Source: Adapted from Saint-Arnaud, S., and Bernard, P. (2003). Convergence or resilience? A hierarchical cluster analysis of the welfare regimes in advanced countries. *Current Sociology, 51*(5), 499–527.

nations. Conservative and Latin nations fall midway between these others in service provision and citizen supports. Table 12.3 shows national membership in the Esping-Andersen welfare state typology.

Sweden, Norway, Denmark, and Finland are social democratic welfare states. These nations have very well-developed welfare states that provide a wide range of universal and generous benefits. As noted, these nations provide a higher percentage of transfers than other nations. Social democratic states are proactive in developing labour, family-friendly, and gender-equity supporting policy. The USA, Ireland, the UK, and Canada are liberal welfare states. Australia and New Zealand are also frequently considered liberal states. Liberal states offer modest universal transfers and modest social-insurance plans. Benefits are provided primarily through means-tested assistance whereby these benefits are provided only to the least well-off.

This liberal approach has also been called a residualist approach to social welfare and service provision. This is a situation where responsibility for well-being falls largely to individuals. When the individual encounters difficulties, it is expected that families and, if necessary, community-based agencies will provide support. Not surprisingly, this approach has resulted in considerably higher poverty rates than where there is commitment to public service provision.

The conservative welfare states include Belgium, France, Germany, the Netherlands, and Switzerland. These states tie benefits to one's occupation and earnings, and tend to stratify citizens rather than promote equality. There is less of an attempt made to support families or women. The vast majority of benefits are earnings-related and contributory rather than universal entitlements as is the case with social democratic nations. Poverty rates of these nations typically fall midway between the social democratic and liberal states.

The Latin cluster consists of undeveloped, more family-oriented versions of the conservative welfare state and includes Greece, Italy, Portugal, and Spain. These nations tend to be less wealthy than the nations found in the other welfare state clusters.

Research has supported the creation of this general typology of welfare states. When cluster of indicators of government spending and organization and distribution of benefits from modern wealthy nations are subject to analyses, these three or four groupings usually emerge.

Research involving Canada, however, is unambiguous. While no less than 12 welfare state typologies are described by Bambra (2007), in six of the seven typologies that include Canada it is found in the group similar to the so-called liberal welfare state: liberal, basic security, or liberal Anglo-Saxon, the exception being for the provision of health care in which Canada is grouped within the conservative cluster.

Further evidence exists that Canada is clearly a liberal welfare state. Even an apparent Canadian conservative outlier as Alberta (more liberal) shows a greater similarity to other Canadian provinces and Canada as a whole—and other liberal states—than it does to the extreme liberal outlier, the USA (Bernard and Saint-Arnaud, 2004). And apparent progressive outlier Quebec shows more similarity to other Canadian provinces and to Canada as a whole—and other liberal states—than it shows to social democratic states such as Norway and Sweden.

An issue of related importance to the nature of the welfare state is its relation to gender equity. This is especially important considering the relationship of gender to poverty in Canada. Bambra (2004) examined the relationship between welfare state type and the extent to which a society engaged in a process of defamilization by which responsibilities related to the family were not left to women but were taken on by the state. She found that there was good correspondence between these two concepts and this was especially the case for the social democratic (high in defamilization) and liberal nations (lower in defamilization).

Welfare States and Population Health Profiles

Navarro and Shi (2002) drew upon Esping-Andersen's insights to identify nations governed predominantly from 1945–1980 by social democratic (Sweden, Finland, Norway, Denmark, and Austria), Christian democratic (Belgium, Netherlands, Germany, France, Italy, Switzerland), or Anglo-Saxon liberal political parties (Canada, Ireland, UK, US). They then compared these nations on a range of political, economic, and population health indicators.

The social democratic regimes presented higher levels of union density—that is, a greater proportion of workers belonged to organized labour unions. Social democratic regimes also had higher levels of social security and public employment expenditures. Between 1960 and 1990, these regimes had the highest public health care expenditures, and the most extensive health care coverage of citizens. These nations implemented full employment strategies, attained high rates of female employment, and showed the lowest levels of income inequality and the lowest poverty rates. Social democratic nations also had the lowest percentage of national income derived from capital investment and the largest from wages—indicating less wealth accumulation by those already wealthy. On a key indicator of population health—infant mortality—these countries had the lowest rates from 1960 to 1996.

The Christian democratic regimes were second to the social democratic regimes in public health care expenditures. These countries had lower public health care coverage of citizens, but levels higher than the liberal regimes. A smaller proportion of the working-age population was employed by governments and a lower proportion of women were employed compared to the social democratic regimes. Christian democratic countries had high income inequalities compared to social democratic countries. This is due to more favourable treatment of wealth and investments and the subsequent lower redistributive effect of the state.

Anglo-Saxon liberal political economies had the lowest health care expenditures and the lowest coverage by public medical care. They had greater incidence of low-wage earnings, higher income inequalities, and the highest poverty rates. These economies derived the greatest proportion of income from capital investment rather than wages. These liberal countries have the lowest improvement rates in infant mortality rates from 1960 to 1996.

Coburn (2010) recently reported an analysis that considered ratings and relative rankings of various welfare states and changes over time on this important indicator of population health—infant mortality. Liberal welfare states have higher infant mortality rates than social democratic nations and the relative gap between these nations is growing. More importantly, these changes show that Canada is falling in relative rank among a set of comparison nations.

Navarro and colleagues (2004) examined how the political orientation of governments operates through labour market and welfare policies to influence social inequalities and health status among the citizens of 18 OECD nations between 1970 and 1996. Power relations (electoral behaviour and trade union solidarity) interact with civic behaviour (trust in government, corruption, and cynicism) to produce labour market and welfare state policies. When these policies ameliorate social and economic inequalities, population health as measured by infant mortality, cause-specific mortality, and life expectancy should improve.

Indeed, they found that characteristics found in well-developed welfare states—especially social democratic political regimes—were reliably associated with declines in infant mortality and increases in both male and female life expectancy over the study period. These declines in infant mortality and increases in life expectancy were related to increases in

- support for social democratic parties;
- the proportion of the population voting;
- public health care coverage;
- the proportion of the population employed;
- female labour force participation;
- income equality; and
- national wealth.

Many of these factors are related to welfare state regime. The findings are also consistent with what is known about public policy-making and how these decisions are related to the incidence of poverty, and income and wealth inequality, within nations. And these findings are especially relevant to Canada, which has seen growing income and wealth inequality, consistently high levels of poverty, and government withdrawal or retrenchment in a range of related public policy areas such as housing, employment benefits, and social assistance benefits.

Finally, Raphael (2010) carried out an extensive analysis of how 12 examples from the four welfare regime clusters fared on a number of poverty-related policy indicators, as well as health and quality-of-life outcomes. Table 12.4 shows how each of these exemplar nations is identified as falling into either the top (best-performing), middle, or bottom (worst-performing) one-third of the 21 OECD nations included in these analyses. Not surprisingly, the social democratic nations are typically among the top-performing one-third of OECD nations in provision of prerequisites of health-related indicators. And, also not surprisingly, the liberal nations—including Canada—are typically among the worst-performing one-third of OECD nations. What is interesting is the very good performance of the conservative nations on many of these indicators. Latin nations show a similar, though less extreme, portrait to that of the liberal nations.

Table 12.4: Placement of Selected Nations as Being among the Top (Best), Middle, and *Bottom* (Worst) One-Third of 21 OECD Nations on Poverty-Related Indicators, Classified as Being Either Social Democratic, Conservative, Liberal, or Latin Welfare States

Welfare State Type	Public Commitments through Expenditures as % of GDP			Key Poverty-Related Indicators				Health and Quality-of-Life Outcomes			
	Public Spending	Active Labour Policy	Early Childhood	Income Inequality	Family Poverty	Union Density	Collective Bargaining	Life Expectancy	Infant Mortality	Suicide Rates	Homicide Rates
Social Democratic											
Finland	Top	Top	Top	Top	Top	Top	Top	*Bottom*	Top	*Bottom*	*Bottom*
Norway	Middle	Middle	Top	Middle	Top	Top	Middle	Top	Top	Middle	Top
Sweden	Top	Top	Top	Top	Top	Top	Top	Top	Top	*Bottom*	Top
Conservative											
Belgium	Top	Top	Top	Top	Middle	Top	Top	Middle	Middle	N/A	*Bottom*
France	Top	Top	Top	Middle	Top	*Bottom*	Top	Top	Middle	*Bottom*	*Bottom*
Germany	Top	Top	*Bottom*	Middle	*Bottom*	*Bottom*	Middle	Middle	Middle	Middle	Top
Latin											
Greece	*Bottom*	*Bottom*	*Bottom*	*Bottom*	Middle	Middle	Top	*Bottom*	Middle	Top	Top
Italy	Middle	Middle	Middle	*Bottom*	*Bottom*	Top	Middle	Top	Top	Top	Middle
Spain	Middle	Middle	Middle	Middle	*Bottom*	*Bottom*	Middle	Top	Middle	Top	Middle
Liberal											
Australia	*Bottom*	*Bottom*	Middle	*Bottom*	Middle	*Bottom*	*Bottom*	Top	*Bottom*	Middle	Middle
Canada	*Bottom*	*Bottom*	*Bottom*	*Bottom*	*Bottom*	Middle	*Bottom*	Middle	*Bottom*	Middle	*Bottom*
UK	Middle	*Bottom*	Middle	*Bottom*	Middle	Middle	*Bottom*	*Bottom*	*Bottom*	Top	Middle

Source: Raphael, D. (2010). *The political economy of health promotion: Moving beyond rhetoric to analysis of public policy.* Toronto: York University School of Health Policy and Management.

Canada falls in the bottom one-third of nations in all of the indicators of public commitments to citizens, the bottom one-third in indicators of poverty and income inequality, and the bottom or middle in indicators of health and quality of life. The implications of Canada being a liberal welfare state are further examined in the remaining chapters of this volume.

Toward the Future

In Chapter 11, analyses of the political factors influencing governments to implement poverty-reducing policies were outlined. These include the presence of proportional representation, strong labour unions, and responsive governments. Support of social democratic political parties is important. In *Politics against Markets*, Esping-Andersen (1985) provides an analysis of the political forces that came together in Scandinavia to produce their unique welfare states. Social democratic governance came about through an alliance between industrial workers and farmers, convincing the middle class of the benefits to them of social democracy, and providing evidence of the improvements in living conditions associated with the development of a responsive welfare state. Does Canada's membership in the liberal welfare state camp preclude such governmental action against poverty?

While Canada is a liberal welfare state, members of the liberal welfare state club are not monolithic in policy approaches. Canada and the UK developed a universal health care system while the USA did not. The UK embarked upon a systematic policy initiative to address health inequalities, social exclusion, and child poverty while Canada has not. Nations systematically shift their basket of public policies to become outliers within their welfare state group. Recent experiences in the UK provide some lessons.

The UK has a long-standing intellectual and academic concern with poverty and health. In 1980, the Black Report revealed that despite a generation of accessible health care, class-related health inequalities had not only been maintained but in many instances had widened (Black and Smith, 1992). The report appeared at the onset of the conservative Thatcher era, and its content and recommendations were ignored for two decades. Instead, numerous policies served to widen income and health inequalities.

The election of a Labour government in 1997 saw the ongoing academic and policy concern with health inequalities translated into a government-wide effort to address health inequalities through the development of public policy.

The Labour government commissioned an inquiry into inequalities in health. The commission considered a wide range of evidence and concluded that

> [t]he weight of scientific evidence supports a socioeconomic explanation of health inequalities. This traces the roots of ill health to such determinants as income, education and employment as well as to the material environment and lifestyle. (Acheson, 1998, p. iv)

The report offered recommendations across a wide range of health determinants: poverty, income, tax and benefits; education; employment; housing and environment; mobility, transport and pollution; nutrition and agriculture policy; mothers, children,

Box 12.2: Evidence Refutes Foes of "Big Government"

Countries with Largest Public Sectors Also Have Healthy Economies

When Canadians went to the polls last June, they chose, in policy terms, new spending by the federal government over shrinking government through more tax cuts. In so doing, they rejected arguments that higher public spending would inevitably undermine Canada's economic performance, or, conversely, that reducing the size of government by cutting taxes would boost the economy.

They made the right choice. Statistically, there is no correlation between economic performance and the size of government. And, to the extent that studies are marshalled in favour of smaller government, closer inspection usually shows that the data have been tortured to wring out a confession.

Canada has tax revenues (an indicator of size of government) of about 36% of GDP, a bit less than the average for the most advanced economies of the OECD (38%), and much smaller than the European countries (42%).

Eleven countries in the OECD are in the same income range as Canada (just under US$30,000 per capita), but have larger public sectors. Topping the list are Sweden and Denmark, the countries with the largest shares of taxes-to-GDP in the OECD (54.2% and 48.8%, respectively).

If "big government" led to weaker economic performance, the Scandinavian countries, which have much larger governments than Canada, should all be economic basket cases. But this is not the case. These countries have among the highest productivity and living standards in the world.

Also in the same income range as Canada are Japan and Australia, countries with shares of taxes-to-GDP closer to the low end (27.1% and 31.5%, respectively). Interestingly, the country with the lowest level of taxes to GDP, Mexico at 18.5%, was second lowest in terms of income. Luxembourg, with a very high average income of US$50,600, nonetheless had taxes that amounted to 41.7% of its GDP.

The same basic result holds for other measures of economic performance and other indicators of the size of government. In a detailed review of the evidence by U.S. economist Peter Lindert, he asks why European welfare states have not had the negative effect on growth that many economists assume it should. He finds that the actual experience of countries with large public sectors has been towards implementing pro-growth taxation and spending policies.

On the tax side, these governments have tended to tax capital lightly to avoid capital flight. They also tend to rely more on consumption taxes, particularly those for gas, alcohol, and tobacco. These taxes, while considered regressive, were introduced as part of a social bargain that the proceeds would fund beneficial social programs.

The flip side of taxation is public spending. On the spending side, welfare state countries have invested in public services, such as health care and child care, that have pro-growth impacts.

A lesson for Canada is that we should press forward with a national early childhood education and care program. Such a program makes good economic sense, both in terms of the labour market impacts for women, and the cognitive impacts for young children. University of Toronto economists Gordon Cleveland and Michael Krashinsky find a two-dollar return for each dollar invested in child care.

The enemies of "big government" fight their battle on ideological rather than economic grounds. Economically, the key questions seem to be not how much tax is taken as a percent of GDP, but what tax mix is used, and what is the money spent on. These considerations dwarf the simple idea that big government is bad for growth.

There is no economic reason why Canada could not expand its public sector by a significant margin. This would invigorate, not kill, the Canadian economy, and could greatly improve it if new expenditures went to pro-growth investments.

What is refreshing about this research is that it reinforces the idea that public policy is about making choices. We can choose to engage in good social policy without fear that the economic sky will come falling down on us.

Marc Lee is an economist in the CCPA's B.C. office, and is the author of *Size of Government and Economic Performance: What Does the Evidence Say?* which is available at www.policyalternatives.ca

Source: From Lee, M. (2004, November 5). Countries with largest public sectors also have healthy economies. *The CCPA Monitor*, p. 5.

and families; young people and adults of working age; older people; ethnicity; gender; and the National Health Service. The most important were: (a) all policies likely to have an impact on health should be evaluated in terms of their impact on health inequalities; (b) high priority should be given to the health of families with children; and (c) further steps should be taken to reduce income inequalities and improve the living standards of poor households.

The government responded quickly to these recommendations. Among the major policy initiatives was the document *Reducing Health Inequalities: An Action Report* (UK Department of Health, 1999). Goals were set for the elimination of health inequalities. The *2002 Spending Review Public Service Agreement*—a kind of business plan for the Department of Health—contained this goal: "By 2010 to reduce inequalities in health outcomes by 10% as measured by infant mortality and life expectancy at birth" (UK Government, 2002). These policy initiatives focused on (a) tackling poverty and low income, (b) improving educational and employment opportunities, (c) rebuilding local communities, and (d) supporting vulnerable individuals and families (Oliver and Nutbeam, 2003). To facilitate action, the government set up "cross-cutting spending reviews." These reviews, focused on health inequalities, were to be used by a number of departments to inform spending plans for 2003–2006.

A 2003 evaluation concluded that significant progress had been made in tackling health inequalities (Exworthy, Stuart, Blane, and Marmot, 2003). Evidence concerning health inequalities had been gathered, health inequalities had been placed on the policy agenda, and a diverse range of activities had been developed. Indicators of outcomes and policy implementation were emerging, though impacts upon health status were not yet apparent. The authors concluded that "[m]any challenges remain but the prospects for tackling inequalities are good" (p. 52). Unfortunately, as Bryant, Raphael, Schrecker, and Labonte (in press) nevertheless point out:

> [r]ecent UK policies under New Labour gave some cause for optimism, including the commissioning of a national follow-up study to the WHO Commission on Social Determinants of Health which contained detailed policy analyses and advice. The election of a coalition Conservative/Liberal Democratic government in 2010, however, corresponded with a deep public deficit, partly a consequence of the global financial crisis and subsequent banking bailouts and counter-cyclical stimulus spending. This has been seized upon by the new government as a basis for advising cuts in most departments of between 25% and 40% and increased marketization of its National Health System, the financial and health burdens of which will be borne disproportionately by women. (p. 1)

Conclusions

Clearly then, Canada's high poverty rates are part of a general approach to resource and social provision to its citizens. Despite Canadians' beliefs about the generosity of Canada's welfare state, it is actually quite undeveloped as compared to most other wealthy developed nations. In just about every area of social welfare and resource and benefit provision, Canada compares poorly to other nations.

In addition, Canada's ratings on a variety of health indicators is in the mid-range and there is evidence that Canada's standings may be slipping in comparison to other wealthy developed nations. Certainly, evidence would indicate that the continuing existence of high levels of poverty is a distinct threat to the future health and quality of life of Canadians.

What are the specific forces that determine the trajectory that a nation takes in its establishment of a welfare state? Esping-Andersen (1999) argues that unique historical and cultural forces set a nation on a general path. For the Nordic nations, the advanced welfare state developed as a result of alliances between workers and farmers, supported by the presence of electoral democracy that applied proportional representation (Esping-Andersen, 1985). In Canada, such an alliance was associated with the development of Medicare and other progressive policies in Saskatchewan. The success of such policies in Saskatchewan saw them extending across Canada. The lack of such political alliances and proportional representation in Canada are responsible in part for Canada's relatively weak welfare state. In addition, Canada's welfare state appears to be under even further threat. These threats and the means of responding to them constitute the contents of the final chapter of this volume.

Critical Thinking Questions

1. How aware do you think Canadians are of Canada's mediocre standings in health status and indicators of the social determinants of health in comparison with other wealthy developed nations? How could this be changed?
2. Should the Canadian approach to provisions of citizen benefits and supports be reoriented to be more like those of European nations? What arguments could be used to support this? What arguments could be used to oppose this shift?
3. What public policies would need to be changed to improve the economic security of Canadians, thereby improving their health and quality of life?
4. What is the likelihood of Canada adopting some of the strategies that were used in the UK to respond to increasing income and wealth inequalities?
5. What are some of the barriers to having Canadians become aware of the importance of public policy in addressing economic and social security as determinants of health and quality of life?

Recommended Readings

Einhorn, E. S., and Logue, J. (2003). *Modern welfare states: Scandinavian politics and policy in the global age.* Westport, CN: Praeger.

>The authors analyze the political, economic, and social challenges facing five small affluent and advanced industrial democracies in Scandinavia: those of Denmark, Finland, Iceland, Norway, and Sweden. This volume emphasizes how global and European developments have affected democratic policy-making.

Esping-Andersen, G. (1990). *The three worlds of welfare capitalism.* Princeton, NJ: Princeton University Press.

Esping-Andersen, G. (1999). *Social foundations of postindustrial economies.* Toronto: Oxford University Press.

Esping-Andersen, G. (2009). *The unfinished revolution: Welfare state adaptation to women's new roles.* Cambridge, UK: Polity Press.

>These three books provide a typology of Western welfare states. This typology considers a range of social polices that are linked with variations in the historical development of Western countries. The author describes how profound differences that exist among liberal (e.g., USA, Canada, UK), conservative (e.g., Germany, France, Italy), and social democratic (e.g. Sweden, Norway, Denmark) political economies translate into widely differing lived experiences among citizens of these nations.

Innocenti Research Centre. (2000). *A league table of child poverty in rich nations.* Florence: Innocenti Research Centre.

Innocenti Research Centre. (2005). *Child poverty in rich nations* (Report Card No. 5). Florence: Innocenti Research Centre.

>These two volumes provide insights as to why some nations have very high child poverty rates and others do not. Much of this has to do with public policies that support citizens and families through the provision of supports and benefits.

Navarro, V. (Ed.). (2002). *The political economy of social inequalities: Consequences for health and quality of life.* Amityville, NY: Baywood Press.

Navarro, V. (Ed.). (2007). *Neoliberalism, globalization, and inequalities: Consequences for health and quality of life.* Amityville, NY: Baywood Press.

Navarro, V., and Muntaner, C. (Eds.). (2004). *Political and economic determinants of population health and well-being: Controversies and developments.* Amityville, NY: Baywood Press.

These three volumes are compilations of contributions to the areas of social epidemiology, health disparities, health economics, and health services research. The overarching theme is analysis of the political economy of health, its relations to public policy, and the politics that spawn these health policies.

Organisation for Economic Co-operation and Development. (2009). *Society at a glance: OECD social indicators.* Paris: OECD.

The OECD sees social indicators as a means of broadly assessing social trends, outcomes, and policies. This volume provides a number of indicators as well as crisp, incisive analyses of their meaning.

Relevant Websites

Innocenti Research Centre (IRC)—www.unicef-icdc.org/
    IRC works to strengthen the capacity of UNICEF and its co-operating institutions to respond to the evolving needs of children and to develop a new global ethic for children. It promotes the effective implementation of the Convention on the Rights of the Child in both developing and developed countries, thereby reaffirming the universality of children's rights and UNICEF's mandate.

Luxembourg Income Study—www.lisproject.org/publications/wpapers.htm
    The Luxembourg Income Study provides working papers on a range of issues related to income and other indicators. Data on Canada and other developed nations are used to produce papers that bear directly on poverty and how pubic policy shapes its incidence. All of the working papers can be downloaded from this site.

Organisation for Economic Co-operation and Development—www.oecd.org/home
    This site provides a wealth of reports, publications, and statistics about every aspect of society in wealthy developed states. Many of its contents are free or available electronically through your local university's library.

Glossary of Terms

Active labour policy refers to policies and programs developed by governments to create or maintain jobs. These range from sheltered workshops and other job creation measures for workers with disabilities to employment in regular public service and public works projects (i.e., building and highway construction). It also covers subsidies to private business to hire new employees or extend seasonal work throughout the year, apprenticeship training, on-the-job training and retraining, work-study programs to ease transition from school to employment, and job transition training for workers facing layoffs.

Family policy refers to policies and programs designed to provide a secure growing environment for children and to ensure that parents have the material and psychological supports for rearing children. Through these policies, usually involving various forms of financial support and a system of child care, society compensates citizens for some of the costs borne by families with children.

Gross domestic product (GDP) refers to the total market value of all goods and services produced in a country in a given year. It is equal to total consumer, investment, and government spending, plus the value of exports, minus the value of imports.

Social democracy is a political ideology that is in favour of stronger labour laws and a strong welfare state. In the modern era, social democrats attempt to reform capitalism to make it more equitable through the creation and maintenance of a strong welfare state. The best examples of where social democratic parties have held power and developed public policies is in Sweden, Norway, Denmark, and Finland. The Labour Party in the UK and the NDP in Canada are social democratic parties.

Welfare state typology describes clusters of wealthy developed nations grouped according to their approach to social provision. These are "liberal," "conservative," "Latin" and "social democratic." Esping-Andersen's typology (1990) and revisions of it offer a "reconceptualization and re-theorization of the basis of what can be considered important about the welfare state" (p. 2). The major difference between the regimes is whether the state (social democratic), the market (liberal), or the family (conservative and Latin) is expected to provide for the welfare needs of its citizens.

References

Acheson, D. (1998). *Independent inquiry into inequalities in health.* London: Stationary Office.

Bambra, C. (2004). The worlds of welfare: Illusory and gender blind? *Social Policy and Society,* 3(3), 201–211.

Bernard, P., and Saint-Arnaud, S. (2004). *More of the same: The position of the four largest Canadian provinces in the world of welfare regimes.* Ottawa: Canadian Policy Research Networks.

Black, D., and Smith, C. (1992). The Black Report. In P. Townsend, N. Davidson, and M. Whitehead (Eds.), *Inequalities in health: The Black Report and the health divide* (pp. 31–218). New York: Penguin.

Black, J., and Shillington, E. R. (2005). *Employment insurance: Research summary for the task force for modernizing income security for working age adults.* Toronto: Toronto City Summit Alliance.

Brady, D. (2009). *Rich democracies, poor people: How politics explains poverty.* New York: Oxford University Press.

Briggs, A. (1961). The welfare state in historical perspective. *European Journal of Sociology,* 2, 251–259.

Bryant, T., Raphael, D., Schrecker, T., and Labonte, R. (in press). Canada: A land of missed opportunities for addressing the social determinants of health. *Health Policy.*

Burstrom, B., Diderichsen, F., Ostlin, P., and Ostergren, P. O. (2002). Sweden. In J. Mackenbach and M. Bakker (Eds.), *Reducing inequalities in health: A European perspective* (pp. 274–283). London, UK: Routledge.

Coburn, D. (2010). Health and health care: A political economy perspective. In T. Bryant, D. Raphael, and M. Rioux (Eds.), *Staying alive: Critical perspectives on health, illness, and health care* (2nd ed., pp. 65–92). Toronto: Canadian Scholars' Press Inc.

Doherty, G., and Friendly, M. (2004). *OECD thematic review of early childhood education and care.* Ottawa: Government of Canada.

Esping-Andersen, G. (1985). *Politics against markets: The social democratic road to power.* Princeton, NJ: Princeton University Press.

Esping-Andersen, G. (1990). *The three worlds of welfare capitalism.* Princeton, NJ: Princeton University Press.

Esping-Andersen, G. (1999). *Social foundations of postindustrial economies.* New York: Oxford University Press.

Esping-Andersen, G. (2009). *The unfinished revolution: Welfare state adaptation to women's new roles.* Cambridge, UK: Polity Press.

Exworthy, M., Stuart, M., Blane, D., and Marmot, M. (2003). *Tackling health inequalities since the Acheson Inquiry.* Bristol, UK: The Policy Press.

Friendly, M. (2009). Early childhood education and care. In D. Raphael (Ed.), *Social determinants of health: Canadian perspectives* (2nd ed., pp. 128–142). Toronto: Canadian Scholars' Press Inc.

Hulchanski, D. (2003). *Housing policy for tomorrow's cities.* Ottawa: Canadian Policy Research Networks.

Innocenti Research Centre. (2000). *A league table of child poverty in rich nations.* Florence: Innocenti Research Centre.

Innocenti Research Centre. (2001a). *A league table of child deaths by injury in rich nations.* Florence: Innocenti Research Centre.

Innocenti Research Centre. (2001b). *A league table of teenage births in rich nations.* Florence: Innocenti Research Centre.

Innocenti Research Centre. (2003). *A league table of child maltreatment deaths in rich nations.* Florence: Innocenti Research Centre.

Jackson, A. (2009). The unhealthy Canadian workplace. In D. Raphael (Ed.), *Social determinants of health: Canadian perspectives* (2nd ed., pp. 99–113). Toronto: Canadian Scholars' Press Inc.

Jackson, A. (2010). *Work and labour in Canada: Critical issues* (2nd ed.). Toronto: Canadian Scholars' Press Inc.

National Council of Welfare. (2004). *Poverty profile 2001.* Ottawa: National Council of Welfare.

Navarro, V., Borrell, C., Benach, J., Muntaner, C., Quiroga, A., Rodrigues-Sanz, M., ... Pasarin, M. I. (2004). The importance of the political and the social in explaining mortality differentials among the countries of the OECD, 1950–1998. In V. Navarro (Ed.), *The political and social contexts of health* (pp. 11–86). Amityville, NY: Baywood Press.

Navarro, V., and Shi, L. (2002). The political context of social inequalities and health. In V. Navarro (Ed.), *The political economy of social inequalities: Consequences for health and quality of life* (pp. 403–418). Amityville, NY: Baywood.

Oliver, A., and Nutbeam, D. (2003). Addressing health inequalities in the United Kingdom: A case study. *Journal of Public Health Medicine, 25*(4), 281–287.

Organisation for Economic Co-operation and Development. (1998). *The battle against exclusion: Social assistance in Australia, Finland, Sweden, and the United Kingdom.* Paris: OECD.

Organisation for Economic Co-operation and Development. (1999). *The battle against exclusion: Social assistance in Canada and Switzerland.* Paris: OECD.

Organisation for Economic Co-operation and Development. (2003). *Transforming disability into ability: Policies to promote work and income security for people with disabilities.* Paris: OECD.

Organisation for Economic Co-operation and Development. (2005). *Pensions at a glance.* Paris: OECD.

Organisation for Economic Co-operation and Development. (2008). *Growing unequal: Income distribution and poverty in OECD nations.* Paris: OECD.

Organisation for Economic Co-operation and Development. (2009a). *Economic policy reforms: Going for growth.* Paris: OECD.

Organisation for Economic Co-operation and Development. (2009b). *Society at a glance, OECD social indicators.* Paris: OECD.

Organisation for Economic Co-operation and Development. (2010). *Social expenditure: Aggregated data.* OECD Social Expenditure Statistics (database). doi: 10.1787/data-00166-en

Raphael, D. (2010). *The political economy of health promotion: Moving beyond rhetoric to analysis of public policy.* Toronto: York University School of Health Policy and Management.

Raphael, D., and Bryant, T. (2010). The political economy of public health: Public health concerns in Canada, the US, UK, Norway, and Sweden. In T. Bryant, D. Raphael, and M. Rioux (Eds.), *Staying alive: Critical perspectives on health, illness, and health care* (2nd ed., pp. 395–434). Toronto: Canadian Scholars' Press Inc.

Smeeding, T. (2005). *Poor people in rich nations: The United States in comparative perspective.* Luxembourg Income Study (Working Paper No. 405). Syracuse, NY: Syracuse University.

Teeple, G. (2000). *Globalization and the decline of social reform: Into the twenty-first century.* Aurora, ON: Garamond Press.

UK Department of Health. (1999, July). *Reducing health inequalities: An action report.* Retrieved October 2006 from www.doh.gov.uk/pub/docs/doh/inequalities.pdf

UK Government. (2002). *SR 2002: Public service agreements.* London, UK: The Treasury Department.

Chapter Thirteen

Anti-poverty Strategies and Programs

The rich will do everything for the poor but get off their backs.—Karl Marx

Learning Objectives

At the conclusion of this chapter, the reader will be able to:

- explain the differences between incremental anti-poverty strategies and programs that aim to bring individuals and families above the poverty line versus structural approaches that aim to create a more equitable distribution of economic and other resources across the population;
- describe the main features of federal and provincial anti-poverty reports, strategies, and programs;
- identify the shortcomings of these anti-poverty strategies and programs;
- identify some specific public policies that would reduce the incidence of poverty in Canada, thereby improving Canadians' health and quality of life; and
- appreciate the need for broader approaches that address the inequalities in power and influence in Canadian society that create poverty.

Introduction

There is little doubt that the issue of poverty has achieved a higher profile in public policy discussions in Canada than has previously been the case. The federal government has programs that serve to reduce the incidence of poverty, and six provinces have initiated anti-poverty strategies. Committees of the Canadian Senate and House of Commons have each produced major reports on means of reducing poverty. Evaluations of the poverty-reducing effects of these federal and provincial activities are becoming available, and there is evidence that they have served to reduce the number of Canadians who would otherwise be living in poverty.

Many of these strategies and programs, however, have been focused on reducing poverty among families with children by providing them with benefits that bring them up to or above the poverty line. The very high poverty rates seen among unattached adults have for the most part been neglected. In addition, there is evidence that, while there have been poverty-reducing effects of these strategies and programs, they have been rather modest. Even before the onset of the 2008 recession, the incidence of poverty continued to be much higher in Canada than in most other wealthy developed nations. These can only have worsened as a result of the 2008 recession and its after-effects.

These anti-poverty strategies and programs have modest poverty-reducing effects because they fail to address the sources of the unequal distribution of resources. These broader issues are intricately related to existing inequalities in influence and power associated with Canada being a liberal welfare state. In a nation where the economic marketplace serves to distribute economic resources with rather little intervention from governments, high poverty rates continue to exist since these inequalities in power and influence persist. There is less inequality in power and influence—and lower poverty rates—in nations where governments take a greater role in managing the economic marketplace. This is not to suggest that anti-poverty strategies and programs are not of value, but rather to argue for the importance of identifying additional means by which poverty rates can be reduced in Canada.

In this chapter, federal, provincial, and some community and municipal anti-poverty strategies and programs are reviewed. The Canadian Senate and House of Commons poverty reports are described. Their components are analyzed and evidence considered as to their assumptions regarding the causes of, and means of reducing, poverty among Canadians. Where possible, evidence of their effectiveness is also considered. Analysis of these anti-poverty measures is grounded in the premise that poverty is a result of inequalities in economic and political power and societal discourses that justify these inequalities. The likelihood of these anti-poverty strategies and programs achieving their goals in the absence of significant structural changes in the operation of the economic and political systems is discussed.

Components of an Anti-poverty Policy

Torjman (2008) acknowledges the upsurge in poverty-related talk among governments. She states that this is good news, but also tells us the bad news: evidence indicates that poverty rates continue to be stubbornly high, and income and wealth inequalities are increasing. Torjman outlines the poverty reduction agenda as involving both *safety net* features that ameliorate the impacts of poverty and *springboard* components that create opportunities for success over time. She then goes on to identify the measures that would constitute the core of a comprehensive poverty reduction strategy (see Box 13.1).

It should not be surprising that many of these core components are areas where Canada has been shown to fall behind other wealthy developed nations. As examples, benefits provided in Canada through employment replacement, social assistance, and spending on employment training and early child development lags well behind amounts provided by other wealthy developed nations (see Chapter 12).

Box 13.1: Core Components of a Comprehensive Poverty Reduction Strategy

- affordable housing which involves the creation of new units, property retrofit and/or rent supplementation
- early childhood development initiatives, including sufficient affordable high-quality child care
- improved high school completion rates and literacy proficiency
- demand-driven customized training that engages the private sector, training institutions and employment programs, and the removal of employment barriers, particularly for foreign-trained workers
- improved minimum wages and enhanced supplementation of low earnings through the federal Working Income Tax Benefit and provincial earnings supplements, and of income through federal and provincial/territorial child benefits
- appropriate replacement of employment earnings through a restored and improved unemployment insurance system
- adequate income and appropriate supports for persons with disabilities
- assistance with the creation of assets for low- and modest-income households and support for the social economy
- strong social infrastructure in the form of community spaces and associated recreation and cultural programs
- place-based initiatives that fashion integrated and effective responses to tackling poverty through creative combinations of resources and approaches

Source: Torjman, S. (2008). *Poverty policy* (pp. 2–3). Ottawa: Caledon Institute.

The Federal Role in Poverty Reduction

While there is no systematic federal initiative that explicitly concerns itself with reducing poverty, there are a variety of programs that effectively serve to reduce poverty rates among Canadians. These include child and family benefits, benefits for seniors, employment benefits, and a set of other measures. Hay (2009) provides a summary of these benefits and argues that these programs serve to reduce the poverty rate among various groups in Canada such that if these programs did not exist, Canada's high poverty rates would be even higher than they are at present.

Drawing upon Boychuk (2004), Hay presents four "policy logics" that explain Canadian governmental provision of social welfare:

- *Universal social provision* for the entire population (e.g., universal programs such as health care, pensions, education);

- *Social insurance* against risk to encourage labour market attachment (e.g., workers' compensation, employment insurance, contributory pensions);
- *Social inclusion* through the establishment of social minimums to mitigate the effects of marginalization (e.g., refundable tax credits, social assistance, social housing);
- *Social cohesion* by fostering social integration in communities, emphasizing "place-based" solutions (e.g., community development programs, programs for "at-risk" groups such as Aboriginal people and immigrants, industrial adjustment programs).

Again, these areas are those in which Canada lags behind other wealthy developed nations. Similar to Torjman (2008), Boychuk distinguishes between *social amelioration* policies that are concerned with the short term and address immediate deficiencies and *social investment* policies of a longer term. These latter policies are concerned with shifting the source of welfare from governmental ameliorative approaches to broader societal institutions, including the employment marketplace.

Examples of the short-term ameliorative approach are unemployment insurance and social assistance. Longer-term investment examples are child benefits and active labour policies that include employment training. It should be apparent—based on the material presented in the previous chapters—that Canada lags in its provision of both ameliorative and investment responses. Hay (2009) provides an overview of these approaches in *Poverty Reduction Policies and Programs in Canada*, which is summarized below.

Child and Family Benefits
The federal government's Canada Child Tax Benefit (CCTB) is a monthly payment made available to qualifying families with children less than 18 years of age. Related to this are the National Child Benefit Supplement (NCBS) and the Child Disability Benefit (CDB), which can be added to the CCTB (Canada Revenue Agency, 2010a).

The actual amount of the CCTB is based upon amounts calculated from income tax returns. For the period from July 2010 to June 2011, the full benefit is available for families whose net income is less than $40,970 in a year and amounts to $1,347 ($112.33 per month) for each of the first two children under 18. The third and each additional child receives a supplement of $94 ($7.83 a month). Once the $40,970 income threshold is reached, benefits are reduced.

The NCBS is available to families whose income is less than $23,855 a year and amounts to $2,088 a year ($174.00 per month) for families with one child, and $1,848 a year for a second child. The benefit for each additional child is $1,758. Benefits begin to be reduced when the $23,855 threshold is reached and are not available once household income reaches $40,726.

The federal government also provides $100 per month to families for each child under the age of six years in what it calls the Universal Child Care Benefit (UCCB). The UCCB, unlike the other child benefits, is treated as taxable income. Finally, there is a GST/HST Credit, which is paid to eligible low-income individuals. Hay points out that in Ontario, a family of two adults and two children with a net income of $41,200 would receive an annual credit of $330. If the family's net income was $26,200, they would receive an annual benefit of $725.

Hay notes that there is some evidence that these benefits and tax credits may have reduced the incidence of family poverty in Canada by about 5–10%. Paterson, Levasseur, and Teplova (2004) state that the "National Child Benefit can be credited with modest decreases in child poverty, [but] the benefit itself is inadequate to reduce child poverty in Canada" (p. 134).

Benefits for Seniors

Hay (2009) points out that, according to the federal government, Canada's "retirement income system" consists of three components: (a) Old Age Security; (b) Canada Pension Plan; and (c) private pensions and savings. Old Age Security (OAS) is a universal plan and itself consists of three parts, those being the OAS monthly pension, the Guaranteed Income Supplement (GIS) for low-income retirees, and an Allowance for spouses of low-income retirees who are 60–64 years of age. These benefits are not automatically provided but must be applied for. The OAS payments are taxable, but the others are not.

The maximum OAS monthly payment is $6,290 a year or $524.23 a month (Service Canada, 2011a). These amounts begin to be reduced once net income hits $67,668 a year and benefits disappear once net income hits $109,607. The GIS is available to families whose income is below $38,112 a year, and the average GIS payment is $370–$450 monthly. The Allowance is available when retirees are 60–64 years of age and their spouse's income is below $29,376 annually. The average Allowance payment is about $390 a month.

The Canada Pension Plan (CPP) is available for those who through employment have paid into the plan. Current benefits are taxable with an annual maximum of $11,520 annually or $960 a month (Service Canada, 2011b). The average benefit is $6,054 a year or $504.50 monthly. Canadians can also contribute to personal Registered Retirement Savings Plans or employer-sponsored Registered Pension Plans. Contributions are deductible from income earned for tax purposes and are sheltered from taxes until they are withdrawn from the plan.

Hay notes that Osberg (2001) has called these programs a "major success story" as they have reduced poverty among older Canadians by a factor of 10 (from about 60% to less than 6% in the early 1990s). Even now, the poverty rate among seniors is very low at about 6%.

Employment Benefits

Commonly termed unemployment benefits in other nations, employment benefits are provided to people who have been working and have become unemployed. Eligibility requirements have become increasingly stringent over the past decade, such that only about half of Canadians who are unemployed now receive these benefits. During the late 1980s, this figure was over 80%.

Canadians are eligible to receive these benefits only if they have lost their jobs involuntarily. Being dismissed for cause or voluntarily leaving your job makes one ineligible for benefits. Hours of required work differ from area to area. Where the unemployment rate is over 13%, one has to have accrued a minimum of about 12 weeks of full-time employment or 420 hours to be eligible. Most have to have worked closer to 20 weeks or 700 hours. If one is working for the first time ever or only in the last two years, 26 weeks or 910 hours of work are needed to qualify.

After a seven-day waiting period and an additional two-week delay in receiving benefits, the maximum—and subject to taxes—benefit is $435 a week for up to 45 weeks, which is calculated as 55% of a maximum of $41,100. Hay points out that an unemployed worker can receive about $1,700 a month for just over 10 months, which is just about at the poverty line for a person in a large Canadian city.

Other programs
Finally, a Working Income Tax Benefit (WITB) provides up to $931 dollars to an individual and $1,690 per annum to families who are low-income earners (Canada Revenue Agency, 2010b). Individuals or families must have earned $3,000, and the benefit is calculated at 20% of earned income up to the maximum benefit level. Once a threshold of $9,500 for individuals and $14,500 for families is reached, the WITB benefits are reduced by 15%.

Provincial Anti-poverty Strategies

Numerous summaries and reviews of provincial anti-poverty strategies and programs are available. A summary overview document is provided by the National Collaborating Centre for Healthy Public Policy (Mendell, 2009). And the Tamarack Institute for Community Engagement (2011) maintains a website that provides an overview of activities and links to provincial documents and reports. These include the original documents outlining provincial anti-poverty strategies, as well as follow-up reports that detail the activities undertaken and attempt to determine their effectiveness. The following review of these provincial anti-poverty initiatives begins with Quebec and Newfoundland and Labrador, which were the first provinces to undertake such programs.

Quebec
Quebec was the first jurisdiction in North America to enshrine poverty reduction into a legislative act or law (Noel 2002). Bill 112, *An Act to Combat Poverty and Social Exclusion*, provides for (a) a national strategy to combat poverty and social exclusion; (b) the establishment of an Advisory Committee made up of various sectors; and (c) a monitoring agency, Observatoire de la Pauvreté et de l'Exclusion Sociale (Government of Quebec, 2002). Noel (2002) provides a history of the Act and describes how it was the result of the development of a broad social movement concerned with reducing "poverty and social exclusion." Noel notes that poverty was examined in light of Quebec's Charter of Rights and Freedoms, thereby bringing a human rights perspective to the reduction of poverty.

The main axes of the Act were: (a) preventing poverty and exclusion; (b) developing potential of individuals; (c) strengthening the social and economic social safety net; (d) promoting access to employment and increasing attractiveness of work; (e) promoting the improvement of society as a whole; and (f) ensuring consistent and coherent intervention at all levels (Mendell, 2009). Torjiman (2010) provides a summary of the initiatives that have been carried out as a result of the law, as does the Quebec government (see Box 13.2).

Government of Quebec reports are available on the initial and current stages of its anti-poverty strategy, its implementation, and identified effects. *Reconciling Freedom and Social Justice: A Challenge for the Future* is the action plan that was laid out by the government in 2004 (Government of Quebec, 2004). It provides a dizzying array of strategies and programs that involve raising the standard of living of social assistance and low-income earners, investments in affordable housing, increasing employment assistance, promoting work, reducing food insecurity, and improving access to medicines, among others.

The Fifth Year Progress Report (Government of Quebec, 2010a) provides an update on the measures taken from 2004 to 2010. It documents increases in the minimum wage, states that 870,000 Quebec households have taken advantage of a refundable tax credit for child assistance, and 514,000 households have benefited from the work premium that encourages low-income families to join the workforce.

It notes that the $1.041 billion invested in affordable housing has delivered 27,000 new affordable social and community housing units. Similar data are provided in relation to improvements in existing private housing, upgrades of public housing, adaptation of housing for people with disabilities, and programs to reduce homelessness. Details are also provided of how those aged 65 years and older now receive free medications, and 313,000 additional low-income people can now access free medications. Many other activities in early child development, food security, and education are described.

The report also provides evidence as to the effects of these strategies upon poverty rates. Using the Market Basket Measure (see Chapter 2), it states that Quebec's poverty rate of 12.7% in 2000 declined to 8.5% in 2007, a 33% reduction. However, it should be noted that Canada's overall poverty rate also declined, from 14.6% to 10.1%, during this same period. This 30% reduction was most likely a reflection of the positive economic times that are part of the ups and downs of the "business cycle."

The report argues that without the 2004 action plan, the Market Basket Measure poverty rate would have been 2 percentage points higher in 2005 and 1.5 percentage points higher in 2006. While these figures indicate that 147,000 more people would have been poor in 2005 and 119,000 more in 2006 without these anti-poverty strategies and programs, these are certainly modest effects for such detailed and varied anti-poverty activities. As noted in Chapter 3, Quebec's pre-tax LICO poverty rate in 2008 was 13.4% overall, 14.7% for children, and 43.8% for female-led lone-parent families, all figures that are well above the rates seen in many other wealthy developed nations.

Newfoundland and Labrador

Newfoundland and Labrador's approach to poverty reduction is found in Reducing Poverty: An Action Plan for Newfoundland and Labrador (2006). It is a sophisticated

Box 13.2: 2004–2010 Quebec Government Action Plan to Combat Poverty and Social Exclusion

The Government Action Plan to Combat Poverty and Social Exclusion brought together a slate of measures worth $4.5 billion over the past six years. These measures had a significant effect on the daily lives of low-income individuals and families. Deployment hinged on close collaboration by all the partners concerned by the fight against poverty and social exclusion.

The first action plan was primarily based on two principles:

- Employment is the leading solution in assuring the economic security and social inclusion of individuals.
- More protection must be granted to individuals with a severely limited capacity for employment.

Acknowledging the value of work through work incentives and assistance measures for low-income workers was the fundamental principle of the action plan. Consequently, a Work Premium to replace the Parental Wage Assistance Program was established for all low-income households as of January 2005. In April 2005, a participation premium was added to support the efforts of social-assistance recipients to enter the workforce. Between May 2004 and May 1, 2010, minimum wage increased from $7.45 to $9.50. The Child Assistance measure, which came into force in January 2005, improved family income, especially that of low-income families.

The action plan also included improvements to the Employment Assistance Program, particularly through the following measures: a baseline threshold for poverty; a personalized youth approach making it possible to provide better-adapted assistance that included coaching; and substantial investment in housing, including the construction of low-cost or affordable rental units.

Insofar as the battle against poverty and social exclusion is a society-wide challenge, the first Action Plan relied on the unity and involvement of local and regional communities through the Fonds québécois d'initiatives sociales, which fostered local action based on an integrated territorial approach and provided financial support for initiatives in the territories deemed priorities.

Lastly, given the importance of civil society's contribution in combating poverty and social exclusion in Québec, creation of the Comité consultatif de lutte contre la pauvreté et l'exclusion sociale, whose members hail from an array of civil society sectors, was among the government's important moves in terms of unity and cooperation at all levels.

This Action Plan, initially intended to cover the period from 2004 to 2009, was extended by a year to enable consultations aimed at laying the groundwork for a second action plan. The 2010–2015 Government Action Plan for Solidarity and Social Inclusion, entitled Québec's Combat Against Poverty, was made public in May 2010. It provides for total investments of nearly $7 billion over five years.

Source: Government of Quebec. (2011). *Fight against poverty and social exclusion*. Retrieved March 11, 2011 from www.mess.gouv.qc.ca/grands-dossiers/lutte-contre-la-pauvrete/plan_en.asp

analysis of poverty and its causes and effects, and notes that "comprehensive approach that includes economic development, as well as social and economic supports, and includes co-operation with key partners (e.g., the federal government, community-based groups) is necessary" (p. 2). The essential details of this approach are outlined by the Tamarack Institute in Box 13.3.

The five goals of the 2006–2010 period consisted of 20 activities classified into five areas: (a) improved access and coordination of services for those with low incomes; (b) a stronger social safety net; (c) improved earned incomes; (d) increase emphasis on early child development; and (e) a better educated population (Mendell, 2009). It proposed to act on issues of poverty through the Newfoundland and Labrador Seniors' Benefit, by reducing taxes for low-income individuals, and by providing a non-refundable tax credit for persons with disabilities. It describes an Income Support Program that provides drug

---

Box 13.3: Newfoundland and Labrador Poverty Reduction Plan

In 2005, the Government of Newfoundland and Labrador committed to pursuing a poverty reduction strategy, and launched the initiative in June, 2006. Their goal was that Newfoundland and Labrador would be the province with the least poverty in Canada by 2014.

The approach is seen as comprehensive, mindful of the special situations of aboriginal people and women in poverty, for example. The strategy connects poverty with many other issues, for example:

- Education
- Housing
- Employment
- Social and financial support
- Health
- Tax measures
- Rural/urban differences

The strategy involves many government departments and agencies and is overseen by about a dozen different ministries and ministers. Key principles include collaborating with community-based groups throughout the process, and a focus on long-term reduction of poverty. After research into best practices and a consultation to help design the action plan, the government started several initiatives in 2006, even before the strategy was ready.

Source: Tamarack Institute for Community Engagement. (2011). *Newfoundland and Labrador's poverty reduction strategy.* Retrieved March 11, 2011 from http://tamarackcommunity.ca/g3s61_VC_2010c.html

cards, medical transportation, vision care, and basic dental care for low-income individuals. It also outlines a medley of career, employment, and youth services programs designed to assist in promoting attachment to the labour force.

Increases to the minimum wage were applied and numerous housing programs that included a Rent Supplement Program and a Home Repair Program were instituted. Much of this took place in consultations with numerous community agencies and groups over an extended period of time.

In 2009 the Government of Newfoundland and Labrador released its first progress report entitled *Empowering People, Engaging Community, and Enabling Success* (Government of Newfoundland and Labrador, 2009). It describes progress made toward meeting the five goals outlined in the 2006 strategy paper, as well as detailing governmental activities and expenditures in support of these activities. For example, for the first goal, that of "improved access and coordination of services for those with low incomes," it reports on the establishment of a Poverty Reduction Division to oversee that strategy. The progress report lists initiatives from all across government that are furthering the aims of the anti-poverty strategy. The *Reducing Poverty* strategy has also assisted numerous community groups that aid low-income individuals. These include funding women's centres, the Canadian Tire Foundation for Families, and numerous community centres across the province.

In relation to the second goal of progress toward "a stronger social safety net," there has been increased funding to persons with disabilities, increased access to the Special Child Welfare Allowance Program, and increased funding to the Newfoundland and Labrador Association for Community Living. The report also considers progress toward achieving the other three goals.

Fifteen comprehensive progress indicators of whether the goals of reducing poverty are being met have been identified. These include *overall indicators*, such as Statistics Canada's after-tax LICOs, after-tax low income measures, and the Newfoundland and Labrador Market Basket Measure. *Income indicators* include median family and personal disposable income measures (both after-tax), and *child and youth indicators* of healthy birth weights, educational achievement scores, and graduation rates. The report states that in 2003, 63,000 fell below the low income cut-off, but by 2007, that number had been reduced to 33,000. Depth of low income for single people declined from $5,500 in 2003 to $4,900 in 2007 and is *now the lowest in Canada* (emphasis in original). An indicator of persistent poverty (poverty over a six-year period) also declined from 3% of the population in 2002 to 2% in 2007. Finally, median after-tax income is seen as having risen significantly, as numbers receiving income support—or social assistance—declined from 36,700 families in 2003 to 31,322 in 2008.

Despite this progress, pre-tax LICO poverty rates in Newfoundland and Labrador were 11.5% overall, 14.8% for children, and 46.9% for female-led single-parent families in 2008. Certainly progress has been made in Newfoundland and Labrador, but, similar to Quebec, poverty rates remain comparatively high as compared to many other wealthy developed nations.

Ontario

Ontario's *Poverty Reduction Act* was passed in 2009. The title of Ontario's anti-poverty strategy, *Breaking the Cycle,* indicates "focus on breaking the cycle of intergenerational poverty by improving opportunities through education" (Government of Ontario, 2008). Consistent with this intergenerational emphasis, the strategy is primarily focused on families with children and sets a goal of reducing the child poverty rate by 25% in five years (see Box 13.4). The success of reaching this target will be assessed through use of Statistics Canada's low income measure.

The components of the strategy as outlined in the initial 2008 document include increases to the Ontario Child Benefit that would provide additional resources to 1.3 million children, tripling the number of Parenting and Family Literacy Centres, investing in an After School Program, and instituting all-day junior and senior kindergarten.

Box 13.4: Ontario's Poverty Reduction Plan

As an over-all goal, Ontario's strategy set a target to reduce child poverty by 25 per cent in five years. The strategy sets out directions and goals in three broad areas:

- Education and Early Learning
- Stronger Communities
- Smarter Government

Initiatives include increasing the number of child care spaces and parenting and literacy centres across the province, funding student nutrition and dental care programs, working with school boards so that all students can take part in activities regardless of income, and helping nonprofit groups have access to schools, so that the schools can become community hubs.

Affordable housing and a provincial rent bank, to help families stay in their homes, received renewed support. There were changes to several income support programs and the Ontario Child Benefit program. The poverty reduction strategy included a commitment to increase Ontario's minimum wage; the 2010 rate is $10.25, which is almost a 50% increase since 2003. The government also proposed a tax package that will exempt many low-income Ontarians from personal income tax.

The poverty reduction strategy also established a Social Assistance Review Advisory Council. Some immediate, short-term changes to social assistance programs have already been implemented. The council has a mandate for a longer-term transformation of Ontario's social assistance system that will increase people's opportunities for work and guarantee security for those who cannot work.

Source: Tamarack Institute. (2011). *Ontario's poverty reduction strategy.* Retrieved March 11, 2011 from http://tamarackcommunity.ca/g3s61_VC_2010f.html

There are also plans to invest in a Community Opportunities Fund and Youth Opportunities Strategy, and fund a Provincial Rent Bank Program.

The document also outlines a plethora of programs and services that are seen as assisting in the poverty-reduction plan. These include a Healthy Schools Strategy, a Student Nutrition Program, a Children in Need of [Dental] Treatment Program, a Mental Health and Addictions Strategy, an Ontario-focused Intervention Partnership, the establishment of Student Success Teams, a Ministry of Education Parent Engagement Office, and so on. In fact, there are over 60 programs listed in *Breaking the Cycle* that demonstrate the Government of Ontario's commitment to poverty reduction. These programs range in focus from providing additional housing to meeting the needs of persons with disabilities, women, Aboriginal people, and others.

The strategy document outlines an impressive set of indicators of progress. These include the low income measure, depth of poverty, school readiness using the Early Development Instrument, educational progress using scores on Ministry of Education tests and high-school graduation rates, birth weights, an Ontario Housing Measure, and a standard of living measure that applies the Ontario Deprivation Index.

A 2010 publication, *Breaking the Cycle: The Second Progress Report*, reviews the poverty reduction strategy, provides details of expenditures, and describes initial assessments of progress (Government of Ontario, 2010). For example, the Ontario Child Benefit now provides up to $1,100 per child to low-income families and now reaches over one million children. The minimum wage has been increased to $10.25 an hour and tax relief worth $12 billion has been provided to Ontarians.

Full-day kindergarten began in September 2010 for 35,000 children and half of children of this age will be receiving this by the fall of 2012 with full implementation by 2015. An investment of $63.5 million in 2010 was able to maintain 8,500 licensed child care spaces that would have been lost as a result of a funding gap left by the federal government's investment withdrawal. Similar information is provided for almost all of the 60-plus programs mentioned above.

Indicators of progress are provided. High-school graduation rates have increased, and scores on the Ministry achievement tests have shown improvement. Unfortunately, poverty rates using the low income measure increased from 2007 to 2008 with 15.2% of Ontario children now living in poverty. The depth of poverty also increased during this period, from 7.5 to 8.5%. (The pre-tax LICO figures provided in Chapter 3 show that, in 2008, 13.4% of Ontarians lived in poverty, 14.7% of children also did so, as did 43.8% of female lone-parent families.) The Ontario Housing Measure showed that the percentage of households with children that have incomes below 40% of the median household income, and spend more than 40% of their incomes on housing, increased from 4.6% in 2007 to 5.4% in 2008.

Nova Scotia

Nova Scotia's anti-poverty program is described in *Preventing Poverty, Promoting Prosperity* (Government of Nova Scotia, 2009), resulting from the passing of Bill 94, *Poverty-Reduction Working Group Act*, in 2007. The anti-poverty strategy identifies four goals: (a) enabling and rewarding work; (b) improving supports for those in need; (c) focusing on children; and (d) improving co-operation and collaboration. Its essential features are outlined in Box 13.5.

Manitoba and New Brunswick

Recent overviews of Manitoba and New Brunswick's anti-poverty strategies are available (Government of New Brunswick, 2008; Torjman, Battle, and Mendelson, 2009; Makhoul, 2010). Manitoba's strategy shows similarities to the other province's programs and include spending on housing, education, jobs, and income supports; raising minimum wages, child benefits, family resource centres, and supports to persons with disabilities. The New Brunswick strategy is just getting underway and is in the consultation stage.

Committee Reports on Poverty

In addition to provincial anti-poverty strategies, it is important to have a federal component to enhance and support these provincial initiatives (Battle and Torjman, 2009). Both Canadian Senate and House of Commons committees have provided comprehensive reports on poverty in Canada and the important role the federal government can play in reducing it. Highlights from these reports are provided in the following sections.

The Senate Report

The Subcommittee on Cities of the Standing Committee on Social Affairs, Science, and Technology released its 282-page report *In from the Margins: A Call to Action on Poverty, Housing, and Homelessness* in December 2009. It is a massive compendium of issues that is based on 35 hearings, five roundtables, and 20 site visits to agencies across Canada.

Box 13.5: Nova Scotia's Anti-poverty Strategy

The Preventing Poverty, Promoting Prosperity strategy has four goals:

1. Improving supports to those most in need
2. Enabling and rewarding work
3. Focusing on children and their families
4. Improved collaboration and cooperation

The first goal alleviates poverty, by improving access to necessities. The second reduces poverty by increasing opportunities to work and removing disincentives. The third goal hopes to prevent poverty by breaking the cycle of poverty through supports for children and families, while the fourth seeks to engage others by developing public awareness as well as coordination and accountability across government and society.

Source: Tamarack Institute. (2011). *Nova Scotia's poverty reduction strategy*. Retrieved March 11, 2011 from http://tamarackcommunity.ca/g3s61_VC_2010e.html

---

The Committee heard from 175 witnesses who constitute a virtual *Who's Who* in the anti-poverty policy and agency community.

The report contains no less than 72 recommendations, which include the federal government adopting a core social policy poverty-eradication goal, modifying all existing federal income security programs, raising minimum wages, reforming employment insurance, establishing a nation-wide initiative on early childhood learning, allocating health care resources to meet the needs of those living in poverty, increasing the National Child Benefit to $5,000, formulating a national housing strategy, and so on and so forth. An accompanying press release provides brief highlights of the full report (see Box 13.6).

The federal government's responded to the report by stating:

> *The Government is taking real action to address many of the issues raised in this report. The Government will take the Committee's recommendations under advisement as it continues to find ways to help Canadians succeed.*

This response was seen as a brush-off by anti-poverty groups: "The response really looked like something a summer student could have pulled together from the Internet, from the site of Human Resources and Skills Development," said Joe Gunn, executive director of Citizens for Public Justice. "We were looking forward to at least an acknowledgement that some of these recommendations would be useful" (Greenaway, 2010).

The House of Commons Report

The Standing Committee on Human Resources, Skills, and Social Development and the Status of Persons with Disabilities (2010) released its 299-page report, *Federal Poverty Reduction Plan: Working in Partnership towards Reducing Poverty in Canada,* in November of 2010. Like the Senate report, it is a massive compendium of poverty-related issues and problems. It heard testimony from over 200 authorities and workers in the anti-poverty, business, labour, and other sectors. It received a multitude of briefs. It contains 60 recommendations that again touch upon a very wide range of issues that include income supports, benefits, taxes, transportation, housing, education, and skills development. The aspects of the report that have been most positively received by the anti-poverty community can be seen in Box 13.7. The government response has been to state that it is already addressing poverty issues and has no plans to address its 58 recommendations (Thespec.com, 2011).

Community-Based Approaches

There are also community-based approaches to reducing poverty in Canada. The best example of this is the approach outlined by the Vibrant Communities initiative sponsored by the Tamarack Institute for Community Engagement. The initiative involves 12 cities across Canada and operates on the assumption that place-based activities can serve to reduce poverty. There is a tendency within Vibrant Communities to downplay the importance of influencing public policy at the provincial and federal levels and a reluctance to

Box 13.6: Senate Anti-poverty Report Press Release

Ottawa (December 8, 2009)—A major Senate report tabled today is declaring that Canada's system for lifting people out of poverty is substantially broken and must be overhauled.

"We began this study by focusing on the most vulnerable city-dwellers in the country, those whose lives are marginalized by poverty, housing challenges and homelessness," stated Senator Art Eggleton, Chair of the Standing Senate Committee on Social Affairs, Science and Technology's Subcommittee on Cities. "As our research evolved, so too did our frustration and concern as we repeatedly heard accounts of policies and programs only making living in poverty more manageable—which essentially entraps people."

The recommendations in the report, *In from the Margins: A Call to Action on Poverty, Housing, and Homelessness*, are the summation of a two-year cross-country study. Committee members heard testimony from more than 170 witnesses, including people living in poverty, several of them homeless, as well as universities, think tanks, provincial and local governments, and community organizations.

Based on the findings of this extensive study, the Committee's first and fundamental recommendation is that Canada and all provinces and territories adopt the goal of lifting people out of poverty. Included among the vast range of measures recommended by the Committee to realize this core goal are the coordination of a nationwide federal-provincial initiative on early childhood education; the development of a national housing and homelessness strategy; and the creation of a basic income floor for all Canadians who are severely disabled.

The Working Income Tax Benefit (WITB) is an existing government program that the report highlights as bearing real promise because it gives people the pure incentive to get a job. To strengthen the WITB's capacity to help Canada's poor, the report recommends that the federal government commit to a schedule of long-term planned increases to bring recipients to the Low Income Cut-off line—as opposed to managing in poverty.

"According to 2007 numbers from Statistics Canada, we spend $150 billion dollars each year in federal and provincial transfer payments to individuals, excluding education and health care costs. So how is it that there are still millions of Canadians weighed down by poverty?" asked Senator Hugh Segal, Deputy Chair of the Subcommittee. "The Committee's recommendations demonstrate the crucial difference between spending, and spending wisely. By breaking the cycle of poverty once and for all, we will be investing in human empowerment—which will drive the health and prosperity of our cities and yield benefits for all of us."

The report and more information about the Committee is available at: http://senate-senat.ca/cities-villes-e.asp

Source: Excerpted from *In From the Margins: A Call to Action on Poverty, Housing and Homelessness.* Accessed on line on March 11 2011 at www.parl.gc.ca/40/2/parlbus/commbus/senate/com-e/citi-e/subsite-dec09-e/Report¬_Home-e.htm

Box 13.7: Reactions to the House of Commons Poverty Report

Government Urged to Respond Favourably to Committee Recommendations

Dignity for All: The Campaign for a Poverty-Free Canada—a coalition of over 430 organizations from across the country—applauds the report from the Human Resources, Skills and Social Development and the Status of Persons with Disabilities Committee which calls for the federal government to immediately commit to a federal action plan to reduce poverty in Canada. The report, *Federal Poverty Reduction Plan: Working in Partnership towards Reducing Poverty in Canada*, is the result of an extensive three-year study on the federal role in addressing poverty.

Key components of a poverty reduction plan the committee recommends the federal government take action on include:

- Raising the Canada Child Tax Benefit and supplement to $5000 within 5 years;
- A long-term national housing and homelessness strategy;
- Measures to help the most vulnerable—a refundable Disability Tax Credit, easing EI qualifications; increasing adult literacy; increasing and indexing GIS for seniors, implementing an early learning and child care strategy; and
- Major help for Aboriginal People for housing, education and social services; including elimination of the two per cent cap on federal funding.

"Depending on the measure used between three to five million Canadians live in poverty. The situation is appalling," says Geraldine King, of the Gull Bay First Nation and President of Canada Without Poverty. "While it is particularly acute among Aboriginal Canadians and people with disabilities, they are not alone. Millions of people in Canada are trapped in low-paying jobs without benefits. Reducing, and eventually eliminating poverty, will require much more than job creation."

Citizens for Public Justice policy analyst and Dignity for All Coordinator, Karri Munn-Venn suggests that the HUMA report is noteworthy for its clarity on the need for a plan, and its focus on significant actions that can—and should—be taken immediately. "We are encouraged," she says, "not only by the content of the report, but by the collaborative approach of parliamentarians that defined much of the work that went into its completion. Now, the consensus among MPs involved in this study must be leveraged into immediate action."

The government has 120 days to table a formal response to this report.

"It is imperative that the government response be substantive. A 'non-response,' such as was issued to the excellent 2009 Senate report In from the Margins, is simply unacceptable," stresses Dennis Howlett, Coordinator of Make Poverty History. Howlett goes on to say, "A potential spring election makes it equally important that all of the parties provide a clear statement on how they intend to act on recommendations—particularly if they form the next government."

Source: Make Poverty History. (2010, November 18). *Dignity for All campaign applauds report calling for federal poverty reduction plan.* Retrieved March 11, 2011 from www.makepovertyhistory.ca/story/dignity-for-all-campaign-applauds-report-calling-for-federal-poverty-reduction-plan-government

put forward critical analyses of the economic and social forces that drive policy-making that creates poverty. Instead they urge and support local economic and social development initiatives related to job training and attracting businesses and developing local attractions. They are very optimistic about the prospects of community development and citizen-engagement activity leading to poverty reduction.

These community-based initiatives have certainly produced varied activities across Canada and much of it has been documented in *Creating Vibrant Communities* (Born, 2008) and in "Vibrant Communities" (Tamarack Institute, 2011). The Edmonton initiative, for example, is described as follows:

> *Vibrant Communities Edmonton centres its framework for change on the keystone of family economic success. We focus on three strategies: family economic support, workforce development and community investments, expressed through projects like the Job Bus, Make Tax Time Pay and partnerships with immigrant and newcomer communities related to workforce development.*
>
> *VCE's role is to be a catalyst for change by brokering multi-sectoral collaborations, sharing knowledge and learning, building on existing assets, advocating, and helping to create comprehensive thinking and action.*

And in Winnipeg, the focus of activity is as follows:

> *The Winnipeg Poverty Reduction Council is based on the understanding that no single group or organization can successfully address poverty on its own. Through a collaborative, community-wide, integrated, and cross-sectoral approach, the WPRC aims to support and enhance current initiatives to create "A City Where Everyone Belongs."*
>
> *WPRC focuses on eight areas: early childhood development; early education; post-secondary education; social infrastructure; asset building and wealth creation; affordable housing; disability income and quality of life benefits; and public education and engagement.*

These activities are extensive and the Tamarack Institute's Vibrant Communities activities are well funded (Tamarack Institute, 2011). Certainly these actions serve to raise public awareness of poverty and suggest local initiatives that can serve to reduce its incidence (Box 13.8).

Municipal Strategies

Cities in Canada have limited powers and must depend in most instances upon the largesse of the provincial and federal governments. In some instances, however, cities can act to provide affordable housing, child care, and free access to recreation facilities. Another approach is for cities to pass "living wage" or "fair wage" policies that ensure that city employees and workers employed under contracts with the city receive wages that keep them above the poverty line. One important instance of this is reported on in Box 13.9.

The question remains as to whether significant reductions in poverty rates in Canada can be accomplished without an explicit focus on shaping public policy—in the service

Box 13.8: Local Initiatives to Reduce Poverty

Vibrant Communities is a pan-Canadian, action-learning initiative that supports and explores promising local solutions for poverty-reduction. On this page you can learn more about our history and approach.

Our Mission
To create and grow a movement of diverse leaders and communities from across Canada who are committed to exploring, challenging and testing ways to unleash the potential of communities to substantially reduce poverty and ensure a good quality of life for all citizens.

Our Approach
Vibrant Communities is a community-driven effort to reduce poverty in Canada by creating partnerships that make use of our most valuable assets—people, organizations, businesses and governments.

It's a unique approach to poverty reduction that allows communities to learn from—and help—each other.

Vibrant Communities links communities across Canada, from British Columbia to Newfoundland and Labrador, in a collective effort to test the most effective ways to reduce poverty at the grassroots level.

We concentrate on four key approaches:

- Comprehensive local initiatives aimed at poverty reduction;
- Grassroots collaboration involving all sectors of the community in these initiatives;
- Identifying community assets and putting them to good use in poverty-reduction efforts;
- A commitment to learning, change and sharing our learning—whether they are the product of our successes or failures.

Vibrant Communities is supported by four project sponsors: The J.W. McConnell Family Foundation, the Caledon Institute of Social Policy, Human Resources and Social Development Canada and Tamarack—An Institute for Community Engagement.

Supports to Trail Builder Communities
Trail Builders are the living laboratories of Vibrant Communities—multisectoral collaborative initiatives in 12 communities across Canada where new ideas about poverty reduction are put to the test.

Once a Trail Builder proposal is approved, the community receives targeted funding support from the McConnell Family Foundation to augment funds already raised locally. Trail Builders also receive coaching, learning and evaluation supports from the Vibrant Communities national office.

As part of their commitment, Trail Builders establish measurable targets they expect to achieve during the life of their project.

Reports from 2002–2006

The experiences and learnings from the first four years of Vibrant Communities' work have been documented in the following reports:

- *In From the Field: Exploring the First Poverty Reduction Strategies Undertaken by Trail Builders in the Vibrant Communities Initiative.*
- *Understanding the Potential & Practice of Comprehensive, Multisectoral Efforts to Reduce Poverty: The Preliminary Experiences of the Vibrant Communities Trail Builders.*
- *Reflecting on Vibrant Communities: 2002–2006.*

A more comprehensive summary of Vibrant Communities can be found in *Creating Vibrant Communities*, a book written to celebrate and document the theory and practice of Vibrant Communities.

Source: Tamarack Institute for Community Engagement. (2011). *What is Vibrant Communities?* Retrieved March 11, 2011 from http://tamarackcommunity.ca/g2_WhatIsVC.html

of more equitable resource distribution—at the provincial and federal levels. This issue is discussed in the following section.

Possibilities and Shortcomings in Provincial and Local Anti-poverty Strategies

The most consistent aspect of provincial and local anti-poverty strategies is their focus on people who are living in poverty as opposed to the structural inequalities in power and influence that lead so many Canadians to live in poverty. For instance, there is usually an assumption—and this is especially the case in Ontario's approach—that the sources of poverty can be found in families—including intergenerational poverty—such that intervening to support low-income families with children offers the best means of reducing the incidence of poverty. There is some attempt to address very low minimum wages and social assistance benefits. However, these efforts are minimal, with increases barely keeping pace with general inflation and increasing housing costs.

Attention will be directed here to four issues especially relevant to these anti-poverty strategies. (This discussion will continue in the concluding chapter.) The first issue is the

---

Box 13.9: Municipal Initiatives to Reduce Poverty

Living Wage Law a Positive Step to Fight Poverty

A British Columbia city council adopted the first municipal living wage policy in Canada last night—a move that will hopefully become a standard for cities across the country.

The New Westminster City Council voted unanimously yesterday for a living wage bylaw based on a calculation of the hourly wage required to keep a family with two children and two working parents above the poverty line.

"This is a great example of the important role municipal governments can play in reducing poverty in their communities and across Canada," said Paul Moist, national president of the Canadian Union of Public Employees (CUPE).

New Westminster's living wage policy will apply to both full-time and part-time employees, and will apply to both direct staff and to contractors performing physical work on City properties.

The Hospital Employees Union (HEU), the health care services division of CUPE in BC, has led a living wage campaign in the province since 2007. The campaign calls on government and health authorities to ensure their private contractors pay a living wage.

To raise awareness in the Vancouver area, the union has partnered with the Metro Vancouver Living Wage for Families Campaign. The New Westminster decision is a great win for the coalition of community organizations.

"Raising the incomes of poor families creates stronger communities, both socially and economically," said Moist. "New Westminster has set a strong example for cities across the country."

Source: Canadian Union of Public Employees. (2010, April 28). *Living wage law a positive step to fight poverty.* Retrieved March 11, 2011 from http://cupe.ca/wages/living-wage-law-positive-step-fight

---

extent to which these strategies are meeting the recommendations offered by anti-poverty advocacy groups and workers. The second issue is their focus on families with children. The third issue is their emphasis on engaging people in the workforce as a primary means of reducing poverty. And the fourth issue is their generally reformist approach, which avoids discussion of modifying structural barriers to reducing poverty in Canada.

Gaps between Anti-poverty Strategies and Desired Actions

The gaps in provincial anti-poverty programs are best illustrated by their failure to reduce poverty rates to those seen in other wealthy developed nations. The increases to minimum wages and social assistance rates are minimal, such that any benefits are quickly eroded by inflation and specific increases in living costs associated with housing and transportation.

Anti-poverty groups may hesitate to criticize governments over these shortcomings as such criticism may threaten even the modest gains attained. The most recent recommendations from Campaign 2000 regarding what is needed to make Canada poverty-free are presented in Box 13.10 and demonstrate what governments would really need to do to reduce poverty yet are so unwilling to do so.

Box 13.10: Campaign 2000's Call for Remedial Action to Address Poverty

A Plan to Make Canada Poverty-Free

Campaign 2000, a network of 120 organizations in all regions of Canada, urges all federal parties to work together and in collaboration with provinces, territories, communities and First Nations, on a Plan to Make Canada Poverty-Free. Secured in legislation, such as Bill C-545, *An Act to Eliminate Poverty in Canada*, this plan will identify key roles for the federal, provincial and territorial governments and recognize the particularities of how Québec pursues social policy in the Canadian context. The plan must include a clear timetable, a transparent accountability structure that can demonstrate progress and a defined role for citizen participation, in particular low-income people.

What Is Needed in the Plan

- An enhanced child benefit for low-income families to a maximum of $5,400 ($2010) per child;
- A system of high-quality early childhood education and child care services that is affordable and available to all children (0–12 years);
- Restored and expanded eligibility for Employment Insurance;
- Increased federal work tax credits of $2,400 per year;
- A federal minimum wage of $11 per hour;
- A strategy for affordable housing, secured in legislation such as Bill C-304, An Act to ensure secure, adequate, accessible and affordable housing for Canadians, including substantial federal funding for social housing;
- Proactive strategies, including employment equity in the public and private sectors, to level the employment playing field for racialized communities and other historically disadvantaged groups;
- Appropriate poverty eradication targets, timetables and indicators for Aboriginal families, irrespective of where they live, developed in coordination with First Nations and urban Aboriginal communities.

Source: From Campaign 2000. (2010). *2010 report card on child and family poverty in Canada 1989–2010: Reduced poverty = Better health for all* (p. 12). Toronto: Campaign 2000.

In fact, in relation to what governments are doing, Torjman (2010) has noted that,

> [i]n fact, many community organizations, researchers and editorialists in Québec have chal-
> lenged the government's commitment to poverty reduction. Their critique even led to a boy-
> cott of a government-led consultation process by many organizations, which argued that the
> strategy's announcements and actions have often fallen short of its stated intent. (p. 1)

Critiques of governmental shortfalls in providing affordable housing and affordable
quality child care are available, as are analyses of the incremental rise in minimum wages
and social assistance benefits across Canada (Swift, Balmer, and Dineen, 2010). The latest recommendations for a poverty reduction strategy involve enshrining poverty reduction and housing provision in federal law. The likelihood of this happening is uncertain
(see Box 13.11).

Focus on Poverty among Children

Anti-poverty strategies and programs frequently focus on children within families. The
National Child Tax Benefit (NCB) is awarded on the basis of the presence of children.
Even this program has not failed to be viewed with suspicion by some anti-poverty
activists.

It has been noted that the program does not deal with the core problems that create poverty in Canada. Jean Swanson (2001) argues that the NCB serves to subsidize
employers who continue to fail to provide decent well-paying jobs. She asserts that its
underlying rationale is one of forcing people living in poverty to take on poor-quality
employment. In her words,

> The Child Benefit is a component of another policy we need to watch out for. The C.D. Howe
> Institute's Thomas Courchene, in Social Canada in the Millennium, suggested in 1994 that
> a good project for the next century would be for provinces to experiment with ending the
> minimum wage. This could be done, he said, if the government was supporting children
> with the Child Benefit and if workfare and trainfare policies were in place for all employ-
> able people, including single parents. In other words, the Child Benefit is part of a corporate
> strategy to justify ending the minimum wage.
>
> Will the Canada Child Tax Benefit make a dent in child poverty? I don't think so. In the
> minds of a lot of powerful people, really ending child poverty would "destroy the incentive" of
> the child's parents to work at low wages. The public stereotypes about lazy, drunk, single par-
> ents help justify a plan that really serves employers who want low-wage workers. The Child
> Benefit is the federal government's part of a network of policies that use the public's concern
> for poor children to force poor parents to flood a cheap labour market that doesn't have work
> for everyone who wants a job. (p. 114)

It has also been noted that the focus on child poverty neglects the very high rates
seen among unattached adults. In fact, an article in the *Hamilton Spectator* suggests that
single poor people have become the "undeserving poor."

Box 13.11: Enshrining Poverty Reduction in Federal Law

History in the Making: "An Act to Eliminate Poverty in Canada" Introduced in the House of Commons, June 16, 2010

On Wednesday, June 16, 2010, the Member of Parliament for Sault Ste. Marie, Tony Martin (NDP), seconded by the Member of Parliament for Chambly-Borduas, Yves Lessard (Bloc Québécois), rose in the House of Commons to introduce Bill C-545—"An Act to Eliminate Poverty in Canada." This private member's bill, if passed into law in its current form, would provide a foundation for federal engagement, leadership and accountability for eliminating poverty in Canada. Key provisions of the bill include the following:

1. Recognition of poverty as a "condition of a human being who does not have the resources, means, choices and power necessary to acquire and maintain economic self-reliance and to facilitate their integration into and participation in society";
2. Recognition of poverty as a human rights issue and anchoring the federal response to poverty in a human rights framework;
3. Imposing on the federal government "the obligation to eliminate poverty and promote social inclusion by establishing and implementing a strategy for poverty elimination in consultation with the provincial, territorial, municipal and Aboriginal governments and with civil society organizations";
4. Requiring the federal strategy to have short, medium and long term targets to eliminate poverty;
5. Establishing the "Office of the Poverty Elimination Commissioner," independent of government and to help hold the federal government to account for progress in addressing poverty; and
6. 6) Amend the *Canadian Human Rights Act* to include "social condition" as a prohibited ground of discrimination.

Bill C-545 aligns with the second goal of *Dignity for All: The Campaign for a Poverty-free Canada*, which calls for "a federal anti-poverty Act that ensures enduring federal commitment and accountability for results." Over the summer, it is expected that individuals and organizations behind the campaign and/or with related efforts will be encouraging all Members of Parliament to support the bill and ensure its passage into history-making law.

Canada Without Poverty and the CWP Advocacy Network congratulate Mr. Martin and Mr. Lessard for helping introduce Bill C-545 into the House. We hope all Members of Parliament and Senators will now work to ensure its passage into law.

Source: Rainer, R. (2010, June 16). *History in the making.* Retrieved March 11, 2011 from Canada Without Poverty website: www.cwp-csp.ca/Blog/history-in-the-making-an-act-to-eliminate-poverty-in-canada-introduced-in-the-house-of-commons-june-16-2010

However, there is still one group that is almost never heard from, even though they represent some of the highest numbers of people currently experiencing poverty in Hamilton: "unattached individuals," that is, adults who live on their own or with roommates. Instead, the focus is almost always on children or children and families.

In 2005, 26,277 unattached individuals in Hamilton were living in poverty. In fact, the rate of poverty for that population was 42 per cent, almost double the rate of child poverty for that same year.

But despite that reality, in Hamilton the aspiration became making this city "the best place to raise a child." The poverty reduction strategy put forward by the provincial government has focused on decreasing the poverty rate by 25 per cent for children; on its website we learn "tackling poverty means providing better opportunities for low-income families."

What if you're not living in what is defined as a family situation? What if you are one of the thousands of seniors living in poverty in Hamilton? The increases to the Ontario Child Benefit won't benefit you! Nor will the funding of student nutrition programs.

It is quite easy to get even the most cynical folks to cough up a few bucks for "poor kids" but talk about their parents or adults who don't have children and all of a sudden the wallet closes. Apparently, there are deserving and undeserving poor. (Pike, 2011, n.p.)

Emphasis on Engaging People in the Workforce

Most anti-poverty strategies and programs have a strong component of labour force engagement. The emphasis is on having low-income people gain paid employment. This is all well and good, but there is little recognition that Canada is among the nations with the highest proportion of low-paid workers among wealthy development nations. This approach represents a social inclusion discourse (see Chapter 1). Ruth Levitas (2005) noted that this approach has a narrow focus on paid work and does not ask why people not working are usually consigned to poverty. Most importantly, it obscures issues of inequality among paid workers and has little focus on women and their receipt of lower pay than men, thereby ignoring both gender and class issues.

The anti-poverty strategies do not address the reality that, in 2008, fully one-third of families living in poverty had at least one parent who worked full time throughout the year. The strategies also say nothing about the profound increases in temporary and other precarious forms of work in Canada, most of which do not provide benefits (Tremblay, 2009). The lack of benefits among those of low income makes the financial situation of many working families even more unstable and moves them closer to living in poverty.

Finally, the emphasis on employment as a means of leaving poverty provides little recognition of the precarious situation of unattached single adults. Unattached adult females and males constitute the largest numbers of Canadians living in poverty. In fact, as noted by Pine, above, these individuals have been described as the *undeserving poor* whose situations are clearly being neglected. It is evident that employment alone is not an effective means of avoiding living in poverty.

Limitations of the Reformist Approach to Poverty Reduction

The economic marketplace—and those classes and institutions that own and manage it—is the dominant institution in Canada's liberal political economy. Hence, it really cannot be expected that current governing authorities will raise and address structural issues responsible for Canada's high poverty rates. The issues this analysis considers include governmental provision of benefits and services to citizens, investments in social infrastructure, and the influence and strength of the labour movement and how this transfers into collective employment agreement coverage. It asks the question: *Who are the representatives of this dominant institution—the market—and what are their positions on governmental action to reduce the incidence of poverty?* Some of these issues are outlined in Box 13.12, which critiques the Ontario anti-poverty plan.

Box 13.12: Key Failings of Canadian Anti-poverty Strategies

What was missing? The list is too long to summarize here, but a few absences were glaring. First, the emphasis on child poverty left the whole issue of adult poverty on the sidelines, as if children can be pulled out of poor families and communities, and lifted out of poverty through child tax credits. The child focus turns attention away from the economic and political forces (read capitalism) that create enduring patterns of inequality within and between communities. Indeed, the rationales for poverty reduction presented are highly liberal: equality of opportunity for children to succeed on the one hand, and producing a high-end competitive workforce on the other.

The failure to confront structural causes could also be seen in its non-engagement with issues of race and gender. For instance, there was no response to the demands of the Colour of Poverty coalition for action on employment equity, anti-racism, public sector hiring diversity and an equitable and inclusive educational curriculum. Beyond a $200 enrichment of the child benefit (from $1100 to $1300/year), there was nothing to ensure liveable incomes, particularly for adults on social assistance or disability. Indeed, beyond a promise to undertake a year-long review of the social assistance system, there was no sign of a concerted plan to improve the quality of life and life chances of recipients. *It was a poverty reduction plan without redistribution.*

The plan's neoliberal orthodoxy of not encumbering public finances with significant new costs was matched in its refusal to challenge the deregulation of labour markets. Again, measures that might allow workers to earn living wages, and thus eliminate in-work poverty, were missing. Not surprisingly, making it easier for workers to form unions, even in the weakest form of returning to card-check certification, was not on the agenda. But even the promises to improve the enforcement of labour standards and to more strictly regulate temp agencies, while important, do more to actualize and enforce existing rights for workers, than to challenge non-standard employment and low wages. Limiting the worst abuses does little to create labour markets providing high and sustainable standards of living.

Source: Excerpted from Graefe, P. (2009, January 3). Breaking the cycle or going around in circles? The Ontario poverty reduction strategy. *The Bullet* (Socialist Project E-Bulletin No. 173). Retrieved March 11, 2011 from www.socialistproject.ca/bullet/bullet173.html

Conclusions: The Issue of Problem Definition and Intervention

Diderichsen, Evans, and Whitehead (2001) outline a model that details the various potential areas of action on health inequalities, but it can be adapted to display the situation of, and responses to, poverty (see Figure 13.1). In their model the social structure contributes to health through a series of stages. First, there is social stratification within a society (I). In Canada, the extent of stratification results in many Canadian living in poverty. As a result of this situation of living in poverty, people become exposed to very adverse living conditions (II). People living in poverty are very vulnerable to the effects of these living conditions (III). The specific exposures associated with these difficult living conditions lead to their experiencing a greater incidence of diseases, injuries, and other problems identified as quality-of-life issues (IV). These greater incidences of diseases, injuries, and quality of life problems then have social consequences.

Those attempting to intervene to improve health and quality of life can do so at a variety of levels. One can direct their attention to the end of the sequence and simply set up new and improved health care and social service systems to make sure that those who fall ill have services that can respond to their afflictions (D). Sadly, most of the current policy responses to poverty in Canada appear focused on such efforts. Higher upstream, one can attempt to decrease the vulnerability of people living in poverty to the development of illness and injuries (C). Resiliency and coping programs are examples. These approaches do little to influence the source of these afflictions: living in poverty as a result of the inequitable distribution of economic and other resources. The emphasis is directed toward making the lives of people living in poverty more palatable through the targeting of services toward these groups. The extent to which these services can achieve success, considering the generally unfavourable living circumstances of people living in poverty, is questionable.

Interveners can also attempt to reduce the negative exposures to which people living in poverty are vulnerable (B). This may involve the establishment of universal affordable child care and the provision of health and social services, as well as educational and recreational opportunities as entitlements rather than commodities requiring payments. This de-commodification of resources, services, and benefits has been the direction taken in many nations to reduce the effects of social stratification in general and the incidence of poverty in particular. Canada scores very low on indices of such de-commodification (Coburn, 2010). Current anti-poverty strategies and programs do little to decrease the adverse exposures that Canadians in poverty experience.

What may be the most efficacious means of reducing the negative health and quality-of-life effects of living in poverty? By reducing the material basis of the poverty experience through the provision of economic and other resources to people such that they do not live in poverty in the first place! This would occur through the provision of employment that pays living wages, raising social assistance and disability benefits to health-sustaining levels, and providing transfers to citizens on the basis of both universal entitlements and identified needs.

Figure 13.1: A Framework for Identifying the Pathways from the Social Context to Health Outcomes and Means of Introducing Policy Interventions

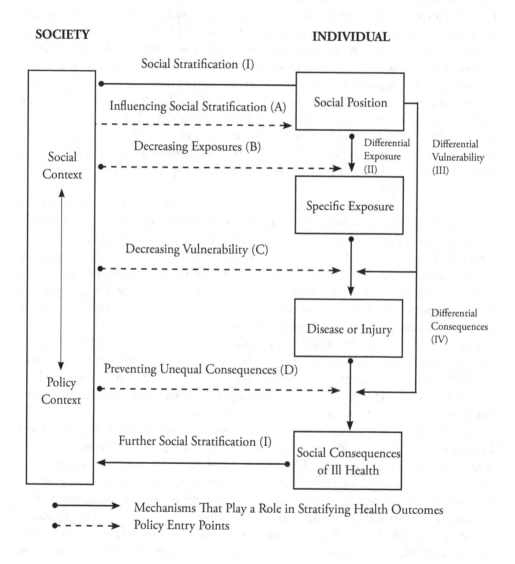

Source: Diderichsen, F., Evans, T., and Whitehead, M. (2001). The social basis of disparities in health. In T. Evans, M. Whitehead, F. Diderichsen, A. Bhuiya, and M. Wirth (Eds.), *Challenging inequalities in health: From ethics to action* (Figure 1, p. 15). New York: Oxford University Press. Adapted from Diderichsen, F., Hallqvist, J. (1998). Social Inequalities in health: some methodological considerations for the study of social position and social context. In Arve-Parès, B. (Ed) *Inequality in Health—A Swedish Perspective*, pp. 25–39. Stockholm: Swedish Council for Social Research.

Brady (2009) argues that the incidence of poverty in wealthy developed nations can best be understood and reduced through an analysis of the politics of a society. The final chapter returns to the politics of poverty and outlines the means by which Canada can become a poverty-free nation.

Critical Thinking Questions

1. What are some of the assumptions about the causes of poverty and the means of reducing them that underlie federal and provincial strategies for reducing poverty?
2. What are some of the issues raised by the Canadian Senate and House of Commons reports on poverty?
3. How much success can we expect from place-based initiatives such as the Vibrant Communities approach? Why?
4. Do you think that there will be a significant reduction in poverty in Canada as a result of these federal, provincial, and local strategies and programs?
5. What are some of the key issues that critics of the federal and provincial plans have raised? How can these be addressed?

Recommended Readings

Born, P. (2008). *Creating Vibrant Communities: How individuals and organizations from diverse sectors of society are coming together to reduce poverty in Canada.* Toronto: BPS Books.
> This volume is a compendium of Vibrant Community projects concerned with place-based anti-policy activities in Canadian communities.

Government of Newfoundland and Labrador. (2009). *Empowering people, engaging community, and enabling success.* Saint John's: Government of Newfoundland and Labrador. Online at www.hrle.gov.nl.ca/hrle/publications/poverty/PRSProgessReport.pdf
> The latest progress report on the province's anti-poverty strategy provides background and progress in Newfoundland and Labrador's attempts to reduce poverty.

Government of Quebec. (2010). *The fifth year progress report.* Quebec City: Government of Quebec. Online at http://tinyurl.com/48u67g9
> This is the latest progress report on Quebec's anti-poverty strategy of *Reconciling Freedom and Social Justice: A Challenge for the Future.* It provides an overview of the strategy, government activities, and achieved results.

Standing Committee on Human Resources, Skills and Social Development and the Status of Persons with Disabilities. (2010). *Federal poverty reduction plan: Working in partnership towards reducing poverty in Canada.* Online at http://tinyurl.com/5snk45r
> This House of Commons report is the result of an extensive three-year study on the federal role in addressing poverty. It contains a wide range of recommendations that have been positively received by the anti-poverty community.

Standing Senate Committee on Social Affairs, Science, and Technology, Subcommittee on Cities. (2009). *In from the margins: A call to action on poverty, housing, and homelessness.* Ottawa: Senate of Canada. Online at www.parl.gc.ca/40/2/parlbus/commbus/senate/com-e/citi-e/rep-e/rep02dec09-e.pdf
>   The recommendations in the report are the summation of a two-year cross-country study. Committee members heard testimony from more than 170 witnesses, including people living in poverty, several of them homeless, as well as universities, think tanks, provincial and local governments, and community organizations.

Relevant Websites

Caledon Institute of Social Policy—www.caledoninst.org/
>   The Caledon Institute seeks to inform and influence public opinion and to foster public discussion on poverty and social policy through research and analysis. It "develops and promotes concrete, practicable proposals for the reform of social programs at all levels of government and of social benefits provided by employers and the voluntary sector." See especially its reports on poverty reduction.
Canadian Social Research Links—www.canadiansocialresearch.net
>   This website contains a wealth of information about poverty and related public policy issues. The former social servant who maintains the site states: "I'm concerned that the Canadian public is over-exposed to the biases of the OECD, the IMF, and the World Bank and under-exposed to the views of the Canadian Council on Social Development, the Canadian Centre on Policy Alternatives and the National Council of Welfare, to name but a few of the 'good guys.' I do, however, set those views aside when it comes to sharing information—you're welcome on this site no matter what side of the ideological fence you're on."
Introspect Poverty Website—http://intraspec.ca/povertyCanada_news-and-reports.php
>   This website provides up-to-date research, statistics, news, and resources on poverty, child poverty, and social policy in Canada, including national and provincial initiatives, local Ottawa services and charities, research and policy organizations, and additional resources.
National Collaborating Centre for Healthy Public Policy—www.ncchpp.ca/en/
>   The interest of the centre is in public policy that potentially affects health by having a positive impact on the social, economic, and environmental determinants of health. Health is influenced by many factors, such as education, social support, income, and the physical environment, and the Centre views public policies as tools to influence these determinants.
Tamarack Institute for Community Engagement—http://tamarackcommunity.ca/
>   The Institute develops and supports collaborative strategies that engage citizens and institutions to solve major community challenges, and to learn from and share these experiences. The Institute sponsors projects and provides learning resources, training, coaching, and strategic consulting that enable people to collaborate and learn with and from each other.

Glossary of Terms

National Child Benefit (NCB) initiative is a partnership among the federal, provincial, and territorial governments and First Nations that aims to help prevent and reduce the depth of child poverty, support parents as they move into the labour market, and reduce overlap and duplication of government programs. The NCB combines two key elements: monthly payments to low-income families with children, and benefits and services designed and delivered by the provinces and territories to meet the needs of families with children in each jurisdiction (National Child Benefit, 2011).

Place-based approaches to poverty reduction are "broad-based collaborations of service providers, residents, advocates, businesses, governments and other stakeholders that come together to develop comprehensive and integrated multi-level service and policy responses to poverty" (Gardner, Lalani, and Plamadeala, 2010). They tend to focus on local conditions and take a rather non-critical approach toward provincial and federal public policy.

Programmatic intervention is "typically achieved through the design and implementation of a specific program or group of programs. Programs can be long term or short term. They can be large scale or small scale. They can be implemented as stand-alone efforts or integrated into a comprehensive framework of complementary programs. They are generally focused on assisting households and individuals to thrive within the economic, political and social systems of society. A program is sustained by a constant renewal of human, financial and other resources" (Loewen, 2009, p. 1).

Systemic intervention is "one which attempts to change one or more aspects of the economic, political and social systems of society. It creates a shift in the way a system works. Whereas a programmatic intervention is generally directed at assisting groups and individuals to adapt to the imperatives of systems, systemic interventions are generally designed to realign a system to accommodate the needs of particular groups and individuals. Systemic interventions, once implemented, may or may not require a constant renewal of resources to be sustained" (Loewen, 2009, p. 1).

References

Battle, K., and Torjman, S. (2009). *The federal role in poverty reduction.* Ottawa: The Caledon Institute.

Born, P. (2008). *Creating Vibrant Communities: How individuals and organizations from diverse sectors of society are coming together to reduce poverty in Canada.* Toronto: BPS Books.

Boychuk, G. (2004). *The Canadian social model: The logics of policy development.* Social Architecture Series. Ottawa: Canadian Policy Research Networks.

Brady, D. (2009). *Rich democracies, poor people: How politics explain poverty.* New York: Oxford University Press.

Canada Revenue Agency. (2010a). *Canada child benefits.* Ottawa: Canada Revenue Agency. Retrieved March 10, 2011 from www.cra-arc.gc.ca/E/pub/tg/t4114/t4114-10e.pdf

Canada Revenue Agency (2010b). *Working income tax benefit.* Ottawa: Canada Revenue Agency. Retrieved March 10, 2011 from www.cra-arc.gc.ca/E/pub/tg/rc4227/rc4227-10e.pdf

Coburn, D. (2010). Health and health care: A political economy perspective. In T. Bryant, D. Raphael, and M. Rioux (Eds.), *Staying alive: Critical perspectives on health, illness, and health care* (2nd ed., pp. 65–92). Toronto: Canadian Scholars' Press Inc.

Diderichsen, F., Evans, T., and Whitehead, M. (2001). The social basis of disparities in health. In T. Evans, M. Whitehead, F. Diderichsen, A. Bhuiya, and M. Wirth (Eds.), *Challenging inequalities in health: From ethics to action* (pp. 12–23). New York: Oxford University Press.

Gardner, B., Lalani, N., and Plamadeala, C. (2010). *Comprehensive community initiatives: Lessons learned, potential and opportunities moving forward.* Toronto: Wellesley Institute.

Government of New Brunswick. (2008). *Overcoming poverty together: The New Brunswick economic and social inclusion plan.* Fredericton: Government of New Brunswick.

Government of Newfoundland and Labrador. (2006). *Reducing poverty: An action plan for Newfoundland and Labrador.* Saint John's: Government of Newfoundland and Labrador.

Government of Newfoundland and Labrador. (2009). *Empowering people, engaging community, and enabling success.* Saint John's: Government of Newfoundland and Labrador.

Government of Nova Scotia. (2009). *Preventing poverty, promoting prosperity.* Halifax: Government of Nova Scotia.

Government of Ontario. (2008). *Breaking the cycle: Ontario's poverty reduction strategy.* Toronto: Government of Ontario.

Government of Ontario. (2010). *Breaking the cycle: The second progress report.* Toronto: Government of Ontario.

Government of Quebec. (2002). *An Act to Combat Poverty and Social Exclusion.* Quebec City: Government of Quebec.

Government of Quebec. (2004). *Reconciling freedom and social justice: A challenge for the future.* Quebec City: Government of Quebec.

Government of Quebec. (2010a). *The fifth year progress report.* Quebec City: Government of Quebec.

Government of Quebec. (2010b). *Governmental action plan for solidarity and social inclusion.* Quebec City: Government of Quebec.

Greenaway, N. (2010). Harper government gives Senate poverty report short shrift: Critics. *Postmedia News.* Retrieved March 10, 2011 from www.canada.com/business/ Harper+government+gives+Senate+poverty+report+short+shrift+Critics/3598069/story. html

Hay, D. (2009). *Poverty reduction policies and programs—Canada.* Ottawa: Canadian Council for Social Development.

Levitas, R. (2005). *The inclusive society: Social exclusion and new labour* (2nd ed.). Basingstoke, UK: Palgrave.

Loewen, G. (2009). *A compendium of poverty reduction strategies and frameworks.* Waterloo, ON: Tamarack Institute.

Makhoul, A. (2010). *New Brunswick's Overcoming Poverty Together plan earns praise and creates hope.* Ottawa: Caledon Institute.

Mendell, A. (2009). *Comprehensive policies to combat poverty across Canada, by province: Preliminary document.* Montreal: National Collaborating Centre for Healthy Public Policy.

National Child Benefit. (2011). *What is the National Child Benefit?* Retrieved March 10, 2011 from www.nationalchildbenefit.ca/eng/06/ncb.shtml

Noel, A. (2002). *A law against poverty: Quebec's new approach to combating poverty and social exclusion.* Ottawa: Canadian Policy Research Networks—Family Network.

Osberg, L. (2001). Poverty among senior citizens: A Canadian success story. In P. Grady and A. Sharpe (Eds.), *The state of economics in Canada: Festschrift in honour of David Slater* (pp. 151–181). Ottawa: Centre for the Study of Living Standards.

Paterson, S., Levasseur, K., and Teplova, T. (2004). I spy with my little eye ... Canada's National Child Benefit. In G.B. Doern (ed.), *How Ottawa spends 2004–2005.* Montreal: McGill-Queen's University Press.

Pike, D. (2011, January 15). Single people: The "undeserving" poor. *Hamilton Spectator.* Retrieved March 10, 2011 from www.thespec.com/opinion/article/474008--single-people-the-undeserving-poor

Service Canada. (2011a). *Old Age Security (OAS) payment rates.* Retrieved March 10, 2011 from www.servicecanada.gc.ca/eng/isp/oas/oasrates.shtml

Service Canada. (2011b). *Canada Pension Plan (CPP) payment rates.* Retrieved March 10, 2011 from www.servicecanada.gc.ca/eng/isp/pub/factsheets/rates.shtml

Standing Committee on Human Resources, Skills and Social Development and the Status of Persons with Disabilities. (2010). *Federal poverty reduction plan: Working in partnership towards reducing poverty in Canada.* Retrieved March 10, 2011 from House of Commons website: http://tinyurl.com/5snk45r

Standing Senate Committee on Social Affairs, Science, and Technology, Subcommittee on Cities. (2009). *In from the margins: A call to action on poverty, housing, and homelessness.* Ottawa: Canadian Senate.

Swanson, J. (2001). *Poor-bashing: The politics of exclusion.* Toronto: Between the Lines Press.

Swift, J., Balmer, B., and Dineen, M. (2010). *Persistent poverty: Dispatches from the margins.* Toronto: Between the Lines Press.

Tamarack Institute for Community Engagement. (2011). *Vibrant communities.* Retrieved March 10, 2011 from http://tamarackcommunity.ca/

Thespec.com (2011). Tories say they won't act on Commons Report on fighting poverty. Retrieved March 11, 2011 from http://www.thespec.com/news/canada/article/497600--tories-say-they-won-t-act-on-commons-report-on-fighting-poverty

Torjman, S. (2008). *Poverty policy.* Ottawa: Caledon Institute.

Torjman, S. (2010). *Poverty reduction in Quebec: The first five years.* Ottawa: The Caledon Institute.

Torjman, S., Battle, K., and Mendelson, M. (2009). *All aboard Manitoba's poverty train.* Ottawa: Caledon Institute.

Tremblay, D. G. (2009). Precarious work and the labour market. In D. Raphael (Ed.), *Social determinants of health: Canadian perspectives* (2nd ed., pp. 75–87). Toronto: Canadian Scholars' Press Inc.

Chapter Fourteen

Poverty and the Future of the
Canadian Welfare State

For those wishing to optimize the health of populations by reducing social and income inequalities, it seems advisable to support political forces such as the labour movement and social democratic parties, which have traditionally supported larger, more successful redistributive policies.—Vicente Navarro and Leiyu Shi

Learning Objectives

At the conclusion of this chapter, the reader will be able to:

- place the prospects of eliminating poverty in relation to the future of the Canadian welfare state;
- apply Saint-Arnaud and Bernard's welfare state typology and Brady's institutionalized power relations theory to explain why Canada's poverty rates are so high and what can be done to reduce them;
- identify the specific political and economic structures that are associated with low poverty rates in other wealthy developed nations;
- understand the specific political, economic, and social forces that present barriers to reducing poverty in Canada and identify means of overcoming them; and
- explain the necessity of supporting left-leaning political parties—and progressive social movements, including the labour movement—as means by which poverty will be eliminated in Canada.

Introduction

Despite the stated intentions of our elected representatives and government policymakers and the efforts of various agencies, organizations, and advocacy groups to reduce and then eliminate poverty in Canada, there has been only limited success in this endeavour. Instead, the past two decades have seen poverty rates remain largely unchanged. Recent improvements have been due in large part to the growth of the Canadian economy, and it is likely that most if not all of these gains have been lost due to the 2008 recession. Anti-poverty strategies and programs that have been implemented have probably kept Canada's high-poverty rates from being even higher than they are.

More ominously, even the sustained growth in the Canadian economy that ended in 2008 was associated with growing income and wealth inequality whereby economic benefits accrued primarily to the already well-off. And since it has been demonstrated that income and wealth inequalities grow during periods of recession and recovery, the figures presented in this volume are certainly underestimates of their extent. In addition, the affordability of basic needs for many Canadians is decreasing, and the social safety net is becoming increasingly frayed.

The most striking effects of these developments have been increasing housing insecurity and homelessness, and growing food insecurity and food bank use (see Box 14.1). Incomes for many Canadians stagnate as meagre minimum wages and social assistance benefits combine with tightened eligibility for unemployment benefits to provide cheap pools of labour that suppress wages. There is a growing gap between the life situations of homeowners and renters and growing divides between low-income Canadians' incomes and their ability to afford housing in virtually every Canadian city. The living conditions of Canadians of colour and recent immigrants become especially more difficult with evidence of a growing Canadian economic apartheid, whereby Canadian of colour are increasingly living in poverty and are concentrated into specific urban neighbourhoods (see Mikkonen and Raphael, 2010 for an overview of these developments).

Canada's high rates of poverty—and its associated health and quality-of-life outcomes—reflect the influence of political and economic forces that shape public policy in numerous policy areas. Active public policy in the service of reducing poverty is but one indicator of the general willingness of a society to meet the needs of its citizens in a systematic and consistent manner. In total, this basket of public policies constitutes the welfare state, and Canada's form of it—like those of other liberal nations—is undeveloped and especially susceptible to threats associated with the resurgence of neoliberalism and increasing economic globalization. In this final chapter, the phenomenon of poverty, and governmental responses to its presence, is examined within the context of the future of the Canadian welfare state.

In Chapter 13, public policies that would reduce the incidence of poverty in Canada and thereby improve population health and quality of life were presented. These policies are not new or unproven. Their Canadian advocates have long presented them for consideration, and they are common in many other wealthy developed nations. Their lack of implementation cannot be due to poverty reduction being a barrier to economic growth and productivity, as many nations with low poverty rates actually outperform Canada. The task, then, is to explain why they have not been implemented in Canada and to identify and overcome the barriers that have prevented this. For example, the powerful Canadian business community and their allies generally oppose public policies that would reduce poverty. Their opposition is a barrier to reducing poverty rates in Canada (Langille, 2009). There are others.

Box 14.1: Facts and Statistics about Food Bank Use in Canada

Hunger Facts 2010

How many are being helped by food banks?
- Number of people assisted by a food bank in March 2010: **867,948**—highest level on record
- Number helped by food banks for the first time: **80,150**—9% of the total
- Change in food bank use since 2009: **+ 9%**
- Change in food bank use since 2000: **+ 19%**
- Number of meals served by food banks in March 2010: **3,459,544**—6.4% higher than 2009
- Number of food banks in Canada: **900+ food banks and 2,900+ affiliated agencies**

Provinces that experienced the largest increases in use compared to 2009:
- Manitoba (**+ 21%**)
- Saskatchewan (**+ 20%**)
- Prince Edward Island (**+ 13%**)
- Quebec (**+ 12%**)
- Nova Scotia (**+ 11%**)
- Alberta (**+ 10%**)

- Number of provinces & territories without a food bank: **0**
- Years since Canada's first food bank opened in Edmonton: **29**

Who are food banks helping?
- **38%** of those helped are children and youth
- **51%** of assisted households are families with children
- **38%** are single people
- **11%** are couples without children
- **17%** of assisted households have income from current or recent employment
- **15%** receive disability-related income supports
- **7%** are on a pension
- **51%** receive social assistance benefits
- **85%** live in rental accommodations
- **6%** own their own home

How are Canadian food banks managing the increase in need?
- **27%** of food banks lack adequate funding
- **31%** of food banks do not have enough food to meet the need
- **50%** of food banks have been forced to give out less food than usual

- **57%** bought more food than usual to meet the need
- Nearly half of food banks in Canada have no paid staff
- **15%** report difficulty recruiting enough volunteers to manage everyday operations

Source: Food Banks Canada. (2010). *Hunger facts 2010.* Retrieved March 11, 2011 from www.cafb-acba.ca/facts-statistics.htm

Poverty, the Welfare State, and Public Policy

The presence of poverty in a wealthy developed nation such as Canada is a failure of the modern welfare state to meet the safety and security needs of its citizens. The welfare state refers to governmental structures that ensure the entitlements of citizenship: meeting basic needs, providing resources for participation in society, and minimizing forces that systematically exclude citizens from these activities (Briggs, 1961).

Scholars are of two minds concerning the origins of the welfare state in nations such as Canada. One view is that the welfare state came about as a result of recognition by governments and policy-makers of the importance of providing safe and secure living environments for the citizenry. In this view, policy-making is a result of democratic processes that reflect responsive governments, a pluralistic society, and societal commitments to principles of fairness and justice.

The alternative view is that the welfare state came about in response to political pressures created by social movements (Teeple, 2000). Here, the welfare state is seen as the result of struggles by working people, women, and other dispossessed groups to gain basic rights and freedoms against the societal forces opposed to such reforms. The first view is a consensus model of society, and the second is a conflict model. Each model has implications for understanding the processes by which progressive public policy comes about. Through such understandings, actions can be taken to reduce the incidence of poverty in Canada.

The consensus model is best expressed by the pluralist model of public policy change (Brooks and Miljan, 2003). Here, those attempting to influence public policy operate on a level playing field where public policy ideas compete with each other for governmental and public acceptance. Policies are endorsed and implemented on the basis of their perceived benefits to society. Policy-making is seen as a rational process carried out by rational policy-makers. The anti-poverty strategies and activities of governments, advocacy groups, and community development organizations presented in Chapter 13 all operate within the parameters of the consensus model of policy change. As shown, while these activities are numerous, their actual impacts upon poverty rates have been modest.

In contrast, the conflict model of public policy change directs attention to the influence of wealthy and powerful elites in society who strive to ensure that governments address their priorities and look out for their interests. In the Canada of the 21st century, these players' priorities include creating corporate and business-supportive environments that serve to maintain and increase company profits and satisfy shareholders. Frequently, such activities involve lobbying for public policies that keep wages low, reduce employment security and benefits, minimize government intervention in the marketplace's distribution of resources, and implement lower taxation rates for the most well-off. Canadian governments have not only implemented policies consistent with these priorities, but they have also acted to reduce the ability of those opposed to these policies to have their voices heard (see Box 14.2).

Each of these public policy models provides insights into, and directions for, developing and implementing public policy. In some public policy situations a pluralist model seems to best handle the facts; in others, the conflict model seems to best explain how public policy is made. The conflict model of society, however, appears most appropriate for understanding the incidence and consequences of poverty in nations within a liberal political economy such as Canada's. This is the case for various reasons. First, the history of the welfare state in Canada and other nations with liberal political economies points to the crucial role played by the labour and other social movements in achieving the reforms associated with the modern welfare state (Mishra, 1990). The institution of public pensions, universal health care, social services and benefits, and better working conditions and business regulation, among other policy areas, came about in response to profound political pressures led by the labour and other social movements.

In Canada, many of these changes occurred during periods of minority federal governments where the party of the left—the NDP—held the balance of power (Russell, 2008). In other cases, innovations developed in provincial legislatures where the NDP led the government, and more recently in Quebec, where the left-leaning Parti Québécois either held power or held the balance of power. In Saskatchewan during the Tommy Douglas CCF-NDP era, numerous reforms were implemented in the health care and pensions areas. The obvious success and public support of these reforms led to their gradual acceptance across the nation. The creation of a universal and affordable child care system in Quebec came about during the left-leaning Parti Québécois's rule and this model is now held out as one to be emulated across Canada.

Second, evidence from Canada and elsewhere indicates policies that maintain high levels of poverty are consistent with the political ideologies and economic interests of the business and corporate sectors. For example, the more difficult it is to organize workers into labour unions—a prime goal of corporate-oriented policy—the lower the unionization rate and the greater the incidence of poverty. And it is these corporate and business sectors that currently appear to have the upper hand in influencing elected representatives across Canada.

For these sectors, high poverty rates—and the policies that maintain these rates—help keep wages down, increase profits, and weaken labour and social movements that threaten the dominance of these elites. Major lobby groups, such as the Canadian Coun-

Box 14.2: The Institutions of Neo-liberalism in Canada: How Corporate Priorities Are Realized

The business sector has been a strong advocate of reducing the Canadian welfare state by reducing expenditures and taxes on the wealthy and ceding control of the economy to the corporate sector. The result of this has been growing inequality and continuing high poverty rates. David Langille outlines the key players behind this resurgence of neo-liberal ideology in Canada.

Business Associations
Canadian Bankers Association: The leading lobby group for the chartered and foreign banks. Nancy Hughes Anthony is president and CEO.
Canadian Chamber of Commerce: A coalition of local chambers of commerce representing the interests of many large and small businesses. Perrin Beatty is president and CEO.
Canadian Council of Chief Executives: The voice of big business, representing the 150 CEOs of the major transnational corporations, formerly known as the Business Council on National Issues. John Manley is president and CEO.
Canadian Manufacturers and Exporters: Canada's oldest business lobby group represents large manufacturers and exporters. Jayson Myers is president.

Think-Tanks
C.D. Howe Institute: The voice of the Bay Street business elite, led by president and CEO William B.P. Robson.
Fraser Institute: Founded in 1974 by Michael Walker to represent the "new right" devotion to free markets. Mark Mullins is the current executive director.
Institute for Research on Public Policy: A liberal response to the economic challenges of the 1970s, allowing more scope for government. Mel Cappe is president.

Citizens' Front Groups
Canadian Taxpayers Federation: A watchdog for the well-to-do against the "special interests" responsible for "runaway spending." John Williamson is the federal director.
National Citizens Coalition: Funded by business leaders to defend individual freedom against government intervention. Peter Coleman is president and CEO.

Lobbyists
"Government relations consultants" hired to help firms increase their influence and gain favours from government. A growth industry in recent years as dozens of firms enter the market. Examples include Earnscliffe, GCI, Hill and Knowlton, and Strategy Corp.

Source: Adapted from Langille, D. (2009). Follow the money: How business and politics define our health. In D. Raphael (Ed.), *Social determinants of health: Canadian perspectives* (2nd ed., Box 20.1, p. 309). Toronto: Canadian Scholars' Press Inc.

cil of Chief Executives, the Fraser Institute, and the C.D. Howe Institute, are funded by corporate interests and all are active—and influential—in shaping public policy in Canada (Langille, 2009).

Third, considering the vast amount of evidence that has accumulated concerning the detrimental effects poverty has upon the health and quality of life of those experiencing it, their communities, and Canadian society in general, and the concerted efforts by numerous groups over the past two decades to have governments address the issue, it is not difficult to attribute governmental neglect of these issues to these powerful political and economic forces. It is not an issue of insufficient evidence being available or needing further research to identify policy solutions to the problem of poverty. Continuing high levels of poverty and the evidence of growing income and wealth inequalities is a result of unwillingness on the part of governments to confront these opposing forces and implement public policies that support poverty reduction and the more equitable distribution of income and wealth.

Fourth, comparative analyses of why poverty rates differ so profoundly among wealthy developed nations shows how societal structures and the political and economic forces behind them shape governmental approaches toward poverty. The balancing of interests between citizen needs and business sector demands is much less likely in nations where the marketplace and its supporters are the primary shapers of the public policy agenda. Nations that have demonstrated the ability to curb the influence of the corporate and business sectors and wealthy elites upon public policy have reduced poverty and limited income and wealth inequalities (Alesina and Glaeser, 2004; Brady, 2009). They do this with the support of broad sectors of the public (Brady, 2003, 2009). As Ed Broadbent describes this process, "They want market-driven economies, but not market-driven societies" (Broadbent, 2006, A12).

The implication of accepting a conflict model of public policy change is recognizing that governments in liberal political economies will usually—unless challenged—implement policies consistent with the dominant views of powerful supporters of the unfettered marketplace. However, political pressures can control these tendencies. How then can these political pressures be created? To help answer this, the forces that shape the form of the welfare state in Canada and elsewhere must be considered.

Ideological Variations in the Welfare State

Figure 14.1 lays out the fundamental forms the welfare state takes in wealthy developed nations. Of particular interest are their guiding principles and dominant institutions. Canada is a liberal welfare state (Esping-Anderson, 1990, 1999; Bernard and Saint-Arnaud, 2004). Liberal welfare states provide the least support and security to its citizens. Canadians consider their welfare state to be much superior to that of the USA. But when viewed within an international perspective, Canada's approach is closer to that of the USA than to European welfare states where poverty levels are lower and greater value is placed upon the economic and social security of citizens.

Figure 14.1: Ideological Variations in Forms of the Welfare State

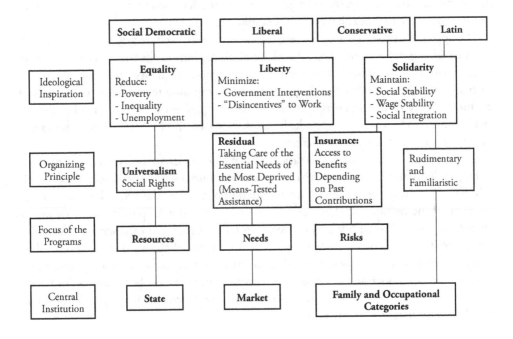

Source: Saint-Arnaud, S., and Bernard, P. (2003). Convergence or resilience? A hierarchical cluster analysis of the welfare regimes in advanced countries (Figure 2, p. 503). *Current Sociology, 51*(5), 499–527.

Within liberal welfare states, the dominant ideological inspiration is that of *liberty*, which leads to minimal government intervention in the workings of the marketplace (Saint-Arnaud and Bernard, 2003). Indeed, such interventions are seen as providing a disincentive to work, thereby breeding "welfare dependence." The results of this ideological inspiration are the meagre benefits provided to those on social assistance, weak supports for the labour movement, undeveloped policies for assisting those with disabilities, and a general reluctance to provide universal services and programs. Programs that exist are residual, meaning they exist to provide the most basic needs of the most deprived. Canada, the USA, the UK, and Ireland are the best exemplars of this form of the welfare state.

Critical social scientists have argued that these welfare states and their ideological characteristics represent those whose interests are allied with their central institution: the market (Coburn, 2010; Teeple, 2000). It is not an accident that these liberal welfare states have the greatest degree of wealth and income inequality, the weakest social safety nets, and the poorest population health (Navarro and Shi, 2002; Raphael, 2011a, 2011b). These states cater to the most well-off in society who either have interests in the business sector or have come to believe that their interests are best represented by this sector. And it is the business sector in Canada that is most vociferously opposed to policies that would reduce poverty, strengthen the social safety net, and improve the lives of the most insecure in Canadian society (Langille, 2009).

The opposite situation is seen among social democratic welfare states. As difficult as it may be to imagine for Canadians, the ideological inspiration for the central institution of these nations—the state—is the reduction of poverty, inequality, and unemployment. Rather than being concerned with governments acting only to meet the basic needs of the most deprived, the organizing principle here is universalism and providing for the social rights of all citizens. Denmark, Finland, Norway, and Sweden are the best exemplars of this form of the welfare state.

Governments with social democratic political economies are proactive in identifying social problems and issues, and strive to promote economic and social security for their citizens. The central institution is not the market but rather the state. The outcome of this form of the welfare state has been the virtual elimination of poverty, the striving for gender and social class equity, and the regulation of the market in the service of citizens. The commitment to these principles and the converting of these principles into public policy action can be readily discerned through review of these nations' public statements and related documents available at government websites. For example, in regard to health care, health, and social issues/insurance, the Swedish Ministry of Health and Social Welfare states the following:

> This area of responsibility is at the heart of welfare policy. It embraces issues concerning people's financial security, social services, health and medical care, public health and the rights of children and persons with disabilities. The Ministry of Health and Social Affairs is responsible for the whole of this area of responsibility. The main tasks of welfare policy are to lessen the gaps between different groups in society while at the same time providing people with security and an opportunity to develop. (Swedish Ministry of Health and Social Welfare, 2011a)

And in regard to public health policy, "The objective … is to create social conditions to ensure good health on equal terms for the entire population" (Swedish Ministry of Health and Social Welfare, 2011b).

A comparison of public policy approaches to citizen economic and social security can be a jarring experience for Canadians accustomed to government inaction on these issues. As two excellent examples of social democratic strategies to anti-poverty, see Sweden's *Strategy Report on Measures to Prevent Poverty and Social Exclusion* (Swedish Ministry of Health and Social Affairs, 2007) and *Report on Measures to Prevent Poverty and Social Exclusion* (Swedish Ministry of Health and Social Affairs, 2005).

Even the conservative and Latin welfare states provide superior economic and social security to their citizens than do liberal welfare states. The ideological inspiration of maintaining social stability, wage stability, and social integration is accomplished by providing benefits based on insurance schemes geared to a variety of family and occupational categories. These well-organized benefits schemes are oriented toward the primary wage earners with rather less concern for promoting gender equity than is the case among social democratic nations. Evidence is available that governmental commitments in these conservative nations, as evidenced through public spending on citizen supports and benefits, in many cases rival those seen for the social democratic nations (Raphael, 2011a, 2001b).

A frequent comment is that Quebec's political and social culture is more similar to European states than to the rest of Canada. Similarly, Alberta's political and social culture at times appears to show closer affinity to the USA than to the rest of Canada. Research, however, contradicts these observations. Bernard and Saint-Arnaud (2004) provide an analysis of numerous indicators of societal organization and functioning, and public policy approaches. They found that the four largest Canadian provinces, Quebec, Ontario, Alberta, and British Columbia, present profiles more consistent with each other than with either the USA or European nations. And these provincial profiles—as well as the overall Canadian profile—fit firmly in the liberal political economy cluster of nations. These findings are consistent with the analyses of Canadian public policy provided in other chapters in this volume.

The form the welfare state takes is important because it shapes the distribution of political, economic, and social resources among the population. Skewed distributions of resources result in significant proportions of the population experiencing material and social deprivation. This experience of material and social deprivation is what living in poverty is all about. Experiences of material and social deprivation are the primary causes of poor health and quality of life among those living in poverty, and the deterioration of health and quality of life observed among deprived communities. These skewed distributions of resources threaten the overall health and quality of life of the entire society.

The outcome of these skewed distributions of economic and social resources is inequitable distribution of the social determinants of health (Raphael, 2009). The experience of limited economic and social resources creates the poverty that impacts negatively upon early childhood development, income, food and housing security, and educational opportunities. When combined with lack of investment in social infrastructure, the resultant weakening of the social safety net, health and social services, and opportunities for education and retraining create a situation that may be unbearable for many Canadians living in poverty. (See Raphael et al., 2010, for studies that document the living situation of people with type 2 diabetes who are living in poverty as one example.)

The Way Forward: The Politics of Poverty Reduction and the Barriers to Such Actions

Canada may be firmly within the liberal political economy camp, but it is important to acknowledge that members of each welfare state type are not monolithic in their policy approaches. Nations have the potential to shift their basket of public policies to become outliers within their welfare state group or even their group completely. How could Canada shift its course? Answering this question requires acceptance of Brady's thesis that "poverty is truly a political problem" (Brady, 2009, p. 181). And as such, it requires a political solution. What are the political factors that lead to high poverty rates in wealthy developed nations, and what would be the political solution that would shift these factors?

Brady (2009) argues that the incidence of poverty in wealthy developed nations can best be understood and reduced through an analysis of the politics of a society. Based on his study of societal structures and rates of poverty among 18 wealthy developed nations—including Canada—he outlines his theory of institutionalized power relations. The components of the theory, that is, the factors that explain the incidence of poverty are: (a) ideologies and interests, (b) welfare generosity, (c) leftist politics, and (d) coalitions for egalitarianism (see Figure 14.2). Each of these is considered in turn.

Ideologies and Interests

At any given point in time the politics of a nation and its manifestation in public policy is molded by the ideologies and interests of various sectors. These ideologies will range from strongly interventionist views that support the redistribution of income and wealth to strong laissez-faire views that oppose any government intervention in the working of the economic system.

Holders of these differing views, however, do not play on a level playing field (Coburn, 2010). In Canada, there is little doubt that the powerful corporate sector—generally holders of the laissez-faire approach to governance—has the upper hand as compared to those favouring more equity-producing policies (Langille, 2009; McQuaig and Brooks, 2010). These imbalances need to be recognized, and the unfair advantages held by the wealthy and powerful need to be addressed. Not surprisingly,

Figure 14.2: Components of Brady's Institutionalized Power Relations Theory

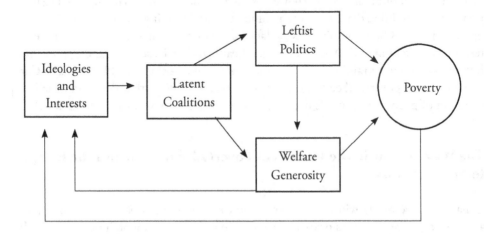

Source: Brady, D. (2009). *Rich democracies, poor people: How politics explain poverty* (Figure 1.2, p. 14). New York: Oxford University Press.

the influence of these laissez-faire supports permeates Canadian public policy and is responsible in large part for Canada's weak welfare state.

Welfare Generosity

There is a profound difference in the extent to which each nation's welfare state provides supports to its citizens. In liberal political economies such as Canada, citizens are in many ways left to fend for themselves. Brady (2009) notes—and it is consistent with the analyses provided in this volume—that social welfare expenditures, social security transfers, extent of de-commodification of necessary supports and benefits, government expenditures, and public health spending are all related to poverty rates. Greater spending and transfers, and greater de-commodification are associated with lower poverty rates.

Brady combines these measures to create a *welfare generosity index* that is found to be far and away the best predictor of poverty rates as compared to the other measures in isolation. (See Chapter 12 to find out how poorly Canada stands on many of the data indicators Brady uses in his index.) Index scores are most strongly related to poverty rates among children and the elderly, but are also very much related to poverty rates for men, women, and working-age adults.

It should be noted that welfare state generosity not only lowers poverty rates but also improves overall life expectancy and numerous other indicators of health and quality of life. Welfare state generosity is an important determinant of the extent of income inequality among nations, a characteristic found to have profound effects upon a bewilderingly wide range of health and quality-of-life indicators (Wilkinson and Pickett, 2009).

Leftist Politics

Brady argues, and his analysis shows, that the generosity of the welfare state—the single best predictor of poverty rates—is strongly related to the strength of institutionalized leftist political influence; that is, the ability of parties of the left, such as the Social Democrats in Europe, Labour in the United Kingdom, and the New Democrats in Canada, to gain and hold political power. It also refers to the ability of these left political parties to influence governing parties to implement public policies under the threat of electoral defeat. This analysis is consistent with data provided in Chapter 11, which shows that greater left Cabinet share is strongly associated with lower poverty rates.

Brady argues that the influence of parties of the left reduces poverty by strengthening the generosity of the welfare state. Parties of the left work closely with organized labour to promote public policies that promote citizen security through better wages, improved employment security, and stronger benefits. Unions contribute to the strength of parties of the left, and parties of the left enable and strengthen the ability of organized labour to form unions.

There is strong support for Brady's views of the importance of organized labour. Within jurisdictions, strong labour movements are associated with higher wages, stronger benefits and greater employment security, and better working conditions (Jackson, 2010). Internationally, nations with stronger labour movements have stronger welfare states, lower rates of poverty, and generally better health and quality-of-life profiles.

The strength of organized labour is an important determinant of the strength of the welfare state, and therefore union density is particularly important. The proportion of the workforce that belongs to unions differs widely among wealthy developed nations. Not surprisingly, union membership is closely related to the proportion of the workforce bound by collective agreements. And, not surprisingly, it is the nations with higher collective bargaining coverage *and* high union membership that show exceptionally low poverty rates (see Figure 14.3).

Figure 14.3 illustrates a number of concepts. First, social democratic welfare states have the lowest child poverty rates; liberal welfare states, the highest. Among the conservative welfare states, the Latin states of Spain, Portugal, and Italy have higher child poverty rates. A key feature is that the social democratic welfare states have both high union density (or membership) *and* high collective bargaining agreement. Generally, the liberal welfare states have low union membership and low collective agreement coverage. These extreme situations are strongly related to child poverty rates.

Figure 14.3: Union Density, Collective Agreement Coverage, and Child Poverty, 2008 (Density and Coverage Rates) and Mid-2000s (Poverty Rates)

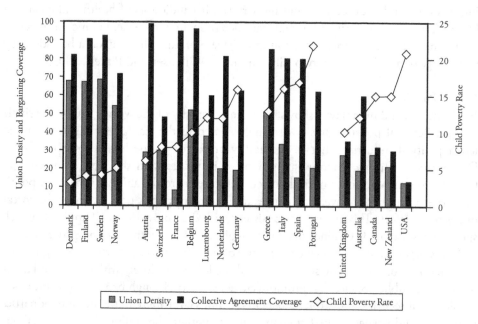

Union Density ■ Collective Agreement Coverage ◇ Child Poverty Rate

Sources: Organisation for Economic Co-operation and Development. (2010). *Trade union density.* Retrieved March 11, 2011 from http://stats.oecd.org/Index.aspx?DataSetCode=UN_DEN; Venn, D. (2009). *Legislation, collective bargaining, and enforcement: Updating the OECD employment protection indicators* (OECD Social Employment and Migration Working Paper No. 89). Paris: OECD; Organisation for Economic Co-operation and Development. (2008). *Growing unequal? Income distribution and poverty in OECD countries.* Paris: OECD.

An interesting aspect is the relatively high collective bargaining coverage of the conservative and Latin welfare states and their relatively low union density or membership. The OECD explains this phenomena—called corporatism by Brady (2009) and others—by pointing out that, in these states, (a) a primary determinant of bargaining coverage is not the share of workers belonging to a union, but the share of employers belonging to employer associations that negotiate collective contracts; (b) it is common practice for a large majority of employers to voluntarily apply the terms of contract to their total workforce; and (c) in some countries, an important additional variable is the administrative extension of agreements, covering all employers in a given sector (Organisation for Economic Co-operation and Development, 2004). In liberal political economies where such agreements do not exist (such as in Canada), there is both low union membership and low collective agreement coverage and high poverty rates. Clearly, poverty reduction is most likely where there is high union membership and broad collective agreement coverage. Strengthening the influence of parties of the left and the organized labour movement are important means of reducing poverty in Canada.

Latent Coalitions

Brady uses the term *latent coalitions* to refer to groups of citizens who may come together under differing circumstances in support of a more generous welfare state. One such taxonomy might involve groups and citizens who are concerned with each and any of the social determinants of health. These latent coalitions could become organized around the social determinants of health of Aboriginal status (Native organizations and Aboriginal people); gender (women's groups and women in general); disability (disability advocates and persons with disabilities); housing (housing advocates and the insecurely housed); early life (child care supporters and families in need of child care); income and income distribution (anti-poverty groups and poor people themselves); education (educators and teachers and families with children in schools); race (anti-discrimination workers and persons of colour); employment and working conditions (labour leaders and workers); social exclusion (social and community workers and their clients); food insecurity (food security and food bank workers and users); social safety net (unemployed and low-income citizens); health services (health care workers and their patients); and unemployment and job security (the unemployed or precariously employed). Clearly the potential for developing latent coalitions in the service of a more generous welfare state—and lower poverty rates—is enormous.

The implications of Brady's analysis for reducing poverty in Canada seem fairly straightforward:

Increase welfare generosity:	→ Advocate for more generous supports and benefits
Strengthen left political actors:	→ Support the New Democratic Party
Build latent coalitions for egalitarianism:	→ Establish active networks of progressive citizens
Ideologies and interests:	→ Recognize important barriers and build support for anti-poverty action

Red Toryism

Brady's analysis of the importance of parties of the left is accurate. However, he neglects the potential poverty-moderating effects of what might be termed *conservative politics*, that is, the politics associated with the conservative regimes and parties of continental Europe. While not as poverty reducing as the social democratic nations, these regimes do provide citizens with policy approaches that provide significantly better security and lower poverty rates than those seen in liberal political economies. In Canada, this brand of conservative politics has been associated with what is called "red Toryism." The term has been defined as follows:

> *Red Tory is a nickname given to a political tradition in Canada's conservative political parties. Red Tories were traditionally fiscally conservative but retained traditional social values of the aristocracy such as noblesse oblige. Modern Red Tories define themselves as "fiscally conservative and socially progressive." (WordIQ.com, 2011)*

However, Wesley (2006) comments:

> *Overall, red toryism implies an easy acceptance of, but a low tolerance for, economic and social inequality, and displays a paternalistic concern for the care of the less-fortunate in society.... [U]nlike the tenets of liberalism, the principles of red toryism do not aim to increase the freedom of the less-fortunate. Nor do they aim to foster greater equality in society, as under socialism. Rather, toryism seeks to increase the security of those of lower status, thus ensuring the stability of the community as a whole. (p. 5)*

While red Toryism as described by Wesley may not sound particularly promising as an ally in reducing poverty, possibilities may exist. For example, Hugh Segal, a Conservative senator, has been calling for the institution of a guaranteed annual income (see Box 14.3). Poverty reduction, therefore, may be able to enlist the support of progressive conservatives, though in a more muted form than might be the case among social democrats. Unfortunately the influence of the "red Tory" tradition in Canada has become limited to the Conservative Party in Maritime Canada.

Proportional Representation

The institution of proportional representation would go a long way toward implementing public policies in support of poverty reduction. It was noted in Chapter 11 that proportional representation is related to a more generous welfare state, a finding replicated by Brady (2009). It has also been implicated as an important contributor to the social democratic welfare states of Scandinavia (Esping-Anderson, 1985).

Institution of proportional representation would ensure that the significant numbers of Canadians in favour of efforts to reduce poverty would see their votes actually translated into seats in elected legislatures. Indeed, it has even been suggested that a Canadian political structure that operated within a proportional representation electoral system would produce a society that would be very close to the social democracies of Denmark, Finland, Norway, and Sweden. (See Box 14.4.)

Box 14.3: A Progressive Conservative Approach to Poverty Reduction

Let's Refocus on a Guaranteed Annual Income
Senator Hugh Segal

It was 40 years ago that a former mayor of Windsor, former provincial minister and Ontario senator issued one of the greatest challenges to Canada's citizens and leaders. Sadly, however, the centre piece of the lifelong work of David Croll remains unfulfilled and his challenge remains unaddressed.

In the introduction to his 1971 report of the Senate committee on poverty, Mr. Croll stated bluntly: "Poverty is the great social issue of our time. The poor do not choose poverty. It is at once their affliction and our national shame. No nation can achieve true greatness if it lacks the courage and determination to undertake the surgery necessary to remove the cancer of poverty from its body politic."

Mr. Croll, one of Canada's greatest Liberal parliamentarians, made his clarion call for the establishment of a guaranteed annual income (GAI) in that report. It was, the committee concluded, the most efficient and least wasteful mechanism for lifting millions of Canadians out of poverty. He was right four decades ago, and he is still right today.

In 1972, the future lieutenant-governor of Ontario, Hal Jackman, introduced Mr. Croll to a well-heeled Toronto Empire Club audience: "For a minister in power [under Ontario premier Mitch Hepburn], David Croll's identification with the dispossessed naturally caused certain uneasiness in government circles, and in 1937, the real crunch came when events so determined themselves that David Croll was forced to choose. In depression-torn Oshawa, housewives were doing alternate duty on bread lines and picket lines, and the issue was whether the government was justified in sending in militia troops and provincial police to break up the pickets of the automobile workers, whose only fault was that they wanted to have their own union. David Croll handed in his resignation and in so doing issued this statement, which has now become part of the folklore of Canadian politics: 'Thousands of working men and women of the province of Ontario have come to look to me as their protector and their champion. I feel that I cannot now fail them. In my official capacity I have travelled the middle of the road, but now that you have put the extreme alternative to me, my place is marching with the workers rather than riding with General Motors.' Croll resigned from the government, but he would not admit that he was beaten."

Mr. Croll remains an inspiring figure to me and many colleagues in the Senate, particularly members such as Liberal Senator Art Eggleton, who chaired the standing Senate committee on social affairs, science and technology, cities sub-committee, of which I was vice-chair. Mr. Croll's work and his words encouraged us and our report, "In from the Margins: A Call to Action on Poverty, Housing and Homelessness," which was released just over a year ago and was passed unanimously and unaltered by the Senate. Those from both parties who worked on that report called on the government to embrace a basic income floor for the disabled and initiate a green paper on welfare reform through a refundable tax credit-based basic income floor.

Very soon, when Parliament resumes, the federal government will have just such an opportunity. Finance Minister Jim Flaherty will rise in the Commons and deliver the government's budget. In that budget there could and should be a green-paper proposal on how to modernize income security once and for all and to put Ottawa on the path of addressing the core challenge that Mr. Croll championed 40 years ago.

Mr. Croll's description of the situation Canada faced in the 1970s still echoes: "If the social welfare business of Canada had been in the private sector, it would have long ago been declared bankrupt. The reasons are not hard to find. Resistance to change, a stubborn refusal to modernize its thinking, a failure to understand the root causes of poverty, inadequate research and the bureaucracy digging in to preserve itself and the status quo, are some of the basic causes of the dilemma in which we find ourselves today."

Forty years later, despite an annual total federal and provincial expenditure of $160-billion on income security, the gap between the most wealthy and the lowest income group has worsened. Liberal and Conservative federal governments, NDP, PQ and other provincial governments have not addressed the challenge at its source. Expensive service and welfare bureaucracies, however well-meaning, run costly, rules-based, micro-managing programs with strong 19th-century anti-poor biases that all fail to reduce poverty in any coherent way. As we celebrate the 40th anniversary of the Croll report, advanced by a proud son of Windsor, we must refocus on the humanity for which he struggled.

Forty years ago Mr. Croll said: "The children of the poor (and there are many) are the most helpless victims of all, and find even less hope in a society where welfare systems from the very beginning destroy their chances of a better life." Forty years later, the time for action on the GAI is upon us. Leaving the challenge of poverty to the side is to deny the essential decency and balance Canadians have always shared.

Source: Segal, H. (2011, January 19). Let's refocus on a guaranteed annual income. *The Globe and Mail.* Retrieved March 11, 2011 from http://tinyurl.com/62w7jb3

Public Opinion and Public Values

Canadian public opinion is of various minds concerning poverty reduction and the means of accomplishing this goal. The information provided in Chapter 11 provides evidence that, for the most part, Canadian recognize that the incidence of poverty is primarily a structural problem that results from political and economic policies. Yet, Canadians do not place poverty reduction high on their public policy agenda. Much of this has to do with

Box 14.4: A Canada with Scandinavian-Style Equality Is Achievable

It's not as if we need to obliterate capitalism. Properly regulated, taxed, and forced to operate in the public interest, business firms can fit constructively into a just society. The wealth that their workers produce can be more fairly distributed. This is evident in several parts of Europe, notably in the Scandinavian nations, where capitalism still thrives. Norway, Sweden, Denmark, and Finland may not have developed idyllic societies—but their economies are far more equitable than Canada's and far less blighted by poverty, hunger, and homelessness. Business firms operate freely and profitably in these countries, but under constraints that make them good corporate citizens....

The tragedy for Canada is that a more equitable Scandinavian-style society has always been achievable, given the resources, the skills, and the values that we share.... Politically, the biggest barrier we face is our outdated, undemocratic, first-past-the-post electoral system, which effectively disenfranchises the millions who cast their ballots for losing candidates. The ensuing allocation of seats in Parliament distorts voters' intent. Had we voted on January 23 under some form of proportional representation (PR), the NDP would now have 59 MPs instead of 29, and the Greens would have a dozen instead of none.

It is no coincidence that, in the Scandinavian and other European countries with the most equitable societies, elections are held on some PR basis. This democratic system produces parliaments that truly reflect the wishes of all voters, not just the majority or plurality. And the governments that emerge tend to be coalitions of the more progressive parties and movements. (Green MPs have even served as Environment Ministers in several European countries.)

A switch to PR in Canada is long overdue. Ours is one of the few major Western nations that still cling to the undemocratic winner-takes-all system. A PR process would open the door to the formation, sooner or later, of a strong left-of-centre coalition government in Ottawa.

How far and how fast such an administration could remodel our society along Scandinavian lines is debatable. Undoubtedly its proposed social and economic reforms would be warmly welcomed by most Canadians, but they would be fiercely opposed by the business community and the wealthiest among us wanting to maintain their privileged status. The commercial media could be expected to fulminate against "tax-and-spend socialists" and cradle-to-grave coddling. But the most formidable and hostile reaction would surely come from our next-door neighbouring superpower....

What I've been projecting here, of course, is a future that may never become a reality. But I'm convinced it could. In fact, if it doesn't—if no such genuinely pro-Canada government emerges, and if no overpowering public demand for social justice, democracy, and national identity develops—then my pessimistic e-mail correspondent will be justified in her despair. Because that will mean that I am indeed living in "a world of wish and fantasy."

Somehow I don't think I am. I think that most Canadians believe in and yearn for a better country and a better world, that we favour fair-sharing over greed, compassion over indifference, peace over war, Canadianism over Americanism.

What we lack is a political system and a political movement that will give voice to our values and reshape our society to embody them.

This is a vacuum that must be filled. If all of us who hold these noble aspirations work together to harness and empower them, we could surprise ourselves with what we can collectively accomplish.

(Ed Finn is the CCPA's Senior Editor)

Source: Finn, E. (2006, March 1). A Canada with Scandinavian-style equality is achievable. *The CCPA Monitor*. Retrieved March 11, 2011 from www.policyalternatives.ca/publications/monitor/march-2006-big-business-bang-theory-iii

the current political and economic discourse that minimizes poverty as a problem, represents the current organization and distribution of economic resources as unproblematic, and in any event blames people living in poverty for their own situations.

As one example of how Canadian public opinion has been shaped to underestimate the importance of poverty as a health and quality of life issue, consider Canadians' views concerning the determinants of health. As noted earlier, when asked both open-ended and closed questions about the importance to health of a variety of health determinants, Canadian overwhelmingly provided the stereotypical responses of diet and exercise. There is little acknowledgement of the much more significant contributions to health of income, education, employment, and quality of early life (Canadian Population Health Initiative, 2004).

These findings are not surprising considering the constant bombardment of messaging Canadians endure concerning the health consequences of the "holy trinity of risk" of tobacco, diet, and physical activity (Raphael, 2009). And sadly, for various reasons, the health care, public health, and health sciences sectors have been complicit in this sophisticated form of "poor-bashing" by saying little to the public of the importance to health of the social determinants of health in general and the experience of living in poverty in particular (Raphael, 2003). How can these public understandings be changed? (See Raphael and Curry Stevens, 2009, for a more extensive analysis of the role that the health care and public health sectors could play in public education concerning the health-threatening effects of poverty.)

Mobilizing the Health Care and Public Health Sectors

The health care and public health sectors could raise the profile of poverty as a health issue. A promising beginning on this has been made by scattered health units across

Canada. In Ontario, the provincial Mandatory Guidelines for Public Health require health units to report on and address the social determinants of health, which includes income and its distribution. Another promising development has been the establishment by the Public Health Agency of Canada of a National Coordinating Centre for the Determinants of Health at St. Francis Xavier University in Nova Scotia. The mandate of this Centre is to raise issues regarding the determinants of health and coordinate action in support of these.

Actual activity would see public health and health care officials, managers, and workers drawing upon developments in the poverty and poverty-related literatures to consider the impacts of policy decisions upon health and quality of life. To date, the public health community has focused virtually all of its attention on behavioural risk factors to the exclusion of poverty and its effects upon health and quality of life. Similarly, the health care community is firmly focused on treatment issues, preventative screening, and managing the health care system and its many components. Both sectors need to raise the profile of poverty as a health threat, build public understanding of its importance, and shift the focus of governments and the public toward improving the living conditions of those living in poverty.

Building Social Movements

Political economists such as Teeple (2000) and Coburn (2004) argue that poverty, increasing income and wealth inequality, and the weakening of social infrastructure result from the concentration of wealth and power within a nation with an attendant weakening of civil society. In response, there are calls for greater equity in political power. How would this come about? Social movements would have to mobilize the public to pressure governments to restore programs and services, and reintroduce more progressive income tax rates. Independent unions are a necessity as is legislation that strengthens the ability of workers to organize (Zweig, 2000). Building a social movement involves educating Canadians about the importance of poverty and the means by which it could be reduced. The strengthening of latent coalitions through support of organizations already advocating for poverty reduction is essential.

The Need for Political Action

The most fruitful avenue to poverty reduction may be to elect representatives who support poverty-reducing policies. As a recent example of such an approach, the advocacy group Campaign 2000 gathered party responses in the lead-up to the 2006 and 2008 federal elections to some key policy options to reduce child poverty (see Chapter 11).

These policy options include making resources available for poor families through higher child benefits and minimum wages, increasing funding for social housing, and providing a national system of early learning and child care. Campaign 2000 found

NDP and Bloc Québécois positions to be consistent with these policy options. The Conservative positions were consistently opposed. The Liberal Party position was supportive of some options but not others.

The national child care issue is particularly relevant to remedying conditions of child deprivation and lack of employment activity. Child care programs along the lines previously agreed to by the federal and provincial governments support childhood development, and allow parents to engage in education, training, and employment (Friendly, 2009). To implement these policy options, it would appear that candidates of parties who support such poverty-reducing policies need to be elected. As noted in Chapter 11, left Cabinet share is the best predictor of poverty rates among modern industrialized nations.

Five years ago, the federal Parliament saw the creation of a national program of child care, increased funding for affordable housing, and a general willingness to address issues related to the social security of Canadian. Unfortunately, virtually all of this was reversed with the election of a minority Conservative government.

What Can You Do?

The primary means of reducing poverty is through the enactment of public policies that provide people with adequate living conditions. Public policies that would reduce poverty are not pipe dreams: they have been implemented in many wealthy developed nations to good effect.

Pressure Government to Act

Governments at all levels have neglected the reduction and elimination of poverty. Since it appears that elected representatives and policy-makers are aware of poverty and its effects yet choose to not act, social and political movements must be developed that will pressure governments and policy-makers to enact poverty-reducing public policy.

There are numerous ways of accomplishing this. One involves educating Canadians about the causes of poverty and its adverse effects and then translating this knowledge into action. Canadians must confront their elected representatives at all levels about what is being done to reduce poverty. Canadians should also raise these issues with agencies, organizations, and institutions whose mandates include promoting health and well-being and preventing illness.

Ask Your Professional or Employee Association or Union to Speak up about Poverty

Almost everyone touched by the issue of poverty has an association or organization that can make themselves heard by elected representatives and policy-makers. Public health workers have the Canadian Public Health Association and their provincial organizations. Nurses, physicians, psychologists, social workers, and others all belong to organizations that have a responsibility to speak up about their members' concerns.

The average worker may have a union or employee association. Local community organizations and agencies are also potential contributors to the debate about poverty in

Canada and how to address it. All of these organizations have a responsibility to "speak truth to power" about what is happening in Canada.

Urge the Health Sector to Get Involved

Public health units, disease associations (such as the Heart and Stroke Foundation, Canadian Cancer Society, and the Canadian Diabetes Association), and health care organizations (such as hospitals and professional associations) must educate themselves and their clients on the role poverty plays in shaping health and quality of life. They should urge governments and policy-makers to create and implement poverty-reducing public policies. Canadians should ask these organizations what they are doing to educate Canadians about poverty.

Get Involved in Politics

Another way to reduce poverty is to support candidates of political parties that are receptive to serious poverty reduction activities. Such candidates can be found in every political party, but are more likely to be candidates of the New Democratic Party. Evidence is abundant that, in Canada and elsewhere, left political parties are more likely to develop poverty reduction policies such as universal health care, public pensions, housing programs, and universal child care that support poverty reduction efforts.

Support the Right to Unionize Workplaces

There is strong evidence that an essential aspect of poverty reduction is the organization of labour. Support is needed to ease the path for Canadians to unionize their workplace (see Box 14.5). In Canada, working under a collective agreement is related to higher wages, better benefits, and improved employment security and working conditions. The strength of labour unions is also related to differences among developed nations in the extent of poverty.

Get Involved with an Anti-poverty Organization

Finally, Canadians can join and/or financially support organizations that work to reduce poverty. These organizations include:

- Campaign 2000—www.campaign2000.ca/
- Canada Without Poverty—www.cwp-csp.ca/
- Make Poverty History—www.makepovertyhistory.ca/
- Canadian Centre for Policy Alternatives—www.policyalternatives.ca/
- Canadian Council on Social Development—www.ccsd.ca/home.htm
- Citizens for Public Justice—www.cpj.ca/

There are also numerous provincial and local anti-poverty organizations that need your help and support. (See Mikkonen and Raphael, 2010, for a list of organizations engaged in working on related issues such as housing, child care, and health and social services.)

Box 14.5: The Importance of Organized Labour in Poverty Reduction

Anti-poverty Arsenal Lacks Key Weapon
Jim Coyle

In its war on poverty, the Ontario government is beginning to sound a little like Saddam Hussein's old spokesman Comical Ali, who rhapsodized about glorious Iraqi victories even as American troops rolled into Baghdad.

"We've set out to take poverty on," Premier Dalton McGuinty boasted again yesterday.

But like Ali, the Liberal government sometimes seems bigger on grand talk than performance.

Two things should give anti-poverty activists cause for alarm in recent days about the government's stomach for the fight.

The first was the start this week of ballyhooed public consultations on poverty reduction and the decision to hold them behind closed doors, ejecting the uninvited with a vigour that made Mike Harris's Common Sense revolutionaries seem like tie-dyed peaceniks.

The only thing worse than hearing Children and Youth Services Minister Deb Matthews defend that embarrassing show—let the excluded use websites! she sniffed—was that last week she was among Liberal MPPs who voted down a private member's bill that offered one of the best anti-poverty tools available.

NDP Leader Howard Hampton's bill would have rolled back a Harris-era crackdown on unions and restored the right of card-membership to Ontario workers as it existed from 1950 to 1996.

True, unions aren't perfect, any more than are corporations. Over the decades, there have been lots of abuses by unions. But it remains true that unionization helped build the postwar middle-class on a solid foundation of good wages, benefits and job security—none of which are easily had by workers in the new millennium.

Statistics Canada data made clear last week that over the last quarter-century the rich have got richer, the poor poorer and the middle-class has shrunk or stagnated.

As *New York Times* reporter Steven Greenhouse says in his new book, *The Big Squeeze: Tough Times for the American Worker*, labour unions, more than any other institution in society, "work to improve the lives of low-wage workers and to reduce inequality."

The labour movement, for all its faults, is the one force "that created some semblance of balance between workers and management during the second half of the 20th century."

Political leaders serious about helping low-income workers, and reducing widening inequality, would make it easier for workers to join unions, he said.

"Labour unions once were, and could be again, the most effective tool to improve the lot of workers," he said. And card-membership such as that proposed by Hampton "would be the single biggest step to enable unions to grow again."

As Hampton said, the people who benefit most are the lowest-paid workers—women, students, younger workers, new Canadians.

"Does it mean that overnight they get huge, whopping pay increases? No. What it means is that they can get, through collective bargaining, a decent wage" and some benefits for their families, he said.

Telling a story common to his generation, New Democrat Peter Kormos said his father was an immigrant from Slovakia with a Grade 8 education, a steelworker able to reach the middle class and send his five kids to university on the strength of a union wage.

For his part, McGuinty noted again yesterday that making good on his poverty reduction promises isn't easy in "challenging" economic times.

But a premier branding himself progressive, and looking for inspiration on leading through difficult times, could do worse than consult the inaugural addresses of Franklin Roosevelt made during the Great Depression.

"The test of our progress is not whether we add more to the abundance of those who have much," he said.

Source: Coyle, J. (2008, May 7). Anti-poverty arsenal lacks key weapon. *Toronto Star*. Retrieved March 11, 2011 from www.thestar.com/printarticle/422233

Quality of Life and Economic Productivity and Innovation

One of the most common objections frequently raised to the poverty-reducing agenda presented here is that such government support to its citizens would threaten Canada's economic competitiveness and thereby Canadians' health and quality of life. Little evidence for such a view has not limited its widespread dissemination, and frequent repetition by those opposed to strengthening the Canadian welfare state and reducing poverty (Jackson, 2000).

The Conference Board of Canada carries out extensive analyses of national performance on several sets of indicators: health, education and skills, environment, society, economy, and innovation (Conference Board of Canada, 2009). In their analyses, they provide ranks for these areas for 17 wealthy developed nations. The Conference Board points out that Canadian performance is in the mid-range among the top 17 performers for most indicators. (See Table 14.1 where nations are ranked by the Society indicator from best to worse.)

The Society indicator consists of measures of jobless youth, confidence in Parliament, disabled income, homicides, elderly poverty, burglaries, child poverty, assaults, working-age poverty, life satisfaction, income inequality, acceptance of diversity, intergenerational income mobility, social isolation, gender income gap, suicides, and voter turnout. The Conference Board states:

Achieving the goal that the Conference Board sets out for Canada—that of providing "a high and sustainable quality of life for all Canadians"—requires much more than economic success. Self-sufficiency, equity, and social cohesion are the three dimensions that are assessed in the Society report card. A high quality of life is defined by communities that ensure the active participation of individuals within society, including its most vulnerable citizens (such as youth and persons with disabilities); minimize the extremes of inequality between its poorest and richest citizens; and are free from fear of social unrest and violence.

It should be no surprise that the Scandinavian social democratic welfare states came in 1st, 2nd, 3rd, and 7th on the set of indicators the Conference Board developed to

Table 14.1: National Rankings on a Range of Indicators—2008, Nations Ranked by Scores on Society Area from Best to Worse

	Society	Health	Education and Skills	Environment	Economy	Innovation
Denmark*	1	15	11	11	5	11
Norway*	2	4	15	3	1	17
Sweden*	3	5	5	1	7	5
Netherlands^x	4	11	8	13	3	8
Austria^x	5	12	12	8	4	13
Switzerland^x	6	2	4	4	2	1
Finland*	7	7	1	2	15	9
Belgium^x	8	n/a	9	12	12	12
Canada^+	9	10	2	15	11	14
France^x	10	6	14	6	9	10
Ireland^+	11	13	13	10	17	2
Germany^x	12	8	7	9	13	6
Italy^x	13	3	17	7	16	16
Australia^+	14	9	6	16	6	15
UK^+	15	14	10	5	10	7
Japan	16	1	3	14	14	4
USA^+	17	16	16	17	8	3

* Social Democratic political economies

x Conservative political economies

+ Liberal political economies

Source: Adapted from Conference Board of Canada. (2009). *How Canada performs: A report card on Canada.* Ottawa: Conference Board of Canada.

cover the Society domain. And four conservative nations also surpass Canada's Society rank of 9th. What is of particular interest is the excellent economic performance of the social democratic welfare states of Denmark, Sweden, and Norway and the conservative states of Netherlands, Austria, and Switzerland. These nations have better Society indicators *and* Economic indicators than Canada. And outside of Norway, all these states that surpass Canada on the Society indicators also surpass Canada on the Innovation indicators.

The Economy indicators include GDP per capita, GDP growth, productivity growth, unit labour cost growth, inflation, deficit-to-GDP ratio, employment growth, unemployment rate, and long-term unemployment rate. Innovation indicators include spending on research and development, technological co-operation, and patents in a range of areas, among others. The argument that reducing poverty and improving quality of life comes at an economic and innovation cost is clearly not supported.

Conclusions

Poverty rates ebb and flow—within a very limited range—as a result of periods of economic growth and recession. Despite the importance of poverty as a health issue, public attention is diverted from this issue toward an inordinate emphasis upon medical treatments, biomedical research, and lifestyle approaches to health. If only a small proportion of current allocations to these activities were devoted to public education and community development activities related to raising the profile of poverty as a public policy issue in the service of health and quality of life, a sea change in attitudes could result. Such a sea change could lead to policy-makers beginning to seriously to address the issue of poverty in Canada. Policy solutions to its presence are available and could be readily applied.

It seems likely that the future of poverty in Canada—and associated indicators of population health and quality of life—primarily depends upon the policy influence of political parties in federal and provincial Parliaments. In the more immediate future, NDP, Liberal, and Bloc strength in the federal Parliament *could* lead to poverty-reducing policies such as the proposed national child care program. Conservative dominance should lead to little if any decline in child poverty rates and—due to greater implementation of market-oriented rather than equity-based policies—may increase these rates.

In the longer term, accumulated empirical evidence on the political economy of poverty in developed nations indicates that the influence of political parties that support reducing poverty is enhanced by implementation of electoral reform. Poverty levels are lower and government commitments to supporting citizens stronger when popular vote is more closely translated into representation in the houses of legislature.

To build support for political action in support of poverty-reducing public policies, continuing action in support of these goals by a range of sectors are required. These actions should provide repeated presentations of the evidence of the importance of

Box 14.6: Canada Slammed During UN Human Rights Review

Ottawa (13 Jan. 2009)—Canada could soon find itself shamed by the United Nations Human Rights Council (UNHRC) as a country that violates international labour and human rights standards.

Fifty submissions slamming Canada—on everything from the state of Aboriginal Peoples to the erosion of labour rights—have been filed with the Geneva-based UNHRC as part of a new Universal Periodic Review (UPR) process. The UPR involves a review of the human rights records of all 192 UN member states once every four years. Canada's human rights record will be officially reviewed at the fourth session of the UNHRC in Geneva which begins Feb. 3, 2009.

The National Union of Public and General Employees (NUPGE) was one of the 50 civil society organizations submitting briefs to the UN Office of the High Commissioner for Human Rights in preparation for the February review.

NUPGE concentrated on the serious erosion of labour rights in Canada over the past 27 years as well as Canada's poor record of ratifying and complying with International Labour Organization (ILO) Conventions.

Summary of 50 submissions

Recently the UN office prepared a summary of the 50 submissions it has received and published Canada's national report prepared by the federal, provincial and territorial governments for the UPR. The first recommendation contained in the summary report was NUPGE's request for the federal government to ratify the three remaining core ILO conventions—No. 29, No. 98 and No. 138—which have not yet been ratified by Canada.

Alex Neve, secretary-general of Amnesty International Canada, said his organization expects Canada to be cited for falling short on human rights issues in a number of areas when the UN human rights arm publishes its final report.

"To be criticized doesn't mean Canada has joined the worst of the worst (abusing nations)," said Neve. "But as a general rule, Canadians are proud this is a country that believes in human rights and do want our governments (federal, provincial and territorial) to do the right thing."

The Amnesty submission highlights several concerns. In a section on indigenous rights, it notes that more children are in the care of the state now than during the century-plus period when they were forcibly removed from communities and sent to Indian residential schools.

"A real disgrace"

"The Canadian record of upholding the rights of indigenous peoples is a real disgrace and a source of national shame," said Neve. "These are not political, economic or natural resource matters. These are issues of human rights."

While only member states can ask questions or make recommendations during the Feb. 3 hearing, written submissions are taken into consideration for the final report. Canada currently sits on the 47-member council, a slot filled by rotation.

Source: National Union of Public and General Employees. (2009, January 13). *Canada slammed during UN human rights review*. Retrieved March 11, 2011 from www.nupge.ca/node/776

reducing poverty that will build public support for such action and counter the forces opposed to poverty reduction. There is a role for a very wide range of actors. The goals of these actors should be to build public support for a concerted public policy agenda of first reducing, and then eliminating, the incidence of poverty in Canada. In the process, the health and quality of life of Canadians will benefit.

This volume began with a 1998 news item on the United Nations Committee on Economic, Social, and Cultural Rights condemning Canada for its treatment of people living in poverty. It seems appropriate to conclude the volume with a 2009 item on Canada's human rights performance—including poverty eradication—as assessed in submissions by numerous Canadian organizations to the United Nations Human Rights Council. It appears that the United Nations will continue to have cause for concern about Canada for some time to come.

Critical Thinking Questions

1. Why do you think most Canadians mistakenly believe Canada has a very well-developed welfare state?
2. What do you believe are the primary reasons why Canada's poverty rate continues to be so high in international comparison?
3. What are some of the reasons most Canadians vote for parties opposed to social democratic approaches to governance?
4. Do you believe that poverty rates in Canada can be substantially reduced without profound political change? How would this be accomplished?
5. What are some of the barriers to poverty reduction in Canada?
6. What are you prepared to do to reduce, and then eliminate, poverty in Canada?

Recommended Readings

Esping-Andersen, G. (1990). *The three worlds of welfare capitalism*. Princeton, NJ: Princeton University Press.

Esping-Andersen, G. (1999). *Social foundations of postindustrial economies*. New York: Oxford University Press.

These books provide a typology of Western welfare states that considers a range of social policies and links these with variations in the historical development of Western countries. The author describes how profound differences that exist among liberal (e.g., USA, Canada, UK), conservative (e.g., Germany, France, Italy), and social democratic (e.g., Sweden, Norway, Denmark) political economies translate into widely differing lived experiences among citizens of these nations.

Esping-Andersen, G. (2002). *Why we need a new welfare state*. New York: Oxford University Press.

Contributors argue that welfare states need to consider issues of social inclusion and justice. The volume focuses on four social domains: the aged and transition to retirement; welfare issues related to changes in working life; risks and needs that arise in households, especially in families with young children; and the challenges of creating gender equality.

Hofrichter, R. (Ed.). (2003). *Social justice and health: Politics, ideology, and inequity in the distribution of disease*. San Francisco: Jossey Bass.

Hofrichter's book outlines the political, economic, and ideological barriers to reducing poverty and promoting health in the USA and Canada. See especially Hofrichter's chapter, "The Politics of Health Inequities: Contested Terrain," and Raphael's chapter, "Towards the Future: Policy and Community Actions to Promote Population Health."

Raphael, D. (Ed.). (2009). *Social determinants of health: Canadian perspectives* (2nd ed.). Toronto: Canadian Scholars' Press Inc.

Each chapter has specific policy options that would help to reduce either poverty or its effects upon health and quality of life. See especially Langille's "The Politics of Health," and Raphael and Curry-Steven's "Addressing and Surmounting the Political and Social Barriers to Health."

Teeple, G. (2000). *Globalization and the decline of social reform: Into the twenty-first century*. Aurora, ON: Garamond Press.

Teeple sees the welfare state as being threatened by the rising strength of economic and political forces associated with global capitalism. He warns that the consequences of weakened welfare states include declining national sovereignty, increasing economic inequality, and increasing insecurity for citizens.

Relevant Websites

Campaign 2000—www.campaign2000.ca/index.html

Campaign 2000 is a cross-Canada public education movement to build Canadian awareness and support for the 1989 all-party House of Commons resolution to end child poverty in Canada by the year 2000. Campaign 2000 began in 1991 out of concern about the lack of government progress in addressing child poverty.

Canadian Centre for Policy Alternatives—www.policyalternatives.ca

The Centre monitors developments and promotes research on economic and social issues facing Canada. It provides alternatives to the views of business research institutes and many government agencies by publishing research reports, sponsoring conferences, organizing briefings, and providing informed comment on the issues of the day from a non-partisan perspective.

Canadian Labour Congress—www.clc-ctc.ca

The Canadian Labour Congress is the national umbrella organization for 2.5 million unionized Canadian workers. The Social and Economic Policy sub-site contains many research papers on labour market issues. The site links to the websites of many unions in Canada and around the world.

Canada Without Poverty—www.cwp-csp.ca

Canada Without Poverty is a federally incorporated, non-partisan, not-for-profit and charitable organization dedicated to the elimination of poverty in Canada.

Make Poverty History—www.makepovertyhistory.ca/

The Make Poverty History campaign is a coalition of organizations that have come together for the common cause of making poverty history both at home and abroad. The campaign is guided by a Steering Committee with representatives appointed by the member organizations. Make Poverty History has over 260,000 individual supporters who have signed on in support of its platform. Many of them are part of an online action network that send messages to decision-makers and take other online actions.

Glossary of Terms

Commodification refers to the production of goods or services for sale in the marketplace. *De-commodification*, in terms of welfare-state issues, refers to the degree to which individuals can live a reasonable life without relying on market wages. Can older people or the unemployed, those not earning a market wage—live a reasonable life? Social democratic states have the greatest degree of de-commodification and the lowest poverty rates. Canada and other liberal nations have the least degree of de-commodification and the highest poverty rates.

Corporate power and influence refers to the dominance of corporate views in shaping public policy. It represents an imbalance between the influence of citizens, labour, and governments, and results in skewed government and societal priorities. Poverty reduction is low on the public policy in large part due to this dominance.

Health promotion represents a comprehensive social and political process. It not only embraces actions directed at strengthening the skills and capabilities of individuals, but also action directed toward changing social, environmental, and economic conditions so as to alleviate their impact on public and individual health. Health promotion is the process of enabling people to increase control over the determinants of health and thereby improve their health. Participation is essential to sustain health promotion action (Nutbeam, 1998).

Noblesse oblige is "honorable behavior, considered to be the responsibility of persons of high birth or rank, to members of the lower class" (Princeton University, 2011). Usually refers to the willingness of conservative politicians and the wealthy to provide charitable and other support to the most downtrodden of society.

Social democracy is a political ideology emerging in the late 19th and early 20th centuries among supporters of Marxism who believed that the transition to a socialist society could be achieved through democratic and evolutionary, rather than revolutionary, means. It emphasizes a program of gradual legislative reform of the capitalist system to make it more equitable, usually with the goal of a socialist society as a theoretical endpoint.

Welfare regimes refers to the different ways in which different nations or societies provide for the well-being of their citizens or compensate for the failures of markets to do so. Social democratic welfare regimes tend to provide more resources, and on a more universalistic basis, than do liberal welfare regimes, which tend to target welfare measures to the poor and to provide less benefits to the fewer that are eligible for such benefits. The conservative regimes provide benefits as a side benefit of working or expect the family to provide support. The Latin regimes are undeveloped versions of the Conservative welfare regimes.

References

Alesina, A., and Glaeser, E. L. (2004). *Fighting poverty in the US and Europe: A world of difference.* Toronto: Oxford University Press.

Bernard, P., and Saint-Arnaud, S. (2004). *More of the same: The position of the four largest Canadian provinces in the world of welfare regimes.* Ottawa: Canadian Policy Research Networks.

Brady, D. (2003). The politics of poverty: Left political institutions, the welfare state, and poverty. *Social Forces, 82*(2), 557–588.

Brady, D. (2009). *Rich democracies, poor people: How politics explain poverty.* New York: Oxford University Press.

Briggs, A. (1961). The welfare state in historical perspective. *European Journal of Sociology, 2,* 251–259.

Broadbent, Ed. (2009). Barbarism lite: The political attack on social rights. Online at http://www.thestar.com/comment/article/590845

Brooks, S., and Miljan, L. (2003). Theories of public policy. In S. Brooks and L. Miljan (Eds.), *Public policy in Canada: An introduction* (pp. 22–49). Toronto: Oxford University Press.

Canadian Population Health Initiative. (2004). *Select highlights on public views of the determinants of health.* Ottawa: CPHI.

Coburn, D. (2004). Beyond the income inequality hypothesis: Globalization, neo-liberalism, and health inequalities. *Social Science and Medicine, 58*(1), 41–56.

Coburn, D. (2010). Health and health care: A political economy perspective. In T. Bryant, D. Raphael, and M. Rioux (Eds.), *Staying alive: Critical perspectives on health, illness, and health care* (2nd ed., pp. 65–92). Toronto: Canadian Scholars' Press Inc.

Conference Board of Canada. (2009). *How Canada performs: A report card on Canada*. Ottawa: Conference Board of Canada.

Esping-Andersen, G. (1985). *Politics against markets: The social democratic road to power*. Princeton, NJ: Princeton University Press.

Esping-Andersen, G. (1990). *The three worlds of welfare capitalism*. Princeton, NJ: Princeton University Press.

Esping-Andersen, G. (1999). *Social foundations of post-industrial economies*. New York: Oxford University Press.

Friendly, M. (2009). *About Canada: Daycare*. Halifax: Fernwood Publishers.

Jackson, A. (2000). *Why we don't have to choose between social justice and economic growth: The myth of the equity/efficiency trade-off*. Ottawa: Canadian Council on Social Development.

Jackson, A. (2010). *Work and labour in Canada: Critical issues* (2nd ed.). Toronto: Canadian Scholars' Press Inc..

Langille, D. (2009). Follow the money: How business and politics shape our health. In D. Raphael (Ed.), *Social determinants of health: Canadian perspectives* (2nd ed., pp. 305–317). Toronto: Canadian Scholars' Press Inc.

McQuaig, L., and Brooks, N. (2010). *The trouble with billionaires*. Toronto: Viking Canada.

Mikkonen, J., and Raphael, D. (2010). *Social determinants of health: The Canadian facts*. Retrieved March 11, 2011 from http://thecanadianfacts.org

Mishra, R. (1990). *The welfare state in capitalist society*. Toronto: University of Toronto Press.

Navarro, V., and Shi, L. (2002). The political context of social inequalities and health. In V. Navarro (Ed.), *The political economy of social inequalities: Consequences for health and quality of life* (pp. 403–418). Amityville, NY: Baywood.

Nutbeam, D. (1998). *Health promotion glossary*. Geneva: World Health Organisation.

Organisation for Economic Co-operation and Development. (2004). *OECD employment outlook 2004*. Paris: OECD.

Princeton University. (2011). Definition of *noblesse oblige*. Retrieved March 11, 2011 from http://wordnetweb.princeton.edu/perl/webwn?s=noblesse%20oblige

Raphael, D. (2003). Barriers to addressing the determinants of health: Public health units and poverty in Ontario, Canada. *Health Promotion International, 18*(4), 397–405.

Raphael, D. (Ed.). (2009). *Social determinants of health: Canadian perspectives* (2nd ed.). Toronto: Canadian Scholars' Press Inc.

Raphael, D. (2011a). *The political economy of health promotion: Part 1, national commitments to provision of the prerequisites of health*. Manuscript submitted for publication.

Raphael, D. (2011b). *The political economy of health promotion: Part 2, national provision of the prerequisites of health*. Manuscript submitted for publication.

Raphael, D., Bryant, T., Daiski, I., Lines, E., Dinca-Panaitescu, S., Dinca-Panaitescu, M., and Pilkington, B. (2010). *Type 2 diabetes: Poverty, priorities and policy, the social determinants of the incidence and management of type 2 diabetes*. Toronto: York University School of Health Policy and Management and School of Nursing. Available online at http://tinyurl.com/ycysb9l

Raphael, D., and Curry-Stevens, A. (2009). Surmounting the barriers: Making action on the social determinants of health a public policy priority. In D. Raphael (Ed.), *Social determinants of health: Canadian perspectives* (2nd ed., pp. 362–377). Toronto: Canadian Scholars' Press Inc.

Russell, P. (2008). *Two cheers for minority government: The evolution of Canadian parliamentary democracy.* Toronto: Emond Montgomery Publications.

Saint-Arnaud, S., and Bernard, P. (2003). Convergence or resilience? A hierarchical cluster analysis of the welfare regimes in advanced countries. *Current Sociology, 51*(5), 499–527.

Swedish Ministry of Health and Social Affairs. (2005). *Sweden's report on measures to prevent poverty and social exclusion.* Stockholm: Swedish Ministry of Health and Social Affairs.

Swedish Ministry of Health and Social Affairs. (2007). *Sweden's strategy report for social protection and social inclusion 2006–2008.* Stockholm: Swedish Ministry of Health and Social Affairs.

Swedish Ministry of Health and Social Affairs. (2011a). Health care, health, social issues/insurance. Retrieved March 11, 2011 from Government Offices of Sweden website: www.sweden.gov.se/sb/d/2197

Swedish Ministry of Health and Social Affairs. (2011b). *Public health.* Retrieved March 11, 2011 from Government Offices of Sweden website: www.sweden.gov.se/sb/d/2900

Teeple, G. (2000). *Globalization and the decline of social reform: Into the twenty-first century.* Aurora, ON: Garamond Press.

Wesley, J. (2006). *The collective center: Social democracy and red tory politics in Manitoba.* Paper presented at the annual meeting of the Canadian Political Science Association, York University, Toronto, Ontario, June 2. Retrieved March 11, 2011 from www.cpsa-acsp.ca/papers-2006/Wesley.pdf

Wilkinson, R., and Pickett, J. (2009). *The spirit level: Why more equal societies almost always do better.* London, UK: Penguin.

WordIQ.com (2011). *Red Tory: Definition.* Retrieved March 11, 2011 from www.wordiq.com/definition/Red_Tory

Zweig, M. (2000). *The working class majority: America's best kept secret.* Ithaca, NY: Cornell University Press.

Copyright Acknowledgements

Boxes

Box 3.3: M. Ornstein, "Toronto Poverty Is Highly Racialized: York University Census Study," from *Ethno-Racial Groups in Toronto 1971-2001: A Demographic and Socio-Economic Profile.* Reprinted by permission of Michael Ornstein.

Box 4.3: C. Wright Mills, "C. Wright Mills on the Key Questions Facing Social Scientists," from *The Sociological Imagination* (Oxford: Oxford University Press, 2000): 6-7. Reprinted by permission of Oxford University Press, Inc.

Box 4.4: S. Baxter, "The Experience of Social Inequality," from *No Way to Live: Poor Women Speak Out* (Vancouver: New Star Books, 1995): 208-209. Reprinted by permission of New Star Books.

Box 4.5: S. Baxter, "The Experience of Social Exclusion," from *No Way to Live: Poor Women Speak Out* (Vancouver: New Star Books, 1995): 92, 141. Reprinted by permission of New Star Books.

Box 5.1: C. Wright Mills, "Explaining Social Phenomena as Individual Phenomena," from *The Sociological Imagination* (Oxford: Oxford University Press, 2000): 67. Reprinted by permission of Oxford University Press, Inc.

Box 5.2: C. Goar, "A Mess Harper Could Easily Fix," from *Toronto Star,* Editorial, A22, February. 15, 2006. Reprinted by permission of Torstar Syndication Services.

Box 5.3: A. Yalniziyan, from *The Problem of Poverty Post-Recession* (Ottawa: Canadian Centre for Policy Alternatives, 2010). Reprinted by permission of the Canadian Centre for Policy Alternatives.

Box 6.1: K. Green, "Desired Community Changes Outlined by Low-Income Mothers Working Together Towards a Healthier Community," from *Telling It Like It Is: The Realities of Parenting in Poverty* (Saskatoon: Prairie Women's Health Centre of Excellence, 2001): 40. Reprinted by permission of Kathryn Green.

Box 6.2: M. Jones, "Melody's Story: They Don't Give It To You Because They Think You Deserve It," from *Women and the Economy — UN Platform for Action Committee.* Reprinted by permission of Melody Jones and UN Platform for Action Committee Manitoba (UNPAC).

Box 6.3: "Trying to Get Off Welfare Is As Hard As Trying to Get On," from *Women and the Economy—UN Platform for Action Committee.* Reprinted by permission of UN Platform for Action Committee Manitoba (UNPAC).

Box 7.1: "Ontarians Can No Longer Count on Employment Insurance to Provide Temporary Income between Jobs: Toronto and Ottawa Have Lowest Coverage in Canada," from *Employment Insurance: Research Summary for the Task Force on Modernizing Income Security for Working-Age Adults,* http://tinyurl.com/s3vjh (Toronto: Greater Toronto Civil Action Alliance, 2005). Reprinted by permission of the Greater Toronto Civil Action Alliance.

Box 7.2: M. Landsberg, "Let's Keep Fighting System for Kim Rogers' Sake," from *Toronto Star,* Life, K01, Saturday January 25, 2003. Reprinted by permission of Torstar Syndication Services.

Box 7.3: "Alberta Settles Lawsuit Launched by Disadvantaged," from *Guelph Mercury,* January 16, 2006. Reprinted by permission of Guelph Mercury.

Box 7.4: B. Wallace, S. Klein, and M. Reitsma-Street, "Restructuring of BC's Social Assistance System," from *Denied Assistance: Closing the Front Door on Welfare in BC* (Vancouver: Canadian Centre for Policy Alternatives, 2006). Reprinted with permission of the Canadian Centre for Policy Alternatives.

Box 13.3: "Newfoundland and Labrador Poverty Reduction Plan," from *Newfoundland and Labrador's Poverty Reduction Strategy* (Waterloo: Tamarack Institute, 2011). Reprinted by permission of Vibrant Communities Canada and Tamarack Institute for Community Engagement.

Box 13.4: "Ontario's Poverty Reduction Plan," from Ontario's *Poverty Reduction Strategy* (Waterloo: Tamarack Institute, 2011). Reprinted by permission of Vibrant Communities Canada and Tamarack Institute for Community Engagement.

Box 13.5: "Nova Scotia's Anti- Poverty Strategy," from *Nova Scotia's Poverty Reduction Strategy* (Waterloo: Tamarack Institute, 2011). Reprinted by permission of Vibrant Communities Canada and Tamarack Institute for Community Engagement.

Box 13.6: "Senate Anti-Poverty Report Press Release," excerpted from *In From the Margins: A Call to Action on Poverty, Housing, and Homelessness* (Ottawa: The Senate of Canada, 2011).

Box 13.7: "Government Urged to Respond Favorably to Committee Recommendations," from *Dignity for All campaign applauds report calling for federal poverty reduction* (Ottawa: Make Poverty History, 2010).

Box 13.8: "Local Initiatives to Reduce Poverty," from *What is Vibrant Communities* (Waterloo: Tamarack Institute, 2011). Reprinted by permission of Vibrant Communities Canada and Tamarack Institute for Community Engagement.

Box 13.9: "Municipal Initiatives to Reduce Poverty," from *Living Wage Law a Positive Step to Fight Poverty* (Ottawa: Canadian Union of Public Employees, 2010). Reprinted by permission of CUPE.

Box 13.10: "A Plan to Make Canada Poverty Free," from *2010 Report Card on Child and Family Poverty in Canada 1989-2010: Reduced Poverty = Better Health For All* (Toronto: Campaign 2000, 2010): 12. Reprinted by permission of Campaign 2000.

Box 13.11: "Enshrining Poverty Reduction in Federal Law," from *History in the Making* (Ottawa: Canada Without Poverty, 2010). Reprinted by permission of Rob Ranier, Executive Director of Canada Without Poverty.

Box 13.12: "Key Failings of Canadian Anti-Poverty Strategies," excerpted from "Breaking the Cycle or Going Around in Circles? The Ontario Poverty Reduction Strategy" in *The Bullet, Socialist Project E-Bulletin*, No. 173 (2009). Reprinted by permission of Socialist Project.

Box 14.1: "Facts and Statistics about Food Bank Use in Canada," from Hunger Facts 2010 (Toronto: Food Banks Canada, 2010).Reprinted by permission of Food Banks Canada.

Box 14.2: "The Institutions of Neo-Liberalism in Canada: How Corporate Priorities Are Realized," adapted from D. Langille, "Follow the Money: How Business and Politics Define Our Health," in *Social Determinants of Health: Canadian Perspective, 2nd Edition* (Toronto: Canadian Scholars' Press, 2009).

Box 14.3: H. Segal, "Let's Refocus on a Guaranteed Annual Income," from *The Globe and Mail*, January 19, 2011. Reprinted by permission of H. Segal.

Box 14.4: E. Finn, "A Canada with Scandinavian-Style Equality is Achievable," *The Monitor* (Ottawa: Canadian Center for Policy Alternatives, 2006). Reprinted by permission of Canadian Center for Policy Alternatives.

Box 14.5: J. Coyle, "Anti-Poverty Arsenal Lacks Key Weapon," from *Toronto Star*, News, May 7, 2008. Reprinted by permission of Torstar Syndication Services.

Box 14.6: "Canada Slammed During UN Human Rights Review," http://nupge.ca/node/776 (Nepean: National Union of Public and General Employees, 2009). Reprinted by permission of NUPGE.

Figures

Figure 1.1: R. Wilkins, "Mortality by neighbourhood income in urban Canada from 1971 to 2001," from the Health Analysis and Measurement Group (HAMG), HAMG Seminar and special compilations (Ottawa: Statistics Canada). Reprinted by permission of Statistics Canada.

Figure 1.2: "Child Poverty in Wealthy Nations, Mid-2000s," adapted from *Growing unequal: Income distribution and poverty in OECD nations* Organisation for Economic Co-operation and Development, http://dx.doi.org/10.1787/9789264044197 (Paris: Organization for Economic Cooperation and Development, 2008). Reprinted by permission of OECD.

Figure 1.3: "Annual Family Income and Percentage of Children with Lower Functional Health, Canada, Includes only Two-Parent Families, 1994–1995," from *Income and Child Well-Being: A New Perspective on the Poverty Debate* (Ottawa: Canadian Council on Social Development, 1999): 24. Reprinted by permission of Canadian Council on Social Development.

Figure 2.1: "Canadian Poverty Rates Over Time, 1984-2008," adapted from Statistics Canada CANSIM Tables 202-0802 to 202-0804 (Ottawa: Statistics Canada). Reprinted by permission of Statistics Canada.

Figure 2.2: D. P. Ross, K. Scott, and P. Smith, "Relationship of Canadians' Views on Getting by with Income Levels Associated with LICOs," from *The Canadian Fact Book on Poverty* (Ottawa: Canadian Council on Social Development, 2000): 31. Reprinted by permission of Canadian Council on Social Development.

Figure 3.1: "Percentage of Canadians Living in Poverty by Age, Gender, and Family Situation, 2008," adapted from Statistics Canada CANSIM Table 202-2802, http://www40.statcan.ca/l01/cst01/famil41a.htm (Ottawa: Statistics Canada). Reprinted by permission of Statistics Canada.

Figure 3.2: "Percentage of All Canadians, Children, and Individuals in Female Lone-Parent Families Living in Poverty, by Province, 2008," adapted from Statistics Canada CANSIM database Table 202-0802 (Ottawa: Statistics Canada). Reprinted by permission of Statistics Canada.

Figure 3.3: "Child Poverty Rates for Selected Social Groups in Canada: Children 0–14 Years, 1996–2006," adapted from Statistics Canada, 2006, 2001 & 1996 Censuses through the Toronto Social Research and Community Data (Ottawa: Statistics Canada; Community Data Consortium). Reprinted by permission of Statistics Canada and Community Data Consortium.

Figure 3.4: "Average Low-Income Gap for All Families and Unattached Individuals for those Living in Poverty, by Province, 2007," adapted from Statistics Canada CANSIM Table 202-2805 (Ottawa: Statistics Canada). Reprinted by permission of Statistics Canada.

Figure 3.5: "Median Total Income for All Families, Unattached Individuals, and Female-Led Families, Canada, 1995-2008," adapted from Statistics Canada publication *Total Income by*

Family Type, 2010, CANSIM Table 202-0403 (Ottawa: Statistics Canada, 2010). Reprinted by permission of Statistics Canada.

Figure 3.6: "Total Average Income by Income Quintile, All Family Units, Canada, 1995-2008," adapted from Statistics Canada publication *Total Income by quintile, 2010*, CANSIM Table 202-0701 (Ottawa: Statistics Canada, 2010). Reprinted by permission of Statistics Canada.

Figure 4.1: J. Percy-Smith, "Social Exclusion in Context," from *Policy Responses to Social Exclusion: Toward Inclusion* (Berkshire, UK: Open University Press, 2000): 5. Reprinted by permission of Open University Press.

Figure 4.2: E. Grabb, "The Major Means of Power, Structures of Domination, and Bases for Social Inequality," from *Theories of Social Inequality* (Toronto: Harcourt Canada, 2002): 212.

Figure 5.1: M. Hatfield, "Percentage of Groups Experiencing Poverty in 1996 and Persistent Poverty from 1996-2001, Canada," from Vulnerability of Persistent Low Income, *Horizons,* 7(2), (2004): 19-26.

Figure 5.2: R. Valletta, "Relative Risks of Short- and Long-Term Poverty Among Canadians As a Function of Family Type, Educational Attainment of Head of Household, and Family Work Attachment," from *The Ins and Outs of Poverty in Advanced Economies: Poverty Dynamics in Canada, Germany, Great Britain and the United States* (Ottawa: Statistics Canada, 2005): 24-26. Reprinted by permission of Statistics Canada.

Figure 5.3: K. Green, "We Did it Together": Low Income Mothers Working Together Towards a Healthier Community (Saskatoon: Prairie Women's Health Centre of Excellence, 2000): 31.

Figure 6.1: R. Lister, "Forms of Agency Exercise by People Living in Poverty," from *Poverty* (Cambridge, UK: Polity Press, 2004): 130. Reprinted by permission of Polity Press.

Figure 7.1: "Percentage of Canadians Indicating Various Health Care Problems by Household Income Quintile, 2002/2003," adapted from *Joint Canada/United States Survey of Health: Findings and Public Use Microdata File*, 82M0022XIE2003001 (Ottawa: Statistics Canada, 2004): Table A7. Reprinted by permission of Statistics Canada.

Figure 7.2: "Percentage of Canadian Population Aged 15 or Older Who Visited a Dentist, by Dental Insurance Status and Household Income, 1979/97," adapted from Statistics Canada publication *Health Reports*, Catalogue 82-003, Volume 11, Number 1, Released date: August 18, 1999, http://www.statcan.ca/bsolc/english/bsolc?catno=82-003-XandCHROPG=1#issue1999001 (Ottawa: Statistics Canada, 1999): 59. Reprinted by permission of Statistics Canada.

Figure 7.3: "Percentage of Lower, Middle, and Higher Income Canadians Having Public or Private Dental Insurance, 2007-2009" from *Report on the Finding of the Oral Health Component of the Canadian Health Measures Survey* (Ottawa: Health Canada, 2010):70.

Figure 7.4: "Percentage of Lower, Middle, and Higher Income Canadians at Differing Ages Reporting Poor Oral Health, 2007-2009," from *Report on the Finding of the Oral Health Component of the Canadian Health Measures Survey* (Ottawa: Health Canada, 2010):71.

Figure 7.5: "Percentage of Lower, Middle, and Higher Income Canadians Reporting a Variety of Oral Health Issues, 2007-2009," from *Report on the Finding of the Oral Health Component of the Canadian Health Measures Survey* (Ottawa: Health Canada, 2010): 12, 79-80.

Figure 8.1: "Infant Mortality, 2001 andLow Birth-Weight Rates, 1996 by Income Quintile of Neighbourhood, Urban Canada," adapted from R. Wilkins, *Mortality by neighbourhood in-*

come in urban Canada from 1971 to 2001 (Ottawa: Statistics Canada, Health Analysis and Measurement Group and R. Wilkins, 2007) and C. Houle, J.M. Berthelot, & D.P. Ross, "The changing health status of Canada's children," from ISUMA, 1(2), p. 61. Reprinted by permission of Statistics Canada.

Figure 8.2: "Odds Ratios for Risk Factors Associated by Self-Rated Fair or Poor Health, and Low Scores (<50 percentile) on the Health Utilities Index (HUI), Ontario," adapted from "Income Inequality and Health in Ontario," by G. Xi et al, *Canadian Journal of Public Health*, 96 (Ottawa: Canadian Journal of Public Health, 2005): 209-210. Reprinted by permission of Canadian Journal of Public Health.

Figure 8.3a: "Diabetes Mortality, Urban Canada, Males 1971-2001," adapted from "Mortality by neighbourhood income in urban Canada from 1971 to 2001," by R. Wilkins from the Health Analysis Measurement Group (HAMG), HAMG Seminar and special compilations (Ottawa: Statistics Canada, 2007). Reprinted by permission of Statistics Canada.

Figure 8.3b: "Diabetes Mortality, Urban Canada, Females 1971-2001," adapted from "Mortality by neighbourhood income in urban Canada from 1971 to 2001," by R. Wilkins from the Health Analysis Measurement Group (HAMG), HAMG Seminar and special compilations (Ottawa: Statistics Canada, 2007). Reprinted by permission of Statistics Canada.

Figure 8.4a: "Where Diabetes Hits Hardest," from *Toronto Star*, using data from Institute for Clinical Evaluation Sciences (Glazier et al., 2007). Reprinted by permission of Torstar Syndication Services.

Figure 8.4b: "Visible Minorities," from *Toronto Star*, using data from Statistics Canada (Charron, 2009). Reprinted by permission of Torstar Syndication Services.

Figure 8.4c: "Poverty in the City," from *Toronto Star*, using data from the United Way of Greater Toronto (2004). Reprinted by permission of Torstar Syndication Services.

Figure 8.5: "Standardized Mortality Ratio for All Deaths and for Four Leading Causes of Death, by Level of Material Deprivation in the Neighbourhood, Quebec, 2000," adapted from Minister of Health and Social Services, *Death registry, Québec*, 2000–2004; and Statistics Canada, *2001 Census, population counts* (Ottawa: Statistics Canada). Reprinted by permission of Statistics Canada.

Figure 9.1: E. Brunner and M.G. Marmot, "Social Organization, Stress, and Health," from *Social Determinants of Health*, (Eds.) M.G. Marmot and R.G. Wilkinson (Oxford: Oxford University Press, 2006): 9. Reprinted by permission of Oxford University Press.

Figure 9.2: M. Benzeval, A. Dilnot, K. Judge, and J. Taylor, "Income and Health: A Life Course Perspective," from Understanding Health Inequalities (Berkshire, UK: Open University Press, 2001): 98. Reprinted by permission of Open University Press.

Figure 9.3: "Living Conditions, Socio-Economic Inequalities, and Children's Health," by H. van de Mheen, K. Stronks, and J. Mackenbach, from "A Lifecourse Perspective on Socio-economic inequalities in health," in The Sociology of Health Inequalities (Oxford: Blackwell Publishers, 1998): 194. Reprinted by permission of Blackwell Publishers.

Figure 9.4: A. Steptoe, (1998). Psychophysiological Bases of Disease, in *Comprehensive Clinical Psychology*, Volume 8: Health Psychology (New York: Elsevier Science, 1998): 39-78.

Figure 9.5: "Summary of Possible Relationships Between Social Comparisons, Other Psychological Factors, Deprivation, and Health," by E. Graham, M. MacLeod, D. Johnston, C. Dibben,

I. Morgan, and S. Briscoe, from "Individual Deprivation, Neighbourhood, and Recovery From Illness," in *Understanding Health Inequalities* (Berkshire, UK: Open University Press, 2000): 177. Reprinted by permission of Open University Press.

Figure 9.6: J. Lynch, "Income Inequality and Health: Expanding the Debate," from *Social Science and Medicine*, 51(7), 2000: 1003. Reprinted by permission of Elsevier.

Figure 9.7: D. Coburn, "Beyond the Income Inequality Hypothesis: Globalization, Neoliberalism, and Health Inequalities," from *Social Science and Medicine*, 58(1), 2004: 44. Reprinted by permission of Elsevier.

Figure 10.1: "Percentages of Children with Various Problems as a Function of Family Income, 1994–1996," from *The Health of Canada's Children: A CICH Profile, 3rd edition* (Ottawa: Canadian Institute of Child Health, 2000): 195.

Figure 10.2: "Difference between Changes in Low Incomes and Changes in Low-End Rents in Various Canadian Municipalities, 1991–2001," from Highlights Report 2004: *Quality of Life in Canadian Municipalities* (Ottawa: Federation of Canadian Municipalities, 2004): 27.

Figure 10.3: "Impacts on Individuals and Neighbourhoods of Processes That Concentrate Disadvantage in Specific Areas," from *Neighbourhood Poverty: Volume 1, Context and Consequences for Children* (New York: Russell Sage Foundation): xvii. Reprinted by permission of Russell Sage Foundation.

Figure 10.4a-d: M. Charron, *Neighbourhood characteristics and the distribution of police-reported crime in the city of Toronto* (Ottawa:Statistics Canada, 2009): Maps 3, 5, 8, and 13. Reprinted by permission of Statistics Canada.

Figure 11.1: "Gini Coefficient for Various Types of Income, Canada, 1980–2007," adapted from Gini Coefficients of Market, Total, and after-tax Income, by Economic Family type, CANSIM Table 202-0705 (Ottawa: Statistics Canada, 2010). Reprinted by permission of Statistics Canada.

Figure 11.2: "Percentage of Canadian Households Spending >30% of Income on Shelter Costs, 1991–2006," from *Housing in Canada online*, available online at http://data.beyond2020.com/CMHC/ (Ottawa: Canada Mortgage and Housing Corporation, 2011). Reprinted by permission of CMHC.

Figure 11.3: L. Rainwater and T. M. Smeeding, "Odds in Fourteen Nations of Escaping Child Poverty, by Left Cabinet Share," (Figure 5.1), from *Poor Kids in a Rich Country: America's Children in Comparative Perspective*. (New York: Russell Sage Foundation, 2003). Reprinted by permission of Russell Sage Foundation.

Figure 11.4: A. Alesina, and E. L. Glaeser, "Degree of Proportional Representation and Extent of Transfers As Percentage of Gross Domestic Product," (Figure x.x), from *Fighting Poverty in the US and Europe: A World of Difference* (Oxford: Oxford University Press, 2004): 86.

Figure 11.5: A. Alesina, and E. L. Glaeser, "Belief That Luck Determines Income and Welfare Spending As a Percentage of Gross Domestic Product," from *Fighting Poverty in the US and Europe: A World of Difference* (Oxford: Oxford University Press, 2004): 187.

Figure 12.1a: "Public Expenditure on Health as % of GDP, 2007," adapted from Social Expenditure: Aggregated data, OECD Social Expenditure Statistics Database, doi: 10.1787/data-00166-en (Paris: Organization for Economic Cooperation and Development, 2011). Reprinted by permission of OECD.

Figure 12.1b: "Public Expenditure on Old Age as % of GDP, 2007," adapted from Social Expenditure: Aggregated data, OECD Social Expenditure Statistics Database, doi: 10.1787/data-00166-en (Paris: Organization for Economic Cooperation and Development, 2011). Reprinted by permission of OECD.

Figure 12.1c: "Public Expenditure on Incapacity-Related Benefits as % of GDP, 2007," adapted from Social Expenditure: Aggregated data, OECD Social Expenditure Statistics Database, doi: 10.1787/data-00166-en (Paris: Organization for Economic Cooperation and Development, 2011). Reprinted by permission of OECD.

Figure 12.1d: "Public Expenditure on Families as % of GDP, 2007," adapted from Social Expenditure: Aggregated data, OECD Social Expenditure Statistics Database, doi: 10.1787/data-00166-en (Paris: Organization for Economic Cooperation and Development, 2011). Reprinted by permission of OECD.

Figure 12.2: "Average Net Replacement Rates over Short Term (1 year) and Long Term (5 years) of Unemployment for Persons Earning 67% and 100% of Average Earnings, 2006," adapted from *Economic Policy Reforms: Going for Growth* (Paris: Organization for Economic Cooperation and Development, 2011). Reprinted by permission of OECD.

Figure 12.3a: "Average Net Incomes Provided by Social Assistance as Percent of Median Equivalent Household Income, Married Couple with Two Children, 2005," adapted from *Society at a Glance: OECD Social Indicators* (Paris: Organization for Economic Cooperation and Development, 2011): 95. Reprinted by permission of OECD.

Figure 12.3b: "Average Net Incomes Provided by Social Assistance as Percent of Median Equivalent Household Income, Lone Parent with Two Children, 2005," adapted from *Society at a Glance: OECD Social Indicators* (Paris: Organization for Economic Cooperation and Development, 2011): 95. Reprinted by permission of OECD.

Figure 12.4: "Net Incomes at Statutory Minimum Wages, Lone Parent with Two Children and Couple with Two Children as Percentage of Median Household Income, 2005," adapted from *Society at a Glance: OECD Social Indicators* (Paris: Organization for Economic Cooperation and Development, 2011): 95. Reprinted by permission of OECD.

Figure 13.1: F. Diderichsen, T. Evans, and M. Whitehead, "A Framework for Identifying the Pathways from the Social Context to Health Outcomes and Means of Introducing Policy Interventions," from *Challenging Inequities in Health: From Ethics to Action.* (New York: Oxford University Press, 2001): 15. Adapted from F. Diderichsen and J. Hallqvist, "Social Inequalities in health: some methodological considerations for the study of social position and social context," from *Inequality in Health—A Swedish Perspective*, (Stockholm: Swedish Council for Social Research): 25–39.

Figure 14.1: S. Saint-Arnaud and P. Bernard, "Ideological Variations in Forms of the Welfare State," from "Convergence or Resilience? A Hierarchical Cluster Analysis of the Welfare Regimes in Advanced Countries," in *Current Sociology* 51(5), 499–527.

Figure 14.2: D. Brady, "Components of Brady's Institutionalization Power Relations Theory," from *Rich Democracies, Poor People: How Policies Explain Poverty* (New York: Oxford University Press, 2009): 14. Reprinted by permission of Oxford University Press.

Figure 14.3: "Union Density, Collective Agreement Coverage, and Child Poverty, 2008 (Density and Coverage Rates) and Mid-2000s (Poverty Rates)," adapted from *Trade Union Density*

(Organization for Economic Co-operation and Development, 2010), *Legislation, Collective Bargaining, and Enforcement: Updating the OECD Employment Protection Indicators*, OECD Social Employment and Migration Working Paper No. 89, and *Growing Unequal? Income Distribution and Poverty in OECD Countries* (Paris: Organization for Economic Cooperation and Development, 2011). Reprinted by permission of OECD.

Tables

Table 2.1: D. Gordon, "Measuring absolute and overall poverty," from *Breadline Europe: The measurements of poverty* (Bristol, UK: The Policy Press, 2000): 66. Reprinted by permission of The Policy Press.

Table 2.2: D. Gordon, "Measuring absolute and overall poverty," from *Breadline Europe: The measurements of poverty* (Bristol, UK: The Policy Press, 2000): 68. Reprinted by permission of The Policy Press.

Table 2.3: "Low Income Cut-Offs For 2009," adapted from Statistics Canada publication *Low Income Line, 2008-2009*, Income Research Paper Series, 75F0002MIE2010005, June 2010, http://www.statcan.gc.ca/bsolc/olc-cel/olc-cel?catno=75F0002MIE&lang=eng#formatdisp (Ottawa: Statistics Canada, 2010). Reprinted by permission of Statistics Canada.

Table 2.4: M. Hatfield, W. Pyper, and B. Gustajtis, "Comparability of Various Measures of Low Income: Market Basket Measure, Low Income Cut-Offs, and Low Income Measure for Various Groups, 2007," from *First comprehensive review of the Market Basket Measure of Low Income* (Ottawa: Human Resources and Social Development Canada; Statistics Canada).

Table 2.5: M. Hatfield, W. Pyper, and B. Gustajtis, " Depth of Low Income for Various Groups in Canada Calculated by Applying Various Measures: Market Basket Measure, Low Income Cut-Offs, and Low Income Measure, 2007," from *First comprehensive review of the Market Basket Measure of Low Income* (Ottawa: Human Resources and Social Development Canada; Statistics Canada).

Table 3.1: "Total Welfare Income as a Percentage of the Poverty Line (After-tax LICOs) for Various Categories, by Province, 2009, " adapted from *Welfare Incomes: 2009*. (Ottawa: National Council of Welfare, 2010): A13-A14. Reproduced with the permission of the Minister of Public Works and the Government Services Canada, 2011.

Table 3.2: "Minimum Wage Income as a Percentage of the Market Basket Measure and LICOs Poverty Lines for the Four Largest Provinces, 200, " adapted from *Income for Living?* (Ottawa: National Council of Welfare, 2004): 16, 25, 35, 45. Reproduced with the permission of the Minister of Public Works and the Government Services Canada, 2011.

Table 3.3: "Percentage of Wage Earners Who Are Low-Paid Workers, Canada, 2000," adapted from Statistics Canada *Low-paid workers: How many live in low-income families? Perspectives on Labour and Income*, 75-001-XIE2004110, Vol.5 No.10; http://www.statcan.gc.ca/bsolc/olc-cel/olc-cel?catno=75-001-XIE&lang=eng#formatdisp (Ottawa: Statistics Canada, 2004). Reprinted by permission of Statistics Canada.

Table 4.1: J. Percy-Smith, "Dimension of Social Exclusion" from *Policy Responses to Social Exclusion: Toward Inclusion* (Berkshire, UK: Open University Press, 2000): 9. Reprinted by permission of Open University Press.

Table 5.1: R. Finnie, "Poverty Rates by Gender and Family Type, Averaged over 1992-1996, Canada," from *Low Income (Poverty) Dynamics in Canada: Entry, Exit, Spell Durations, and Total Time* (Ottawa: Human Resources and Social Development Canada, 2000).

Table 5.2: R. Finnie, "Annual Rates of Entry into and Exit out of Poverty Averaged over 1992-1996 as a Function of First- and Second-Year Family Status and Gender," from *Low Income (Poverty) Dynamics in Canada: Entry, Exit, Spell Durations, and Total Time* (Ottawa: Human Resources and Social Development Canada, 2000).

Table 5.3: R. Finnie, "Percentage of Total Number of Canadians either Never, Sometimes, or Always Living in Poverty Contributed by Each Family Situation by Gender, 1992-1996," from *Low Income (Poverty) Dynamics in Canada: Entry, Exit, Spell Durations, and Total Time* (Ottawa: Human Resources and Social Development Canada, 2000).

Table 7.1: National Council of Welfare, "Liquid Assets Allowable for Receipt of Social Assistance or Welfare," *from Welfare Incomes: 2009* (Ottawa: Minister of Public Works and Government Services of Canada, 2011): Table 6.1. Reproduced by permission of the Minister of Public Works and the Government Services Canada, 2011.

Table 7.2: "Age-Standardized Hospitalization Rates for 33 Census Metropolitan Areas by Socio-economic Status, 2006," adapted from *Hospitalization Disparities by Socio-Economic Status for Males and Females* (Ottawa: Canadian Institute for Health Information, 2010): 15. Reprinted by permission of Canadian Institute for Health Information.

Table 7.3: "Characteristics of Residents and Hospitalization Rates for Heart Attacks by Affluence of Neighbourhood, Canada, 2006," adapted from *Health Indicators 2010* (Ottawa: Canadian Institute for Health Information, 2010): 2, 11. Reprinted by permission of Canadian Institute for Health Information.

Table 7.4: "Characteristics of Residents, Health Indicators, and Physician Contract Rates by Relative Affluence of Neighbourhood, Winnipeg, 1992," adapted from "Variation in Health Care Use by Socioeconomic status in Winnipeg, Canada: Does the System Work Well? Yes and No," by N. Roos and C.A. Mustard, from *Milbank Quarterly ,75*(1), 1997 (New York: Milbank Quarterly, 1997):89-111. Reprinted by permission of John Wiley & Sons Inc.

Table 8.1: "Age-Standardized Mortality Rates per 100,000 Population, for Both Sexes and for Males and Females for Selected Causes of Death by Neighbourhood Income Quintile, Urban Canada, 2001," adapted from Statistics Canada, *Mortality by neighbourhood income in urban Canada from 1971 to 1996*, Health Reports – Supplement, 82-003-SIE2002001, Vol. 13, July 2002; http://www.statcan.gc.ca/bsolc/olc-cel/olc-cel?catno=82-003-SIE&lang=eng (Ottawa: Statistics Canada, 2002). Reprinted by permission of Statistics Canada.

Table 8.2: R. Lessard, D. Roy, R. Choinière, J. Lévesque, and S. Perron, "Life Expectancy and Mortality Rates for Four Leading Causes of Death by Gender and Income Quintile, Montreal, 1994-1998," from *Urban Health: A Vital Factor in Montreal's Development*. Copyright © Direction de la santé publique, 2002.

Table 8.3: "Key Demographics Characteristics and Various Health Outcomes of Differing Income Quintiles within Toronto, 2006," adapted from D. McKeown, K. MacCon, N. Day, P. Fleiszer, F. Scott, and S. Wolfe , *The Unequal City: Income and Health Inequalities in Toronto* (Toronto: Toronto Public Health, 2008). Reprinted by permission of Toronto Public Health.

Table 10.1: "Percentage of Canadians Expressing a Great Deal or Quite a Lot of Confidence in Selected Public Institutions As a Function of Household Income," adapted from Statistics Canada publication *2003 General Social Survey on Social Engagement, Cycle 17: An Overview of Findings,* Catalogue 89-597, Released date: July 6, 2004, http://www.statcan.gc.ca/bsolc/olc-cel/olc-cel?catno=89-598-X&chropg=1&lang=eng (Ottawa: Statistics Canada, 2004): 50. Reprinted by permission of Statistics Canada.

Table 10.2: "Percentage of Interviewees Living in Poverty (n = 59) and Not Living in Poverty (n = 60) Participating in Various Types of Activities, and Percentage Wishing to Participate in Activities but Unable to Do So Because of Financial Issues," adapted from *Left out: Perspectives on social exclusion and social isolation in low-income populations: Final report* (Edmonton: University of Alberta, 2003).

Table 10.3: A. Jackson, "Twenty-Five Key Indicators of Social Development," from *Canada Beats USA — But Loses Gold to Sweden,* http://www.ccsd.ca/pubs/2002/olympic/indicators.htm (Ottawa: Canadian Council on Social Development, 2002). Reprinted by permission of Canadian Council on Social Development.

Table 11.1: "Federal Party Positions for the 2006 Federal Election on Issues Identified by Campaign 2000 as Essential to Eliminating Child Poverty," adapted from *Addressing Child and Family Poverty in Canada: Where do the parties stand?* (Toronto: Campaign 2000, 2006): 2. Reprinted by permission of Campaign 2000, a cross-Canada network working to end child and family poverty in Canada.

Table 11.2: "Federal Party Positions for the 2008 Federal Election on Issues Identified by Campaign 2000 as Essential to Eliminating Child Poverty (only national parties included)," adapted from *Addressing Child and Family Poverty in Canada: Where do the parties stand?* (Toronto: Campaign 2000, 2008): 2. Reprinted by permission of Campaign 2000, a cross-Canada network working to end child and family poverty in Canada.

Table 11.3: L. Reutter et al., "Percentage of Albertans Providing Various Attributions for Why Poverty Is Related to Health," from *Canadian Journal of Public Health* 90 (1999): 14. Reprinted by permission of Canadian Journal of Public Health.

Table 11.4: L. Reutter et al., "Percentage of Toronto and Edmonton Residents Providing Various Attributions As to the Causes of Poverty," from *Canadian Review of Sociology and Anthropology* 43 (2006): 9. Reprinted by permission of John Wiley & Sons Inc.

Table 12.1: "Relative Poverty Rates by Type of Household in 11 Wealthy Industrialized Nations, 1999, 2000," adapted from *Poor People in Rich Nations: The United States in Comparative Perspective,* Luxembourg Income Study Working Paper #419 (Syracuse, NY: Syracuse University, 2005): 30. Reprinted by permission of Timothy Smeeding.

Table 12.2: "The Anti-Poverty Effect of Government Spending – Percent of All People Living in Poverty, 1999, 2000," adapted from *Poor People in Rich Nations: The United States in Comparative Perspective,* Luxembourg Income Study Working Paper #419 (Syracuse, NY: Syracuse University, 2005): p. 33. Reprinted by permission of Timothy Smeeding.

Table 12.4: D. Raphael, "Placement of Selected Nations as Being among the Top (Best), Middle, and Bottom (Worst) One-Third of 21 OECD Nations on Poverty-Related Indicators, Classified as Being Either Social Democratic, Conservative, Liberal, or Latin Welfare States,"

Photographs

Index